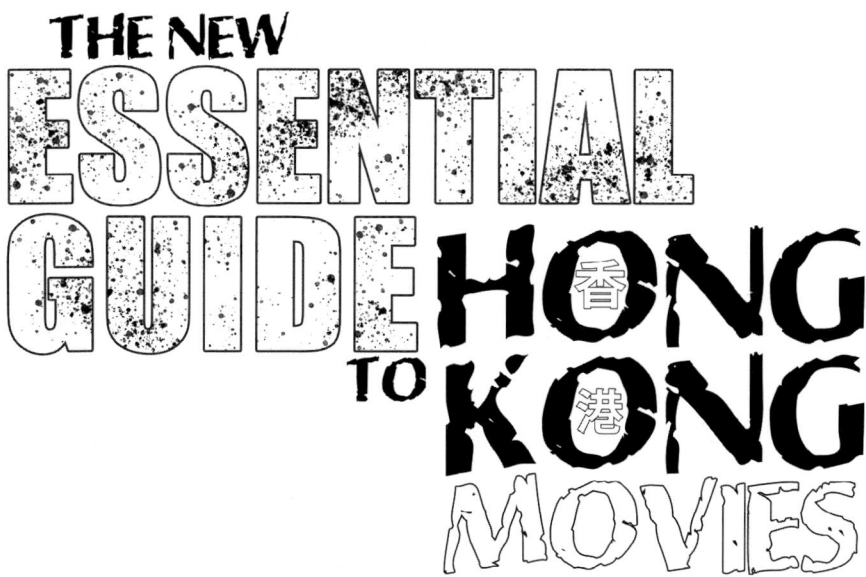

THE NEW ESSENTIAL GUIDE TO HONG KONG MOVIES

RICK BAKER & KEN MILLER

Foreword by
JACKIE CHAN

Afterwords by
CYNTHIA ROTHROCK & VINCENT LYN

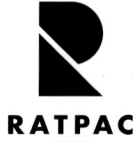

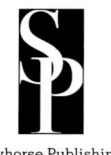

RATPAC
PRESS   Skyhorse Publishing

New York, New York

Produced and written by Rick Baker and Ken Miller
Edited by Ken Miller
Images © the copyright owners
Foreword © 2024 Jackie Chan
Afterword © 2024 Cynthia Rothrock
Afterword © 2024 Vincent Lyn
Special thanks to Brett Ratner, Toby Russell, and Lisa Tilston

This book includes film reviews that originally appeared in the first edition of *The Essential Guide to Hong Kong Movies*, courtesy of these contributors: John Brennan, Malcolm Dome, Howard Lake, Chris Mercer, Jude Sleeman, Liam Sanford, Tim Greenwood, Mike Leeder, and Peter Smith. Some of those reviews were originally featured in *Eastern Heroes Magazine*, *Imaginator Magazine*, and *Film Extremes Magazine*.

Published by RatPac Press and Skyhorse Publishing.

Skyhorse® and Skyhorse Publishing® are registered trademarks of Skyhorse Publishing, Inc.®, a Delaware corporation.

RatPac Press logo is a registered trademark of RatPac Press, LLC.

Visit our website at www.skyhorsepublishing.com.
Please follow our publisher Tony Lyons on Instagram @tonylyonsisuncertain.

10 9 8 7 6 5 4 3 2 1

Library of Congress Cataloging-in-Publication Data is available on file.

Cover image collage by Tim Hollingsworth
Cover design by Brian Peterson

Print ISBN: 978-1-64821-016-7
Ebook ISBN: 978-1-64821-017-4

Printed in China

ABOUT THE AUTHORS

Rick Baker

Began publishing *Eastern Heroes* magazine in 1988, sharing his love for Hong Kong cinema with enthusiasts worldwide.

Organized many martial arts triple bill movie events in renowned venues including London's esteemed Scala Cinema and the iconic Prince Charles Cinema in Leicester Square. Over the course of five years, from 1988 to 1993, Rick curated more than 40 events, attracting special guests such as Hong Kong movie superstars Chow Yun-Fat, Donnie Yen, Jet Li, Gordon Liu, Maggie Cheung, Cynthia Rothrock, and John Woo, among others.

Adviser on the cult TV series *The Incredibly Strange Picture Show*, most notably working on the Jackie Chan episode, which was hosted by top UK presenter Jonathan Ross.

Established the highly regarded cult label Eastern Heroes Distribution in 1994, specializing in the release of Hong Kong movies on video and DVD. Releases included *The Victim*, *The Last Blood*, and *Shaolin Temple*.

Cocreated the six-part TV series *Stop! Kung Fu!*, presenting the show with Jonathan Ross, light-heartedly delving into the world of martial arts movies. Organized numerous events, including a major gathering at London's O2 arena in 2014, with the legendary super-kicker Hwang Jang-Lee as the main guest, followed by another spectacular gathering in 2016, showcasing Hwang In-Shik.

Initiated the Kung Fu Café in 2017, a regular meeting place for like-minded Hong Kong movie fans, providing a space for discussion, appreciation and camaraderie.

Launched Eastern Heroes Publishing in 2020. This venture saw the relaunch of the *Eastern Heroes* magazine and the publication of books and magazines dedicated to Hong Kong cinema.

Presented awards and was a panel guest at the 2022 Urban Action Showcase International Action Film Festival, in Times Square, NYC.

Has been interviewed for productions including *The Golden Boy—Harvesting a Major New Martial Arts Maverick* (a documentary on the early years of Jackie Chan's career), *VHS Forever? Psychotronic People*, and a documentary overview of *Game of Death Redux*.

Rick appears in the feature length, theatrically released documentary *Scala!!! Or, the Incredibly Strange Rise and Fall of the World's Wildest Cinema and How It Influenced a Mixed-Up Generation of Weirdos and Misfits*, talking about the popular kung fu triple bill film shows he hosted at the venue.

Ken Miller

Published *Imaginator* magazine, which covered horror, fantasy, sci-fi, kung fu and action films, especially those from Hong Kong. Also copublished *Film Extremes* magazine.

Hosted multiple *Film Extremes* all-day events at London's legendary Scala cinema with Rick Baker. These movie festivals included rare UK cinema screenings of such Hong Kong films as *Nocturnal Demon* and *A Better Tomorrow III*.

Cocreated the six-part BBC entertainment show *Stop! Kung Fu!* (2001), a series hosted by Jonathan Ross, featuring a delirious deluge of awesome kung fu movie clips.

Consulted on the three-part BBC documentary *Asian Invasion* (2006), which was presented by Jonathan Ross and focused on films from Hong Kong, Japan and South Korea.

Consulted on *Japanorama* (2002), a six-part series celebrating Japanese films, anime, manga and culture, hosted by Jonathan Ross. As with *Asian Invasion*, Ken advised on what film clips should be used in the episodes.

Wrote the screenplay for *Kill 'Em All* (2012), a contained martial arts action thriller starring Hong Kong movie royalty Gordon Liu as the kung fu–skilled villain.

Continues to contribute articles and film reviews to *Eastern Heroes* magazine.

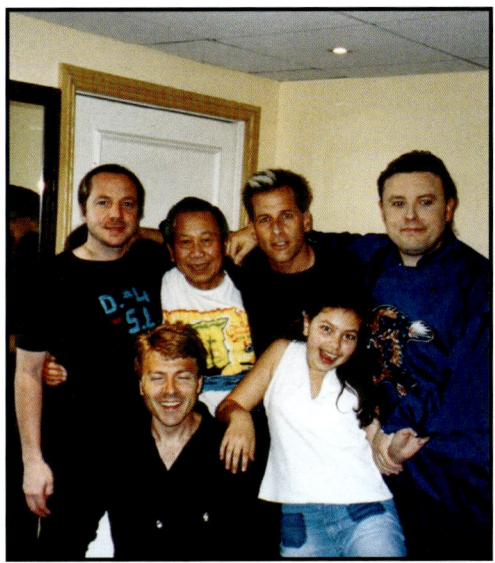

BEHIND THE SCENES ON STOP! KUNG FU! FAR LEFT: KEN MILLER, FAR RIGHT: RICK BAKER, NEXT TO RICK: HONG KONG ACTION GUY STEVE TARTALIA

FOREWORD
BY JACKIE CHAN

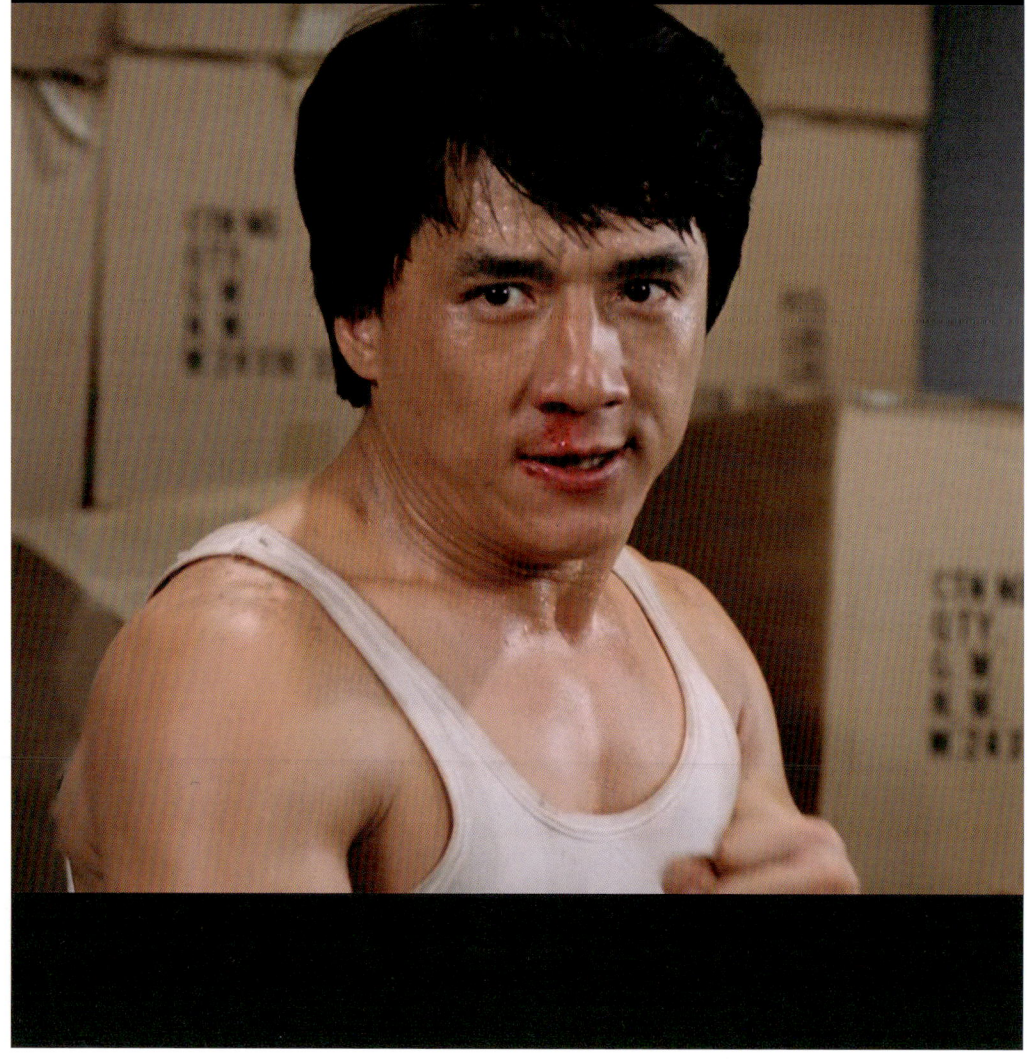

As a kid, I wanted to grow up to be a policeman, a boxer, or a secret agent. And thanks to my career in Hong Kong cinema, I have been able to live out those dreams and many others. Being the director, I could hire a screenwriter to turn my dreams into a reality.

If you've seen one of my films, and you probably have if you're reading this book, then you may have an idea of the things that make my movies different from American action movies. And, if you haven't seen one of my movies, you should put this book down and go watch one!

In most movies, the hero is usually a perfect fighting machine—a killer who never loses and walks away without a scratch. But in my movies, the hero gets beaten up all the time. But that's life. You lose, and lose, and lose, and then, with any luck, you eventually find a way to win. It's like the difference between martial arts tournaments and real fighting. In a tournament, the winner is the person who tallies up the most points. In real fighting, the winner is the person who throws the last punch. You can be beaten to a pulp and about to fall over, but if you can reach inside yourself for the energy to throw the final blow, you win.

My characters aren't perfect, and usually, they don't even like to fight. But they fight when they have to, and they win when they have to. That's what counts.

Another difference between the movies I've made and American action movies is that American movies always cut away from the action during stunts. Someone will fall out a window and the camera will cut to a reaction shot. Then it cuts back to the body on the ground. The obvious reason is that no Hollywood actor is going to jump out a three-story window. These movies also use stunt doubles, special protective equipment, or CGI. It's safer, but it's fake—and no matter how good the effects are, people can tell.

So, in my movies, there is no faking it. What you see on the camera is exactly what we did, even if it almost killed us!

I remember working on *Rush Hour* in America, and it seemed that the dialogue scenes would always take forever. We would spend ten days doing dialogue, and only two days doing action. In Hong Kong, twenty days would be spent doing action, and only two days on dialogue.

I spent much of my career shooting movies in Hong Kong and engaging in death-defying feats. In the movie *Police Story*, one of the most dangerous and most memorable scenes was the final battle that took place in a crowded shopping mall. Glass was everywhere and was scattered from the fists and bodies that had broken through the countless panes of glass.

To make it look as real as possible, I ordered special breakthrough glass from a supplier in America, asking for it to be made twice as thick as ordinary "sugar glass." This also made it twice as dangerous, as people were bruised and cut all the time. But anything less would not have had the same effect.

The movie's last stunt, "The Great Glass Slide," where I had to chase the boss gangster before he escaped with condemning evidence, entailed a desperate leap from five stories up, grabbing onto a chandelier made of twinkling lights strung along a series of thick wires. I would then slide down the wires, sending sparks and broken glass flying on my way down, and finally crash through a series of glass overhangs before hitting the ground.

We had only one chance to make the stunt work. The cameras started rolling and the mall went quiet. I leaped from the balcony, slid, fell, and crashed. Glass exploded in all directions and, there I was, flat on my back on the hard floor of the ground level. Everyone held their breath until they knew I was okay. And, despite the pain, I managed to stand up. Everyone began to clap without even hearing the word "cut," and I knew the stunt was a success.

Working with Golden Harvest Studios was always a moving experience. When I first showed up at Golden Harvest as a kid, I'd risk my life for pennies, quietly waiting to make my mark. My manager, Willie Chan, liked my prospects working with Golden Harvest. He thought they'd be able to build my career and make me an international star, the biggest Chinese icon in the world after Bruce Lee.

Leonard Ho and Raymond Chow had set up this company together. Mr. Chow was expanding the business, while Mr. Ho took care of making the movies. They'd met while working at Shaw Brothers and were a perfect duo. It was their collaboration that filled Golden Harvest with new possibilities, and me with confidence about working with them.

The first movie I made after joining Golden Harvest was *The Young Master*, the story of a man who goes off on his own mission to find his lost brother. I wanted to make a good film, and I wanted everything to look perfect to repay the trust these two had put in me. Golden Harvest was making an investment in me, assuming that I would become a superstar, and I couldn't let them down.

For one small scene, I shot more than fifty takes. I had to kick my fan into the air and catch it with one hand. Even though it was a lot of work to go through so many takes, that one scene turned out beautiful.

Back when I started making films in Hong Kong, shooting anything on location meant turning a public space into a movie set. While filming *Project A*, there was a stunt where I found myself dangling from a clock tower. Holding on as long as I could, I let go and crashed through a series of cloth canopies before smashing into the ground. We filmed in the parking lot and caused a major disruption for the people who lived and worked nearby. Luckily everyone was understanding, and no one complained. Instead, many people showed up to watch!

Raymond Chow and Leonard Ho were at the set one day. They climbed the tower and saw how dangerous the stunt was. They urged me to reconsider, offering to get a stunt double. But I had to do it. I climbed out onto the tower and hung from the minute hand of the clock. If you watch that scene now, you'll see that I'm clinging on for dear life until I can't hold on any longer. There was no acting—it was all real. When I heard "Action," I waited until my hands ran out of energy and throbbed with pain before loosening my grip and sending my body into a free fall.

That's what makes these movies so special— the stunts do not take a back seat to anything else, and they are done with an intensity and authenticity that can't be found in any other type of movie. The Hong Kong film industry has produced so many great movies, and I'm glad that they are able to be showcased here for everyone to enjoy.

—Jackie Chan

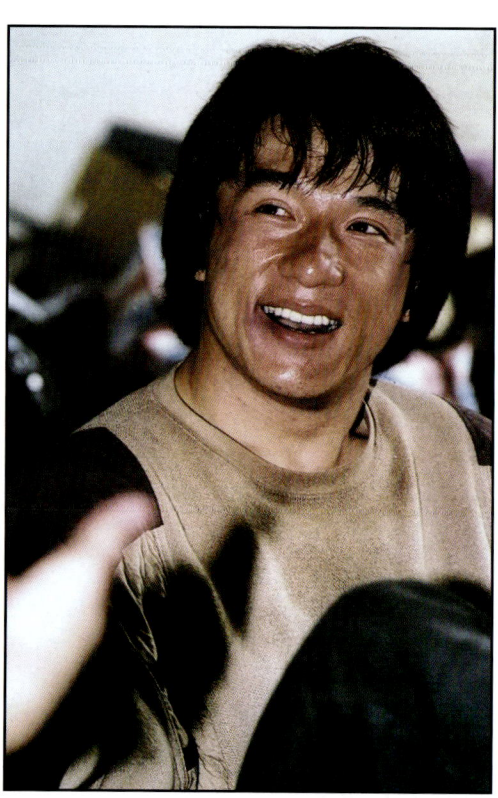

INTRODUCTION BY RICK BAKER AND KEN MILLER

It is with great pleasure that we bring you this updated edition of the *Essential Guide to Hong Kong Movies*, a publication brimming with hundreds of reviews of the most dynamic, exciting, fantastic, oddball, funny, twisted, violent, strange, kinetic, and downright enjoyable movies you are ever likely to see.

In the three decades that have passed since the original guide was published in 1994 it is easy to see the significant impact Hong Kong moviemaking has had on the global cinematic stage. Its influence can clearly be seen in Hollywood blockbusters, where energetic, intense and intricate action choreography, always a staple of Hong Kong's films, now forms an integral part of most Western-made actioners. In the time since the first edition came out, John Woo, who pioneered the heroic bloodshed genre, gained international recognition, while stars like Chow Yun-Fat and Jet Li went on to appear in American films to much acclaim, with Jackie Chan and Michelle Yeoh still continuing to be successful international stars.

This is all a testament to the enduring legacy of this remarkable, vigorous film industry, which we, of course, continue to enthuse about in this new book. Whether expertly performed kung fu flicks, sweeping wuxia swordplay epics, nihilistic, slick, ultraviolent gangster pics, gritty crime dramas, outlandishly imaginative fantasy films, taboo-breaking CAT III releases, or off-the-wall horror movies, we delve into the sometimes quite outrageous storylines and highlight what each production has to offer.

The reviews we've curated all stem from the Hong Kong film genres we adore the most, so the chapters remain the same as before, encompassing kung fu and swordplay films, modern day actioners, heroic bloodshed and crime dramas, plus a smorgasbord of fantasy, erotic, horror, and assorted Category III films.

Beyond the obvious classics, what we love about these movies is that even far lesser productions almost always have something to enjoy: it could be thanks to an unexpectedly kick-ass final fight, a jarring change of tone, a jaw-dropping example of truly inappropriate humor or perhaps a refreshingly different cultural take on a horror movie trope.

This edition's new material covers Hong Kong (and Taiwanese) movies released up until the year 2000 (three years after Hong Kong's handover to China), as well as additional reviews of 70s and 80s films that were not included in the first book. Working on this guide gave us an excuse to rewatch and revisit these Hong Kong "golden age" films, which we have such deep affection for. In fact, we enjoyed this experience so much we are definitely planning a third volume, that'll encompass Hong Kong movie releases up until the present day.

So, let's dive now into the mind-boggling "reel" world of Hong Kong, a place of beautiful ghosts, supercool hit men, stoic monks, high-kicking female cops, well-dressed gangsters, sword-wielding warriors, bizarre ceremonies, unspeakably evil villains, and hopping vampires, where practically every man and woman in the region is an amazing martial artist. It's going to be a fun ride . . .

—Rick Baker & Ken Miller

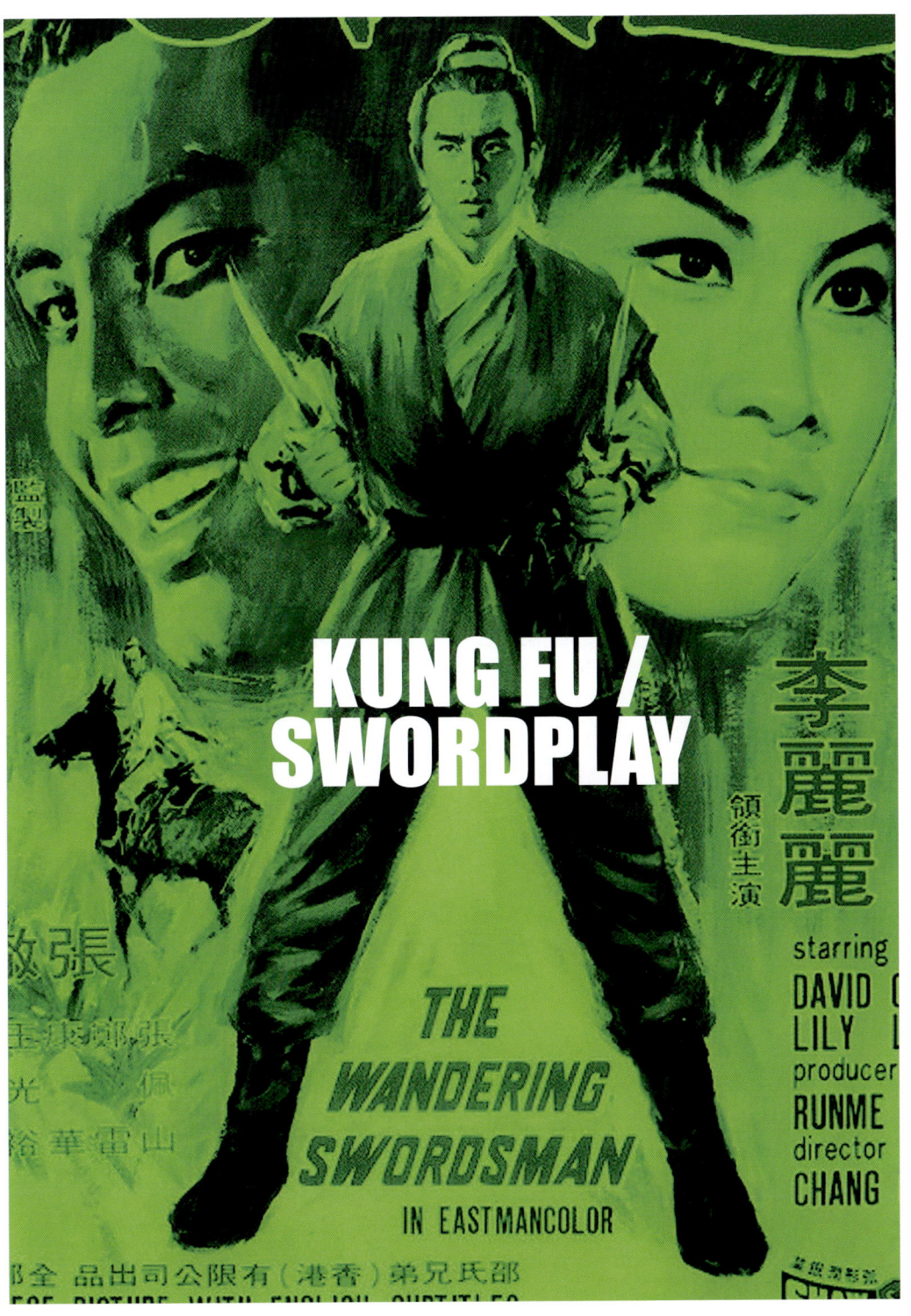

KUNG FU /
SWORDPLAY

ALL MEN ARE BROTHERS (1974)
*Starring David Chiang, Chen Kuan-Tai, Fan Mei-Sheng,
Ti Lung*
Directed by Chang Cheh, Wu Ma
Produced by Runme Shaw
Shaw Brothers

Also titled *Seven Soldiers of Kung Fu*, this Shaw
Brothers epic came out earlier in Taiwan before it
was released in Hong Kong. David Chiang, Ti Lung,
and Chen Kuan-Tai star in this classical swordplay
tale, leading their heroic clan into action against
rebel Fang La, who aims to overthrow the emperor.

The action, choreographed by Chen Chuan, Lau
Kar-Leung, Lau Kar-Wing, and Tang Chia, is fast,
furious, and frenzied, featuring broad canvases of
martial fare. And the climax, inside Fang's fortress,
is a masterful mix of chivalry, honor and bloodshed.

ASHES OF TIME (1994)
*Starring Leslie Cheung, Jacky Cheung,
Tony Leung Chiu-Wai, Brigitte Lin, Tony Leung Ka-Fai,
Maggie Cheung, Carina Lau, Charlie Yeung*
Directed by Wong Kar-Wai
Jet Tone Production/Scholar Films Company

In ancient China, Ouyang Feng (Leslie Cheung) is a
heartbroken and cynical man who spends his days
in the desert in exile, spinning tales that connect
expert swordsmen with those seeking revenge and
willing to pay for it.

Attracting many characters to his bolthole on the
edge of the Gobi desert, Cheung, as Ouyang Feng,
acts as the only constant in the movie, narrating
each story as it unfolds. These tales feature a stellar
cast, including Tony Leung Ka-Fai as Huang Yaoshi,
Brigitte Lin as twin sisters Murong Yang and Murong
Yin, Tony Leung Chiu-Wai as the Blind Swordsman,
and Maggie Cheung as Ouyang Feng's sister-in-law,
who appears in flashbacks throughout the film.

As one can expect with a Wong Kar-Wai movie,
the cinematography is sumptuous. The action scenes
are often edited quickly, and the constant movement
of the camera can make it sometimes hard to focus.
The plot, if you're not paying full attention, can be
a little confusing, but, despite its shortcomings, it's
another masterpiece from Wong Kar-Wai. Unlike
the swordplay kung fu movies one might normally
watch, this is more of a thinking man's kung fu film,
where you must concentrate as much on the storyline
as you do to the fight action.

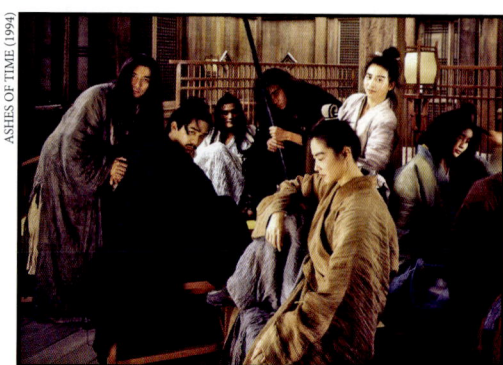

ASHES OF TIME (1994)

THE AVENGING EAGLE (1978)
*Starring Fu Sheng, Ti Lung, Ku Feng, Shih Szu, Eddy Ko,
Dick Wei*
Directed by Sun Chung
Produced by Run Run Shaw
Shaw Brothers

An evil group of bandits known as the 13 Eagles
are hunting a former top member, Chik Ming Sing
(Lung). Chik is determined to stop the Eagles'
misdeeds and meets a wanderer (Sheng) who helps
him in his cause. However, Chik later finds out there
is more to this wanderer than meets the eye.

This is a film of revenge, love, and comradeship,
with towering performances from the superb Fu
Sheng and Ti Lung. The two are ably supported by
an awesome cast, with Ku Feng in stunning form as
the Eagles' evil leader. The fight scenes are in keeping
with the film as a whole: powerful and brilliant.

THE BARE-FOOTED KID (1993)
*Starring Aaron Kwok, Ti Lung, Maggie Cheung,
Wu Chien-Lien, Kenneth Tsang*
Directed by Johnnie To
Produced by Mona Fong
Action by Lau Kar-Leung
Cosmopolitan Film Productions

Aaron Kwok stars as Kuan, an illiterate peasant boy
who comes to the Four Seasons Weavers dye factory
looking for employment. Tuan (Ti Lung), a friend
of his father, gives Kuan his first pair of shoes and
teaches him to perfect his already impressive martial
arts skills. Meanwhile, Ke (Tsang), a villainous
business rival, sets out to take over the Four Seasons,
owned by Miss Ho (Maggie Cheung), and after
witnessing Kuan's fighting talent in a tournament,
persuades him to go and work for him. But when
Kuan discovers he has been tricked into hurting the
people who befriended him, his fury turns against Ke.

Aaron Kwok is excellent as the peasant boy determined to better himself by learning to write his name, yet too shy to admit it. His fighting is equally assured and stylish. It's always satisfying to find a film that's so well-acted and captivating in its plot yet has enough action to satisfy the most hardened fight flick fan!

BASTARD SWORDSMAN (1983)
Starring Tsui Siu-Keung, Alex Man, Tony Liu, Wilson Tong, Wang Jung
Directed by Lu Chin-Ku
Shaw Brothers

Yun Fei Yang (Siu-Keung) is a human punching bag (or should that be dagger bag?) humiliated by all his Wu Tang classmates in this classic Shaw Brothers wuxia epic. Secretly, however, Yun is being taught by one of the Wu Tang masters, who is actually his father. Wu Tang is challenged by Chief Dugu (Man) of the Wu Di clan, and Yun's father is sent to face the challenge. He is injured by Dugu's deadly skill and, on his journey back to Wu Tang, he is attacked by the blood edict. A swordsman in white intervenes, saves his life, and helps him make it back to Wu Tang, where secret love and subplots complicate matters. The Wu Tang chief is a master of silkworm technique, an extremely advanced form of martial art, but his failing abilities are becoming a worry for all concerned, besides which there is a traitor in the camp. Due to tricks and traitorous tactics, Yun is forced to flee and Wu Tang is overthrown by Fu Yu Shu (Liu) and his cronies. On his travels, Yun meets his mother, who is Dugu's wife and owner of the silkworm skill book, which Yun learns and masters before returning to Wu Tang, batteries recharged, to exact his revenge.

This is a really fun, bizarro movie which many of the modern sword fantasies have tried to recreate

BEACH OF THE WAR GODS (1973)

without nearly as much style. What really sticks in the mind, of course, is the fantastical silkworm kung fu technique!

BEACH OF THE WAR GODS (1973)
Starring Jimmy Wang Yu, Lung Fei, Tien Yeh, Shan Mao, Wang Yung-Sheng
Directed by Jimmy Wang Yu
Produced by Raymond Chow
Golden Harvest

Wang Yu bursts back onto the big screen with this spectacular that is his take on *The Seven Samurai*.

Yu plays Feng, a famous knight who rallies the people of a small fishing village in Hang Chow to fight against the tyranny of invading Japanese pirates. The villagers have been told that they must pay a sum of 200,000 taels of silver to the Japanese warlord Hashimoto (Fei) or their village will be razed. Rather than see the loot fall into enemy hands, Feng suggests that the money can be put to better use and he embarks on his quest to seek out some fierce warriors to help him in his just cause. On the way Feng meets five top fighters, whom he, sometimes with difficulty, signs up. The heroes gather at the small village and plan their strategy. Within days, Hashimoto and his 1,000-strong army land at the beach of the war gods . . .

What follows is half an hour of nonstop chivalry and bloodshed that will leave you totally breathless. Oh, and how awesome is this film's title?!

THE BIG BOSS (1971)
Starring Bruce Lee, Nora Miao, James Tien, Han Ying-Chieh, Maria Yi, Billy Chan
Directed by Lo Wei
Produced by Raymond Chow
Action by Han Ying-Chieh
Golden Harvest

Bruce Lee plays Cheng, a migrant worker, who has traveled to Thailand in search of a job. He finds refuge with a group of Chinese workers who find him employment at the local ice packing factory. Mysteriously, members of the group start to disappear, causing a mutiny within the factory with workers demanding an explanation for the disappearance of their colleagues. In a bid to quell the rising tempers, Cheng is promoted to foreman. The management hope that this gesture will calm the workers, but this is short-lived when people continue to vanish. Cheng investigates the factory,

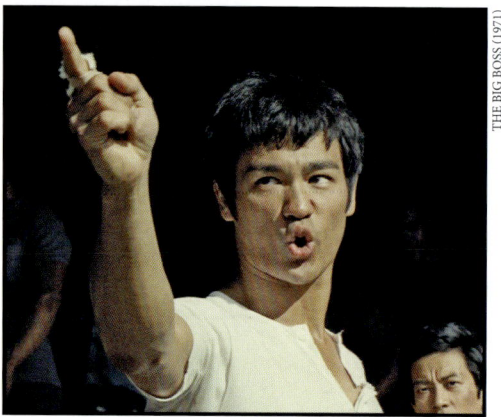

THE BIG BOSS (1971)

BIG BOSS OF SHANGHAI (1979)
Starring Chen Kuan-Tai, Lung Fong, Chen Sing,
Cheng Kang-Yeh
Directed by Chen Kuan-Tai
Produced by Lo Wei
Action by Chen Mu-Chuan
Lo Wei Motion Picture Company

In the 1930s, two good friends are forced to flee to Shanghai after killing a local mobster while coming to the aid of a friend. Working on the docks, they once again find themselves defeating a gang boss and this time their humble lives take a change of direction. Their new position as owners of the docks not only brings wealth but also forces the two men to review where their loyalties lie.

Like *Chinatown Kid* and *The Big Rascal*, this movie concerns itself with the pressures that wealth can put on friendships and the ways crime can decay even the simplest understanding of morality. Emotionally charged, the many fight scenes complement this film perfectly. The plot and performances are suitably strong and the violent action scenes are inventive.

When you take into account the leads that this film boasts, with their combined experience and talent, you know you can expect quality from this production.

looking for clues, and discovers a drug trafficking operation, plus the bodies of several of the missing men packed within the ice. Cheng decides to go to the big boss' lair for the explosive showdown . . .

It would have been impossible for director Lo Wei, producer Raymond Chow, and lead star Bruce Lee to have predicted the massive success of *The Big Boss*. In fact, in this, Lee's first completed film, he is redundant in the first half of the movie, as his conscience will not allow him to fight while wearing a jade amulet given him by his mother, reminding him that his kung fu skills should not be abused. Lee is only triggered into action when, during a scuffle, it is ripped from around his neck.

Despite its low budget, *The Big Boss* rocketed Lee to fame beyond his wildest imaginings. On reflection, *The Big Boss* is the weakest of the four completed Lee films, perhaps due to a change of directors, Wu Chia Hsiang, the original choice, being replaced by Lo Wei. This is the reason some extra footage can be found in certain trailers but not in the finished movie, such as a scene which shows Bruce naked, as he visits a second prostitute. Lee's martial arts persona had not yet been perfected but his screen presence and charisma blasted off the screen and boosted an otherwise no-hope picture into the annuls of Hong Kong history.

THE BIG RASCAL (1979)
Starring Chi Kuan-Chun, Lu Ti, Chiang Yang, Wang
Chen, Peng Kang
Directed by Chi Kuan-Chun
Kuan Chun Film Company

A moral tale about Ho, a young man from a simple background, whose kung fu skills win him the favor of the local gambling house owner. At first his appointment as bodyguard is a means by which he can support himself and his brother, but slowly Ho is sucked deeper into the ways of the criminal empire he serves. After his ambitions lead to moral deterioration, it takes the murder of his brother at his wedding to show Ho the error of his ways. Thus, the stage is set for a showdown, as Chi Kuan-Chun, as Ho, strips to the waist to take on the title character in an expertly choreographed duel.

The film, also known as *Dragon Force*, is full of excellent action from the "in front of red" credit sequence through to the final confrontation. An interesting subplot and effective symbolic use of a watch (as in *Chinatown Kid*) help to round off a well-crafted kung fu film.

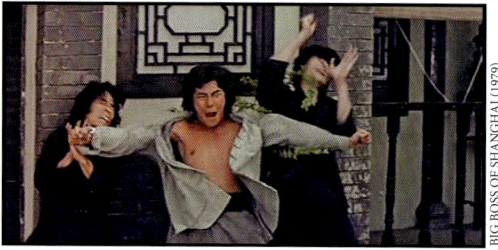

BIG BOSS OF SHANGHAI (1979)

BLACK BELT KARATE (1979)
Starring Li Chin-Kun, Lo Lieh, Bruce Leung,
Billy Chong, Chiang Tao, Peter Chan
Director Suen A-Foo
China Films (H.K.) Co

This takes us on a journey through the world of Japanese martial arts, specifically the art of karate, with Li Chin-Kun playing a country boy who finds work at a karate school. However, he soon finds himself entangled in a dangerous world of local thugs. Billy Chong costars, in his screen debut, as the school head's son.

The film's action scenes are predominantly set on the front lawn of the karate school, with bustling traffic serving as a backdrop, but, despite its amateurish execution, the film boasts some impressive fight scenes, showcasing the stars' martial arts prowess.

The film also features two Hong Kong cinema legends, Lo Lieh and Bruce Liang, who add to the film's overall appeal. Although *Black Belt Karate* may not offer much else in terms of plot or character development, it's a must-watch for fans of martial arts films and provides a glimpse into the earliest days of Billy Chong's career.

THE BLACK TAVERN (1972)
Starring Shih Szu, Tung Li, Ku Feng, Chiang Ling,
Yu Feng, Wu Ma
Directed by Yip Wing-Cho
Shaw Brothers

One wintry evening various unsavory characters arrive at the Gao Family Inn (run by cannibal owners) to await the arrival of an official who, it is said, has a trunk full of wonderful loot. These exotic lowlifes include: a trio of brigands (Tiger, Leopard, and Bear) known as the Three Headed Cobra, Whipmaster

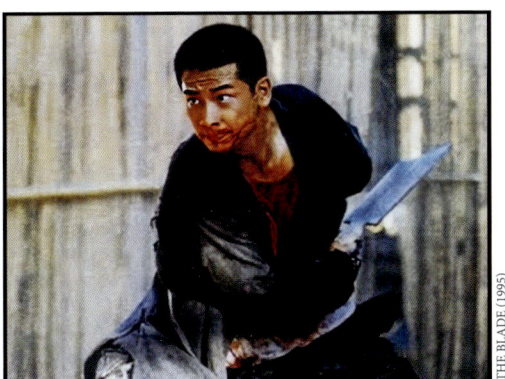

THE BLADE (1995)

Zheng Shoushan, Brother Hu (who wears a horned helmet) and a group of bandits called the Five Ghosts of Xiang Xi, who pretend to be hopping vampires!

Into this den of inequity come two loner heroes, the cool, suave-looking swordman Zha Xiaoyu (Li) and mysterious, white-clad woman warrior Zhang Caibing (Szu). Confrontations, bogus identities, and fights abound, until it is revealed that the information concerning the official and his trunk of treasure is merely a ruse to flush out all these bad guys.

The action, including swordplay, beheadings, and poison gas bomb attacks, is handled with skill by Yip Wing-Cho (aka Yeh Yung-Tsu), who infuses this enjoyably dark Shaw Brothers wuxia with gleeful horror overtones.

THE BLADE (1995)
Starring Vincent Zhao, Moses Chan, Song Lei,
Hung Yan-Yan, Austin Wai, Chung Bik-Ha, Valerie Chow
Directed by Tsui Hark
Film Workshop/Golden Harvest

While working at a local foundry, On (Zhau), a highly skilled swordsman, overhears a conversation between the foundry master's daughter Ling (Lei) and her grandmother, revealing that On's father was brutally murdered by a ruthless swordsman called the Flying Dragon. Hungry for vengeance, he quits the foundry to seek retribution. However, his actions are short-lived when a group of bandits set upon Ling and, despite his best fighting skills, On ends up badly beaten, losing one of his arms in the battle. On becomes very disillusioned, now that he is unable to avenge his father's death, but his fate changes when a young woman called Blackie (Bik-Ha) passes him an old martial arts training book owned by her parents, offering him a chance to upgrade his skills. With determination, and a training sequence reminiscent of classic martial arts movies, On's confidence rises from the ashes to enable him to have the showdown he craves with the Flying Dragon, armed only with the broken sword of his father.

Any martial arts movie fan will instantly recognize Tsui Hark's nod to the classic *One-Armed Swordsman*. Hark brings the tale up to date with the modern style of filming that he helped develop in the 90s for wuxia and martial art movies and he also incorporates CGI, to give the lost arm a much more realistic look (as opposed to being tied behind the actor's back).

The sword action is well-choreographed, with some very slick set pieces, and the camera often weaves

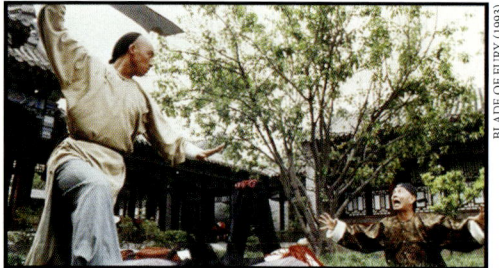

BLADE OF FURY (1993)

in and out frenetically, capturing the multiple battle scenes leading up to the spectacular showdown with the Flying Dragon. This frenzied battle, however, is slightly let down by the speed at which some scenes are filmed, creating far-fetched moves rather than the grounded fighting we saw earlier. That said, this is a furious, fabulous, breathtaking wuxia.

BLADE OF FURY (1993)

Starring Ti Lung, Cynthia Khan, Yang Fan, Ngai Sing,
Sammo Hung, Rosamund Kwan
Directed by Sammo Hung
Produced by Lo Wei
Action by Sammo Hung
Grand March Movie Production Company Ltd/
Changchun Film Studio

This stands head and shoulders above most of the new wave of traditional-style movies, mainly due to its stunning cinematography, excellent performances and brilliant fight action. The movie opens with a superb broadsword form performed by legendary patriot Brother Wong, head of the Black Flag troupe: a group dedicated to the removal of all foreigners from China. This is the day of their biggest mission, to destroy a Japanese munitions cache located in the middle of a heavily guarded camp. The cache is destroyed but so is the troupe, except for Brother Wong. Years later, Tan (Lung) and his servant Nine Catties (Khan) arrive in a small desert town which is besieged by a group of bandits trying to ambush Yuan, a rising official. Tan and Nine Catties save the townspeople, helped by the local blacksmith who is identified by his tattoo as Brother Wong. They go to the capital, where Wong opens a kung fu school, Tan becomes the emperor's right-hand man, and Yuan becomes the governor's aide. But their friendship is strained when Tan is framed for treason by the governor and Wong is pushed into action against Yuan.

Some superb martial artistry is on display here, with highlights including a mesmerising Drunken Sword form, the blistering attack on the Japanese camp, the epic sword fight between Wong and Sammo Hung's character, plus the intense bloodbath finale involving swords, fists, spears, and rope-darts.

BLOOD BROTHERS (1973)

Starring Ti Lung, David Chiang, Chen Kuan-Tai,
Ching Li
Directed by Chang Cheh
Produced by Run Run Shaw
Action by Lau Kar-Leung, Tang Chia
Shaw Brothers

Considered to be Chang Cheh's finest achievement, this epic tale of brotherhood and betrayal features Ti Lung in one of his best-ever roles. The story, told retrospectively by condemned prisoner Chang (Chiang), relates how he and his brother Huang (Kuan-Tai), who are both highwaymen, befriend Ma (Lung), a dropout government official, after attempting to rob him. The three blood brothers form a private army under the instructions of the idealistic Ma, then tension is created with the arrival of Huang's wife (Li). Years later, Ma, now a man of high standing in the military, sends for his two brothers and their army. The victories are many and they are showered with wealth and fame, but love once again intervenes, as Ma, still besotted with Huang's wife, uses his

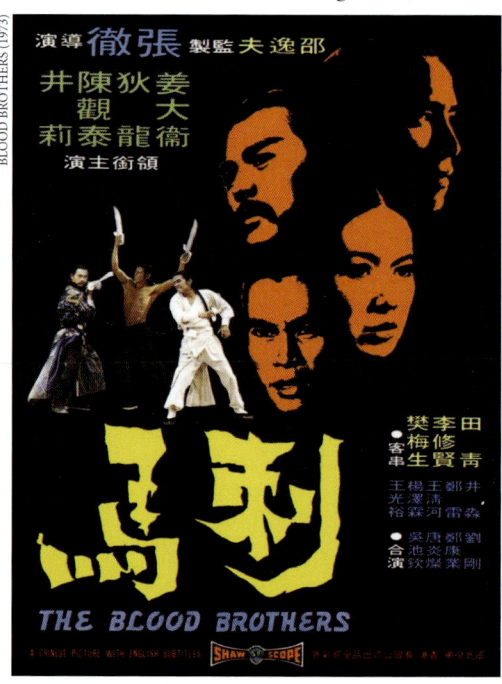

position and cunning to devise a plot to get rid of Huang, the simpler of the two brothers. Ma succeeds, but comes under scrutiny from Chang . . . and what follows is a one-man war against a cast of thousands.

When released, this made an instant star of real-life martial arts expert Chen Kuan-Tai, and the film enjoyed much success and critical acclaim.

BLOOD TREASURY FIGHT (1979)
Starring David Chiang, Tan Tao-Liang, Wang Chung,
Michael Chan Wai-Man
Directed by Pao Hsueh-Li
Action by Yuen Cheung-Yan
Yen Shing Film Company

Ex-Shaw Brothers director Pao Hsueh-Li captains an all-star cast in this Taiwanese hardboiled treasure caper, also known as *Blooded Treasury Fight*.

A group of Ming Patriots have hidden a large cache of booty in an old mill in a remote corner of China. The Ching government officials are aware of this and send out a party of spies to get it! After a treacherous journey, our million-dollar double-crossing cast get ready for the fight of their lives in the mill.

David Chiang shines as the intrepid supersleuth who schemes his way to victory, but it is the flashy legwork of Tan Tao-Liang that remains the high point of this not-so-action-packed movie.

THE BONE CRUSHING KID (1979)
Starring Pan Yin-Tze, Chin Lung, James Tien,
Chen Hung-Lieh
Directed by Hsieh Hsing
Family Film Company

A young orphan working as a cook in a prestigious kung fu school is finally given a chance to prove his worth when an old man he befriends teaches him a rare style of fighting. His newfound skills are put to use in several run-ins with local thugs, but it is when an evil master, intent on wiping out all martial arts experts, comes in pursuit of his teacher that he must put his monkey style to the test and his neck on the line.

Also known as *Monkey in the Master's Eye*, this movie has a manic, childish plot containing many elements similar to Jackie Chan's Seasonal Film Corporation hits, here combined with a level of buffoonery unparalleled in kung fu movies. The impressive fight scenes, however, make this flick worthy of a watch.

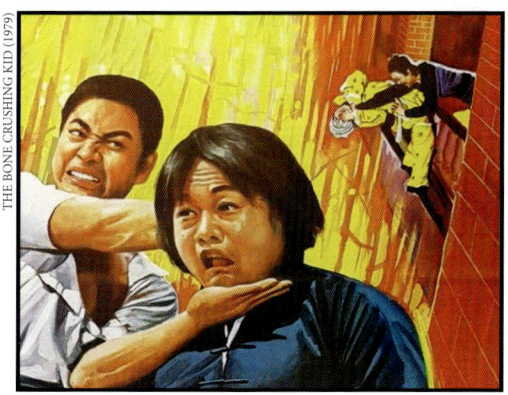

THE BONE CRUSHING KID (1979)

BORN INVINCIBLE (1978)
Starring Carter Wong, Lo Lieh, Jack Long,
Mark Long, Nancy Yen
Directed and produced by Joseph Kuo
Action by Yuen Woo-Ping
Hong Hwa International Films

Carter Wong gives a dazzling performance as the laughing white-haired kung fu expert who wreaks havoc in the martial world. Three young avengers discover the weak spot of this seemingly invincible fighting force, but hitting it isn't going to be easy . . .

Combined with Wong's awesome villainy is Jack Long's martial arts mastery, making this a well-above-average kung fu flick from independent movie mogul Joseph Kuo.

THE BOXER FROM THE TEMPLE (1979)
Starring Wu Yuan-Chun, Lam Fai-Wong, Kuan Feng,
Wang Sha, Chiang Cheng
Directed by Lo Mar
Produced by Mona Fong
Action by Hsu Hsia, Tsui Fat, Yuen Tak
Shaw Brothers

A young orphan is brought up by Shaolin monks and taught the art of Buddhist Fist and Palm. When the lad comes of age, he leaves the temple and starts a new life in a sleepy town. In time he marries a widow and, along with her young son, they live happily until their tranquil bliss is shattered when a villainous master (Feng) and his men kill the wife and stepson. The hero now transforms himself from village cook to Buddhist Palm avenger in a highly stylised end fight sequence.

Beautiful Buddhist Fist forms and the fast fight action of Kuan Feng are the high points of this otherwise average Shaw Brothers production.

BROKEN OATH (1977)

Starring Angela Mao, Bruce Leung, Sammo Hung
Michael Chan Wai-Man, Kwan Shan, Dean Shek
Directed by Chang Cheung Wo
Produced by Raymond Chow
Action by Yuen Woo-Ping, Hsu Hsia
Golden Harvest

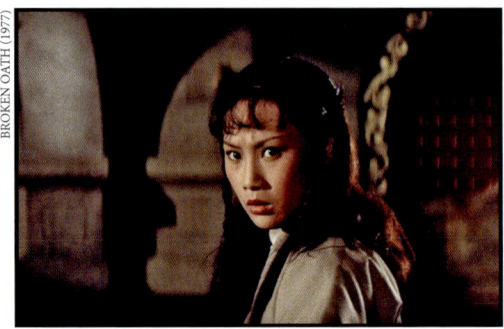

BROKEN OATH (1977)

A beautiful woman is raped by a gang led by a vicious general, who has her banished to an island prison after she refuses to be his concubine and subsequently blinds him in one eye. While on the island prison she gives birth to his illegitimate child, Lotus, who is sent from the island to be brought up by monks. Twenty years later Lotus, now a striking young woman, leaves the religious order in search of the gang who brought about her mother's tragic demise. Joining her in her search are a pickpocket and a government agent, Chang (Leung), who wants the evil general on suspicion of treason. Together they catch up with the gang and twenty years of supressed rage is let loose, with the help of a bag of scorpions!

Angela Mao gives the performance of a lifetime as the young woman filled with hate in this classic tale of vengeance, Chinese style. Basic plot, great action, terrific viewing!

BRUCE LEE AGAINST SUPERMEN (1975)

Starring Bruce Li, Fei Lung, Hei Ying, Chang Yi-Kuei
Directed by Wu Chia-Chun
Alpha Motion Picture Company/Alpha Motion Pictures

The inspiration for this Bruce Lee exploitationer comes from the sixties TV series *The Green Hornet*, which was characterised by its mix of humor, fight action, and a total disregard for realism. Here these ingredients are blown totally out of proportion and inserted into a brainless plot about a scientist who discovers a way of producing food from petroleum. He concludes that his breakthrough will solve the world's hunger problems. The boss of a crime gang intent on global domination kidnaps the aging boffin, so it's down to our hero (Li) to save the day.

Although unintentionally ridiculous, the film does boast some well-staged fights, notably Bruce Li's confrontation in a forest with four masters of monkey kung fu. It's a pity that such bizarre creativity should be wasted on a project where the main villain is a forty-something kung fu master who calls himself Superman!

BRUCE LEE, THE LEGEND (1984)

Starring Bruce Lee (archive footage), Lee Hoi-Chuen
(archive footage), Linda Lee Cadwell, Robert Clouse,
Nora Miao, James B. Nicholson (narrator)
Directed by Leonard Ho
Produced by Raymond Chow
Golden Harvest

The earlier part of this documentary is of most interest, with B&W footage of 6-year-old Lee in *My Son Ah Cheun*, starring alongside his father, actor Lee Hoi-Chuen, plus some photos of Bruce winning a Hong Kong Cha-Cha championship.

Written by Russell Cawthorne, this doc shows one of Lee's early films, *The Thunder Storm*, where Bruce doesn't do any fighting, because he plays a real wimp! There's also the wonderful sequence showing Bruce doing a screen test for the proposed TV series *Number One Son* where, after asking him some questions, the interviewer gets Bruce to exhibit his prowess in Jeet Kune Do. With his blows, missing a nervous member of the crew by centimeters, Lee showed what a brilliant exponent of his art he was. He needed no camera trickery or snappy editing, he was simply breathtaking to watch in action whenever he was on-screen, even for this statically filmed screen test.

Obviously, this documentary contains clips from Lee's main movies, like *The Big Boss*, plus outtakes from *The Game of Death*.

Lee's death, in July of '73, is gone into, of course, with shots of him lying in an open coffin and his funeral. His mourners included James Coburn, Steve McQueen and Jim Kelly.

It's ironic to think that Lee, who was such a skilled martial artist, was turned down by the makers of the *Kung Fu* television series. This example of shortsighted decision-making is highlighted in the documentary, as is the story surrounding Lee's proposed project *The Silent Flute*. Lee was offered

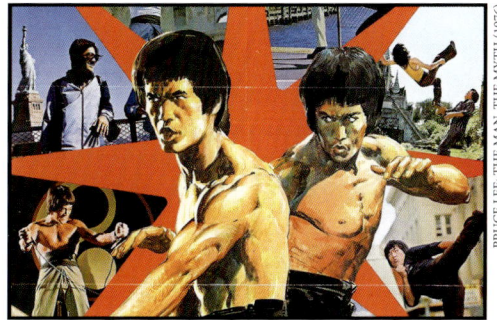

BRUCE LEE: THE MAN, THE MYTH (1976)

peanuts to do *Flute*, but the film wasn't actually made until after his untimely death, resulting in the casting of David (*Kung Fu*) Carradine in the lead role.

As is usually the case with films that delve into Bruce Lee's life and career, *Bruce Lee, The Legend* leaves you with so many "if only" thoughts, as you ponder what other great films and shows could have been made under different circumstances.

An interesting documentary. Bruce was the best!

BRUCE LEE: THE MAN, THE MYTH (1976)

Starring Bruce Li, David Chow, Little Unicorn, Mars, Lynda Hirst
Directed by Ng See-Yuen
Eternal Film Company

Bruce Li (Ho Tsung-Tao) plays the late martial arts movie star in this "done in good taste" biopic. It traces Bruce Lee's life from his arrival in the States to his untimely death in July 1973.

Some action-packed reconstructions make this by far the best of the Lee biopics, not that that's saying much! Interestingly, this took more money in its first run in certain territories than some of the actual Lee films did.

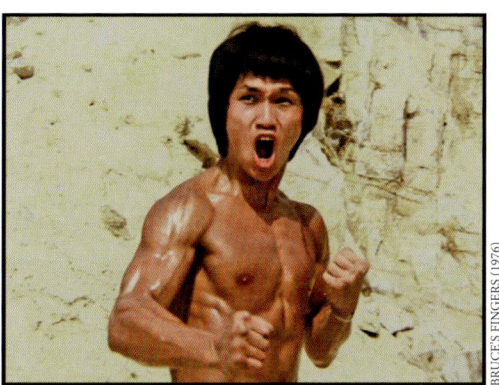

BRUCE'S FINGERS (1976)

BRUCE'S FINGERS (1976)

Starring Bruce Le, Lo Lieh, Chan Wai-Man, Nora Miao, Bolo Yeung, Cheung Nik
Directed by Joseph Kong
Produced by Joseph Kong, Lau En Tzi
Action by Cheng Kay Ying, Wong Hung
United Cine-Production Enterprises

Wong, a disciple of the late martial arts icon Bruce Lee, arrives in Hong Kong from the United States to inherit a manual of kung fu finger techniques bequeathed to him by his late master. Also after the book is a ruthless triad overlord, who will stop at nothing to get his prize. Aiding him in his unscrupulous quest are some formidable exponents of martial arts, including Bolo Yeung and Ching Tao.

This silly but above-average cash-in yarn features some good fight action and training scenes, plus a rare screen appearance from Bruce Lee's real-life friend and tutor, Wong Shun-Leung.

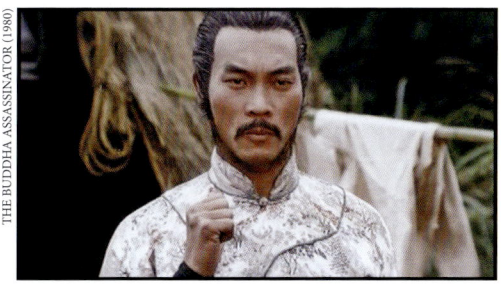

THE BUDDHA ASSASSINATOR (1980)

THE BUDDHA ASSASSINATOR (1980)

Starring Meng Hoi, Hwang Jang-Lee, Lung Fei, Chin Yuet-Sang
Directed by Tung Kan-Wu
Action by Corey Yuen, Chin Yuet-Sang
Fortuna Film Company/
Golden Princess Film Production limited

The Buddhist Fist is divided into two factions: the Buddha's Palm, which was preferred by the Mings, and the Buddhist Fist, which was favored by the unpopular Manchus. A prince (Hwang Jang-Lee) has used his Buddhist Fist expertise to destroy a great many Ming patriots. One day, when visiting a temple, he is ambushed by a group of Ming freedom fighters, but is saved by a naive kung fu fanatic called Shao (Hoi). The prince repays Shao by employing him as his personal guard and teaches him some forms of Buddhist Fist. Shao is, however, already a student of a Ming monk (Yuet-Sang). After accidentally killing his aunt on behalf of the prince, Shao decides to help the Ming patriots. Knowing that Shao is no match for the prince, the old monk teaches him the Five Element Buddha's Palm so that he can match the prince blow for blow. After defeating the best of the prince's men, the young avenger must face the might of the Buddhist Fist in an epic showdown, where only one will emerge victorious.

Fresh from the success of *Hell's Windstaff*, Meng Hoi and Hwang Jang-Lee deliver an ace, low-budget kung fu fest that has a fine final fight.

THE BUDDHIST FIST (1980)
Starring Tsui Siu-Ming, Yuen Shun-Yee,
Chen Shao-Peng, Lee Hoi-Sang
Directed by Yuen Woo-Ping, Tsui Siu-Ming
Produced by Yuen Woo-Ping
Action by Yuen Clan
Bang Bang Films/Peace Film Production Co

A Shaolin monk adopts two young boys and decides to bring them up differently. The older child, Ming (Siu-Ming), is brought up as an ordained monk within the monastery. The younger, Hsiang (Shun-Yee), is sent to the city where he is brought up by a kindly old man. But both boys are taught the classic and beautiful art of the Buddhist Fist. The cruelty of fate, however, means that the orphans, now young men, must confront one another after Ming is led astray by some bizarre villains and forced to commit various criminal acts.

Kung fu movie genius Yuen Woo-Ping combines his talents with child star and popular singer Tsui Siu-Ming for a picture that's filled with amazing, energetic, and beautifully choreographed fight scenes.

This kung fu gem is also known as *Secret of the Buddhist Fist*.

BUDO WING (1979)
Starring Ng Ming-Tsui, Hon Kwok-Choi, Jason Pai Piao,
Lee Hoi-Sang
Directed by Chin Ming, Lu Bai-Sheng
First Films Organisation

Far more attention is paid to the precision of fight choreography than to historical detail in this retelling of what is in essence the Wong Fei-Hung legend. The film concerns itself with Wing (Ming-Tsui), the town butcher, and his fishmonger friend, their training in kung fu under the Fei-Hung (portrayed by Pai Piao as a righteous sadist) and their confrontation with a gang of opium smugglers.

The leader is the ubiquitous white-haired villain played by Lee Hoi-Sang, who utilizes the Fist of the Hungry Tiger style to destroy his adversaries.

Comic relief is on hand to soften the impact of some of the more brutal scenes, and the plot moves along at a steady pace, serving as a means by which the cast members can display their impressive skills to good effect.

The film is also known as *Butcher Wing* and *Death Stroke*.

BURNING PARADISE (1994)
Starring Willie Chi, Carmen Lee, Wong Kam-Kong
Directed by Ringo Lam
Produced by Tsui Hark
DLO Films Production/Silver Medal Productions Ltd

After dominating the modern-day scene for the previous six years, Ringo Lam made an unexpected change to the kung fu genre. In this dark, morbid, and probably accurate account of the evil Red Lotus sect, we see legendary Shaolin heroes Fong Sai Yuk and Hung Shi Kwan battling their way through labyrinths of deadly mantraps, poisonous gases, lethal fighters, and bottomless pits in order to free hundreds of incarcerated Shaolin monks from the murky depths of this unholy temple, itself a major character of the film. Finally, the Shaolin duo must face their most difficult obstacle, the self-proclaimed demigod of the perverse order, the red lotus high priest.

Ringo Lam proves himself to be a master auteur yet again. The finished work is a unique blend of action and master storytelling, making this an instant classic. Definitely a major contribution to nineties Hong Kong action cinema.

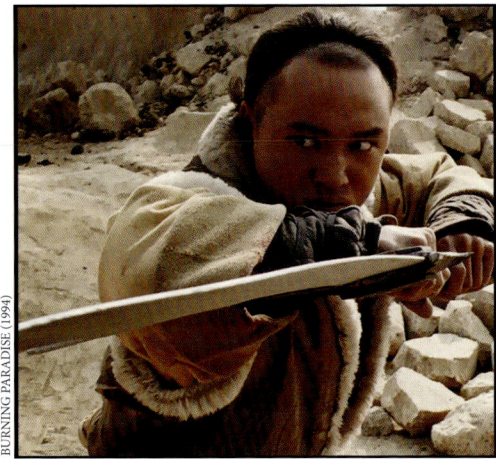

BURNING PARADISE (1994)

BUTTERFLY & SWORD (1993)

Starring Tony Leung Chiu-Wai, Donnie Yen,
Michelle Yeoh, Joey Wong, Elvis Tsui
Directed by Michael Mak
Produced by Chu Yen-Ping
Action by Ching Siu-Tung
Chang Hong Channel Film & Video

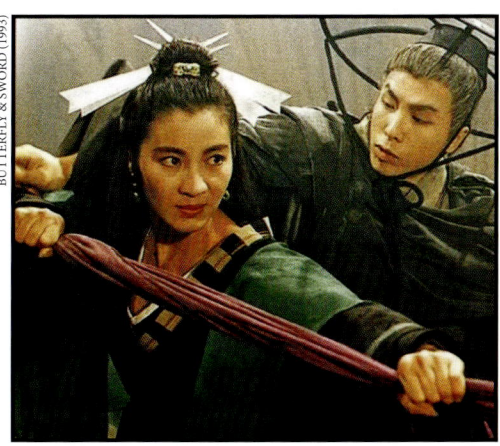

Michelle Yeoh plays Lady Ko, hard as nails but soft-centered head of the Happy Forest clan, a group of fighters who swore a blood oath of allegiance when children. Her sidekicks are po-faced swordsman Yip (Yen) and happy-go-lucky swordsman Meng (Leung), who longs to retreat from the martial world and live in pastoral bliss with girlfriend Butterfly (Wong). The clan are sent to secure a letter which is proof of a planned rebellion by kung fu warrior Suen Yuk Pa (Tsui).

The plot takes more twists and turns than a roller coaster, but the visuals are spectacular and the action choreography is supercharged. Classic moments from other movies are blatantly borrowed, and added to the mix are flying scythes, a human bow and arrow formation and a villain whose weapon owes more to Edward Scissorhands than any Chinese creation.

Lush locations, excellent performances and fine fighting make this mature swordplay movie a real winner.

CHALLENGE OF DEATH (1978)

Starring Don Wong Tao, Tan Tao-Liang, Chang Yi,
Chin Ming
Directed by Lee Tso-Nam
Action by Chin Ming
Yung Tai Film Company

In this worthy sequel to *The Hot, The Cool and The Vicious*, the cast and crew reunite for a fun, hard-hitting flick. Chang (Tao), a gambler and a playboy, has been arrested by lawman Lu (Tao-Liang) for meddling with underaged girls. We learn that this is just an excuse and, actually, Lu needs help to catch an unscrupulous arms dealer (Yi) from Mongolia, who is among, other things, a master of the extremely rare "Spider Fist." Chang and Lu are no match for the deadly spiderman alone and must combine their snake and dragon fist styles to quash the evil venom.

Wicked kicking from the cool Tan Tao-Liang, high-power punching from matinee idol Don Wong Tao, plus inventive use of ropes that aid Chang Yi's Spider Fist technique, all combine to make this a movie worth watching for the set piece fights.

Also known as *Dragon & Snake in the Spider's Web*.

THE CHALLENGER (1979)

Starring David Chiang, Tsui Siu-Keung, Lily Li,
Phillip Ko
Directed by Eric Tsang
Lo Wei Motion Picture Company

Chin (Siu-Keung) is searching for an evil kung fu expert, to right a wrong done to his wife. To find this elusive fellow he goes around challenging all the kung fu masters in the area. A chancer called Yu Kit (Chiang) aids this quest to find dastardly Pao Shen Chang (Ko) for his own reasons . . . namely money!

This is a fist-tastic flick, with David Chiang shining as a cash-obsessed, quick-witted, smart-mouthed fighter who, refreshingly, is willing to run away from a fight he knows he's going to lose. Phillip Ko almost steals the show, however, as the awesomely villainous fighting machine Pao, who gives our heroic duo a serious thrashing, forcing them to unite their skills to overcome him during the finale.

There's a completely unexpected sequence that's shot like a silent movie comedy, followed immediately by a far more serious flashback showing what really happened to Chin's wife. A violent encounter in a moodily lit derelict temple is worth looking out for, as is an entertaining staff battle, with Yu and Chin taking turns to scrap with multiple headscarf-wearing opponents, who swap their staffs for wooden rings mid-fight.

Chin's serious, vengeance-focused character is nicely contrasted against Yu's ever-smiling personality, the standard of choreography in the film is high, and the overall execution is flawless.

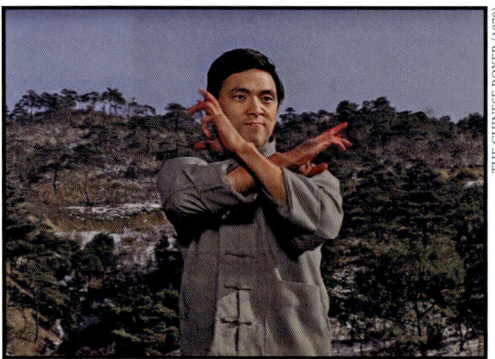

THE CHINESE BOXER (1970)

CHINATOWN KID (1977)
Starring Fu Sheng, Sun Chien, Phillip Kwok, Lo Meng,
Wang Lung-Wei, Shirley Yu
Directed by Chang Cheh
Produced by Run Run Shaw
Shaw Brothers

When Tan Tung (Sheng) runs afoul of a local triad boss (Lung-Wei), he escapes to San Francisco. Once there, his hot temper lands him in the middle of a gang war between White Dragon (Kwok) and Green Tiger (Meng), and he soon rises up within the criminal ranks, but he finally finds a conscience . . .

As the lead in this moral tale of a man redeeming himself for his past crimes, Fu Sheng brings forth an astonishing performance, handling his character's complexities with ease. A Shaw Brothers classic!

THE CHINESE BOXER (1970)
Starring Jimmy Wang Yu, Lo Lieh, Chao Hsiung,
Wang Ping, Fang Mien
Directed by Jimmy Wang Yu
Produced by Runme Shaw
Action by Tang Chia
Shaw Brothers

The imaginative genius of Wang Yu was allowed to blossom when he was given the greenlight to write, star and direct this highly entertaining kung fu flick.

This was the first time movie audiences had seen empty hand fighting and intense training sequences presented in such a way. Wang Yu plays Lei Ming, sworn to avenge the murder of his teacher by Japanese karate experts. To do so he must undergo months of intense training to master the deadly Iron Palm technique. In the snow-capped mountains of Korea, Wang Yu faces off with his deadly Japanese foes for a no-holds-barred death match.

Top-notch stuff.

THE CHINESE DRAGON (1973)
Starring Barry Chan, Meng Ting, Yi Yuan, Sun Yueh
Directed by Wu Chia-Chun
Lucky Star

Barry Chan plays a man who becomes involved with the boss of a small (and I do mean small) casino, leading to confrontations with the killer of his father. This guy is a nasty piece of work, who also stole the rights to the family gold mine, although most of this information is not revealed until near the end of the film.

A bike and car chase takes place that makes the stunt driving in *Kung-Fu Gangbusters* look good (and that's really saying something!) Another piece of vehicular action sees the hero bashing through the villain's gates on a teeny 50cc Honda bike, in a scene that, let's be honest, lacks impact.

With the director utilizing lots of Dutch angles, the film features two women having a kung fu punch-up in flared trouser suits, plus more scenes involving that lil' Honda motorbike, but the film does ratchet up a few notches on the enjoyability scale when a staff & spear fight takes place in the Japanese baddie's home.

The hero's bare hands, in the midst of one martial arts scrap, are suddenly inside white gloves and then, as the scuffle ends, he's not wearing the gloves any longer. Okay, maybe continuity isn't this movie's strong point.

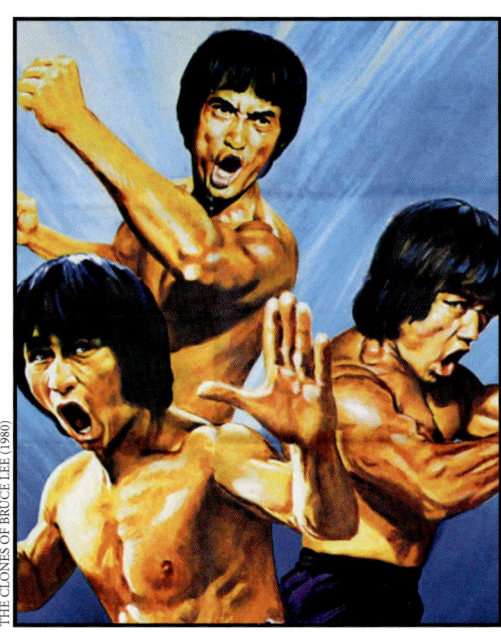

THE CLONES OF BRUCE LEE (1980)

CINEMA OF VENGEANCE (1994)

*Starring Bruce Lee (archive footage), Joe Lewis (self),
Jackie Chan (self), Sammo Hung (self)*
Directed by Toby Russell
Produced by George Tan
Vengeance Productions

This is more of a novice's guide to Hong Kong cinema,
rather than an in-depth study, but it is informative
and interesting. Stars like the legendary Wang Yu talk
about their careers and Bruce Li speaks of his success
portraying Bruce Lee in countless exploitation
films. Director Lau Kar-Leung explains how fight
choreography has changed from the Shaw Brothers
days to much faster-paced editing and why he
would like to see a return to the traditional method.

Sammo Hung and John Woo also talk, plus there
is behind-the-scenes footage from *City Hunter*
and *Hard Target*. Also featuring: Jackie Chan, Don
Wilson, Chow Yun-Fat, Simon Yam, Donnie Yen,
Sophia Crawford, Terence Chang, Yukari Oshima,
Cynthia Rothrock, Yuen Biao, Kirk Wong, Carter
Wong, and many, many more!

CLAN OF THE WHITE LOTUS (1980)

*Starring Gordon Liu, Lo Lieh, Kara Hui, Hsiao Hou,
Wilson Tong*
Directed by Lo Lieh
Produced by Run Run Shaw
Action by Lau Kar-Leung
Shaw Brothers

Essentially, this sort-of sequel to the Shaw Brothers
classic *Executioners from Shaolin* is kung fu cinema
at its most absurd and most fun.

Lo Lieh plays the dastardly white-eyebrowed
monk Pai Mei who, besides being able to achieve
weightlessness (so he simply floats away from his
attacker's blows), can also suck his testicles into his

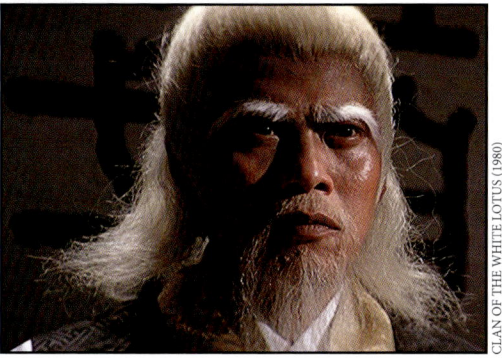

CLAN OF THE WHITE LOTUS (1980)

abdomen (a useful technique for cyclists!) Our hero,
played by Gordon Liu, receives a sound thrashing
from Pai Mei early on, but later masters the graceful
embroidery technique thanks to Kara Hui. Needless
to say, he finally gets his revenge when, after some
spectacular fight scenes, he attacks Pai Mei's "vital
spot." Ouch!

Also known as *Fists of the White Lotus*, this movie
is ninety-five minutes of pure bliss.

THE CLONES OF BRUCE LEE (1980)

*Starring Bruce Le, Dragon Lee, Bruce Lai, Bruce Thai,
John T. Benn*
Directed by Joseph Kong
Produced by Dick Randall
Action by Bruce Le
Filmline Enterprises/Wai Leng Film Company

This insane but enjoyable low-budget film sees
Professor Lucas (Benn) extract a sample of blood
from Bruce Lee's still warm corpse and create a series
of Bruce Lee clones. This new generation of Lees are
under the control of a government agency. Bruce Lee
number one is sent to smash a gold smuggling ring
while Lees two and three are sent to eliminate a mad
doctor in Bangkok. There they are joined by a fourth
Bruce. Eventually Lucas, corrupted by his power,
tries to use the Lee clones for his own evil ends . . .

Let's be honest, if nothing else, this flick has an
awesome title!

COME DRINK WITH ME (1966)

*Starring Cheng Pei-Pei, Yueh Hua, Chen Hung-Lieh,
Yang Chih-Ching*
Directed by King Hu
Shaw Brothers

When a group of vicious bandits raid a government
event, their mission is to abduct a high-ranking
official and exchange him for their imprisoned leader.
In response, the authorities decide to dispatch their
most renowned swordsman, Golden Swallow (played
by Cheng Pei-Pei), to take on the mission. When
the two groups eventually encounter each other
at an inn, the bandits discover Golden Swallow's
outstanding martial arts skills, realizing that their
task is not going to be easy, with Golden Swallow
determined to prevent them from succeeding in
their nefarious plans at all costs.

Come Drink with Me has definitely stood the test
of time. Beautifully filmed, with graceful action

scenes, it is regarded as "the film that started it all" in the wuxia genre.

King Hu's vision made this one of the most iconic films to come out of the Shaw Brothers stable. Despite her obvious beauty, Cheng Pei-Pei's character is portrayed as a man, which became quite a popular plot staple in the wuxia films that followed.

COWARD BASTARD (1980)

Starring Meng Yuen-Man, Yuen Wah, Yu Tsui-Ling, Wang Sha, Lin Hui-Huang, Wang Lung-Wei, Kuan Feng
Directed by Kuei Chih-Hung
Produced by Runme Shaw
Action by Hsu Hsia, Tsui Fat, Yuen Tak, Poon Kin-Kwan
Shaw Brothers

Ah Chi (Yuen-Man) works for Mr. Su (Sha) as a waiter in his restaurant. He is ill-treated by Mr. Su and bullied by rich eccentric customer Hung (Hui-Huang). Chi wants to get even and secretly acquires a unique martial arts technique from the chef Chang Piao (Wah).

Badly wounded by Chi, Hung wants revenge and consults his elders Hei Chin-Kang (Lung-Wei) and Tieh Chin-Kang (Feng). Chi falls into their hands shortly afterward and Hei and Tieh recognize his kung fu style as that of Chang Piao, who they themselves have been seeking vengeance on for some time. Chi escapes, runs into Chang Piao, and offers to assist him in fighting off the two criminals. Chang rejects Chi's offer and suggests, instead, that only one person, known as the Drunkard, can overcome them with his own particular martial technique. Chi rests in a derelict temple and, by coincidence, finds the Drunkard, who is on the point of being attacked by bandits . . .

Coward Bastard, by the director of such Shaw Brothers horror yarns as *The Killer Snakes, Hex, The*

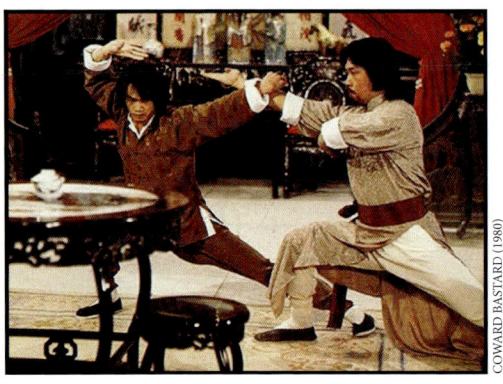

COWARD BASTARD (1980)

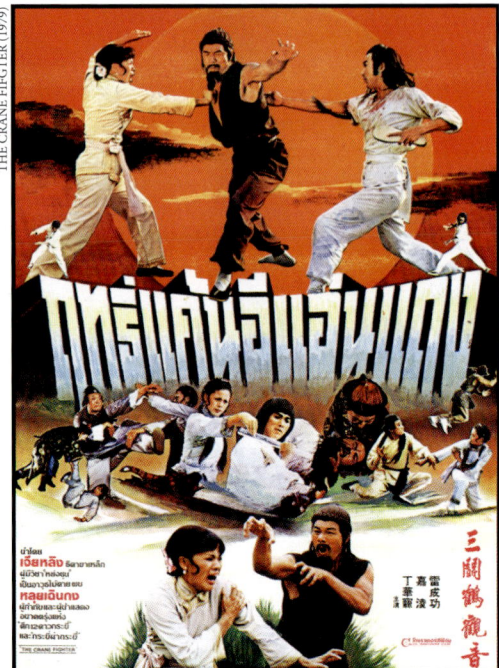

THE CRANE FIGTER (1979)

Boxer's Omen and *Corpse Mania*, has some fights that, although few and far between, are superbly performed by the operatic cast. However, far too much time is spent on tedious slapstick comedy routines, leaving the viewer robbed of true martial fulfillment.

THE CRANE FIGHTER (1979)

Starring Chia Ling, Raymond Liu, Chin Kang, Ting Hua-Chung
Directed and produced by Raymond Liu
Action by Raymond Liu
Success Film Production Company

In this ambitious production, Chin Kang plays Kao, a ruthless Manchu tyrant who brings about merciless destruction to the Shaolin movement. There is a sole survivor, named Liang, who sets up a bean curd stall in a small provincial town. His daughter (Ling), meanwhile, is studying crane fist against his wishes. An alliance follows with a cool cavalier (Liu), a formidable pugilist in his own right. The combination of the two martial artists worries the notorious Kao, who, along with his lackeys, storms the town in search of the deadly duo, destroying anything that gets in his way. Finally, Kao comes face-to-face with the pair of crane fighters . . .

During the latter part of the seventies, entrepreneur Raymond Liu produced, directed and starred in several movies. *The Crane Fighter* is by far the best of these, mainly due to Chia Ling's superb performance as the lovely but deadly heroine.

CRAZY GUY WITH SUPER KUNG FU (1978)

Starring Li Yi-Min, Peng Kang, Dean Shek,
Wei Ping-Ou, Mark Long Kuan-Wu
Directed by Hwang Lung
Yangtze Productions Ltd

In this tacky, tasteless Taiwanese kung fu comedy we follow Li Yi-Min and his two buddies, who are all failed street acrobats. Unable to keep jobs as waiters for more than a day or two, the unlikely trio return to performing in the streets, only to find themselves moved on by the local big boss (played by Peng Kang) and his mob. Fearing for their lives, the trio seek refuge with an old kung fu master, but he refuses to teach them unless they can produce a substantial amount of cash for him. They approach town headman Fu, who has put up a reward on the gang leader's head. The trio return once again to the kung fu master with the money and prepare for a wacky end fight with the big boss and his cronies.

A long, acrobatic end fight, plus a great cameo from Mark Long Kuan-Wu as a trilby-hatted avenger, are this lame piece of Taiwan schlock-fu's only redeeming features.

CRIPPLED AVENGERS (1978)

Starring Chen Kuan-Tai, Chiang Sheng, Lo Meng,
Philip Kwok, Lu Feng, Sun Chien
Directed by Chang Cheh
Shaw Brothers

When the Tien Nan Tigers murder Tu's wife and cut off his son's arms, Tu becomes a vindictive, cruel warlord. His son, now an adult and equipped with gauntlet-like iron arms, is just as spitefully vicious as Tu, leading to the father and his son inflicting petty punishments on several fighters, resulting in one being blinded, another losing his legs, a third man becoming deaf and mute, while a fourth warrior's head is constricted in a metal band until brain damage causes him to become childlike. After three years of training, these four disabled fighters set out to avenge what was done to them, which will mean taking on Tu's allies first.

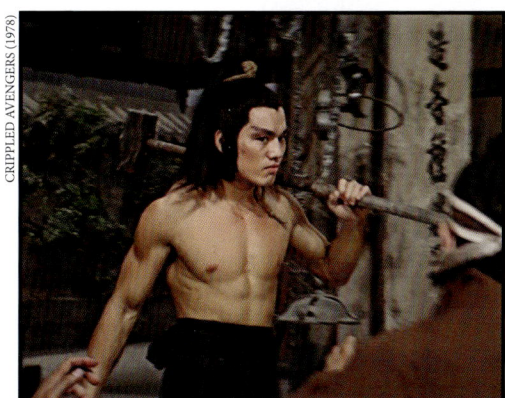

CRIPPLED AVENGERS (1978)

This is a widescreen, colorful, set-based Shaw Brothers revenge-action-drama, in which the brutal mutilations of Tu's wife and son in the opening scene trigger a cycle of bullying, crippling punishments and confrontations that culminate in a series of showdowns and killings.

Director Cheh delivers some memorable moments, including a silent sequence that effectively illustrates the soundless world one newly deafened character now dwells in, plus novel fights involving cymbal-shields, metal hoops, and large drums. The film, which features such exotic weapons as dart-firing (and extendable) metal hands, a bow that shoots ball bearings, and an iron-ball-on-chain, ends with a nifty three-against-one clash. Great stuff!

CROUCHING TIGER, HIDDEN DRAGON (2000)

Starring Chow Yun-Fat, Michelle Yeoh, Zhang Ziyi,
Cheng Pei-Pei, Chang Chen
Directed by Ang Lee
Columbia Pictures Film Production Asia/
China Film Co-Production Corporation

During the Qing dynasty, renowned swordsman Li Mu Bai (Yun-fat) plans to retire, but when his fabled sword, Green Destiny, is stolen, he is drawn into a dramatic conflict involving his friend Yu Shu Lien (Yeoh), the vengeful Jade Fox (Pei-Pei), masked thief and skilled fighter Jen (Ziyi), and her lover, the bandit Lo (Chen).

With wire-fu courtesy of Yuen Woo-Ping, a marvelous score by Tan Dun, stunning location shooting, great performances from the leads, and a script that neatly melds Western arthouse dramatics with Eastern-style philosophizing and action, *Crouching Tiger, Hidden Dragon* is a sumptuous delight for the eyes, ears and heart.

For diehard wuxia fans, of course, the wirework fighting is nothing new, but for general Western audiences unaware of this genre, this film's set pieces, including gravity-defying wall-climbing and gliding through the canopy of a bamboo forest, were something really novel and new, helping to make it a massive success in the West. Winning many awards, the film had a significant impact on the global film industry, helping to raise the profile of Hong Kong/Asian cinema, paving the way for other foreign-language films to gain acceptance and recognition.

CRYSTAL FIST (1979)
Starring Billy Chong, Yuen Siu-Tin, Chu Tiet-Wo, Hau Chiu-Sing, Corey Yuen, David Wu
Directed by Hua Shan
Action by Corey Yuen, Chin Yuet-Sang, Yuen Shun-Yee, Brandy Yuen
Eternal Film Company

Indonesian teen idol Willy Dohzan changed his name to Billy Chong and burst onto cinema screens in a series of martial arts movies. For many fans, *Crystal Fist* is regarded as his best.

Ah Wen, played by Billy Chong, witnesses the slaying of his father by Phoenix Eye Fist exponent Master Yen (Tiet-Wo). Many years later Ah Wen, now a full-fledged wanderer, gets a job working in the kitchen of a kung fu gym and it is here that he befriends an old cook (Siu-Tin). One day the gym is raided by Deaf Man and Blind Man, lackeys of Yen, who has a clan feud to settle with the old cook. Ah Wen sustains serious injury from the attackers, and the old cook takes pity on him, teaching him the Shadow Eagle Claw, a new technique designed to beat Yen and his flunkies. After rigorous training,

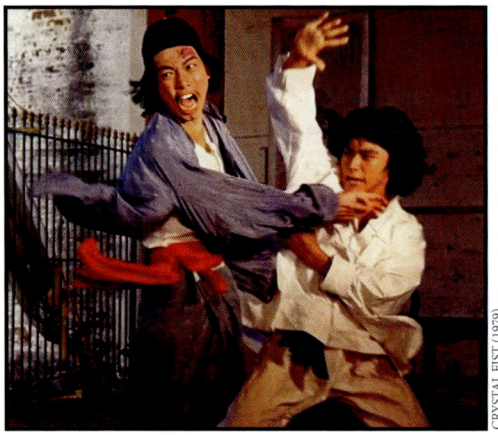

CRYSTAL FIST (1979)

Ah Wen is ready to confront the deadly Phoenix Eye Fist . . .

Also known as *Jade Claw*, this is the best of the Jackie Chan cash-in movies of the late seventies, brilliantly choreographed by Corey Yuen and the Yuen brothers. It made Billy Chong an overnight martial arts sensation, and the film still remains one of the all-time kung fu classics.

DAGGERS 8 (1980)
Starring Meng Yuen-Man, Lilly Li, Wilson Tong, Alan Chui Chung-San
Directed by Cheung Sum, Wilson Tong
Action by Wilson Tong
Honest Films Company

Baby-faced boxer Meng Yuen-Man stars in this bright and light martial arts showcase. Chi (Meng) is forbidden to study martial arts by his grandfather, because his brother was killed in a contest. But the young prodigal grows tired of studying books and takes leave of his comfortable home in search of a kung fu teacher. He finds three different masters and studies diligently under them but, as soon as his training is complete, the masters are mysteriously murdered by a hired killer (Wilson Tong) whose concealed eight daggers are his weapons of surprise and destruction. The enraged Chi sets out to avenge his three masters and discover the identity of the secret paymaster.

Some fine martial arts action, including "woman-style" kung fu courtesy of Lilly Li, makes this worth a viewing.

THE DAMNED (1977)
Starring Don Wong Tao, Angela Mao, Lo Lieh, Phillip Ko, Wang Hsieh, Wen Chiang-Lung
Directed by Kao Pao-Shu
Park Films

This compelling tale of morality, love, honor, and greed, told well on a low budget by ex-Shaw Brothers starlet Kao Pao-Shu, stars Don Wong Tao as Li, a poor but hardworking carriage driver who falls in love with a prostitute. Li is also a formidable fighter, and his skills catch the eye of a brigand called Sparrow (Chiang-Lung), who approaches him after a fight at an inn. Sparrow explains that he needs a cart driver for a bullion robbery. After much debate, Li accepts the job, needing the money to free his loved one from her life of vice, but, of course, matters become complicated and deadly . . .

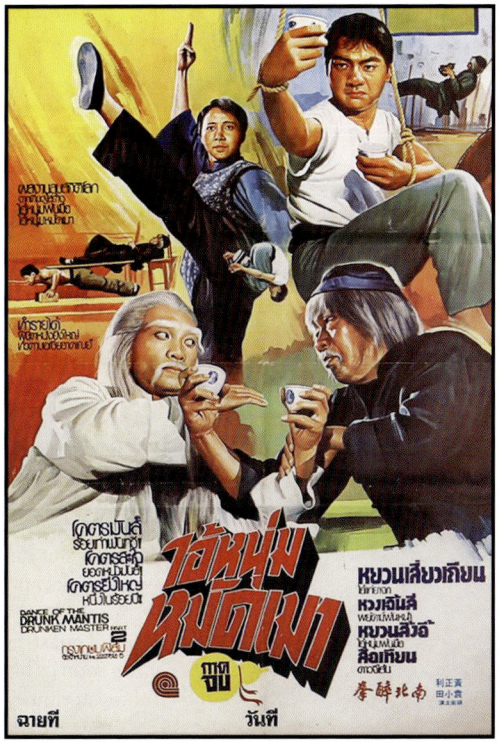

DANCE OF THE DRUNK MANTIS (1979)

Also known as *Bandits, Prostitutes and Silver*, *Battle of Shaolin* and *Snake in the Eagle's Shadow 3*, the film includes some novel weapons, with Angela Mao using spinning-blades footwear and Lo Lieh wielding a head-severing chain-device.

DANCE OF THE DRUNK MANTIS (1979)

Starring Yuen Shun-Yee, Yuen Siu-Tin, Hwang Jang-Lee, Linda Lin Ying, Corey Yuen, Yen Shi-Kwan
Directed by Yuen Woo-Ping
Produced by Ng See-Yuen
Seasonal Films

After many years of wandering, Sam Seed (Siu-Tin) returns home to find that his wife has adopted a son in his absence. Sam dislikes the lad, called Foggy (Shun-Yee), and tortures him both mentally and physically. Devastated, the boy runs away and takes a job at an inn, where he meets Rubber Legs (Jang-Lee) and his student (Yuen). He discovers that they are looking for Sam Seed and want to eliminate him, to make Rubber Legs' northern Drunk Mantis boxing style supreme. Foggy runs back to warn Sam Seed, who is then injured by Rubber Legs in a magnificent duel involving fighting

with cups. Sam sends Foggy to Sickness Teacher (Shi-Kwan) for herbs to cure him, and the doctor teaches Foggy the unconventional art of Sickness boxing. Now armed with this sick form of fighting, Foggy is ready for the Drunk Mantis and his student.

This spin-off sequel to *Drunken Master* boasts exceptional kung fu scrapping, with Yuen Woo-Ping's creation of new fighting gimmicks making it a must-see.

THE DAREDEVILS (1979)

Starring Philip Kwok, Lo Meng, Chiang Sheng, Wang Li, Lu Feng, Sun Chien
Directed by Chang Cheh
Produced by Run Run Shaw
Action by Robert Tai, Chiang Sheng, Philip Kwok, Lu Feng
Shaw Brothers

After General Yeng is murdered by Han (Li), an ambitious officer, Yeng's son Yang (Meng) sets out for vengeance. He fails and General Han kills him, so Yang's childhood friends, played by Philip Kwok, Chiang Sheng, Lu Feng and Sun Chien, unite and set in motion an elaborate plan to avenge their friend.

This is undoubtably one of the more complex of Chang Cheh's "Venoms" films, although there is no shortage of action. The fighting is great and the Venoms are awe-inspiring. The finale is a remarkably lengthy mix of brilliant kung fu and jaw-dropping acrobatics.

The movie is also known as *Magnificent Acrobats*, *Daredevils of Kung Fu*, *Shaolin Daredevils*, and several other titles.

THE DEADLY BREAKING SWORD (1979)

Starring Ti Lung, Fu Sheng, Shih Szu, Lily Li, Michael Chan Wai-Man, Ai Fei
Directed by Sun Chung
Produced by Run Run Shaw
Action by Tang Chia, Huang Pei-Chi
Shaw Brothers

There have been long swords, short blades, twin swords, flying swords and even circular ones. Then veteran Shaw Brothers director Sun Chung came out with the "deadly breaking sword." This sumptuous-looking film opens with eccentric swordsman Tuan (Lung) possessing a special sword blade which breaks a piece of itself into the body of the opponent, causing

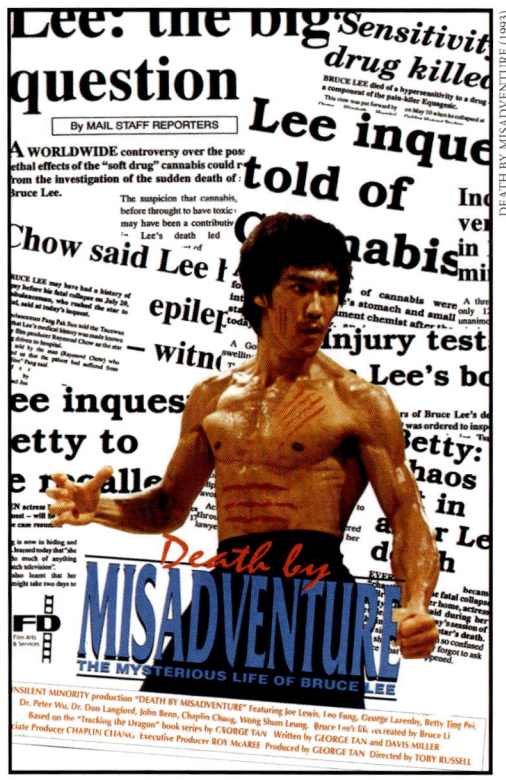

DEATH BY MISADVENTURE (1993)

This documentary contains rare and unseen material, including footage of early Bruce Lee films, Bruce practicing his Wing Chun form, Bruce on TV with a very young Brandon, rare footage of Bruce demonstrating his one-inch punch and doing forms at martial arts exhibitions, interviews with George Lazenby, who was waiting for Bruce with Raymond Chow on the night of his death, an interview with Betty Ting Pei, an exclusive interview with the doctor who examined Bruce just months before his death, plus a Canadian doctor who had also treated Bruce earlier and was called when his card was found in Bruce's wallet.

There are also interviews with Jhoon Rhee and Joe Lewis, and behind-the-scenes footage of Brandon on the set of *The Crow*. The documentary uses footage from Bruce Li movies to help reconstruct the last hours of Bruce's life, as we hear accurate and detailed accounts of what happened that night.

DEATH DUEL OF KUNG FU (1979)

Starring John Liu, Don Wong Tao, Han Ying,
Chen Yao-Lin, Chan Lung, Chung Fat
Directed by William Cheung Kei
Action by Chin Yuet-Sang, Meng Hoi
Kee Woo Film Co

The stars of *Secret Rivals* reunite in this action-packed film. Don Wong Tao and John Liu play a pair of Ming patriots who are trying to stop the Ching Army from crossing the Formosa Straits and attacking the remnants of the Ming troops residing in Formosa (Taiwan). Their plight is made difficult as news of their presence spreads to the capital. The emperor orders Lord Lan (Ying), a Manchu kung fu expert, along with several other top fighters, to bring the Ming patriots to justice.

What follows is nearly an hour of superb fight choreography set against the beautiful backdrop of South Korea. Great music and the introduction of super villain Han Ying as the Mantis Fist master from Manchuria make for a tremendous viewing experience.

untold hours of agony and suffering before the final death. Tuan becomes famous and gets himself an invite from top courtesan Liu (Szu) in a brothel, but she has ulterior motives. Meanwhile, Tuan's comrade Xiao Dao (Sheng) is manipulated by foxy casino owner Luo (Li) . . .

Ti Lung's humorous performance and the sword fighting skill displayed here make this an entertaining watch.

DEATH BY MISADVENTURE: THE MYSTERIOUS LIFE OF BRUCE LEE (1993)

Starring Brandon Lee (archive footage), Bruce Lee
(archive footage), Peter Wu (self), Ron Van Cleef (self),
Jim Kelly (self), Bruce Li (self), George Lazenby (self),
Don Langford (self)
Directed by Toby Russell
Produced by George Tan
Unsilent Minority Productions/Golden Media Group

Many, many years after the death of Bruce Lee, rumors are still rife as to what the events were during the last hours of his life and the cause of his death.

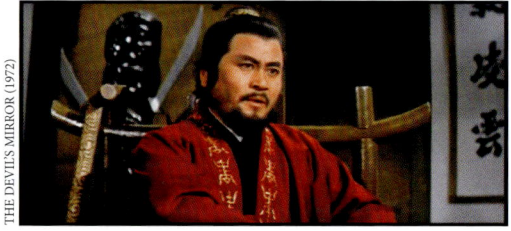

THE DEVIL'S MIRROR (1972)

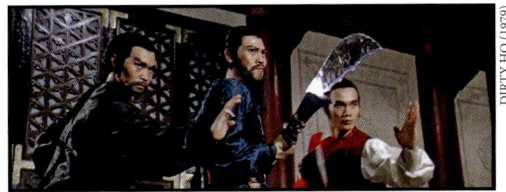

DIRTY HO (1979)

THE DEVIL'S MIRROR (1972)
Starring Shu Pei-Pei, Lau Dan, Li Chia-Chien,
Wang Hsieh, Ching Miao, Tung Lin
Directed by Sun Chung
Shaw Brothers

The sexy Jiuxuan Witch (Chia-Chien), leader of the Bloody Ghouls Clan, sets out to steal the Wind Magic Mirror and Thunder Magic Mirror: powerful artifacts that will enable her to access Emperor Wu's tomb and take the legendary Fish Intestines Sword. But the clans of the region have joined forces against her, so the Witch must sow seeds of division among them, forcing the heroic Wen Jianfeng (Dan) and the feisty Xiaofeng (Pei-Pei) to team up and thwart her schemes.

Sun Chung's first wuxia is hugely enjoyable, showcasing some well-choreographed sword fighting action! A standout sequence involves the assault on the Phoenix Tower at the Jixian Mansion, which sees black-clad, ninja-like warriors hacking and stabbing their way through all opposition to take the Wind Magic Mirror. The action is fluid and exciting and bloody.

This being a Shaw Brothers movie, there are some fine-looking sets, the best one being the luscious, large, fantastical Bloody Ghouls Clan chamber with its skull-themed back wall and an alcove for bewigged drummers.

Keeping the fantastical elements to the forefront, the Jiuxuan Witch can fly, there are fighters with infected, leprous faces caused by the forced ingestion of Corpse Worm Pills and we hear much talk concerning the power of the two combined magic mirrors, which will produce rays of cosmic power. Ultimately, these mirrors are never really wielded to devastating effect, merely being used to open Emperor Wu's tomb, but this is a minor quibble in a movie that's thoroughly enjoyable throughout, full of blood-splattered fights and absurdly great moments, like the scene in which the one-legged Jixian Chief (Hsieh) transfixes a double-dealing villain on his wooden peg leg, before revealing, of course, that he's only been pretending to be disabled all along.

DIRTY HO (1979)
Starring Wong Yue, Gordon Liu, Kara Wai, Lo Lieh
Directed by Lau Kar-Leung
Produced by Run Run Shaw
Action by Lau Kar-Leung
Shaw Brothers

A breakthrough film for prominent auteur and martial arts master Lau Kar-Leung. The story recounts a legend: the eleventh son of an emperor, while traveling incognito, is assisted by a rascal called Dirty Ho to return to the palace in time for the naming of the emperor's successor.

Dirty Ho humorously subverts the typical master-student yarn, with Lau Kar-Leung concentrating on some stunning fight choreography and the relationship between the two main characters, which has led to the movie being described as the first introspective kung fu movie.

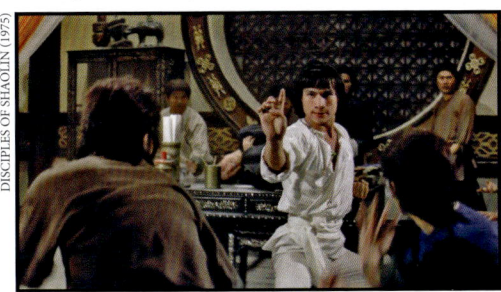

DISCIPLES OF SHAOLIN (1975)

DISCIPLES OF SHAOLIN (1975)
Starring Fu Sheng, Chi Kuan-Chun, Chiang Tao,
Fung Hark-On
Directed by Chang Cheh
Action by Lau Kar-Leung
Shaw Brothers/Chang's Film Company

Martial art superstars Fu Sheng and Chi Kuan-Chun have never been better than in this classic tale of greed and retribution. Fu Sheng plays Feng Yi, a naive young bumpkin arriving in the big city searching for his old friend and martial arts brother, who is employed in a local textile mill. Due to his martial arts prowess, Feng Yi gains fame and power overnight when he sends the lackeys of a rival boss packing. Unable to beat Feng Yi, the rival boss showers him with wealth and Feng Yi ends up becoming just another spoilt lackey. The boss eventually gains control of the mill, which he has long desired, Feng Yi realizes his mistake and has to fight back to regain his friends and his own self-respect . . . only to face his tragic destiny.

Directed with sensitivity, *Disciples of Shaolin* is one of Chang Cheh's most acclaimed movies. The story was adapted by Johnny To for the masterpiece *The Bare-footed Kid* (1993).

DRAGON DIES HARD (1975)

Starring Bruce Li, Lung Fei, Shan Mao, Wu Ho
Directed by Li Kuan-Chang
Produced by Liu Hsiao-Ling
Artist Productions

A martial arts teacher is shocked to hear of Bruce Lee's death and drowns his sorrows in drink. When asleep he has a bizarre dream in which the spirit of the deceased kung fu star urges him to investigate the circumstances surrounding his death. Acting upon the advice of a monk, the teacher prepares himself both physically and spiritually before following the trail, which leads to the boss of a powerful crime syndicate.

The exploitative plot allows for as many fight scenes as possible, which, although well-choreographed, occasionally suffer from the use of poor editing and atrocious camera angles.

Despite being made with less-than-noble intentions, the film is humorous (often unintentionally) and, while obviously not intended to be taken seriously, it does lend itself to conspiracy theories popular at the time of production. For this reason, it may be of interest, but it is trashy stuff! The movie is also known as *Golden Sun* and *Bruce Lee, We Miss You!*

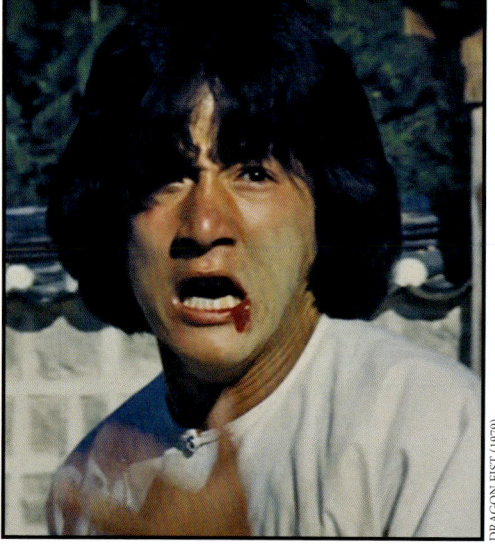

DRAGON FIST (1979)

DRAGON FIST (1979)

Starring Jackie Chan, Nora Miao, Yen Shi-Kwan,
Peng Kang, Hsu Hsia
Directed by Lo Wei
Produced by Lo Wei
Action by Jackie Chan
Lo Wei Motion Picture Company

Shot back-to-back with *Spiritual Kung Fu*, this serious offering has Jackie Chan playing the role of a dishonored student of the Dragon Fist Sect, bent on getting revenge for his teacher who was murdered by an uninvited challenger from the north. Jackie travels far and wide to seek out and settle the score with the northerner, only to find on his arrival that the man he hates is engaged in a bloody feud with local mobsters. Not only that, the man has also reformed and is powerless, after severing his own leg as compensation for his wrongdoing. Jackie is now caught in the middle of local infighting and his own emotions as he decides which way to turn.

Dragon Fist was a gamble that didn't pay off for Lo Wei, as audiences would not accept Jackie in such a serious and heavy role. The fight scenes, however, are some of the best Jackie has ever done, filled with speed, power and anger, leaving the audiences begging for more.

DRAGON INN (1967)

Starring Pai Ying, Shang-Kuan Ling-Feng,
Han Ying-Chieh, Shih Chun, Miao Tien
Directed by King Hu
Action by Han Ying-Chieh
Union Film Company

Master storyteller King Hu crafts an epic tale of patriotism and chivalry in this magnificent siege picture filled with intrigue and atmosphere. A condemned minister's children are to be exiled to Dragon Gate on the day of their father's execution. Although the distant and dusty town of Dragon Gate lies far away on the Chinese-Tibetan frontier, the powerful eunuch Tsao (Ying) fears that the children will become heroes and cause him unnecessary grief in the future. He sends a party of spies to Dragon Gate to kill them, but he hasn't counted on a band of patriots opposed to the eunuch's rule, who have taken the children into safe custody.

What follows is a lengthy siege of the famous Dragon Inn, with the patriots playing mind games with the eunuch's spies. Eventually the white-haired, all-powerful eunuch arrives at Dragon Gate to take care of the crisis himself, but a feisty young swordswoman (Ling-Feng) has other ideas as to how this should turn out.

Fantastic debut performances from Shang-Kuan Ling-Feng and Pai Ying, under the careful direction of King Hu, lift this interesting film into a league of its own.

DRAGON LORD (1982)
Starring Jackie Chan, Mars, Shirley Yim, Hwang In-Shik, Michael Chan Wai-Man
Directed by Jackie Chan
Produced by Leonard K.C. Ho, Raymond Chow
Action by Jackie Chan
Golden Harvest/Lo Wei Motion Picture Company/ Authority Films

Jackie Chan plays Dragon, the son of a wealthy man who spends his time chasing girls and taking part in local sporting events. One day, while out flying kites with his mates, he accidentally stumbles upon a band of villains planning to sell off the country's national treasure. After many dangerous and highly original encounters, Dragon brings the gang to justice.

Dragon Lord marked the birth of a new form of action comedy for Jackie. Gone were the flashy, intricate fight scenes of his earlier movies, replaced by mad stunts and quick-cut, straightforward punching

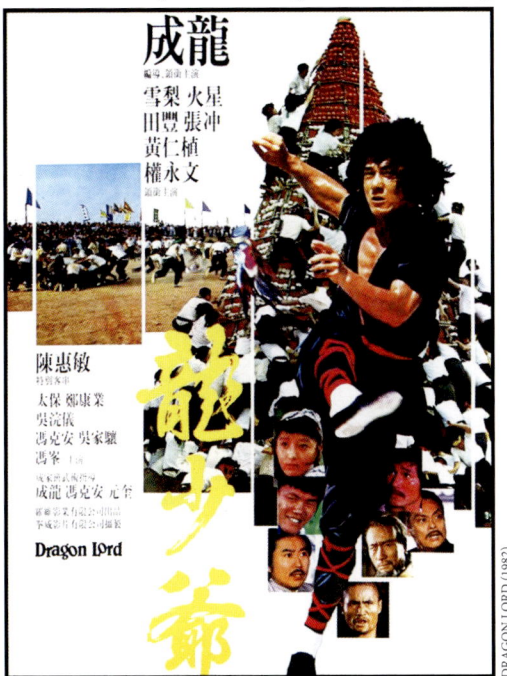

DRAGON LORD (1982)

and kicking: the new trademarks that would later make him a recognized talent all over the world.

At the time *Dragon Lord* held the world record for the most takes for any one shot. Over 1,000 takes were shot during the shuttlecock kick sequence!

THE DRAGON, THE HERO (1979)
Starring John Liu, Tino Wong, Phillip Ko, Dragon Lee, Bolo Yeung, David Wu
Directed by Godfrey Ho
Produced by Joseph Lai, Tomas Tang
Action by Tang Tak-Cheung
Asso Asia Films

The undisputed boss of cut-and-paste productions, Godfrey Ho, deviates from his usual filmmaking techniques and delivers some explosive, old-school martial arts mahem.

Wanderer John Liu and angry young man Tino Wong are direct descendants of the Strike Rock Fist masters who, once the best of friends, died the worst of enemies. Now the legacy of hate and revenge continues into the next generation, until the two feuding warriors discover that they have a mutual enemy in the form of a perverse kung fu master (Ko), who specializes in the dangerous art of Sun Ta. To quash this evil menace, the duo must forget the past and unite to fight as one solid rock.

This colorful and at times bizarre picture, featuring great performances from John Liu and Phillip Ko, is well worth a watch.

THE DRAGON, THE LIZARD AND THE BOXER (1977)
Starring Tan Tao-Liang, Meng Fei, Ramon Zamora, Edna Diaz
Directed by Lo Chi, Ngai Lai
Action by Chin Ming
Jowell Films

If you long for a high-class martial arts adventure . . . then this is not your film. It is not hard to imagine that this movie looked a lot better on paper, and its start is promising enough: Ting, a sailor, rushes from Hong Kong to Vietnam after the fall of Saigon in order to save his younger brother. At the same time, Raymond travels to Saigon to rescue the woman he plans to marry. Their overcrowded ship is sunk in a storm and various survivors (from priest to bank manager) are washed up on a desert island. A gang of villains just happens to have hidden their store of gold on the same island and a confrontation swiftly ensues . . . only it doesn't . . .

You have to wait for what seems like an eternity before anything truly interesting happens. The final ten minutes of this Hong Kong-Philippines co-production are worth waiting for, however, when Tan Tao-Liang goes into action under the expert direction of the white-haired Chin Ming.

DREADNAUGHT (1981)
Starring Yuen Biao, Yuen Shun-Yee, Kwan Tak-Hing,
Leung Kar-Yan, Phillip Ko, Lily Li
Directed by Yuen Woo-Ping
Produced by Raymond Chow
Action by Yuen Clan
Golden Harvest

Tiger (Shun-Yee) is an insane killer and when a group of cops corner him and kill his wife, he becomes even crazier. He links up with an old accomplice (Ko) and becomes obsessed with killing laundry boy Mousy (Biao). Luckily, Mousy has master Wong Fei-Hung (Tak-Hing) and student Foon (Kar-Yan) to help him, and they start hunting Tiger.

Though the movie could do with less of the silly Hong Kong–style humor, Yuen Woo-Ping directs with his customary excellence, and his choreography is never sharper, just check out the awesome lion dance sequence for proof. Yuen Biao turns in a great performance, making timidity an art form, while Kwan Tak-Hing is wonderful as the wise Wong. Look out for the "laundry-fu!"

DRUNKEN MASTER (1978)
Starring Jackie Chan, Yuen Siu-Tin, Hwang Jang-Lee,
Hsu Hsia, Linda Lin Ying
Directed by Yuen Woo-Ping
Produced by Ng See-Yuen
Action by Yuen Woo-Ping, Hsu Hsia
Seasonal Film Corporation/Golden Harvest

In a fresh twist to tradition, Chan portrays legendary folk hero Wong Fei Hung in a comic light. After disgracing the family name twice in one morning, Fei Hung's father decides that his mischievous son must be severely punished by sending him to his uncle Sam Seed, renowned for crippling his students. Fei Hung, realizing that this is a fate worse than death, flees the Wong house only to come face-to-face with Sam after a run-in with a group of angry waiters. After numerous escape attempts, Fei Hung becomes Sam's martial arts prisoner and the torture training

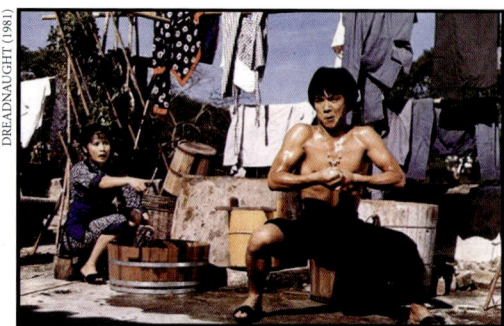

DREADNAUGHT (1981)

commences! In one last desperate attempt, Fei Hung finally manages to escape Sam's clutches. He then crosses paths with a hired assassin (Jang-Lee), who beats him senseless and humiliates him. Fei Hung, hungry for revenge, returns to old wino Sam Seed to improve his half-baked skills . . . and now he begins to learn in earnest.

This was both Jackie Chan and Yuen Woo-Ping's second film for Seasonal. It was a huge hit and outgrossed even *Snake in the Eagle's Shadow*, with a cool HK$8,000,000 in its first run. The novel, comic end fight with Chan staging the eight drunken immortals was a hit all over Asia.

Kung fu comedy was here to stay, and kung fu cinema had found a new king in Jackie Chan.

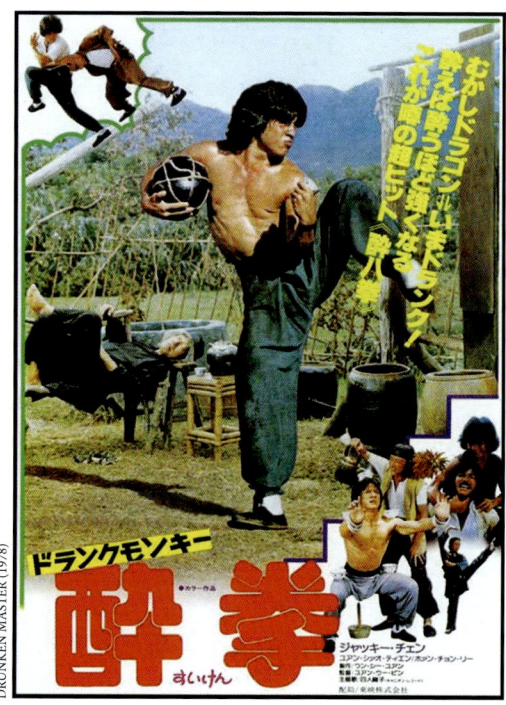

DRUNKEN MASTER (1978)

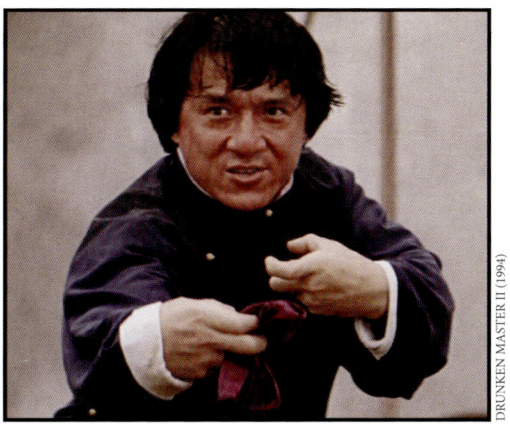

DRUNKEN MASTER II (1994)

DRUNKEN MASTER II (1994)
Starring Jackie Chan, Ti Lung, Anita Mui,
Lau Kar-Leung, Felix Wong, Ken Lo
Directed by Lau Kar-Leung, Jackie Chan
Action by Lau Kar-Leung, Jackie Chan
Golden Harvest/Hong Kong Stuntman Association

In *Drunken Master II* Jackie once more plays young Wong Fei Hung, who helps his father (Lung) out at his medical practice. He and his mother (Mui) have a close alliance: he covers for her gambling debts and she covers for his blunders with the patients. After several highly amusing encounters, the plot switches to a more serious note, when it is discovered that local gang bosses are using a foundry and its workers as a front to smuggle antiques out of China.

Although the plot is a little convoluted and the change of directors halfway through (when Lau Kar-Leung walked off set) obviously didn't help matters, Jackie Chan still manages to deliver the film of his career, turning it into a huge box office success on its Chinese New Year release.

The term "best film" is probably bandied about quite a lot in Hong Kong cinema, but this really is every kung fu film fan's dream and establishes Jackie once again as a martial arts movie genius. Considering Jackie was only a few months away from his fortieth birthday when this was completed, his stamina and physique are that of a man half his age, which is quite incredible when you consider the amount of physical punishment he had put himself through over the last couple of decades.

Also known as *The Legend of the Drunken Master*, one of the highlights of this film, of which there are many, is the end fight with Ken Lo, which is a jaw-dropping, edge-of-seat experience.

DRUNKEN MASTER III (1994)
Starring Andy Lau, Michele Reis, Adam Cheng, Simon
Yam, Willie Chi, Lau Kar-Leung, Gordon Liu
Directed by Lau Kar-Leung
Action by Lau Kar-Leung, Lau Kar-Yung,
Lai Shing-Kwong
Modern Films Distribution

After being dismissed by Jackie Chan during the shooting of *Drunken Master II*, Lau Kar-Leung set off for China to shoot his own version of the drunken legend.

Michele Reis plays Sam, a young maiden in desperate need to rendezvous with the Manchu general and would-be emperor Shi-Kai. If she presents him with a jade ring, he will make her his queen. Trying to prevent this is Yeung, a nationalist revolutionary, played by Andy Lau. After clashing with Manchu guards, Yeung and the wounded Sam find safety in the house of Wong Kei Ying (Cheng), a famous doctor and kung fu master. Not wanting the Manchu officers to discover the identity of the maiden, he pretends he has taken a young bride, much to the dislike of his young tearaway son, Wong Fei Hung (Chi). The young master is ordered by his father to escort the lady to a restaurant where he will be met by Yeung and more nationalist patriots who plan to overthrow the Manchu stronghold. Along the way, the couple run into a gay fencing expert (Yam) and a wine blender (Kar-Leung), who teaches Fei Hung the finer points of drunken boxing. Training complete, the trio set off for the city and the restaurant. But before they reach their destination, Sam breaks free and rushes to the court of Shi-Kai. She presents him with the ring and, delighted, he organizes a banquet. He is outraged, though, when he finds that the ring, which he has given her as an engagement ring, is broken in two. He summons his deadly ally, the high priest of the White Lotus Sect, giving orders for Sam to be sacrificed. Now it is up to Yeung, the blender, and the two Wongs to save the maiden from the Manchus, the White Lotus Sect and the three-section staff angels!

This is a film that could have been a classic, but it doesn't quite make it, spending far, far too much time on tedious slapstick and weedy attempts to develop the two main characters. What fighting we get is excellently shot, so it's a shame more time wasn't spent on the action rather than the daft plot. But be sure to watch out for the Gordon Liu versus Andy Lau confession box fight: its wild!

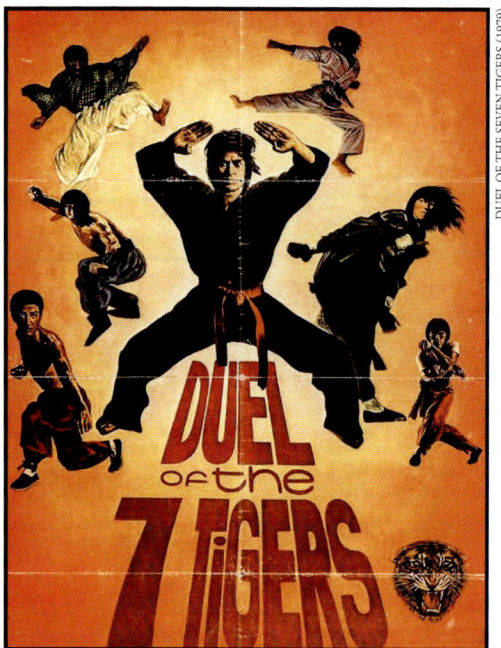

DUEL OF THE SEVEN TIGERS (1979)

area with the aid of a giant wheel. Eventually the killer catches up with Donnie, who uses the softly softly approach to tackle this most insane of foes.

More innovative action choreography from the Yuen brothers, plus a brilliant debut performance from Donnie Yen, means this is a flick that fu-fans shouldn't miss.

DUEL OF THE MASTERS (1983)
Starring Tsui Siu-Keung, Sonny Yue, Emily Chu,
Brandy Yuen, Fung Hark-On
Directed by Wilson Tong
Action by Wilson Tong and Yuen Clan
Dai Dai Film Company

This inferior *Miracle Fighters* cash-in sees Brandy Yuen and Fung Hark-On play two feuding disciples of a magical sect. Since childhood they have been trying to outsmart each other. Now they have adopted two young followers, Tsiu Siu-Keung and Sonny Yue, in the hope that this younger generation will carry on their endless childish squabble.

Despite the impressive cast list, this picture comes as a real disappointment. The miraculous Sonny Yue is given hardly any screen time and far too much of the story focuses on the comic antics of the elders. A magical rocking horse and the hard fighting fists of Tsiu Siu-Keung are the only redeeming qualities of this otherwise wasted outing.

DRUNKEN TAI CHI (1984)
Starring Donnie Yen, Yuen Cheung-Yan, Yuen Shun-Yee,
Yuen Yat-Chor, Don Wong Tao
Directed by Yuen Woo-Ping
Action by Yuen Clan
Peace Film Production Co

In 1983 American-born Donnie Yen stopped off in Hong Kong on his way back to the States after completing his Wu Shu studies in Beijing. During his brief visit to Hong Kong, he auditioned for director Yuen Woo-Ping, who was impressed by what Donnie had to offer . . . and Donnie was given the lead role in Yuen's next picture, *Drunken Tai Chi*.

When the son of a nobleman is turned into a basket case by Donnie Yen and his brother (Yat-Chor), the nobleman employs a sadistic killer (Shun-Yee) to do away with the boys. Donnie escapes the massacre but his brother and the grumpy old miser of a father are burnt to death in an almighty inferno caused by the killer. Donnie, now homeless, wanders the streets looking for scraps to eat and trying his best to stay clear of the mad assassin. Later, he helps a very peculiar old man (Cheung-Yan) in a fight with some street acrobats. The grateful old man takes him home to stay with him and his wife. The two grouchy old Taoists teach Donnie the gentle but deadly art of tai chi to prepare him for the maniac killer who is still patrolling the

DUEL OF THE SEVEN TIGERS (1979)
Starring Cliff Lok, Yeung Pan Pan, Phillip Ko,
Chen Yao-Lin
Directed by Yeung Kuen
Produced by Alex Guow
Action by Chan Siu-Pang
Goldig Film Company

Two Shaolin priests contest the vacant leadership of the temple. The loser of the combat leaves the order and flees to the distant island of Okinawa, where he creates his own fighting system, karate. Years later, his descendant (Ko) returns to China to avenge his master's shame. Martial turmoil erupts as all the masters of various Chinese systems are mortally wounded by this new form of empty hand combat. A famous fighter (Lok) is persuaded out of retirement to deal with the foreign menace. He is trained by six wounded masters in the hope that the unification of their respective styles—Choy Lee Fat, Dragon, Lama, Wing Chun, Monkey, and Hung (tiger and crane)—will be enough to defeat the karate fighter.

The Hong Kong Kung Fu Federation helped finance this lavish production, which features many real-life masters.

Also known as *Shadow of the Tigers* and *Return of the Scorpion*, this film, with its multiple fighting styles, is a must for martial art fans and action film buffs alike.

DUEL TO THE DEATH (1983)
Starring Tsui Siu-Keung, Damian Lau, Flora Cheung,
Paul Chang Chung, Cheng Mang-Ha
Directed by Ching Siu-Tung
Produced by Raymond Chow
Action by Ching Siu-Tung
Golden Harvest

In ancient China a duel is held every ten years between its own greatest swordsman and one from neighboring Japan.

This is an outstanding swordplay movie from Hong Kong New Wave director Ching Siu-Tung. It has a complex plot that leads up to the final duel, fought on a huge, mist-shrouded rock jutting out from the sea. Breathtaking set pieces include: a Chinese fighter attacked by dozens of ninjas swooping out of the night sky on bamboo kites, a Shaolin monk pursued by a twenty-foot-high ninja which explodes into myriad mini-ninjas, and a samurai attacked by his own master in a devilish disguise.

Hinting at what was to come, *Duel to the Death* reveals the kind of fantastical, kinetic visuals and highly creative action choreography and directional skills that Ching Siu-Tung would refine as he made a string of classics including the *A Chinese Ghost Story* trilogy and *Swordsman* movies.

DUEL WITH THE DEVILS (1977)
Starring Tan Tao-Liang, Angela Mao,
Lung Chun-Erh, Lung Fei
Directed by Lin Pai
Taam Jeung

Japanese imperialists invade China, leaving death and destruction in their bloody wake. One young man bitterly affected by the atrocities is Lin (Tao-Liang), whose father and son were killed by soldiers and his wife abducted as a general's concubine. Armed only with a yo-yo, Lin travels far and wide in search of his foes . . .

Even though "Flash Legs" Tan Tao-Liang was one of the producers, this film still fails to showcase his

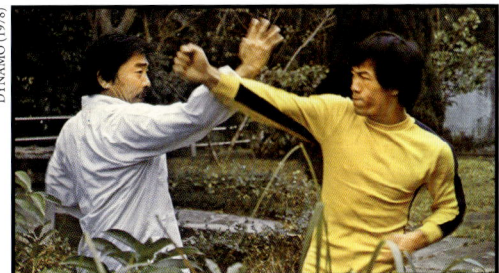

DYNAMO (1978)

kicking talents. However, the final sequence in a *Game of Death*-style pagoda is worthy of attention, as Flash Legs kicks, flips, whips, and yo-yos his way to a fiery finish.

DYNAMO (1978)
Starring Bruce Li, Ku Feng, Mary Hon, Lau Dan,
Chiang Tao
Directed by Hua Shan
Action by Yuen Cheung-Yan
Eternal Film Company

Lee (Li) is a happy-go-lucky taxi driver whose close resemblance to the late Bruce Lee is spotted by Mary, an advertising executive. Soon Lee finds himself sucked into the world of show business, but with a rival ad agency causing trouble, hiring fighters to attack our hero, Lee is going to have to train hard with his kung fu teacher (Feng) and fight back.

This is actually an above-average Bruceploitation film, from the director of *Crystal Fist*, *The Super Inframan* and *Kung Fu Zombie*.

EAGLE'S CLAW (1977)
Starring Chi Kuan-Chun, Don Wong Tao, Chang Yi,
Hwa Ling, Phillip Ko, Leung Kar-Yan
Directed by Lee Tso-Nam
Action by Chin Ming
Tai Seng Video Marketing

After being fatally wounded in a death duel by a Mantis Fist Master called Ma-Wu (Chang Yi), the Eagle Claw patriarch bequeaths his school to his second most senior student (Don Wong Tao). The senior student is enraged by the master's decision and storms off to join the Mantis Fist school. A blood feud rages between the two factions and, more importantly, the two brothers. After many confrontations and double crosses, the plot reaches its epic conclusion, with Eagle Claw vs Mantis Fist.

Lee Tso-Nam directs with flair, style, and his usual quick-paced storytelling. Chin Ming (aka Tommy

Lee), choreographer extraordinaire, orchestrates quite beautifully the seven Eagle Claw styles. The cast is first rate: the laconic Chi Kuan-Chun puts in one of his best performances ever, Don Wong Tao is at his matinee idol best, Phillip Ko and Leung Kar-Yan are added treats as the villain's hired help, but it is Chang Yi, as the Master of Mantis Fist, with his white hair and pointed boots, who really steals the show.

THE EAGLE'S KILLER (1979)
Starring John Cheung, Hwang Jang-Lee,
Cheng Kang-Yeh, Fan Mei-Sheng, Chiang Kam
Directed by William Cheung Kei
Action by Chin Ming
Sun Wah Film

Orphaned and homeless, Tai (Cheung) sets out to find a master to teach him kung fu. But every time he finds someone suitable to fill this role, things never quite work out. Until, that is, a beggar kung fu expert rescues Tai from a gang of local, if slightly inept, thugs and subsequently takes Tai under his ample wing and teaches him effective martial arts techniques. But things turn sour when Tai's teacher is killed by Lo (Jang-Lee), a hired assassin whom Tai had earlier asked to be his master. The scene is thus set for a climactic showdown between Tai and Lo.

Also known as *Kung Fu Maniac*, this is a so-so *Snake in the Eagle's Shadow* knockoff that has a lot of slapstick humor and, as a big plus point, features lethal bootman Hwang Jang-Lee playing the villain.

THE 8 DIAGRAM POLE FIGHTER (1984)
Starring Gordon Liu, Fu Sheng, Lily Li, Kara Wai,
Lau Kar-Leung, Wong Yue, Yeung Ching-Ching
Directed by Lau Kar-Leung
Produced by Mona Fong
Action by Lau Kar-Leung, Hsiao Hou, Lee King-Chu
Shaw Brothers

Set during the mid-Song dynasty, General Yang, along with his seven sons, are much praised and honored by the imperial court for their patriotism and martial arts skills. General Pan Mei is resentful of their success and conspires with the Tartars to trick the family into a siege and, at the same time, convinces the emperor that the warriors are really traitors. Hopelessly outnumbered, the Yangs suffer heavy casualties. Only the sixth son (Sheng) is able to return home after witnessing the massacre of his brothers and father. The fifth son, Wu-Lang (Lui),

has also survived, and is rescued by a hunter (Kar-Leung), who sacrifices his life to protect him from the Tartars. Wu-Lang is so grief stricken that he becomes a monk and learns the eight diagram pole technique, which he plans to use for his revenge.

This was Lau Kar-Leung's final film for Shaw Brothers, and it's one of his finest, though tragedy did strike midway through production, when Fu Sheng died in a car crash, which resulted in major script changes, entailing putting Kara Wai in the lead role alongside Gordon Liu.

The film has many memorable moments, with the superbly executed pole fight between Gordon Liu and Phillip Ko yet to be surpassed.

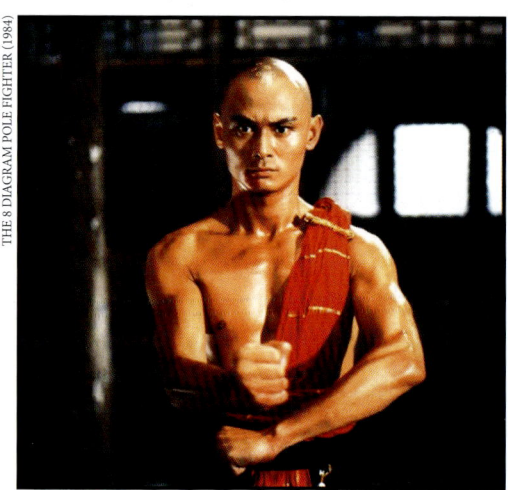

THE 8 DIAGRAM POLE FIGHTER (1984)

EIGHT ESCORTS (1980)
Starring Michael Chan Wai-Man, Tan Tao-Liang,
Hsu Feng, Lily Li, Wu Ma
Directed by Pao Hsueh-Li
Action by Chen Mu-Chuan
Yen Shing Film Company

Yet another tedious heist movie with a double cross plotline from big-budget Shaw Brothers director Pao Hsueh-Li. Eight escorts, each with his or her own lethal style of kung fu, embark on the journey of a lifetime when they are commissioned to guard the "Eight Rarities," a priceless treasure that no man can resist getting his greedy paws on.

Sounds exciting? Well, it isn't. *Eight Escorts* is long and wordy with the kung fu spread thinly through its dull plot. The best part of the film is the opening title sequence, where we see the escorts demonstrating their stuff in front of different colored backdrops.

THE 18 BRONZEMEN (1976)
Starring Carter Wong, Tien Peng, Chang Yi,
Polly Shang-Kuan Ling-Feng
Directed and produced by Joseph Kuo
Action by Chan Siu-Pang, Cliff Lok,
Huang Fei-Lung
Hong Hwa International Films

At the end of the Ching dynasty and during the time of the Manchurian invasion, a Ming general sends his son to Shaolin Temple to avoid being slaughtered. Eighteen years roll by, and the boy, now a fully grown man and master of the Shaolin martial arts, requests to leave the temple and help fight the Manchu invaders. To leave the sacred order he must first face a test of immense skill, courage and daring. Along with his classmate Wan (Wong) he must enter a labyrinth of martial arts mayhem. Before them lie corridors of traps and huge bronze men, some wielding clubs, staffs and swords, others dressed in huge armor-plated suits, who will destroy anything which crosses their path. Once through the dreaded chambers, the Shaolin disciples have the Shaolin crest of the dragon and tiger burnt into their forearms as they lift a huge bronze pot. Outside, our heroes meet up with more patriots and fight against tyranny.

Joseph Kuo hits the mark with this spellbinding big-budget offering, a great movie that spawned a sequel and several imitations.

ENTER THE DRAGON (1973)
Starring Bruce Lee, John Saxon, Jim Kelly, Shih Kien,
Angela Mao, Ahna Capri, Bob Wall, Bolo Yeung
Directed by Robert Clouse
Produced by Fred Weintraub, Raymond Chow
Action by Bruce Lee
Concord Productions/Golden Harvest/Warner Bros

Every ten years the notorious renegade monk and underworld bossman Mr. Han (Kien) holds a tournament of martial arts on his privately owned island. Lee (Bruce Lee) is approached by Braithwaite, a British intelligence operative, who wants to know more about Han's suspected drug-running operation. Asked to enter the tournament and act as Braithwaite's agent, Lee accepts the assignment, but, in fact, he has his own secret reason for doing this: his sister (Mao) was driven to her death by Han's right-hand man O'Hara (Wall). Lee arrives on the island, along with a host of international martial artists including supercool Williams (Kelly) and

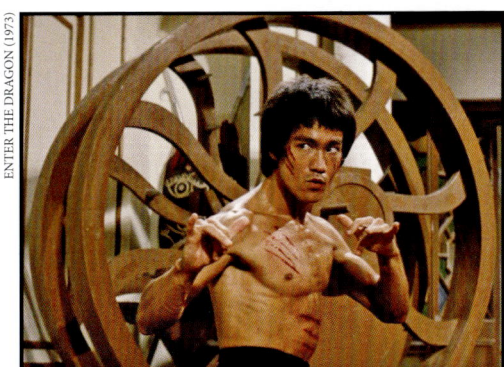

ENTER THE DRAGON (1973)

the laconic Roper (Saxon), ready to do whatever it takes to deal with Han and O'Hara . . .

What follows is a series of now-legendary sequences, including kung fu contests, deadly punishments meted out by muscled henchman Bolo (Yeung), Lee's astounding underground battle with Han's goon army, and an iconic showdown in a room of mirrors.

Still considered to be the greatest martial arts movie of all time, and certainly the most widely seen, *Enter the Dragon* is endlessly rewatchable, with a good screenplay, a superb score by Lalo Schifrin, Kelly, Saxon, and Kien on fine form, and, anchoring it all, a charismatic central performance by Bruce Lee. He is utterly electric, demanding the viewer's attention whenever he's on the screen.

Bob Wall, Angela Mao, and Bolo Yeung are a brilliant supporting cast, and the fighting is crisp, all adding up to a kung-fu-action-adventure classic: James Bond, Hong Kong style!

For those of you watching this movie for the umpteenth time, a good exercise to test your Hong Kong cinema knowledge is to see how many of Hong Kong's leading stars you can recognize in early roles: Jackie Chan, Sammo Hung, and Yuen Biao are the obvious ones, but many other youthful faces are hidden in the crowd scenes.

EXECUTIONERS FROM SHAOLIN (1977)
Starring Chen Kuan-Tai, Wong Yue, Lilly Li, Lo Lieh,
Cheng Kang-Yeh
Directed by Lau Kar-Leung
Produced by Runme Shaw
Action by Lau Kar-Leung
Shaw Brothers

Pai Mei (Lieh) kills the top Shaolin disciples while Manchu troops raze the temple to the ground. A survivor of the massacre is Hung, one of Shaolin's most formidable fighters. Hung travels the country posing as a member of an opera troupe, until he takes a bride, Yung-Chun (Li). The two lovebirds settle down and, before long, they are blessed with a son, Wen-Ting (Yue). With revenge still at the back of his mind, Hung practices the art of the Tiger Subduing style day and night, hoping to be able to defeat the white-eyebrowed priest Pai Mei one day. Twice he tries, and twice he fails. Now it is down to his crafty son Wen-Ting to bring down this most lethal of menaces.

A brilliant example of vintage Shaw Brothers, this film, helmed by connoisseur of martial arts mythology Lau Kar-Leung, boasts an awesome display of kung fu styles.

FASTER BLADE, POISONOUS DARTS (1982)

Starring Leung Kar-Yan, Mang Fei, Yang Chun-Chun, Phillip Ko, Chang Fu-Chien
Directed by Wang Yu
Yi Teng Motion Picture Company

Madam Liu is torn between love for her husband and the feelings she still has for her childhood sweetheart Show (Kar-Yan), who is a vagabond fighter currently being framed for the murders of various martial arts warriors by a mysterious gold-caped religious group, led by its vengeance-seeking chief.

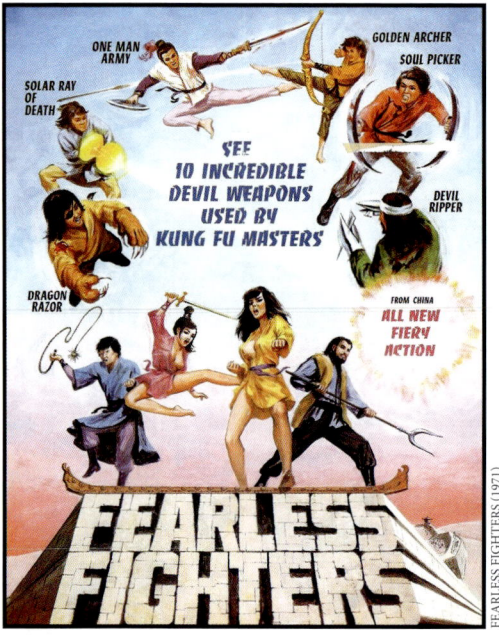

ONE MAN ARMY
GOLDEN ARCHER
SOUL PICKER
SOLAR RAY OF DEATH
DEVIL RIPPER
DRAGON RAZOR

SEE 10 INCREDIBLE DEVIL WEAPONS USED BY KUNG FU MASTERS

FROM CHINA ALL NEW FIERY ACTION

FEARLESS FIGHTERS

FEARLESS FIGHTERS (1971)

Also known as *Sheng Tiao Hero*, *The Great Massacre* and *Shaolin Hero*, this Taiwanese film presents us with some vigorous, pacy combat scenes, a dart-hurling villainess, many "thinking aloud" moments, music borrowed from *The Thing* (1982) and a unique team of blind fighters, who kidnap a bathing beauty by carrying her away while she's still in her bath! She responds by composing some romantic poetry!

This watchable wuxia culminates with Madame Liu taking her own life, and a one-against-two showdown, as the religious cult leader fights the combined forces of Liu's husband and vagabond hero Show.

FEARLESS FIGHTERS (1971)

Starring Yi Yuan, Chang Ching-Ching, Chen Hung-Lieh, Wu Min-Hsiung, Ma Chi
Directed by Wu Min-Hsiung
Sun Wah Motion Picture Company

Also known as *A Real Man*, this Taiwanese wuxia movie details the events that spin out of control after corrupt members of the Eagle Claw clan, led by To Pa (Min-Hsiung), rob a shipment of imperial gold from the Lightning Whipper (Chi), who gets mortally wounded. Virtuous Eagle Claw clan member Lei Peng (Yuan) takes hold of the loot and decides to give the gold back to the government. But evil To Pa frames Lei Peng, murders most of his family and retakes the gold. Now the stage is set for Lei Peng, the adult children of the dead Lightning Whipper, plus a white-clad female fighter called Lady Tieh, to go on a mission of vengeance.

Shot mainly in fairly forgettable countryside locations, with somewhat slapdash fight scenes, *Fearless Fighters* makes up for these shortcomings by piling on incident after incident. There are nonstop confrontations, as the heroes make their way toward To Pa's base of operations, taking on various villains, including top swordsman One Man Army and a despicable, long-haired dude called Soul Picker.

With characters who can jump super-high, lots of exotic weapons (such as the lightning whip, gloves with metal talons, and shiny disc-shields that cause explosions) and a protagonist who has an arm and a leg replaced with fake limbs that can be fired at opponents, the production certainly keeps you entertained.

One sequence that sticks in the mind takes place in a temple, where black-faced, vampire-fanged "statues" turn out to be yet more killers, who have been patiently waiting for the right moment to launch their attack on the heroes!

The English dubbed version adds to the fun by using the main theme and incidental music from US sci-fi TV series *The Invaders* (1967–1968) during fight scenes.

THE FEARLESS HYENA (1979)

Starring Jackie Chan, Yen Shi-Kwan, James Tien,
Li Kun, Dean Shek, Chen Hui-Lou
Directed by Jackie Chan
Action by Jackie Chan
Good Year movie Company

After the huge success of *Drunken Master*, Lo Wei gave Jackie Chan carte blanche on his next film. Jackie's directorial debut is an action-packed kung fu comedy filled with gimmickry. Jackie plays Lung, the scheming grandson of a rebel fighter and master of the Hsing Yi technique, played by James Tien. Lung, with his half-polished skills, takes on a job as a kung fu instructor in a bogus gym run by Li Kun. Lung's flair for showing off his secret techniques attracts the attention of the ruthless General Yen (Shi-Kwan), the archenemy of the Hsing Yi sect. Yen follows Lung to his grandfather and eliminates him. Lung, desperate for immediate revenge, is fortunately stopped by mysterious clan elder Unicorn (Hui-Lou). The elder teaches Lung the extremely rare Iron Wire technique, a unique form of combat that uses the human emotions of crying, joy, laughter and anger as its basis. After incredible no-holds-barred training, Lung is ready to face General Yen and his three deadly spearmen.

When released in 1979, this film, written by Lo Wei and Jackie Chan, was a great success and was the second-highest-grossing film of the year. Jackie

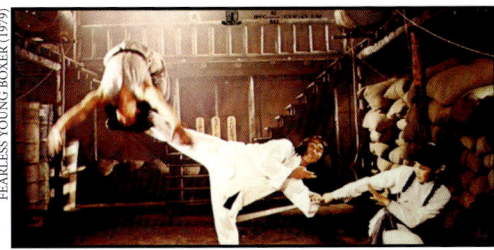

FEARLESS YOUNG BOXER (1979)

had proved himself a competent director as well as a box office superstar.

Incidentally, two out of the three spearmen (Peng Gang and Wang Chi-Sheng) were the same two who fought Jackie in *Snake and Crane Arts of Shaolin* (1978). Jackie, realizing that few people had seen that epic showdown, decided to revamp the sequence with added comic touches. The fight never loses its magic, no matter how many times you see it in either film.

FEARLESS YOUNG BOXER (1979)

Starring Peter Chang Chi-Lung, Casanova Wong,
Chia Kai, Chen Hui-Lou, Hwa Ling
Directed and produced by Jimmy Shaw
Action by Huang Kuo-Chu
Hong Kong Alpha Motion Pictures Co

This is an uninteresting story about a boy, Lung (Chi-Lung), who joins an acrobat troupe in the hope of improving his kung fu skills, so that he can defeat the merciless killer Pa Fong (Wong), who took his father's life in an old clan feud.

Although the story is a common one, the action is pretty original, with high-performance acrobatics, real knife fights, and the mighty kicks of Casanova Wong, which always leave you begging for more.

Also known as *The Avenging Boxing*, *Avenging Boxer* and *Method Man*.

THE FEMALE CHIVALRY (1975)

Starring Chia Ling, Barry Chan, Tsui Fu-Sheng,
Shan Mao
Directed by Yang Ching-Chen
Mei Hung Organization Production/
Kam Hoi Film Company

The second in a trilogy of films starring Taiwanese Opera beauty Chia Ling (aka Judy Lee) as undercover agent Iron Phoenix. On this outing she befriends a young knave in order to get close to his uncle, a big-time crime boss.

Sadly, sloppy directing and run-of-the-mill fighting sink this Taiwanese production.

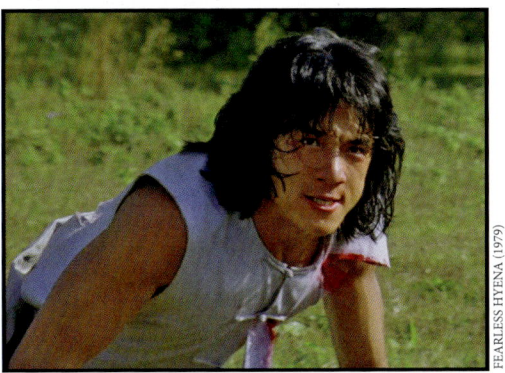

FEARLESS HYENA (1979)

FIST FROM SHAOLIN (1993)

Starring Wang Qun, Ji Chunhua, Sharon Kwok,
Gabriel Wong
Directed by Lau Kwok-Wai, Chang Hsin-Yen
Mei Ah Entertainment/Sil-Metropole Organization

In this *Once Upon a Time in China* cash-in, we see
Wong Fei Hung saving his fellow countrymen from
being branded, packed into wooden crates and
shipped overseas, where they will be sold as slaves.
Masterminding this sordid operation is an opium
smuggler and master of Eagle Claw, who gives the
fast-kicking, multi-flipping Wong Fei Hung a good
run for his money.

This film will come as a great sigh of relief for
those who like to see their action clearly and at a
realistic pace, rather than the quick-cut, speeded-
up wirework of other films in this genre. Good,
solid choreography and decent cinematography
turn this relatively low-budget production into an
enjoyable fight fest.

FIST OF FURY (1972)

Starring Bruce Lee, Nora Miao, Lo Wei, Li Kun,
Maria Yi, James Tien, Robert Baker
Directed by Lo Wei
Produced by Raymond Chow
Action by Han Ying-Chieh, Bruce Lee
Golden Harvest

Following the colossal success of *The Big Boss*, Bruce
Lee and Lo Wei were reunited for a second feature.
This time Lee was given more control over the fight
action, the end result being an awesome action-
packed fu-fest.

Set in Shanghai in the 1930s, the founder of the
Ching Wu kung fu school is reported to have
died from a sudden illness. Chen Zhen (Lee),
the master's most formidable student, attends the
funeral, becomes suspicious of the circumstances
surrounding his teacher's untimely death, and his
subsequent investigations draw him into a violent
and tragic adventure against Japanese antagonists.

When released, this magnificent production, which
deals with the sensitive issue of Japanese colonialism
while showcasing outstanding martial arts set pieces,
broke all box office records throughout Southeast
Asia, previously set by *The Big Boss*.

Bruce Lee's tour de force performance, overflowing
with charisma and martial arts genius, captivated
moviegoers worldwide.

Also known as *The Chinese Connection*.

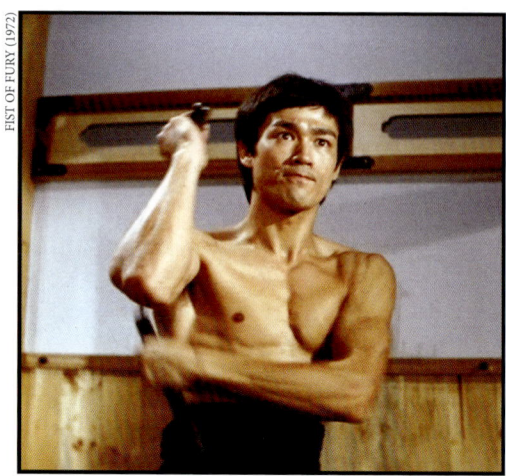

FIST OF FURY (1972)

FIST OF FURY II (1977)

Starring Bruce Li (Ho Chung-Tao), Lo Lieh, Tien Feng,
James Nam, Tsao Chien
Directed by Jimmy Shaw, Lee Tso-Nam
Produced by Jimmy Shaw
Alpha Motion Picture Company

After the tragic death of Chen Zhen, the morale of
the Ching Wu school plummets to an all-time low.
Constantly picked on by Japanese oppressors, they
become the mockery of Shanghai, until avenging
brother Chen Shen (Li) arrives to settle the score
with the Japanese and reestablish the glory of the
Ching Wu school.

A bravado performance from Li, plus a terrific
supporting cast and decent fight scenes, make this
exploitational venture one of the best of its kind.

Also known as *Chinese Connection 2* and *Fist of
Fury Part 2*.

FIST OF FURY III (1979)

Starring Bruce Li, Ku Feng, Tang Yen-Tsan, Fang Yeh
Directed by Tu Lu-Po
Shin Shin Film Enterprise

In this installment of the Ching Wu legacy, we see
Bruce Li as Chen Zhen's younger brother, who,
after avenging his bro's death, returns home to the
countryside to settle down and lead a peaceful life.
But a corrupt Japanese gang have other ideas and
involve Chen Shen in a series of crimes. Chen tries
desperately to stay clear of trouble, but, when his
mother is beaten to death by the ruthless Japanese
villains, his hands change into fists of fury, and the
bloodshed and human carnage finally commences.

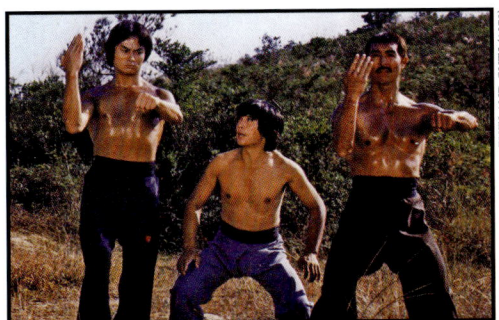

FISTS AND GUTS (1979)

on the trail are five former pupils, each an expert in a mystic reptilian style: The Centipede, The Snake, The Scorpion, The Lizard, and The Toad. Yang must determine who, if any, of these martial marvels he can trust to aid him in his task.

Chang Cheh directs this fiercely fought movie with style, verve and no little wit, complemented by some excellent choreography. Also going by the titles *The Five Venoms* and *The 5 Deadly Venoms*, this is a hugely enjoyable Shaw Brothers mystery kung fu yarn.

Also known as *Jeet Kune the Claws and the Supreme Kung Fu* and *Chinese Connection 3*, this ho-hum production's only real saving grace is an okay fight finale.

FISTS AND GUTS (1979)
Starring Gordon Liu, Lau Kar-Wing, Lo Lieh,
Lee Hoi-Sang
Directed by Lau Kar-Wing
Action by Lau Kar-Leung, Lau Kar-Wing
Liu Brothers Film Company

Lau Kar-Wing follows in the footsteps of his brother Lau Kar-Leung and goes behind the camera to direct this action-packed caper. Gordon Liu plays Ah San, a man apparently pursuing his former housekeeper, a master of disguise, in an effort to recover family heirlooms and riches. At least, that's the story he tells a couple of loveable rascals he persuades to help him in his quest. But, in truth, Ah San is the abbot of the Shaolin Temple, determined to recover valuable holy artifacts stolen by a Tibetan lama (Lieh).

Also known as *Fist and Guts*, the film has a supple mastery of martial arts technique, as well as a welcome brand of slapstick humor.

THE FIVE DEADLY VENOMS (1978)
Starring Chiang Sheng, Philip Kwok, Lo Meng, Lu Feng,
Wei Pai, Dick Wei
Directed by Chang Cheh
Produced by Runme Shaw
Action by Robert Tai, Leung Ting, Lu Feng
Shaw Brothers

The dying master of the esoteric Poison Clan sends his last pupil Yang out on a crucial mission. He must track down a retired colleague of his master and persuade him to donate the fortune he made from the clan to charity, before it can be put to criminal use. But Yang isn't alone in seeking these riches: also

FIVE ELEMENT NINJAS (1982)
Starring Cheng Tien-Chi, Lo Meng, Lung Tien-Hsiang,
Chu Ke, Chen Pei-Hi, Michael Chan Wai-Man
Directed by Chang Cheh
Produced by Mona Fong
Action by Cheng Tien-Chi, Chu Ke
Shaw Brothers

Chang Cheh sets an outrageous, over-the-top tale of vengeance, betrayal, and ambition against the backdrop of warring ninja clans.

When his school is destroyed and his colleagues are slaughtered by supreme ninja Cheng Yun and his five element ninjas, Hao sets out to take his revenge. But stopping the elemental ninjas (gold, wood, water, fire, and earth) is an awesome task.

So, Hao studies the secrets of the ninja under the guidance of his old teacher and, thus armed, Hao and three new cohorts challenge the five element ninjas in a climactic gore-tastic battle to the death.

Once again, Chang Cheh displays his unique talents for marshaling aggression, violence, and balletic, bloody grace within an inventive yarn. Also known as *Super Ninjas* and *Chinese Super Ninjas*, this film proves that fight flicks are always made better with the inclusion of ninjas. Fact.

FIVE SUPERFIGHTERS (1979)
Starring Wu Yuan-Chun, Austin Wai, Hou Chiu-Sing,
Kuan Feng, Leung Siu-Hung
Directed by Lo Mar
Shaw Brothers

China's kung fu teachers are gripped by fear as the Corrector of Bad Kung Fu (Feng) traverses the land, giving out his painful lessons. One such victim is an elderly Monkey Fist teacher (Chiu-Sing), who, after his beating, is left a drunken, demoralized wreck. His three students apparently decide to abandon their teacher. In reality, they leave to search out new skills needed to defeat the Corrector's kung fu, to win back their teacher's self-respect.

Another slice of Lo Mar lunacy, this is stuffed to capacity with serious martial artistry and acrobatics. Kuan Feng gets one of his best character roles as the insane Corrector, while still getting many chances to display his awesome weapons mastery. A classic.

THE FLAG OF IRON (1980)
Starring Philip Kwok, Lu Feng, Chiang Sheng,
Lung Tien-Hsiang, Wang Li
Directed by Chang Cheh
Produced by Run Run Shaw
Action by Lu Feng, Chiang Sheng
Shaw Brothers

Chang Cheh unleashed his "second team" (including Wang Li, Lu Feng, Chiang Sheng and Philip Kwok) on this tale of betrayal and vengeance. The Master of the respectable and honored Iron Flag clan is murdered by the mysterious Spearman, an assassin hired by the elder brother of the clan, Chow Fang. He takes over the clan and turns their energies toward immoral activity. However, in order to cement his position, Chow must kill the virtuous brother Lo (Kwok). To this end he hires the nefarious Ten Killers of the Underworld (including the Book Keeper, the Fortune Teller, and the Killer Butcher) to remove Lo, who somewhat surprisingly teams up with the Spearman in order to defeat these masters of death and exact suitable revenge.

What unfolds is a well-paced and vibrant battle of wits and weaponry between Chow on the one hand and the Lo/Spearman team up on the other, all of which is kept moving nicely under Chang Cheh's expert control.

Also known as *The Spearman of Death*.

THE FLASH LEGS (1977)
Starring Tan Tao-Liang, Lung Chun-Erh, Lo Lieh,
Lu Ti, Lung Fei, Kam Kong
Directed by Wu Ma
Produced by Kuan Shan
Wha Tai Motion Picture Co

When eight brutal thieves steal a priceless treasure, they hide it and engrave the location on a map, giving one part to each thief. A top police chief (Tao-Liang) goes undercover to track them down, one by one.

Tan Tao-Liang's kicking is stunning and, with so many fights, his martial artistry is fully displayed. The plot may not be up to much, but the fights

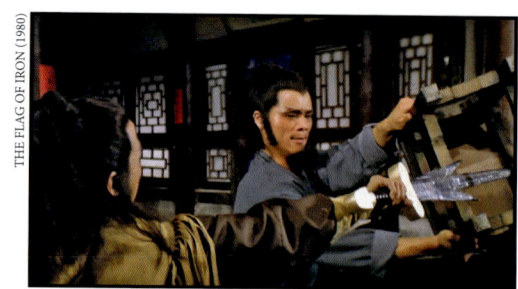

THE FLAG OF IRON (1980)

themselves are excellent and the finale with top thief Lo Lieh is a mega-nasty affair. It's bootwork heaven! The movie is also known as *Shaolin Deadly Kicks*.

FLYING DAGGER (1993)
Starring Tony Leung Ka-Fai, Jimmy Lin, Cheung Man,
Jacky Cheung, Maggie Cheung, Ng Man-Tat, Gloria Yip,
Pauline Chan
Directed by Chu Yen-Ping
Action by Ching Siu-Tung
Chang Hong Channel Film & Video

Chu Yen-Ping and Wong Jing (who scripted this) combine their insane talents to bring you yet another laugh-a-minute action spectacular.

Big Dagger (Leung) and Little Dagger (Lin) are a pair of bounty hunters commissioned by a warlord to bring him the head of Nine Tail Fox (Jacky Cheung), who reportedly killed his daughter and forty servants. Also after the same bounty are Big Bewitchment (Man) and Little Bewitchment (Yip). Soon the double double acts catch up with the Fox and, after many hilarious escapades, finally bag him up. The Fox's mate, Flying Cat (Maggie Cheung), is none too pleased by the proceedings and, with her posse of kittens, is hot on their tails. The respective parties meet at a rather peculiar inn run by a sex pervert (Ng Man-Tat). Here they discover that they have been fooled by the warlord, who is working in cahoots with Japanese pirates. Together our hovering heroes join forces and descend upon the warlord's stronghold.

It's all pretty silly, but it's a fun, entertaining romp.

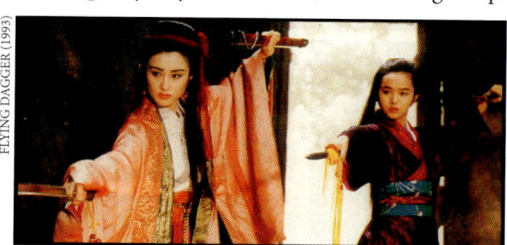

FLYING DAGGER (1993)

FONG SAI YUK (1993)

Starring Jet Li, Sibelle Hu, Josephine Siao,
Michele Reis, Chen Sung-Yung, Vincent Zhao
Directed by Corey Yuen
Produced by Jet Li
Action by Corey Yuen, Yuen Tak
Eastern Productions

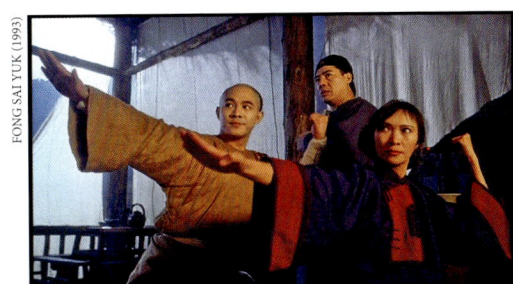

FONG SAI YUK (1993)

Also known as *The Legend*, this film reinvents the Fong Sai Yuk story in much the same way as Jet Li and Tsui Hark reworked the Wong Fei Hung story. Liberties with the legend are really taken when boxer Tiger Lui (Sung-Yung) issues a challenge. Rather than being a straight fight challenge, here contenders must fight Tiger's wife, Siu Wan (Hu), to win their daughter's hand. Fong Sai Yuk accepts the challenge and defeats Siu Wan, but then throws the fight when he mistakes an unattractive maid for the daughter. Wishing to prove the supremacy of the family style of kung fu, Fong Sai Yuk's mother then enters the competition, disguised as a man . . .

Jet Li portrays Fong Sai Yuk as a mischievous tearaway, making full use of his high-kicking Wu Shu style, rather than the historically accurate Southern Shaolin style. While not traditional then, this is a brilliant action movie with top-notch comedy. The choreography is superb, employing hand-to-hand techniques as well as wire stunts and kicks. But don't call it a classical kung fu film: it's a classic in an entirely different sense of the word.

FONG SAI YUK 2 (1993)

Starring Jet Li, Adam Cheng, Josephine Siao,
Michele Reis, Ji Chunhua, Corey Yuen
Directed by Corey Yuen
Produced by Jet Li
Action by Corey Yuen, Yuen Tak
Eastern Productions

Another dose of lighthearted kung fu comedy with the legendary hero being portrayed as more of a happy-go-lucky romantic and less as the hot-tempered patriot he was in reality. This time Fong Sai Yuk is sent by the sect chief to woo the emperor's daughter in order to obtain the Sacred Box, which contains important information regarding a claim for power. When Fong Sai Yuk's wife and mother hear that another woman is involved, they set out to stop him. While Fong must cope with the nagging pair and his complex mission, he must also face up to the problem of a crazed kung fu fighting rebel who, while supposedly working with the sect, has great ambitions for himself.

Packed with intense wire-aided action and much effective humor, this film, also known as *The Legend II*, is recommended, despite the fact that the final confrontation is somewhat disappointing in the light of the many more impressive and atmospheric fights featured elsewhere in the film.

THE FOUR INVINCIBLES (1979)

Starring Hon Kwok-Choi, Ku Feng, Cheng
Kei-Ying, Sung Gam-Shing
Directed by Hua Jen
Produced by Tsai Wen Hua
Action by Hon Kwok-Choi, Sung Gam-Shing
Yat Sun Productions

A struggle for leadership within the Lung clan erupts when the old master dies. A notorious, ruthless student, Chen-Hai (Kei-Ying), stops at nothing to gain control. He cripples his only real threat, Lei (Feng), and subsequently takes over the clan with his demonic Devil's Palm technique. Now dejected, Lei wanders the countryside, seeing life through a bottle, until he befriends three disabled men. Reluctant at first to seriously accept Lei's teaching, they finally join forces. The Devil's Palm must now combat the bizarre, zombielike Four Invincibles technique . . .

The portrayal of the disabilities is certainly very much of the time in this cheap knockoff of *Crippled Avengers*, though enjoyment can certainly be gleaned by watching some decent fighting and trying not to

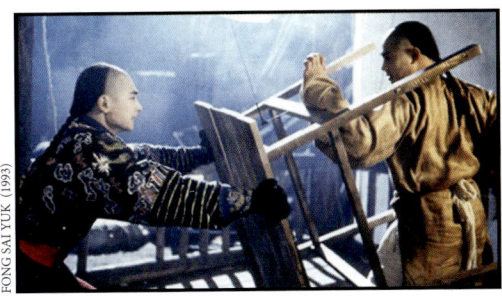

FONG SAI YUK (1993)

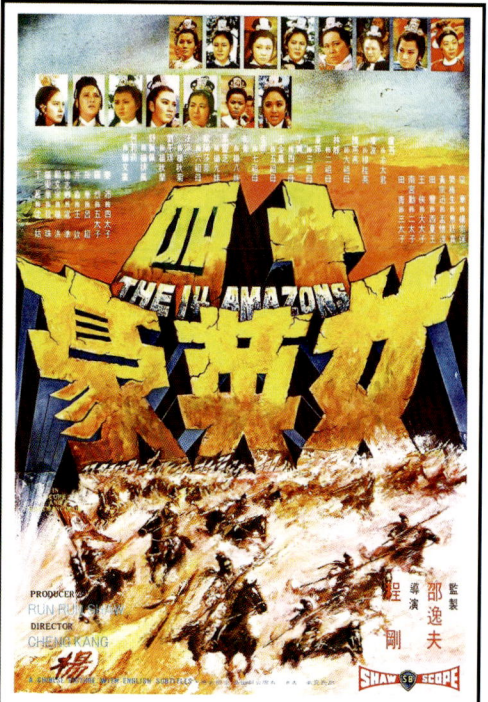

THE 14 AMAZONS (1972)

The costumes and sets are wonderful and it's great to see the actresses holding their own in the action. *The 14 Amazons* was a box office smash and won a clutch of awards, including Best Supporting Actress for Lisa Lu at the 11th Golden Horse Awards, the Best Director gong for Cheng Kang at the same awards ceremony, and Outstanding Female Lead Performance for Lily Ho at the 19th Asian Film Festival.

GAME OF DEATH (1978)
Starring Bruce Lee, Gig Young, Dean Jagger, Colleen Camp, Hugh O'Brien, Dan Inosanto, Kareem Abdul-Jabbar, Bob Wall, Ji Han-Jae, Tong Lung, Yuen Biao
Directed by Robert Clouse
Produced by Raymond Chow
Action by Bruce Lee, Sammo Hung
Concord Productions/Golden Harvest/Columbia Pictures

Years after it first went into production, *Game of Death* finally found its way to its audience in 1978. As Bruce died during the making of the movie, only a small part of it actually features him, with his character being played by stand-ins. The story follows Billy Lo, played by Bruce Lee (and stand-ins, including Tong Lung), who is shot for refusing to join an international management syndicate. Billy feigns his own death as an opportunity to hunt down the gang in secret, with a buildup to the finale in which the real Bruce Lee does combat with a different master of martial arts on each floor of what should have been a pagoda.

The story bears very little resemblance to the original concept and one would probably be better off watching *The Silent Flute* in order to grasp Bruce's philosophy. The film's international cast and decent budget did little to supress Lee fans' disappointment in the final production. It can be very annoying viewing such things as the infamous photo-of-Bruce's-face-taped-on-the-mirror moment or the

notice "one-armed" Sung Gam-Shing's arm, which is tucked into his shirt, while also marveling at villain Cheng Kei-Ying's impressive sideburns.

THE 14 AMAZONS (1972)
Starring Ivy Ling Po, Lisa Lu, Lily Ho, Tien Feng, Yueh Hua, Li Ching, Lo Lieh
Directed by Cheng Kang
Shaw Brothers

This Shaw Brothers film follows several generations of a family as they seek revenge for the death of their patriarch, who was killed while defending the Chinese border against Mongolian attackers. The family includes the widow Mu Kuei Ying and her great-granddaughter, among others. Despite facing much danger and starvation, the family heads to the front, disobeying official orders.

Okay, the plot is somewhat confusing, with a big cast of characters who are sometimes difficult to differentiate from each other. It doesn't help that the male heir, Yang Wen Kuan, is played by a female actress too, Lily Ho. However, the film is pretty damn entertaining and is quite a spectacle, with battle sequences that are impressively handled by director Cheng Kang.

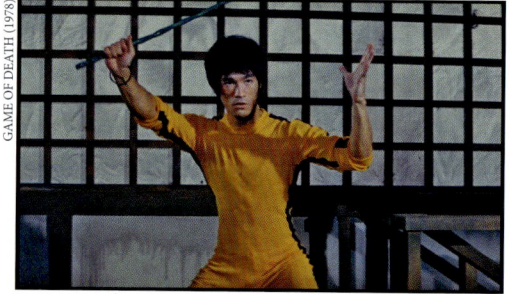

GAME OF DEATH (1978)

bad-taste use of real footage of Bruce Lee's corpse in his open casket. It's doubly frustrating because it is obvious that this movie could have been one of Bruce Lee's finest pieces of work if it'd been completed by Bruce: the eleven or so minutes of footage in which Lee himself features demonstrates this. There's a unique nunchaku battle with Dan Inosanto and an amazing David and Goliath fight, where Lee takes on towering student Kareem Abdul-Jabbar. Wonderful stuff indeed. Oh, and it must be admitted that the title sequence, showing footage from Lee's previous films, accompanied by a stirring John Barry theme tune, is really bloody awesome.

A film that actually gets better with age somehow.

GOLD CONSTABLES (1978)
Starring Carter Wong, Lo Lieh, Nancy Yen, James Tien
Directed by Wang Chung
Man Nien Film Company

Intrigue abounds as disparate characters become entangled in the mystery that surrounds stolen government gold. Who are the criminals out to get the loot? Who are the constables secretly working for the government? Who is here looking for revenge?

Predating *The Dark Knight* (2008) by thirty years, *Gold Constables* begins in a similar fashion, showing a robbery in which criminals kill one another in a series of betrayals. The story then becomes a slow burner, which really pays off as you get to know the characters well before they reveal their true identities and take part in a very enjoyable, action-packed finale, where the skirmishes are nonstop! This extended resolution is full of great fight choreography, as waves of different foes, including tonfa-wielding dudes and fighters in gold masks, take on the heroes.

Crisp, nimble clashes involve swords, spears and staffs, music from *Billion Dollar Brain* (1967) works

well as part of the soundtrack, a big boss villain uses razor-toothed shields, a strange bell-shaped lantern weapon at a monastery fires multiple darts at intruders and, well, the cool combat at the end just goes on and on, making this a wonderful wuxia to watch!

THE GOLD CONNECTION (1979)
Starring Ho Tsung-Tao, Hon Kwok-Choi, Chiu Chi-Ling, Phillip Ko, Shan Kuai
Directed by Kuei Chih-Hung
The Eternal Film Company

Also known as *The Iron Dragon Strikes Back*, this is a thrilling action movie that's vastly underappreciated. The film features Ho Tsung-Tao, popularly known as Bruce Li in the Bruceploitation genre, as Ah Wai, one of four friends who discover a stash of gold during a scuba diving trip. Realizing that the gold might belong to smugglers, they return it to the ocean depths. However, one of them is unable to resist temptation and retrieves the gold, putting a target on his back and everyone associated with him.

The movie's choreography is pretty impressive and the performances are top-notch. Shan Kuai, who played the hunchback in *The Buddhist Fist*, leads a group of henchmen in the first half, resulting in an unforgettable brawl in a quarry. The action scenes mix styles and tones, ranging from frantic and messy to fights featuring shapes and weapons, and the camerawork is lively and often handheld.

The film's narrative takes some unexpected turns, and Phillip Ko's entrance is completely out of left field. The cuts in some scenes may be abrupt and confusing, but they don't detract from the movie's overall excellence. Worth seeking out.

GOLDEN MASK (1977)
Starring Chi Kuan-Chun, Wang Kuan-Hsiung, Tung Wei, Lung Chun-Erh, Chia Kai
Directed by Ting Chung
Good Friends Motion Picture Co/
Great China Film Company

An assassin is hired by the mysterious Golden Mask to kill a man, who turns out to be the killer's own brother. The protagonist (Kuan-Chun), who is certainly not much for small talk, carries his dead brother's lute around with him as he sets out to hunt down Golden Mask. Meanwhile, it is announced that Eagle House, owned by a former bandit, is going

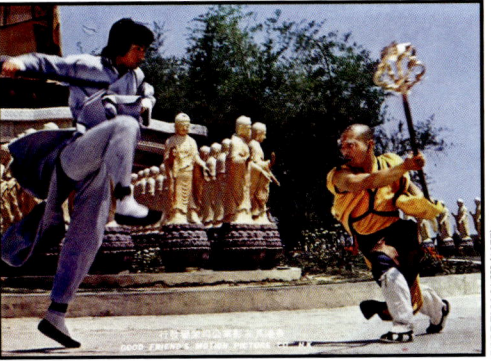

GOLDEN MASK (1977)

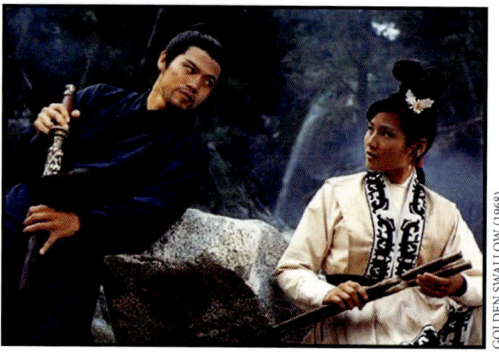

GOLDEN SWALLOW (1968)

to be opened to the public ... and a lot of folks seem intent on finding out what's inside the place.

This Taiwanese movie, also known as *Bad Ninjas Wear Gold*, is constructed like a whodunit, with dead bodies found all around Eagle House, and the riddle of Golden Mask's true identity used as the central mystery. There are twists too, including dead characters proving to be alive and secret family ties revealed.

Starring former Shaw Brothers actor Chi Kuan-Chun, this is a brisk, slightly batty actioner with some interesting moments, such as a fight with assailants wearing red hoods in a bamboo forest and a pretty inventive final showdown between the hero and six Golden Masks, who are all armed with spinning, serrated, circular-saw shield-weapons!

GOLDEN SWALLOW (1968)
Starring Jimmy Wang Yu, Cheng Pei-Pei, Lo Lieh, Wu Ma
Directed by Chang Cheh
Produced by Runme Shaw
Action by Lau Kar-Leung, Tang Chia
Shaw Brothers

Sometimes known as *The Girl with the Thunderbolt Kick*, this follow-up to King Hu's *Come Drink with Me* is another winner from director Chang Cheh. Jimmy Wang Yu stars as the brooding Silver Roc, a lone, ruthless master swordsman who is cutting a bloody swath through the land. Expert swordswoman Golden Swallow (Pei-Pei), who becomes implicated in this rampage, is forced to get involved and a love triangle eventually develops between her, Silver Roc and chivalrous warrior Golden Whip Han Tao.

The atmosphere of ultimate tragedy is beautifully choreographed, as Silver Roc's unrequited love is balanced against the mayhem. The final battle scene, as the swordsman stands alone, mortally wounded,

against an army of his archenemies, the Golden Dragon bandits, is magnetic in its nihilistic idealism.

Watch out for Lo Lieh in the supporting role of the moralistic Golden Whip, who inadvertently leads Silver Roc to his doom.

GREAT SHANGHAI 1937 (1986)
Starring Xu Xiao-Jian, Du Yu-Ming, Dong Zhi-Hua, Liu Li-Jun
Directed by Chang Cheh
San Yang Film Productions/Sil-Metropol Organization

The great city of Shanghai has been occupied by foreign governments, who have divided the city into territories, each governed by the foreign power residing there. A group of Chinese patriots rise up against the foreign influence. The patriots meet stiff opposition when they lock horns in the powerful Japanese-held territory.

Although the cast are all unknowns, they are exceptionally talented martial artists and acrobats, handling the superb fight choreography with ease. The film's patriotic viewpoint is also vividly realized.

GREEN DRAGON INN (1977)
Starring Yueh Hua, Polly Shang-Kuan Ling-Feng, Lo Lieh, Lan Chi, Sze-Ma Lung, Su Kuo-Liang
Directed by Wu Min-Hsiung
Action by Ma Chang, Su Kuo-Liang
Yao Lei Film Production Company

After the son of a warlord murders an entire family, a marshal and a group of royal officers begin a treacherous journey, transporting the killer to the capital ... but the warlord vows to get his son back.

Also known by the misleading Bruceploitation title *Bruce is Loose*, this Taiwanese period martial arts actioner is fairly watchable, with the straightforward plot providing opportunities for lots of confrontations, as the hero leads his team through enemy territory.

The marshal, for some reason, decides it's a good idea to stop off at the Green Dragon Inn, which is in the middle of a town controlled by the warlord, so it comes as no surprise that a siege situation soon develops. Luckily, our hero is aided by a hood-wearing female fighter and a warrior (Lieh), who is already staying at the inn.

After a fun sequence where the inn is booby-trapped with lots of ropes and sword blades embedded in tables and window shutters, there's some more fighting, then the movie reaches a final showdown,

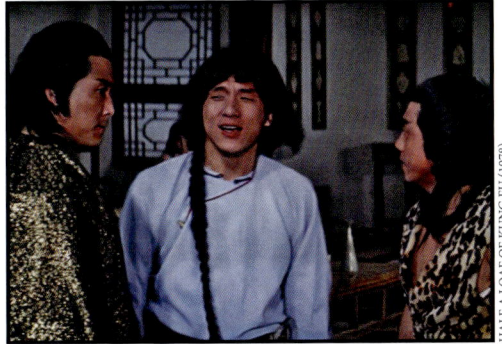

HALF A LOAF OF KUNG FU (1978)

as the silver-haired warlord strips his shirt off to fight barechested and the various protagonists and antagonists battle to the death. Cue sudden freeze-frame ending!

HALF A LOAF OF KUNG FU (1978)

Starring Jackie Chan, Kam Kong, Lung Chun-Erh, James Tien, Dean Shek
Directed by Chan Chi-Hwa
Produced by Lo Wei
Action by Jackie Chan
Lo Wei Motion Picture Company

Daunted by the poor box office receipts for *Snake and Crane Arts of Shaolin*, Jackie Chan and his close friend, director Chan Chi-Hwa, decided to throw in their lot and mess about with producer Lo Wei's money, hoping that a new approach to the genre might improve box office.

Chan portrays a bumbling buffoon obsessed with martial arts, the only problem being that he can't fight to save his life. Eventually, the hapless idiot gets a job as an escort where he befriends a kung fu master who eventually manages to knock some sense into him. The tedious storyline, with its camp comedy, finally reaches a point on a dusty road where Chan makes comic mincemeat of a notorious robber, who is after some priceless jewels under Chan's protection.

Only innovative choreography and pretty kung fu

THE HAND OF DEATH (1976)

forms save this otherwise turgid mess. When Lo Wei viewed the finished product, he went ape and shelved the picture, but Chan and Chi-Hwa were right about their hunch concerning kung fu comedy, because Jackie's next film was the successful *Snake in the Eagle's Shadow*.

THE HAND OF DEATH (1976)

Starring Tan Tao-Liang, James Tien, Jackie Chan, Sammo Hung, John Woo, Yang Wei
Directed by John Woo
Produced by Raymond Chow
Action by Sammo Hung
Golden Harvest

Flash Legs Tan stars as a young Shaolin student who, after proving himself worthy, embarks on a mission to bring to divine justice a Shaolin renegade turncoat (Tien), who is working for the Ching government in a position of high authority. Joining him on his quest are a spearman (Chan), a swordsman (Wei) and a regal scholar (Woo).

Don't miss the epic showdown! Although this amiable film bears no resemblance to Woo's later works, it still features the hallmarks of a professional filmmaker. It's also well worth watching for an early Jackie Chan performance: although in a supporting role he ends up stealing the picture.

HAPKIDO (1972)

Starring Angela Mao, Sammo Hung, Carter Wong, Hwang In-Shik, Ji Han-Jae
Directed by Huang Feng
Produced by Raymond Chow
Action by Sammo Hung
Golden Harvest

Angela Mao, Sammo Hung, and Carter Wong are instructed by their teacher to flee from Japanese-occupied Korea and return to China to spread the teachings and art of Hapkido there. After successfully opening a Hapkido school in China, they pay their respects to the neighboring school in the area, which happens to be a Japanese school.

The Black Bear Association does not take kindly to the Hapkido students, and a blood feud rages throughout the rest of the action-packed film.

Only standard direction, which restrains Angela Mao from being totally unleashed, prevents *Hapkido*, also known as *Lady Kung Fu*, from becoming an all-time classic. Check out the blink-and-you'll-miss-it cameo from Jackie Chan.

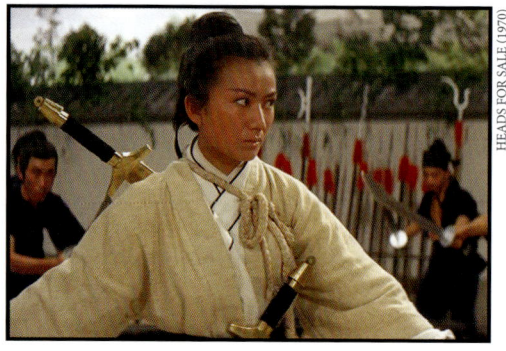
HEADS FOR SALE (1970)

HEADS FOR SALE (1970)

Starring Chiao Chiao, Wang Hsia, Helen Ma,
Chen Liang
Directed by Cheng Chang-Ho
Produced by Runme Shaw
Shaw Brothers

Hold on to your heads and prepare for a roller-coaster ride into the Shaw Brothers world of chivalry and righteousness. The multitalented Shaws beauty Chiao Chiao stars as a spoilt brat of a swordswoman who, after jilting her lover, decides to rescue him when he is captured by a rival clan. She uses a genius scheme to gain entrance to the enemy's stronghold, which involves the selling of severed heads in the town square. Chiao Chiao manages to release her lover from the clutches of the evil warlord, and the action escalates as the warlord and his lackeys give chase to the fleeing lovers.

In an epic finale, the brave swordswoman fights on a rope bridge suspended 400 feet up between two mountains. Good overpowers evil and the spoilt brat is now a true swordswoman of the world.

A vibrant and witty script is supported by intelligent direction and fine acting from all involved, making this one of the finest swashbucklers of the time.

HELL'S WINDSTAFF (1979)

Starring Meng Yuen-Man, Meng Hoi, Hwang Jang-Lee,
Jason Pai Piao, Kwon Young-Moon
Directed by Lu Chun-Ku, Tony Wong Yuk-Long
Action by Corey Yuen, Hsu Hsia, Chin Yuet-Sang,
Brandy Yuen, Yuen Shun-Yi
Yuk Long Movies

Hong Kong comics artist, publisher and actor Tony Wong Yuk-Long brought his most popular comic book heroes to life in this movie.

Tiger Wong (Yuen-Man) and Stone Dragon (Hoi) are two mischievous boys who discover that their townspeople are being sold without their knowledge as slave laborers to Indonesia by a group of bandits headed by a man named Lu (Jang-Lee). While trying to stop the activities, the boys are forced to kill one of the Four Snakes, Lu's deadly lackeys. As a result, the father of Dragon, along with his kung fu teacher, are killed by Lu's Hell Windstaff, a highly evolved form of staff-fighting never known to have been defeated. The two boys manage to escape and seek refuge with Shek (Young-Moon), the master of Stone Dragon. Attempting to curb the boys' desire for revenge, the old master teaches them White Dragon Fists and Paddle Staff to combat not only Lu's Hell Windstaff, but his Sky Eagle Claws as well. After overcoming many obstacles, the boys finally confront Lu's Hell Windstaff in a battle that has now become a screen classic among fu fans.

Also known as *The Dragon and the Tiger Kids* and *Hell'z Windstaff*, the film's villain, Hwang Jang-Lee, is a force to be reckoned with, as usual.

HERO AT THE BORDER REGION (1981)

Starring Chang Ling, Yuen Cheung-Yan, Tsai Hung,
Ti Lung
Directed by Pao Hsueh-Li
Yu Feng Film Company

Princess Ching Chin (Ling) returns to her Sun sect, to find her father has left, and the Moon Legate in temporary charge. In reality, the Legate has imprisoned Ching Chin's father and is trying to find the whereabouts of the sect's treasure store. When the princess discovers this, a bloody struggle ensues.

This is a sequel to *The Inheritor of Kung Fu* (aka *The Heroic One*) that all but does away with Ti Lung's central character, only using regurgitated shots from *Inheritor*. The story is pretty lame, although the fight action is okay.

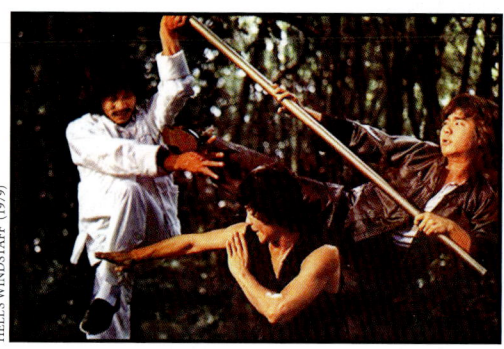
HELL'S WINDSTAFF (1979)

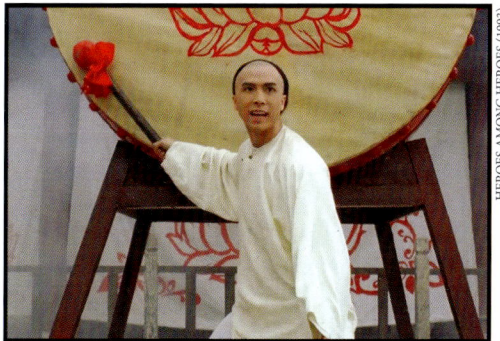

HEROES AMONG HEROES (1993)

THE HEROES (1980)

Starring Ti Lung, Shih Szu, Tan Tao-Liang,
Michael Chan Wai-Man
Directed by Wu Ma, Pao Hsueh-Li
Action by Robert Tai
Yen Shing Film Company

In order to underline their stranglehold on the country, the Ching dynasty bans kung fu teachings and outlaws all students of the Shaolin temple who are loyal to the Mings. Yang (Ti Lung), a former Shaolin student who has turned traitor and is now in the Ching's employ, is ordered to wipe out the temple and its disciples. However, he spares the lives of selected pupils, hoping that the application of severe torture techniques will persuade them to spurn their beliefs and join the Ching army. But why are his torture devices seemingly designed to strengthen the Shaolin prisoners? And why, when one hapless captive agrees to join the Ching, does Yang kill him? Could there be more to Yang than meets the eye?

Shih Szu puts in a fine performance in this Wu Ma–directed epic of unrequited heroism and noble destinies.

Also known as *Story of Chivalry, The Shaolin Heroes, The Unforgiven of Shaolin* and *Wu Tang Clan.*

HEROES AMONG HEROES (1993)

Starring Donnie Yen, Wong Yuk, Fennie Yuen,
Ng Man-Tat
Directed by Yuen Woo-Ping, Chan Chin-Chung
Produced by Yuen Woo Ping, Chan Chin-Chung,
Lam Shu-Kin
Art Sea Films

Yuen Woo-Ping sheds more light on Sam Seed (Beggar So), the character his late father brought to life in the classic *Drunken Master*. This time we catch Sam (Yen) in his younger years. Rather than being a nasty old man, he is a rich young man of virtue, until there's a misunderstanding with master Wong Fei Hung (Yuk). From this moment on, he sides with the Manchu twelfth prince and foolishly helps him push opium, much to the disgust of Wong. The devious prince gets Sam hooked on opium and uses him to rid himself of his toughest obstacle . . . Wong Fei Hung. After an assassination attempt while under the influence, Wong captures Sam and cures his drug addiction with the help of a high-kicking Korean herbalist. Once revived, Sam teams up with Wong to wage a righteous war on drugs.

This excellent new wave kung fu movie is full of great fights and gimmickry, but is sadly marred by tedious slapstick comedy routines.

HEROES OF THE EAST (1978)

Starring Gordon Liu, Yuka Mizuno, Yasuaki Kurata,
Lau Kar-Leung,
Directed by Lau Kar-Leung
Produced by Run Run Shaw
Action by Lau Kar-Leung
Shaw Brothers

This is one of the best choreographed kung fu films made under the Shaw Brothers banner. A pretty Japanese girl (Mizuno) marries a handsome Chinese man, Toa (Liu), and their marriage is initially blissfully happy, but it turns into a nightmare when Toa discovers that his wife is an ardent kung fu trainee. He disapproves of her tough fighting style with high-flying kicks but she will not change to his gentler martial art. Their household is turned into a battleground as they frequently fight to prove their superiority. Toa gains the upper hand each time and the humiliated girl returns to Japan to perfect her skills. He challenges her to return but his letter falls into the hands of an expert instructor who comes to China with seven other masters to teach Toa a lesson.

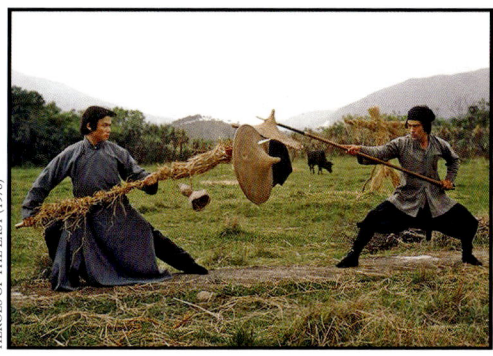

HEROES OF THE EAST (1978)

The remarkable display of swords, drunken kung fu versus karate, Chinese boxing against judo, and ninjitsu are a feast for the eyes as Chinese and Japanese skills are tested against each other.

Also known as *Shaolin Challenges Ninja*, *Challenge of the Ninja* and *Drunk Shaolin Challenges Ninja*.

HEROES TWO (1974)
Starring Chen Kuan-Tai, Fu Sheng, Chu Mu,
Fung Hark-On
Directed by Chang Cheh
Produced by Run Run Shaw
Action by Lau Kar-Leung, Tang Chia
Chang's Film Company/Shaw Brothers

Fervent Ming patriot Fang Shih Yu (Sheng) inadvertently helps the Ching to capture rebel leader and fellow patriot Hung Hsi Kuan (Kuan-Tai). For this, Fang finds himself disliked by the rest of the patriots. To redeem himself, Fang swears to rescue Hung from the Ching army . . .

This movie is flavored with strong scenes of brotherhood between Hung and Fang and the other Ming patriots, while the excellent fight scenes bear the trademarks of choreographer Lau Kar-Leung's ongoing quest for authenticity.

THE HEROIC ONES (1970)
Starring David Chiang, Ti Lung, Chin Han,
Ku Feng, Chen Sing, Lily Li, Bolo Yeung
Directed by Chang Cheh
Produced by Run Run Shaw
Action by Lau Kar-Leung, Lau Kar-Wing
Shaw Brothers

Ti Lung and David Chiang are once again teamed as the eleventh Prince and thirteenth Prince, sons of the Tartar King. The Tartars, hard drinkers and fighters all, are embroiled in a bloody internal feud for control of the throne of China. To this end, they come face-to-face with treachery wherever they turn . . .

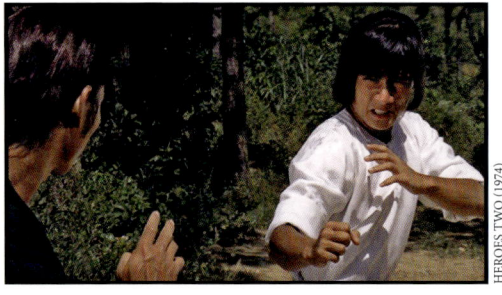

HEROES TWO (1974)

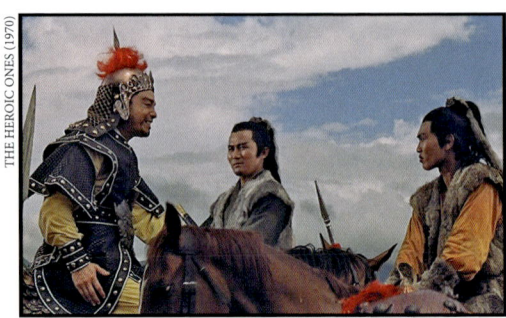

THE HEROIC ONES (1970)

The climactic scene inside the villain's fortress leaves a huge body count, as the king and his sons are forced to fight their way out of an ambush, making this another classic Shaw Brothers swordplay movie.

HIDDEN HERO (1990)
Starring Dong Zhi-Hua, Du Yu-Ming, Li Bing,
Wu Xi-Wei
Directed and produced by Chang Cheh
Action by Dung Chi-Wa, Du Yu-Ming,
Mu Li-Xin
Chang He Film Company/Xi'an Film Studio

Mu (Zhi-Hua) was a top weaponsmith and martial artist until a client cut him across the back. This incident forced Mu to disappear and become an ordinary blacksmith. But his peace is destroyed by a group of thieves who cause much trouble and strife in the martial world, then appear on his doorstep.

Basically, Chang Cheh has remade his earlier classic *Life Combat*, but adds some more twists to the story. The action is stunning. Dong Zhi-Hua, as Mu, is superb, performing some mind-blowing acrobatic martial artistry. Yet another classic from Chang Cheh.

THE HIMALAYAN (1976)
Starring Angela Mao, Tan Tao-Liang, Chen Sing,
Ho Pak-Kwong, Corey Yuen
Directed by Huang Feng
Produced by Raymond Chow
Action by Han Ying-Chieh, Sammo Hung
Golden Harvest

Power-mad Kao Chu (Sing) has his younger brother marry the beautiful daughter of a wealthy man in order to take over the man's huge estate. After the wedding, Kao kills his brother and frames his sister-in-law for the murder. The girl's father flies into a rage and has her tied to a board and thrown into the river. Luckily, she is rescued by one of the house servants, Hsu (Tao-Liang), who is her secret admirer. They find sanctuary in a lamasery high up in the Himalayas, where they are taught Lama breath-control and kicking techniques to prepare them for their inevitable onslaught on Kao's mansion.

A solid performance from Chen Sing, plus the swift kicking skills of Flash Legs Tan, lift this slightly above-average film.

HIS NAME IS NOBODY (1979)

Starring Lau Kar-Wing, Leung Kar-Yan,
Dean Shek, Chung Fat, Karl Maka
Directed by Karl Maka
Action by Lau Kar-Wing
Sharp Films Company

The wild and predominantly wacky adventures of a foundling with no name are chronicled in this inventive comedy. The Nobody Kid (Kar-Wing), as he becomes known as, teams up with both a con artist and a professional killer, as he learns the fine art of survival through martial expertise. The Nobody Kid picks up streetwise trickery from the con artist and the power of instinct from the killer. However, when the latter is murdered by his vicious rival, Dreg (who lists necrophilia among his more salubrious pastimes), the Nobody Kid and the conman combine forces to exact revenge.

The film, which is for die-hard fans of the kung fu comedy genre only, ends with the pair emigrating to America, which left the way open for a possible sequel.

HITMAN IN THE HAND OF BUDDHA (1981)

Starring Hwang Jang-Lee, Fan Mei-Sheng, Tino Wong,
Eddy Ko, To Siu-Ming
Directed and produced by Hwang Jang-Lee
Action by Corey Yuen, Chin Yuet-Sang, Meng Hoi
Hwang Jang-Lee Production Company

Tired of playing villains, Hwang Jang-Lee turned his hand to directing, producing and starring in this action-packed kick-fest.

Hwang plays Wong Chin, a bumpkin who has come to live with his brother, who works in a rice trading company in a small town. They learn that Wan Li rice-trading company, their competitors, are cheating the public into buying rice under false pretenses. The Wan Li group hire a fighter to deal with our hero, but Wong literally makes mincemeat out of him. "I've made a mess of your dragon and snake dish,"

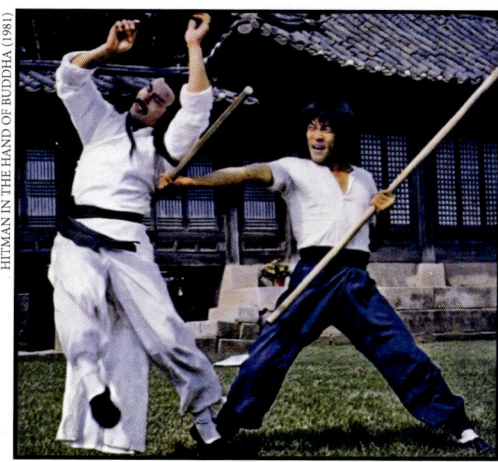

HITMAN IN THE HAND OF BUDDHA (1981)

he says at the end of the teahouse duel. The killer, shamed by his defeat, seeks the help of his master, Uncle 33 (Ko), to deal with Wong. Uncle 33 tears Wong to bits with his Eagle Claw style, but, luckily, Wong is saved by Beggar Fan (Mei-Sheng), who sends Wong to the temple to seek the guidance of the high abbot. His training complete, Wong returns to discover that his brother has been murdered by Uncle 33's gang. Buddha's hand watching over him, Wong seeks out Uncle 33 in the ultimate challenge.

Although the film drags in places, and the comedy routines are tedious beyond belief, Hwang Jang-Lee's charisma and martial arts expertise lift this otherwise average film into the realms of a classic. He showcases not only his entire kicking repertoire, but also his ability in staff-wielding, boxing, chopsticks and, of course, Eagle Claw.

If you like your action fast, hard and violent, then this is for you!

THE HOT, THE COOL AND THE VICIOUS (1976)

Starring Don Wong Tao, Tan Tao-Liang, Chin Ming,
Sun Chia-Lin
Directed by Lee Tso-Nam
Action by Chi Ming
Tung Hai Film Company

The town of Black Stone is thrown into martial arts turmoil when a counterfeiting ring, run by the mysterious golden-haired Lung (Chin Ming), comes under the close scrutiny of undercover agent Pai (Don Wong Tao), a reformed assassin and Southern Fist boxing expert. Aiding him in his fight against corruption is security chief Lu (Tan Tao-Liang), an upright and honest man, who's an expert in kicking. Together they smash the ring, but are they a match for Lung, who is an expert in both Mantis Fists and Dragon Kicks? Watch the vicious end duel to find out . . .

This is a fast-paced movie with some of the best two-on-one fights ever filmed: from the opening credit sequence to the ball-busting ending, footwork and fist-shapes are on full display.

THE INCREDIBLE KUNG FU MASTER (1979)

Starring Tung Wei, Sammo Hung, Lee Hoi-Sang, Phillip Ko, Meng Hoi
Directed by Joe Cheung
Action by Sammo Hung Action Group
First Films Organization/Hong Kong Wei Kuen Film Company

Pretty boy Tung Wei, who will always be best remembered for his role as Bruce Lee's disciple in *Enter the Dragon*, gets a chance to showcase his acrobatics in this action-crammed kung fu comedy.

Ching (Wei) gets expelled from two kung fu schools after breaking his vows of secrecy. Now masterless, he befriends a kung fu vagabond (Hung), who compares martial arts to food. This unorthodox and practical teacher tutors Ching well and the lad soon becomes an expert. Ching then returns to his former masters, who are caught in the middle of a death duel with Mongolian expert Yang (Hoi-Sang), who has an old score to settle. Ching fights off Yang's tiger men before finishing off the Mongol in a funny and slippery way.

There's not much of a plot to this film, also known as *They Call Me Phat Dragon*, but the training scenes showing Sammo putting Tung Wei through torturous opera exercises with Greek bouzouki music playing in the background make the whole adventure seem worthwhile.

INCREDIBLE KUNG FU MISSION (1980)

Starring John Liu, Robert Tai, Chui Chung-San
Directed by Chang Hsin-Yi
Action by Robert Tai
Golden Sun Films/Yangtze Film Company Ltd

A famed revolutionary, Ching, is taken prisoner by a warlord, Lu Ping (Tai), so a concerned "revolutionary" hires Ting (Liu) to train five men to rescue Ching from the warlord's territory.

An excellent martial cast gather around John Liu

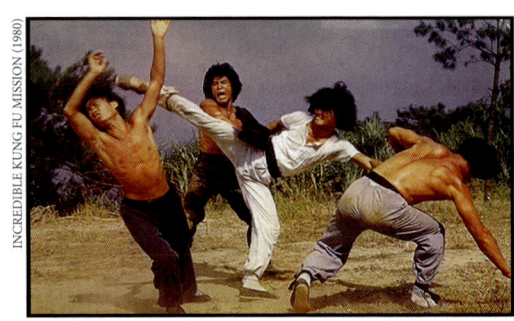

INCREDIBLE KUNG FU MISSION (1980)

for this all-out fight-fest. Liu dominates with utterly wondrous leg techniques, but is matched by the villainous brilliance of Robert Tai. The twist ending is an added bonus.

THE INHERITOR OF KUNG FU (1981)

Starring Ti Lung, Chang Ling, Kwan Yung-Moon, Tsai Hung
Directed by Pao Hsueh-Li
Yu Feng Film Company

A kung fu manual goes missing in the middle of a huge clandestine battle for supremacy between all the clans. Caught in the middle is a mountain clan member, Fan (Lung). He is framed, accused of taking the manual and is forced to fight his own clan and the other 129 clans. Fan befriends a border tribe princess, Chin Chin (Ling), and the two fight back, while trying to discover the truth about the manual.

Also known as *The Heroic One*, this movie has an incredibly complicated storyline and stunningly oddball characters, combined with exceptional fight action. Ti Lung is superb, as always, and handles the fights with effortless style.

THE INSTANT KUNG FU MAN (1978)

Starring John Liu, Hwang Jang-Lee, Yeh Fei-Yang, Corey Yuen
Directed by Tung Chin-Hu
Action by Yuen Woo-Ping, Yuen Cheung-Yan, Yeh Fei-Yang, Corey Yuen
Fortuna Film Company

Two identical twins wreak havoc in the quiet Chinese countryside. Hu, the younger of the pair, is a naughty Shaolin disciple who escapes from the temple under false pretences by infesting the 108 wooden men with woodworm, making it easy for him to smash his way out of the restrictive world of the Shaolin order. John Liu plays Kam, the martial monk with the task of bringing back

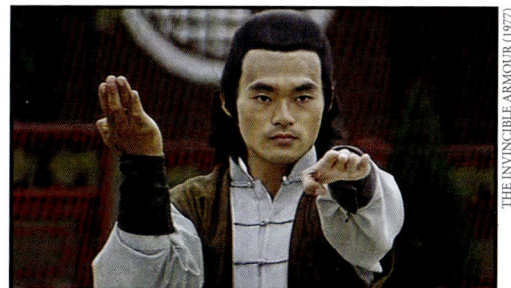

THE INVINCIBLE ARMOUR (1977)

the young tearaway. Fu, the older of the brothers, is a notorious bandit renowned for his ruthless kung fu techniques. Hwang Jang-Lee, meanwhile, plays Yi Lang, a hardened criminal who is out for Fu's blood after being crossed by him in a jewel heist. The twins, both played convincingly by Taiwanese actor Yeh Fei-Yang, have a great time outwitting all and sundry in this madcap martial arts outing. The fights between "Northern Leg" John Liu and "Silver Fox" Hwang Jang-Lee are some of the best-ever captured on celluloid, but then, with kung fu ace Yuen Woo-Ping at the helm, it's hardly surprising.

The mistaken identity plot, added to the great fights, make this a cheap, cheerful, enjoyable flick.

THE INVINCIBLE ARMOUR (1977)

Starring John Liu, Hwang Jang-Lee, Tino Wong,
Phillip Ko
Directed by Ng See-Yuen
Produced by Hsia Fan
Action by Yuen Woo-Ping, Hsu Hsia
Lai Wah Film Company

Set in the days of the Ming dynasty, *Invincible Armour* sees Hwang Jang-Lee play Cheng, a ruthless court official who, for his own advancement, frames Chow (Liu) for murder. Chow is intent on exposing the real killer and clearing his own name, but, as Cheng is a master of Eagle Claw and the coveted Iron Armor technique, he's going to be a foe that's hard to beat. Finally, Chow, along with Shen (Tino Wong), do battle with Cheng in one of the most imaginatively ruthless end fights in martial art movie history.

The use of the enthralling spaghetti western soundtrack, lifted from the classic *Day of Anger* (1967), works really well here, plus, let's face it, any film that features both Hwang Jang-Lee and John Liu is definitely going to be worth watching.

Ng See-Yuen holds the helm, while top fight choreographers of the calibre of Yuen Woo-Ping and Hsu Hsia shape the splendid action.

INVINCIBLE SHAOLIN (1978)

Starring Philip Kwok, Lu Feng, Chiang Shang,
Chan Shen, Lo Meng, Wang Lung-Wei, Dick Wei
Directed by Chang Cheh
Produced by Run Run Shaw
Action by Robert Tai, Leung Ting, Lu Feng
Shaw Brothers

An evil Ching warlord (Lung-Wei) comes up with a brilliant plan to rid the Ching Empire of the Shaolin masters. He invites three North Shaolin dudes to his mansion and has them fight it out with three South Shaolin novices. Of course, the Northerners win and accidentally kill the Southerners. News of the incident reaches Shaolin, where the elder dispatches three top fighters to deal with this Shaolin infighting crisis. The plot is finally exposed and North and South Shaolin fight alongside each other, but not without tragic loss to both camps.

In this film, also known as *Unbeatable Dragon*, the "Venoms" actors are in top-notch form, under the beady eye of madman Robert Tai, with the crisp storytelling of maestro Chang Cheh guaranteeing high-quality viewing.

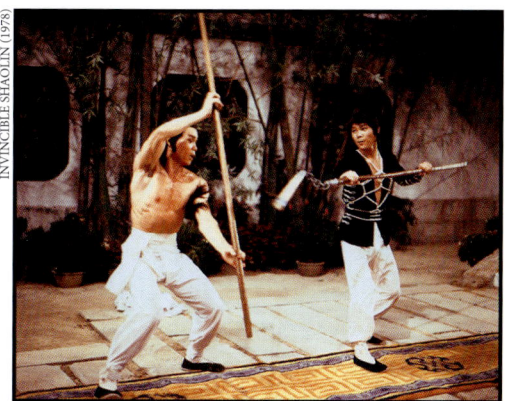

INVINCIBLE SHAOLIN (1978)

IRON FIST ADVENTURE (1972)

Starring Jimmy Wang Yu, Tien Yeh, Paul Chang Chung,
Li Hsiang, Li Su, Fan Ling
Directed by Li Su
Hua Feng Film Company

Guan (Jimmy Wang Yu), leader of the 6th Union, becomes involved in the treacherous infighting of a family clan in an isolated town, which is linked to the death, years earlier, of Guan's boss.

Also known as *The Adventure*, this Taiwanese movie mixes fists, swords, guns, and knives into its action scenes. Wang Yu looks great in a fur hat, as

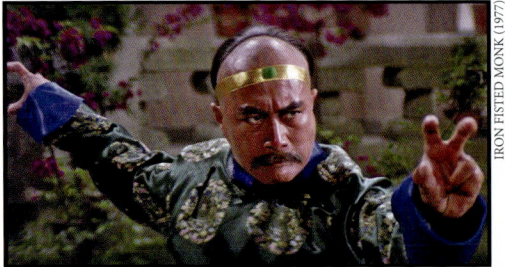

IRON FISTED MONK (1977)

Mantis Boxing, sends for help and, after a successful raid and another gruesome rape, the Manchus return home to celebrate. But, joining the party are two Shaolin avengers, Husker and monk San Te (Sing). In the magnificent finale, the duo take-on a meteor man, a Mongol head-crusher, two saber fighters, two warriors, an Eagle Claw master, and, finally, the sick Mantis master.

Kung fu cinema's hard man, Chen Sing, is brilliant here in a good guy role and *Iron Fisted Monk* proves to be a must-see warm-up to *Warriors Two*.

IRON MONKEY (1977)

Starring Chen Kuan-Tai, Chin Kang, Chi Kuan-Chun,
Wilson Tong, Leung Kar-Yan
Directed by Chen Kuan-Tai
Action by Chen Mu-Chuan
Chin Hua Film Company/Wing Tai Film Co

Iron Monkey is the nickname of a young gambler who becomes the sole survivor of a Manchurian massacre. After burying his family, a fate-filled road leads Iron Monkey to the confines of Shaolin Temple. Full of vengeance, the young victim of circumstance endures humiliation from his classmates and rigorous training from the infamous Bitter Monk. All hardship is painfully accepted, to finally explode into a merciless confrontation with the chief of the Manchus, who is a master of Eagle Claw.

With great costumes, an excellent cast, and the raw, youthful talent of Chen Kuan-Tai, this is an outstanding example of the genre.

IRON MONKEY (1993)

Starring Donnie Yen, Yu Rongguang,
Tsang Sze-Man, Yuen Shun-Yee
Directed by Yuen Woo-Ping
Produced by Tsui Hark
Action by Yuen Clan
Film Workshop/Golden Harvest/Long Shong Pictures

During the late Ching Dynasty a renowned herbal doctor, Dr. Yang (Rongguang), becomes disenchanted with the corrupt political system. In order to help the poor and needy, he takes matters into his own hands, becoming a Robin Hood–type figure: Iron Monkey. Pursued by the government's mightiest fighters, Yang manages to elude capture at every obstacle and finds an able ally in the form of Wong Kei-Ying (Yen), one of the most acclaimed kung fu warriors of the region. When Wong's son, Wong Fei Hung (Sze-Man), is captured by the Iron Monkey's nemesis,

he uses pistols or his boot knives or just his feet & fists to hunt down the traitor that's paying bandits to kill off other members of the local bigwig family.

One character melodramatically takes ages to die from a gunshot wound and pleads with Guan to mercifully finish him off, which Guan does, but our fur-hatted hero is eventually falsely accused of being a traitor, is captured, then blinded with daggers. This, though, doesn't deter Guan from battling the villain in a final showdown, where Guan is repeatedly slashed by the knife-wielding traitor, but the bloody, blind Guan still manages to mortally wound his opponent with an iron nail he pulls from a wooden post.

The hand-to-hand fighting is rather basic and unflashy, and much of the dialogue in the dubbed print is purely expositional, but the use of the Bergmann-Bayard-style pistols adds a novel angle to the action in this flick, there's atmospheric use of Taiwanese locations, and the purloined music featured in the overbearing soundtrack is really good.

IRON FISTED MONK (1977)

Starring Sammo Hung, Chen Sing, Fung Hark-On,
James Tien, Dean Shek, Mars
Directed by Sammo Hung
Produced by Raymond Chow
Action by Sammo Hung
Golden Harvest

Sammo Hung's directorial debut is a vibrant and colorful action-gorged kung fu fest, a style which would mature and become synonymous with his name. Kung fu legend Husker (Sammo) is the most mischievous disciple within the Shaolin Temple. Impatient for revenge on those who killed his boss, he sneaks out of the temple under cover of darkness. Once outside, he befriends Liang, a dye factory worker who shares his hatred of the Manchus, because they raped his sister and are trying to take over the factory. The evil local Manchu warlord (Hark-On), who specializes in necrophilia as well as the Monk, the two have to face the might of the corrupt dynasty's armies in an all-out action finale.

A remake of the 1970s film of the same name, *Iron Monkey* has an engrossing storyline and is a roller-coaster ride of action. Hong Kong superstar Donnie Yen has plenty of opportunities to demonstrate the high-kicking martial arts he is best known for, and here he is joined by rising action star Yu Rongguang.

Also known as *Iron Monkey: The Young Wong Fei Hung*, the spectacular choreography and excellent performances really pack a punch.

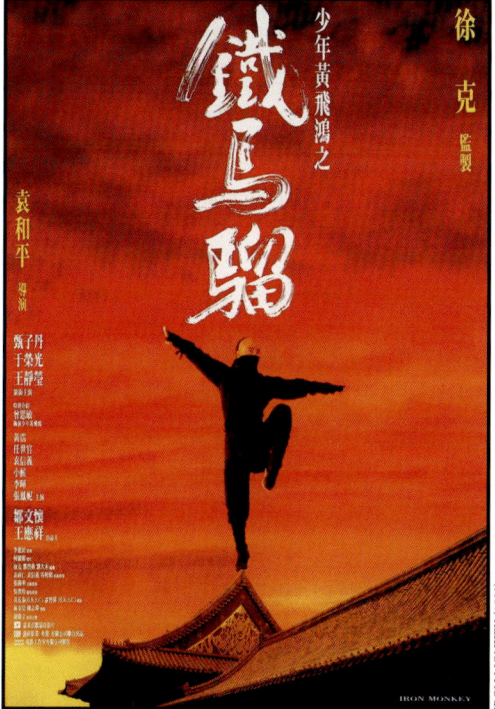

IRON MONKEY (1993)

IRON MONKEY 2 (1996)

Stars Donnie Yen, Chang Jian-Li, Billy Chow, Wu Ma, Steve Benson
Directed by Chao Lu-Chiang
Gold Rush Film Co

Iron Monkey (Yen) and his visually impaired companion Jin team up to track down the Tiger (Jian-Li), a notorious underworld agent. However, things take a dramatic turn when Jin's son enters the picture and becomes involved in the conflict. Tragically, Jin loses his life in the midst of the chaos, leaving his son to join forces with Iron Monkey

to bring Tiger to justice, but they have to get past his brother (Chow), which won't be an easy task.

Despite the title *Iron Monkey 2*, this is not a true sequel but more of a distant cousin to the original. The only similarity is that Donnie Yen is back, with plenty of speeded-up action and wirework. Though nowhere near as good as the original, the strength of this film lies in some of the inventive fight pieces, including a flying guillotine that looks like a spaceship with a very visible wire attached to it, and some great action using ladders. Any movie that casts Billy Chow as a villain, of course, is sure to have at least some hard-hitting action.

KICKBOXER (1993)

Starring Yuen Biao, Yen Shi-Kwan, Lu Hsiu-Ling, Yuen Wah, Wu Ma
Directed by Wu Ma
Produced by Yuen Biao
Action by Yuen Biao
Regal Films Company Ltd

Yuen Biao takes a break from fantasy flicks to star in this traditional movie, which gets better with each viewing. His athleticism lends itself to a great performance in both character and combat.

Yen Shi-Kwan, complete with beard and gold shoes, looks great, and there are a bunch of attention-grabbing scenes, including Biao and Shi-Kwan's battle of wits across a giant chessboard and Yuen Biao's demoralization after being framed for opium smuggling.

Biao's versatility is pushed to the limit in this excellent martial arts gem, which is also known as *Once Upon a Chinese Hero*.

THE KID WITH THE GOLDEN ARM (1979)

Starring Sun Chien, Philip Kwok, Lu Feng, Chiang Sheng, Lo Meng, Wang Lung-Wei, Yang Hsiung, Wei Pai, Helen Poon
Directed by Chang Cheh
Produced by Runme Shaw
Action by Robert Tai, Chiang Sheng, Lu Feng
Shaw Brothers

Yang (Chien) is asked by the government to escort a cargo of gold into a famine area. However, he must contend with the vicious Chi Sha gang, who boast the individual talents of leader Golden Arm (Meng), plus Silver Spear (Feng), Iron Robe (Lung-Wei), and Brass Head (Hsiung). In order to protect the gold from their attentions, Yang hires the services of swordsman Li Chin-Ming (Pai) and his girlfriend Leng (Poon), an axe-wielding duo, and drunk master Hai To (Kwok).

What follows is a clash of wits and strength between everyone, with the mysterious character Iron Feet making his appearance. But who is Iron Feet? The answer comes as something of a surprise. Great stuff.

KIDNAP IN ROME (1974)
Starring Bruce Leung, Meng Hoi, Cinzia Bruno,
Enzo Monteduro
Directed and produced by Ng See-Yuen
Action by Bruce Liang
Seasonal Film Corporation

A young man working as a waiter for a Chinese restaurant finds his considerable skill in martial arts put to use in helping to find the kidnapped son of an Italian millionaire. He is helped by a fellow waiter and three bungling Europeans. Fight fans may wish that less time was spent on the buffoonish humor and more time was focused on the action.

When the opportunity for combat does arrive, the results are fun: Leung's kicking is simply divine and Hoi's use of nunchakus is both skilled and amusing. The producers were adventurous enough to make this film outside Asia, and the wonderful Italian locations definitely prove to be one of the movie's main assets.

KID'S ACE IN THE HOLE (1979)
Starring John Liu, Kwon Young-Moon, Lung Chun-Erh,
Cheng Ching, Han Su, Wu Ma
Directed by Chang Chih-Chao
Action by Wang Chi-Sheng, Cheng Tien-Chi
Fong Cheng Film

John Liu plays an orphan in search of the perfect kung fu master, thus enabling him to take revenge on the crazed martial arts master who killed both his parents. On his travels John meets up with

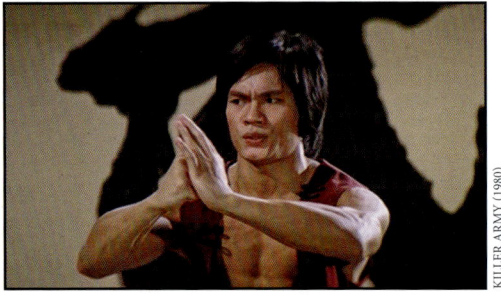

KILLER ARMY (1980)

some amazing masters of the martial arts, the most formidable being the leg fighter played by Kwon Young-Moon (an 8th Dan in both Taekwondo and Hapkido). The scenes of these two bootmen training are worth the price of admission alone.

Also known as *Kung Fu Ace* and *Fighting Ace*, this is a highly entertaining little kung fu movie that's not too demanding on the brain.

KILLER ARMY (1980)
Starring Philip Kwok, Lo Meng, Chiang Sheng,
Lu Feng, Wang Li
Directed by Chang Cheh
Produced by Runme Shaw
Action by Chiang Sheng, Lu Feng, Philip Kwok
Shaw Brothers

In this film, also known as *The Rebel Intruders*, China is ripped apart by a civil war, and thousands of displaced refugees swarm into towns not yet ravaged by war. Three such refugees (Kwok, Meng and Sheng) arrive in one town, only to get caught up in a web of intrigue, deception, and death.

This is a lavish film, with stunning acrobatic martial artistry, and an excellent story. Philip Kwok is top notch as an alpha fighter forced to bend his own moral code, due to the circumstances he finds himself in. Awesome stuff.

KILLER CONSTABLE (1980)
Starring Chen Kuan-Tai, Jason Pai Piao, Ku Feng,
Ai Fei, Dick Wei
Directed by Kuei Chih-Hung
Produced by Mona Fong, Run Run Shaw
Shaw Brothers

When two million taels of gold are stolen from the imperial treasury, ruthless yet honest chief constable Ling Tian Ying (Kuan-Tai) is ordered to get back the gold and to deal with the five robbers responsible—and he's given just ten days in which to discharge this difficult task. Overcoming personal injuries and the gradual loss of his five cohorts on the mission, Ling eventually finds the main culprit, only to discover that it is his own commander!

Kuei Chih-Hung, director of horror flicks like *Hex* and *Corpse Mania*, imbues this swordplay movie, which is also known as *Lightning Kung Fu*, with dark, rainy atmospherics, keeping the tale stark, nihilistic, and brooding.

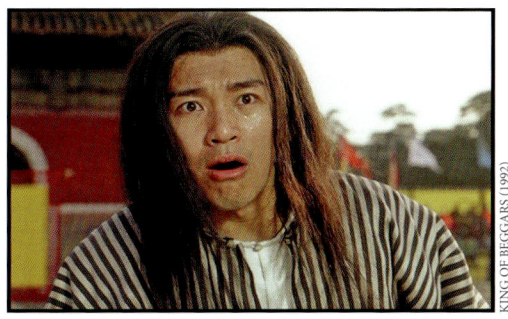

KING OF BEGGARS (1992)

KING BOXER (1972)

Starring Lo Lieh, James Nam, Wang Ping, Tien Feng,
Wang Chin-Feng, Fang Mien
Directed by Cheng Chang-Ho
Produced by Run Run Shaw
Action by Lau Kar-Wing, Chan Chuan
Shaw Brothers

Considered by many to be the movie that started it all. Lo Lieh plays Chao, a young martial arts student who dreams of winning the all-China martial arts tournament. After defeating a notorious headbutting challenger sent by the rival Meng school, Chao is given the privilege of learning the secret of Iron Fist. Master Meng (Feng) learns of Chao's prowess and tries to do away with him with the aid of three Japanese bushido experts. Chao manages to overcome all the obstacles Master Meng can throw at him and he finally wins the tournament, defeating Master Meng's son in the finale.

This influential kung fu movie, known also as *Five Fingers of Death*, still holds up to this day and is a firm favorite among film fans worldwide.

KING OF BEGGARS (1992)

Starring Stephen Chow, Ng Man-Tat, Cheung Man,
Tsui Siu-Keung, Lam Wai, Lawrence Cheng, Ng Yuk-Shu
Directed by Gordon Chan
Win's Entertainment Ltd

Box office king Stephen Chow plays Chan, the playboy son of a wealthy conniving general (Man-Tat) in this Qing dynasty comedy. While visiting a whorehouse, Chan accidentally foils a plot to kill Chui (Siu-Keung), an evil, scheming warlord, by falling for the ample charms of revolutionary femme fatale Yu-Shang, played by Cheung Man. She refuses to succumb to his advances unless he achieves the position of top kung fu scholar. Chan beats all opponents in the martial arts tournament,

reaching the final against a Mongolian bootman (Yuk-Shu), who unfortunately is related to the judges. The two battle it out with bows, maces, spears, three section staffs and nunchakus, and somehow Chan seizes victory, only to have it snatched away on a technicality. He and his father are then stripped of their possessions and forced to join the legions of beggars roaming the countryside. Chan finds himself in the unlikely role of leader of the beggars and must battle the power-hungry Chui for the sake of the beggars' good name and the love of Yu-Shang.

This is an excellent comedy poking fun at everything from the class system to traditional kung fu movies, and it also has an ample supply of excellent action. Highlights include Chow against Lam Wai in the brothel, with Lam playing praying mantis against Chow's crane and tiger, some worthy kicking and mastery of the nunchaku from Chow at the martial arts contest, plus the deadly finale between Tsui Siu-Keung's flaming dragon style and Chow's "dragon suppressing stance."

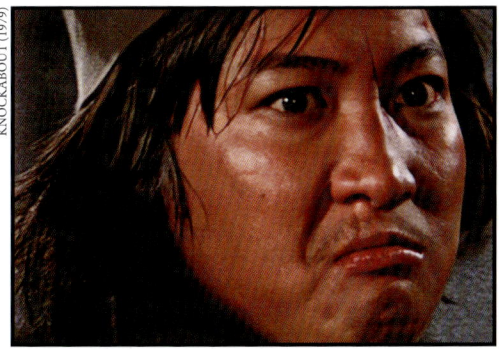

KNOCKABOUT (1979)

KNOCKABOUT (1979)

Starring Yuen Biao, Leung Kar-Yan, Lau Kar-Wing,
Sammo Hung
Directed by Sammo Hung
Action by Sammo Hung
Golden Harvest

Dai Pao (Kar-Yan) and Yipao (Biao) are two happy-go-lucky schemers who, in trying to cheat an old man (Kar-Wing), only end up being beaten by him. Impressed by the old fox's skills, the duo beg him to adopt them as students. But the old fox is in fact a hardened criminal on the run, and he uses the two lads to fight for him. When Yipao learns who the fox is he tries to escape to inform Dai Pao. In a cruel twist of fate, it is Dai Pao who is killed, and Yipao escapes. He runs into a beggar

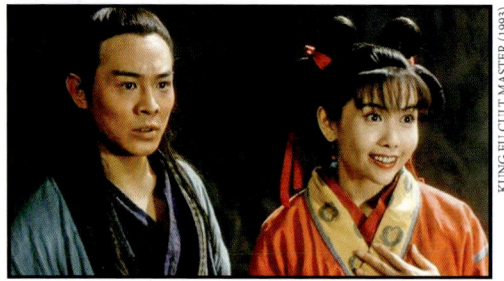

KUNG FU CULT MASTER (1993)

(Hung), who teaches him a special combination of Mantis, Monkey, Choy Lee Fat, Wing Chun and Hung Fists. Together they seek revenge for Dai Pao.

This fun kung fu comedy features Yuen Biao in his first starring role, showcasing some of his outstanding skills, signposting the fact that he was a talent destined to star in many blockbusters.

KUNG FU CULT MASTER (1993)
Starring Jet Li, Chingmy Yau, Sammo Hung,
Ngai Sing, Cheung Man, Ekin Cheng
Directed by Wong Jing
Action by Sammo Hung
Win's Film Productions

Set when various clans, notably Wu Tang and Shaolin, battled for supremacy, this story follows the plight of a young man, orphaned as a child when his parents met their deaths at the hands of the clan leaders. Although told to take revenge, he is uncomfortable with fighting but discovers that he must learn kung fu in order to reverse the effects of a delayed death blow he received. He takes lessons from an old Shaolin monk embedded in a boulder, then sets out to find his parents' killers, but he must put his retributive urges on hold and unite with the clans to fight a far greater evil, when he discovers that there is a more immediate threat to be dealt with.

This is an extremely bizarre, surreal martial arts flick, also known as *The Evil Cult*, which combines

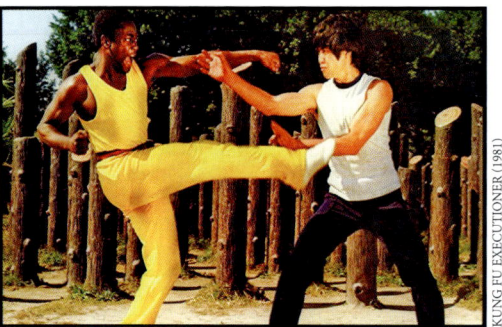

KUNG FU EXECUTIONER (1981)

the visual style of *Zu: Warriors from the Magic Mountain* with top class fight action. The style of humor may be a little too much for Western audiences sometimes, but there is much to appreciate in its originality and pace.

THE KUNG FU EMPEROR (1981)
Starring Ti Lung, Tan Tao-Liang, Shih Szu,
Chen Sing, Fang Mien
Directed by Pao Hsueh-Li
Produced by Phillip Ko
Action by Chen Mu-Chuan
Yi Peng Film Co

Another big-budget movie from Pao Hsueh-Li, filled with pageantry and an all-star cast. The 4th prince (Lung) is the favorite to take the throne of the dying emperor (Mien), but Lord Long also covets it. Unlike films *Rebellious Reign* and *Lady Assassin*, *The Kung Fu Emperor* has the 4th prince flee the royal

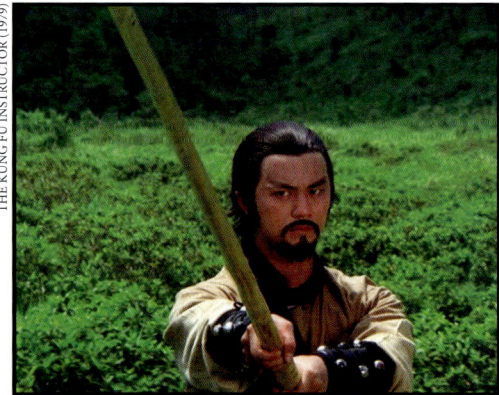

THE KUNG FU INSTRUCTOR (1979)

court in fear of becoming a victim of Lord Long's elaborate schemes to discredit him. The 4th prince takes on the mantle of a civilian and, on his travels, he befriends many top swordsmen and martial artists. On one occasion he finds himself incarcerated by his own loyal subjects. After a narrow escape from some of Lord Long's lackeys, our hero flees with a lady from a brothel (Szu). They find sanctuary in a remote cottage and from here the prince plans his return to the court, only to find, on his arrival, that the emperor is in his death throes. Martial mayhem now breaks out as the dying ruler reads his will: who will become the kung fu emperor?

Great sets, costumes, a vast potpourri of martial arts and fine performances from Ti Lung and Shih Szu make this martial arts epic worthy of a watch.

KUNG FU EXECUTIONER (1981)

Starring Billy Chong, Carl Scott, Chen Sing,
Chiang Tao, Chu Li
Directed by Lin Chan-Wei
Action by Leung Siu-Chung
Eternal Film Company

This sees the second teaming of Billy Chong and Carl Scott as kung fu soul brothers in this hard-hitting action thriller set in Shanghai in the 1930s. Li (Chong) returns from studying in Europe to find his family caught in a deadly web of triad violence and intrigue. After his father refuses point blank to lend his ships to help import raw opium, gang boss Hung (Sing) has Shima (Tao) beat him up. When he still refuses to comply with the gangster's wishes, Hung has the old-timer killed, along with other members of his family. Now, totally against his father's wishes, Li will have to face Hung and his army of assassins. Together with Donny (Scott), they storm Hung's mansion hideout in a martial arts fight to the finish.

Billy Chong pulls out all the stops in this martial arts revenger, using a wide range of weapons, flashy kicks and some unusual Indonesian Silat systems. Watch for the fight with the four samurai assassins: it's a winner! Carl Scott is in top form too, proving that you don't have to be Bruce Lee to look good with a pair of nunchakus.

Unfortunately, cheap sets and awful costumes stop this period gangster saga from becoming a better-regarded film.

THE KUNG FU INSTRUCTOR (1979)

Starring Ti Lung, Wong Yu, Ku Feng, Chao Ya-Chih,
Tien Ching
Directed by Sun Chung
Shaw Brothers

Martial arts instructor Wang Yang (Lung) is framed into training the men of unscrupulous Chief Meng, in a town that is strictly divided between the Meng and Zhou clans. Helped by Chief Meng's adopted daughter Jia Jia and hindered by his right-hand flunky Meng Fa, Wang is finally attacked and wounded for wanting to leave the Meng clan's employ, forcing him to go into hiding, to tutor promising student Zhou Ping (Yu) in preparation for the eventual showdown with Chief Meng.

Ti Lung has real screen presence as the righteous master of staff fighting, Chao Ya-Chih inhabits her role of orphan Jia Jia well, though her character gets sidelined in the second half of the movie, Tien Ching

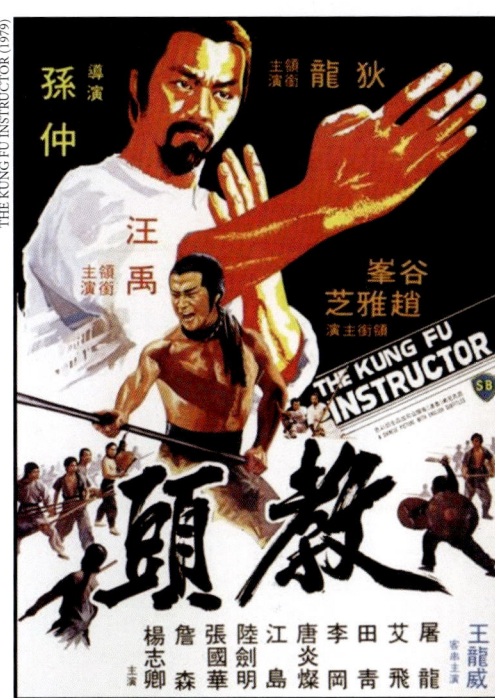

THE KUNG FU INSTRUCTOR (1979)

is his snidely best as the sneaky Meng Fa, and Ku Feng is imposing as the robust, gray-haired main villain Chief Meng.

There are some instances of fluid camerawork following characters as they pace through corridors, alleys and rooms, which makes it a shame that this shooting style isn't really used for the fight scenes, but don't worry, the combat sequences are fine as they are, plus there's a lot other stuff to enjoy, including Wang's novel training methods, using various contraptions to get Zhou Ping fit for purpose to become a master of the staff. It all ends solidly with a finale in which Wang & Zhou do battle with Chief Meng, who brandishes a Pudao polearm weapon.

KUNG FU KID (1994)

Starring Lam Ching-Ying, Chin Kar-Lok,
Kwan Hoi-San, Wu Ma
Directed by Lee Chiu
Golden Sun Films Distribution

Hong (Lam Ching-Ying) is hunted by Ching soldiers and the Wu-Tang clan. While trying to escape, Hong meets a young fighter, Feng Shi-Yu (Chin Kar-Lok), whose mother is Hong's kung fu sister. Hong leaves a rebel name list with her, but the Ching soldiers discover this and kill Feng's family, including his

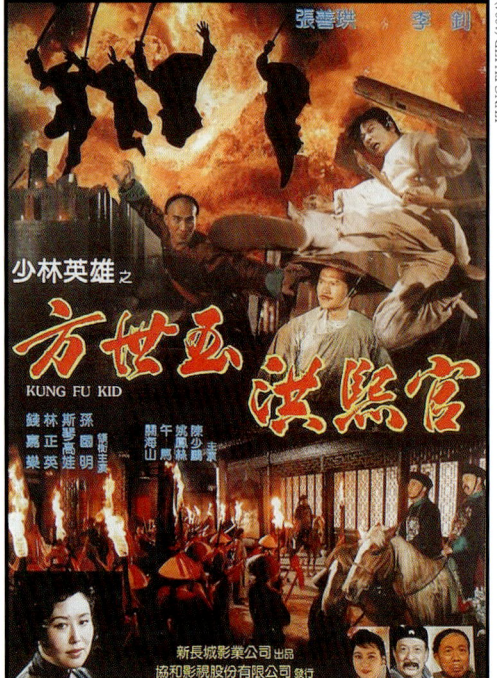

KUNG FU KID (1994)

THE KUNG FU SCHOLAR (1994)

Starring Aaron Kwok, Leung Kar-Yan, Dicky Cheung,
Gordon Liu, Ng Man-Tat
Directed by Norman Law
In-Gear Film Production

Escaping the East Chamber eunuchs, Lee Man Lung (Kar-Yan) is entrusted with taking the ninth prince to safety. Coming upon a small town, Lee decides to use a disguise so he can move unnoticed. He becomes a teacher at the local school run by headmaster Heung (Man-Tat). In the class are two good martial artists, Liu (Kwok) and Lun (Cheung). Matters worsen when the town's rival school challenges them to a competition and then a monk (Liu) starts hunting for Lee and the prince. The monk questions Lun, who refuses to cooperate and is beaten, but is saved by the arrival of a masked Lee. Lun confides with Liu about the incident and his suspicions that Lee was the masked man. When these suspicions are proven right, the three set out to beat the monk and the eunuchs, and while they're about it, win the competition.

The film is full of spellbinding fight action, Aaron Kwok's kicking skills are a revelation and his swordplay is excellent. However, the film belongs to Beardy (Leung Kar-Yan), and Gordon Liu, both looking like they did in their prime. The two men

new wife, to get the list. The Ming patriots, of course, swear vengeance . . .

Chin Kar-Lok's awesome ability just gets better with every film, while Lam Ching-Ying gets a chance to leave the hopping vampire and ghost movies alone for a bit to sink his teeth into a proper role. Also known as *Shaolin Avengers*, this fast-paced movie showcases some decent performances.

KUNG FU OF SEVEN STEPS (1979)

Starring Cheng Tien-Chi, Chang Shan, Chia Kai,
Lung Fei
Directed by Ting Chung, Wang Chung-Kuang
Action by Chin Ming
Great China Film Company

A subversive military group, known as the Five Hands League, plans to overthrow a small trading town, but their plot is thwarted when town pickpocket Tiger (Tien-Chi) learns of their attempted coup. Together with his teacher Li San Pei (Kai), he takes out all the members of the Five Hands League. Finally, they must face the dreaded leader of the gang, white-haired Kong (Shan) in an intense end duel.

Also known as *Seven Steps of Kung Fu* and *Shaolin Raiders of Death*, this is an above-average indie from Taiwan.

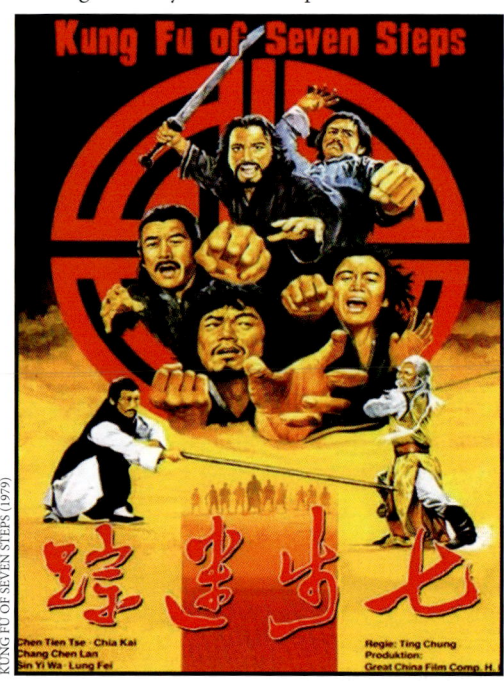

KUNG FU OF SEVEN STEPS (1979)

have a superb duel during the finale, with Beardy swinging a lethal Kwan Do against Liu's monk's spade. The flowing choreography is a throwback to the good ol' days, and a far cry from the fast-edit fight action of newer films.

KUNG FU VS. YOGA (1979)
Starring Chin Yuet-Sang, Alan Hsu, Michelle Yim, Dupar Singh
Directed by Chen Chuan
Action by Meng Hoi, Tsui Fat
Cheung Brothers Film Company

Two wily kung fu fanatics, Tiger (Yuet-Sang) and Wu Shing (Hsu), enter a kung fu contest without knowing what the prize is. Tiger, after many hard bouts, emerges victorious and claims his prize, the beautiful Miss Ting's hand in marriage. In order for the marriage to take place, Tiger has to embark on a martial arts odyssey to prove himself worthy. With the aid of Wu Shing, Tiger starts his quest, and the first trophy they must obtain is a book of secret Shaolin techniques kept by a monk. The second one is an infamous prostitute's gold brooch. The third and final obstacle is their toughest challenge: to steal the priceless ruby from the turban of a yoga expert.

The focal point of this action kung fu comedy is the unorthodox climactic confrontation between Tiger, Wu Shing, and the yoga master, played by Dupar Singh. You will not believe your eyes when you see Singh's out-of-this-world flexibility. Good crisp fights and funny plot twists make this well worth watching.

KUNG-FU GANGBUSTERS (1973)
Starring Jason Pai-Piao, Ingrid Hu Yin-Yin, Lu Chun-Ku
Directed by Sun Chia-Wen
Yangtze Film Company Ltd

A local man, whose brother was killed by gangsters, sets out to make the mob boss pay. Though adept at kung fu, he is finally helped by a young policeman, who is an even better martial artist.

The fighting, which is, of course, the main attraction for such a flick, is okay, although sometimes the blows are obviously pulled. It does become irritating when none of the characters actually stay down, they always get back up, no matter how many times they receive a foot or fist in the face.

This is a routine piece of kung fu fodder, featuring an anemic car chase, uncredited use of the *Shaft* theme and a lead protagonist who attempts some

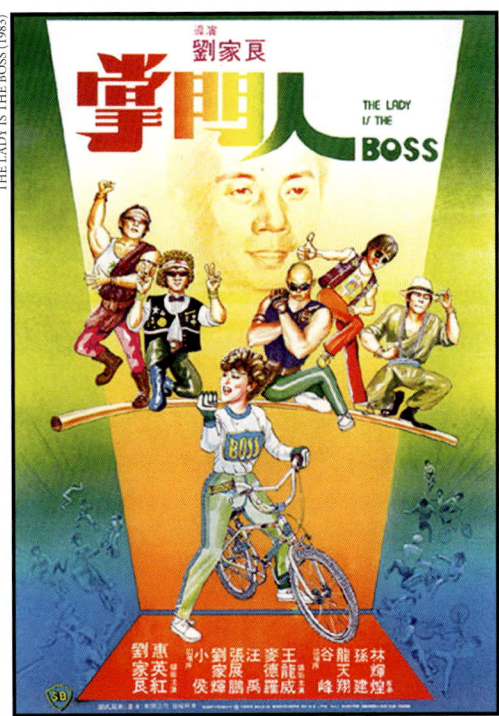

THE LADY IS THE BOSS (1983)

of Bruce Lee's mannerisms. There is a very realistic arm breaking shot, though, and some of the later punch-ups are well handled.

THE LADY IS THE BOSS (1983)
Starring Kara Hui, Hsiao Hou, Lau Kar-Leung, Gordon Liu
Directed by Lau Kar-Leung
Produced by Mona Fong
Action by Lau Kar-Leung, Hsiao Hou
Shaw Brothers

When Hua Chiang gym opens its new premises, the founder of the clan is invited to return from America to personally oversee the ceremony. However, being too ill to travel back to Hong Kong, the old man sends his daughter Chen Mei Ling (Hui) in his stead. Much to the consternation of the traditionalist Hua Chiang master Hsieh Yun (Kar-Leung), Chen then attempts to modernize the gym, importing American marketing methods and training values. A battle of vastly differing gender, social, and cultural attitudes ensues between Chen and Hsieh in this Asian comedy of manners. The two, though, are brought closer together when Chen inadvertently runs afoul of the local vice boss.

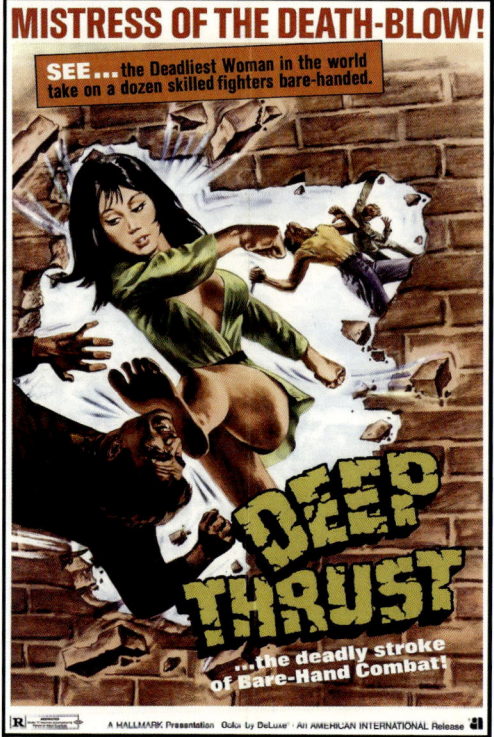

MISTRESS OF THE DEATH-BLOW!

SEE... the Deadliest Woman in the world take on a dozen skilled fighters bare-handed.

LADY WHIRLWIND (1972)

DEEP THRUST

...the deadly stroke of Bare-Hand Combat!

A HALLMARK Presentation Color by DeLuxe® An AMERICAN INTERNATIONAL Release

Director Lau Kar-Leung brings his usual mastery of fight choreography to this movie, though he seems slightly ill at ease with the generally lighthearted atmosphere.

LADY WHIRLWIND (1972)
Starring Angela Mao, Chang Yi, Chin Yuet-Sang,
Bai Ying
Directed by Huang Feng
Produced by Raymond Chow
Golden Harvest

A young woman, Tien (Mao), skilled in kung fu, sets out to find the man who drove her sister to suicide. The culprit, Ling Shih-Hua (Yi), has been in hiding for the past three years, perfecting his fighting skills in order to destroy a gang of opium traders. By coincidence, Tien has already had a run-in with the same gang's lackeys and, realizing Ling's plight, she is forced to put her feelings of retribution behind her and concentrate on defeating the gang.

The fight scenes and plot may well seem dated to today's legion of action fans, but it was films such as this which created the winning formula for many of Hong Kong's classics. Indeed, many of the most

popular filmmakers in Hong Kong today can be seen in bit parts in this flick, which is also known as *Deep Thrust*.

LAST HERO IN CHINA (1993)
Starring Jet Li, Cheung Man, Leung Kar-Yan,
Gordon Liu
Directed by Wong Jing
Produced by Charles Heung, Jet Li
Action by Yuen Woo-Ping
Win's Film Productions/Golden Harvest

Jet Li once again plays folk hero Wong Fei Hung in this excellent period piece. It opens in turn-of-the-century Hong Kong, with Wong provoking an attack by three members of the Boxer Society, an anti-foreigner peasant uprising. After kicking their respective butts into oblivion, Wong returns to Canton to find his clinic and gym has become unbearably overcrowded. Students set out to look for more spacious accommodation and unwittingly rent out a very unsuitable property from an obnoxious pimp. Wong is less than delighted to find the premises for his "Moral Reform Society" are slap-bang next to a brothel! Wong's troubles are doubled when he becomes the victim of a vendetta planned by Boxer Society leader Lui. Thickening the plot are priest Hung (Lui), who is stealing and selling girls to raise money for the Boxer Society, and a woman who is searching for her abducted sister. The scene is set for some truly rib-tickling comedy and adrenaline-pumping action.

Scorching skirmishes include a final duel, where Wong combats Lui's iron-spike vest with drunken boxing in a barnstorming battle. Lovers of acrobatic kung fu will appreciate the restrained wirework, aerial spins and handstand kicks, as well as Chicken Beak versus Centipede kung fu.

LAST HURRAH FOR CHIVALRY (1979)
Starring Damian Lau, Wei Pai, Fung Hark-On,
Lee Hoi-Sang
Directed by John Woo
Produced by Raymond Chow
Action by Fung Hark-On
Golden Harvest

When virtually every member of a man's family is murdered, he sets out to exact revenge and, to this end, he persuades Chang (Pai) to take up the fight against the invincible killer on his behalf. Chang joins forces with the irrepressible Tsing Yi

(Lau), a swordsman rather fond of his wine, and together the wise-cracking pair fight their way into the villain's stronghold, overcoming a series of diabolical tests before homing in on their objective.

John Woo, better known for his later, celebrated bullet-spitting epics like *Hard Boiled* and *The Killer*, here focuses on swordplay rather than gunplay. The film features a series of twists and surprises, with entertaining, surreal opponents, including the Sleeping Wizard, who fights while slumbering!

THE LEG FIGHTERS (1980)

Starring Tan Tao-Liang, Hsia Kuang-Li, Peng Kang,
Sun Jung-Chi
Directed by Lee Tso-Nam
Action by Peng Gang, Sun Jung-Chi, Wang Yao
Magnificent Tower Film Company/
Wa Nam Films Company

This simple tale deals with master kicker Tan Hai-Chi (Tao-Liang). After defeating a challenger from the "ground kicking sect," Tan goes on his way, but the brother of the beaten man, Pan Pak (Kang), is busy planning to take vengeance and wipe out all who are proficient in Tan's style of kung fu. Tan is employed by a wealthy widower to train his spoilt daughter, Phoenix (Kuang-Li). The beautiful young girl is at first desperate to be rid of the turbulent master but begins to realize that he is the only man who can show her the genuine benefits of martial arts training. After learning several lessons in humility, she begins to learn Tan's style and, in the tradition of such films, proves to be a natural. Once proficient in his art, Phoenix joins Tan in facing the villainous Pak, who has reared his silver-haired head again.

Also known as *The Invincible Kung Fu Legs*, this is essentially a lighthearted feature with some scenes of combat, with Tan's footwork the highlight of the flick.

LEGEND OF A FIGHTER (1982)

Starring Leung Kar-Yan, Yasuaki Kurata, Yuen Yat-Chor,
Fung Hark-On, Phillip Ko, Chen Yao-Lin
Directed by Yuen Woo-Ping
Produced by Ng See-Yuen
Action by Yuen Clan
Seasonal Film Corporation

This highly engrossing tale of courage and morality, masterfully told by Yuen Woo-Ping, looks at the life of one of China's most formidable fighters, Fok Yun Gap (also known as Huo Yuanjia). Gap's family's kung fu is renowned throughout China and many

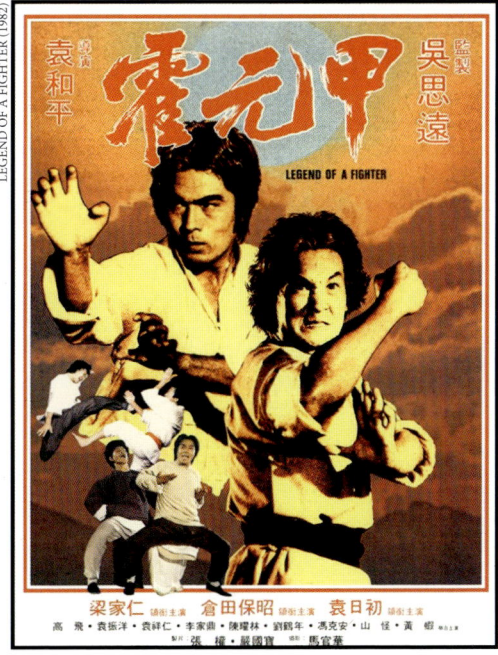

LEGEND OF A FIGHTER (1982)

wish to learn it. But if you are a stranger, a cheat, or a weakling, you are forbidden to learn. The young Gap (Yuen Yat-Chor) falls into the last category and is forced to study by his strict father (Ko), who has employed a teacher from Japan to further his son's academic abilities. But, in fact, the teacher (Kurata) is a master of Japanese bushido and wants to further his knowledge of Chinese martial arts. Aware of Gap's yearning, he decides to teach him martial arts as well as books. The years roll by and Gap (Kar-Yan), older and stronger, is a learned young man and the time comes for his teacher to return to Japan. One day a challenger arrives at the household, and Gap's father is now too old to fight, so has his students fight the challenger, but they are not his match. In steps Gap and, much to everyone's surprise, he demolishes the aggressor. News of his skill travels far and wide, and challengers come and go. After beating a Japanese karate man, who commits suicide after the shame of defeat, Gap receives a death challenge from a Japanese man wanting revenge for his ally in combat. When the challenger arrives, Gap's past catches up with him, and a cruel twist of fate ends this epic tale.

Moving and convincing performances from Yasuaki Kurata and Leung Kar-Yan, within a series of bone-smashing fight sequences, plus a superb screenplay, ensure first-rate viewing.

LEGEND OF THE DRUNKEN TIGER (1991)

Starring Alexander Lo Rei, Kara Wai, Hso Tung
Directed and produced by Robert Tai
Action by Robert Tai
Chi Movie Production Company Limited

Toward the end of the Ching dynasty, China is besieged by foreign powers stripping the country of its treasures. Only the drunken tiger and his warrior allies can stop the tyranny of the foreign besiegers.

Alexander Lo Rei heads a competent cast, with Kara Wai solid in a supporting role, though the film itself becomes less and less convincing as the story progresses.

LEGEND OF THE WOLF (1997)

Starring Donnie Yen, Dayo Wong, Carman Lee,
Ben Lam, Edmond Leung, Mak Wai-Cheung
Directed by Donnie Yen
My Way Film Company/Bullet Films

Donnie Yen stars as Fung Man Hin, a retired assassin who was once feared by all. Ben Chan (Leung), an aspiring assassin, searches for Fung with the dream of taking his place as the number one killer. Wai (Wong) knows where Fung is hiding, as a recluse, and leads

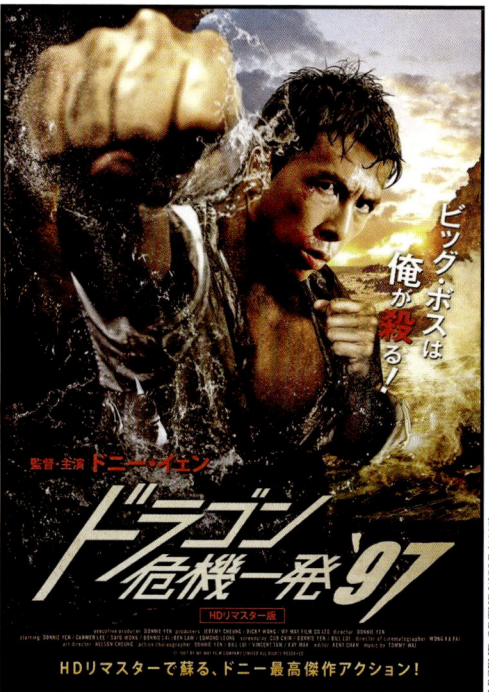

LEGEND OF THE WOLF (1997)

Ben to him. When they find Fung, he's sitting alone in an empty building, sleeping. Through a series of flashbacks, Wai recounts the memories that explain why Fung is the tortured soul he is today.

Legend of the Wolf was Donnie's directorial debut, and he delivers a good story. However, if there's anything to fault, it would be some of the ways the action was shot. The quick editing and sometimes hazy background can make the fight scenes feel too sped up. For example, in the opening scene, where Fung takes on a multitude of gangsters to save a girl from being raped and killed, the atmospheric lighting makes it difficult to keep up with the speed. The outdoor fights are better, but Donnie still seems to be experimenting with finding his own style. As a great movie fighter, it's unclear why he needs to film at such a fast shutter speed, which takes away from his on-screen abilities.

The film was retitled *The New Big Boss* in some territories. Was this because Donnie, being a huge Bruce Lee fan, somehow thought this would appeal to Bruce fans, as the cover depicts him wearing the trademark T-shirt similar to the one Bruce wore? Whatever the reason, the original title, *Legend of the Wolf*, works better. Overall, this was a good, solid attempt at starting Donnie's directing career.

LEGENDARY WEAPONS OF CHINA (1982)

Starring Lau Kar-Leung, Kara Wai, Hsiao Hou,
Gordon Liu, Lau Kar-Wing
Directed by Lau Kar-Leung
Produced by Mona Fong, Run Run Shaw
Action by Lau Kar-Leung, Hsiao Hou, Lee King-Chu
Shaw Brothers

This is widely regarded as one of the greatest genre movies ever made. It is set at the turn of the century, during the Boxer Rebellion, when gun-toting foreigners are invading China. In a bizarre ritual, kung fu masters meet to test their powers against the dreaded gun. Four bare-chested students stand before aimed rifles. Chinese mystics and a Shaolin monk dance and mouth incantations. As the action (and the strident score) rises to a frenzy . . . the rifles fire. The monk prays, the men remain standing. The Grandmasters smile at their success . . . and then the four men drop dead. Guns can defeat even the greatest kung fu warrior! Only one master is willing to admit the defeat. He is Lei Kung, played by director Lau Kar-Leung, who promptly disbands his school

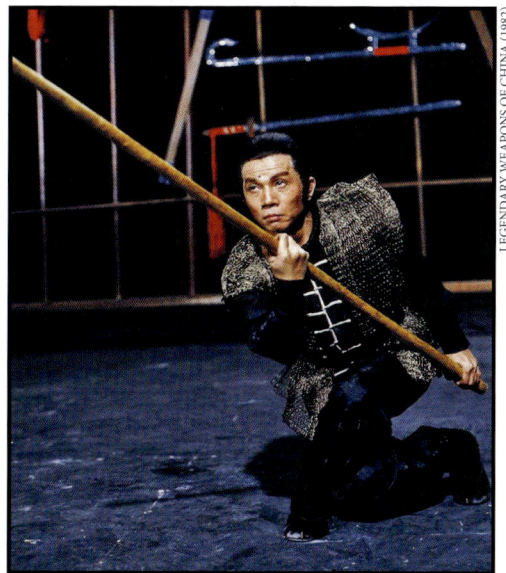

LEGENDARY WEAPONS OF CHINA (1982)

LEGEND OF THE LIQUID SWORD (1993)

Starring Aaron Kwok, Tsui Sui-Keung, Chingmy Yau, Gordon Liu, Cheung Man
Directed and produced by Wong Jing
Win's Film Productions

This film is a series of comic sketches and action scenes, held together by a tenuous plot, although Aaron Kwok does cut a dash.

Kwok plays Swordsman Chu, who sets off on his adventures after his master (Sui-Keung) selects him to duel with Shaolin monk Flowerless. Accompanied by his three sisters, our hero crosses paths with a variety of bizarre characters, including a sniggering swordsman called Metal Flower, a mystic called Seaweed and a bloodsucking villain called Batman. In one scene Chu must combat Flowerless without touching the ground. Unfortunately, after this, things get unspeakably silly, lapsing into a camp parody of the genre.

and leaves! The other schools want him silenced to prevent foreigners from discovering his doubts, so they send three killers after him. The scene is now set for some wild action, culminating in a twenty-minute duel in which Lei Kung fights his informer brother using every Chinese weapon bar the kitchen sink!

Everything about this movie is crisp: the plot, the well-developed characters and, of course, the stunning choreography, enhanced by terrific "fire-cracker" sound effects.

Also known as *Legendary Weapons of Kung Fu*, you should beg, steal, or borrow this film and watch it now!

LIFE GAMBLE (1979)

Starring Philip Kwok, Fu Sheng, Wang Lung-Wei, Kara Wai, Lu Feng, Lo Meng
Directed by Chang Cheh
Produced by Run Run Shaw
Shaw Brothers

Zi-Yu (Kwok) was a former top weaponsmith and fighter, but after a client (Feng) tried to kill him, Zi-Yu retired and became an anonymous blacksmith. But, when a group of thieves cause uproar, Zi-Yu finds out that he cannot retain his anonymity any longer.

Chang Cheh fills this movie, also known as *Life Combat*, with some odd characters and superb action, stirring it all into a rather complicated plot concerning sneaky motives, betrayal, a dart-firing metal gauntlet, and subterfuge.

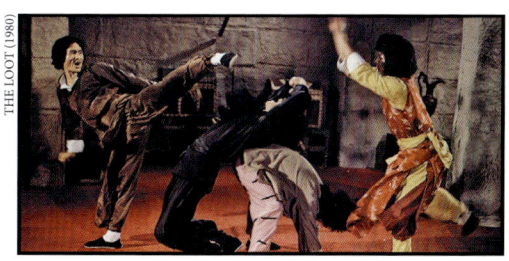

THE LOOT (1980)

THE LOOT (1980)

Starring David Chiang, Tsui Siu-Keung, Lily Li, Phillip Ko
Directed by Eric Tsang
Good Year Movie Co

When a spate of robberies is linked to the infamous thief known as the Spider, who disappeared twenty years before, a group of former accomplices get jumpy. Fortune-chaser Yang Wei (Chiang) gets caught up in this intrigue when he is employed as a guard to one of these accomplices. Yang teams up with the mysterious Fang Tsung (Siu-Keung), whose father was a victim of the Spider, to find out the Spider's bloody secret.

Featuring the same awe-inspiring team behind *The Challenger* (1979), this is an all-out comic fight fest, with top-notch kung fu displayed time and again, ending with a jaw-dropping finale that's made up of two lengthy, stunning fight scenes. Brilliant stuff.

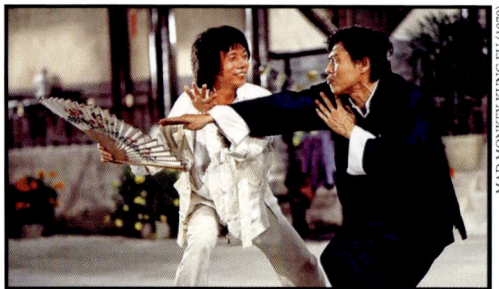

MAD MONKEY KUNG FU (1979)

MAD MONKEY KUNG FU (1979)
Starring Lau Kar-Leung, Hsiao Hou, Lo Lieh,
Kara Wai
Directed by Lau Kar-Leung
Produced by Mona Fong, Run Run Shaw
Action by Lau Kar-Leung
Shaw Brothers

Lau Kar-Leung stars as successful kung fu stage performer Chen, who has his hands smashed by the villainous Tuan (Lieh) while he's drunk. Tuan also traps Chen's sister into becoming his concubine. Forced by his injuries to give up the martial arts, Chen opens a street show with a monkey as his "partner." However, when local criminals kill the monkey, Chen and his pupil, the clownish petty thief Little Monkey (Hou), are led to an inevitable confrontation with Tuan, where their monkey style kung fu is put to the ultimate test.

Lau Kar-Leung directs the movie with the right balance of humor, ferocity and humanity.

MAFIA VS. NINJA (1985)
Starring Alexander Lo Rei, Philip So, Tang Lung,
Lan Hai Han, Eugene Trammel
Directed by Robert Tai
Action by Robert Tai
Golden Sun Films

More martial arts mayhem from madcap director Robert Tai! Jack Do (Lo Rei) leaves his hometown for the bustling streets of Shanghai. He finds work as a coolie and he meets Wu (So). They become friends, refusing to pay two villains who try to extort protection money from them, and discover that the two bandits belong to an evil organization. They join the rival Hung triad gang, who have vowed to rid the city of this corruptive force, but to do so they must first defeat the organization's hired killers, including Western boxers, Italian knife throwers, Japanese Samurai, karate fighters and, last but not least, the ninjas.

Crazy nonstop action on a grand scale and the usual kitsch pageantry that goes with all of Robert Tai's movies makes for ninety minutes of pure entertainment. And, hey, it's a great title for a movie, right?

Incidentally, the movie was so well received in some territories that the cast and crew were recalled to make the story into a three-part miniseries.

MAGIC SWORD (1993)
Starring Tuo Tsung-Hua, Emily Chu, Liu Chun,
Don Wong Tao
Directed by Ting Shan-Hsi
Taiwan Film Culture/Han Hsing Broadcasting

Imagine, if you will, an old Shaw Brothers classic like *The Last Woman of Shang* wedded to new wave cinematography and martial arts and you will get some idea of the feel and look of *Magic Sword*. Set in 500 BC, a time of rival kingdoms, the main thrust of the story is of Lord Kwan's attempts to secure the secret of the manufacture of steel swords in order to gain political and military ascendancy. This is the time of bronze and iron (known to contemporary Chinese writers as "the lovely metal" and "the ugly metal"), so our metalsmith hero is under some pressure to succeed!

With astonishing ease, this hitherto relatively realistic film, with its beautifully designed and lit steel furnaces, breaks into stunningly animated fantasy following the suicide of the metalsmith's wife. She throws herself into the furnace to ensure the success of the swords and emerges as a spirit-bird with ensuing nonstop action. Perhaps this works so well because the film is set in a time when the old legends were still mingled with the reality of an emerging Chinese nation.

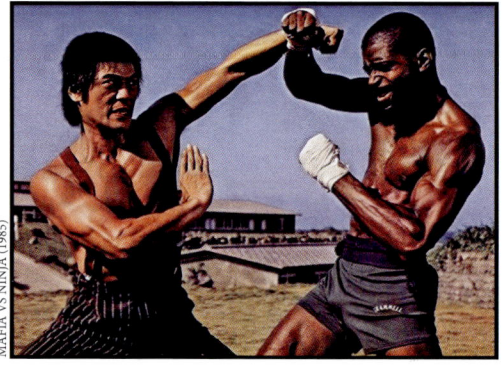

MAFIA VS NINJA (1985)

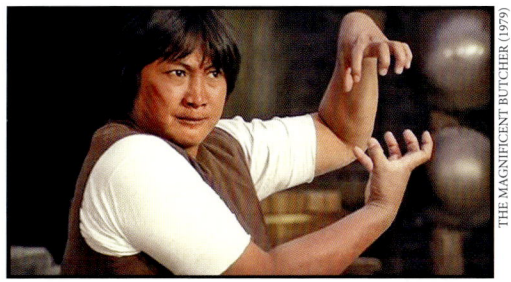

THE MAGNIFICENT BUTCHER (1979)

MAGNIFICENT BODYGUARDS (1978)

Starring Jackie Chan, Bruce Leung, James Tien,
Wang Quen
Directed by Lo Wei
Lo Wei Motion Picture Company

Three bodyguards (Chan, Leung and Tien) are hired by a rich maiden to escort her sick brother through a bandit-ridden gorge of death. The dynamic trio take on the assignment, unaware that the person within the sedan chair is none other than the bandit king himself, who has been banished by the girl's mother. A violent and bloody reunion awaits and the bodyguards will have to fight their way out from the middle of it.

Better-than-average fights and the charismatic Jackie Chan saves this otherwise dull actioner.

THE MAGNIFICENT BUTCHER (1979)

Starring Sammo Hung, Kwan Tak-Hing, Yuen Biao,
Lee Hoi-Sang, Fung Hark-On, Lam Ching-Ying,
Chung Fat, Wei Pai, Fan Mei-Sheng
Directed by Yuen Woo-Ping
Action by Yuen Clan, Sammo Hung
Golden Harvest

Butcher Wing (Hung) is master Wong Fei Hung's top student. He is also the most trouble-bound. His good intentions cause a feud between Wong Fei Hung (Tak-Hing) and master Ko of the Five Dragon sect. In a test of calligraphy that escalates into a fanciful fight, master Ko is sent off with the word "respect" printed on his forehead. More trouble is afoot when Butcher Wing's brother Lam arrives, searching for his bro, who he hasn't seen in over ten years. With him is his pretty wife, who catches the eye of master Ko's prodigal son Tai Hoi (Hark-On). He manages to capture her, leaving poor Lam destitute and suicidal. In the nick of time, Sam Seed (aka Beggar King), after a magnificent fight with Butcher Wing, reunites the portly brothers. Together they think up a plan to get Lam's wife back, but, as usual, Butcher

Wing botches things up and, in saving the young wife, also drags along the goddaughter of master Ko, mistaking her for the prisoner. Things go from bad to worse when Tai Hoi kills the goddaughter and frames Butcher Wing. Master Ko and his assassins storm Wong Fei Hung's school and, after a fierce fight, Wing, Chat (Pai) and Foon (Biao) escape. Wing gets badly injured by Ko's cosmic palm, but Sam Seed teaches him the secrets of Hung boxing. When Tai Hoi murders Lam, Butcher Wing confronts him in a violent and bloody duel: an epic showdown with Butcher Wing's five animals style going up against master Ko's five elements.

This movie was originally set to star Yuen Siu-Tin in the Sam Seed role, but, sadly, he passed away during the early stages of production. The film was completed with Fan Mei-Sheng in the role, and has become an enduring kung fu classic.

The Magnificent Butcher is a must-see for all Hong Kong kung fu film buffs.

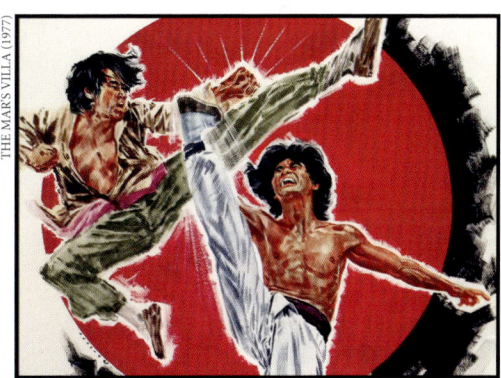

THE MAR'S VILLA (1977)

THE MAR'S VILLA (1977)

Starring John Liu, Phillip Ko, Tung Wei, Chia Kai,
Tang Bao-Yun
Directed by Ting Chung
Good Friends Motion Picture Co

Super-kicker "Northern Leg" John Liu plays Mar Tien-Liang. On his wedding night, Mar's villa is attacked by the evil, bloodthirsty Kang (Ko), who robs Mar of his stock and kills his men. Mar engages in a death duel with Kang and kills him. Mar's wife Ling (Bao-Yun), distraught because of the killings, begs her husband not to fight again, but this promise is soon broken as Kang's brother Tang (also played by Phillip Ko) is now out for vengeance. He and his nephew Fan (Wei) make Mar's life hell, kidnapping his wife's brother, torturing Mar in an iron cage to drive him mad, and eventually luring Mar's wife away to live with the wicked and envious pretty boy Fan. Mar, now totally mad, wanders the streets begging for bread. Luckily, he is found by his old and trusted servant (Kai), who shelters him and, after some rigorous training, Mar fully recuperates, ready for the climactic challenge of death.

The Mar's Villa, also known as *Rocky Lee* and *Wu Tang Magic Kick*, is a 70s Taiwanese independent production that sticks in the memory thanks to Liu's fine legwork, good use of locations, lots of fights and a cool, cheeky soundtrack that borrows from Dominic Frontiere's *Hang 'Em High* score.

MARTIAL ARTS MASTER WONG FEI HUNG (1992)

Starring Chin Kar-Lok, Lam Ching-Ying, Jacqueline Ng
Directed by Lee Chiu
Great Audience Film & Television Production

The early years of the real-life hero are represented here as full of mischief and confrontation, portraying the young Wong Fei Hung as an unintentional trouble maker. While coming to terms with his father's death in a duel with a Japanese warrior, Fei Hung has a run-in with a gang of opium traders that are destroying the village. To add to his troubles, the new love of his life is the killer's sister, who is having to cope with her brother's vast hunger for vengeance. Thrown into a battle of loyalties, Fei Hung must decide between his honor, his love and the welfare of the village.

Also known as *Great Hero from China*, the film shows the unlikely partnership of Fei Hung and his father's killer to destroy the opium gang and the corrupt officials that guard it. Although factually inaccurate, this movie is still worth a view: Chin Kar-Lok is an impressive performer here, who needs no wires to look fantastic. Jet Li, take note!

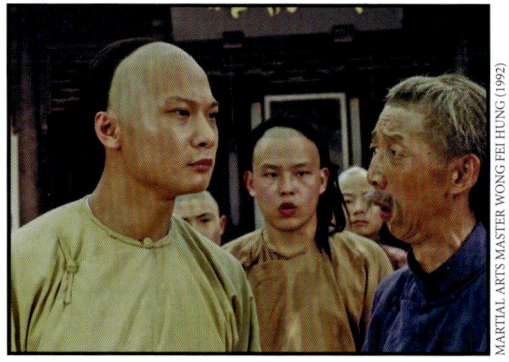

MARTIAL ARTS MASTER WONG FEI HUNG (1992)

MARTIAL ARTS OF SHAOLIN (1986)

Starring Jet Li, Yu Hai, Yu Cheng-Hui,
Hu Jian-Qiang, Ma Chen
Directed by Lau Kar-Leung
Shaw Brothers

More mainland martial arts magic, with the defiant Shaolin baldheads conspiring with rebels to bring a violent, out of control warlord to justice.

This, you'll be pleased to know, comes in the form of many spectacular displays of Wu Shu wizardry. There's mesmerising Mantis style, captivating calligraphy-fu and prodigious pole-handling.

This ambitious picture, known also as *Shaolin Temple 3* and *North & South Shaolin*, ratchets up its production values with the inclusion of hundreds of extras in vividly colored costumes and the effective use of luscious landscapes. In every sense of the word a stunner: it's staff-swinging, shape-pulling, back-flipping good!

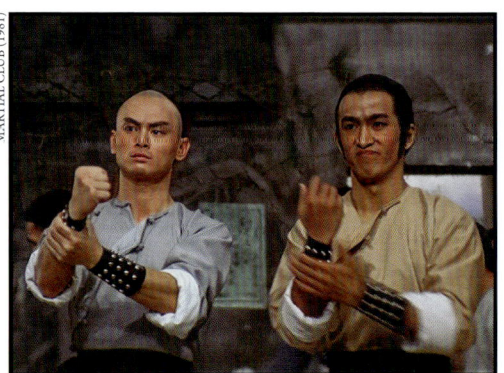

MARTIAL CLUB (1981)

MARTIAL CLUB (1981)

Starring Gordon Liu, Kara Wai, Robert Mak,
Wang Lung-Wei, Chu Tiet-Wo, Ku Feng, Robert Mak
Directed by Lau Kar-Leung
Produced by Mona Fong
Shaw Brothers

More martial arts mastery from Mr. Kung Fu, Lau Kar-Leung. In Canton there are three famous martial clubs, Wong, Chan and Lu. While the Wong and Chan schools are both friendly and hold mutual respect for one another, the Lu school is unfriendly and devious by comparison. Master Lu (Tiet-Wo) invites his friend, Master Su (Lung-Wei), a highly skilled Ching Wu exponent from the north. Lu's cunning attempts to pit Master Su's skills against Master Wong's school are thwarted when Wong's son, Wong Fei Hung, matches blows with the northerner in a battle of wits, strength and morality. The northerner leaves Canton a wiser and improved man, while Master Lu is excluded from the New Year lion dance festivities.

Aka *Instructors of Death*, this nonviolent look into the moral code of Cantonese folk hero Wong Fei Hung, superbly portrayed by Gordon Liu, is funny, exciting and extremely well-crafted by director Lau Kar-Leung, himself a former master in Canton. Magnificent fights and the good supporting performances of Kara Wai, Robert Mak, and Ku Feng guarantee an awesome viewing experience.

THE MASKED AVENGERS (1981)
Starring Philip Kwok, Lu Feng, Chiang Sheng,
Chu Ke, Wang Li
Directed by Chang Cheh
Produced by Mona Fong
Action by Philip Kwok, Lu Feng, Chiang Sheng
Shaw Brothers

Another epic tale of vengeance and betrayal from director Chang Cheh. The insidious Mask Gang of hired killers have been terrorizing the countryside, with their mastery of the trident and an inherent brutality. But who are these men, and what are the identities of the three chiefs in the gold masks? The answers inevitably lead to a few surprises, as battle is joined.

Chiang Sheng, Chu Ke, Lu Feng, Philip Kwok, and Wang Li head the cast in this quick-fire tale that boasts a stunning climax at the Mask Gang's headquarters, housed inside an abandoned Buddhist temple.

THE MASTER (1980)
Starring Yuen Tak, Chen Kuan-Tai, Wang Lung-Wei,
Wen Hsueh-Erh, Chan Lau, Lau Hok-Nin
Directed by Lo Chun Ku
Produced by Mona Fong
Action by Hsu Hsia
Shaw Brothers

Three gangsters make a surprise attack on Chin Tien-Yun (Kuan-Tai), a renowned and skilled martial artist of strange character. Chin is badly wounded and takes refuge with Kao Chien (Tak), who is already a pupil of Shi Chen Chung (Hok-Nin). Chin teaches his own martial skills to Kao out of gratitude. One day, during practice at Shi's gym, Kao accidentally reveals his new expertise. In order to protect Chin, his secret new master and also an enemy of Shi,

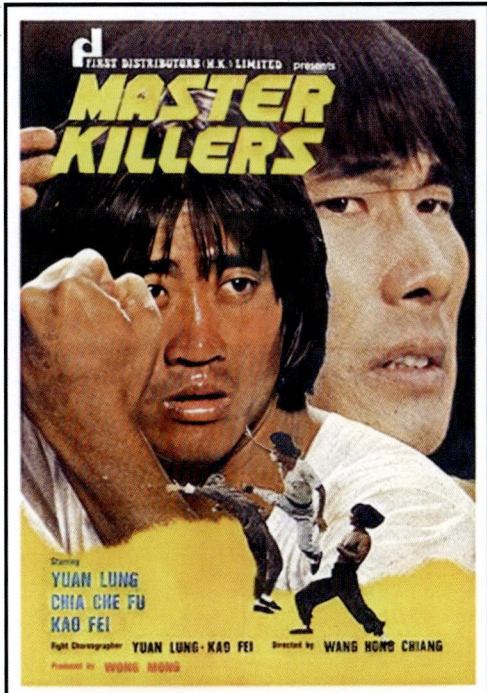

MASTER KILLERS (1980)

Kao endures brutal treatment. Chin reveals his presence, a fight breaks out, and, as Chin flees for his life, he falls into the hands of the same three gangsters who this time kill him. Kao is expelled in disgrace and seeks work at a small restaurant, where he continues to improve his kung fu. He learns that Shi's gym is being taken over by the three gangsters and immediately sets out to take revenge.

Also going by the title *3 Evil Masters*, this flick is martial arts entertainment at its best. Yuen Tak shines as the kindly student who saves the charismatic Chen Kuan-Tai from the three evil masters, and there are kung fu styles and weapons aplenty.

MASTER KILLERS (1980)
Starring Phillip Ko, Casanova Wong, Chan Lau,
Yuen Lung, Bolo Yeung
Directed by Wang Hung-Chiang
First Distributors

Betrayal and deceit are the themes of this actioner. Two long-lost siblings, Yuen Lung and Casanova Wong, are pitted against each other by an evil kung fu doctor (Ko), who fears that they might be descendants of a man he once killed. The tables are turned when the two young men finally realize they are brothers

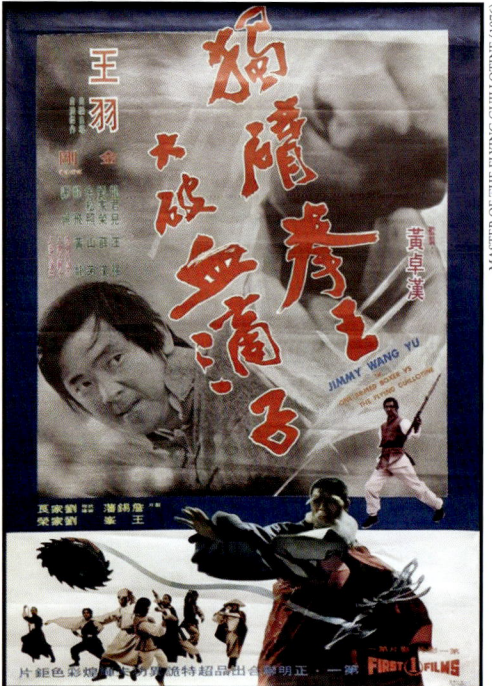

MASTER OF THE FLYING GUILLOTINE (1976)

and, together with the help of an old beggarman who teaches them the delicate art of Concubine Fist, they take their revenge on the ruthless doc.

Also known as *The Master Avengers*, the film's dull storyline is lifted by the final fight, which has Casanova Wong and Phillip Ko operating at their best. Watch out for Bolo Yeung not looking as he tackles the avenging duo!

MASTER OF THE FLYING GUILLOTINE (1976)

Starring Jimmy Wang Yu, Kam Kong, Lung Chun-Erh, Lau Kar-Wing, Tony Sum, Wang Yung-Sheng
Directed by Wang Yu
Produced by Wong Cheuk-Hon
Action by Lau Kar-Leung, Lau Kar-Wing
First Films Organisation

In this sequel to *One-Armed Boxer* (1972), the blind master of the flying guillotine searches for the one-armed boxer (Wang Yu) in the year 1730. The boxer is a Ming supporter presently attending a martial arts tournament, so to help with the hunt, the guillotine master secures the aid of two attendees. One of these dudes is an Indian fighter (actually Wang Yung-Sheng in turban and brownface), who can stretch out his arms to ever-extending lengths (quite

a technique). The one-armed boxer defeats the two hirelings and eventually battles the blind master in an undertaker's room that's booby trapped with axe-throwing devices. After the master receives an axe through his body, he is punched through the ceiling and, as he rolls down the roof, our boxer hero kicks one of the coffins out of the undertaker's room, and the blind dead master neatly falls into it!

The title weapon, the flying guillotine, as you no doubt know, resembles a quilted tea cosy on a chain. The master throws it over a victim's head, blades flick out to sever the neck, and a net then drops down to hold the detached head, while the master yanks on the chain to return his handy deadly weapon to his grasp.

Jimmy Wang Yu's awkward martial arts style may not make him the prettiest of fighters, but his films are very entertaining and this production, also known as *The One Armed Boxer Vs. the Flying Guillotine* and *One-Armed Boxer II*, is full of enjoyably weird incidents: strangulation by ponytail, a guy with testicles impervious to kicks due to his protective spirit (which falters when his eyes get poked out), a man hopping from sword-tip to sword-tip without being cut, and the one-armed boxer being able to walk over the ceiling because of his breathing technique! The Indian fighter, of course, is one of the more memorable moments in this movie, as his arms lengthen absurdly to help him beat his foes.

If nothing else, watch the opening of this film, featuring inspired use of the tunes "Super" and "Super 16" by German band Neu! This is, dare I say, one of the paciest, coolest credit sequences ever.

MASTER OF ZEN (1994)
Starring Derek Yee, Fan Siu-Wong, Wu Ma
Directed and produced by Brandy Yuen
Action by Brandy Yuen
Brandy Film Production

With untold numbers of movies having been centered around folk such as Wong Fei Hung and the Shaolin heroes Fong Sai Yuk and Hung Si Kwan, and a fair few made about the originators of the Wing Chun system, it is quite surprising that there have been so few concerned with the creator of Shaolin kung fu, the Indian monk Tamo (Bodhidharma).

A cast of what appears to be hundreds were employed as part of this production, which is definitely an epic, where the fights are secondary to an essentially simple but engrossing plot. Western viewers may find the film's atmosphere too surreal

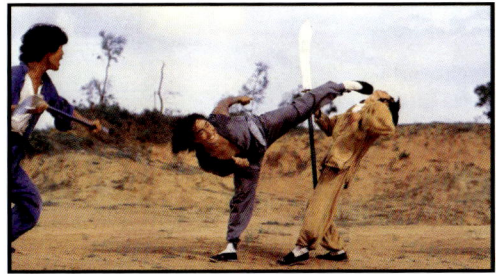

THE MASTER STRIKES (1980)

and kung fu enthusiasts may wonder why, when Tamo was the art's originator, he has to float about aided by wires. The point of the film is, however, that Tamo was more than merely an excellent fighter but rather an important spiritual leader: while Jesus was content to walk on water, Tamo bounces across it!

THE MASTER STRIKES (1980)

Starring Casanova Wong, Eddy Ko, Ching Siu-Tung,
Yen Shi-Kwan, Meng Yuen-Man
Directed by Kao Pao-Shu
Action by Ching Siu-Tung
Park Films

When escort Chen (Wong) loses a valuable jade horse, the owner, Lung (Shi-Kwan), who in reality is a master crook, forces Chen out of business with his excessive compensation demands. This drives the uncomprehending Chen mad. Two conniving conmen, played by Yuen-Man and Siu-Tung, use the mad kung fu expert to lead them to Lung's money.

Casanova Wong gets his finest ever role, as a gibbering lunatic who just happens to have some of the most devastating legwork around. Meng Yuen-Man and Ching Siu-Tung are both superb, especially when they let off the "heaven and earth" kung fu style. Also known as *Super Tiger*, the overall results are awesome.

MASTER WITH CRACKED FINGERS (1979)

Starring Jackie Chan, Hon Kwok-Choi, Dean Shek,
Yuen Siu-Tin
Directed by Mu Chu
Produced by Lee Leung Kao
Soon Lee Films

This cheap offering was actually created using footage from the obscure film *The Cub Tiger from Kwang Tung*, which featured a young Jackie Chan, with extra material, focusing on Dean Shek and Yuen Siu-Tin, added to the mix. This was done,

obviously, to cash in on Jackie's success after films like *Snake in the Eagle's Shadow* and *Drunken Master*.

The story sees Jackie undergoing training courtesy of a beggar/master and getting into trouble with a bunch of hoods. This tatty flick also goes by the title *Snake Fist Fighter*.

MING PATRIOTS (1976)

Starring Bruce Li, Michael Chan Wai-Man,
Chang Chin, Lung Fong, Chia Ling, Chang Yi
Directed by Tsai Yang-Ming
Produced by Wong Cheuk-Hon
Action by Lau Kar-Leung, Lau Kar-Wing
First Film Production Company

After the Ching forces overthrow the Ming dynasty, a small group of skilled fighters attempt to escort a Ming princess and her treasure to the safety of loyal forces. Hot in pursuit is a large Ching army, led by Chang Yi. The patriots hide the treasure in a dead pig, which they float down a river parallel to their route. The journey is fraught with danger, as friendships are put to the test.

Chang Yi, as the archvillain, puts in a particularly memorable performance as the sadist with a snuff

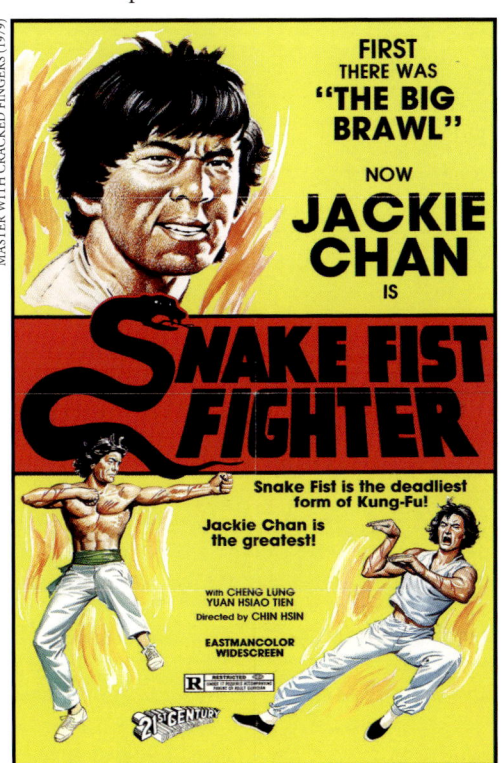

MASTER WITH CRACKED FINGERS (1979)

FIRST THERE WAS "THE BIG BRAWL" NOW JACKIE CHAN IS

SNAKE FIST FIGHTER

Snake Fist is the deadliest form of Kung-Fu!

Jackie Chan is the greatest!

WITH CHENG LUNG
YUAN HSIAO TIEN
Directed by CHIN HSIN

EASTMANCOLOR
WIDESCREEN

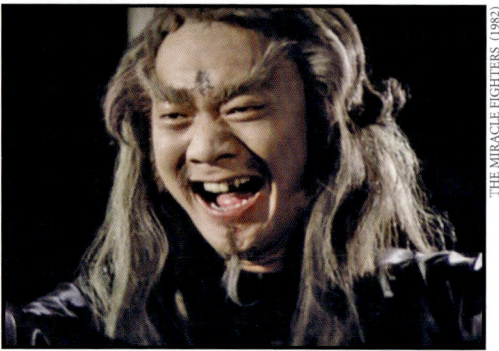

THE MIRACLE FIGHTERS (1982)

bottle and a gift for kung fu. Also known as *Revenge of the Patriots* and *Dragon Reincarnate*, this movie has copious amounts of decently choreographed fights, which is good, but it also has some animal cruelty (the pig was killed for real), which isn't so good.

THE MIRACLE FIGHTERS (1982)
Starring Yuen Yat-Choh, Leung Kar-Yan,
Yuen Shun-Yee, Yuen Cheung-Yan, Brandy Yuen
Directed by Yuen Woo-Ping
Produced by Leonard K.C. Ho, Raymond Chow
Action by Yuen Clan
Golden Harvest/Peace Film Production Co

In this weird and wonderful offering from Yuen Woo-Ping, set in seventeenth-century China, the Bat Master (Shun-Yee) captures a young orphan (Yat-Choh), who resembles a long-lost prince. He tattoos the royal birthmark onto the sole of the boy's foot and keeps him in his palace, guarded by a poor slave who is incarcerated in a large jar with holes for his arms and legs. After an amusing fight with the bottle baby, the boy escapes and seeks refuge with a pair of Taoist magicians (Leung Kar-Yan and Yuen Cheung-Yan), who, despite their many years of marriage, can't see eye to eye on anything. Each wants the lad as their own student, but, tired of the squabbling, he learns from both. Meanwhile, the Bat Master sends his rodent-like assassins after the youth, knowing that his capture will assure him an important position in the government. The assassins are no match for the Taoists and are killed by their own tricky schemes, so the Bat Master must face the wrath of the Taoists in a hilarious duel, with the boy transformed into a foot-high kung fu midget. The Taoists urge the boy to enter the contest at the annual wizards conference, where he must defeat many other wizards, fighters and obstacles of madness to become the acclaimed miracle fighter.

This is one of the most original, inventive and well-directed comedy-kung-fu movies ever and was hugely successful.

MONKEY KUNG FU (1980)
Starring Chen Mu-Chuan, Chang Yi, Yueh Hua,
Eddy Ko
Directed by Lo Chi
Sky Melody Film Company

An expert of the floating snake style terrorizes the martial arts community, destroying the lives of those who refuse to follow him. To protect the future of his own style, an expert of monkey kung fu conceals his identity by working as a barber in a small village. An enthusiastic young man, wanting to study martial arts, discovers the old man's skill and, after much begging, convinces the Sifu to teach him. Months of training equip the young man with the skills to confront the evil master of the snake and to finally put an end to his reign of terror.

Also known as *Drunken Monkey* and *Monkey Fist, Floating Snake*, this film is obviously influenced by Jackie Chan's *Snake in the Eagle's Shadow* and *Drunken Master*, but it's definitely a vapid knockoff of those better Seasonal Film hits.

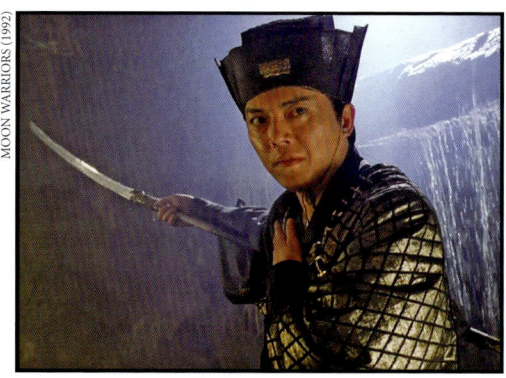

MOON WARRIORS (1992)

MOON WARRIORS (1992)
Starring Andy Lau, Anita Mui, Kenny Bee,
Maggie Cheung
Directed by Sammo Hung
Action by Corey Yuen, Ching Siu-Tung
Team Work Motion Pictures

The valiant 13th Prince of the empire is embroiled in a bitter struggle to wrest back the crown from his nefarious younger brother, the rebellious 14th Prince. Along the way, the 13th Prince (Bee) is saved

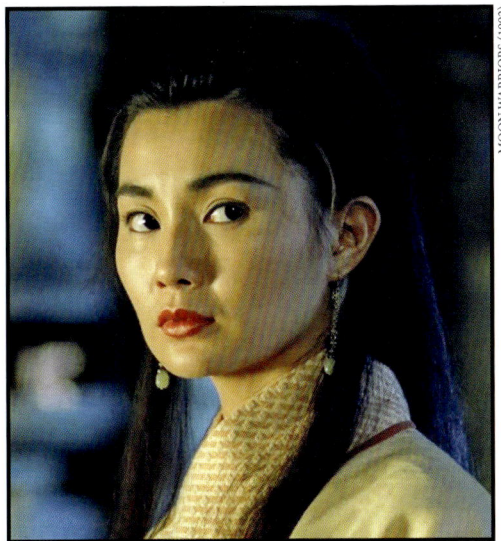

MOON WARRIORS (1992)

Sheng's last films before his tragic death in the summer of 1983. Here he showcases his extended kung fu repertoire, using three-section staff, samurai sword, butterfly knives, boxing, and Chinese Mantis style too.

MY SON (1970)

Starring Jimmy Wang Yu, Margaret Hsing Hui,
Tien Fong, Ku Feng, Wu Ma
Directed by Lo Chen
Produced by Runme Shaw
Shaw Brothers

Only die-hard Wang Yu buffs will find something in this dated tragic teen rebellion movie, in which he plays Kuo-Liang, the motherless son of a police commissioner. He falls in love with a bunny girl, whose father has been missing at sea for the past seven years. The tormented Kuo-Liang leaves his comfortable home, wanting nothing more to do with his estranged father, who he never forgave for letting his mother die. As the naive Romeo's love deepens, so do his debts. In desperation, the lovers turn to gambling, only to find themselves drawn deeper into the endless spiral of debt.

Some stylish direction, psychedelic sets and a few rough fights from Wang Yu provide relief from this otherwise tedious film.

NEW DRAGON GATE INN (1992)

Starring Tony Leung Ka-Fai, Maggie Cheung, Brigitte
Lin, Donnie Yen
Directed by Raymond Lee
Produced by Tsui Hark
Action by Ching Siu-Tung, Yuen Bun
Seasonal Film Corporation/Film Workshop

Aka *Dragon Inn*, this reworking of the King Hu classic opens in mid-Ming dynasty, at a time when powerful eunuchs have taken control of the Imperial court, ushering in a reign of terror. The despotic head eunuch Cho (Donnie Yen), in a bid for supreme rule, proceeds to eliminate all obstacles in his way. After torturing to death the imperial military commander, he sets out to eliminate Chow (Tony Leung Ka-Fai), a military instructor who has set up a makeshift group of resistance fighters. Using the dead commander's orphans as bait, Cho sets up a trap to snare Chow, but fails when the resistance army save the children. Chow tells his band and his lover Yau to meet up with him later at the Dragon Gate Inn, run by an outlaw hostess (Cheung) and her merry band of

from an ambush by naive fisherman Fei (Lau), who becomes a close friend of the regal hero.

Moon Warriors contains some interesting plot developments. Firstly, the 13th Prince's inner sanctum is breached by Hsien (Cheung), a swordswoman ordered by the evil 14th Prince to kill his brother, but she secretly loves her intended victim. Meanwhile, Fei is charged by the 13th Prince with bringing a princess (Mui), who his future bride, safely through enemy lines, but the pair fall in love on the journey.

This Sammo Hung–directed swashbuckler is a solid, vibrant affair, featuring romance, acrobatic wirework fighting and even a killer whale!

MY REBELLIOUS SON (1982)

Starring Fu Sheng, Ku Feng, Michael Chan Wai-Man,
Wang Lung-Wei
Directed by Sun Chung
Produced by Mona Fong
Shaw Brothers

Fu Sheng portrays Chang Siu Tai, the crafty son of a famous doctor (Feng). When not causing havoc at his father's clinic, Chang can be found picking on local mobsters or entering kung fu tournaments under false pretences. Chang's skills are put to good use when a group of foreigners, aided by Japanese samurai, take a priceless gold statue of the goddess of mercy from the town's temple. In a dazzling display of martial arts, Chang sends the bad guys packing and the statue is returned to her place in the temple.

This knockabout kung fu comedy was one of Fu

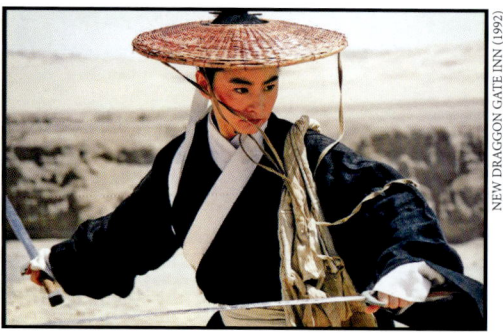

NEW DRAGON GATE INN (1992)

barbarians. An enraged Cho assigns some of his best secret police to hunt down Chow. The good guys and the bad converge at the Dragon Gate Inn, with Chow unable to escape unless the outlaw landlady reveals the location of a secret passage.

Although some comical incidents occasionally lighten the mood, the general atmosphere is tense and claustrophobic, with revenge and hatred forever simmering. It's great, nail-biting stuff, and the action scores high on the adrenaline-ometer, most notably the final battle, which was shot on location in the Gobi Desert. It was a nightmare to shoot and injuries were frequent, but it looks terrific. The love triangle between the flirtatious innkeeper, high-minded Chow, and his soulmate Yau also allows for some ingenious character development and amusing, flirtatious moments.

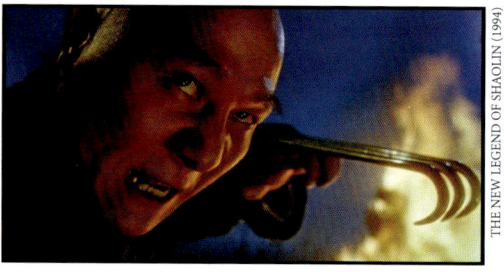

THE NEW LEGEND OF SHAOLIN (1994)

THE NEW LEGEND OF SHAOLIN (1994)

Starring Jet Li, Chingmy Yau, Wang Lung-Wei, Xie Miao, Deanie Ip, Wong Jing
Directed by Wong Jing
Action by Corey Yuen
Upland Films

The tale of Shaolin folk hero Hung Hei-Kwun and his son Man-Ting is told here in a very different light. Hung (Li) and his son (Miao) are fugitives trying to stay one step ahead of ruthless Manchu officers and renegade Shaolin traitors. Hung and Man-Ting come to the aid of young pupils who survived the massacre

at Shaolin and must present a map (tattooed on their backs) detailing the whereabouts of Manchu treasure to a monk. Hot on the trail of the Shaolin kids is Ma Ling-Yee, a poisonous, corrupt Shaolin ex-monk who rides around in a customized armored car. Finally, in the finale, Hung and Man-Ting confront Ma Ling-Yee, who gets kicked into an acid-filled vat.

Also going by the title *Legend of the Red Dragon*, the many comic outbursts mar this movie, though the fight scenes, courtesy of an underutilized Jet Li, are cool and make the film watchable.

THE NEW ONE-ARMED SWORDSMAN (1971)

Starring David Chiang, Ti Lung, Lee Ching, Ku Feng, Chen Sing
Directed by Chang Cheh
Produced by Runme Shaw
Action by Lau Kar-Leung, Tang Chia
Shaw Brothers

This classic tale of chivalry and retribution stars David Chiang as a young swordsman, Lei Li, who loses his right arm after being tricked in a duel with the corrupt warlord Lung (Feng). Lei flees and takes a menial job as a waiter in a small and remote inn. Here he meets a wandering swordsman, Feng (Lung), who tries to encourage Lei to take up arms and storm Lung's mountain fortress. Lei is not persuaded, and continues about his tasks, but when Feng fails to return, our one-armed avenger transforms from passive waiter into a raging death force, which ultimately leads to a blood-spattered ending.

This is really worth checking out, especially for Lei's battle with multiple opponents on the magnificent Bridge of Death, constructed especially for this film.

NEW SHAOLIN BOXERS (1976)

Starring Fu Sheng, Wang Lung-Wei, Jenny Tseng, Leung Kar-Yan
Directed by Chang Cheh
Chang's Film Company

Jian (Sheng) is the only man to stand up against the town's gang boss (Lung-Wei) and his lackeys, but, as Jian painfully discovers, his kung fu isn't good enough to beat the boss. Jian's Sifu sends him to a Shaolin monk to learn Choy Lay Fat, with devastating consequences.

Fu Sheng rises above the rest of the cast with an excellent performance, as the only man to give a

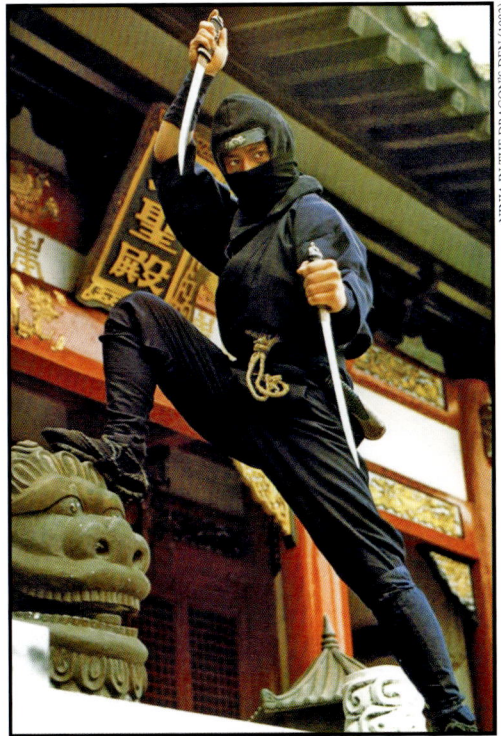

NINJA IN THE DRAGON'S DEN (1982)

damn about his town. The action is consistently superb, with Fu Sheng's use of Choy Lay Fat style standing out. Also known as *Demon Fist of Kung Fu*, this film is a classic of its kind.

NINJA HOLOCAUST (1985)

Starring Michael Chan Wai-Man, Mabel Kwong,
Casanova Wong, John Ladalski, Phillip Ko
Directed by Yeung Chun-Bong, Choi Young-Chul
First Films

Also known as *City Ninja*, this is a Hong Kong production where the rather acrobatic sex scenes are often more inventive than the fight choreography. Casanova Wong, one of Hong Kong cinema's best kickers, and veteran hardman Michael Chan Wai-Man appear in this action film, which concerns the quest for a necklace upon which the numbers of a Swiss bank account have been inscribed. Rival gangs hit each other a lot, boxers copulate with their managers' wives, and ninjas run around and disappear whenever they feel so inclined.

The reason for the oddness of this plot is due to the fact that it's actually a cut-and-paste flick, merging footage from a softcore-sex-and-boxing film

called *Rocky's Love Affairs*, material from a Korean martial arts picture called *Hwa-ya*, plus newly shot ninja scenes. These disparate elements are all added together to create this vortex of demented, inspired awfulness.

NINJA IN ANCIENT CHINA (1993)

Starring Dong Zhi-Hua, Du Yu-Ming, Chan Yee-Gong,
Lu Feng
Directed and produced by Chang Cheh
Chang He Film Company

A Han dynasty general is tricked into killing a Taoist priest and ninja teacher, forcing his students, the Five Element Ninja, to seek vengeance. Two join the general's household, where they spy on the layout and guard placements, and wait for their chance to avenge their teacher's death.

This is a return to traditional kung fu filmmaking, bursting with urgent fight action and colorful costumes, showcasing Chang Cheh's interest in brotherhood and morality in a production, also known as *The Prowess*, which turned out to be his final film.

NINJA IN THE DRAGON'S DEN (1982)

Starring Conan Lee, Hiroyuki Sanada,
Hwang Jang-Lee, Chin Lung
Directed by Corey Yuen
Produced by Ng See-Yuen
Action by Corey Yuen, Meng Hoi
Seasonal Film Corporation

With such a tradition of anti-Japanese sentiment in Chinese action films (take Jimmy Wang Yu's movies, for example) it is good to see a positive change. In this fast-paced tale of a ninja taking revenge on Chinese fighters for his father's death, Hiroyuki Sanada does not play an insidious villain, rather, he is a heroic victim of circumstances. Conan Lee plays the Chinese hero who collaborates with Sanada in a

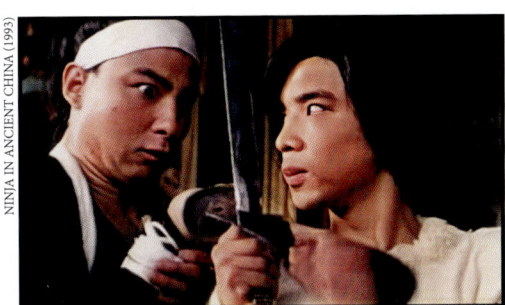

NINJA IN ANCIENT CHINA (1993)

final, absurd battle against the mystical "God sect."

This cool movie just bristles with energy and there are some great set pieces, including an acrobatic fight performed entirely on stilts, plus a blistering duel at the top of a Chinese pagoda.

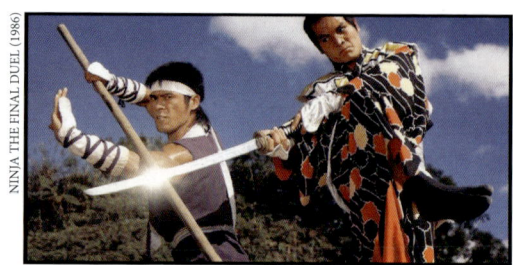

NINJA THE FINAL DUEL (1986)

NINJA THE FINAL DUEL (1986)
Starring Alexander Lo Rei, Alice Tseng, Li Yi-Min,
Eugene Trammel, Toby Russell, William Yen
Directed by Robert Tai
Action by Robert Tai
Sheng Hsien Moviedom Ltd

After the success of *Shaolin Vs Ninja*, madcap director Robert Tai bounces back with an insane sequel. The full version has a running time of eight hours; the version here is the first of two ninety-minute features.

Alexander Lo Rei plays a young Japanese monk well versed in the ways of Bushido. He is sent to China to warn the Shaolin high abbot about a proposed ninja onslaught of the Holy Temple. On his travels he encounters monks from India and Tibet and, after initial misunderstandings, they unite and help protect Shaolin from the deadly wrath of the ninjas.

Lots of bizarre fights, a nude kung fu skirmish, a ninja attack team that bounces about on huge, inflatable water spiders, a jive-talking black monk, plus the schlocky pageantry synonymous with Robert Tai's movies, combine to make this disjointed actioner a must-see for fans of trash-tastic ninja flicks and lovers of unhinged, mad moviemaking.

NINJA WOLVES (1979)
Starring Yueh Hua, Chang Yi, Chen Mu-Chuan,
Chin Po, Wang Hsieh, Eddy Ko
Directed by Lo Chi
Magnificent Tower Film Co

Silver-haired court eunuch Ma Tung (Yi) abuses his high position to take tributes intended for the emperor, using the palace bodyguards to enforce his will. Japanese warrior Ti Yung, recruited into the bodyguards via a series of grueling tests, loyally follows Ma Tung's orders, showing no mercy to those who find themselves in his master's crosshairs. Yung ruthlessly works his way up the ranks of the bodyguards, becoming Commander, and it seems Ma Tung's corrupt rule is set to continue with Yung's support, but a rebel group begins to meet in secret . . .

Also known as *A Pretended Rebel* and *The Wolf-Boxer*, this middling martial arts film, starring Shaw

Brothers actor Yueh Hua as Yung, makes it difficult for viewers to know who to root for, as nearly all of the characters are pretty despicable, with anyone possessing scruples getting murdered. It isn't until the rebels appear later in the story, and a main character is eventually revealed to be on a secret mission, that you understand the film isn't quite a morally bleak as it initially seems.

ODD COUPLE (1979)
Starring Sammo Hung, Lau Kar-Wing,
Leung Kar-Yan, Mars, Chung Fat, Dean Shek
Directed by Lau Kar-Wing
Produced by Karl Mak
Gar Bo Films Company

An eternal conflict is the premise for this martial arts masterpiece as Sammo Hung and Lau Kar-Wing portray old rivals who meet every ten years to find out whose weaponry skills are better: the sword (Sammo) or the spear (Lau). As the contests always end in a draw, the two aging warriors decide to take on pupils to continue the once-a-decade duel. In a novel twist, Sammo plays Lau's younger student and vice versa, thus making way for untold comic possibilities.

There has never been anything like *Odd Couple* before or since, nor is there likely to be, so skilful are the balletic duels between the sword and spear. It would be impossible for anyone else, barring Jackie Chan and Lau Kar-Leung, to pull off such intricate work.

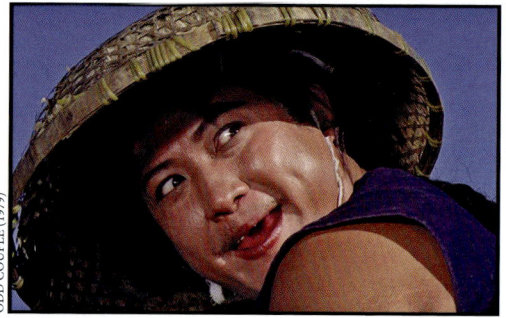

ODD COUPLE (1979)

OF COOKS AND KUNG FU (1979)
Starring Chan Siu-Lung, Chia Kai, Chang Shan,
Wu Ma
Directed by Ting Chung
Action by Chan Siu-Lung
Great China Film Company

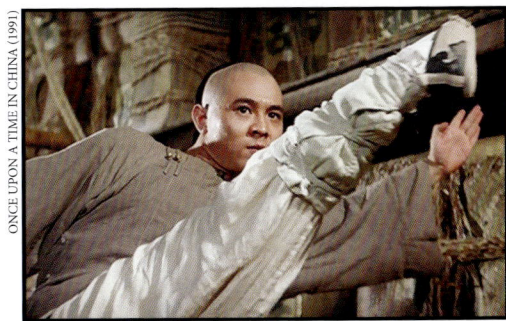

ONCE UPON A TIME IN CHINA (1991)

In this offbeat outing, Tawian's answer to Lee Van Cleef, Chai Kai, portrays Master Glutton: a master chef who once served up culinary delights to the Empress Dowager. His banquet was sabotaged and Master Glutton was exiled to a remote corner of China and falsely accused of murder and treason. All the other members of his clan, including his family, are mysteriously annihilated by a basket hat-wearing assassin. Only Master Glutton and his grandson (Siu-Lung) survive the massacre. The lad grows up under the strict discipline of his grandfather and soon becomes a master of the extremely rare Glutton Clan kung fu. Once again, the assassin rears his ugly baskethead when he learns of Master Glutton's whereabouts. Now it is up to the youth of the Glutton Clan to stop the massacre and take revenge for the elders.

This insane, ultralow-budget movie is saved by terrific training sequences between old man Glutton and Hong Kong's top TV choreographer, Chan Siu-Lung.

ONCE UPON A TIME IN CHINA (1991)
Starring Jet Li, Yuen Biao, Rosamund Kwan, Kent Cheng,
Jacky Cheung, Yen Shi-Kwan
Directed and produced by Tsui Hark
Action by Lau Kar-Wing, Yuen Cheung-Yan
Golden Harvest/Film Workshop

Jet Li brought new life to the role of Cantonese folk hero Wong Fei Hung in this fists-and-feet kung fu movie. Set in the 1870s, China looks set to be carved up by imperialist powers. Gunboats gather ominously off the coast and Chinese patriots realize that desperate times lie ahead. Martial arts master and herbalist Wong Fei Hung runs a clinic with sidekicks Porky (Cheng) and Buck Teeth So (Cheung). Besides treating locals wounded by foreign bullets, Wong is in charge of a Black Flag army, a local militia set up to defend the town against aggression. But an equally dangerous threat to the town comes from the Shaho gang, a vicious group of bandits running a protection racket. A fight between the Black Flag army and the Shaho gang erupts and spills over into a foreign settlement. To appease the foreigners, the local Manchu commander puts Wong under house

arrest and disbands the militia. Meanwhile, Yim (Shi-Kwan), a down-and-out master of the fearsome Iron Robe style, hears of Wong's fighting prowess and challenges him to a contest. When Wong refuses, Yim sides with the Shaho gang, but, when the evil alliance seizes Wong's beloved Thirteenth Aunt (Kwan), the scene is set for a serious showdown.

This is an unusually powerful movie because it pays pretty close attention to historical detail, particularly the oppression of the Chinese by a terrifying new weapon: the gun. Jet Li, in top form, portrays Wong Fei Hung as the embodiment of traditional Chinese values and moral rectitude at a time of great danger and exploitation. The choreography is masterful, with Wong taking on hoodlums armed only with an umbrella, in a thunderstorm and atop a tower of bamboo ladders.

Jet Li's superfluid and graceful kung fu makes the action soar. He leaps, flips, spins, flies up in a whirling crescent kick and lands in full splits. This masterful action merges with the interesting historical backdrop to make a wonderfully paced, outstanding kung fu movie.

ONCE UPON A TIME IN CHINA II (1992)
Starring Jet Li, Mok Siu-Chung, Donnie Yen,
Rosamund Kwan, David Chiang, Zhang Tielin
Directed and produced by Tsui Hark
Action by Yuen Woo-Ping
Golden Harvest/Film Workshop

Proof that not all sequels are cursed! Late 19th century China, weakened by corruption, poverty and the invasion of imperialist forces, is thrown off balance again by a new invasion of foreign culture, beliefs and technology. While for revolutionaries like Sun Yat-Sen (Tielin), this is a time to adapt or die, legendary martial artist Wong Fei Hung (Li) remains puzzled by Western culture and clings to tradition.

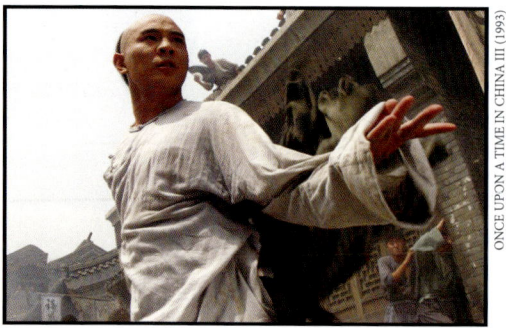

ONCE UPON A TIME IN CHINA III (1993)

Although lighter in tone and with more comedy than the first part, this sequel still conjures up some sobering images. The ransacked language school, full of massacred teachers and covered in xenophobic spells, is a shocking sight. Martial arts are incidental to the plot, but there is still plenty of hair-raising kung fu action, notably a cracking pole fight between Jet Li and Donnie Yen, performed at breakneck speed. Even more thrilling is the showdown at the temple of the White Lotus, where Wong uses his umbrella to whip and whack his way through hordes of incensed disciples. He then fights the high priest, precariously balanced on a tottering tower of wooden tables.

Flawlessly combining art and commercialism, this is exciting, dynamic escapism.

ONCE UPON A TIME IN CHINA III (1993)

Starring Jet Li, Rosamund Kwan, Mok Siu-Chung, Xiong Xin Xin, Lau Shun
Directed by Tsui Hark
Produced by Tsui Hark, Ng See-Yuen
Action by Yuen Bun
Golden Harvest/Film Workshop

This third installment in the life and times of Wong Fei Hung is a sad disappointment after the first two films. With his sidekick Leung Foon (Siu-Chung) and 13th Auntie (Kwan), who is now his fiancé, Wong Fei Hung (Li) goes to visit his father, who runs a medicine factory in Beijing. Every martial arts society in town is preparing for a lion dance contest, and Hung tries to restore harmony between the rival factions. But his troubles are doubled when 13th Auntie's old flame shows up and gang leader Chiu makes an attempt on his life. Hung joins the contest, aided by Chiu's former henchman Club Foot, and the scene is set for a spectacular showdown.

Unfortunately, it seems as if Tsui Hark ran out of steam a little with this one: the plot ties up nicely but the more serious sociopolitical overtones of the first two parts are missing, which is a shame as they made the movies so much more than mere actioners. However, there are redeeming qualities, including 13th Auntie's creation of a film within a film on the cine camera that her old flame gives her and some excellent comic sketches.

One of the other letdowns in this film is the fact that Jet Li's fight skills are not matched by those of any of his opponents, and the action mainly consists of him sweeping his way through a legion of inferior martial artists without any decent dueling. The mammoth fight scene at the end is certainly very impressive, but much of the movie seems to be a waste of so much fine talent.

ONCE UPON A TIME IN CHINA IV (1993)

Starring Vincent Zhao, Mok Siu-Chung, Jean Wang, Lau Shun, Xiong Xin Xin
Directed by Yuen Bun
Produced by Tsui Hark, Ng See-Yuen
Action by Yuen Bun
Film Workshop/Golden Harvest

In this fourth episode of the Wong Fei Hung saga, newcomer Vincent Zhao replaces Jet Li as the star.

Set in 1900, during the Qing dynasty, the powerful allies have been putting enormous pressure on the ever-weakening country. With the possibility of war breaking out at any stage, conflicts are occurring in various cities, with the civilians rising up against the foreigners. To demonstrate their power further, the allies organize their own allied team to take part in an important lion dance competition. Their aim is to demolish the morale of the Chinese people by incorporating Western science with traditional kung fu. The Qing government select the previous winner, kung fu master Wong Fei Hung, to participate on their behalf in the competition. Wong Fei Hung

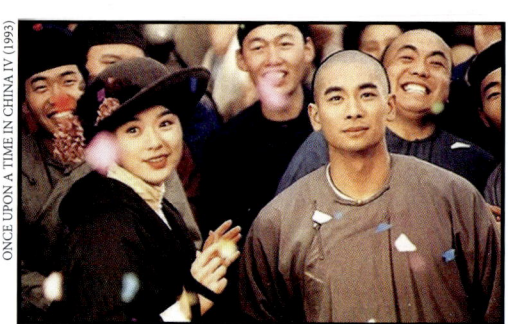

(Zhao) and his student Leung (Siu-Chung) had been planning a trip, but they are forced to stay in Beijing to help reestablish the reputation of their government and defend their country by winning the lion dance.

Newcomer Zhao's skills and fighting ability make him an excellent replacement for Jet Li, while director Yuen Bun delivers several excellently executed fight scenes without the help of hidden wires. One exceptional sequence is the fight set inside the local prison, when Wong Fei Hung delivers a devastating series of kicks and blows! On its release in Hong Kong, the film did well, proving that not even Jet Li is indispensable in the Hong Kong film industry.

ONCE UPON A TIME IN CHINA V (1994)

Starring Vincent Zhao, Rosamund Kwan,
Mok Siu-Chung, Kent Cheng, Roger Kwok, Jean Wang
Directed by Tsui Hark
Film Workshop/Golden Harvest

Wong Fei Hung (Zhao) sets about freeing a coastal town from the threat of local pirates, while also finding himself the focus of the affections of 13th Aunt (Kwan) and her younger sister (Wang).

Beginning with overly generous helpings of farce and romantic complications, which really do outstay their welcome, this sequel finally kicks into gear and delivers copious amounts of action, handled with kinetic pizazz by Tsui Hark.

Vincent Zhao may lack the charisma of Jet Li, but the movie as a whole is enjoyable, stuffed with breakneck brawls as various pirate villains come face-to-face with Wong Fei Hung and his loyal band of fighters. In one standout action sequence, Wong Fei Hung competes against an elder pirate chief who can expertly balance on the many swaying jars and containers they are battling on top of.

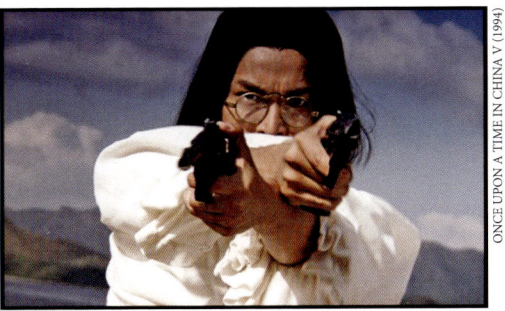

ONCE UPON A TIME IN CHINA V (1994)

ONCE UPON A TIME IN CHINA AND AMERICA (1997)

Starring Jet Li, Rosamund Kwan, Xiong Xin Xin, Chan Kwok-Pong, Jeff Wolfe
Directed by Sammo Hung
Produced by Tsui Hark
Win's Entertainment Ltd/Film Workshop/Golden Harvest

On a trip to America, Wong Fei Hung (Li) has an accident, causing him to suffer a bout of amnesia, and he gets separated from his companions, 13th Auntie (Kwan) and his sidekick Club Foot. Wong finds salvation when he is rescued by a tribe of Native Americans, who take him back to their village, where he is met with some hostility by the younger warriors of the tribe. His memory might have gone, but his fighting skills are very much intact as he fights for acceptance, defending the tribe from rival warriors.

Reunited with his companions, they head to a nearby corrupt town, where Wong and his friends are set up and accused of robbing the local bank. It is here they chance upon Billy (Wolfe), a gunslinger who helps them fight back and find justice.

The film's plot is very uneven, but this is easily forgiven because of the excellent action, including a great bar fight, large-scale battles with Native Americans, plus the end fight against a gang leader who wears deadly spurred boots. Jet Li is in top form, under the guidance and choreography skills of Sammo Hung, and there's some excellent madcap kicking action from Club Foot.

ONE ARMED HERO (1994)

Starring To Siu-Chun, Lilly Li, Fennie Yuen, Yang Lin
Directed by Wai Hon-To
Action by Philip Kwok
Citimedia

At the start of this sequel to *Sam the Iron Bridge—Champion of Martial Arts*, Sam Liang (Siu-Chun) is now Canton's navy commander and has just married his sweetheart Butterfly. His animosity toward Prince Mu has not improved any, and his feelings for Keke (Yuen) are just as confused. Mu is now Canton's main official, and has been joined by Prince Ting, a top kung fu man. Mu and Ting set Sam up, he loses an arm and then his wife as a result, forcing him to seek revenge.

To Siu-Chun once more impresses in both the action and acting departments, the fights are good examples of bone-crunching Wu-Shu, but the film gets bogged down with the drama, making it a somewhat plodding affair. Also known as *Sam the Iron Bridge 3*.

ONE-ARMED BOXER (1972)
Starring Jimmy Wang Yu, Lung Fei, Tien Yeh, Tang Hsin
Directed by Jimmy Wang Yu
Produced by Raymond Chow
Golden Harvest

This makes most martial art films look mediocre by comparison. The loss of a limb leaves Wang Yu a blackened soul, but after he is treated with a special elixir, he soon becomes an iron fist of vengeance. He faces fighters from all over the world, including Tibetan lamas, a mystical yoga master and, ultimately, a karate man who chops limbs away with his bare hands.

This epic production is utterly exhilarating, with carnage aplenty, as the one-armed boxer becomes a one-man demolition squad. Outrageous, over-the-top awesomeness!

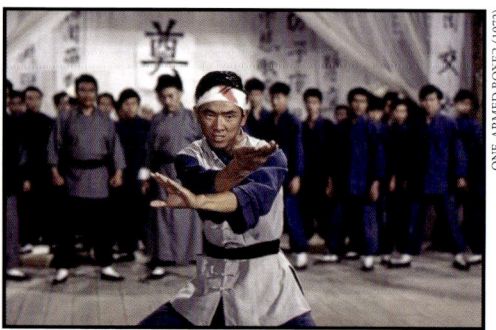

ONE-ARMED BOXER (1972)

ONE-ARMED SWORDSMAN (1967)
Starring Jimmy Wang Yu, Chiao Chiao, Tien Feng, Pan Yin-Tze
Directed by Chang Cheh
Produced by Runme Shaw
Action by Lau Kar-Leung, Tang Chia
Shaw Brothers

Jimmy Wang Yu is cast as Fang Kang, the diligent disciple of a sword-master, whose spoilt brat of a daughter (Yin-Tze) enjoys teasing the self-righteous Fang. He feels that he is an outcast and decides to leave the sword sect, but he is stopped in the snow-covered woods by the master's daughter and fellow disciples. Fang is forced to fight and defeats the mob easily. The master's daughter throws an

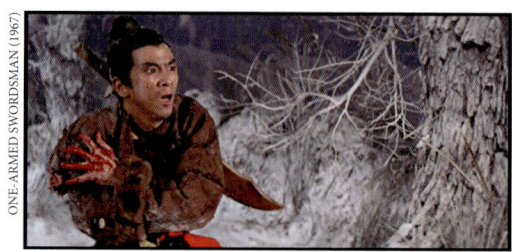

ONE-ARMED SWORDSMAN (1967)

almighty tantrum and slashes Fang's right arm off. Fang flees the scene in agony and later collapses by a small brook. There he is discovered by a simple, kindhearted country girl (Chiao), who nurses him back to health. She grows fond of him and makes him a gift of her father's sword-fighting manual, which Fang studies assiduously, becoming a master one-armed swordsman. Meanwhile, a ruthless villain known as Long-Armed Devil is wreaking havoc in the martial world with a new secret and deadly weapon known as the "sword lock." Fang learns that his master is next on the villain's list and rushes back to save him from the ruthless killer . . .

When Chang Cheh embarked on this little project, he had no idea of the effect it would have on Asian moviegoers. This seminal martial arts film, boasting some good production design, broke all previous Shaw Brothers records, and Jimmy Wang Yu became an overnight superstar. The picture spawned several sequels, the best known being *New One-Armed Swordsman*.

THE POSTMAN STRIKES BACK (1982)
Starring Leung Kar-Yan, Chow Yun-Fat, Yuen Yat-Chor, Cherie Chung, Eddy Ko
Directed by Ronny Yu
Action by Brandy Yuen, Yuen Shun-Yee
Golden Harvest/Peace Film Production Co

During the early years of the Republic, a corrupt warlord dispatches his envoy to employ four men to escort a consignment of arms for him. The envoy seeks out four hardened professionals to undertake the mission, a postman (Kar-Yan), a pickpocket (Yat-Chor), a dynamiter and a conman (Yun-Fat). The gang of four take on the task without knowledge of what they are carrying, since they are forbidden to open the cases. All they know is they have seven days to get to Lo Yang Pass. On route, after many ambush attempts, the party realize they have embarked upon a mission with an unjust and unpatriotic cause, and the arms are to be delivered to a notorious warlord intent on using them to fight against the Nationalist guard. Now the escorts must transform themselves into patriotic warriors, but not without tragic loss.

First-class acting, swift direction and plenty of gimmicky fights, including some ninjitsu, make for excellent viewing.

THE PRODIGAL BOXER (1972)
Starring Meng Fei, Li Lin-Lin, Yasuaki Kurata,
Pai Hung, Wong Ching
Directed by Tsai Yang-Ming
H.K. South Sea Film Company

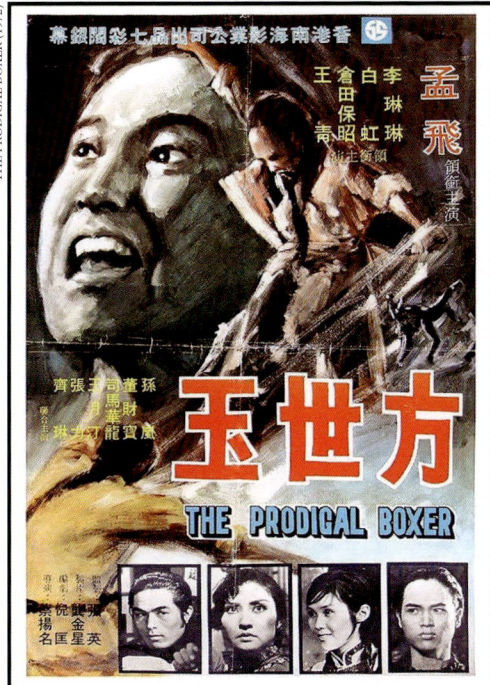

The youthful Fang Shi-Yu (Fei) accidentally kills someone in a fight, causing a tit-for-tat reprisal, resulting in the murder of his father. Fang becomes obsessed with defeating the two very skilled martial arts teachers responsible for the revenge killing, but Fang will need to really develop his skills to have any chance of ultimately beating these foes.

Also known as *Death Punch* and *Kick of Death*, this film has some effective emotional story beats, as we follow a protagonist who is his own worst enemy, continually trying to fight the formidable twosome, even though he is not ready for these face-offs. Luckily for Fang, his strong, firm-but-fair mother (Hung) is there to help him heal and prepare himself, utilizing a bunch of novel training regimes to really knock Fang into shape.

Of its kind, *Prodigal Boxer* is an adeptly handled kung fu yarn with awesome legwork courtesy of Yasuaki Kurata playing one of the dastardly teachers, some lively, roving camerawork, and a decent character arc for the hero, who finally learns to refrain from fighting until the time is right, leading up to a very satisfying final showdown.

PRODIGAL BOXER 2 (1976)
Starring Meng Fei, Tan Tao-Liang, Lung Chun-Erh
Directed by Tsai Yang-Ming
H.K. South Sea Film Company

In this weak two-films-spliced-together *Prodigal Boxer* follow up, Meng Fei once again returns to play the role of legendary Shaolin folk hero Fang Shi-Yu. This time Shi-Yu gets a job as a houseboy for an evil lord who has committed many heinous crimes in the region. Shi-Yu's cover is nearly blown by a rival martial artist, Kow Lee (Tao-Liang). Kow agrees to keep his mouth shut if Shi-Yu will oblige him with a friendly duel. After the fight, which lasts a full day, the two pugilists become friends and Kow Lee aids Shi-Yu in bringing the evil tyrant to justice.

Only a strong supporting role from flashy Tan Tao-Liang saves this film from being a dud. Also known as *Enter the Whirlwind Boxer*, *Young Hero of Shaolin* and *Pork Chopper: The Kung Fu Butcher*.

THE PRODIGAL SON (1981)
Starring Sammo Hung, Yuen Biao, Frankie Chan,
Lam Ching-Ying, Dick Wei
Directed by Sammo Hung
Produced by Raymond Chow
Action by Sammo Hung, Yuen Biao, Lam Ching-Ying,
Billy Chan
Golden Harvest

Leung Chang (Biao), the only son from a wealthy family, believes himself to be the best fighter in Fat San town. But, in reality, his father pays for all the fights to be fixed, without Leung's knowledge. However, when Leung is badly beaten by Peking Opera actor Leung Yee Tai (Ching-Ying), the truth finally comes out. A contrite and humbled Leung determines to persuade the reluctant Yee Tai to take him as a pupil and teach him the rudiments of Wing Chun kung fu. But it's only after Leung rescues the actor from a bunch of hired killers that he gets his wish.

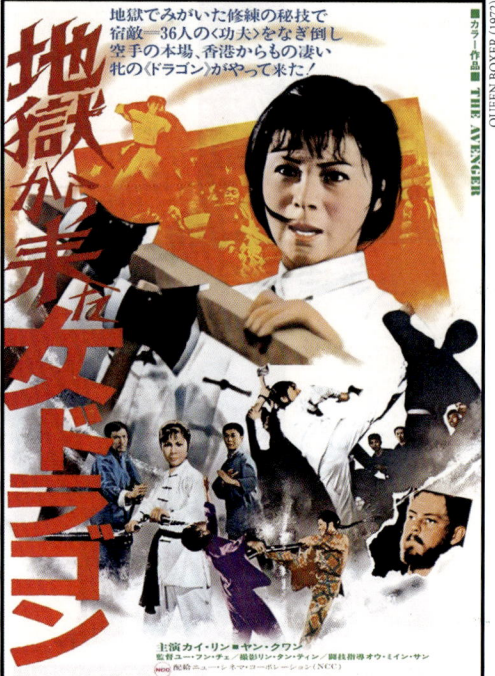

QUEEN BOXER (1972)

THE AVENGER

Undoubtedly one of the greatest kung fu classics to be committed to celluloid, Sammo Hung's pioneering fight choreography and direction were responsible for the new wave of kung fu action flicks that were to follow. The awe-inspiring end fight sequence will have you rewatching it repeatedly!

Also known as *Pull No Punches*, this movie is unmissable.

QUEEN BOXER (1972)

Starring Chia Ling, Yang Chun, Lee Ying, Lan Yun
Directed by Florence Yu
H.K. Fong Ming Motion Picture Company

Peking Opera starlet and classmate of Angela Mao, Chia Ling (Judy Lee), breaks away from her operatic background and enters the film world for a prosperous career. In this, her debut film, she portrays Ma Su Chen, who travels to the busy port of Shanghai searching for her brother's waterfront murderers, who, before tossing his carcass to the fish, burnt his eyes out with cigarettes. After several encounters and some detective work, Su Chen learns that the man she is after is notorious boss Pai Li Lei (Ying), who lives in a mansion protected by the fifty-strong axe gang. Su Chen enters the mansion

at dusk and, by dawn, leaves a wake of blood and death, before finally gouging out the eyes of boss Pai.

The pedestrian plot is elevated by Chia Ling's tour de force performance: you'll marvel at the way she moves in long takes around boss Pai's mansion, slaying anyone who gets in her way.

Shot on a low budget and completed in eighteen days, *Queen Boxer* fared well at the box office in Taiwan and Japan, and made the lovely-but-deadly Chia Ling an overnight sensation.

Also going by the title *The Avenger*, this is highly recommended, with great US dubbing.

THE REBELLIOUS REIGN (1980)

Starring Lung Fong, Tsui Siu-Keung, Li Kuen,
Alan Hsu, Kwan Yung-Moon
Directed by Fong Chiung
Produced by Lo Wei
Action by Alan Hsu
Good Year Movie Company

During the Ching dynasty, with the king dying after a long reign, the struggle between princes for the throne is long and rebellious. The movie opens with Nien Keng Yao (Fong) being taken through his martial paces by four of his uncles. With his kung fu perfected, he must leave to find his own

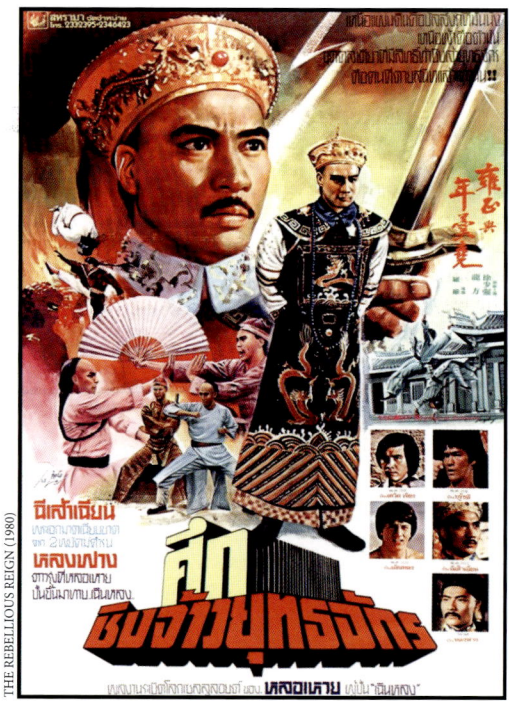

THE REBELLIOUS REIGN (1980)

life. On his way to the capital, he meets Tai (Alan Hsu), who is on the verge of a confrontation with the 14th prince and his lackeys. Objecting to having to work for the Ching government, Tai is forced into a fight, which develops into a superb sequence. Tai and Nien then fight each other, interrogating each other mid-fight in a magnificently inventive scene. On reaching the capital, Nien runs into the notorious 4th prince (Siu-Keung). One of the prince's henchmen (Yung-Moon) wrongly accuses Nien of stealing a piece of jade, swiftly setting about him with an awesome array of kicks. But Nien cunningly decides to work for the 4th prince, and helps him reach the throne, gaining full military power for himself. However, Nien falls out with the prince and is gradually demoted to security guard, the lowest rank. Meeting with his uncle, Tai and other patriots, Nien decides it is time to strike against the Ching government, and the Ming patriots fight off their enemies in a courageous display of martial artistry, which builds up to a formidable fight finale.

The characters and choreography put this on a par with anything in the field. Incidentally, this was originally written for Bruce Lee.

THE RESCUE (1971)
Starring Lo Lieh, Shih Szu, Ku Wen-Chung, Fang Mian, Ling Ling, Bolo Yeung, Chan Shen
Directed by Shen Chiang.
Shaw Brothers

It's 1279 AD, and China has been invaded by the Mongols. With the Sung Dynasty on the verge of collapse, and the Prime Minister (Mian) imprisoned after a failed uprising, a group of survivors, led by a young warrior girl named "White Duck" (Szu), embark on a dangerous mission to free him. Along the way they are joined by a mysterious wandering swordsman (Lieh) on his own mission.

Director Shen Chiang delivers a captivating movie in which the two heroes fight against the odds, often taking on small armies in large-scale battles that are well-choreographed for the period. Lo Lieh, the No. 1 box office star at the time, gives a great performance as both an actor and on-screen fighter, and he's well-paired with Shih Szu, who demonstrates stunning swordsmanship as she battles her way through a sea of soldiers. There's an early appearance from Bolo Yueng, and actress Ling Ling adds to the glamor.

Another solid period piece from the Shaw Brothers studio stable.

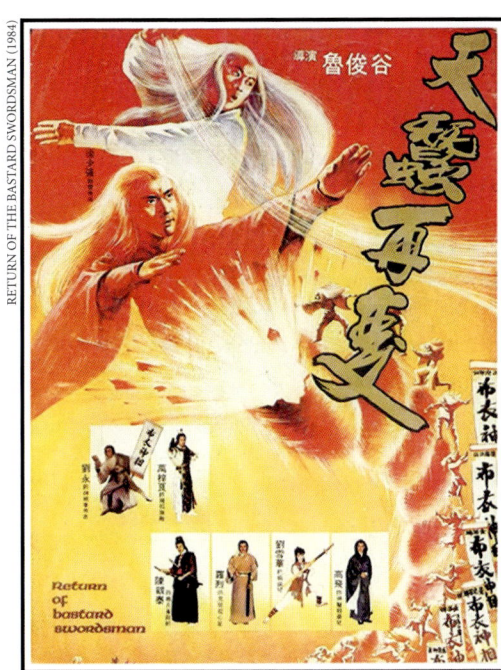

RETURN OF THE BASTARD SWORDSMAN (1984)

RETURN OF THE BASTARD SWORDSMAN (1984)
Starring Tsui Siu-Keung, Alex Man, Leanne Lau, Chen Kuan-Tai, Phillip Ko
Directed by Lu Chin-Ku
Produced by Mona Fong
Shaw Brothers

This starts where *Bastard Swordsman* left off, with the unresolved battle between Dugu (Alex Man in an excellently demented performance) of Wu Di clan and Yun Fei Yang of Wu Tang. Also trying to get in on the act is Mochitsuki (Kuan-Tai) of the Japanese Ega clan. They are all striving to be number one in the martial world. Yun deals with Dugu and is injured by his fatal skill. A mysterious fortune teller comes to his rescue and takes Yun to see Doctor Lai (Ko), who heals Yun. Meanwhile, Mochitsuki and the Ega clan attack Dugu and the Wu Di clan, showing off their phantom skill, known as "killing heartbeat," which has to be seen to be believed. Yun Fie Yang finally comes out of his cocoon and plots the downfall of Mochitsuki with the help of his fortune teller friend.

Once again Shaw Brothers comes up with quality choreography, wirework and martial arts styles with fantastic names (this film could be called Silkworm Vs Phantom Skill), to produce a highly entertaining viewing experience.

RETURN OF THE DEADLY BLADE (1981)

Starring David Chiang, Yasuaki Kurata, Tsui Siu-Keung,
Yeung Pan-Pan, Lo Lieh, Hwang Jang-Lee
Directed by Taylor Wong
Action by Ching Siu-Tung
Champion International Films Company

News that the famous swordsman Lee Wai has returned after many years causes much disturbance in the martial world. In reality, the man calling himself Lee is Siu Wan (Chiang), a young fighter assuming the name of his father's killer in order that he might find him and take revenge. Following the path of vengeance, he meets the mysterious Lonely Winner (Kurata), a fighter whose style, despite being unorthodox, is familiar to Siu Wan . . .

Also known as *Shaolin Fighters vs. Ninja*, this is a visually stunning adventure packed with many magnificent fights and featuring appearances by stars including Hwang Jang-Lee, Bruce Leung and Lo Lieh. Despite its fast pace, sufficient time is also given to character development. All in all, a fresh change from the more formulaic martial arts movies.

RETURN OF THE ONE-ARMED SWORDSMAN (1969)

Starring Jimmy Wang Yu, Chiao Chiao, Tien Feng,
Ku Feng, Lau Kar-Leung
Directed by Chang Cheh
Produced by Runme Shaw
Shaw Brothers

In this action-packed, bloodthirsty sequel to *One-Armed Swordsman*, maimed warrior Fang Kang (Wang Yu) is forced out of retirement in order to save a large party of swordsmen who have been lured into the deadly labyrinth of a nemesis (Tien

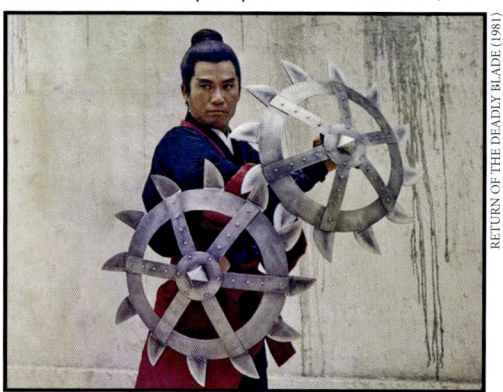

RETURN OF THE DEADLY BLADE (1981)

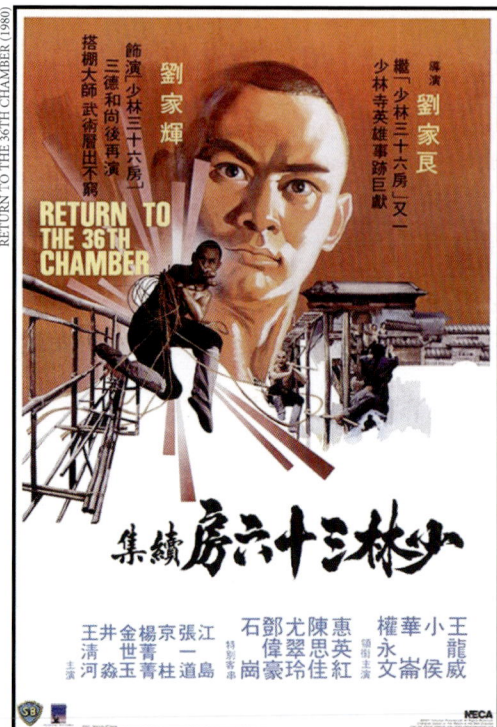

RETURN TO THE 36TH CHAMBER (1980)

Feng) on the pretext that they are entering a sword competition. Can Wang Yu save the incarcerated knights and will he be able to defeat the deadly array of swordsmen that guard the villain's fortress? Watch to discover the outcome in this nonstop feast of action from the pope of martial arts, Chang Cheh.

Points of interest include a cameo from a very debonaire Ti Lung as a young swordsman and terrific action cameos from Lau Kar-Leung, Lau Kar-Wing, Yuen Cheung-Yan, Tang Chia, and Ku Feng as five element swordsmen.

RETURN TO THE 36TH CHAMBER (1980)

Starring Gordon Liu, Kara Wai, Wang Lung-Wei,
Kwon Young-Moon
Directed by Lau Kar-Leung
Action by Lau Kar-Leung
Shaw Brothers

This is not in fact a direct sequel to the classic *36th Chamber of Shaolin*, but follows a young man who must watch his friends at the local mill being terrorized by a vicious gang. When the villains' tactics progress from simple bullying to murder, he decides that he has seen enough and sets off to study kung fu at the Shaolin Temple in order to solve the problem. On his arrival at Shaolin, he meets the famed monk San Te (Liu's character in the original) but is disappointed to find that the only physical work he will be doing will involve repairing the temple's thirty-sixth chamber.

Unlike the first film, this is lighter in tone and, at times, pretty humorous. Nevertheless, it is just as engrossing and there is much to marvel at. Also known as *Return of the Master Killer*, for Shaw Brothers fans this film is a must.

REVENGE OF A SHAOLIN MASTER (1978)
Starring Tan Tao-Liang, Chan Sing, Chang Fu-Chien, Lung Fei, Liu Shan, Kong Tao
Directed by Lo Chen
Cineconcord Film Company

Chief escort Lin (Tao-Liang) is ambushed and robbed of his shipment of food, which was being sent to a famine area. Lin is accused of conspiring with the robbers and imprisoned. After being freed by his sister (Shan), he spends the rest of the film trying to clear his name, dodging aggressors and getting recaptured more than once.

Also known as *Ninja Thunderkicks*, this lackluster Taiwanese flick has nothing much to offer other than some nifty kicking from Flash Legs Tao-Liang. Chan Sing fans will be disappointed, though, as he only gets going five minutes from the end.

REVENGE OF THE SHOGUN WOMEN (1977)
Starring Pai Ying, Han Hsiang-Chin, Liang Hsiu-Shen, Lin Di
Directed by Chang Mei-Chun
Central Motion Picture Studio

Village women who were raped by bandits become shaven-headed warrior nuns. When the masked bandits return, pitilessly raiding the area, the nuns must decide whether to involve themselves in the conflict, even though they have now sworn to serve Buddha and keep out of the affairs of the outside world. But with the bandit leader seeking the secret formula for a type of sulfur-based explosive, known only by the local doctor, the nuns eventually take up arms for a bloody confrontation.

Even viewed flat, there's no mistaking the fact

that *Revenge of the Shogun Women*, aka *13 Golden Nuns*, was originally shot in 3D by Chang Mei-Chun, who also directed the previous 3D kung fu opus *Dynasty*. The tips of weapons and fighters' feet seem to be continually poking into your face!

The bandit leader's dextrous use of his long, weaponised, almost prehensile ponytail is a great touch, but the fighting in general ain't all that hot, though the novelty of seeing 3D weapons swooshing right between your eyes partly makes up for this.

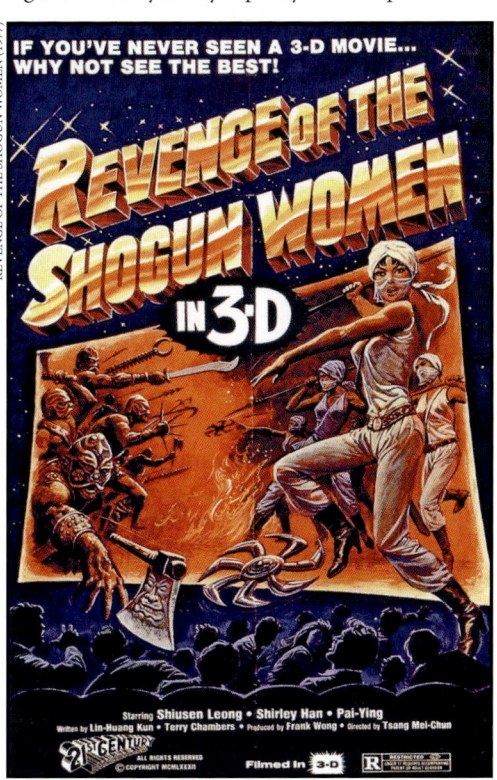

REVENGE OF THE SHOGUN WOMEN (1977)

THE REVENGER (1980)
Starring Ti Lung, Shih Szu, Tan Tao-Liang, Wong Ching
Directed by Pao Hsueh-Li
Yu Feng Film Company

Chou Tu (Lung) is a top fighter who spends his time disturbing the evil work of a fighter alliance led by Master Mao. After a few run-ins, Mao expends great effort to kill Chou. However, Chou's pregnant wife escapes and later bears a son. Eighteen years later, Chou Shu (Ti Lung again) sets out for revenge.

The plot is rather difficult to follow, but Ti Lung does his best with his dual role, trying his hardest to

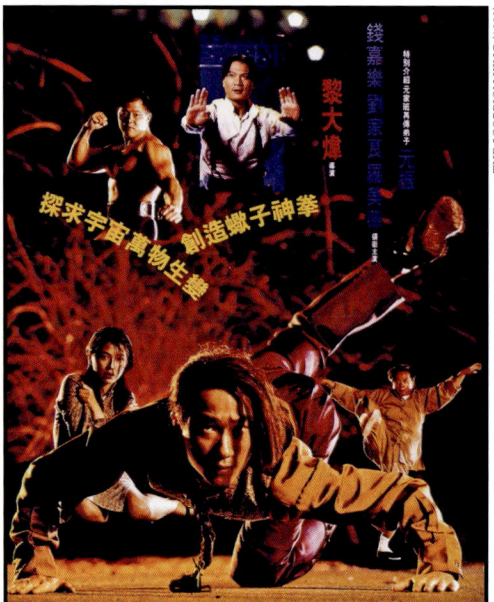

THE SCORPION KING (1992)

distinguish the two different characters, though it's a big ask to buy him as a teenager, and he handles the many fight scenes effortlessly, of course.

THE RING OF DEATH (1980)
Starring Cliff Lok, Hwang Jang-Lee, Shih Kien, Dean Shek, Wang Lai
Directed and produced by Ng See-Yuen
Action by Corey Yuen, Meng Hoi, Hsu Hsia
Seasonal Film Corporation

When country boy Ah Niu (Lok) accidentally kills a man, his aunt (Lai) sends him to his father, a general, who refuses to recognize Ah Niu, but keeps him as a servant. The General's three sons bully Ah Niu

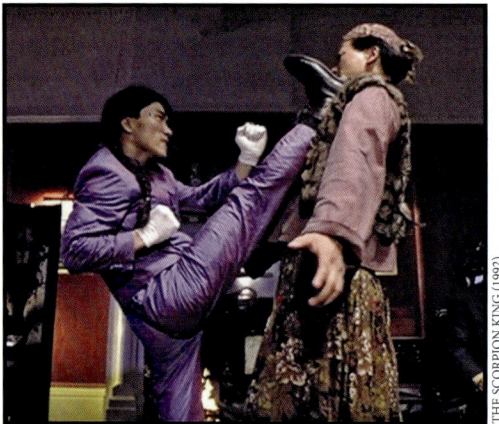

THE SCORPION KING (1992)

until he finds himself a kung fu teacher, eventually becoming tough enough to beat a Russian fighter (Jang-Lee), who has been deriding Chinese kung fu.

The fight action is superb, and Cliff Lok is totally believable, both as the downtrodden youth and the supreme fighter he becomes. Hwang Jang-Lee is as awesome as ever.

SAM THE IRON BRIDGE—CHAMPION OF MARTIAL ARTS (1993)
Starring To Siu-Chun, Yu Hai, Lilly Li, Fennie Yuen, Wong Kam-Kong
Directed by Fung Pak-Yuen
Action by Philip Kwok
Citimedia/Long Shong Pictures

To pay off a friend's debts, Sam Liang (Siu-Chun) enters the Canton martial arts tournament. The money will also help pay for Sam's forthcoming wedding to Butterfly. After winning, his victory brings him into the service of a local official trying to stop the import of opium, which then puts him into conflict with Prince Mu (Kam-Kong), who controls Canton's opium supply. To make matters worse, Mu's daughter Keke has the hots for Sam . . .

To Siu-Chun is a superb Wu Shu player and a talented actor to boot. He's supported by an excellent cast of Hong Kong and mainland actors and martial artists, the action is awesome, and the movie as a whole is well-executed and beautifully shot.

THE SCORPION KING (1992)
Starring Chin Kar-Lok, Won Jin, Lau Kar-Leung, May Law, Frankie Chin
Directed by David Lai
Action by Yuen Tak
Golden Harvest/Bo Ho Film Company Ltd

Yu Shu (Kar-Lok), who aspires to be a swordplay comic book artist, rescues a servant girl from the clutches of a slave trader and, soon after, he's sheltered by restaurant owner Master Lo (Kar-Leung). When Lo's noodle restaurant is burned down and the girl recaptured, Yu Shu and Lo, who is revealed to be a retired assassin, take on the slave trader's bodyguard . . . Sonny, the Scorpion King.

Also known as *Operation Scorpio*, this film gave Won Jin the chance to become one of the most exciting Hong Kong movie villains ever. He plays the son and bodyguard of the slave trade boss, sporting a long braid, skintight suit, and white gloves as he scuttles around the floor on his hands and knees with one leg raised high, ready to strike. Think you've seen everything? Well, wait till you've seen "scorpion style" kung fu! Displaying an amazing athleticism, Won Jin leaps off walls, does triple forward somersaults, and pulls off eye-boggling aerial kicks. He takes the upside-down kick perfected by Sammo Hung and Yuen Biao in *Pedicab Driver* and *Iceman Cometh* one step further: when he's finished, he just scuttles backward up the wall and stays there! He basically transforms an entertaining kung fu movie into something far more memorable.

THE SECRET OF SHAOLIN KUNG FU (1979)

Starring Li Yi-Min, Hsu Pu-Liao, Ko Chun, Shih Ting-Ken
Directed by Ko Shih-Hao
Ocean Films Production

Plotwise, this is yet another variation on the Jackie Chan success *Snake in the Eagle's Shadow*. Li Yi-Min plays an orphan (aren't they always?) working in a restaurant, whose only worry is how to deal with the bullying headwaiter. What time he has spare, he spends on his kung fu (don't they all?), which he studies under his stern, blind grandfather. He defeats a gang of thugs with the help of a local tramp, who he befriends and, in exchange for his friendship (and the wine Li gives him), the old beggar teaches him his own method of martial arts. The orphan's exceptional fighting skills make him ready to come to the defense of the beggar population when a crazed killer starts to bump them off for fun.

The storyline is obviously lacking, though this does mean it has one redeeming feature: it leaves ample time for Li Yi-Min to show his stuff. He is a pleasure to watch, whether being pushed to his limits when training or when battling hordes of

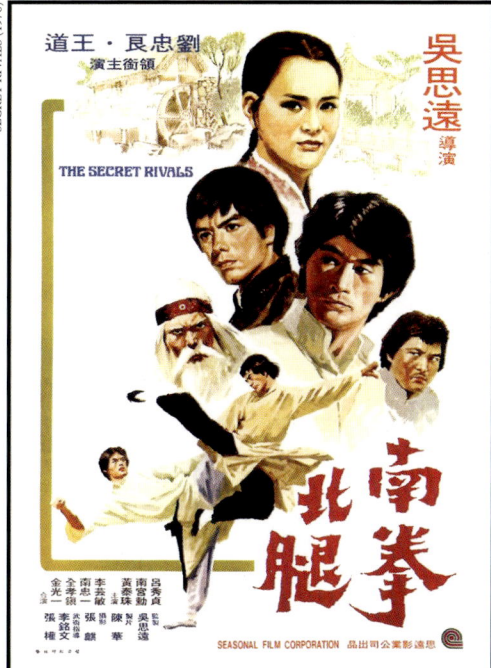

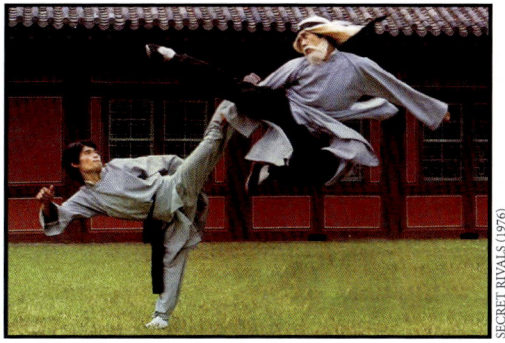

villains. The English version is further enhanced by some atrocious dubbing which is so bad it's good. As to how "Shaolin" comes into it, your guess is as good as ours.

SECRET RIVALS (1976)

Starring John Liu, Don Wong Tao, Hwang Jang-Lee, James Nam
Directed by Ng See-Yuen
Action by Chin Ming
Seasonal Film Corporation

John Liu and Don Wong Tao play rivals in search of a mutual foe, the dreaded martial arts expert and killer Silver Fox (Jang-Lee). Liu plays Shao Yi-Fei, a loner who has created his own deadly form of combat, the Northern Leg. He seeks revenge on Silver Fox for having murdered both his parents. Don Wong Tao plays Sheng Ying-Wei, otherwise known as Southern Fist, a government law officer who is after the Silver Fox for his part in a bullion robbery. In the quest for justice, the secret rivals' fate becomes intertwined and the duo end up confronting each other more than once. However, it turns out that, when alone, the rivals are no match for Silver Fox. Only by teaming up can Northern Leg and Southern Fist have any hope of overcoming the Fox's might.

Not only is this an all-time classic, but it was a groundbreaking film in the way it presented martial arts conflict on-screen, setting new standards in fight choreography. Gone were the flailing sporadic arm movements of the early seventies: now, in their place, were flashy high kicks combined with acrobatics, stylish, crisp hand moves, and jumping combination kicks . . . a new style of fighting was born. All the cast went on to enjoy lucrative careers in this new genre they helped create.

Ironically, *Secret Rivals* was shelved for nearly a year after its completion as distributors felt it had no star power. Only when a slot appeared between bookings did one brave distributor play the film, and audiences loved it so much it had to be held over for several weeks.

SECRET RIVALS 2 (1977)
Starring John Liu, Hwang Jang-Lee, Tino Wong, Chan Yao-Lin, Corey Yuen
Directed and produced by Ng See-Yuen
Action by Yuen Woo-Ping
Seasonal Film Corporation

This action-gorged sequel marked the first fruitful collaboration between Ng See Yuen and Yuen Woo-Ping. The story is a direct continuation from part one: Gold Fox (Jang-Lee) grieves at the sight of his brother Silver Fox's corpse. Gold Fox swears vengeance on the two who brought about his demise:

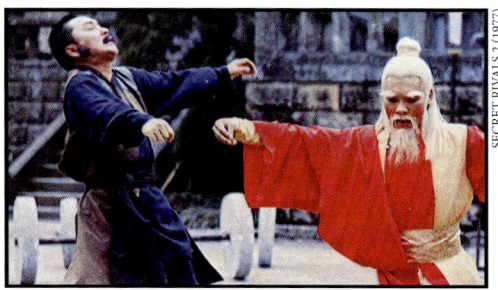

SECRET RIVALS 2 (1977)

Northern Leg and Southern Fist. His thirst for blood will not be easy to satisfy as Southern Fist has been posted to far-off Szechuan Province, while nobody knows where mysterious wanderer Northern Leg is. Gold Fox, however, must have his revenge, so he attacks Southern Fist's brother (Wong), but, luckily, Northern Leg shows up on the scene to save him. The pair must now team up to have a chance of beating Gold Fox, though this won't be easy, because Gold Fox (who is also searching for hidden treasure) has

eight elite guards, four of whom specialize in kicking and the other four are experts in fists.

Probably the only problem you might find with this production is that there is so much excellent fighting you eventually become numbed by it!

THE SEVEN COMMANDMENTS OF KUNG FU (1979)
Starring Lee Yi-Min, Chang Yi, Ma Chin-Ku, Ching Kuo-Chung
Directed by Ko Shih-Hao
Produced by Annie Wang
Action by Shiao Di, Shiao Po
Ocean Films Production

The often-seen staple of the youngster and wise old master duo is used to decent effect in this martial arts yarn from Taiwan. Lee Yi-Min plays the young and eager-to-learn student, with Chang Yi as the experienced old-timer. The twosome form a strong bond as the story develops, with the youngster learning the seven commandments of combat from the white-haired warrior. However, tragedy strikes when the youngster learns that the old master harbors a deep dark secret. Now student must rise above master in a tragic confrontation where only one will survive.

This low-budget film draws its plot and characters from the spaghetti western *Day of Anger* (1967).

SEVEN GRANDMASTERS (1977)
Starring Jack Long, Li Yi-Min, Alan Chui Chung-San, Corey Yuen
Directed and produced by Joseph Kuo
Action by Corey Yuen, Yuen Cheung-Yan
Hong Hwa Motion Picture Company

Taiwanese movie mogul Joseph Kuo, the man who brought you *The 18 Bronzemen* and *Born Invincible*, delivers yet another powerhouse of a film. Jack Long plays Sang Kuan Chun, an aging kung fu master who, before his retirement, wants to prove himself the grandmaster of all China. He spends the next few years traveling around China challenging various masters and defeating them all. Along the way he and his followers and his daughter are joined by an easygoing fellow (Yi-Min), who, after months of persuasion, is finally accepted by the master, much to the dislike of the other students. The young man quickly becomes proficient in the art of Pak Mei, and he soon outshines the other students. Having defeated all the other masters,

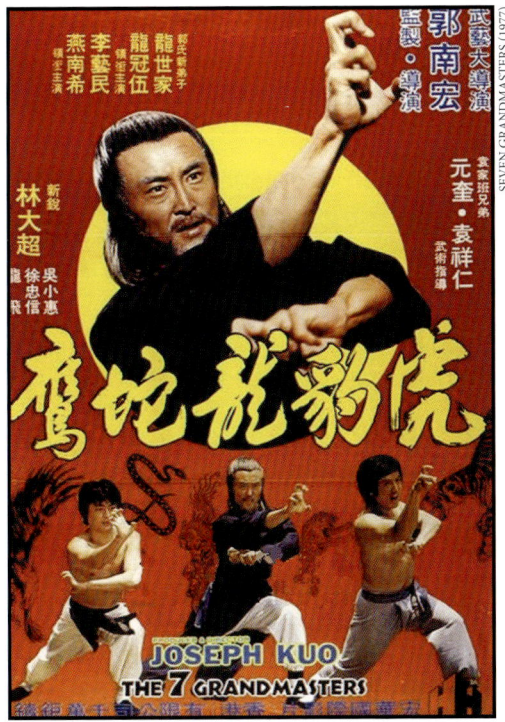

Up against this bunch of no-goods stand an agent for the emperor, a fighter named Ghost Killer (who, at one point, rams two of his fingers through someone's hand), the Blind Swordsman, the One-Armed Swordsman (okay, it's an actor with one arm hidden under his clothes) and the daughter of a murdered general.

There are various fun moments to watch out for, especially any scenes involving the grotesque mega-monk (Siu Kam). In one incident a general stabs at the monk's face, only to have the sword locked between the baddie's golden gnashers. Biting off the tip of the blade, the monk spits it into the general's forehead! The monk then laughs and, wow, he is one weird-looking dude. This huge monk also doesn't get too fazed when a pile of rocks is dumped on him or when he tumbles down a cliff. He even bites the One-Armed Swordsman in the throat like the Bond villain Jaws did to a victim in *The Spy Who Loved Me*.

A bizarre, pretty decent Taiwanese tall tale with adequate action scenes.

THE SHADOW WHIP (1971)

Starring Cheng Pei-Pei, Yueh Hua, Ku Feng, Kao Ming
Directed by Lo Wei
Produced by Run Run Shaw
Shaw Brothers

Directed by Lo Wei, who of course made his name working with Bruce Lee, this is a swordplay movie with a difference: two of the main protagonists, Shadow Whip Fang and his ward Miss Yun, wield whips rather than swords. Add the fact that much of the action takes place in the snow, and you have an unusual costume swashbuckler.

Fang has been in hiding for fifteen years because he has been wrongly suspected of masterminding a robbery. However, he is forced into the open when various factions come looking for him, seeking either revenge or the booty he is supposed to have

Sang returns home, only to find that there is still one more challenge: from his new adopted follower. Extremely disappointed and curious, Sang accepts the challenge. Why has the young man issued the challenge and what dark secrets does he hide? All is revealed in the breathtaking twist ending.

An unusual storyline, five-star direction, fight scenes that will leave you begging for more, convincing performances from all involved and the triumphant music of Laurence Rosenthal (*Return of a Man Called Horse*) make *Seven Grandmasters* one of the best independent fu films of the seventies.

THE 72 DESPERATE REBELS (1978)

Starring Bai Ying, Chan Sing, Miao Tian, Siu Kam
Directed by Lin Bing
Li Yun Film Company

In the middle years of the Ming Dynasty a notorious robber lord, Master Wolf, ravages the coastline with his band of outlaws, known as the seventy-two fighters. This Master Wolf guy certainly knows how to protect himself: among his men are thirty-six personal bodyguards, including 9 "Goldmen," four Chiefs, eighteen monks known for their cruelty, three spike-fingered Killers, and a huge monk with golden teeth.

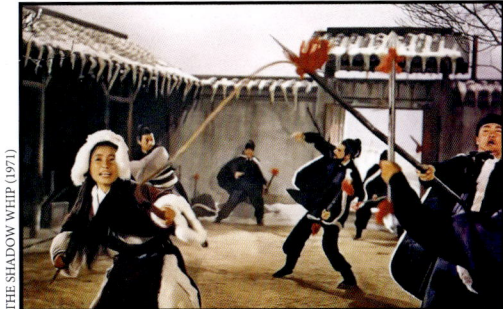

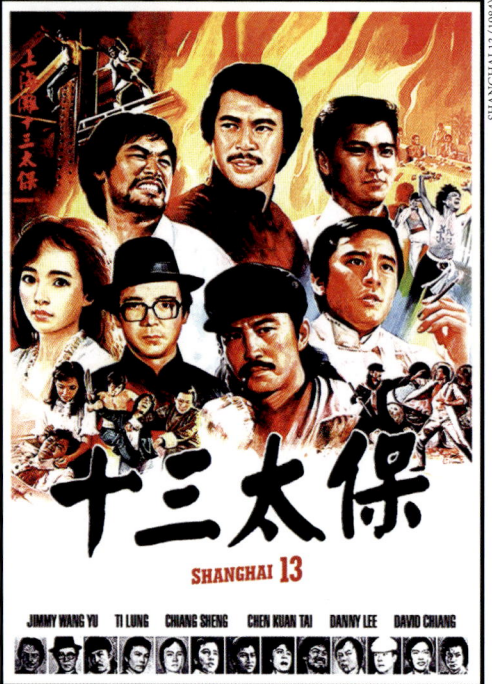

SHANGHAI 13 (1984)

SHAOLIN CHASTITY KUNG FU (1983)
Starring Alexander Lo Rei, Liu Hao-Yi, Tang Lung,
Li Hai-Hsing, Robert Tai
Directed by Robert Tai
Shing Hsien Production Company

The ruthless Nine Devil gang intercepts a shipment of gold bullion near a small village. In their greedy ecstasy they decide to level the village and kill all its inhabitants, but one of the men, Ah Tien (Lo Rei), escapes along with the women and children. Together they make for the mountains where they encounter a wandering monk, who teaches the nomads the secret art of Shaolin Chastity kung fu. Training complete, Ah Tien leads the baby warriors into a bizarre battle against the Nine Devils.

Also known as *Revenge of the Dragon*, this flick boasts totally insane fight action, innovative use of wires and a kid-fu finale, making this mad offering pretty memorable.

SHAOLIN EX-MONK (1978)
Starring John Liu, Yuen Lung, Alan Hsu,
Cecilia Wong, Jack Long
Directed by Chang Hsin-Yi
Action by Yuen Lung, Alan Chui Chung-San
Golden Sun Film Company

A former Shaolin monk turned thief murders a number of people in a local town, then disappears. The town's police captain (Liu) vows to bring him to justice. He picks up a student (Lung) along the way and the duo set off to find the killer.

John Liu's kicking is superb, as usual, and he brings his customary style to the proceedings. Yuen Lung, also a stunning martial artist and acrobat, nearly steals the show. The fights are excellent and the story moves along at a breakneck pace. Also known as *A Notorious Ex-Monk* and *Renegade Monk*.

SHAOLIN INVINCIBLE STICKS (1978)
Starring Don Wong Tao, Chang Yi, Cheng Ching,
Hsia Kwan-Li
Directed by Lee Tso-Nam
Action by Chin Ming
Ocean Shores Video

stolen all those years ago, thus the search begins to find the real culprit, so that Fang can clear his name.

This entertaining vehicle for Cheng Pei-Pei, who looks fetching in her fur gear, features a fair bit of wirework and uses chunks of John Barry's *Goldfinger* score on the soundtrack.

SHANGHAI 13 (1984)
Starring Ti Lung, David Chiang, Jimmy Wang Yu,
Chen Sing, Leung Kar-Yan, Andy Lau
Directed by Chang Cheh
Hong Kong Chang He Motion Picture Company/
Winner's Video Entertainment

Mr. Gau, a minister with the new government, is suspicious of his superior's links with the Japanese, so he investigates and finds that the government is selling China out. The superiors set out to catch Mr. Gau, who employs the services of a group of fighters, the Shanghai 13, to help him escape and spread the news of the country's betrayal.

The brotherhood theme of most Chang Cheh movies is definitely less to the fore here. Instead, we are treated to lots of well-staged fight scenes. Though the film lacks the budget of Chang Cheh's Shaw Brothers pictures, everyone involved here gives 100 percent.

Don Wong Tao plays Chen Ku Yung, the only son of the late king of sticks Lord Chen. Cocky and playful, the young Chen thinks he is a natural staff fighter and doesn't bother to train. His three uncles know otherwise and make him take a clan test. He fails,

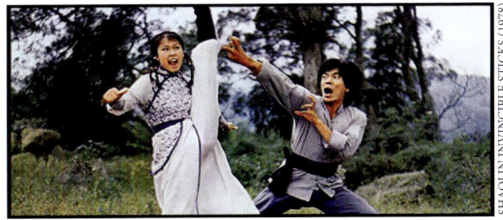

SHAOLIN INVINCIBLE STICKS (1978)

of course, and is exiled until he can pull himself together. On his travels Chen meets up with many staff-wielding allies and foes, then he learns that the sworn enemy of his family, northerner Lu Tai Yeh (Yi), is on the warpath and plans to smash the Chen household. The young master rushes home to find that he is too late. Most of his uncles and servants have been killed by Lu's mouse tail stick. Lu has also left a note for Chen, challenging him to deadly staff combat in the bamboo grove. Can the young prodigal defeat the might of the white-haired northerner, or will he come to a sticky end?

More martial mayhem from the master blaster Lee Tso-Nam. This time staff fighting is on the agenda, whether it be long staff, short stick, three-section staff, the mouse's tail, the monk stick, nunchaku, or double sticks, this decent fight flick will have a staff for you.

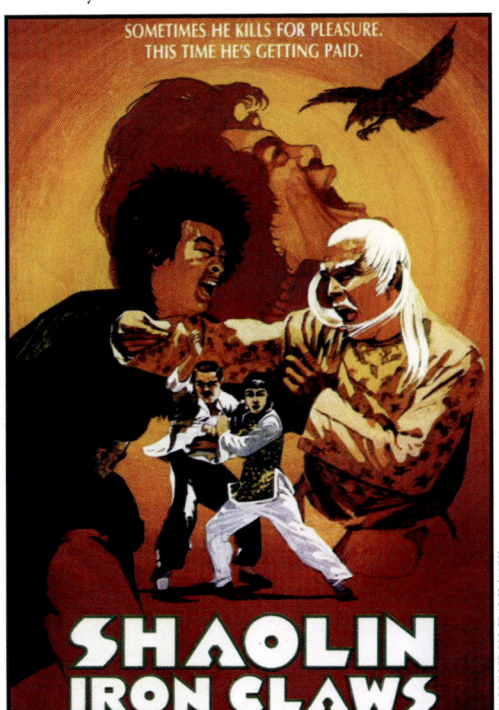

SOMETIMES HE KILLS FOR PLEASURE. THIS TIME HE'S GETTING PAID.

SHAOLIN IRON CLAWS

SHAOLIN IRON CLAWS (1978)

THE SHAOLIN INVINCIBLES (1977)

Starring Carter Wong, Chia Ling, Lung Chun-Erh, Tan Tao-Liang
Directed by Hou Cheng
Produced by Keung Chung-Ping
Hai Hua Cinema Company

This threadbare and unoriginal revenge swordplay movie is lifted to the stratosphere of silliness with the introduction of two long-tongued magicians, who present the emperor with a couple of moth-eaten gorillas that practice kung fu. In one mad moment one of our heroines sees these two apes for the first time and sternly announces: "Look out, there are two gorillas coming this way and they look like they know kung fu!"

This film is, obviously, hard to take seriously, but if you want to witness the moment when blood fountains out of the heads of the wounded men-in-suit-gorillas, or see Carter Wong de-tongue the wizards, oh Lord, you'll just have to watch this movie!

SHAOLIN IRON CLAWS (1978)

Starring Don Wong Tao, Li Yi-Min, Chang Yi, Chan Sing
Directed by Ko Shih-Hao
Fu Tu Film

At the beginning of the Republic, an ex-Ching lord (Sing) coerces a group of former Ching ministers into signing a declaration for the reestablishment of the Ching dynasty. This declaration falls into the hands of a provincial police chief (Wong Tao) and all hell breaks loose.

Also known as *Hawk's Fist*, this is a pretty fine kung fu movie, with an outstanding cast. The fight action is superb, with Don Wong Tao on serious form and Li Yi-Min also adding martial sparkle. However, the true star is Chang Yi as the top villain, who unleashes some mean mantis moves.

SHAOLIN KUNG FU MASTER (1978)

Starring Wang Kuan-Hsiang, Don Wong Tao, Chang Yi, Chi Kuan-Chun, Lung Fei
Directed by Huang Fei-Lung
Hong Kong Alpha Motion Pictures Co

A paranoid Manchu prince orders his five most trusted guards to hide a cache of treasure for fear of any Ming patriots getting their hands on it. After the prince fails to show up on the agreed date, the five guards decide to split the loot among themselves. Now, one by one, the guards are mysteriously

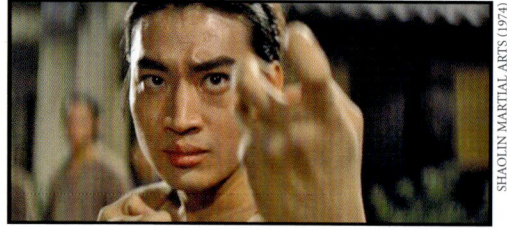

SHAOLIN MARTIAL ARTS (1974)

murdered. Who is the secret assassin and what happens when the white-haired prince reappears? Watch this martial arts whodunit to find out . . .

However, don't be misled by the large ensemble cast advertised on the glossy poster: Don Wong Tao and Chi Kuan-Chun only appear as guests in the picture, playing the parts of the elite guards.

Also goes by the name *The Five Invincible Guards*.

SHAOLIN MARTIAL ARTS (1974)
Starring Fu Sheng, Chi Kuan-Chun, Gordon Liu
Directed by Chang Cheh
Action by Lau Kar-Leung, Tang Chia
Chang's Film Company

More masterful storytelling from the maestro of mayhem, Chang Cheh. In this highly engrossing film, Shaolin disciples are trained in Eagle Claw and Shaolin Fists to combat the wicked Manchu tyrants who murdered their kung fu brothers. Unfortunately, their newfound skills prove too inferior to the Manchu's mighty Iron Robe technique. Realizing a massacre is at hand, the teacher and clan elder sends the two senior students, played by Fu Sheng and Chi Kuan-Chun, to learn Tiger and Crane and Wing Chun styles respectively, in the hope that these techniques can match the Manchu wrath. Months of dedicated training over, the deadly Shaolin duo set off for a bloody showdown with the Manchu masters of disaster!

Some brilliant characterisations and a great music score all add up to 106 minutes of viewing delight. Also known in the UK as *Five Fingers of Death*.

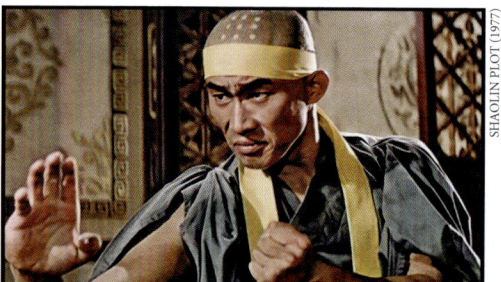

SHAOLIN PLOT (1977)

SHAOLIN PLOT (1977)
Starring Chen Sing, James Tien, Casanova Wong,
Sammo Hung, Yen Shi-Kwan, Kam Kong
Directed by Huang Feng
Produced by Raymond Chow
Action by Sammo Hung
Golden Harvest

Wicked Manchu Prince Daglen (Sing) collects martial arts manuals. The only books absent from his vast library are the Shaolin and Wu Tang manuals. He sends his lackeys (Hung and Shi-Kwan) out to obtain these rare documents, only to have the Wu Tang clan leader burn the manual before his savage death. His son, Little Tiger (Tien), flees and finds refuge with a blind Shaolin monk (Kong), who teaches him Shaolin Fists. Daglen and his army storm Shaolin and demand their secret training manual but they are turned away empty-handed. Not wanting a bloodbath on his hands, Daglen disguises himself as a poor, handicapped monk and infiltrates the temple and, subsequently, the holy library. His devious plot is uncovered by Little Tiger, who tells the abbot. Daglen, realizing his cover is blown, takes the abbot hostage and flees the temple. Eight Shaolin warriors are selected to march to Daglen's palace and, after a magnificent, kick-filled end fight, peace is restored to Shaolin and the martial world.

Suffering from an uneven plot, the film makes up for this with wonderful combat scenes choreographed by Sammo Hung, with Casanova Wong's skills showcased to perfection, plus there's some very good use of locations too.

SHAOLIN RESCUERS (1979)
Starring Jason Pai Piao, Lu Feng, Philip Kwok, Lo Meng,
Sun Chien, Chiang Sheng
Directed by Chang Cheh
Produced by Mona Fong
Action by Robert Tai, Lu Feng, Chiang Sheng
Shaw Brothers

After a bloody massacre at Hsin Shan temple, Shaolin hero Hung (Pai Piao) escapes, badly wounded, and finds shelter in a dye mill run by Chu (Chien), who is an expert kicker. Chu and his buddies from the market, played by Lo Meng, Philip Kwok and Chiang Sheng, who are also excellent martial artists, protect Hung from the evil Kao (Feng) and his army of Manchurian fighters.

This movie from the latter days of the Venoms mob has a terrific end sequence with Lu Feng taking on all of the Venoms simultaneously. His engrossing performance won him the Outstanding Supporting Actor award at the 25th Asian Film Festival.

The movie is also known as *Avenging Warriors of Shaolin*.

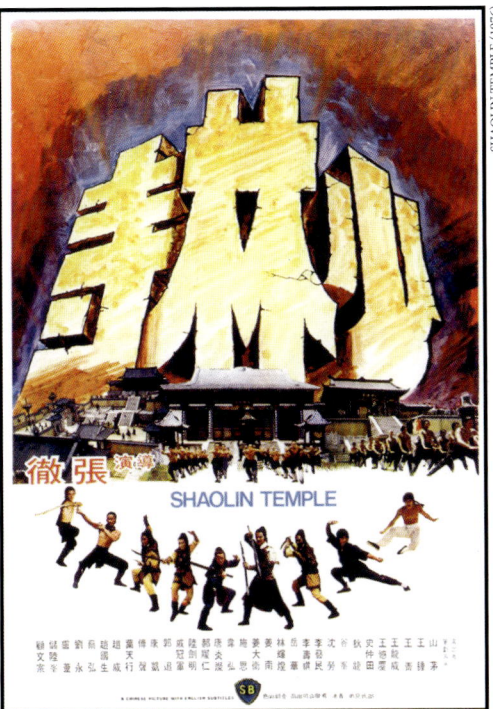

SHAOLIN TEMPLE (1976)

SHAOLIN TEMPLE (1976)

Starring Fu Sheng, Chi Kuan-Chun, Li Yi-Min, Philip Kwok, Ti Lung, David Chiang
Directed by Chang Cheh
Produced by Runme Shaw
Action by Hsieh Hsing, Chen Hsin-I
Shaw Brothers

Also known as *Death Chamber*, this colossal production looks at the final years of the magnificent Shaolin Temple before it was burnt to the ground by evil Manchus. The bulk of the film concentrates on the training of the famous Shaolin disciples: Fong Sai Yuk, Hu Hui Chin, Chu Tu, Hung Shi Kwan and Fang Ta Lung. Fong and Hu manage to break through the wooden alley, freeing themselves from the Shaolin order. Once outside it, they learn that there is a traitor within the temple who has advised the Manchu generals to attack the temple, so Fong and Hu rush back to inform the abbot that a massacre is on hand. The temple is assaulted,

casualties are many, finally the temple is destroyed and the surviving disciples flee to different parts of China to spread the teachings of Shaolin.

This fantastic production not only contains superb training and fight sequences (probably more than any other Shaws film) but it also marked the departure of David Chiang and Ti Lung from the Chang Cheh camp and the arrival of the Venoms mob.

SHAOLIN TEMPLE STRIKES BACK (1983)

Starring Chen Chien-Chang, Mark Long, Chang Shan, Chiang Nan
Directed and produced by Joseph Kuo
Kam Production Studios

During the final days of the Ming dynasty, one princess escapes the palace with an escort of guards, heading for Taiwan. At San Hai gorge their escape is cut off and all but the princess and one guard (Chien-Chang) die. The two run to the Shaolin Temple, and the guard trains with the monks as they await the final, bloody conflict with the army.

This fun Taiwanese fu flick is fast-paced, with a lot of fight sequences, climaxing with a huge battle in the Shaolin courtyard.

SHAOLIN VS. LAMA (1983)

Starring Alexander Lo Rei, Chang Shan, William Yen, Wang Chi-Sheng, Li Wei-Yun
Directed by Lee Tso-Nam
Produced by Keung Chung-Ping
Tin Ping Film Company

Yu Ting (Lo Rei) is a kung fu fanatic in search of the ultimate master. When he saves a young Shaolin monk, Hsu Shi (Yen), from a group of mobsters, Ting sees it as a golden opportunity to enrich his kung fu skills further and persuades the young novice monk to smuggle him into the holy gates of Shaolin. However, Ting's presence isn't welcome at the temple and he is

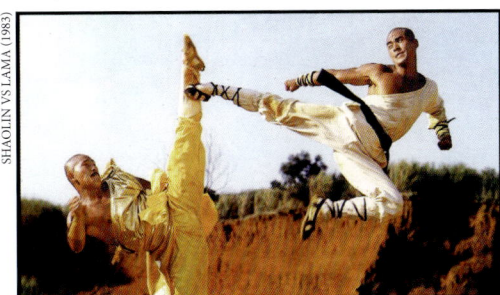

SHAOLIN VS LAMA (1983)

driven out, but remains close to the temple, liaising with Hsu Shi. One night, Ting rescues a girl from the clutches of the Flying Eagle gang, the leader being the infamous Golden Wheel Lama. Ting is no match for the Lama and is defeated by him in a furious fight. Luckily, the young novice monk saves Ting and the girl and sneaks them into the temple. Recognizing his kind nature and diligence for the arts, the abbot decides to bring Ting into the Shaolin order and teach him the deadliest techniques to prepare him for the Lama's merciless fury.

Taiwanese maverick director Lee Tso-Nam churns out yet another superb fist-fest that achieves what it set out to do: entertain us with copious quantities of kung fu skirmishes in a story featuring Alexander Lo Rei playing a likeable protagonist.

SHAOLIN VS. WU TANG (1983)
Starring Gordon Liu, Adam Cheng, Wang Lung-Wei, Ching Li
Directed by Gordon Liu
Produced by Lau Kar-Leung
Action by Lau Kar-Leung
Hing Fat Film Company

A Manchu prince (Lung-Wei) uses trickery to coax the secret fighting skills out of the Shaolin and Wu Tang masters. Then he creates a rift between two young students, played by Gordon Liu and Adam Cheng, who were once the best of friends despite their respective backgrounds of Shaolin and Wu Tang. The two disciples return to their temples to seek advice from their superiors. When later they reunite, their differences forgotten, Shaolin and Wu Tang team up to fight the Manchu menace.

The pedestrian storyline is rescued by beautifully choreographed fight scenes, with the opening credit scene worth the admission price alone. The temple training is an updated version of *The 36th Chamber of Shaolin* and the Wu Tang sword training is a real eye-opener.

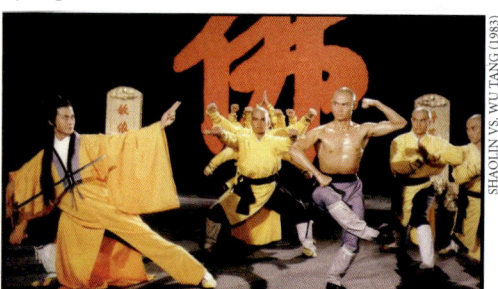

SHAOLIN VS. WU TANG (1983)

Also known as *Shaolin and Wu Tang*, samples from this film's English dub are used in Wu-Tang Clan's debut hip hop album "Enter the Wu-Tang (36 Chambers)."

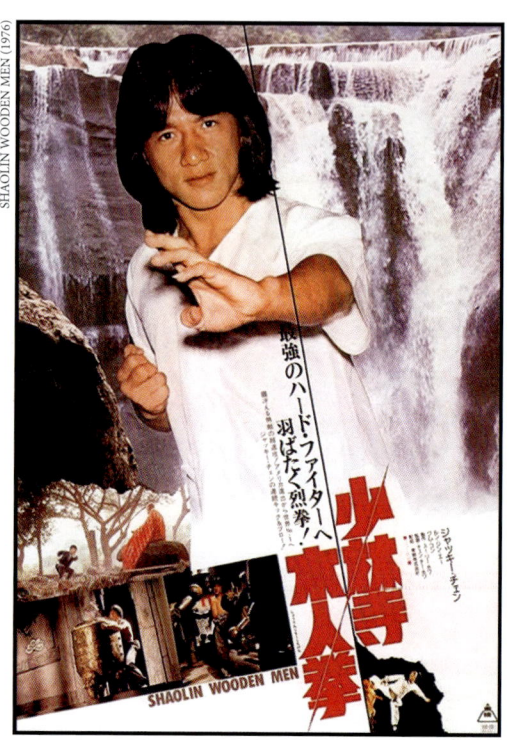

SHAOLIN WOODEN MEN (1976)

SHAOLIN WOODEN MEN (1976)
Starring Jackie Chan, Kam Kong, Lung Chun-Erh, Chiang Kam, Yuen Biao
Directed by Chen Chi-Hwa
Produced by Lo Wei
Action by Chin Ming, Jackie Chan
Lo Wei Motion Picture Company

After witnessing the murder of both his parents at the hands of a masked assassin, Jackie, or Brother Mute as he becomes known, takes a vow of silence, until he can avenge his parents' deaths.

Jackie makes for the Shaolin Temple for obvious reasons. There he encounters many weird masters: a drunk monk, a snake fist nun, and a wild and crazy man (Kong), who teaches Jackie how to defeat the wooden men, an army of robot-like, automated wooden dummies that stomp, clobber, and bash anything in their path. After successfully emerging from the alley of wooden men still in one piece, Jackie ventures into the busy world outside Shaolin,

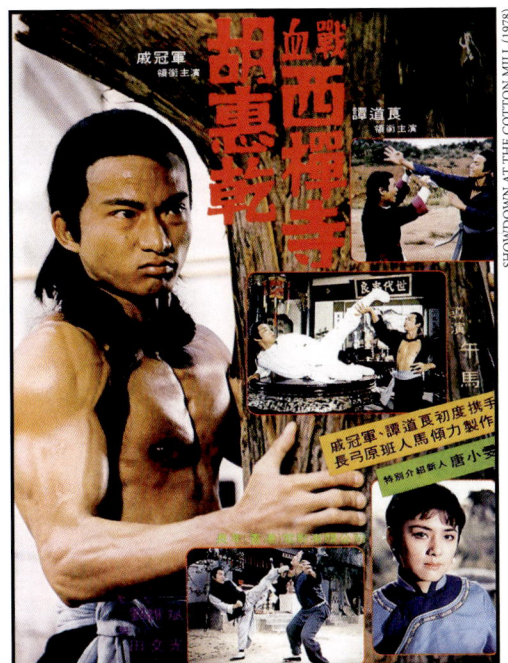

SHOWDOWN AT THE COTTON MILL (1978)

where he encounters many martial artists. In an ironic twist of fate Jackie avenges his parents' death and is freed from his vow of silence.

When released, this film, also known as *36 Wooden Men*, created a lot of gossip in the Hong Kong movie industry. People were surprised by this young, awesome, stylish talent that seemed to emerge from nowhere. Jackie displays five animal styles, staff and acrobatics, all stamped with his flashy trademark, the likes of which had never been seen before. Credit should also go to Chin Ming (Tommy Lee) for allowing Jackie such freedom with the fight scenes.

SHOWDOWN AT THE COTTON MILL (1978)
Starring Chi Kuan-Chun, Tan Tao-Liang, Chang Peng, Ching Kuo-Chung
Directed by Wu Ma
Produced by Lih Wei-Bin
Action by Chang Peng
Long Year Film Company Production

The Ching government assigns Kao Chin-Chung (Tao-Liang) to deal with Shaolin revolutionary Hu Hui-Chien (Kuan-Chun). To accomplish his task Kao uses a disguise to fool the Shaolin brethren and gain their trust, biding his time for the right chance to strike. Kao succeeds in badly injuring Hu, but Hu,

mortally wounded, returns for a final, deadly face-off.

Tan Tao-Liang plays the bad guy for once, bringing to the screen a charismatic villain who exudes subtle menace. His kicking is awe-inspiring, as to be expected, and Chi Kuan-Chun is in top form too, showcasing the five animal styles to full effect. Powerful stuff.

SLAUGHTER IN XIAN (1990)
Starring Dong Zhi-Hua, Xu Xiao-Jian, Du Yu-Ming
Directed and produced by Chang Cheh
Chang He Film Company/Xi'an Film Studio

One of Xian's top police inspectors, Ho Yuan-Hsin (Zhi-Hua), finds himself up to his neck in corruption involving Xian's local crime family and his own colleagues, who prove to be involved. Ho makes a stand against the corruption, but it's a stand that costs him everything.

Chang Cheh's new crew yet again amaze, as they strut their amazing talents in this mainland-made, relatively low-budget late offering from Cheh. The fights are superb and are coupled with an involving storyline and an excellent performance from Dong Zhi-Hua, who comes across as a kung fu fighting Dirty Harry.

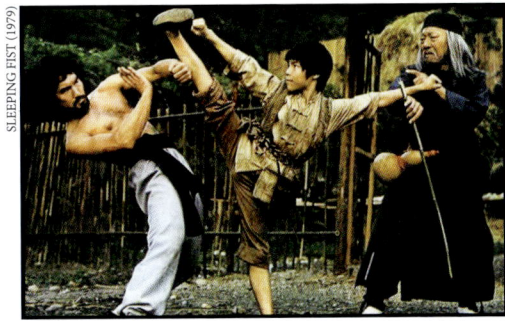

SLEEPING FIST (1979)

SLEEPING FIST (1979)
Starring Leung Kar-Yan, Wong Yat-Lung, Yuen Siu-Tin, Eddy Ko
Directed by Yip Wing-Cho
Produced by Chow Fook-Leung
East Asia Film Company

After providing the music scores for hundreds of movies, maestro Chow Fook-Leung turns to producing. Plainclothes policeman Chin (Kar-Yan) is seriously wounded in a fight with some ruffians. A young wise guy, The Kid (Yat-Lung), comes to his aid and brings him to visit his master, Old Fox

(Siu-Tin). While he recuperates, he watches the old master put The Kid through extreme martial arts tutoring, which the young lad seems to relish. One day, while buying wine for his master, The Kid comes to the aid of a young girl being accosted by a motley bunch of thugs. The Kid is no match for the gang and is thrashed within an inch of his little life. Old Fox decides to teach The Kid the secret art of the sleeping fist, and Chin, now fully recovered, learns too. Training complete, the trio march to the Shang Wei martial arts school to take revenge on the thugs. After an amusing fight, the sleepy trio emerge victorious. The mob don't take defeat easily and, in a last desperate attempt to get even, they call on Eagle Claw master Kao to sort out the snoozers.

Following his success in *Drunken Master* (1978), Yuen Siu-Tin made several cash-in movies. *Sleeping Fist* remains by far the best of these, thanks to the great on-screen chemistry between Wong Yat-Lung and Leung Kar-Yan. The film fared well at the box office and a sequel, *Thundering Mantis*, soon followed.

SNAKE AND CRANE ARTS OF SHAOLIN (1978)

Starring Jackie Chan, Nora Miao, Kam Kong,
Kim Chin Lan, Lee Wing-Kwok
Directed by Chan Chi-Hwa
Produced by Hsu Li Hwa, Lo Wei
Action by Jackie Chan, To Wai-Wo
Lo Wei Motion Picture Company

Once every decade, the various martial art factions meet in the Hwa mountains to create new systems. This time the art of Snake and Crane is developed, but no sooner has the new style been documented than all the masters, along with the book, mysteriously disappear. Enter Hsu Yin-Fung (Chan), a young martial artist who claims to possess the coveted book of the Snake and Crane. Dozens of dastardly martial artists try to scheme the book away from Hsu, but his martial arts and cunning are too good for his aggressors, most of whom end up befriending him. It turns out, after many breathtaking fights in which Hsu uses chopsticks, swords, bamboo, window frames, stalls, paper and acrobatics, that he is in fact the student of the sole surviving master from the Hwa mountains conference. The master explains that he gave Hsu the book in order to lure out the culprit who poisoned the other masters. By this time Hsu and the gang have a pretty good

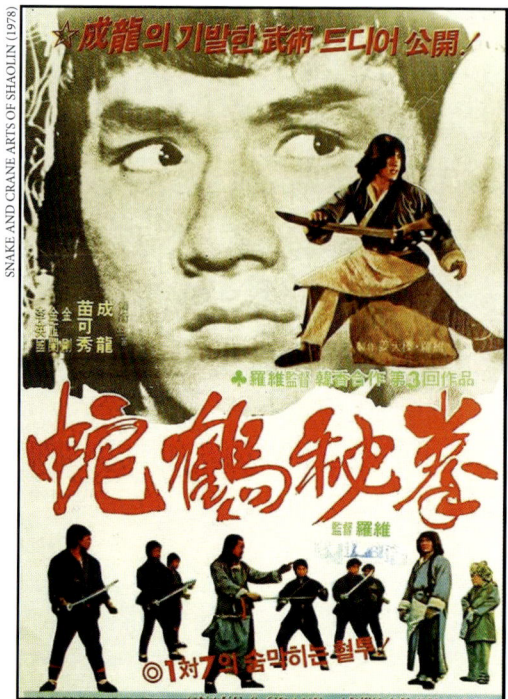

SNAKE AND CRANE ARTS OF SHAOLIN (1978)

idea who the masked culprit is and challenge him to a duel at the Hwa mountains. Before Hsu can fight Master Chin (Kong), the leader of the Black Dragon Gang, he must fight three spearmen in what can only be described as the most intricate piece of choreography ever filmed. The spearmen finally done with, Hsu combines the Snake and Crane arts in order to destroy Chin's Iron Armor technique.

This is without doubt the best Jackie Chan period film as far as showcasing his martial arts is concerned, from the opening credits, where Jackie displays his prowess with spear, sword and tonfa, to the epic ending. Two of the spearmen (Peng Gang

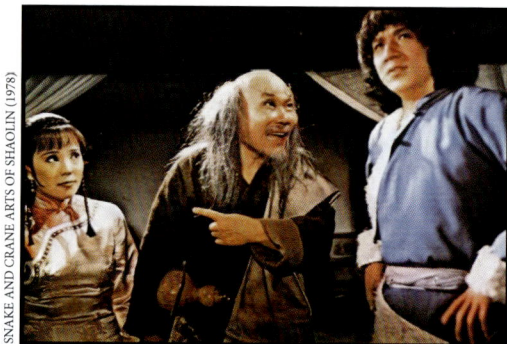

SNAKE AND CRANE ARTS OF SHAOLIN (1978)

and Wang Chi-Sheng) returned as spearmen in Jackie's blockbuster *The Fearless Hyena*.

This movie, unfortunately, did very bad business when released in Hong Kong in 1978 due to a lack of advertising. Upset at seeing all that hard work go to waste, Jackie made the classic kung fu send-up *Half a Loaf of Kung Fu* as his statement on the whole kung fu genre at that time.

SNAKE DEADLY ACT (1980)
Starring Ng Kwan-Lung, Wilson Tong, Fong Hark-On, Angela Mao, Michael Chan Wai-Man, Phillip Ko
Directed by Wilson Tong
Produced by Lee Ching
Action by Wilson Tong
Million Film Company

Chung (Kwan-Lung) is the happy-go-lucky son of a wealthy businessman, Kuo (Tong). Because of his upright moral character, Chung often finds himself getting into fights with gangsters. He is nearly killed when he comes to the aid of a prostitute, but is saved by Yueh (Hark-On), a mysterious snake fist fighter. Yueh shows up a second time after Chung starts on a casino boss (Wai-Man). Chung takes lessons from the snake fist exponent and he soon masters the art. Chung learns from Yueh that his father is not all that he's cracked up to be, and that he actually owns the brothel and the casino. Disgusted by this revelation, Chung sets up a meeting, only to discover that he has been used by his master

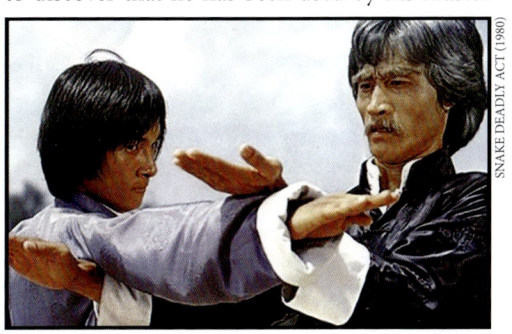

SNAKE DEADLY ACT (1980)

to lure his father out into the open. The two old-timers were, in fact, both disciples of the snake fist sect, but Kuo turned to evil and even raped and killed Yueh's wife. Now, after years of waiting, Yueh will have his revenge, but what of Chung? Watch the three-against-three ending to find out.

Although the plot is a bit on the lame side, the fighting, as you might expect from Wilson Tong,

is first rate, and the film even includes "lobster-style" kung fu! Newcomer and real-life martial arts master Ng Kwan-Lung showcases his expertise in the dozens of fight scenes he's in (so it's a shame he decided not to make any more movies). There are also great cameos too, from Angela Mao as the sword-wielding brothel owner, Michael Chan Wai-Man and the cool Phillip Ko.

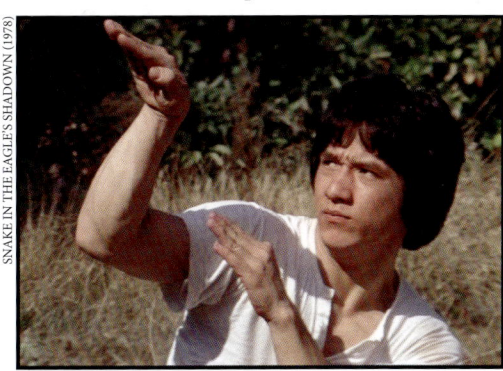

SNAKE IN THE EAGLE'S SHADOWN (1978)

SNAKE IN THE EAGLE'S SHADOW (1978)
Starring Jackie Chan, Yuen Siu-Tin, Hwang Jang-Lee, Tino Wong, Roy Horan
Directed by Yuen Woo-Ping
Produced by Ng See-Yuen
Action by Yuen Woo-Ping, Hsu Hsia
Seasonal Film Corporation

Jackie Chan plays a dogsbody, Chien Fu, at a small kung fu gym where he is bullied and beaten by his seniors. One day, while on his rounds, Chien Fu comes to the aid of an old beggar (Siu-Tin), the old man is grateful and the two become close friends. The beggar is, in fact, Pai Chang Tien, the last of the snake fist masters, the rest of whom have been wiped out by eagle claw masters from Manchuria. Chien tells the beggar of his plight, and the old man teaches him how to escape, but is reluctant to teach him snake fist. Only after being severely injured by two eagle claw lieutenants does the old man decide to teach Chien the deadly art. But the snake fist alone is no match for the king of eagle claw, Shang Kuan (Jang-Lee). Chien has to incorporate new techniques of cat's paw (his own creation) before he can hope to beat the dreaded eagle king.

After being unable to get Fu Sheng for the role of Chien, director Yuen Woo-Ping picked Jackie Chan and the result was a big hit, reinvigorating the stagnating kung fu genre.

SNAKE IN THE MONKEY'S SHADOW (1979)

Starring John Cheung, Wilson Tong, Pomson Shi, Chen Yao-Lin
Directed by Cheung Sum
Produced by Alex Gouw
Action by Wilson Tong
Goldig Film Company

Liang (Cheung) gets a job running errands for a kung fu gym. Too poor to pay for lessons, Liang steals techniques whenever the master's back is turned. In time he becomes quite proficient in the arts. The master, much impressed by Liang's diligence, decides to teach him drunken boxing. When tit-for-tat violence occurs, due to the gym's master clashing with the rich Yan family, two killers become involved. These guys, Hsia (Yao-Lin) and Lun (Tong), are both exponents of the snake style. Together they storm the gym, killing the master and most of the students. Liang manages to escape and seeks refuge with his friend Koo, a monkey fist expert who defeated one of the snake fighters several years before. Liang soon recovers and learns the art of monkey boxing. The two killers eventually track Liang down and murder Koo, but Liang runs to safety. While burying Koo, Liang notices a monkey

fighting a snake and, from this observation, he invents a new technique combining monkey and drunken fists, then sets about exacting his revenge . . .

This classic actioner from the seventies still packs a punch with martial arts fans. Well worth tracking down.

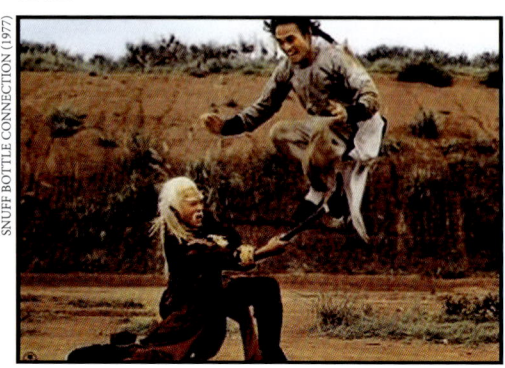

SNUFF BOTTLE CONNECTION (1977)

SNUFF BOTTLE CONNECTION (1977)

Starring John Liu, Hwang Jang-Lee, Roy Horan, Yip Fai-Yang, Phillip Ko, Yuen Biao
Directed by Lily Lui Li-Li, Tung Chin-Hu
Produced by Richard Tu Chin
Action by Yuen Woo-Ping
Fortuna Film Company

When a corrupt magistrate (Jang-Lee) conspires with the Russians, who want to possess a map highlighting weak points within China's territories that will allow them to invade, a secret agent, Chow Tien (Liu), and his friend Ko (Fai-Yang) are tasked with spying on the magistrate. They discover that the link between the magistrate and the Russian general (Horan) is a rare snuff bottle, which acts as a form of identification between Russia and China. Chow steals it, and they have to fight their way out in a bid to save China and bring the traitors down.

With its heavyweight cast featuring legendary kickers John Liu and Hwang Jang-Lee, who had been paired together to do battle in some of the best kung Fu movies of the 70s, including *Secret Rivals 1 & 2* and *Invincible Armour*, this film is also up to snuff and is deemed by many to be "kung fu movie late-night cinema gold" at its best.

With a decent plot and the skilled action choreography of Yuen Woo-Ping delivering pull-no-punches action, and great supporting roles from Yip Fai-Yang, plus an early cameo from Yuen Biao, this is a movie that will feed the appetite of the most hardened kung fu movie fan.

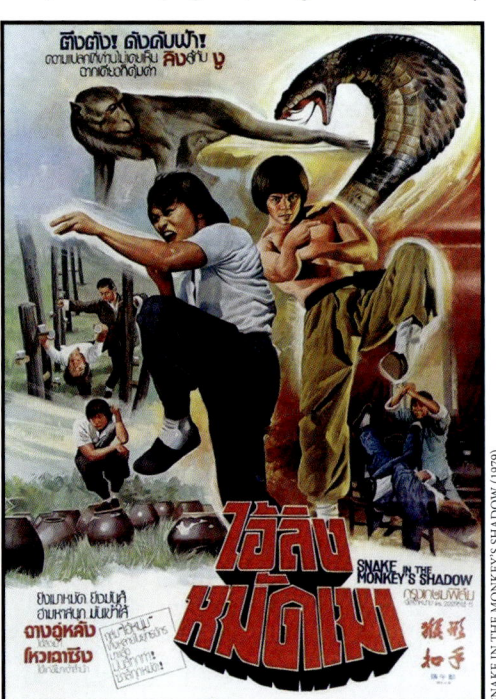

SNAKE IN THE MONKEY'S SHADOW (1979)

SPIRITUAL KUNG FU (1978)
Starring Jackie Chan, James Tien, Wu Wen-Siu,
Li Tung-Chun
Directed by Lo Wei
Produced by Lo Wei
Action by Jackie Chan
Lo Wei Motion Picture Company

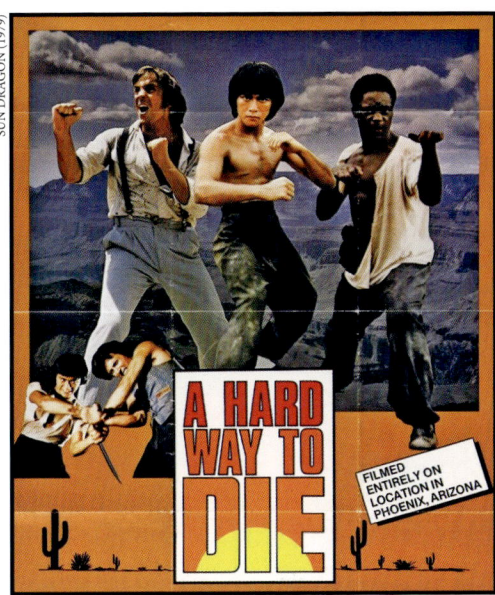

Jackie Chan plays a young Shaolin layabout who is always getting into trouble with the abbot. One of his punishments is to guard the library after the book of the Seven Fist technique is stolen. Jackie encounters five spirits here, who teach him the long-lost art of Five Fists kung fu. Once Jackie has mastered the art, he decides he wants to leave the temple to search for the renegade monk that stole the Seven Fist book. To leave the temple he must first pass the eighteen Lo Han formation, a deadly array of Shaolin's most formidable fighters. With the aid of a pair of tonfas Jackie amazingly defeats all eighteen of the Lo Hans. Once outside

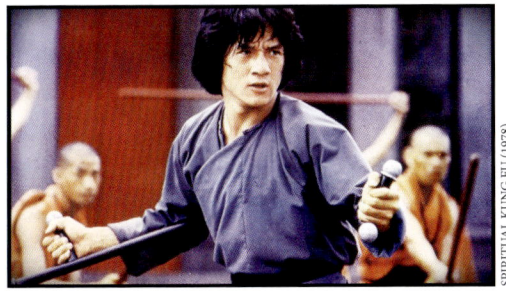

the temple he discovers the identity of the renegade and, with the help of his friends from the spirit world, the Shaolin traitor is brought to justice.
  Dazzling choreography from Chan the Man makes this one of the best Lo Wei films.

STONER (1976)
Starring George Lazenby, Angela Mao, Betty Ting Pei,
Whang In-Shik, Sammo Hung
Directed by Huang Feng
Produced by Raymond Chow
Action by Sammo Hung, Chan Chuen
Golden Harvest

Lazenby plays a hardened Australian cop on the trail of a Hong Kong-based operation smuggling a lethal new drug, which is being aimed at the young. Aided by an Asian policewoman, they finally locate and penetrate the gang's headquarters, as in *Enter the Dragon*, and are subsequently captured. Staging

a break out, despite having been used as guinea pigs for the drug, they confront the boss and his army of kung fu cronies.
  This is a mindless, clichéd attempt at making a martial arts star out of Lazenby. He is, however, no screen fighter—a deficiency his acting skills cannot disguise. Mao is underused, probably because it was feared she would outshine her leading man, which she does anyway. Her fight scenes are up to standard, especially her duel with super-kicker Whang In-Shik.
  Also known as *The Shrine of Ultimate Bliss* and *A Man Called Stoner*.

SUN DRAGON (1979)
Starring Billy Chong, Carl Scott, Leung Siu Sung,
Ma Chung-Tak, Louis Neglia
Directed by Hua Shan
Produced by Pal Ming
Eternal Film Company

Martial arts heart-throb Billy Chong bursts back onto the big screen in yet another flashy, incident-filled martial arts flick. In this outing Billy is westward bound after fleeing China due to a run-in with the mayor's son. On arrival in Arizona, Billy looks up his uncle and finds work doing odd jobs. Billy strikes up a friendship with a black rancher called Tom (Carl Scott), who learns martial arts from Billy's uncle so that he can avenge the death of his family, who were killed by land-greedy mobsters. In no time

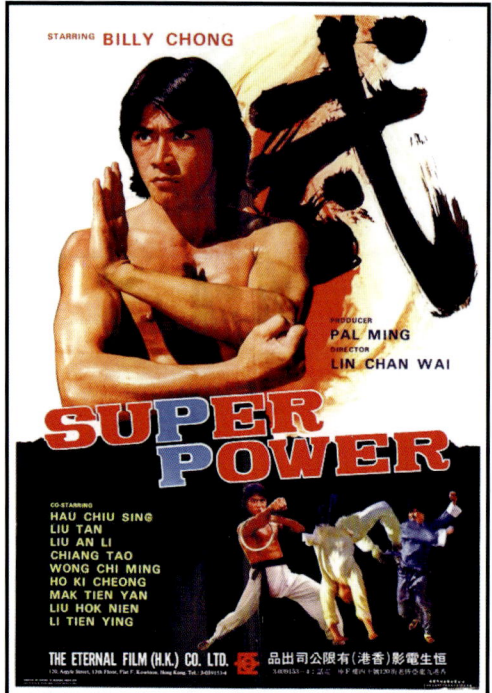

STARRING BILLY CHONG

SUPER POWER

PRODUCER PAL MING
DIRECTOR LIN CHAN WAI

CO-STARRING
HAU CHIU SING
LIU TAN
LIU AN LI
CHIANG TAO
WONG CHI MING
HO KI CHEONG
MAK TIEN YAN
LIU HOK NIEN
LI TIEN YING

THE ETERNAL FILM (H.K.) CO. LTD.

SUPER POWER (1980)

at all Tom becomes an expert and they team up to right the wrongs.

Despite the hokey production values and dire English dubbing, this movie, also known as *A Hard Way to Die*, succeeds in being an entertaining B movie kung-fu-western that's delightfully diverse. Billy Chong is as dazzling as ever, but the film belongs to young star Carl Scott, who proves himself to be an outstanding Western martial artist.

SUPER POWER (1980)

Starring Billy Chong, Liu On-Lai, Hau Chiu-Sing, Lau Dan, Wong Chi-Ming
Directed by Lin Chan-Wei
Action by Tang Tak-Cheung, Wong Chi-Ming
Eternal Film Company

Kang, an obsessed Manchu fighter, seeks revenge on all Chinese martial artists for having humiliated Manchu boxers. Enter Billy Chong as the easygoing Chun, a kung fu fanatic who will undergo hours of intense training to save the honor of Chinese boxing.

Indonesian kung fu idol Chong dazzles audiences yet again with his unique brand of flashy fighting and exquisite forms. The end confrontation against Kang's Manchu horse boxing is a real eye-opener.

THE SWORD (1971)

Starring Jimmy Wang Yu, Chen Pei-Ling, Wang Lai
Directed by Jimmy Wang Yu, Pan Lei
Action by Kwan Hung
Yangtze Film Company Ltd

This is a splendidly atmospheric Jimmy Wang Yu starrer, notable for the rich cinematography of the sumptuous sets and some terrific costume design for a dynasty not usually portrayed on the screen, thus giving the simple tale of an obsessive swordsman's attempts to collect the greatest blade in the land a strong pictorial edge.

The acting is more restrained than usual, making the character development more convincing, and the bursts of swordplay become all the more effective because of the plotting between each bout. Particularly effective is the final battle in the snow, complete with delayed reaction deaths. Note the size and weight of the swords as well as the style of swordplay used here.

SWORD OF SWORDS (1968)

Starring Jimmy Wang Yu, Li Ching, Tien Feng, Ching Miao
Directed by Cheng Kang
Produced by Runme Shaw
Action by Tang Chia, Lau Kar-Leung
Shaw Brothers

A Jimmy Wang Yu vehicle in which the sword in question acts more like a Hitchcockian MacGuffin than a centerpiece, although when it comes into play the results are cheerfully devastating. There are several neat touches, such as our hero's refusal to fight because he believes his enemies to be better than he is, archers who make William Tell look inaccurate and a sword fight interrupted by the need to tend the baby!

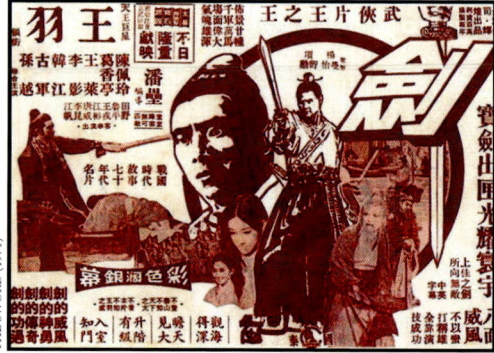

THE SWORD (1971)

In this film, which gets bloodier and bloodier, Wang Yu loses his eyesight, which makes a change from his usual lost appendages (though he does lose his sight again in *Iron Fist Adventure*).

Wang Yu cleverly retrains himself by listening for the movements of the family cat, but there's a disturbing sequence at the climax, when gagged members of his family are used as human shields . . . you have been warned!

THE SWORD STAINED WITH ROYAL BLOOD (1993)

Starring Yuen Biao, Danny Lee, Cheung Man, Ng Man-Tat, Anita Yuen, Elizabeth Lee
Directed and produced by Cheung Hoi-Ching
Action by Brandy Yuen
Production Line Films

If acrobatic martial arts action and mental swordplay are your thing, then this flick is for you. Mind you, if an easily comprehensible plot is also an essential requirement, then you're probably better off looking elsewhere. With that said, *The Sword Stained with Royal Blood* is a rollicking medieval super-powered bash 'em up, where exposition is rarely allowed to interfere with the serious business of full-on blade-action from start to finish.

Plotwise, it's your fairly standard saga of a mystic warrior seeking vengeance against a repressive feudal emperor, but, by the time you've tossed in all manner of oddballs and red herrings, from identity confusion to faked madness to poison-administering vampire spider people, you're liable to start feeling pretty weary just keeping up with who's got it in for who and, instead, you're just concentrating on some impressive fight sequences and marveling at a movie where the protagonists seem to spend about fifty percent of the time flying through the air with mayhem in mind.

Despite the odd severed head, violence is strictly on the biff-bang-pow level and this, with its strained plotline, makes this movie primarily one for tree-hopping Peking Opera devotees (which, luckily, I am).

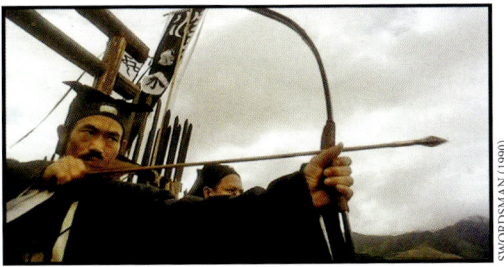

SWORDSMAN (1990)

SWORDSMAN (1990)

Starring Sam Hui, Lam Ching-Ying, Cecilia Yip, Jacky Cheung, Yuen Wah, Wu Ma
Directed by Tsui Hark, Ching Siu-Tung, King Hu, Raymond Lee, Ann Hui, Kam Yeung-Wah
Produced by Tsui Hark
Action by Ching Siu-Tung, Lau Chi-Ho
Long Shong Pictures, Golden Princess Film Production Ltd/Film Workshop

Set in the Ming Dynasty, *Swordsman* follows the adventures of roving sword-hero Chung and his admiring sidekick Kiddo (Yip), who stumble into a fierce power struggle in which it seems everyone, including ambitious royal eunuchs, wants to gain possession of the Sunflower Scriptures: an ancient scroll of do-it-yourself instructions for developing the highest form of martial arts.

Memorable scenes include a clash of swords on the deck of a rammed junk, tribeswomen healing Chung and saving him from villain Zhor (Wah), who is attacked by a swarm of killer bees, and the final, awesome duel in which Chung uses all his midair sword tactics to combat his treacherous master's invisible sword energy.

Employing the now-familiar swooping camera flights, up-shots, tilted angles, special effects and atmospheric use of outdoor locations, this wuxia did surprisingly well at the box office, although nobody could have predicted the phenomenal success of its sequel.

SWORDSMAN 2 (1992)

Starring Jet Li, Brigitte Lin, Rosamund Kwan, Waise Lee, Michelle Reis
Directed by Ching Siu-Tung
Produced by Tsui Hark
Action by Ching Siu-Tung, Yuen Bun, Cheung Yiu-Sing, Ma Yuk-Sing
Film Workshop/Long Shong Pictures

This opened in Taipei during Chinese New Year, a time of fierce box office wars, and wiped the floor with all the opposition. It was still playing to packed theaters three months after opening.

At the start we find Chung (Li) and Kiddo (Reis) on their way to a meeting with the rest of the Hua Mountain swordsmen. Disillusioned with a life of martial chivalry after their master betrayed them, they plan to retreat, but, on the journey, Chung decides to pay a visit to Ren (Kwan), the beautiful Chief of the Sun Moon sect, who saved his life in

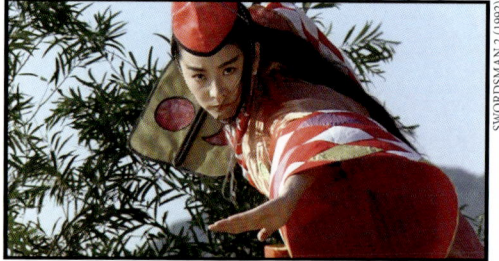

SWORDSMAN 2 (1992)

an earlier adventure. But the place is deserted and Ren explains that the Sunflower Scriptures have fallen into the hands of an ambitious warrior who, to master the devastating martial arts technique, has castrated himself and is now transitioning into a woman known as Invincible Asia (Lin). Asia plans to overthrow the ruling Ming court and has imprisoned Ren's father. Chung agrees to help, but he unwittingly sets in motion a series of events which will bring another deranged despot to power.

Besides having a well-developed storyline, this is such a feast for the eyes, with a relentless barrage of mind-blowing imagery. The action choreography is peerless, with fluid swordplay, ingenious wirework and innovative sfx. Jet Li displays his excellent Wu Shu skills and also gets the chance to develop his comedy skills (far more than usual) in this exceptional movie.

SWORDSMAN III: THE EAST IS RED (1993)

Starring Brigitte Lin, Joey Wong, Yu Rongguang, Eddy Ko
Directed by Ching Siu-Tung, Raymond Lee
Action by Ching Siu-Tung, Dion Lam, Ma Yuk-Sing
Long Shong Pictures, Golden Princess Film Production Ltd/Film Workshop

Ming government official Koo (Rongguang) leads a Spanish expedition to the grave of Invincible Asia at the foot of Black Cliff, where, we presume, she met her doom at the end of the last chapter. After being forced to plunder the grave by the Spanish adventurers, Koo is abducted by a silver-haired woman. This mysterious figure is none other than Invincible Asia (Lin), who reveals to Koo that she never died, but became a recluse. She states her intention of ridding the world of all the "fake" Asias that have sprung up and have been forming their own clans using her name. Asia promises not to kill these imposters (a promise which is quickly broken and leads to much brilliantly staged carnage) if Koo vows not to reveal her identity. Joey

Wong, meanwhile, plays Snow, Invincible Asia's former concubine, who has re-established the Sun Moon sect in an effort to regain its former glory. Soon events will lead to a third act naval battle . . .

Stylistically, this is more of the same from the Film Workshop school of brash, flash aesthetics: the blue filters, dust and dry ice, firelight, split-second editing and rushing camera swoops. Although the end section is full of empty spectacle, sound and fury, the first half is crammed full of visual inventiveness and spine-tingling images including, for example, Japanese kite-flying warriors and a grotesque ninja regurgitating a live pigeon! The movie doesn't quite live up to the previous part, but it's still well worth seeing.

THE SWORDSMAN IN DOUBLE FLAG TOWN (1991)

Starring Gao Wei, Zhao Mana, Chang Jiang, Sun Haiying, Wang Gang
Directed by He Ping
Xi'an Film Studio

A teenage swordsman, Hai Ge (Wei), goes to Double Flag Town, a barren, dusty village in China's harsh desert, in search of Hao Mei (Mana), a girl he has never met but to whom he is betrothed. But the townspeople do not take kindly to strangers. The notorious bandit Lethal Swordsman (Haiying) and his gang terrorize the countryside, and the only way to survive is to mind one's own business. Trouble develops when one of the gang tries to rape Hao Mei and Hai Ge kills him. The townspeople are furious that he has exposed them to the wrath of Lethal Swordsman, so when Hai Ge and his bride try to leave, they are begged to stay . . . not because the townspeople want to rally around them but because they are frightened that if Hai Ge escapes they will bear the brunt of Lethal Swordsman's rage.

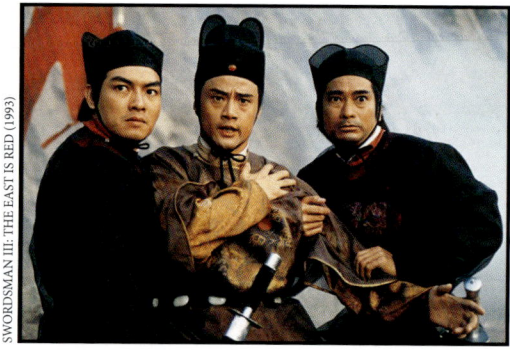

SWORDSMAN III: THE EAST IS RED (1993)

In the world of this film there is no sense of the public good or the rule of law in Double Flag Town, just the ability to defend oneself. The duel between Hai Ge and his nemesis is a masterpiece of tension, with the stillness of the bleak village creating the atmosphere of a John Ford western. Stylistically, *The Swordsman in Double Flag Town*, a mainland Chinese production, is the polar opposite of typical Hong Kong swordplay movies. Rather than blind us with kinetic, hyper-choreographed fights and wirework, this film goes for more of a cool Kurosawa aesthetic, with lengthy buildups ending in sudden sword-strikes. It is a breath of fresh air in an often cliché-plagued genre and it certainly sticks in the memory.

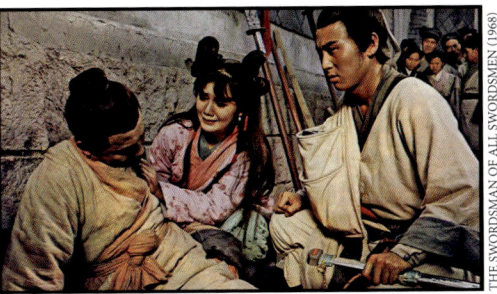

THE SWORDSMAN OF ALL SWORDSMEN (1968)

THE SWORDSMAN OF ALL SWORDSMEN (1968)

Starring Tien Peng, Miao Tien, Chiang Nan,
Polly Shang-Kuan Ling-Feng, Liu Chu
Directed by Joseph Kuo
Union Film Company

Single-minded swordsman Tsai (Peng) is hell-bent on avenging the murder of his father, but during his quest he's hit with a poisoned dart and an arrow. Fortunately for him he's helped by Flying Swallow (Ling-Feng), who gives him an antidote for the poison. She's feeling very conflicted, however, because she has saved Tsai out of guilt for what her father did to his dad . . . but now Tsai will be well enough to go off and hunt for her father. Tsai does, indeed, track down Flying Swallow's dad, who feels a lot of regret for what he did all those years ago, so much so that Tsai refrains from killing him. But now the warrior Black Dragon (Nan) requests a fight-to-the death showdown with Tsai by the sea in a sandy bay. The story ends with Tsai pacing away, aware of the futility of constant fighting.

Joseph Kuo handles the directing chores expertly, showing a lot of control, knowing when to keep

things still, knowing when to keep events at a distance, knowing when a close-up will be effective, using long tracking shots well. The way Kuo shoots the film actually gives it something of a Japanese movie vibe. He films everything with a certain amount of restraint, keeping the usual high jumping-style fight moves, such as during the beach skirmish with Black Dragon, to a minimum.

The film excels in its location choices, which include waterfalls and beaches, using the real landscapes excellently, differentiating this production from the more set-bound, theatrical-looking Shaw Brothers wuxia films.

TAI CHI BOXER (1996)

Starring Jacky Wu, Christy Chung, Sibelle Hu,
Billy Chow, Mark Cheng, Darren Shahlavi, Yu Hai
Directed by Yuen Woo-Ping
Film Can Production/Upland Films Corporation Limited

Set in the 1830s, we see Hawkman, a young kid who is easily distracted from his studies, preferring to sneak out with his friend to secretly watch his father, Yeung Shan-Wu (Hai), demonstrating his lion dance skills. Suddenly, the mood is disrupted by an impromptu challenge from Wong (Chow), better known as The Great North Kick. His father, not wanting to disrupt the day's events, tries to defuse the situation. His wife (Sibelle Hu) suggests that, as skilled fighters, they should tell each other the moves that they planned to use, like a chess battle. Wong agrees, and they start to shout their moves at each other, using terminology like "Bear's Paw" and "Steel Broom." But, not satisfied by this, Wong attacks Yeung, only to be defeated. The young Hawkman, impressed, wants to learn his father's skills and become a great fighter.

Moving forward in time, we now see an older Hawkman (Wu) practicing with old manuscripts based on the tai chi of the Kwan family. During a lion dance, which he and his friend have gate-crashed, he chances upon the lovely Rose (Chung). Enchanted by her beauty, his youthful hormones are immediately focused on pursuing her. Their romance is interrupted, though, when Rose's fiancé, Lam Wing (Cheng), finds out, leading to a fight which Hawkman wins. With Lam's ego bruised, he heads home only to be ambushed and murdered. This results in Hawkman being accused of killing Lam and he must now do everything in his power to clear his name.

As always in Yuen Woo-Ping movies, the fight action is full-on, well-executed and enhanced by the use of wirework. In one inventive scene we see Hawkman fighting while wearing roller skates, making the action look like he is using Drunken Style Boxing. He also has a Shaolin monk braid that he whips about by rotating his head, using it to great effect in the fight action.

Tai Chi Boxer, also known as *Tai Chi Master 2* and *Tai Chi II*, was a follow-up to the hugely successful *Tai Chi Master* with Jet Li and Michelle Yeoh, who are replaced here by Jacky Wu and Christy Chung. Along with a decent cast, including Billy Chow (you always know you're in for a good fight when he plays a villain), Sibelle Hu and Mark Cheng, the film also features British martial artist Darren Shahlavi, who sadly passed away just as his career was taking off.

This was a very early outing for Jacky Wu (Jing Wu), but already you could see that he was somebody to watch out for, and he is now currently one of Hong Kong's biggest action stars.

An excellent film that will satisfy even the hardest-to-please kung fu movie fans.

TAI CHI MASTER (1993)

Starring Jet Li, Michelle Yeoh, Chin Siu-Ho,
Fennie Yuen
Directed by Yuen Woo-Ping
Produced by Jet Li, Chui Bo-Chu
Eastern Productions

This is an excellent example of how wirework can complement rather than detract from martial arts expertise. Chin Siu-Ho plays Tienbao and Jet Li plays Junbao, two young men raised in the Shaolin Temple. While Junbao is content to comply with the rules set down by the Buddhist way of life, his friend is ambitious and longs for fame and fortune. Conflict rears its ugly head when Tienbao's aggression leads to him being driven out of the temple after a furious pole battle. Junbao comes to his friend's aid and they try to adapt to life in the world beyond Shaolin. While begging they

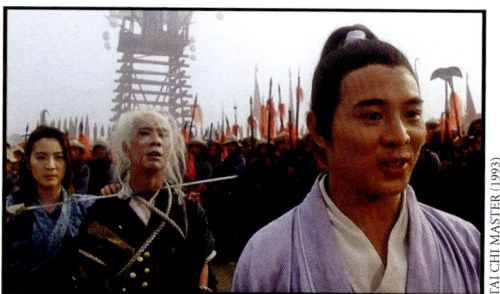

TAI CHI MASTER (1993)

meet two women who are rebelling against Eunuch Jin's taxation policies. Junbao joins the rebels while Tienbao becomes a member of the eunuch's army, betraying his former companion to gain promotion. This leads to a huge battle between the army and the rebels, with heroic fights and exotic weaponry worthy of a Venoms mob movie. After a dramatic broadsword duel with Tienbao, Junbao loses his memory. During this period of amnesia, he creates the fighting style of tai chi, which is adapted to react perfectly to Tienbao's Iron Palm technique.

The training sequences in this movie are refreshing and inventive and, while the fight choreography is escapist, there's enough genuine martial arts expertise to dazzle the most jaded viewer.

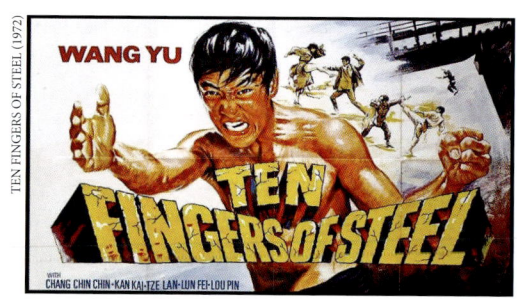

TEN FINGERS OF STEEL (1972)

TAOISM DRUNKARD (1984)

Starring Yuen Yat-Chor, Yuen Cheung-Yan,
Yuen Shun-Yi, Yen Shi-Kwan, Liu Hao-Yi
Directed by Yuen Cheung-Yan
Produced by Lo Wei
Action by Yuen Clan
Lo Wei Motion Picture Company

Old Devil (Shun-Yi) seeks revenge on the miracle fighters for having him banished from the clan and depriving him of his identity by having his palms removed by a grotesque torture device resembling a roller coaster. Old Devil escapes from the box in which he is incarcerated and causes havoc in the region. Old Granny Wu and Taoist Drunkard, who rides around in a giant mouse-shaped shoe (both played by Yuen Cheung-Yan) train Wu Shun-Chiu (Yat-Chor) to tackle Old Devil. After many totally insane fights Old Devil has to face the wrath of the miracle fighters once more.

The imagination of the Yuen clan reaches new heights in this madcap movie, which is the third installment in the *Miracle Fighters* series. Highlights including the "watermelon/banana monster" (a spherical robot who munches at peoples' groins), giant pipe kung fu, a handheld cluster bomb, untold stunts, magic, and general wackiness make the world of the miracle fighters a must see.

TEN FINGERS OF STEEL (1972)
Starring Jimmy Wang Yu, Lung Fei,
Chang Ching-Ching, Ma Chi
Directed by Chien Lung
Chin Hua Film Company

Jimmy Wang Yu portrays a young Chinese avenger in this first-frame-to-last action ballbuster. After the family of Tai Yung (Wang Yu) are massacred by Japanese pirates, the young avenger travels to Japan to track down his ruthless foes, whom he knows neither by name nor by sight. His encounters along the way give him (and the audience) an opportunity to see how well the ancient Chinese fighting arts stand up against the more modern Japanese systems. After defeating dozens of exponents, Tai Yung meets up with his ultimate nemesis (Fei), the man who brought about the demise of his family. In one of Wang Yu's most dangerous fights, aboard a steaming locomotive, vengeance strikes the final blow . . .

Also known as *The Screaming Tiger*, *Wang Yu, King of Boxers* and *The Screaming Ninja*, this movie features mad, mad fights from Jimmy Wang Yu and Lung Fei, making this a must-see for seventies fu film fans.

THIRTEEN COLD-BLOODED EAGLES (1993)
Starring Cynthia Khan, Waise Lee, Yan Shi-Kwan,
Chung Fat
Directed and produced by Tsui Fat
Action by Tsui Fat Stunt Group
Cheung Yau Production Co

Cynthia Khan leads the way in this action-crammed period piece drama. The 13 Cold-Blooded Eagles are a band of highly skilled martial artists who are instructed by their leader, the Foster Father (Shi-Kwan), to destroy surrounding kung fu schools in search of the Skills Book. By possessing this he will unlock its martial arts secrets and become invincible. On their quest they face many obstacles, including the Shinshu monster, who practices the star bleeding skill, which allows his body to be penetrated by daggers and swords without being killed.

An engaging movie with lots of wire-fu fight sequences, *Thirteen Cold-Blooded Eagles* features a

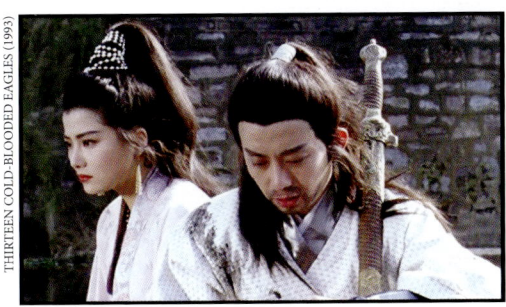

THIRTEEN COLD-BLOODED EAGLES (1993)

range of weaponry and fast-paced kung fu. The movie also goes by the title *The 13 Cold Blooded Eagles*.

THE 36 CRAZY FISTS (1979)
Starring Leung Siu-Hung, Lau Kar-Yung,
Yen Shi-Kwan, Ku Feng
Directed by Chen Chi-Hwa
Action by Jackie Chan
United Enterprise Corporation

After a severe beating at the hands of a senior Manchu officer, Wong (Siu-Hung) is rescued by Shaolin monks. Once fully recovered he asks that he might train in Shaolin kung fu but, at first, his pleas are rejected. When he is finally accepted as a student, he finds that he learns far more from a local drunk beggar friend than from any of the esteemed monks. As the result of much training, his skills enable him to beat his master and Wong leaves Shaolin in order to avenge his father, who was murdered by the Manchus. Wong's troubles do not end once he defeats a senior Manchu, however, and he and the beggar find that they must combine their kung fu styles in order to defeat an extremely powerful villain.

This film contains nothing new in terms of plot, but its strength lies in its decent, solid fight scenes. Note: some versions have an additional opening, showing Jackie Chan choreographing the main title.

THE 36TH CHAMBER OF SHAOLIN (1978)
Starring Gordon Liu, Lo Lieh, Yung Wang Yu,
Wilson Tong, Lee Hoi-Sang, Lau Kar-Wing
Directed by Lau Kar-Leung
Produced by Run Run Shaw
Shaw Brothers

Gordon Liu plays the real-life Shaolin disciple San Te, a young rebel whose father is killed by Manchu troops. After a confrontation with the assassins, he is seriously wounded and seeks refuge in the Shaolin Temple. San Te plans to study kung fu so that he can take revenge, but his hot temper and yearning for retribution make him stand out from the other monks. His education in the martial arts takes him on a journey through the temple's thirty-five chambers, each specializing in a particular area of combat. Completing his formal training, San Te proves his proficiency in a rigorous duel utilizing a three-sectioned staff to counter a pair of butterfly swords. San Te is offered the stewardship of a chamber of his choice but, instead, he opts to leave the temple in order to recruit suitable men to form a resistance force against the Manchus' evil. San Te finally returns to Shaolin to create his own 36th chamber, to be used to teach martial arts to the common man.

Also known as *Master Killer*, this film has all the elements of a martial arts classic (which it is): the fights are excellently executed, the villain is suitably cruel, the training sequences are original and inventive and San Te is a hero the audience really cares about. *Return to the 36th Chamber* followed.

THUNDERCLAP (1984)
Starring Chen Kuan-Tai, Leung Siu-Hung,
Mok Siu Chung, Liao Li-Ling, Ku Feng
Directed by Leung Siu-Hung
Produced by Mona Fong
Shaw Brothers

Another bonkers fantasy martial art extravaganza from the Shaw Brothers stable. This one's got the lot, and even takes place in a comic writer's head!

The three evils create two pills: the ice pill and the fire pill, which revive and give great strength to whoever takes them. One problem, however, is that they have to be taken together, otherwise there will be a massive imbalance in the recipient's Yin/Yang. They have been created for Shen Chun (Kuan-Tai), who has been put in a coma by the Chao Yung clan. The clan manage to stop Shen Chun's followers feeding him both pills to revive him. They intercept the fire pill and place it inside a pigeon, which flies off to become the unsuspecting dinner of a guy called Frog (Siu-Hung), who suddenly develops the power to electrocute things and some pretty nifty footwork too. The two clan leaders track him down, but Frog and his inventor friend (Siu-Chung) escape in a balloon! Shen Chun sends Kuan Yin, Mistress of Poison, to kill the Chao Yung clan boss (Feng).

Shen Chun then destroys the rest of Chao Yung and starts to hunt for his pill and the escapees.

Cutting between the comic writer and the story works okay and, though the plot drags slightly in places, this madcap, cartoonish flick is a fun watch.

THE THUNDERING MANTIS (1980)
Starring Leung Kar-Yan, Chang Hai-Fen, Eddy Ko,
Wong Yat-Lung, Chin Yuet-Sang
Directed by Yip Wing-Cho
Produced by Chow Fok-Leung
Action by Robert Tai
East Asia Film Company

Ah Chi (Kar-Yan) is obsessed with martial arts and, more often than not, his kung fu antics get him into trouble. Chi has a fight with a local tough guy who is a henchman of boss Hsia (Ko) of the Jade Gang and, as a result, his master has him expelled from the gym. Now masterless, Chi carries on working as a delivery boy for a fishmonger. One day Chi bumps into a crafty kid (Yat-Lung) and the two become fast friends. The kid introduces Chi to his uncle (Yuet-Sang), who is a master of insane mantis fist. But the uncle is a bad-tempered old man and refuses to teach Chi. However, this does not stop Chi from learning what he can in secret. Armed with his half-baked knowledge of insane mantis, Chi gets involved in a fight with more of Hsia's henchmen. Chi takes a beating and looks set to be killed, but the kid intervenes. Using trickery, the kid persuades his uncle to accept Chi as his student. Hsia and his lackeys are still on the warpath, however, and they kill the uncle. Chi and the kid hide in the fishmonger's shop, but in time Hsia tracks them down and proceeds to kill the fishmonger. Hit with even more adversity, driven over the edge by rage, Chi is eventually able to merge his insanity with the mantis style to really make Hsia pay . . .

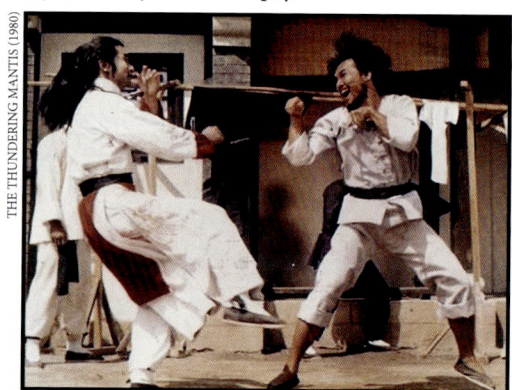
THE THUNDERING MANTIS (1980)

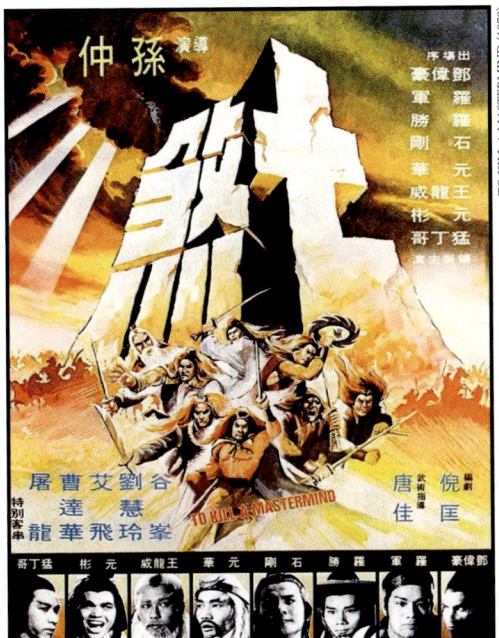

TO KILL A MASTERMIND (1979)

TO KILL A MASTERMIND (1979)

Starring Wang Lung-Wei, Lo Sheng, Shih Kang, Yuen Wah, Yuen Bun
Directed by Chung Sun
Action by Tang Chia
Shaw Brothers

The Chi Sha clan is a notorious organization that the Imperial Court would like to take down, but there's a mystery surrounding the identity of the clan's mastermind: even the Chi Sha clan's own members don't know who he really is. So, the protagonists decide to sow seeds of doubt among this syndicate of martial arts-skilled criminals, who begin to fear there's a traitor among them . . . and they soon start killing each other.

The wuxia-tastic weapon fights, of which there are many, are overseen by stunt coordinator Tang Chia, and Chung Sun, director of *The Deadly Breaking Sword* and *The Kung Fu Instructor*, makes sure that the double crosses and other mystery aspects of the story nicely counterbalance the action scenes.

The box office success of *Sleeping Fist* saw Leung Kar-Yan and Wong Yat-Lung reunited for this movie. Although this has nothing to do with *Sleeping Fist*, it is still an entertaining flick with fights brilliantly choreographed by "martial arts madman" Robert Tai, which are fast and furious and even kung fu cannibalism gets introduced for the first time! Pretty training sequences and strong supporting roles from the ever-reliable Chin Yuet-Sang and Eddy Ko make *Thundering Mantis* a meaty entertainment.

TIGER & CRANE FISTS (1976)

Starring Jimmy Wang Yu, Lau Kar-Wing, Lung Fei, Ma Chi
Directed by Jimmy Wang Yu
First Films

Two rival martial arts schools put their differences aside to confront Lu Ting Chu, a despicable villain working for the Japanese invasion forces.

Also known as *The Savage Killers*, as an example of grindhouse-style kung fu pulpiness this movie does just fine, though many viewers may find it hard to take it seriously as footage from this movie was used in Steve Oedekerk's comedy flick *Kung Pow! Enter the Fist* (2002). The dastardly Lu Ting Chu is definitely no laughing matter, however, just check out his haircut: it has an evil demeanor all of its own!

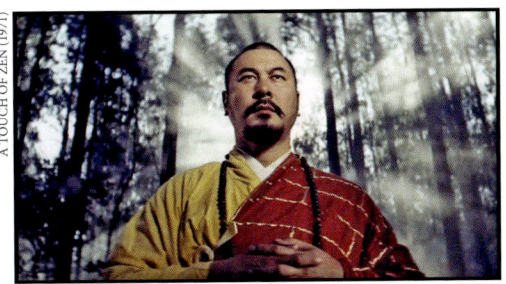

A TOUCH OF ZEN (1971)

A TOUCH OF ZEN (1971)

Starring Shih Chun, Hsu Feng, Pai Ying, Roy Chiao, Tien Peng, Miao Tien
Directed by King Hu
Action by Han Ying-Chieh, Pan Yao-Kun
Union Film Company/International Film Company

King Hu's critically acclaimed wuxia is based on a story from writer Pu Songling's *Strange Tales from a Chinese Studio*, which was also the source material for many other movies, including *A Chinese Ghost Story* (1987).

A Touch of Zen tells of a group of political refugees fleeing the East Chamber guards. A local scholar comes up with a plan that involves taking cover in a supposedly haunted fortress, where the guards can be defeated. Although a classic swordplay film, the plot is not centered around a typical action-oriented martial arts format, but instead delivers a gripping tale of romance, enlightenment and adventure, with a memorable finale, featuring a monk (Chiao) getting treacherously stabbed by a villainous commander, resulting in the image of the holy man silhouetted against the sun, bleeding gold.

A Touch of Zen is structured in a novel way, is beautifully conceived and shot, is epic in length and epic in quality.

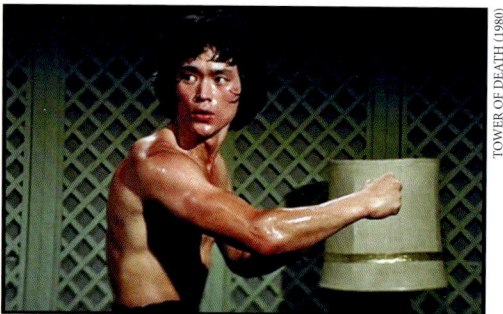

TOWER OF DEATH (1980)

TOWER OF DEATH (1980)

Starring Tong Lung, Hwang Jang-Lee, Roy Horan, Roy Chiao, Lee Hoi-Sang, Bruce Lee, Tiger Yang
Directed by Ng See-Yuen
Action by Yuen Woo-Ping
Golden Harvest

This production is a follow-up to *Game of Death* and stars Tong Lung, aka Kim Tae-Jeong (who was one of Bruce's stand-ins in *Game of Death*), playing Bobby Lo. His brother, Billy Lo (Bruce Lee via archive footage), is murdered while attending the funeral of sensei Chin Ku (Hwang Jang-Lee), so Bobby travels to Japan to investigate the mysterious murder. There he meets Lewis (Roy Horan), a strange American with a taste for raw meat, who talks of a hidden underground temple. With a mounting death toll, Bobby eventually enters the Tower of Death beneath the temple . . .

This exploitational flick features just a few sequences of Bruce Lee himself, via unused footage and outtakes from *Enter the Dragon*, with Tong Lung doubling for the Billy Lo character while also playing brother Bobby. With Billy getting bumped off early in the story, this gives the filmmakers the freedom to just concentrate on creating a watchable B movie fu flick without the need to keep splicing in old, obvious clips of Bruce, resulting in this film becoming a fight-filled guilty pleasure.

Note: there are other versions of the film with different clips and scenes added.

TRAIL OF THE BROKEN BLADE (1967)

Starring Jimmy Wang Yu, Chin Ping, Chiao Chiao, Chen Hung-Lieh, Tien Feng
Directed by Chang Cheh
Produced by Run Run Shaw
Action by Tang Chia, Lau Kar-Leung
Shaw Brothers

Jimmy Wang Yu plays the ill-fated Li Yueh in this epic tale of doomed lovers. Li is a master swordsman forced to become a fugitive after killing a government official who was responsible for his father's disgrace. He becomes an obscure groom under an assumed identity. However, Li's childhood sweetheart Chen Erh (Ping) persuades the chivalrous Lord Fang Chun Chao to seek out her lost love. Fang agrees to this despite his own deep affection for the lady. The Flying Fish gang provide the villainous intrigue and, on the gang's well-fortified island, there's a climactic battle, where the star-crossed lovers are united in death.

Chang Cheh's direction provides an atmosphere of inevitable tragedy in this solid wuxia that boasts an exciting climax.

THE TRAITOROUS (1976)

Starring Carter Wong, Polly Shang-Kuan Ling-Feng, Chang Yi, Sammo Hung
Directed by Sung Ting-Mei
Produced by Yen Wu-Tung
Action by Chen Chuan, Ko Shih-Hao
Fortuna Films

During the Ming Dynasty the government is overrun by dozens of wicked eunuchs. One such eunuch is Tin Erh Keng (Chang Yi), who is backed by a band of warriors, including First Head (Sammo Hung) and the Tien Lo Set. These villainous dudes go around the country killing all those who oppose Keng. The son of one of the victims escapes unharmed and finds sanctuary in the Shaolin temple. Ten years roll by and the young man, Shang Yung (Carter Wong), is fully versed in the ways of Shaolin. After managing to defeat the legendary 18 bronze men, Yung is allowed to leave the temple. On arriving in a small town, Yung engages in fights with some of Keng's subordinates and Keng's adopted daughter Hsiao (Polly Shang-Kuan Ling-Feng), realizing who Yung is, tells the men to back off. Yung leaves, vowing vengeance on the evil Keng. Days later, Yung is invited to a death duel at Yellow Sands. Yung is nearly killed by the Tien Lo Set, but he is saved by Hsiao. She confesses to Yung that she is also out for

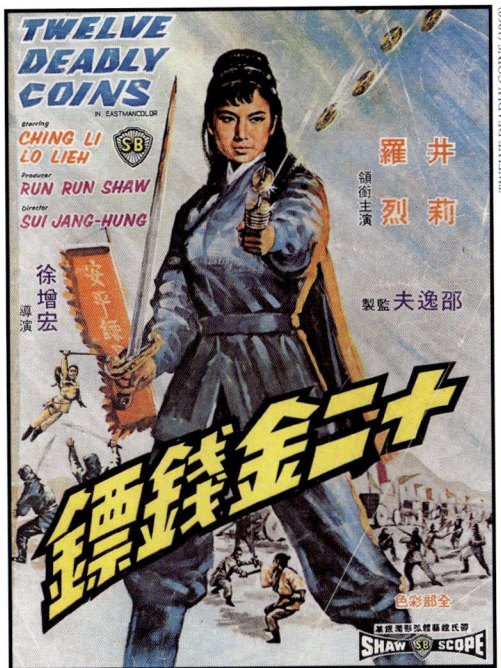

TWELVE DEADLY COINS (1969)

TWELVE DEADLY COINS (1969)

Starring Lo Lieh, Tien Feng, Wu Ma, Lau Kar-Leung
Directed by Hsu Tseng-Hung
Produced by Runme Shaw
Action by Lau Kar-Leung, Tang Chia
Shaw Brothers

The future of the Peace Security Bureau, run by Yu Chien Ping (Feng), is put in serious jeopardy when it becomes the victim of a well-planned robbery. Yu's only hope is to catch the villains, but where to begin the search? And could his star pupil and most experienced employee, Chiao Mao (Lieh), really be in league with the guilty party?

Melodrama, tragedy, and romance, laced with deftly handled martial contests, which often involve throwing weapons, make this a solid wuxia that culminates in a rain-soaked end fight. It's well worth your time.

TWO ASSASSINS OF THE DARKNESS (1977)

Starring Don Wong Tao, Chang Yi, Lung Chun-Erh, Tung Wei
Directed by Ting Chung
Action by Chin Ming
Great China Film Company

A couple of assassins arrive in a town and cross paths due to a mix-up relating to the intended targets. Eventually the two hit men team up, and the tale ends with a finale involving a fight with rope-swinging fighters.

Also going by the name *Kung Fu Killers*, this film combines decent, old school indoor and outdoor scraps with a plot involving hidden agendas and double crosses.

TWO CHAMPIONS OF SHAOLIN (1980)

Starring Chiang Sheng, Lo Meng, Lu Feng, Chin Siu Ho
Directed by Chang Cheh
Produced by Mona Fong, Run Run Shaw
Action by Lu Feng, Chiang Sheng, Philip Kwok
Shaw Brothers

To avenge his father's death, Shaolin expert Hu (Sheng) kills two Wu Tang clansmen. This action pits Shaolin against the Ching-backed Wu Tang clan. Tung (Meng) joins Hu in Canton, just as Wu Tang sends their top man Kao (Feng) to kill the Shaolin men . . .

This is yet another in Chang Cheh's long line of variations on the Shaolin legend and, like the

vengeance, since Keng butchered her family when she was a baby. Now, with careful planning, the avenging duo must prepare for their ultimate test and face pure, white-haired fury . . .

Also known as *Shaolin Traitorous*, this movie is worth a watch because, despite the rather generic revenge plot, it features such neat elements as bronze men, a cool training sequence, well-staged fights, monks, the Tien Lo Set, Sammo Hung with full white hair and deadly eunuchs!

TREASURE HUNTERS (1981)

Starring Fu Sheng, Chang Chan-Peng, Gordon Liu, Wang Lung-Wei
Directed by Lau Kar-Wing
Produced by Mona Fong
Action by Lau Kar-Wing
Shaw Brothers

Conman Chi Ta Po (Sheng) joins forces with rich dude Chow Su Chi (Chan-Peng) to hunt for hidden treasure. The bumbling duo soon find themselves up to their necks in trouble because a monk (Liu) and evil Lord Mo (Lung-Wei) are after the gold too.

Aka *Master of Disaster*, this entertaining film boasts a fine, fu-tastic cast, inventive fight scenes on lavish Shaw Brothers sets and maybe too much knockabout comedy.

others, it's an instant classic that doesn't disappoint, stuffed full of superb kung fu action and classic performances from Lo Meng as the hot-headed Tung and Chiang Sheng as the cooler Hu.

TWO CRIPPLED HEROES (1980)
Starring Jack Conn, Frankie Shum, Pao Chan-Feng
Directed by Hsiao Yao
Distributed by Ocean Shores Video

The main protagonists in this movie are an armless kung fu fighter and his chimp, a paraplegic friend, and a girl (Chan-Feng) who is temporarily blind. The hero with no arms keeps small knives attached to his ankles, pulling them from their sheaths if attacked, gripping them with his toes. The paraplegic dude, meanwhile, trundles along on a board with wheels. This basic form of transport contains two hand-grips, which can also be used as large hooks on lengths of rope, with which he uses as nifty weapons. Even though he keeps his small legs constantly crossed and must walk on his hands, this character is agile when fighting, in combat sequences that utilize a fair bit of stunt wirework.

The simple story concerns the duo (and the chimp) saving a girl from a corrupt mayor, who is selling guns to a despised warlord. After our heroes thwart several attacks by the mayor's men, it is left to the Major, who serves the warlord, to deal with the tough pair. Firstly, the Major's brother is sent over to bump them off and a protracted fight ensues, in which the villain comments: "Who the hell d'you think you are? You're not Bruce Lee, I can see that. Huh, you're just two lousy cripples." What a bastard! But don't worry, the Major's brother is knifed, axed, cut with a hook, hung upside down from a tree and knifed again. That will show him!

The girl, who'd been blinded for a while by lime, finds her sight returning and discovers that her two rescuers are actually disabled. After initially being surprised by the true nature of her mates, she pulls herself together and, on the soundtrack, we hear her thoughts: "Even though one has no arms and one has no legs, they have both got noble hearts." Proving to be crafty as well as noble, the two heroes remove the firing pins from the guns of the Major's men, but the Major, who has a gun that still works, shoots the mayor, then the townsfolk attack the soldiers and the two protagonists battle the kung fu–skilled Major. There follows a knife-tipped staff fight, until the Major, dazzled by the sun reflected off a piece of broken glass, is finally transfixed by a spear.

Let's just say that this film is definitely a product of its time . . .

The two feisty protagonists, played by Conn & Shum, are portrayed as personable characters who fight on the side of good in a story that highlights the message that people should be accepted for who they are and not how they look, but there's no denying the fact that the filmmakers rely rather a lot on the sideshow nature of the production, rather than attempt to create any really worthwhile set pieces or stylish sequences.

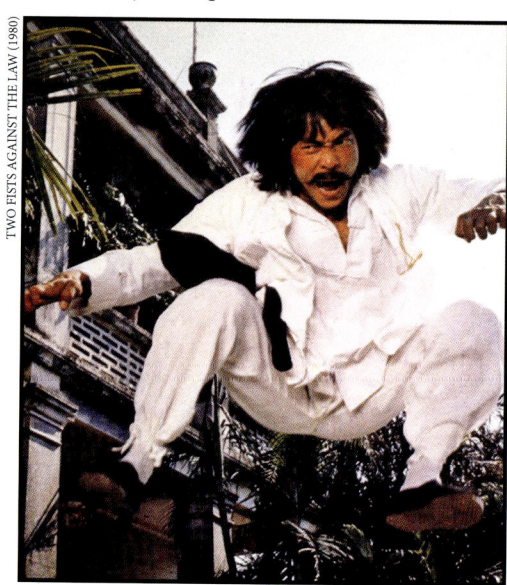

TWO FISTS AGAINST THE LAW (1980)

TWO FISTS AGAINST THE LAW (1980)
Starring Chui Chung-San, Hwang Jang-Lee,
Melvin Wong
Directed by Chen Chuan
Produced by Ng See-Yuen
Seasonal Film Corporation

Two unscrupulous conmen decide to rob master Tai (Jang-Lee) of his new consignment, rumored to be worth seven million. The local police captain (Wong) tries to change their ways and the duo do see the light when they discover the consignment is actually opium . . .

Hwang Jang-Lee shows that he is the best when it comes to viciously awesome legwork. This low-budget punch-'em-up-comedy has an entertaining fight finale, though the humor that fills much of the running time is an acquired taste.

TWO ON THE ROAD (1980)

Starring Leung Kar-Yan, Phillip Ko, Wang Lung-Wei
Directed by Lei Chiu
Produced by Alex Gouw
Goldig Film Company

When a large amount of gold is stolen, a couple of conmen (Phillip Ko and Leung Kar-Yan) are blamed. The two men decide to investigate the chief of the security bureau (Wang Lung-Wei) responsible for moving the gold and, finally, they reveal the identity of the mysterious antagonist.

Aka *The Fearless Jackal* and *Fearless Dragons*, the film sometimes strays too far into farce territory, but it does have impressively choreographed fight scenes, and the three stars are in awesome form.

TWO WONDROUS TIGERS (1979)

Starring Phillip Ko, John Cheung, Tiger Yang,
Wilson Tong, Yeung Pan-Pan
Directed by Cheung Sum
Produced by Alex Gouw
Action by Wilson Tong
Goldig Film Company

Robert Ko (Phillip Ko) returns home from America and meets Tiger (John Cheung), a vagrant. The two strike up a friendship and Tiger becomes involved with a girl (Yeung Pan-Pan) from a family of fighters. The girl arouses the interest of the local boss (Tiger Yang), who kidnaps her, so the Two Wondrous Tigers come to the rescue.

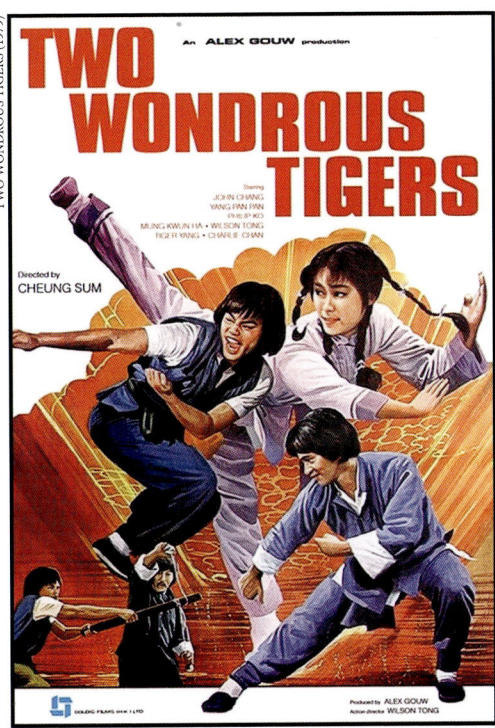

TWO WONDROUS TIGERS (1979)

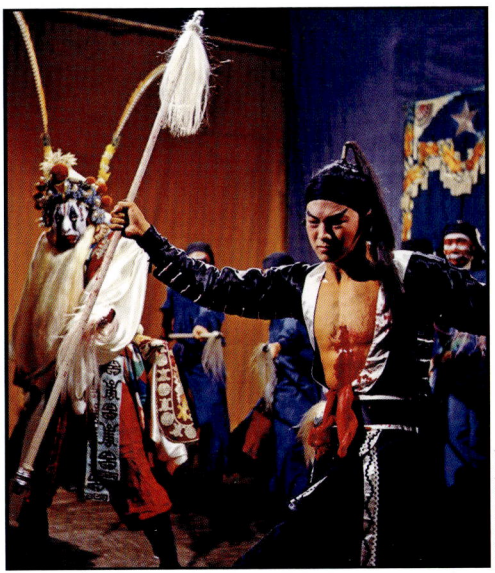

VENGEANCE! (1970)

Goldig had a habit of making enjoyable kung fu flicks and this one, though sketchily plotted, is certainly a likeable affair, with some decent fighting femme action courtesy of Yeung Pan-Pan. John Cheung lets off some serious Tiger shapes and Phillip Ko is as great as ever.

VENGEANCE! (1970)

Starring David Chiang, Ti Lung, Wang Ping, Ku Feng
Directed by Chang Cheh
Produced by Runme Shaw
Action by Tang Chia, Yuen Cheung-Yan
Shaw Brothers

Chang Cheh pays homage to John Boorman's classic *Point Blank* with this tale of betrayal and revenge. David Chiang returns home from afar to find his brother murdered by the fifty-strong Axe Gang, who were employed by a jealous rival. He systematically tracks down those responsible for his brother's cruel demise and, one by one, he takes them on, starting with his brother's unfaithful wife and finishing with an epic onslaught against the Axe Gang.

Blood and guts galore, a tight script, a brilliantly haunting musical score and the superb direction

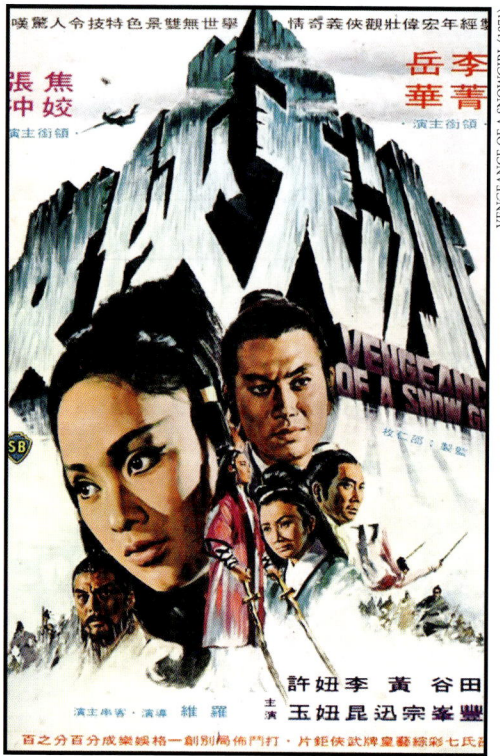

VENGEANCE OF A SNOWGIRL (1971)

a unique pearl, but to access this pearl will require entering a hot, volcanic zone in a suit of heat-resistant armor. But this armor resides in the treasure house of a prince . . . and so a quest for these items begins.

Shen Bing Hong, as played by Li Ching, is a great movie character, unwilling to show appreciation to others just for the sake of it, stubbornly striving to avenge her dead parents, while also being flexible enough to accept help from others she knows are being sincere. She glides along when using her special crutches, rather than limping, and can leap about when required, brandishing the Jade Phoenix Sword that she keeps in one of her crutches!

Feelings do start to blossom between Shen and Tin Ying, who is incredibly understanding, sincere and chivalrous. Tin Ying knows Shen is intent on killing his equally fair-minded father, but hopes that he can change Shen's mind by helping to mend her legs. The story culminates in the freezing area in which the special pool is located (a typically theatrical, large Shaw Brothers sound stage set), but a confrontation with characters who want Shen dead leads to a rather touching ending, with Tin Ying fulfilling his promise never to leave Shen's side, even if it means them freezing under a coating of ice.

This is a wonderful wuxia from Shaw Brothers, made particularly memorable because of its well-sketched, unique female protagonist.

THE VICTIM (1980)

Starring Sammo Hung, Leung Kar-Yan, Chang Yi,
Fanny Wang, Karl Maka, Wilson Tong
Directed by Sammo Hung
Action by Sammo Hung, Lam Ching-Ying, Yuen Biao,
Billy Chan
Graffon Film Company/Yung Hwa film Company

Sammo Hung plays the carefree Chan Wing, who is searching for a suitable master to teach him kung fu. Unfortunately, he chooses the unwilling Leung Chung Yau (Kar-Yan) and he walks straight into a feud between Leung and his spoilt, vicious elder brother, Jo Wing (Yi). This feud harks back to the latter's attempt to rape Leung's wife on their wedding night, thereby forcing the married couple into hiding. Complicating matters is an unknown assassin, who has been blackmailed by Jo into killing Leung. As a game of surprising double and triple bluffs unfolds, the inevitable showdown between brothers provides the movie with a fitting climax.

of Chang Cheh, which won him the Best Director Award at the 16th Asian Film Festival, ensure viewing satisfaction. David Chiang is especially good in this, with his performance earning him the Best Actor Award at the 16th Asian Film Festival. This film is also known as *Kung Fu Vengeance*.

VENGEANCE OF A SNOWGIRL (1971)

Starring Li Ching, Yueh Hua, Ku Feng, Tien Feng,
Chiao Chiao
Directed by Lo Wei
Shaw Brothers

Shen Bing Hong (Ching) is the daughter of Shen Dun and Madam Fa, who were both murdered when she was a child. Now an adult, walking with the help of crutches, Shen is laser-focused on making everyone involved in the death of her parents pay with their lives. Some of these people want nothing more than to kill her and get her out of the way, but Gao Yun and his two sons, Tin Wai and Tin Ying (Hua), seek to make peace with Shen, offering to help heal her damaged legs. This will involve Shen bathing in a special pool in an area of snow fields, but to withstand the harsh temperatures she will need to be holding

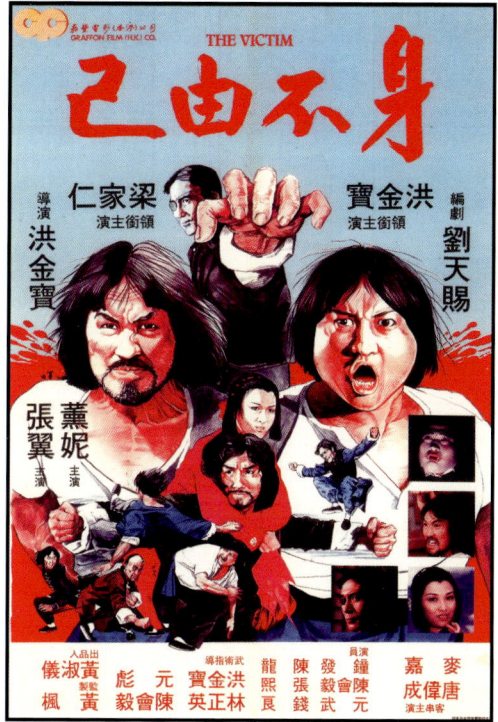

THE VICTIM (1980)

The many plot twists ensure that the film, which is also known as *Lightning Kung Fu*, always keeps the viewers on their toes, while Sammo's comedic performance is both engaging and convincing.

THE WANDERING SWORDSMAN (1970)

Starring David Chiang, Lily Li, Chang Pei-Shan,
Cheng Lei, Wang Kuang-Yu, Wu Ma, Bolo Yeung
Directed by Chang Cheh
Shaw Brothers

The Wandering Swordsman becomes involved in a gang's plan to rob the Wei Sheng Security Bureau's undercover escort team, which is transporting valuable goods hidden in fruit carts.

David Chiang is charismatic as the title character, who is affable, ever-smiling and quick-witted, robbing from lowlifes and giving the spoils to the needy. He leaps around effortlessly like a wuxia Peter Pan, always ready with a witty retort. Lily Li plays spirited Bureau agent Jiang Ning, Wu Ma is whip-cracking casino owner Jiou and Bolo Yeung makes his screen debut as tough guy Unicorn.

Though the Wandering Swordsman is smart in his dealings most of the time, writer Ni Kuang, in order to push the plot forward, shows our hero

getting rather easily tricked by a criminal big-brain, nicknamed Fail-Safe, into taking part in the attack on the security team. Matters become more serious now, with the Wandering Swordsman getting badly hurt by a flexible sword and a bloody fight kicking off in a pumpkin garden.

The steely, driven side of the Wandering Swordsman comes to the fore in these latter scenes, as he determinedly hunts for Fail-Safe, despite being seriously injured and bleeding. But even then, after getting run through by two swords, this charming swordsman still manages to smile impishly.

Thanks mainly to David Chiang's portrayal of the very likeable lead character, *The Wandering Swordsman* is an extremely enjoyable Shaw Brothers wuxia, which possesses a rather touching ending, as the hero's earlier comments to Jiang Ning are repeated with new meaning: "I'd rather die than see you cry." Sniff.

WARRIORS TWO (1978)

Starring Sammo Hung, Casanova Wong,
Leung Kar-Yan, Fung Hark-On, Tiger Yang
Directed by Sammo Hung
Produced by Raymond Chow
Action by Sammo Hung
Golden Harvest

This impressive martial arts movie begins with Tsang (Kar-Yan) and his student Wah (Wong) demonstrating their graceful and versatile techniques in a beautifully choreographed sequence.

In the town of Fatshan, during the Ching dynasty, a gangster called Mo opens a bank with the aim of controlling the whole town. Wah discovers his plan, but is set up and confronted with four broadsword-wielding guys. Wah's fighting skills, although competent, are no match for these dudes, who include killing machine Thunder and spear

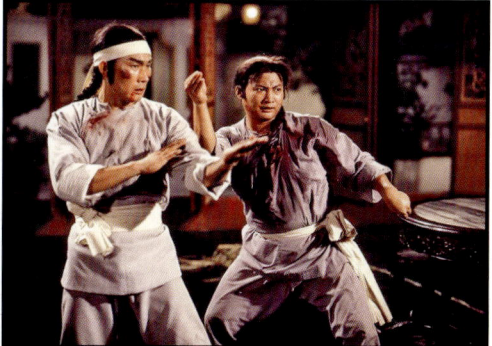

WARRIORS TWO (1978)

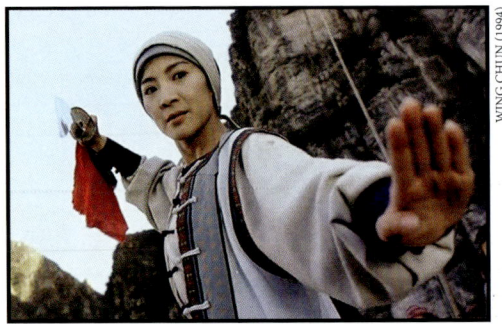

WING CHUN (1994)

fighter Tiger. Luckily for Wah, his friend Cheun (Hung) helps him escape death, and then the pair try to warn the town chief about the trouble to come. Inevitably, matters escalate and, when Mo has Wah's mother killed, Wah decides to master the art of Wing Chun so that he can seek revenge on his enemies.

The excellent training scenes are complemented with some fine comedy, before momentum gathers for some brutally breathtaking battles in this true kung fu classic.

THE WAY OF THE DRAGON (1972)

Starring Bruce Lee, Nora Miao, Chuck Norris,
Bob Wall, Whang In Shik, Little Unicorn
Directed and produced by Bruce Lee
Action by Bruce Lee
Golden Harvest/ Concord Productions

Bruce Lee plays Tang Lung, who arrives in Rome from the New Territories with a mission to protect a restaurant under threat from a syndicate that wants to buy the property. After he thwarts several attempts, in which the gang terrorizes customers and owners of the restaurant, the syndicate decides to hire professional fighters, including Colt, an American martial artist played by Chuck Norris. Tang and Colt finally fight a duel to the death at a venue where many battles have been fought over the centuries: the Colosseum in Rome. After Tang beats Colt, there's a final confrontation that leads to the arrest of the mob boss.

The Way of the Dragon was Bruce Lee's directorial debut and, although its script is far from unique, Bruce uses this vehicle to explore new areas, filming a Hong Kong production in Rome, tapping into the spirit of the place's long history of heroic battles. Rather than settling for the Hong Kong fighters and studio sets available, his passion for the martial arts drove him to seek out Western practitioners, a vision that paid off as his death duel with karate champion

Chuck Norris is one of his most memorable and exciting confrontations committed to celluloid.

The Way of the Dragon also allowed Lee to take one of his trademarks, the use of nunchakus, one step further when, in a scene at the back of the restaurant, he takes on a dozen or so hoods using not one but two sets. It's a scene that has inspired much audience adulation over the years!

The Way of the Dragon maintains all the motifs seen in Lee's work, crystallizing them into a new presentation, and it makes one yearn for the more representative picture which Lee, alas, was never to make.

WING CHUN (1994)

Starring Michelle Yeoh, Donnie Yen, Waise Lee,
Tsui Siu-Keung, Cheng Pei-Pei
Directed by Yuen Woo-Ping
Peace Film Production Co/Wo Ping Films Company
Limited

In a small town, a destitute widow named Yim Wing Chun (Michelle Yeoh) finds herself, due to her beauty, the focus of the townspeople's attention. She's far more than a pretty face, though, as she possesses unbeatable Wing Chun skills. This is demonstrated when her friend Wong Hok Chow (Waise Lee) is attacked by bandits. Yim Wing Chun effortlessly beats them while sitting in a chair, using poor old Wong as a puppet. With the aid of a cane, she taps

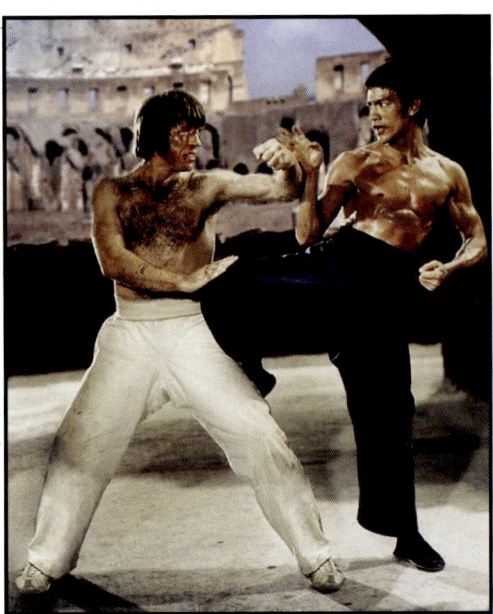

THE WAY OF THE DRAGON (1972)

certain parts of his body with precision, executing moves like a skilled fighter. The real comedy and action begins, however, when Leung Pok To (Donnie Yen) arrives in town and mistakenly believes Yim Wing Chun is his long-lost love.

Despite Donnie Yen's remarkable on-screen fighting abilities, he doesn't have as much to do in this film, as most of the main action is carried out by Michelle, who delivers some stunning, well executed fight moves. There are also great supporting performances from Waise Lee, Tsui Siu-Keung and veteran female martial arts star Cheng Pei-pei.

THE WOMAN AVENGER (1980)
Starring Hsia Kwan-Li, Peng Gang, Wang Chi-Sheng, Shih Ting-Ken, Mao Ching-Shun, Chang Kuan-Lung
Directed by Lee Tso-Nam
Action by Peng Gang, Yuen Lung
Hong Kong Jade Dragon Film Company/Yung Hwa Film Company

In this kung fu revenge story, Taiwanese opera star Hsia Kwan-Li plays Lo Ling Chi, a deadly and determined martial arts-skilled avenging angel.

After being raped and seeing her husband murdered before her eyes, Chi sets out on a one-woman vengeance trail. But, before she can take on the deadly scumbags, she must perfect her martial arts skills. After being taught the "Deadly Kicks" by a lame kung fu nun, she is ready to take on the ugly mob. The first to go is Butterfly Knives (Ching-Shun). Second is the Spearman of Death, Chi San (Chi-Sheng). Then comes womanizer Lung (Kuan-Lung) and then, last but by no means least, the madman of the bunch, golden-haired Wu (Gang).

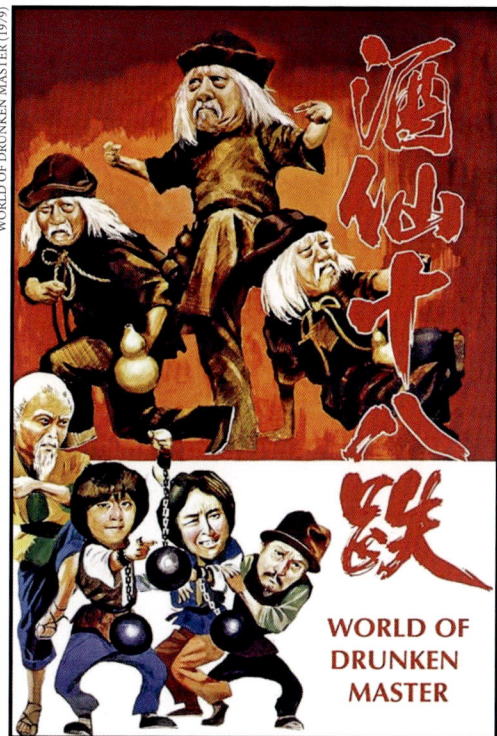

WORLD OF DRUNKEN MASTER

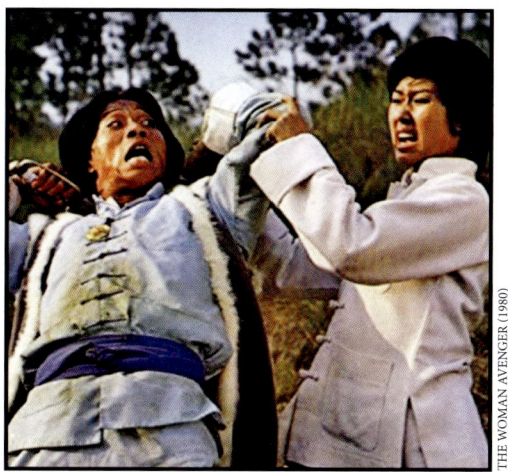

Lee Tso-Nam directs this punchy flick with his usual quick-paced, no-nonsense style, showcasing Hsia Kwan-Li's amazing kicks as she transcends the dreary rape-revenge plot to light up the screen with her amazing opera-trained acrobatics, aided by Peng Gang's martial arts choreography.

WORLD OF DRUNKEN MASTER (1979)
Starring Li Yi-Min, Jack Long, Chen Hui-Lou, Lung Fei, Yuen Siu-Tin
Directed and produced by Joseph Kuo
Action by Yuen Cheung-Yan
Hong Hwa International Films

Two orphans, Sam Seed/Beggar Su (Yi-Min) and Ta Pei (Long), are caught stealing grapes from an orchard by wine blender Chang (Hui-Lou), who puts the two lads to task in his distillery as compensation. In time boss Chang takes a shine to the twosome and teaches them Drunken Boxing. They soon become experts in the art and decide to test out their new skills on the unsuspecting town toughs. But the duo do not know that the leader of the thugs is none other than Yeh (Fei), who happens to be an archenemy

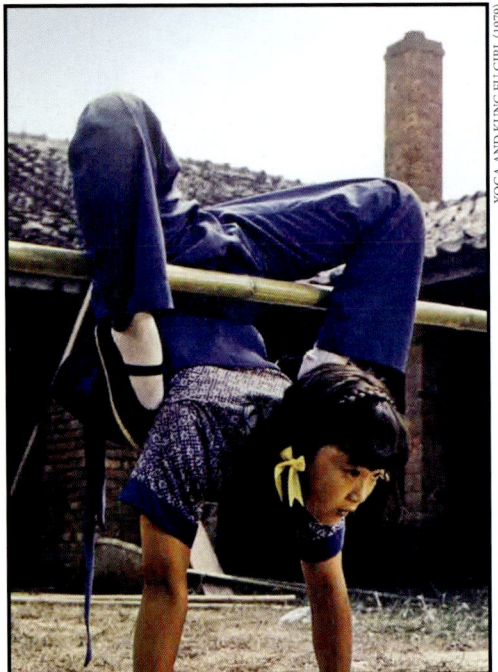

YOGA AND KUNG FU GIRL (1979)

of boss Chang. Yeh gathers up all his minions and storms the distillery. The rest is drunken history . . .

Aka *Drunken Dragon*, this Joseph Kuo offering is one of the better *Drunken Master* cash-ins to come out of Taiwan. The film, told in flashback by the two reminiscing old beggars, is packed to the gills with top-notch fight work and some off-the-wall training sequences by Taiwan's dynamic duo of Jack Long and Li Yi-Min.

YOGA AND KUNG FU GIRL (1979)
Starring Chi Kuan-Chun, Phoenix Chen, Pai Ying
Directed by Sun Yang
Long Sun Film

Regarded as an oddity, this feature, with its poor excuse for a storyline, did no favors to Chi Kuan-Chun's career and succeeds only in serving as a showcase for the amazing flexibility of a young woman by the name of Phoenix Chen. The fight choreographer's determination to stretch Chen to her limit by showing her in the most bizarre contortions of the human body imaginable means that her fighting techniques have little practical application. Nevertheless, the viewer is wowed by Chen as she battles with the owners of a gambling house. One may wonder why she was cast as a mute as she can

act, but it seems her actions were meant to speak louder than her words.

While the superior talents of Chi Kuan-Chun are wasted in a routine role, we do get to witness parodies of popular martial arts heroes: a blind swordsman, a drunken master and a Jackie Chan clone.

Those who admire Chi Kuan-Chun from his Chang Cheh days will wish more time was spent on the muscled maestro and less on the buffoonery which, unfortunately, does little to forward the slim plot of this film, which is also known as *Octagon Force*.

THE YOUNG AVENGER (1980)
Starring Wong Yu, Wilson Tong, Tsui Siu-Keung, Chiang Tao
Directed by Wilson Tong
Action by Wilson Tong, Wong Siu-Yu
Fei Tang Film

Wong Yu plays Fu Yua, a young schemer who works in a funeral parlor. He earns his dishonest crust by robbing the corpses. On one occasion a ghost actually appears and a petrified Fu listens as the apparition tells him a story of betrayal and murder. A grave robber Fu may have been, but he will not stand for injustice. He makes a pact with the ghost, agreeing that, in return for kung fu lessons, Fu will help the ghost get even with those who wronged him . . . but is this spirit actually a ghost?

This comedic fu film definitely becomes more involving once the hunt starts for the bad guys (Tsui Siu-Keung and Wilson Tong) and the decently done fights begin in earnest, ending with an entertaining martial arts showdown.

THE YOUNG MASTER (1980)
Starring Jackie Chan, Wei Pai, Lilly Li, Yuen Biao, Shek Kin, Shih Kien, Tien Feng
Directed by Jackie Chan
Produced by Raymond Chow
Action by Jackie Chan, Fung Hark-On
Golden Harvest

In 1979 Jackie Chan left Lo Wei and signed himself over to Raymond Chow's Golden Harvest Group. His first project there was a true milestone in the annals of kung fu cinema. Chan made a brave move and deviated from the "master training student/learning secret style" storyline, the very formula that made him an overnight star. Instead, he crafted a highly original and amusing action-packed story. Chan plays Dragon, the younger of two orphans who are

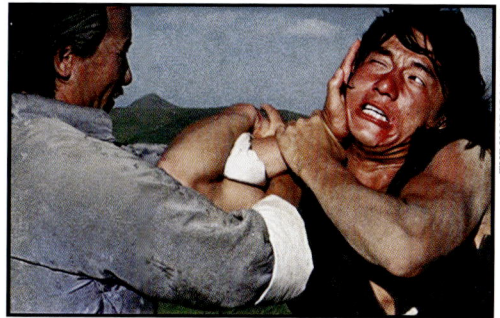

THE YOUNG MASTER (1980)

fight scenes, which include a lion dance duel, a fan fight, a bench fight, broadsword-wielding and a Chaplin-esque pipe fight. This movie is a major treat and is always worth revisiting.

ZEN KWAN DO STRIKES IN PARIS (1981)

Starring John Liu, Alan Hsu, Tino Wong, Jack Long, Roger Paschy, Dan Schwarz
Directed by John Liu
Action by Alan Hsu, John Liu
John Liu's Film Corp

In this supposedly biographical film, John Liu would have us believe that his father, who is a top aerospace scientist, has been kidnapped by a ruthless syndicate. John is called away from shooting kung fu movies in Hong Kong to travel to Paris, where he must discover his father's whereabouts.

brought up by a kind but strict master. The elder of the pair (Pai) becomes greedy and betrays his master by working for a rival school, but ends up doing dirty work for them. Dragon sets out to bring his wayward brother back but becomes embroiled in various hijinks involving a criminal called Kam and a sheriff (Kin) and his children (Yuen Biao and Lilly Li). Everything comes to a head when Dragon faces off against Kam for a stupendous final face-off that lasts nearly twenty minutes.

Young Master was released during Chinese New Year 1980 and broke all box office records throughout Asia and Chinatowns worldwide. Audiences couldn't get enough of Chan's comic antics and unbelievable

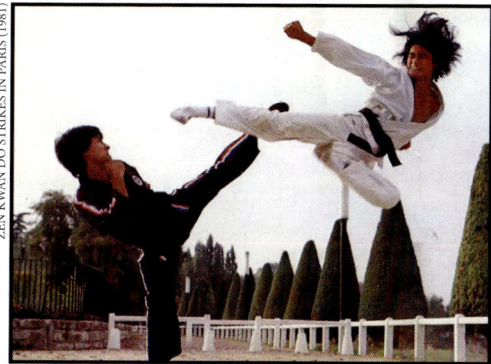

ZEN KWAN DO STRIKES IN PARIS (1981)

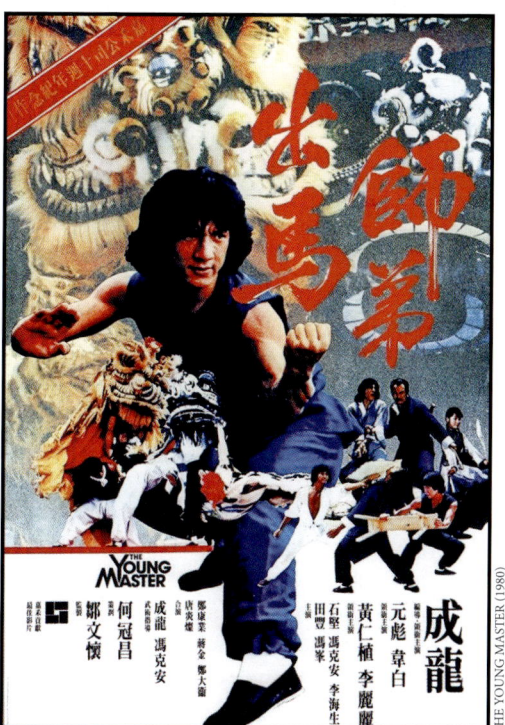

THE YOUNG MASTER (1980)

This film is one long, amazing ego trip for John Liu who, when not fighting, seems to be in a perpetual state of reminiscence, as one jaw-dropping flashback follows the other. Bikini-clad women swoon over him (one becomes a nun!), mind-numbing expository dialogue is frequently uttered, there is the occasional erratic camera zoom, and flared trousers, big collars and hideous ties insult the eyes of the viewer.

Accompanied by some incredible martial chanting music, Liu walks around Parisian landmarks, jogs, uses some nifty legwork in his frequent fights, but never really attempts to find his dad! The film ends with the poor aerospace expert still held captive!

Though the movie finally begins to outstay its welcome, the action scenes are well mapped out by veteran choreographer Alan Hsu, with the fights between full-contact world champion Roger Paschy and John Liu coming across as both flashy, realistic, and probably the best John Liu has ever done.

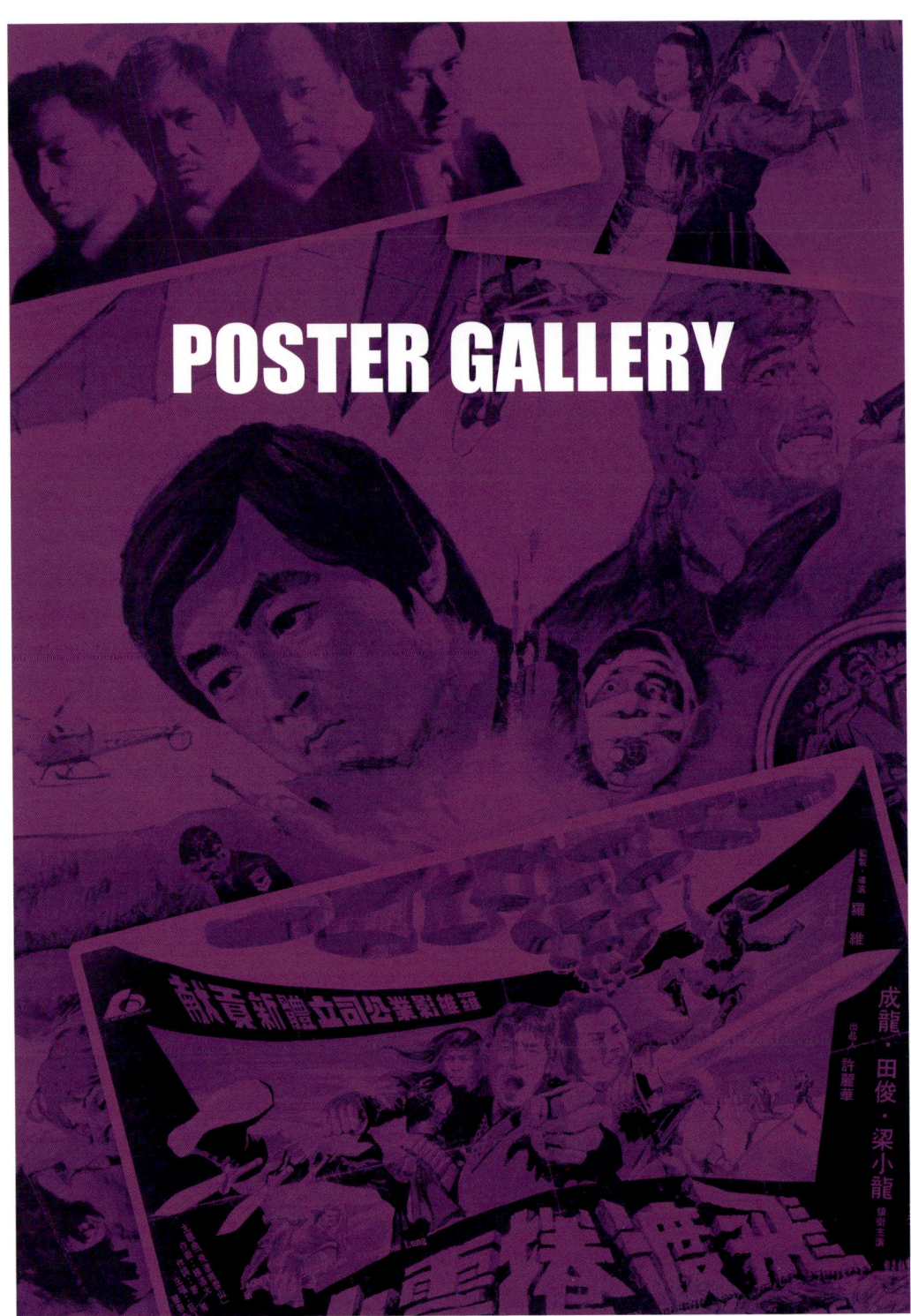

POSTER GALLERY

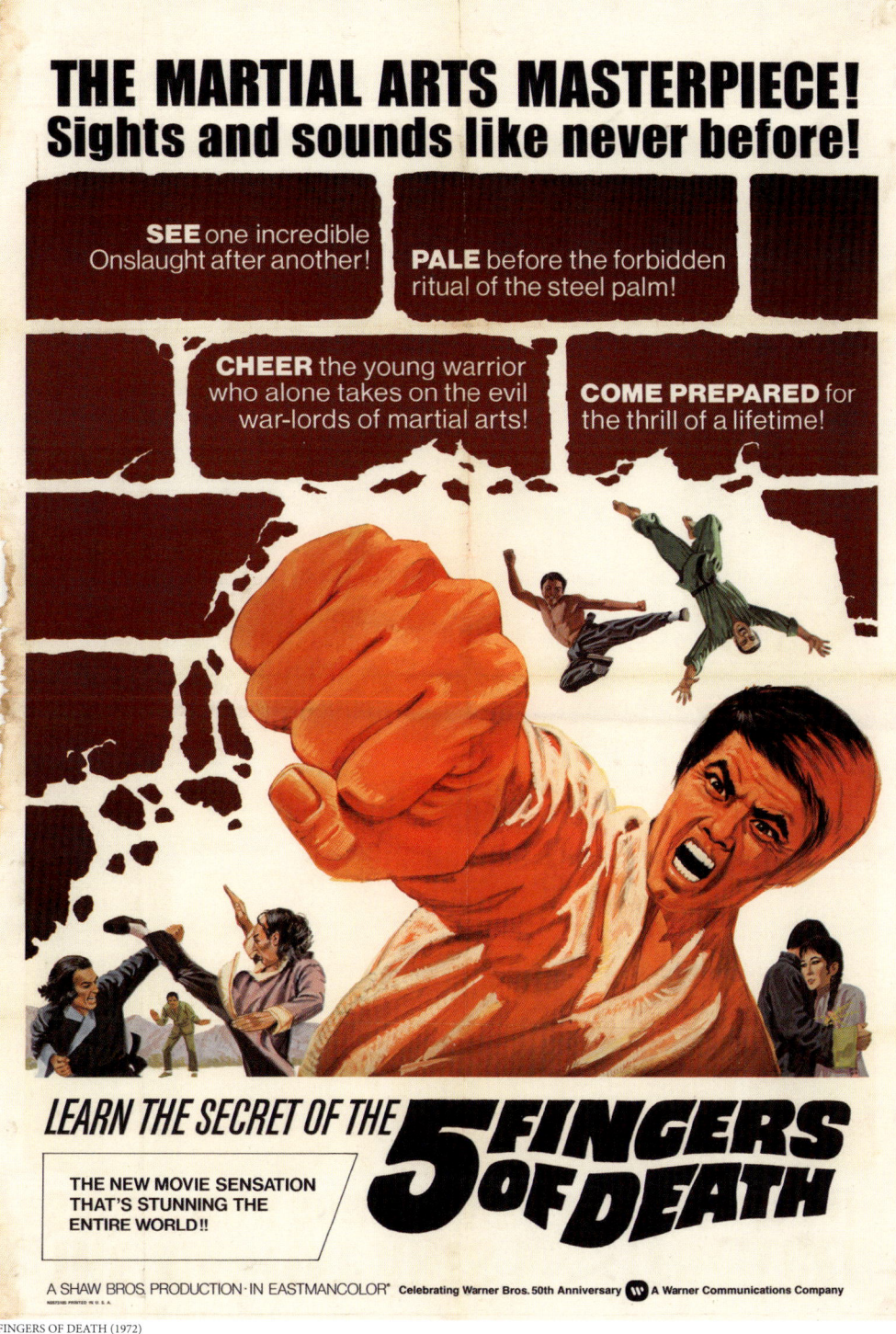

5 FINGERS OF DEATH (1972)

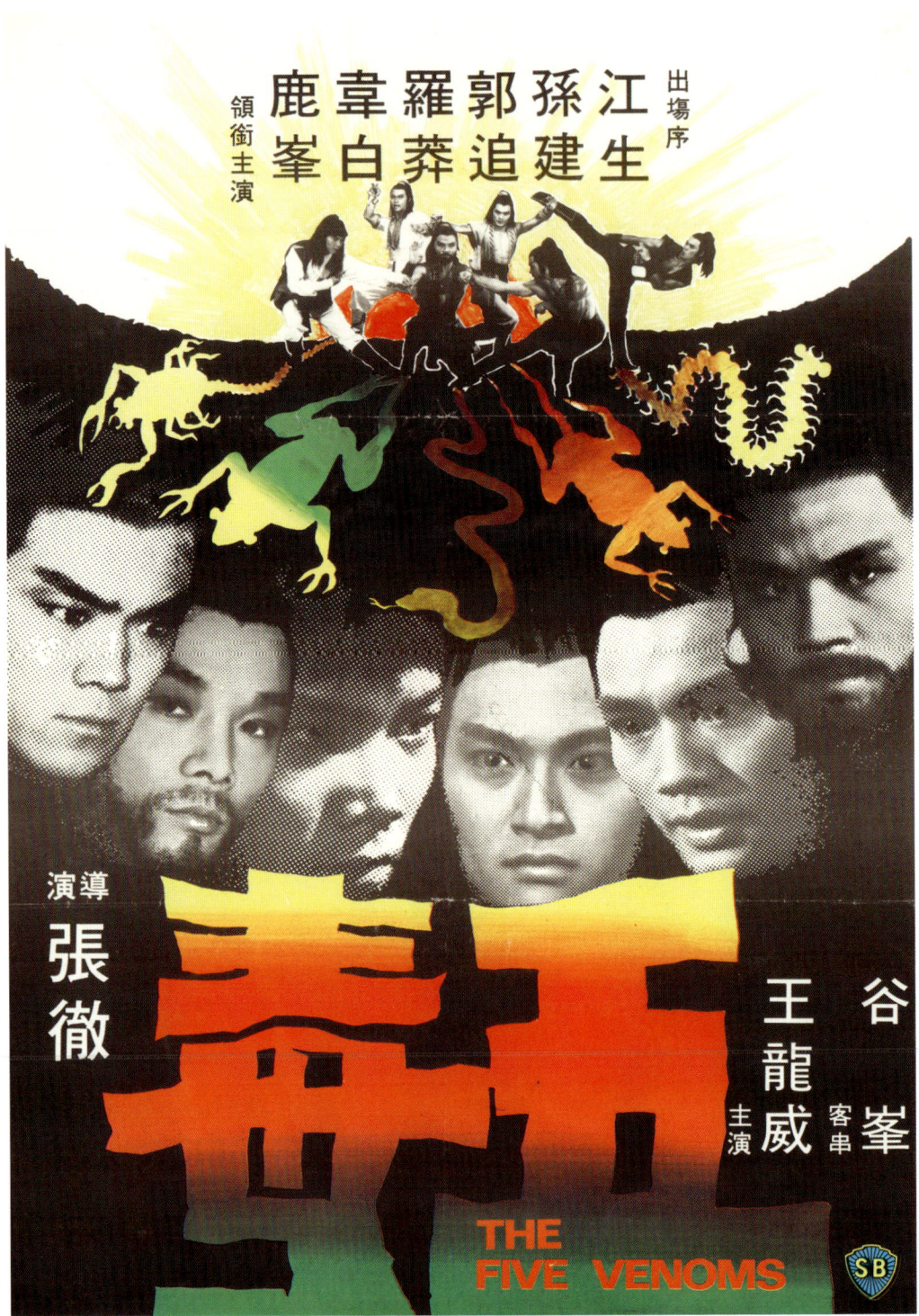

THE FIVE DEADLY VENOMS (1978)

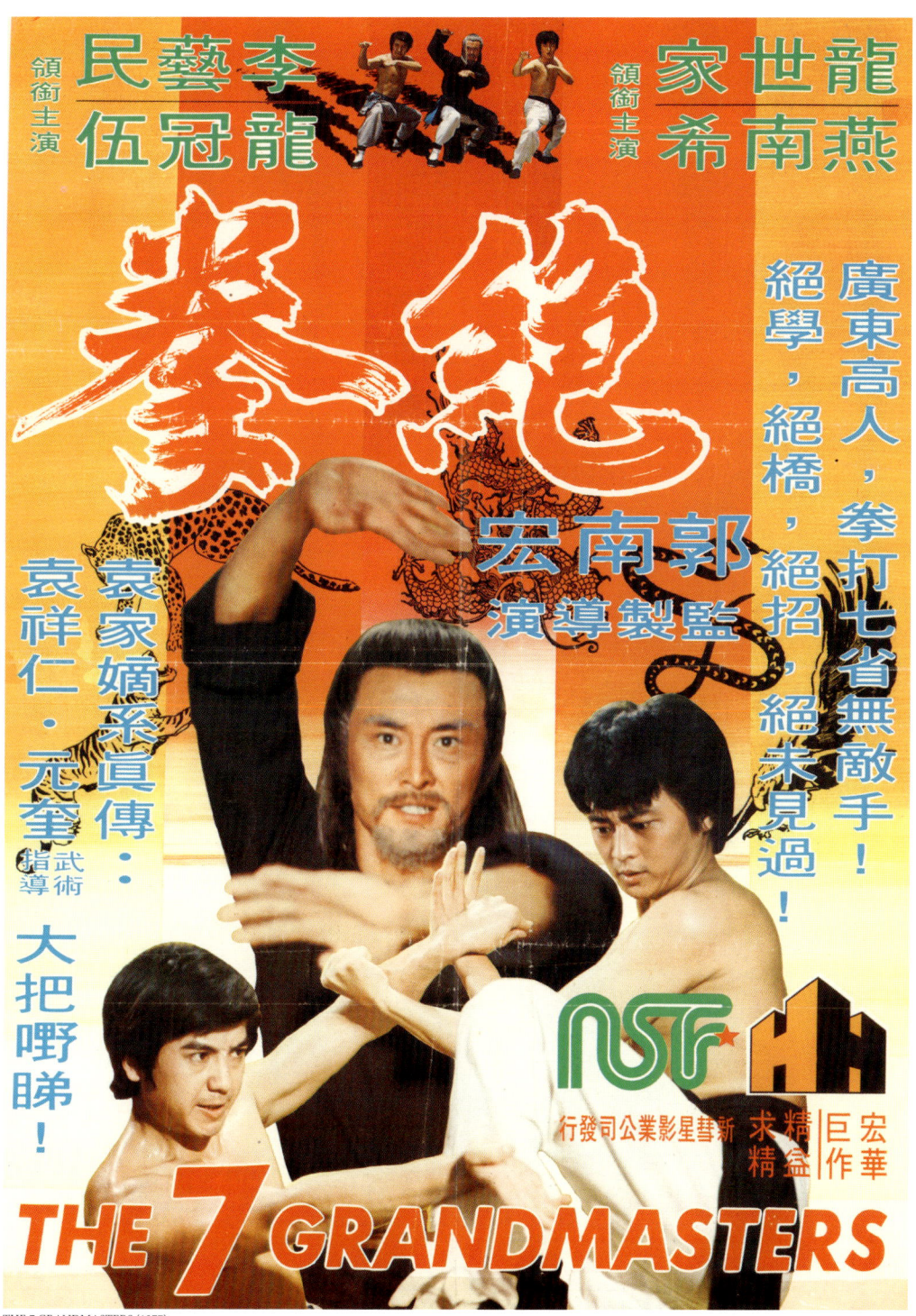

THE 7 GRANDMASTERS (1977)

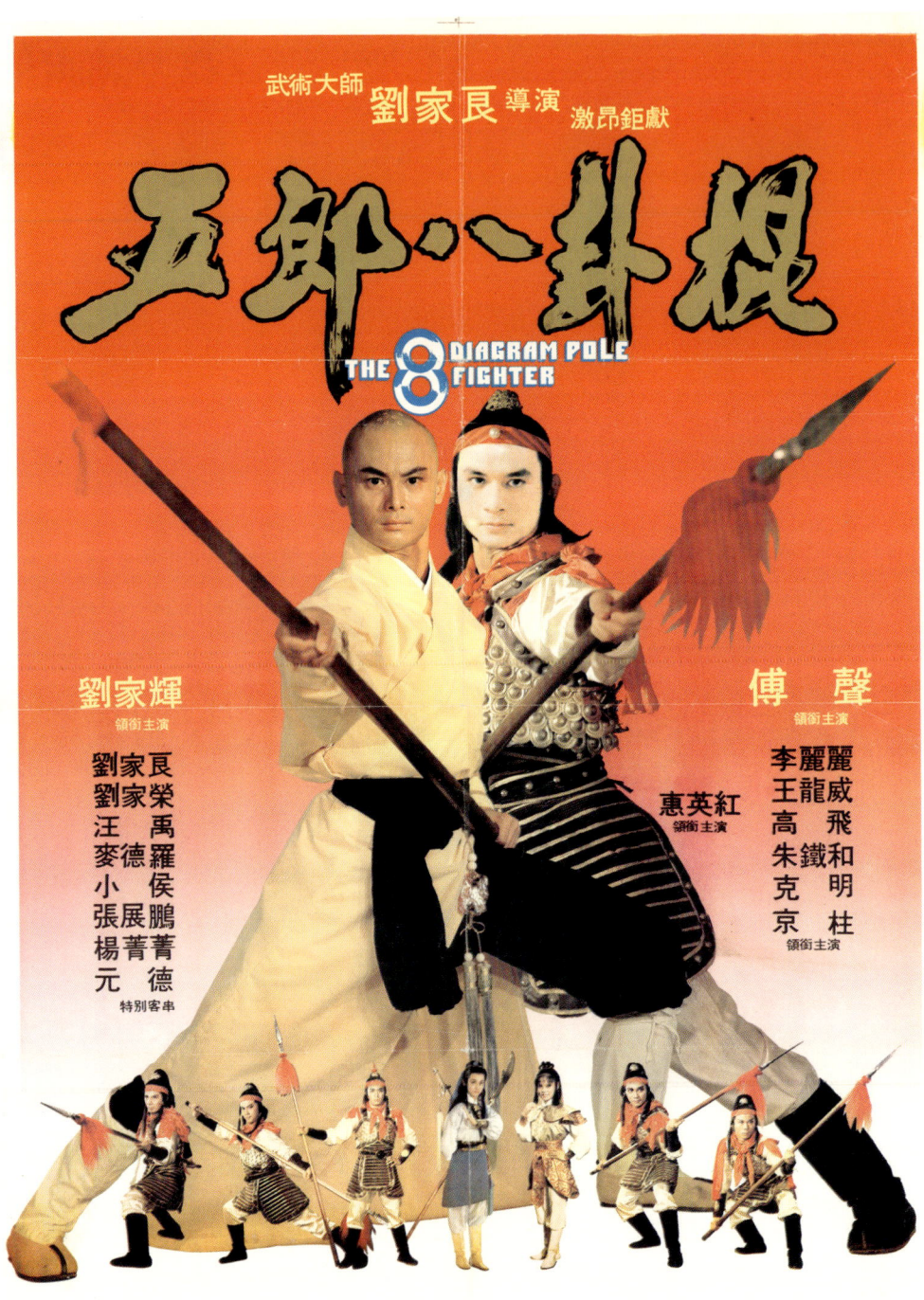

THE 8 DIAGRAM POLE FIGHTER (1984)

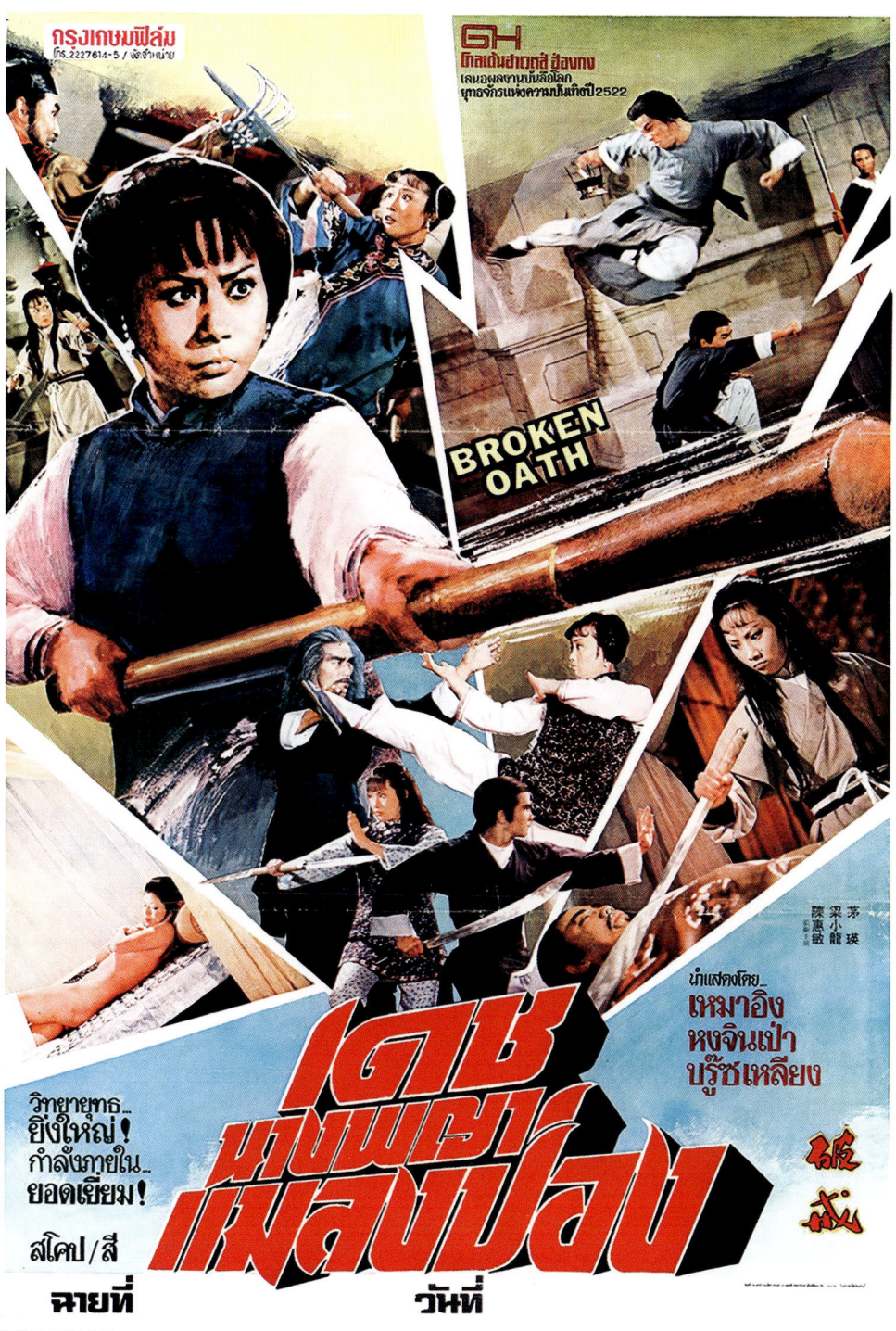

BROKEN OATH (1977)

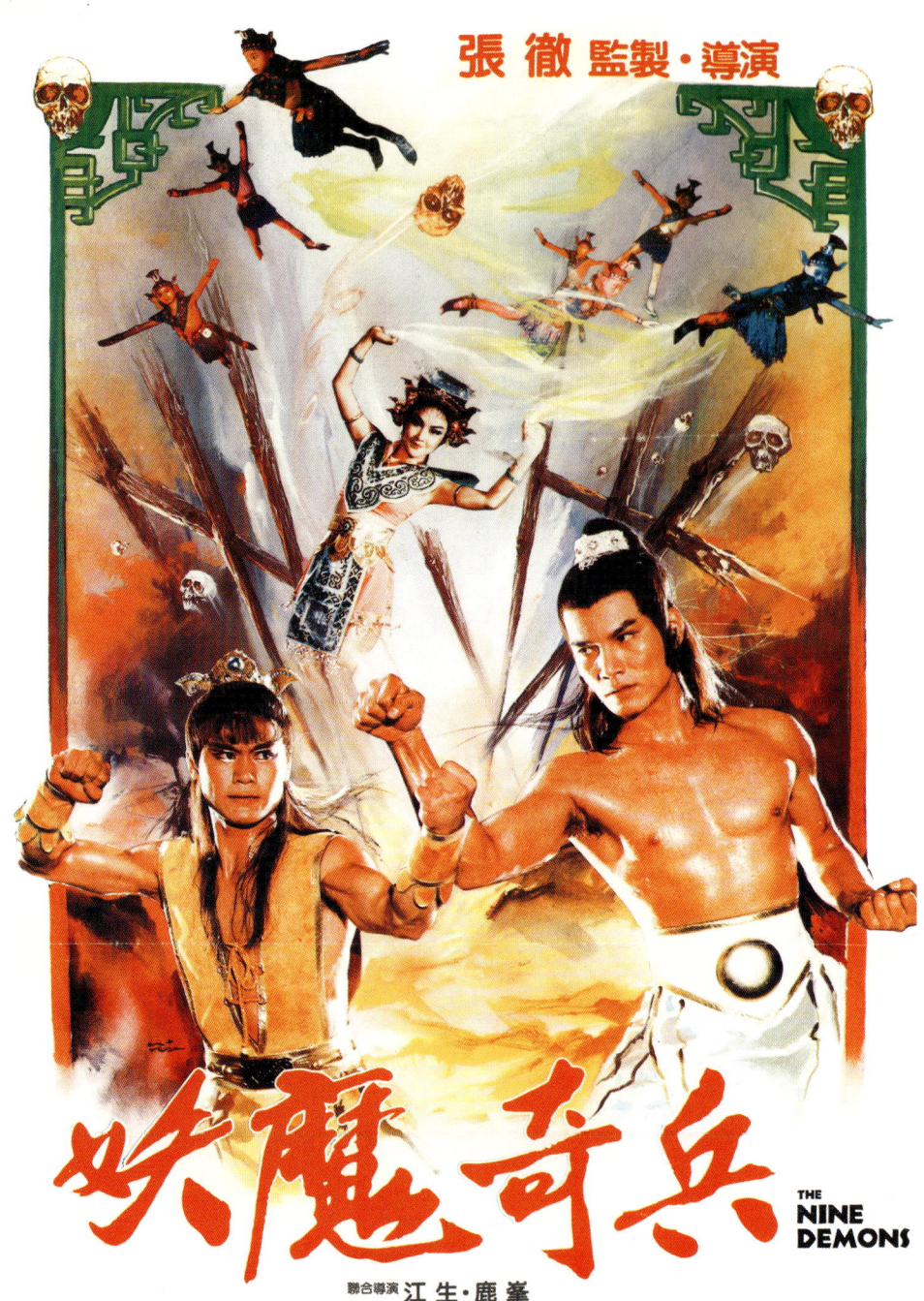

THE NINE DEMONS (1984)

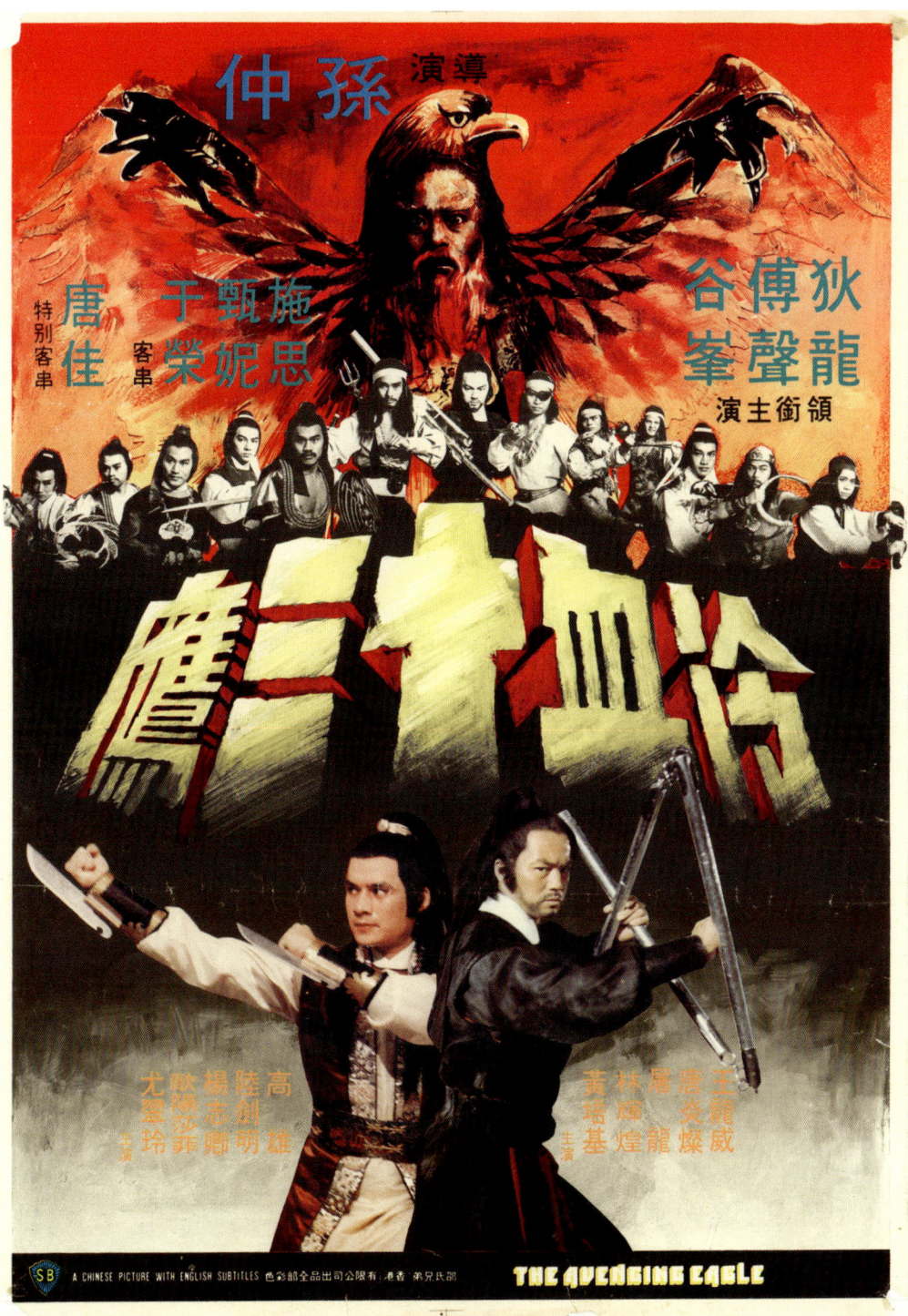

THE AVENGING EAGLE (1978)

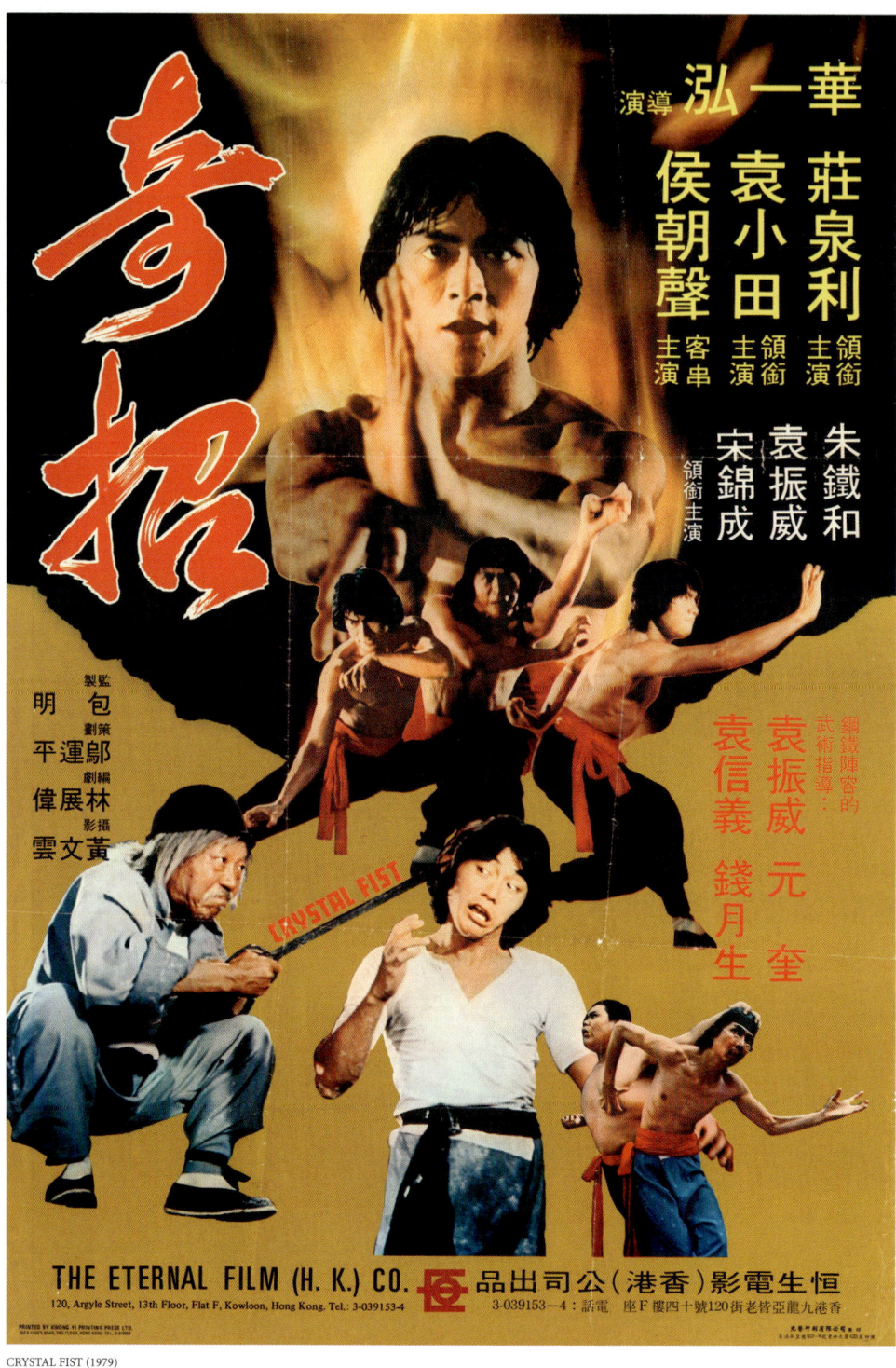

CRYSTAL FIST (1979)

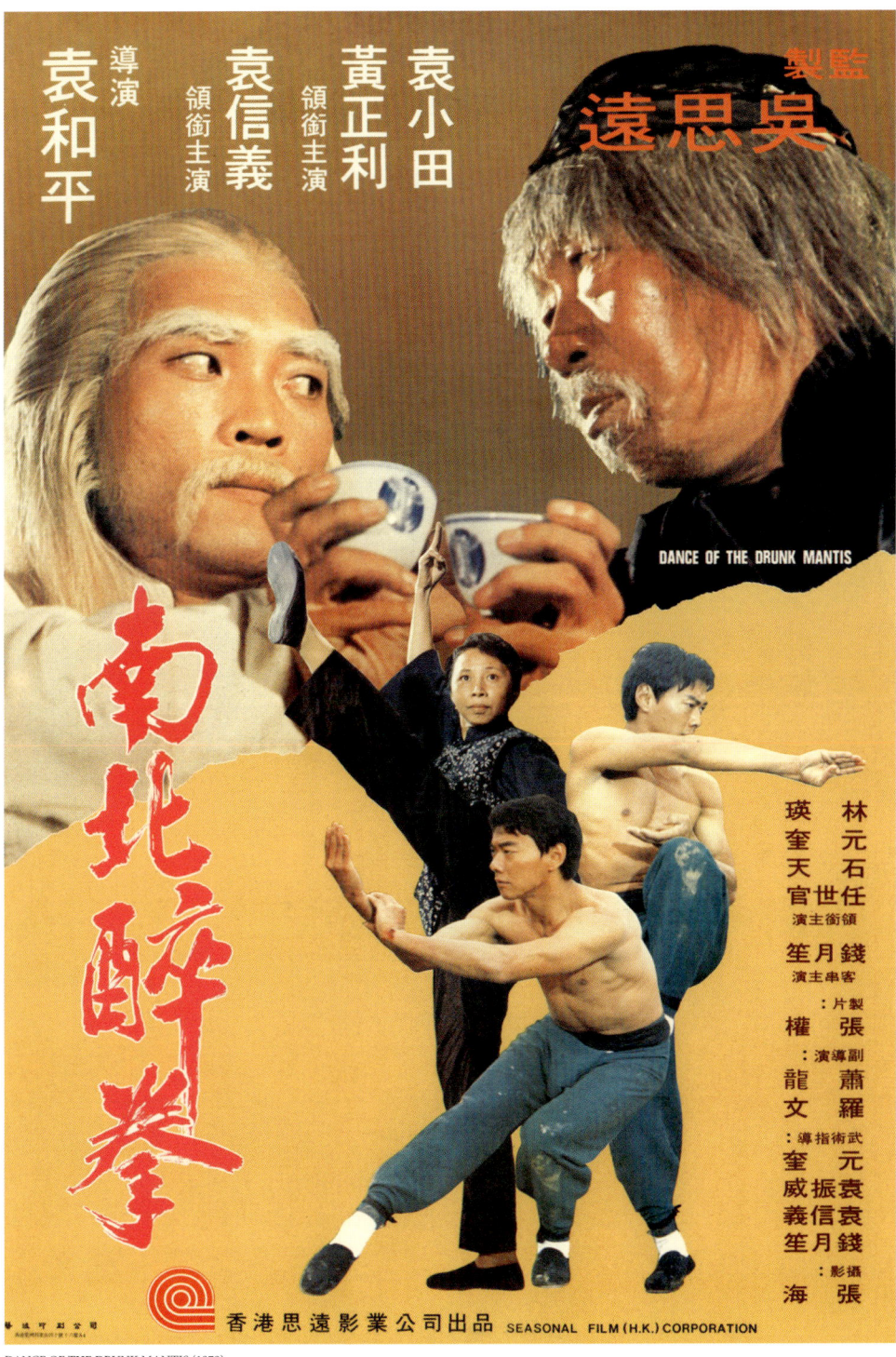

DANCE OF THE DRUNK MANTIS (1979)

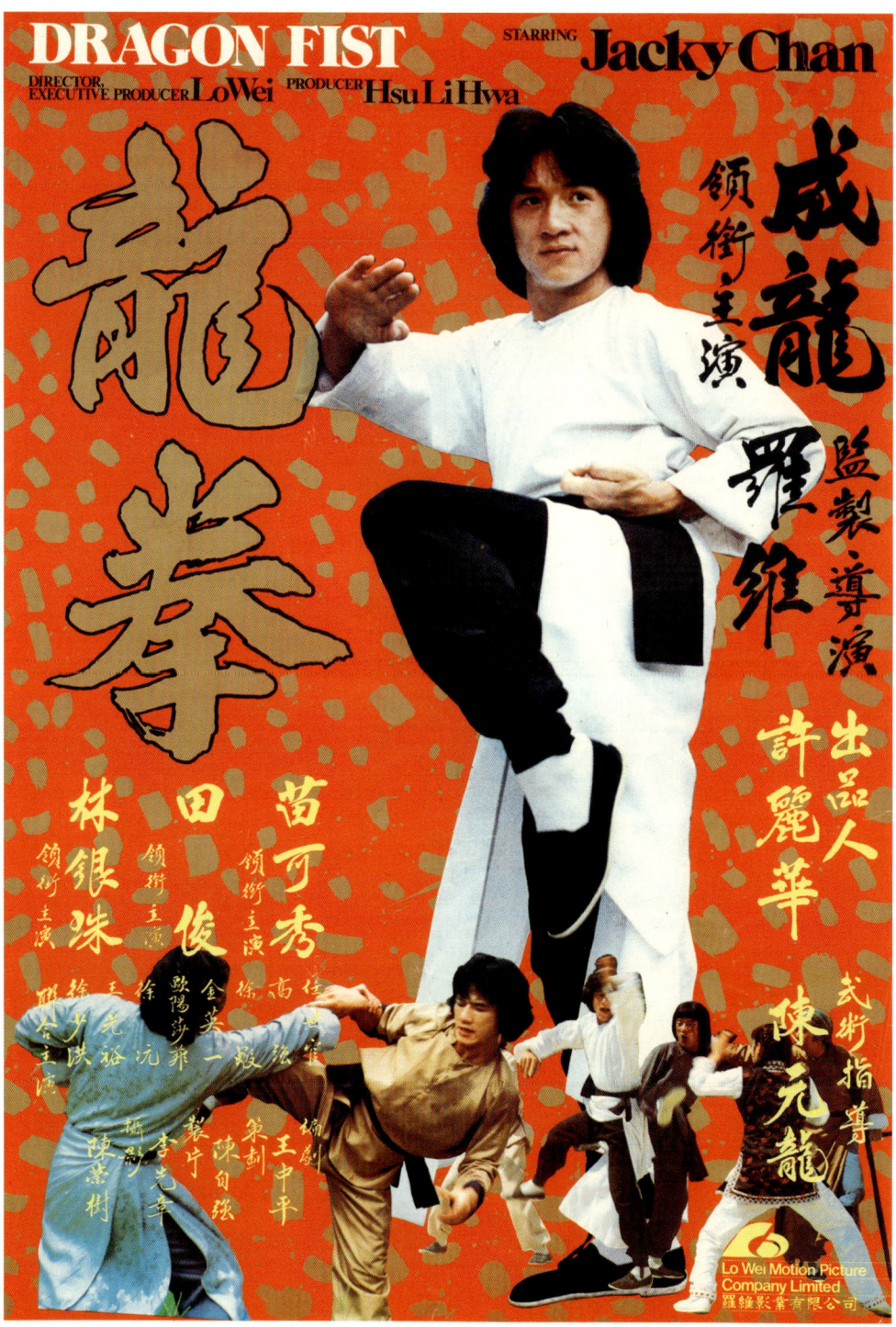

DRAGON FIST (1979)

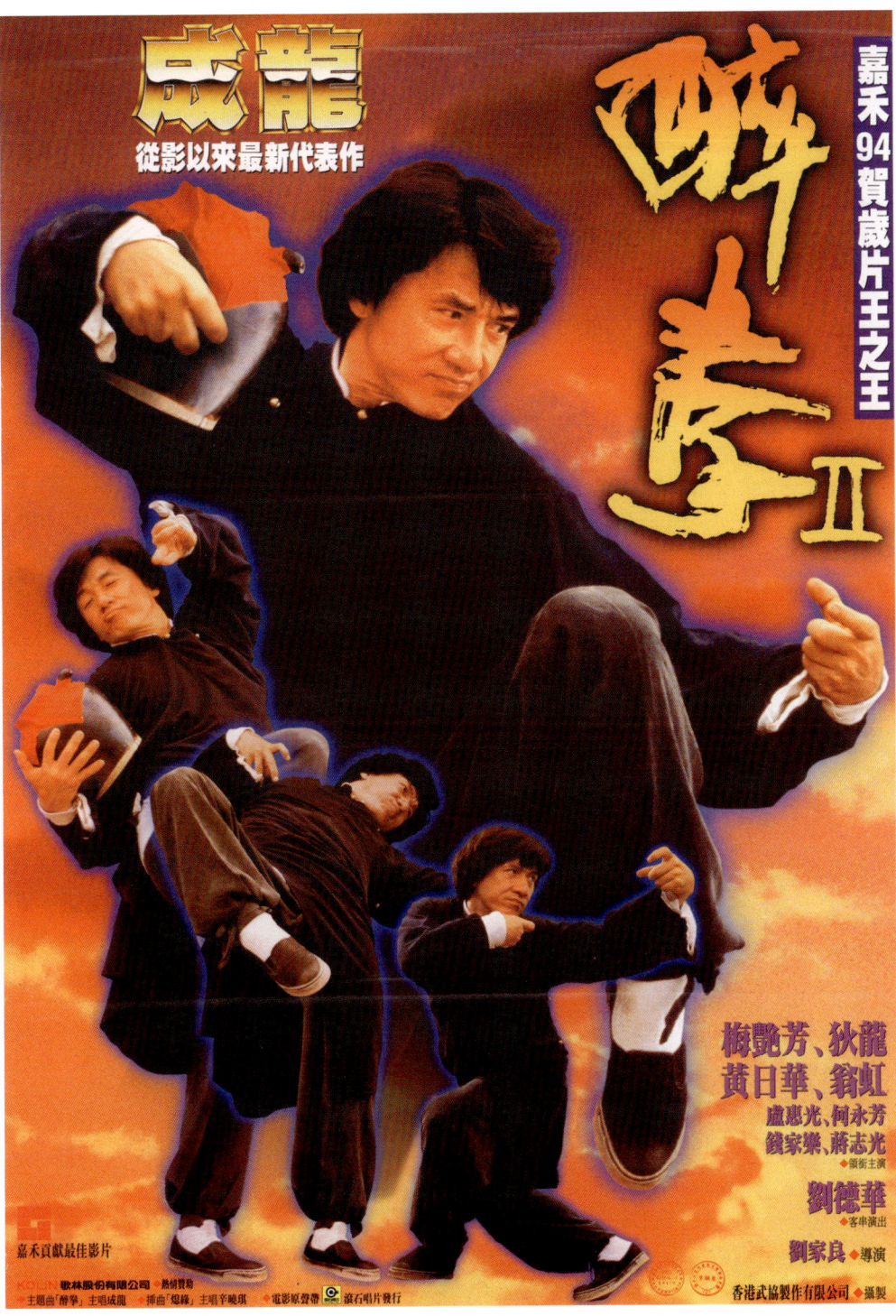

DRUNKEN MASTER II (1994)

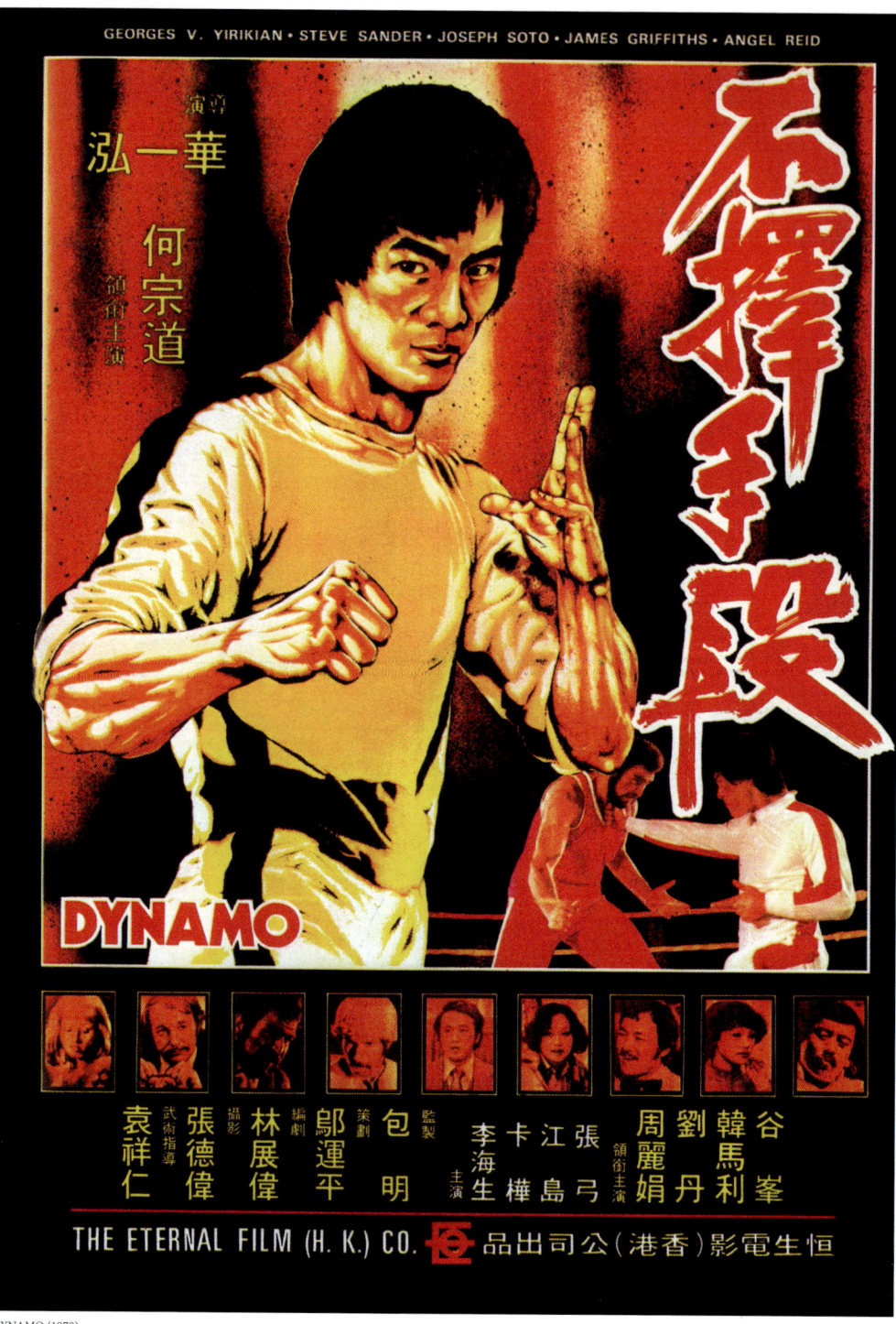

DYNAMO (1978)

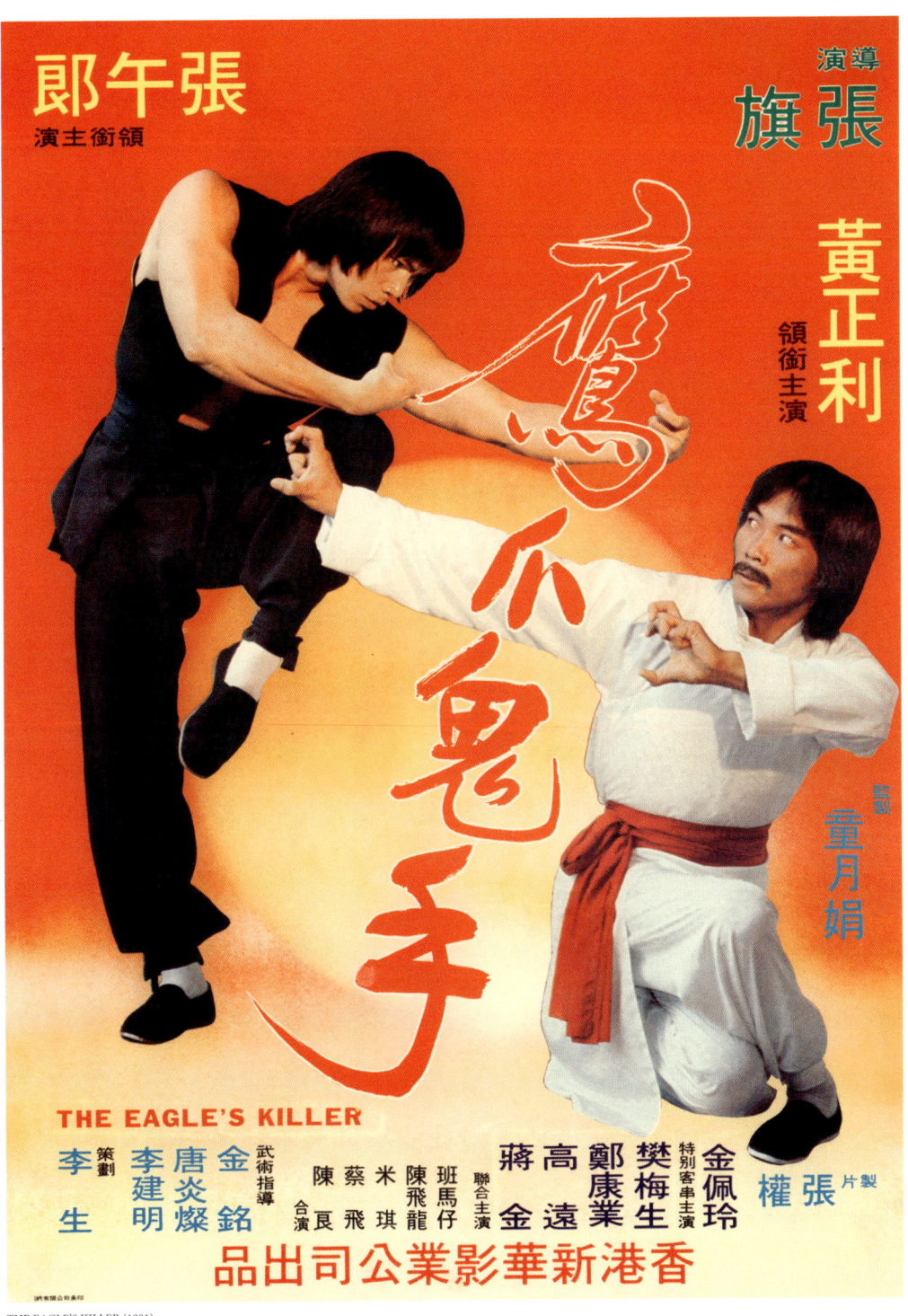

THE EAGLE'S KILLER (1981)

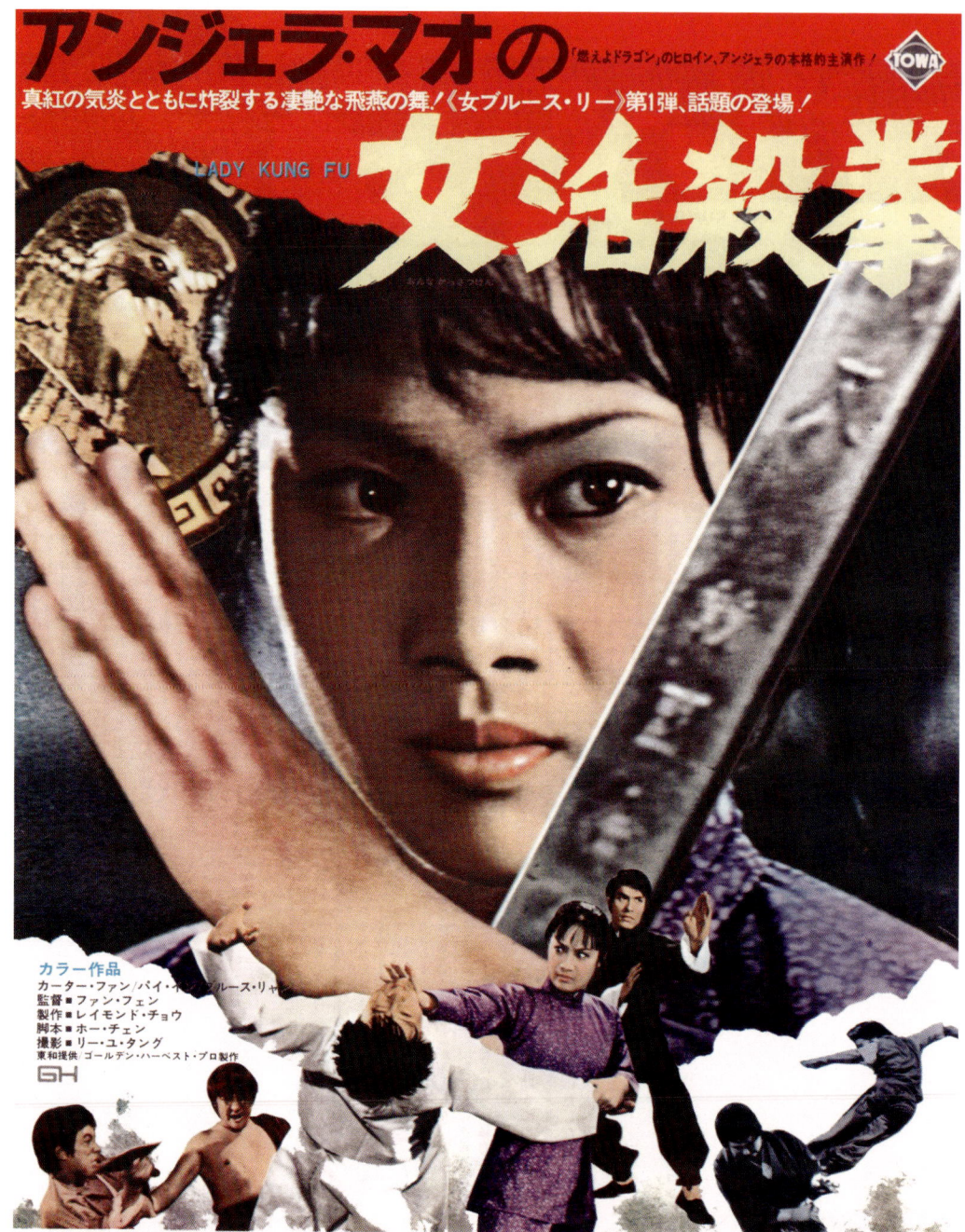

HAPKIDO (1972)

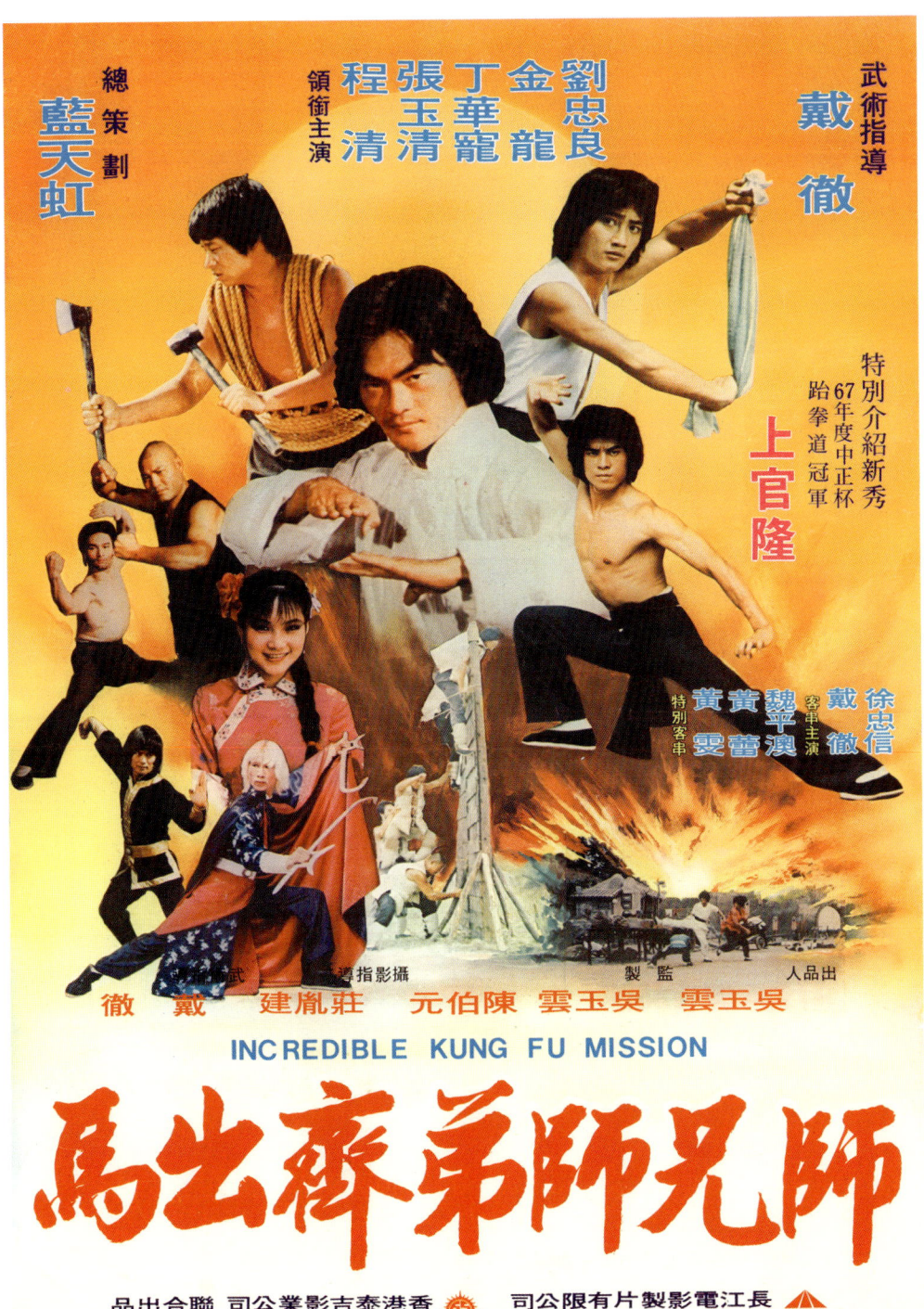

INCREDIBLE KUNG FU MISSION (1979)

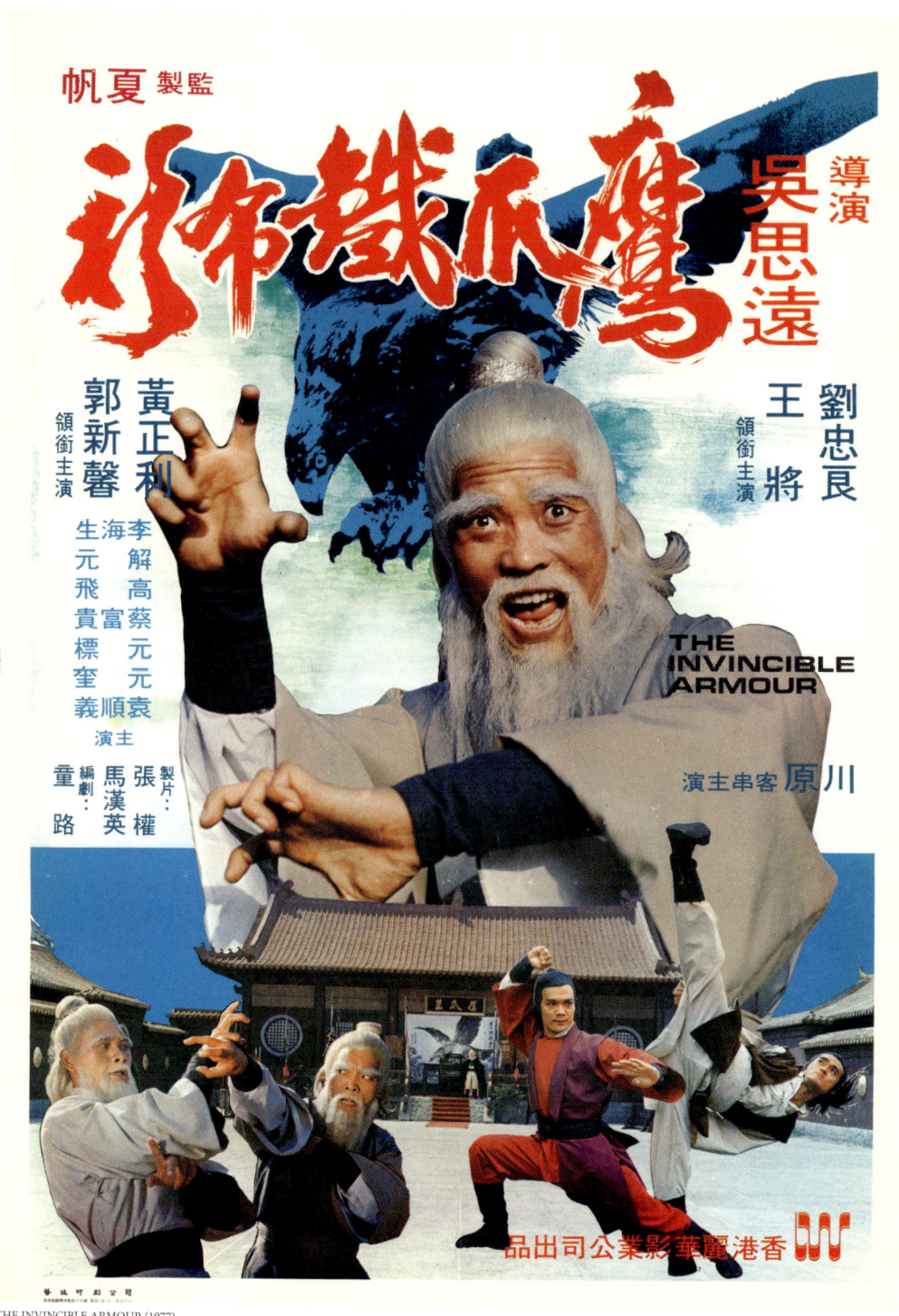

THE INVINCIBLE ARMOUR (1977)

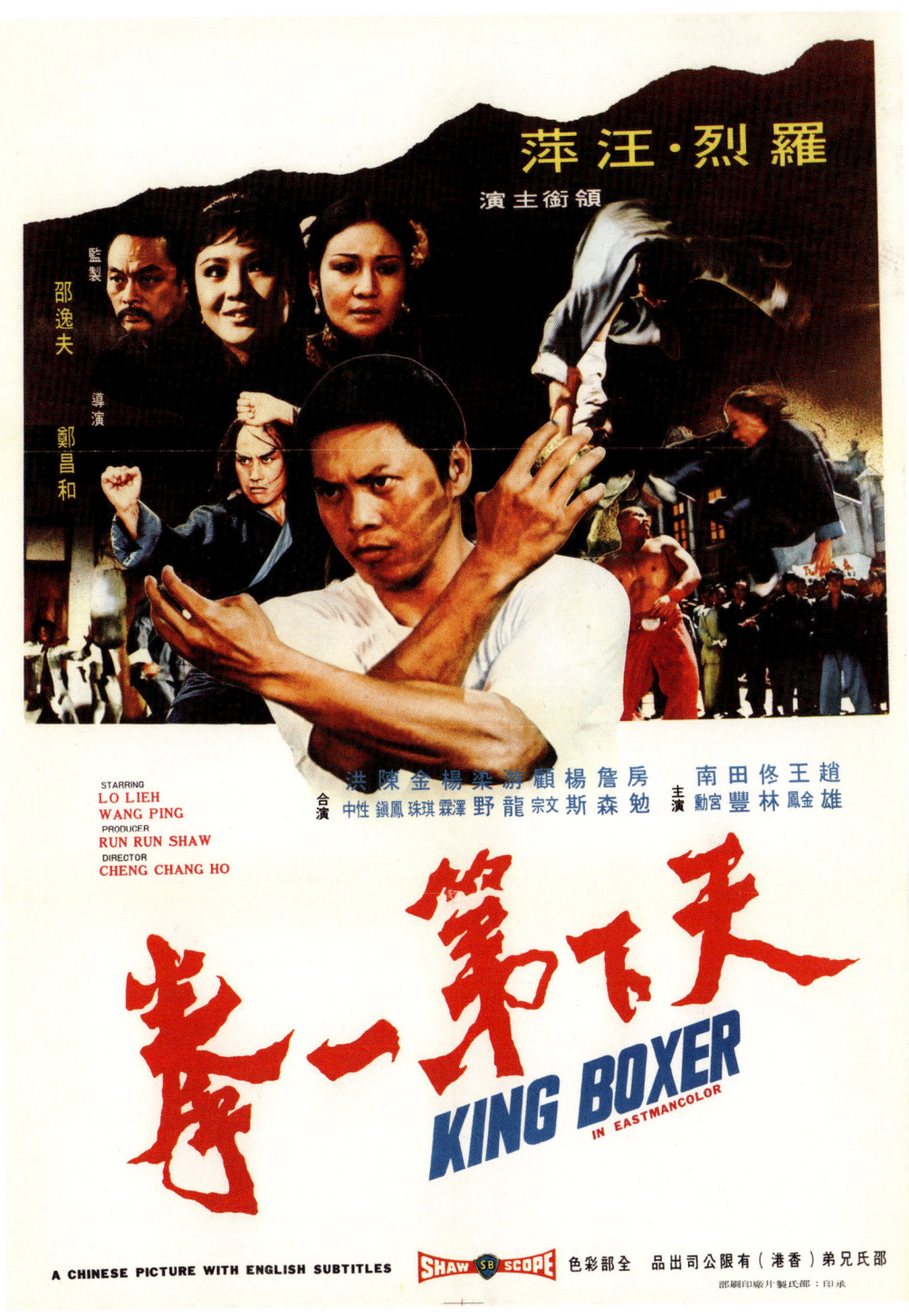

KING BOXER (1972)

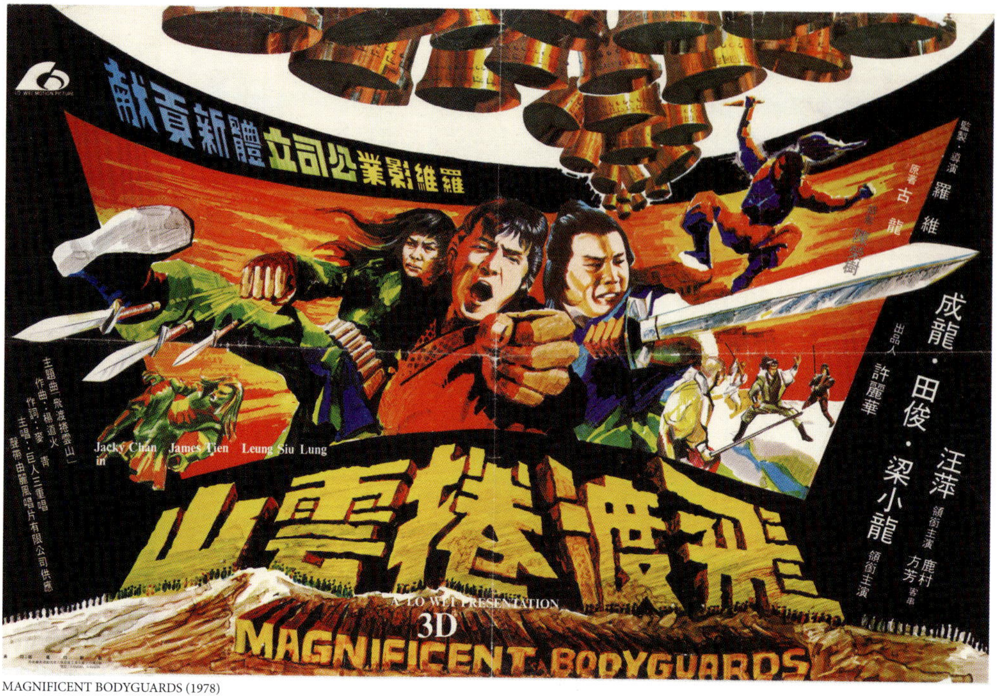

MAGNIFICENT BODYGUARDS (1978)

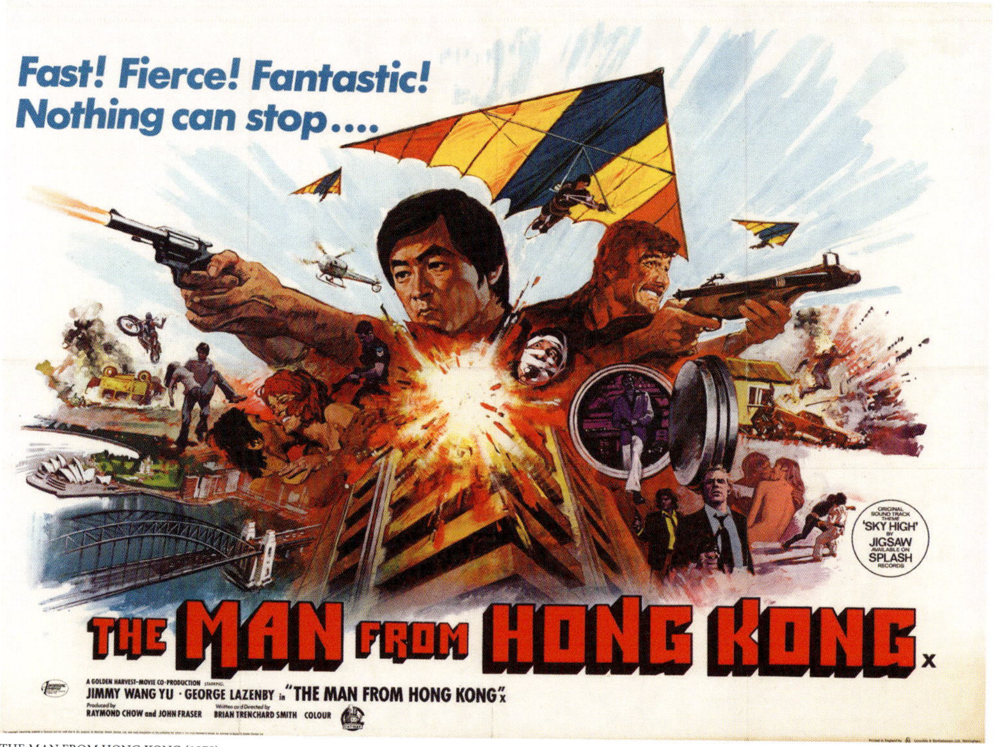

THE MAN FROM HONG KONG (1975)

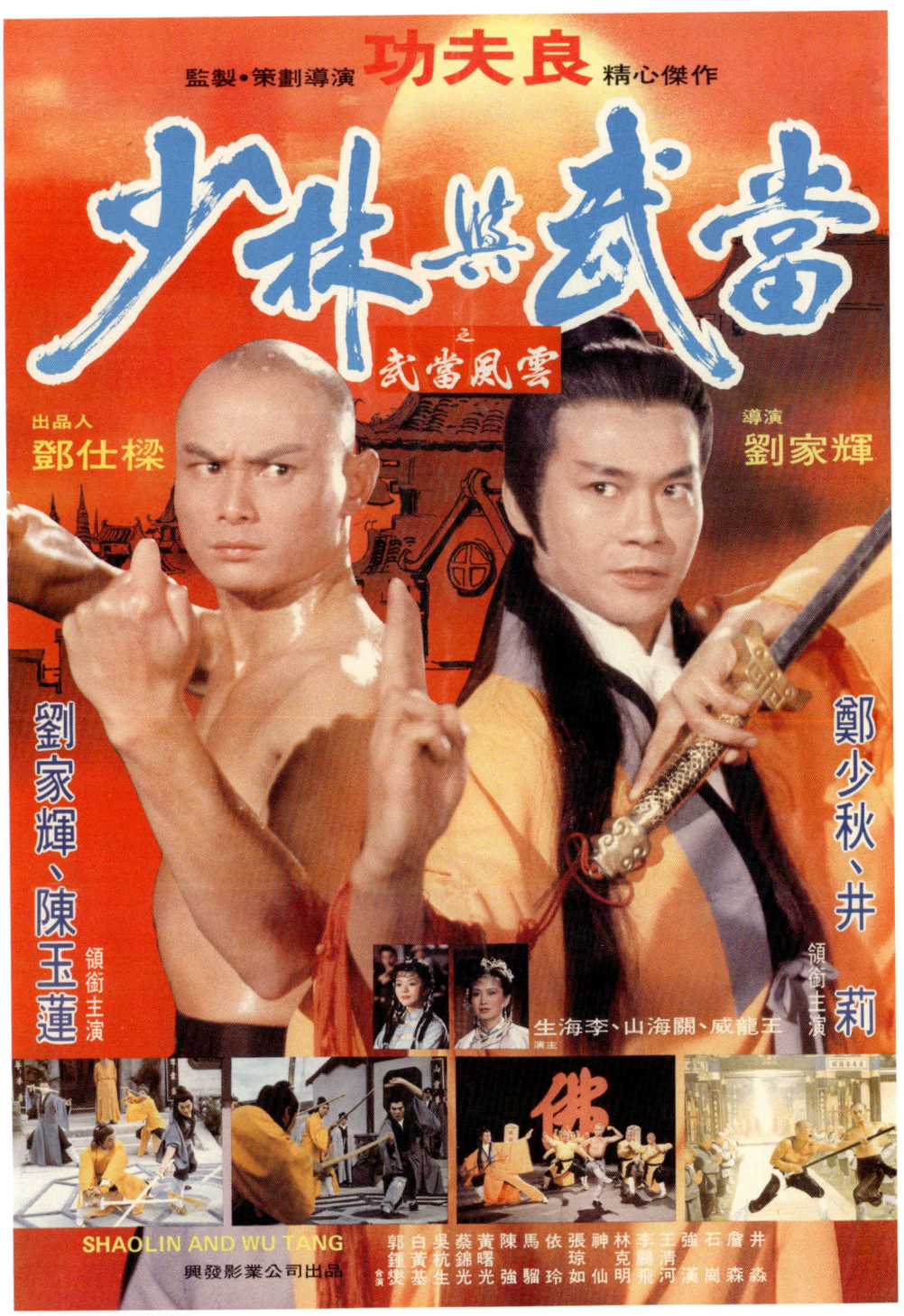

SHAOLIN AND WU TANG (1983)

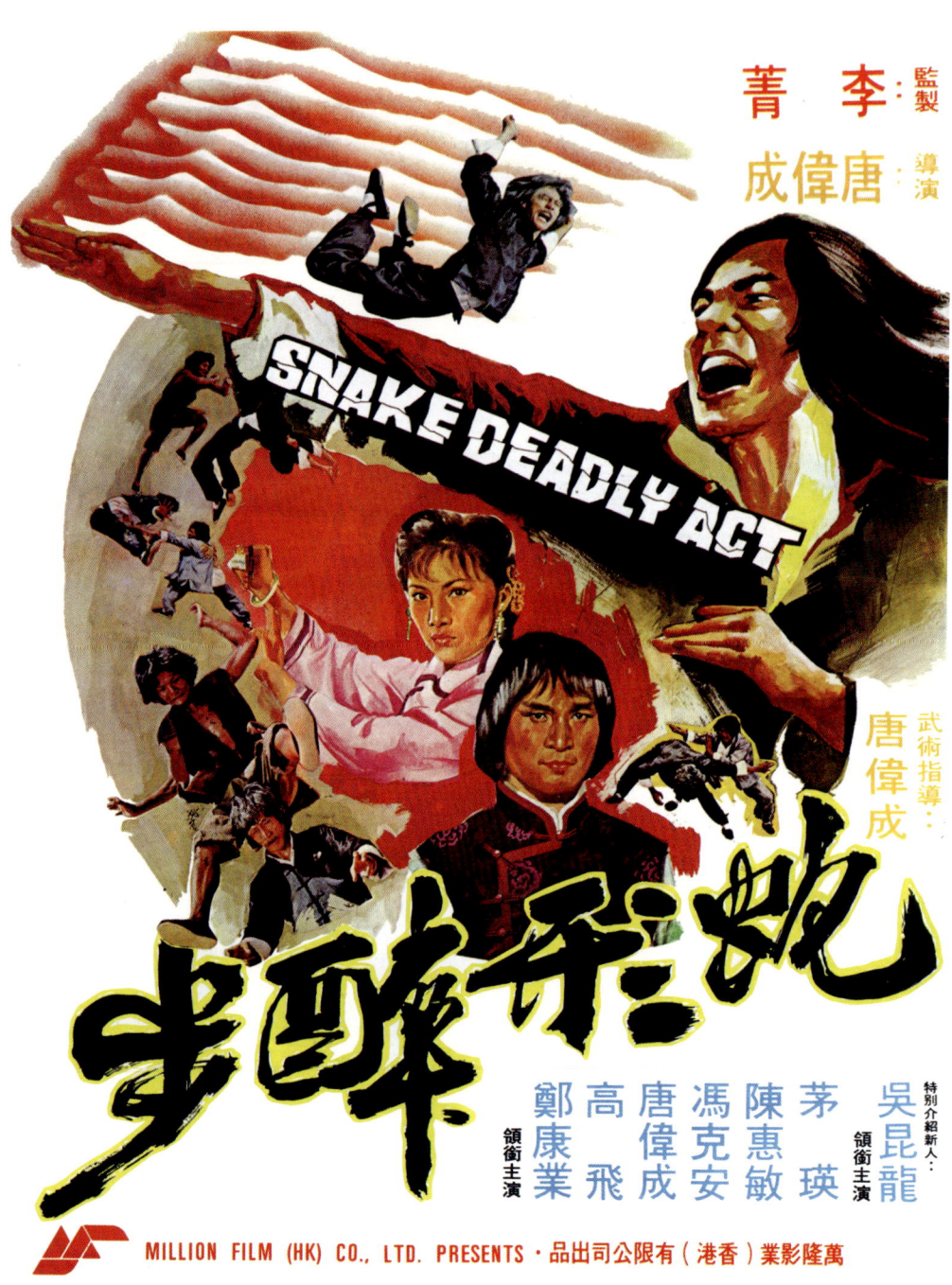

SNAKE DEADLY ACT (1980)

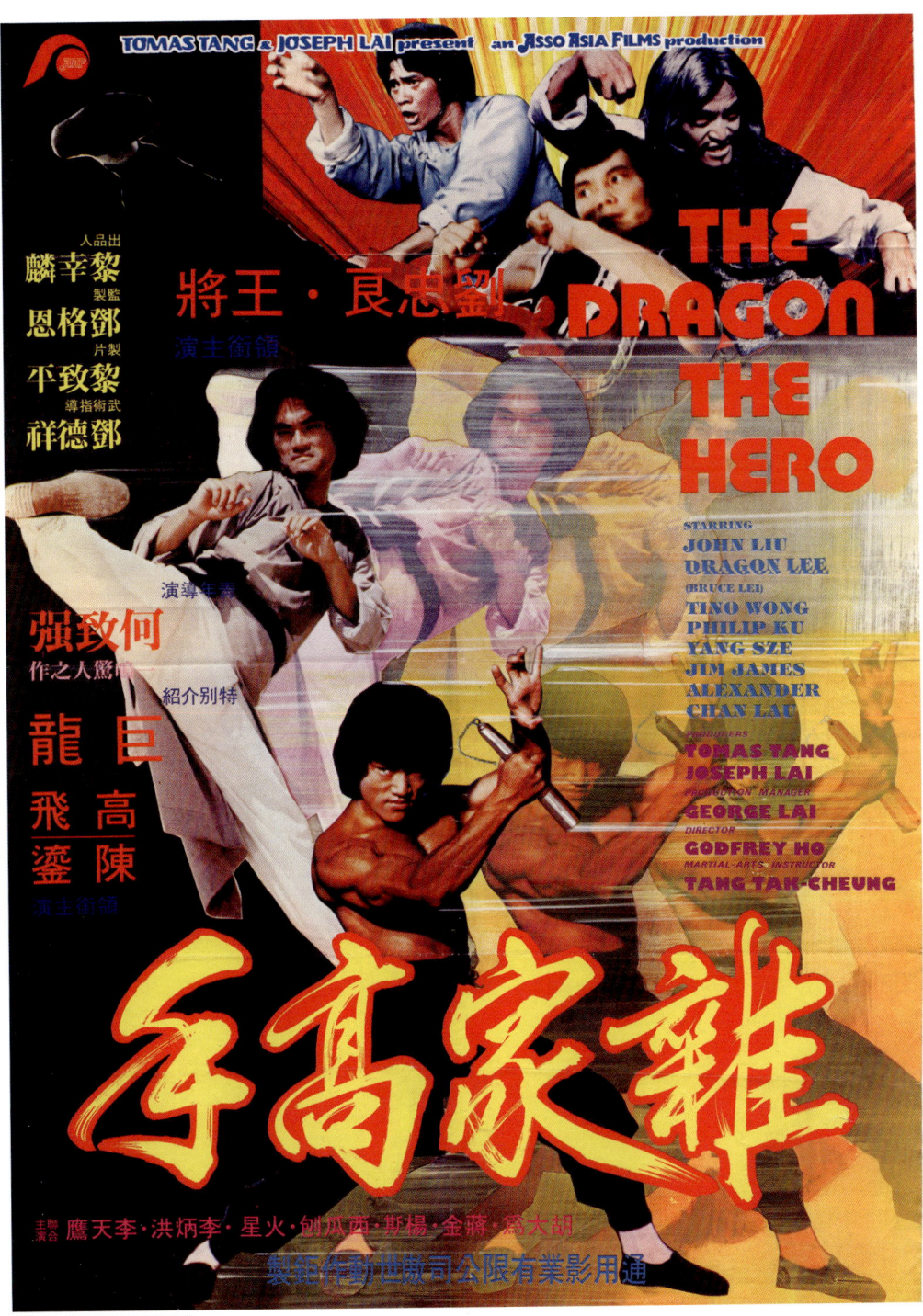

THE DRAGON, THE HERO (1979)

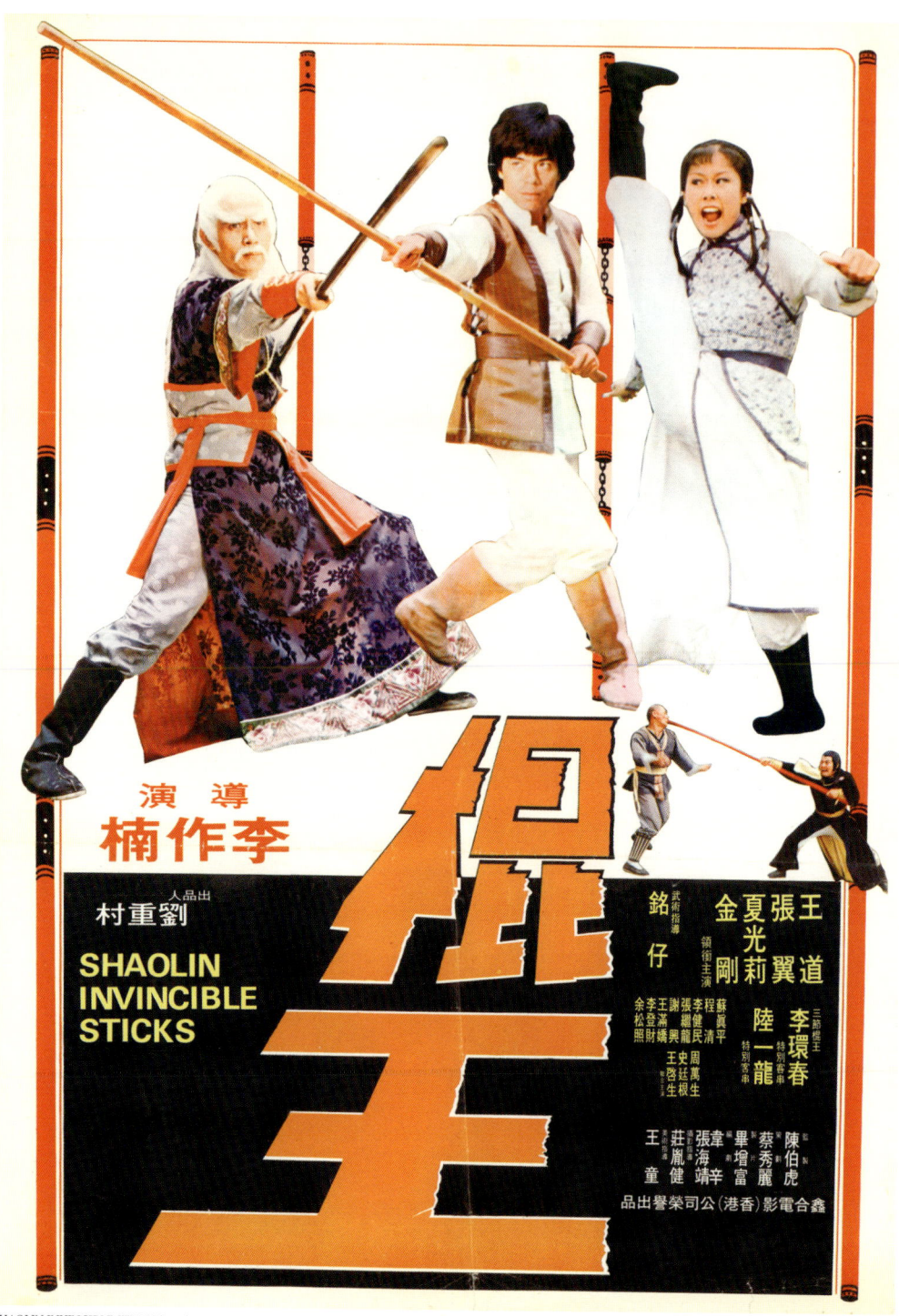

SHAOLIN INVINCIBLE STICKS (1978)

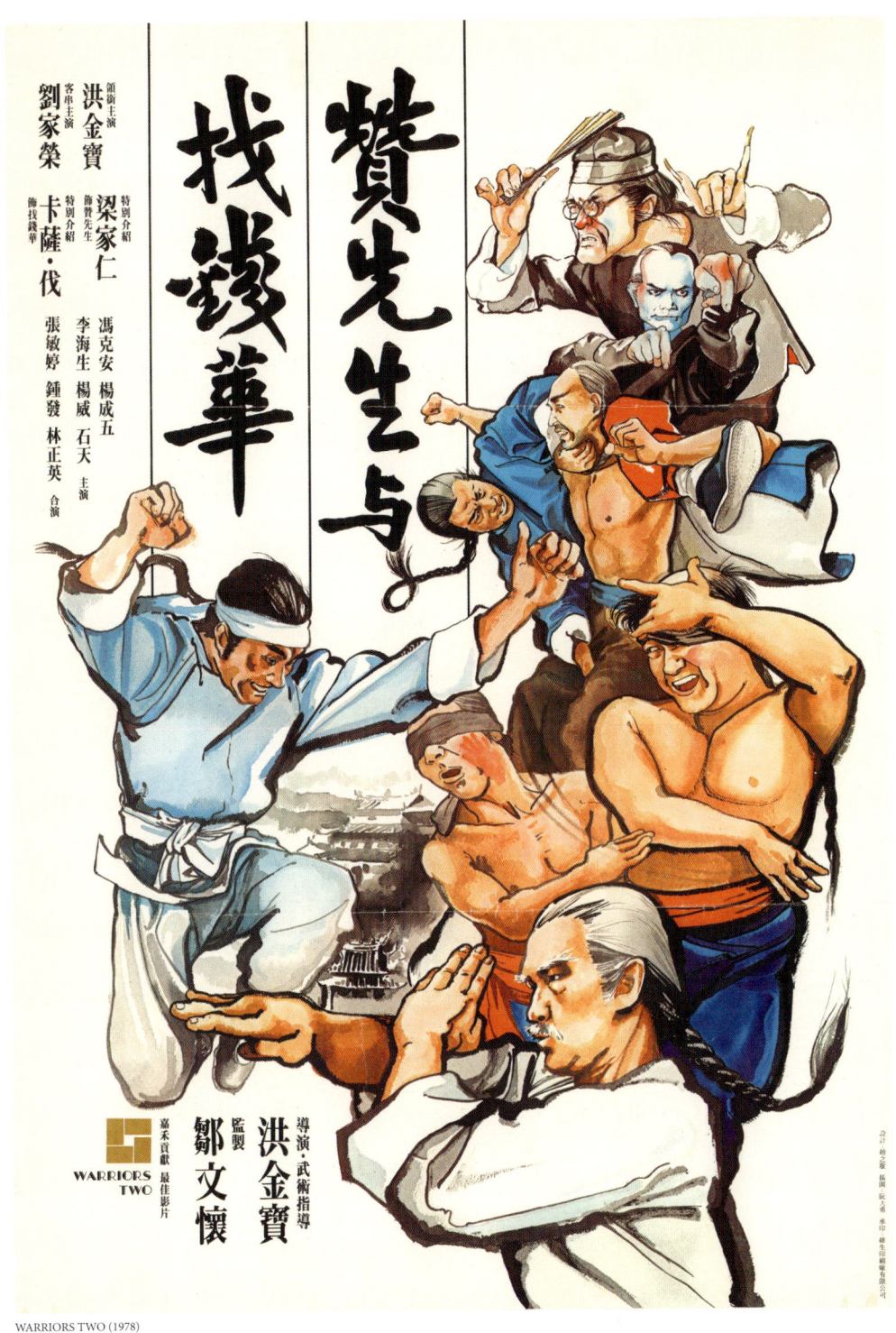

WARRIORS TWO (1978)

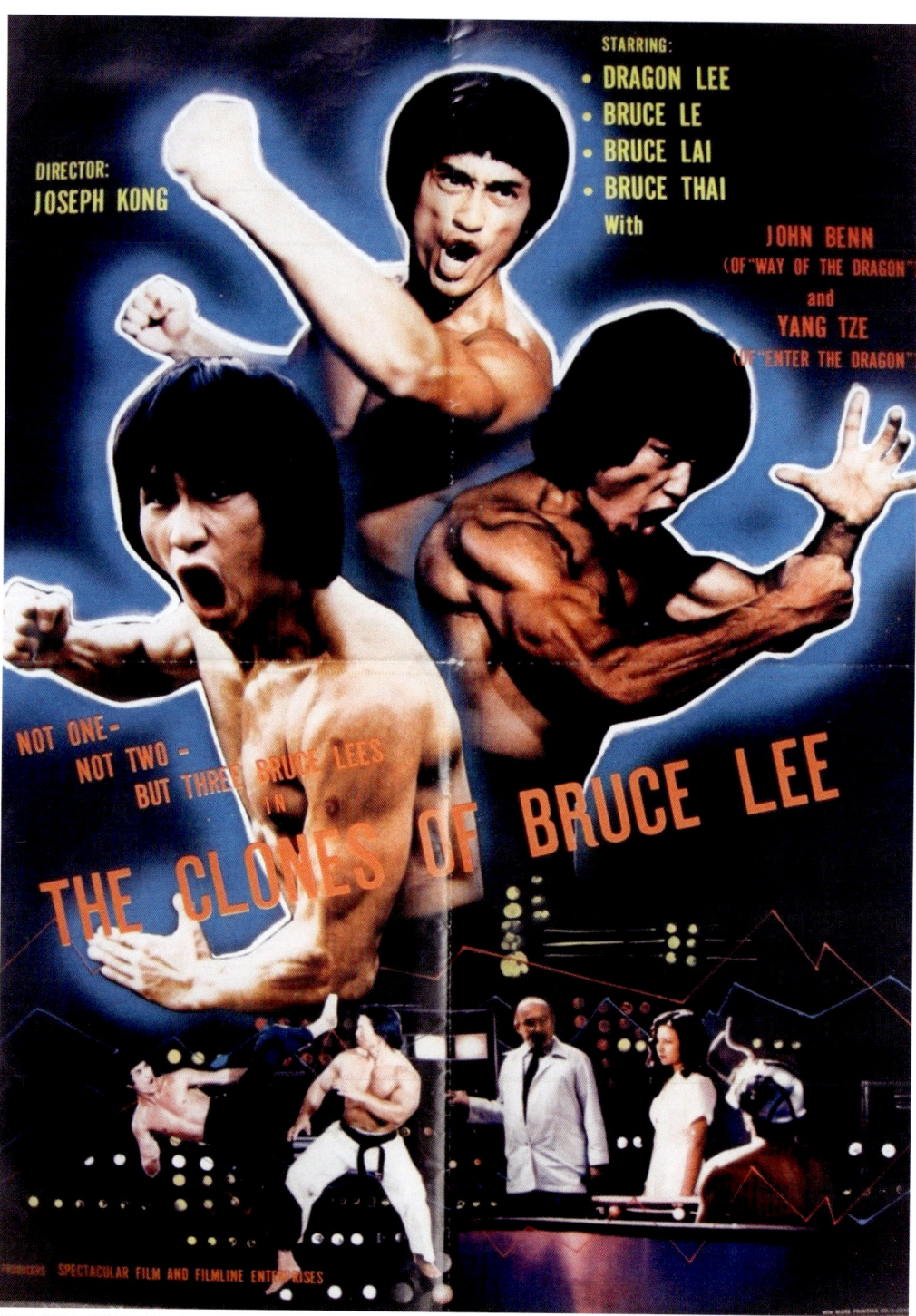

THE CLONES OF BRUCE LEE (1980)

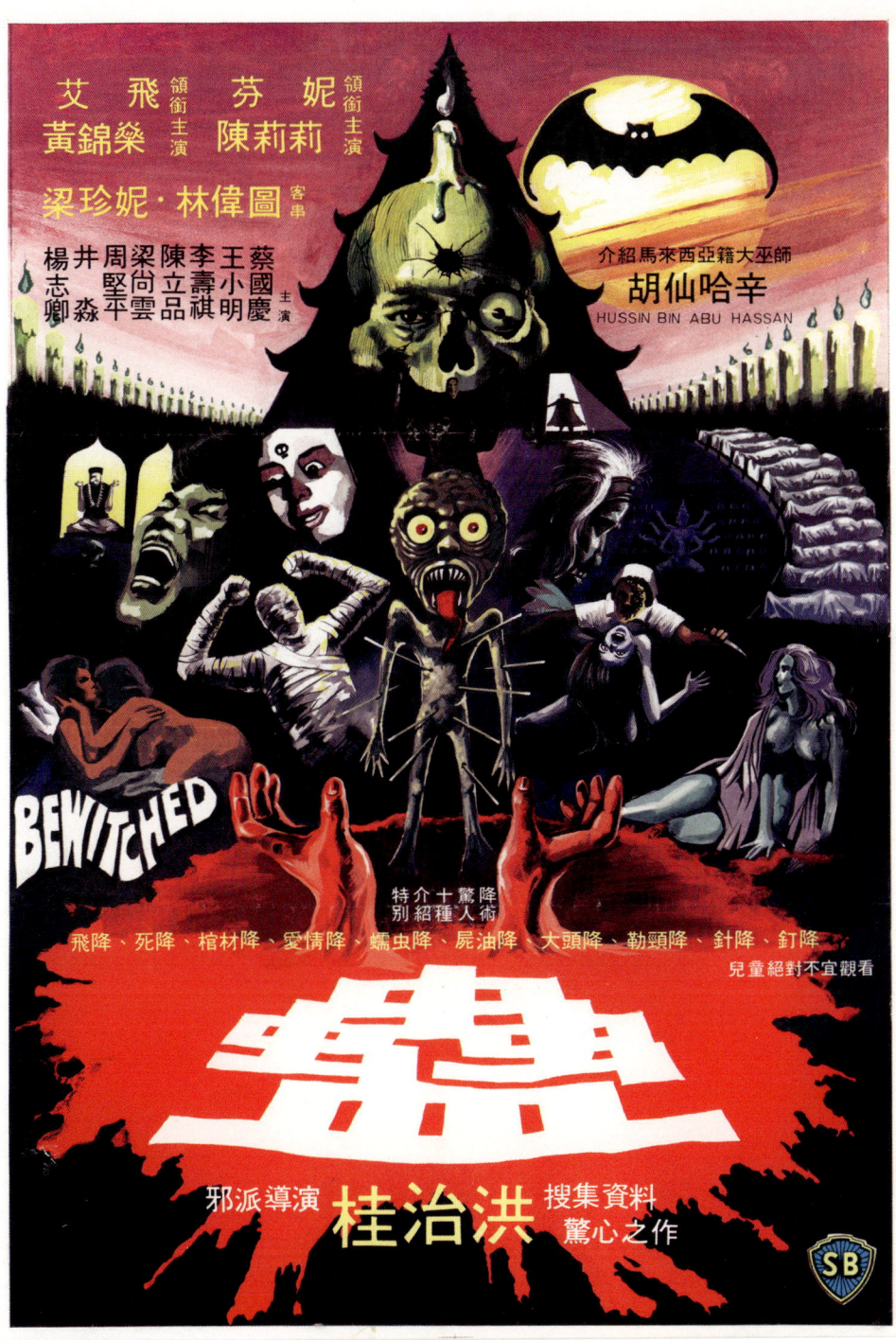

BEWITCHED (1981)

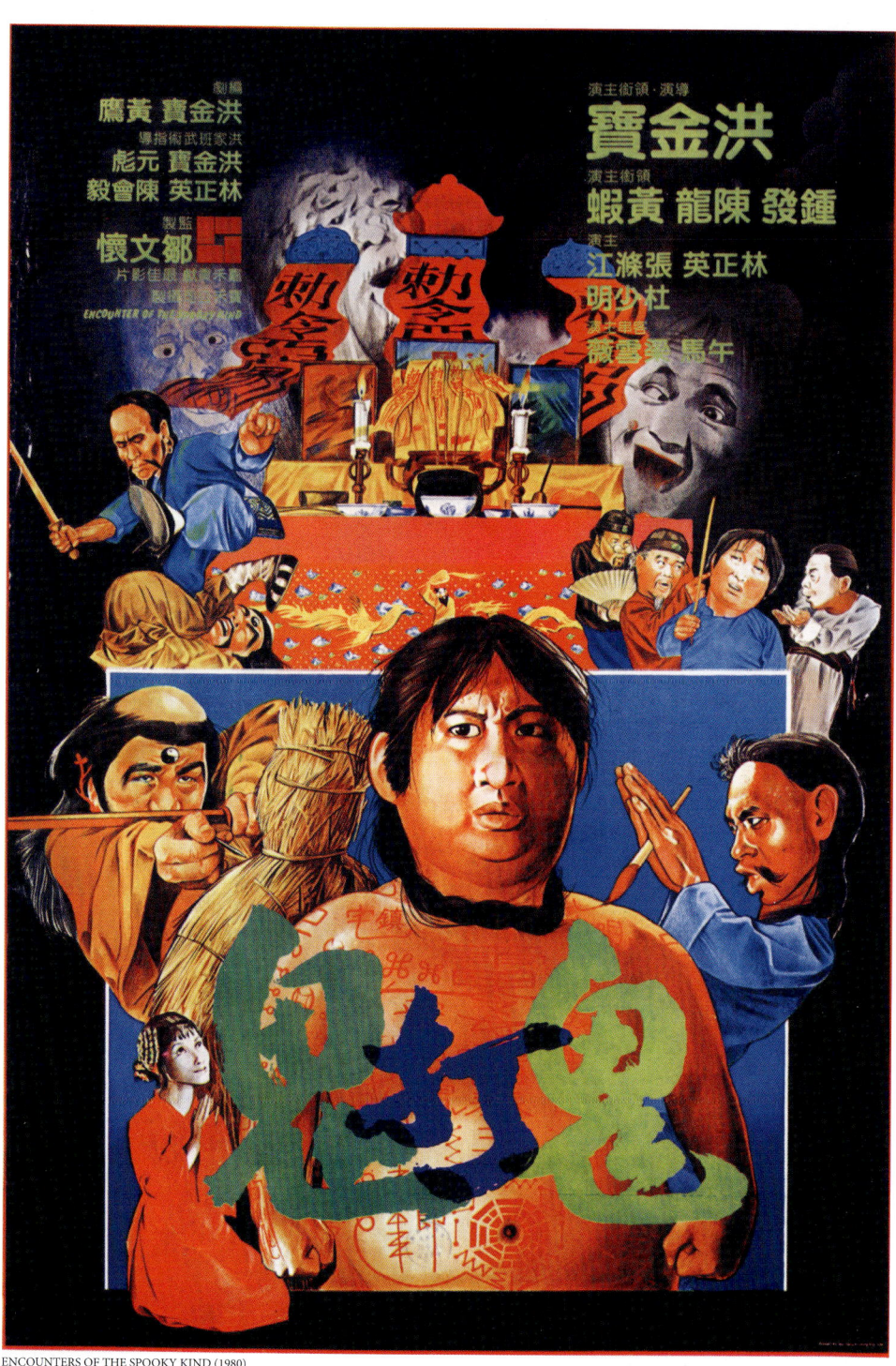

ENCOUNTERS OF THE SPOOKY KIND (1980)

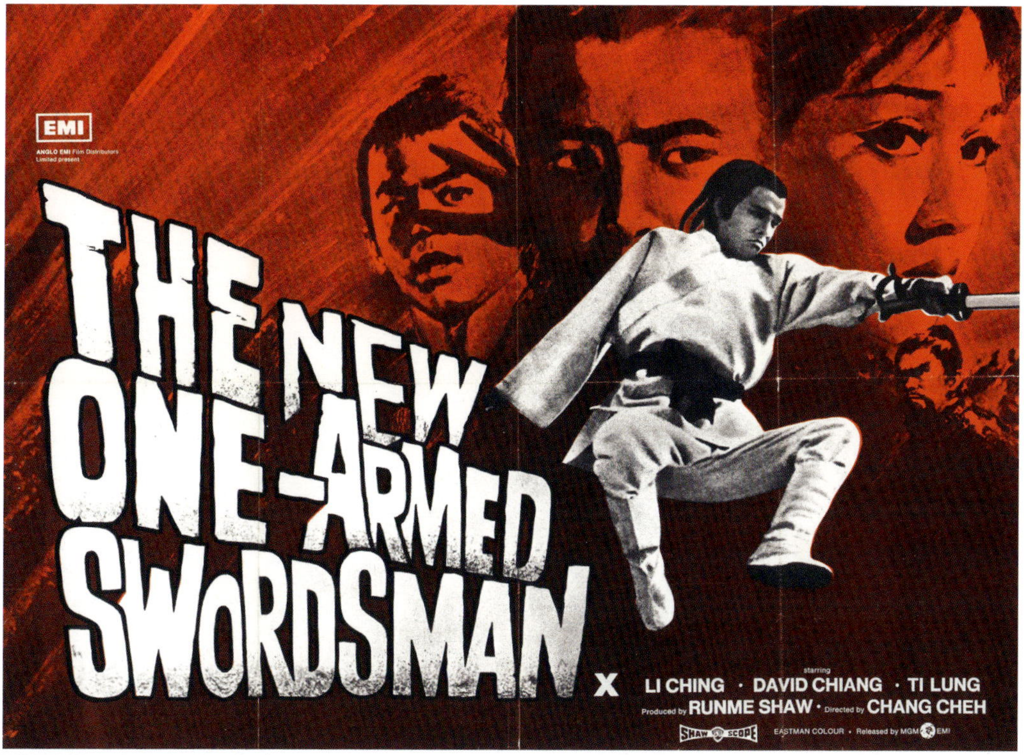

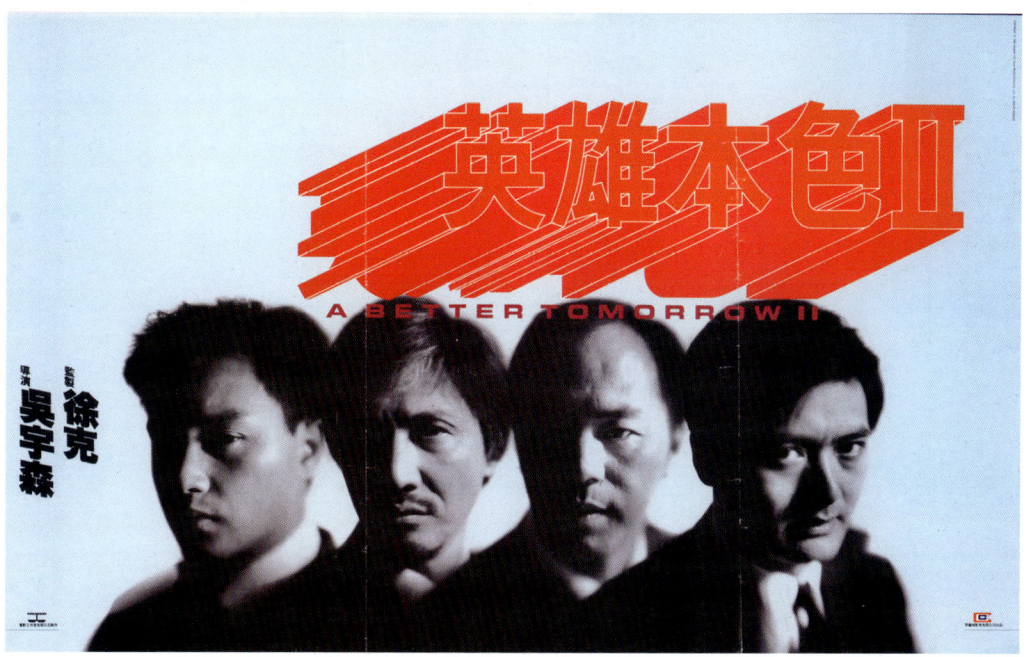

THE NEW ONE-ARMED SWORDSMAN (1971)

A BETTER TOMORROW II (1987)

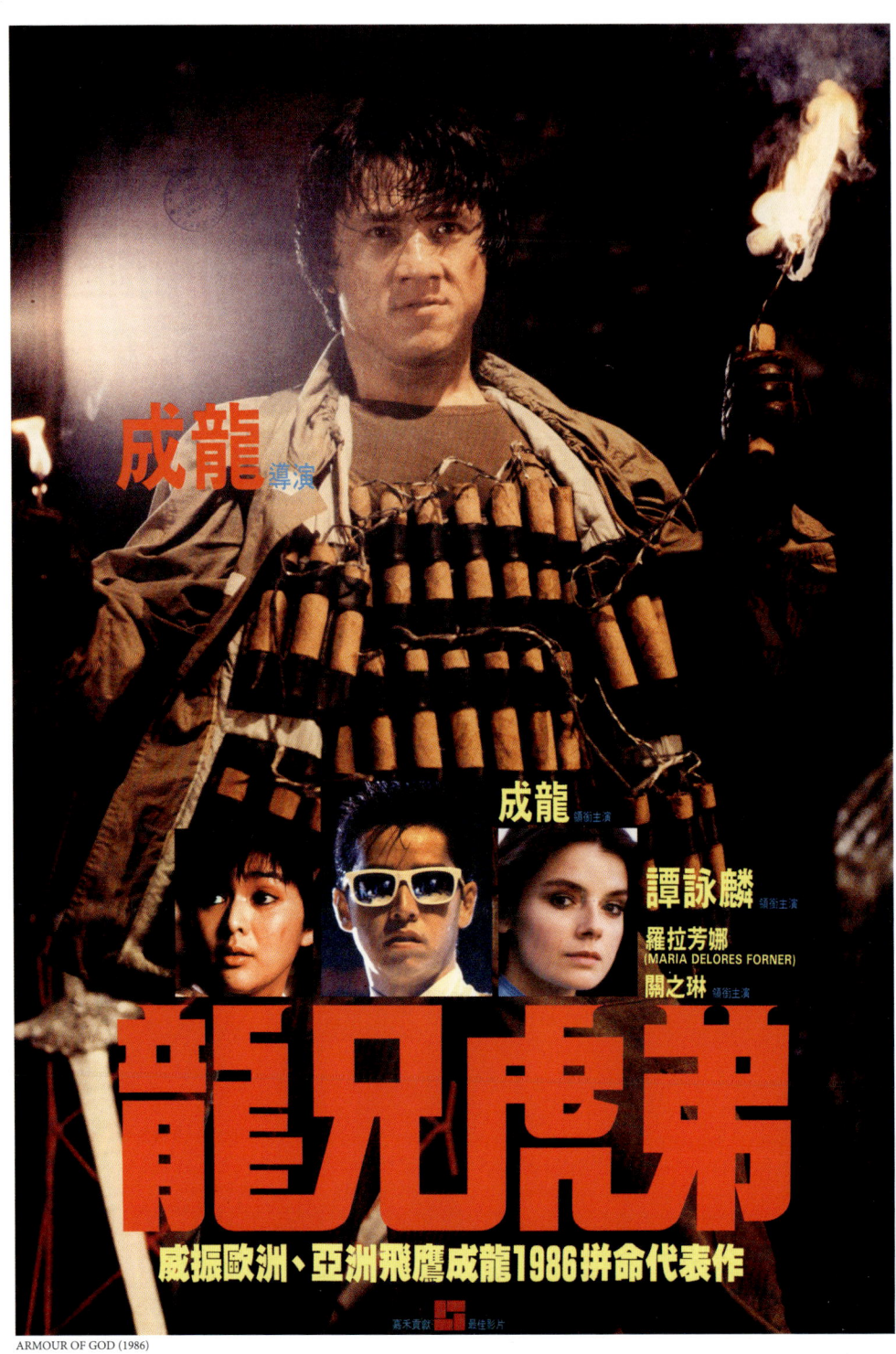

ARMOUR OF GOD (1986)

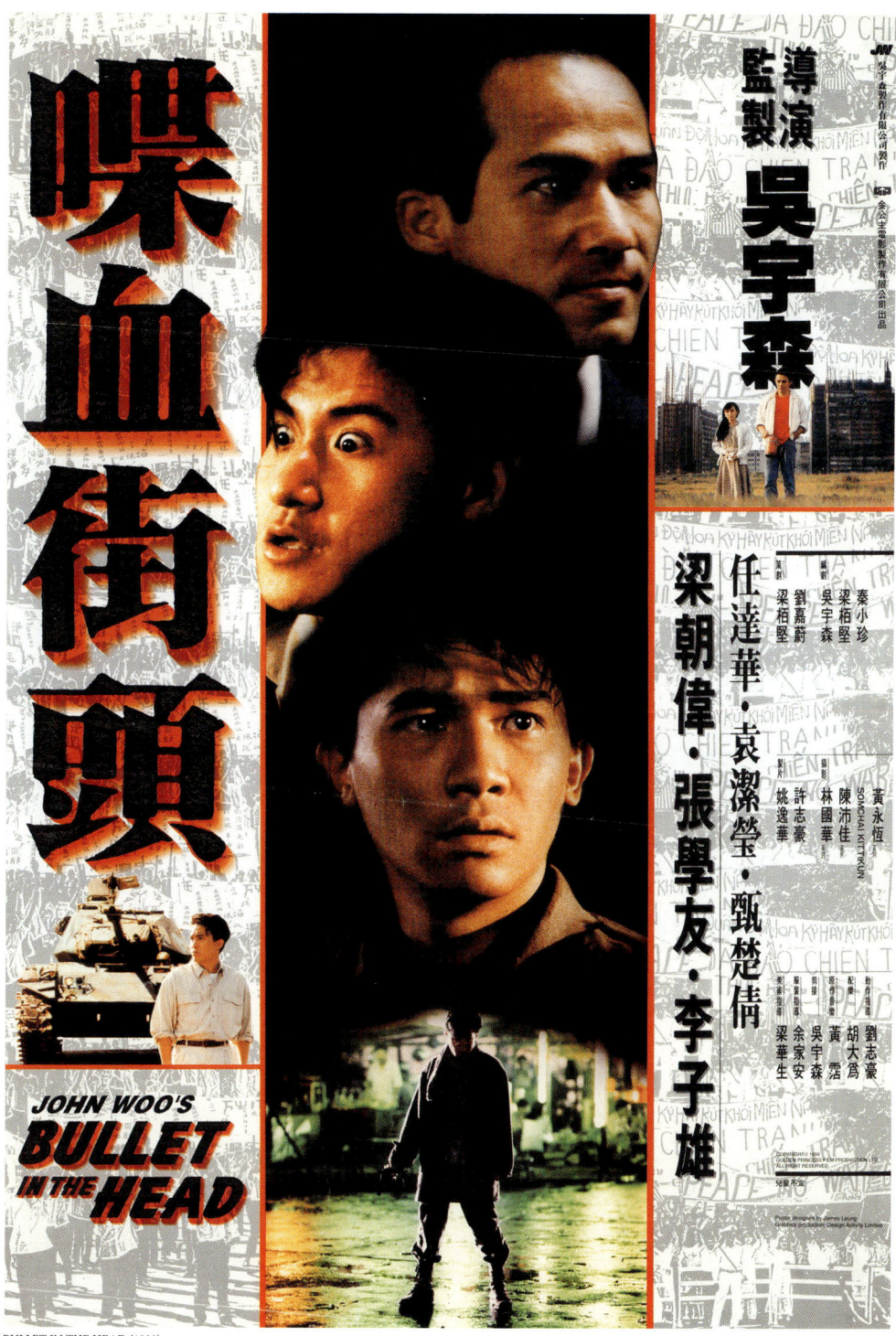

BULLET IN THE HEAD (1990)

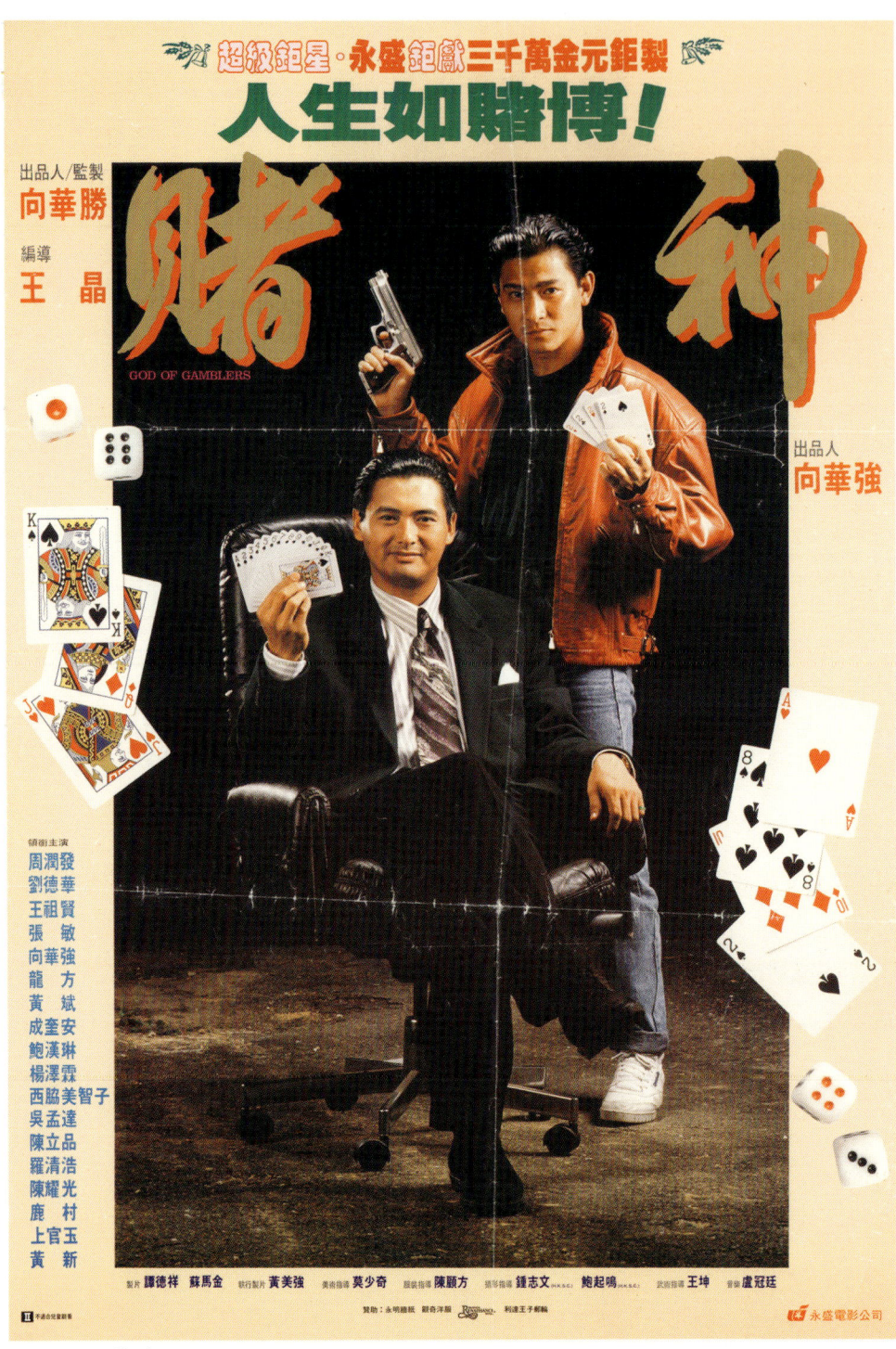

GOD OF GAMBLERS (1989)

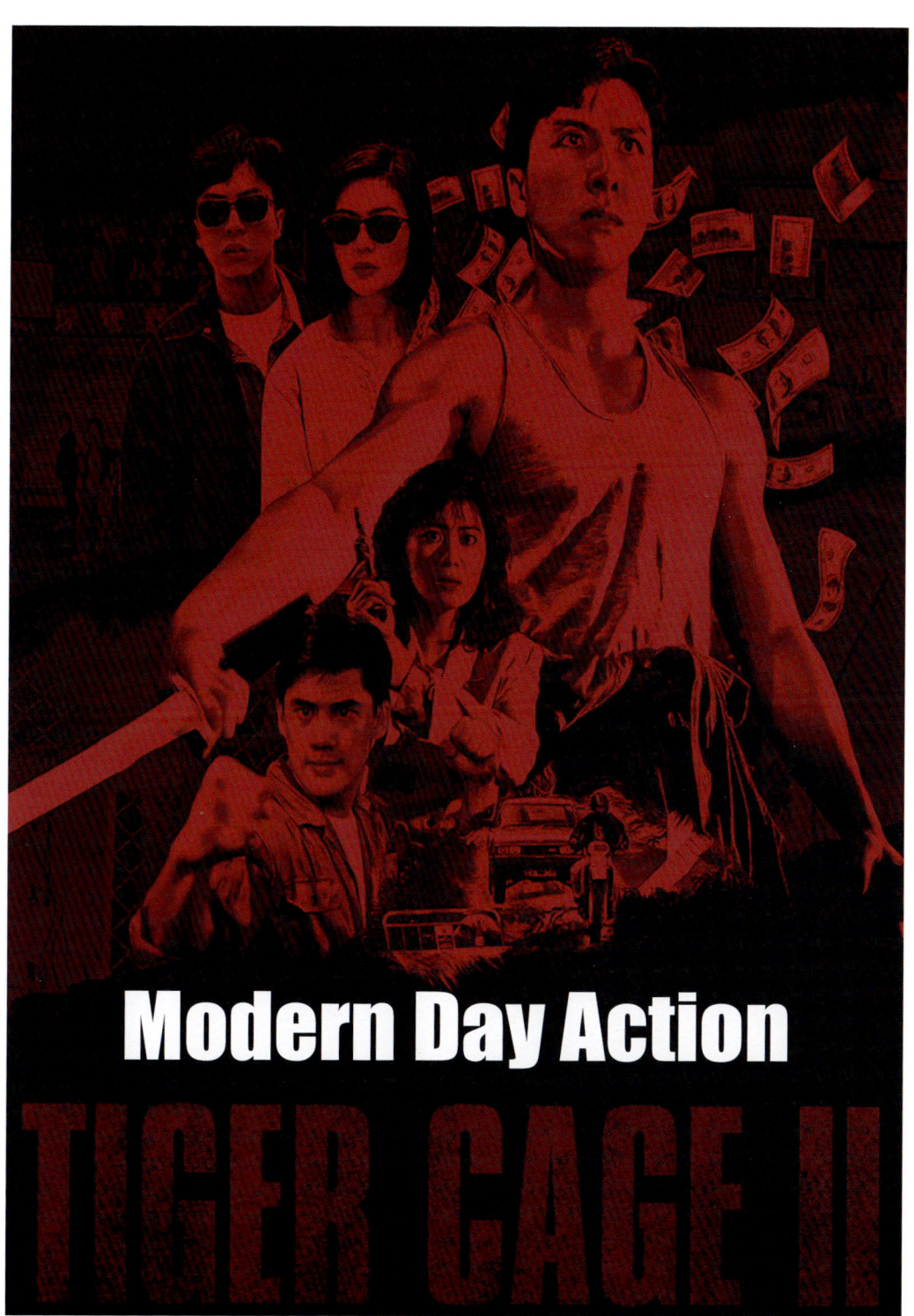

Modern Day Action

TIGER CAGE II

ABOVE THE LAW (1986)

*Starring Yuen Biao, Cynthia Rothrock, Melvin Wong,
Karen Sheperd, Roy Chiao*
Directed by Corey Yuen
Action by Corey Yuen, Meng Hoi
Golden Harvest/Bo Ho Film Company Ltd

Also known as *Righting Wrongs*, this top-notch action-drama casts Yuen Biao alongside fighting femme star Cynthia Rothrock. Biao plays lawyer Jason Chan, who is about to prosecute his first big case. The two on trial are known drug traffickers and Chan is confident that he and his star witness will put them behind bars. But things are thrown into turmoil when the witness and his family are brutally murdered, allowing the two criminals to get away scot-free.

Chan now turns vigilante and kills one of them, but comes under the suspicion of Detective Inspector Sandy Jones (Rothrock). Oblivious to her monitoring, he goes to the second criminal's house to kill him, only to find somebody has beaten him to it. Unfortunately, Chan is the suspect for this murder too, so he now has to convince Sandy of his innocence and discover the identity of the assassin.

This is an excellent showreel for Yuen Biao, who wows and dazzles us with his full repertoire of martial arts skills. Rothrock (when not being doubled by Meng Hoi) delivers an impressive performance, which was responsible for making her the household name she is today.

There are many high points in this movie, including the memorable fight between Rothrock and hired assassin Karen Shepherd. The film has two endings: in the Chinese version Rothrock actually gets killed, but both retain the awe-inspiring stunt in which Biao plummets from an airborne plane into the sea. Highly recommended viewing.

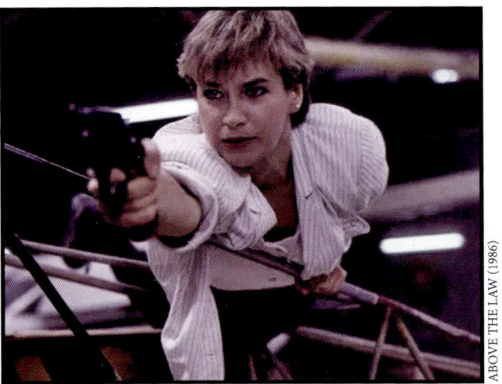

ABOVE THE LAW (1986)

ACES GO PLACES (1982)

Starring Sam Hui, Karl Maka, Sylvia Chang
Directed by Eric Tsang
Produced by Karl Maka, Dean Shek
Cinema City

King Kong (Hui), an amiable jewel thief, steals a collection of priceless diamonds from the mafia and ends up in a whole lot of trouble. In order to help with the investigation, a bungling, bald New York cop (Maka) teams up with outspoken female police officer Nancy Ho to try and get information about the mob from King Kong, while the mob are after King Kong for the diamonds and his life. King Kong joins forces with the police and together they run headfirst into the biggest (and silliest) bust-up in history.

Boasting an all-star line-up of funnymen and funnywomen, and featuring countless crazy stunts, this movie is recommended to viewers searching for laughs: if you don't find them, you've either had a sense-of-humor bypass, or you're dead!

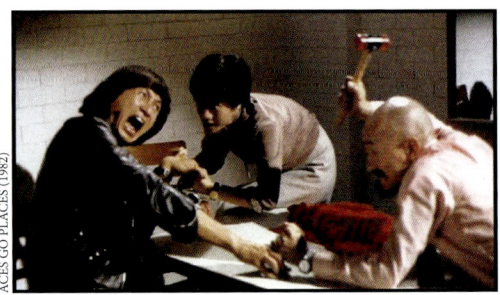

ACES GO PLACES (1982)

ACES GO PLACES 2 (1983)

Starring Sam Hui, Karl Maka, Sylvia Chang
Directed by Eric Tsang
Cinema City

King Kong (Hui), having stolen a cache of diamonds from the mob, is being pursued by men from both sides of the law. Filthy Harry is a tough dude who drives a Rolls Royce with a few optional extras (rocket launchers) and Bozo is the head of a vast criminal empire, intent on getting *his* diamonds back, whatever the cost. What's more, Bozo is not the kind of man to be deterred by clichés!

Also known as *Mad Mission Part 2: Aces Go Places*, this movie delivers plenty of humor and crazy stunts by way of a plot where sense is secondary to humor.

Watch out for a recurring cameo by Tsui Hark and a cool, giant Transformer robot!

ACES GO PLACES 4 (1986)

Starring Sam Hui, Karl Maka, Sally Yeh, Sylvia Chang
Directed by Ringo Lam
Cinema City

More action-comedy mayhem, but this time the mission has a science-fiction flavor to it. When King Kong (Hui) is required to save a genius professor (and, of course, the world), he has no idea what he's letting himself in for. The professor has invented a crystal which has the potential to turn men into superhumans, and it's no surprise that the villains want it for their own gain. Aided, as ever, by his faithful cop buddy, played by Karl Maka, King Kong pursues the crystal-snatchers across the globe, taking time out for car chases, explosions at sea and helicopter crashes.

In a change of style from the previous three films of the series, there are fewer send-ups of film genres and more cameo appearances: veteran of the jade screen Kwan Tak-Hing is present, but more memorable is the late Ronald Lacey as his *Raiders of the Lost Ark* character.

If you expect brainless buffoonery, you'll find this very enjoyable.

THE ADVENTURERS (1995)

Starring Andy Lau, Simon Yam, Rosamund Kwan, Paul Chun, David Chiang, Jacklyn Wu, Paul Chun, Daniel Ng
Directed by Ringo Lam
China Star Entertainment/Win's Entertainment Ltd

This is an action-packed thriller that will keep your attention. The film centers on Wai Lok Yan, played by Andy Lau, who witnessed his parents' murder as a child and was raised by his father's best friend. As an adult, Andy's character becomes a pilot and seeks revenge against Ray Liu (Chun), the double agent who killed his parents.

Ray is a wealthy and powerful man in Vietnam, making it difficult for Wai Lok Yan (now going by the name Mandy) to get close to him. However, after an unsuccessful assassination attempt, our hero decides to gather criminal evidence against Ray for the CIA in America. The protagonist's only link to Ray is his daughter, who he begins to court while pretending to be a criminal boss.

As the plot thickens, Wai/Mandy finds himself in a love triangle with Ray's daughter and his mistress, Mona. He is torn between his loyalty to the CIA and

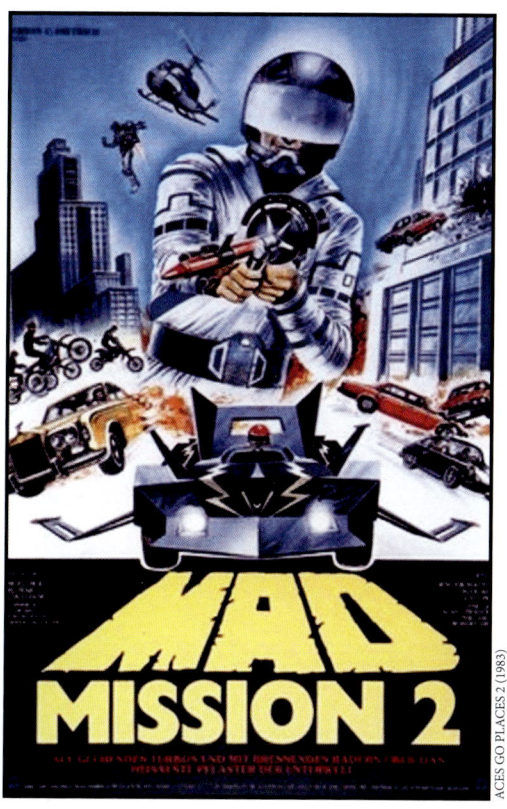

ACES GO PLACES 2 (1983)

ACES GO PLACES 3 (1984)

Starring Sam Hui, Karl Maka, Richard Kiel, Peter Graves, Sylvia Chang
Directed by Tsui Hark
Action by Corey Yuen
Cinema City

Tsui Hark, never a director to do things by halves, begins this Bond spoof with jewel thief King Kong (Hui) dodging a rocket attack, fighting Richard "Jaws" Kiel and "Oddjob" atop the Eiffel Tower lift, parachuting off the tower, diving into the River Seine, and getting swallowed by a shark-shaped submarine with gnashing teeth!

Peter Graves receives a tape which will "self-destruct in five seconds," jewel thieves impersonate the Queen and James Bond, and wacky gadgets include a rocket-powered skateboard and a jet glider that flies through the Hong Kong subway.

The film, also known as *Mad Mission 3: Our Man from Bond Street*, is rather patchy, but wacky ideas like a reversible submarine, which turns inside out to become a liner, do keep it from ever being dull.

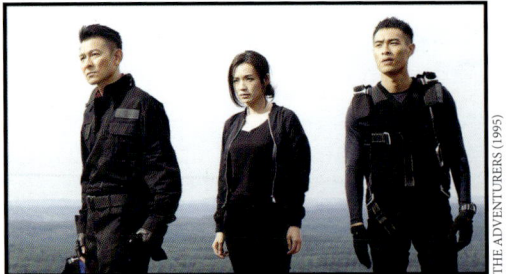

THE ADVENTURERS (1995)

his love for Ray's daughter, making for a thrilling and emotionally charged story.

The cast is led by Andy Lau as Wai Lok Yan/ Mandy, who delivers a very convincing performance as a conflicted and determined protagonist. Paul Chun's menacing presence on screen as Ray Liu is a testament to his acting abilities and Rosamund Kwan also delivers a strong performance as Ray's daughter, adding a fair bit of depth to her character. It was also good to see Shaw Brothers veteran actor David Chiang as Ray Liu's war comrade, who is now working for the CIA.

If you're a fan of action thrillers with complex characters and a compelling story that blends action, romance and drama, then *The Adventurers* is definitely worth a watch.

ALL'S WELL, ENDS WELL '97 (1997)

Starring Stephen Chow, Raymond Wong, Francis Ng, Roy Chiao, Christine Ng, Jacklyn Wu, Christy Chung
Directed by Alfred Cheung
Eastern Bright Motion Picture/Mandarin Films Distribution

Lo Kung, the ultimate man-child, pulls off the performance of a lifetime as he pretends to have a mental illness in order to swindle his hardworking brothers out of their inheritance. While Lo Leung (Raymond Wong) slogs away building his empire of greasy spoon restaurants and Lo Fei (Francis Ng) buries himself in books and financial disasters, Kung sits back and plays the role of the invalid to perfection. But don't be fooled by his act, this guy is about as sane as a sock puppet on acid.

Meanwhile, Leung's love life is about as stable as a one-legged table, and Fei's attempts to win his father's approval are about as successful as trying to make a soufflé in a hurricane. As the chaos unfolds, and the lies pile up, one can't help but wonder if this family has any sanity left to lose. But, as they say, all's fair in love and inheritance fraud.

One of the charms of *All's Well, Ends Well '97* is its central performance by Stephen Chow, who is hilarious and likable as the film's lead character. One of the pitfalls of the film, however, is that it is somewhat formulaic, following a familiar romantic comedy structure that may not be particularly original. Additionally, some of the jokes in the film may not land so well with all audiences, plus the film's portrayal of women is somewhat problematic.

Overall, *All's Well, Ends Well* is a lighthearted and entertaining film that is worth checking out for fans of Hong Kong comedies. While it may not be an innovative work of art, it is a fun and enjoyable film that will leave audiences smiling.

ANGEL (1987)

Starring Hideki Saijo, Yukari Oshima, Moon Lee, Elaine Lui, Hwang Jang-Lee, Alex Fong, David Chiang
Directed, written and produced by Teresa Woo
Action by Leung Siu-Hung
Molesworth Ltd

Yukari Oshima, as the revenge-fixated, sadistic villainess Madam Sue, certainly steals the show in this Hong Kong spy yarn, although this was also a groundbreaking movie for Moon Lee, whose

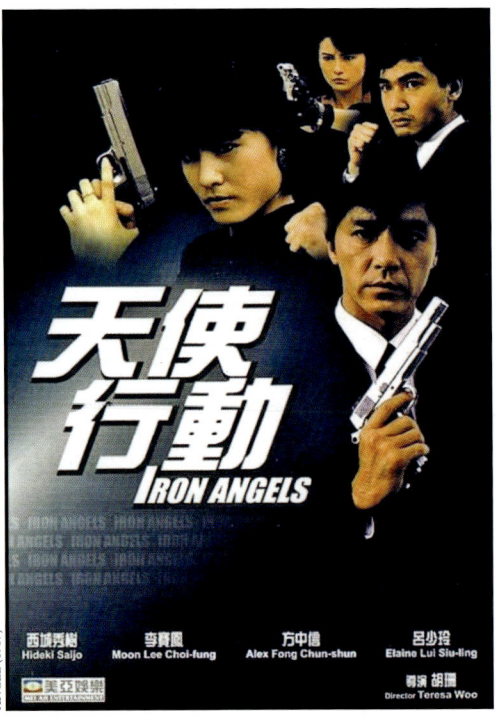

ANGEL (1987)

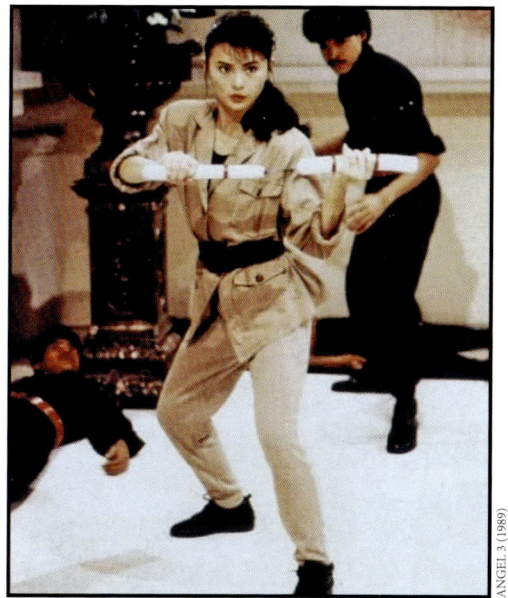

ANGEL 3 (1989)

attempts at screen fighting will not please hardened fans, but the sight of the lovely Moon Lee and Elaine Liu in action more than compensates. Also known as *Iron Angels 2*.

ANGEL 3 (1989)
Starring Moon Lee, Alex Fong, Ralph Chen, Kharina Isa
Directed by Stanley Tong, Teresa Woo
Molesworth Ltd

Also known as *Return of the Iron Angels* and *Iron Angels 3*, this third outing for Moon Lee and friends is slightly disappointing, without Elaine Lui now, though the film is at least heavy with fighting femme action.

The movie features several moments of Bond-ish gimmickry and there's a well-executed nunchaku fight scene, which allows Moon Lee to let her singing rods of iron dispose of countless assailants in several minutes of high-voltage carnage.

A fun film that breaks no new ground, but is appealing because of its main lead.

battling babe image spawned a flurry of sequels. It also showcased the beautiful Elaine Lui.

Aka *Iron Angels*, this has high-octane shoot-outs and well-choreographed fight scenes, especially the three-way end fight, proving to viewers everywhere that gals with guns are always a force to be reckoned with.

ANGEL 2 (1988)
Starring Moon Lee, Alex Fong, Elaine Liu
Directed, written and produced by Teresa Woo
Molesworth Ltd

The angelic trio take a break from their crime-busting exploits to go on holiday in Malaysia. No sooner have they arrived than Alex is reunited with Peter, an old high-school buddy, who seems to be doing very well for himself. Peter invites them to stay with him as his guests but it's just their bad luck that, since his school days, Peter has become a revolutionary who idolizes Hitler and is intent on ruling the world! As Elaine (Liu) falls for the charismatic psycho, Billy (Fong) and Mona (Lee) wise up to his schemes, and it's down to them and a local transgender character they have befriended to destroy Peter and his loyal army of skilled combatants.

The expertly handled climax, which incorporates all the elements of jungle warfare (guns, explosions, helicopters, more explosions) with top-class martial arts choreography, makes up for the fact that the storyline itself is not too hot. Alex Fong's lousy

ARMOUR OF GOD (1986)
Starring Jackie Chan, Alan Tam, Rosamund Kwan, Lola Forner
Directed by Jackie Chan and Eric Tsang (uncredited)
Golden Way Films Ltd/Golden Harvest

Jackie Chan plays the Asian Hawk, a bounty hunter who must save his old flame Lorelei (Kwan) from a cult. In exchange for her freedom, they want the Armour of God, a collection of weaponry dating back to the dark ages. The wealthy collector who owns the pieces is content to lend them, on condition that his beautiful but spoilt daughter (Forner) travels with the Hawk.

The Asian Hawk's quest, aided by Lorelei's fiancé Alan (Tam), takes him across Europe and involves car chases, hot air balloons and some very mean Amazon women, not to mention the cult of power-hungry maniacs.

It is no surprise that, internationally, this is one of Jackie Chan's highest-grossing films. It has all the ingredients of a classic action-adventure comedy, and Chan's stunt work is incredible. Although this picture has the feel of an Indiana Jones feature, you know that Harrison Ford wouldn't dream of performing the outrageous stunts Jackie Chan does! Making this film nearly cost Jackie his life—and the accident footage is included in the end credits! Ouch!

ARMOUR OF GOD II: OPERATION CONDOR (1991)

Starring Jackie Chan, Do Do Cheng, Ikeda Shoko, Eva Coba, Aldo Sambrell
Directed by Jackie Chan
Golden Way Films Ltd/Golden Harvest

A fast-paced, hard action comedy which shamelessly raids *Raiders of the Lost Ark* and recalls *Total Recall*.

Jackie plays an international adventurer hired by the United Nations to retrieve some stolen gold that was buried by the Nazis in a secret base in the African desert. He is hampered by three female partners, a pair of joke Arab characters and a gang of mercenaries led by the wheelchair-bound Adolf.

The action ranges from a frenetic car and bike chase, through a mix of bedroom farce and roughhouse fighting at an inn, to the final showdown in a giant wind tunnel at the Nazi base, where our hero battles Adolf's guards, played by a bunch of Western stunt-fighters, including Vincent Lyn, who stands out as scar-faced bad guy Mark.

The plot is uninspired, but the action is excellent, as it should be on a film that went way over budget and over schedule. Also known as *Operation Condor: Armour of God II* and *Operation Eagle*.

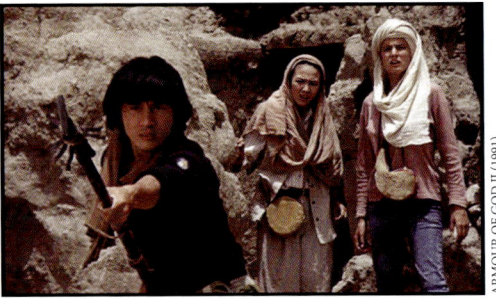

ARMOUR OF GOD II (1991)

ASIAPOL (1966)

Starring Jimmy Wang Yu, Fang Yin, Wang Hsia, Nintani Hideaki, Asaoka Ruriko
Directed by Matsuo Akinori
Shaw Brothers/Nikkatsu

Following the international success of *You Only Live Twice*, Shaw Brothers teamed-up with a Japanese studio to produce a highly entertaining James Bond cash-in picture, with Wang Yu playing Yang, a very 007-style role. His covert mission is to bust up an international smuggling ring, aided, of course, by two Asian beauties.

Wang Hsia plays a mystery gunman on Yang's tail, while Wang Yu puts in a flamboyant performance in this enjoyable but dated sixties spy romp.

It's a must-see for any Bond/UNCLE fans who think they've seen it all. Aka *Asiapol Secret Service*.

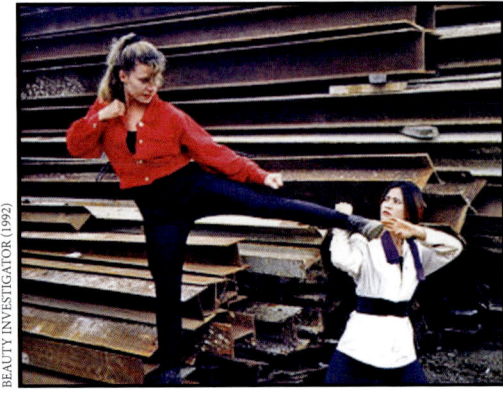

BEAUTY INVESTIGATOR (1992)

BEAUTY INVESTIGATOR (1992)

Starring Yukari Oshima, Moon Lee, Sophia Crawford, Melvin Wong, Gam Chi-Gei
Directed by Lee Tso-Nam
New Treasurer Films Company

There's a sex killer on the loose, and two beautiful policewomen, Moon Lee and Yukari Oshima, go undercover as club hostesses. They overhear the manager speaking to the club owner, who is the head of an arms smuggling syndicate, who wants the manager to hire an assassin to murder three of his associates. The manager obliges and a third femme fatale lights up the screen: Tanaka, a lethal lady assassin, who poses a new problem for our "beauty investigators."

The popular fusion of Moon Lee and Yukari Oshima always grabs the attention of audiences, and their figure-hugging catsuits and fist-to-fingernail fights definitely assure them reasonable box office success!

From the director of *Kung-Fu Wonderchild*, *The Hot, The Cool and the Vicious* and *Eagle's Claw*.

BEYOND HYPOTHERMIA (1996)

Starring Jacklyn Wu Chien-Lien, Lau Ching-Wan, Han Jae-Suk, Shirley Wong, Han Sang-Woo
Directed by Patrick Leung
Milky Way Image Company/Sanqueen Limited

This is an outstanding action film focusing on a nameless female killer, played by Jacklyn Wu. Rescued and raised by Mei (Wong), the wife of a former assassin, we learn that our hitwoman heroine has a body temperature that's five degrees below normal, which may explain her ice-cold attitude when performing hits on crime bosses. The story takes a turn when she forms a friendship with the owner of a local noodle bar, played by Lau Ching-Wan. During one of her visits, she reveals her vulnerable side to him. However, their newfound feelings are cut short when a Korean hit man, played by Kim Ki-Ju, shows up, seeking revenge.

This movie may have gone under the radar for many people, but it is a slick and well-made action film. While we never really understand why Jacklyn Wu's character has such a low body temperature, it gives the filmmakers an excuse to use icy cold blue tints during her cold-blooded executions of targets.

The action in this movie is elevated, with some excellent shoot-out scenes, from the opening credits to the high-octane finale. This Hong Kong/Korean collaboration clearly shows the influence of John Woo, which is very probably down to the fact that Patrick Leung was second unit director on *Hard Boiled* and first assistant director on *The Killer*.

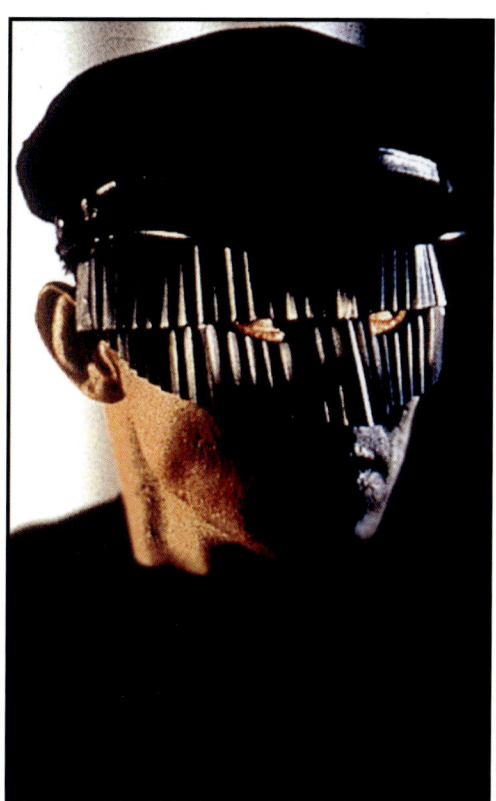

BLACK MASK (1996)

BLACK MASK (1996)
Starring Jet Li, Lau Ching-Wan, Karen Mok
Directed by Daniel Lee
Film Workshop/Distant Horizon/Win's Entertainment Ltd

Jet Li plays mild-mannered Tsui Chik, a librarian intent on living a normal life. But he is actually a "701," an artificially enhanced super-soldier, who helped others of his kind escape a government attempt to terminate them. Now he is forced back into action, as the vigilante-hero Black Mask, when a ruthless gang of 701s starts wiping out drug lords and causing much mayhem.

Black Mask is more than happy to use automatic weaponry when he takes on his opponents, so this violent Hong Kong superhero movie features lots of high-body-count action scenes and doesn't shy away from nastier details, such as a bomb being surgically inserted into a drug lord's body, an antagonist fighting on after losing part of his arm, and computer CDs thrown like shuriken.

Martial arts director Yuen Woo-Ping delivers some gravity-defying, acrobatic choreography, Lau Ching-Wan provides solid support as a tough Hong Kong detective who at first hunts down Black Mask and then aids him, Karen Mok is geekily appealing as library colleague Tracy, and Jet Li is on top physical form as the titular hero.

Though the domino mask Jet Li wears looks like two pieces of corrugated cardboard stuck together (maybe this is intended to look homemade), it is still pretty cool seeing Jet kicking ass dressed in black chauffer's gear, just like Kato from *The Green Hornet* television series.

The film is very much a Tsui Hark production, showcasing some sizeable showdowns that must have taken time to plan, so it's a shame that the script, cowritten by Hark, doesn't seem to have been given the same amount of care and attention. The movie does end satisfyingly, though, as it shifts from the earlier bigger-scale confrontations and treats us instead to some hand-to-hand face-offs, including a Wu Shu-style fight between Black Mask and the main villain, who both use sparking, live electrical cables to lash out at each other in the big, dank basement beneath the police HQ.

A dubbed version of *Black Mask* (Jet Li's character is renamed Simon), with a brand-new hip-hop soundtrack, was released in America in 1999 to cash in on Jet Li's increased fame due to his role in 1998's *Lethal Weapon 4*.

THE BLACKSHEEP AFFAIR (1998)

Staring Vincent Zhao, Shu Qi, Ken Wong Hap-Hei,
Andrew Lin Hoi, Joe Cheung Tung-Cho,
Kenneth Tsang Kong, Lau Shun, Xiong Xin-Xin
Directed by Lam Wai-Lun
China Star Entertainment/Win's Entertainment Ltd

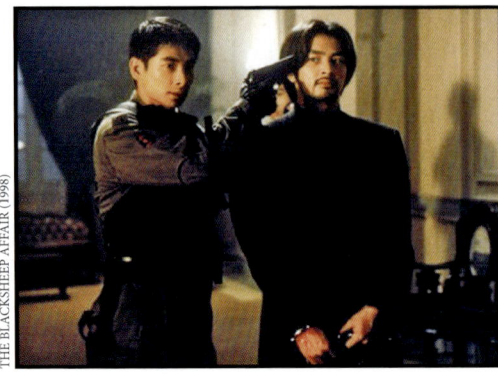

Disobeying orders on a mission, Yim Dong (Zhao), a skilled member of an elite Special Forces squad, is sent to Lithuania, where he reunites with his ex-girlfriend, Chan Pun (Qi), who has fled the country in fear of violence. Witnessing the brutal killings of Interpol agents at the airport, Yim Dong is tasked with uncovering the identity of those behind the attack. Keizo Mishima (Lin), a terrorist and crazed cult leader who has launched a bombing campaign, becomes the target for Yim Dong to track down. In a bid to stop him, Mishima kidnaps Chan Pun, but this only intensifies Yim Dong's need to bring his adversary down.

After replacing Jet Li in *Once Upon a Time in China IV*, Vincent Zhou was touted as the next big star. He certainly possesses the necessary on-screen fighting skills and looks, but, despite this, he never quite managed to leave his mark. Andrew Lin delivers an excellent performance as the crazed Keizo Mishima, making for an exceptional villain who can both act and display some impressive on-screen fighting. As expected with Ching Sui-Tung on fight action, you get some brutal violence, plus some great set piece fights, littered with his signature wirework. The final scrap between Vincent and Andrew is explosive, making up for the sometimes quite flawed script. It's also great to see some UK talent, in the form of Jude Poyer and Mike Lambert, among the fight scenes.

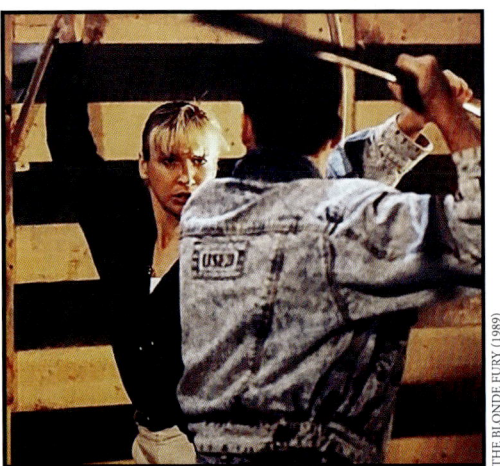

THE BLONDE FURY (1989)

Starring Cynthia Rothrock, Meng Hoi, Elizabeth Lee,
Chin Siu-Ho, Roy Chiao, Billy Chow, Jeff Falcon
Directed by Meng Hoi
Action by Meng Hoi
Golden Harvest/Bo Ho Film Company Ltd

Rothrock, at the height of her Hong Kong action career, plays Cindy, an intrepid crime reporter, who takes on some ruthless criminals from the world of high finance. When top banker Wong is accused of fraud, Cindy senses that the chief crown prosecutor (Chiao) has been nobbled by villains. She decides to follow the story, aided by the prosecutor's daughter Judy (Lee), and it isn't long before they find themselves the target of repeated murder attempts as they try to uncover the truth.

Also known as *Lady Reporter*, the movie has a slightly incoherent plotline, possibly due to the fact that filming stopped halfway through and wasn't resumed for some time (watch out for Rothrock's new hairstyle!), but this doesn't detract from some excellent fight sequences, including a great performance from Billy Chow as the kickboxer with an attitude. There's also a classic end fight scene where Cindy comes fist-to-fingernail once again with Jeff Falcon, in an ingenious battle taking place on a spiderweb of rope.

THE BODYGUARD FROM BEIJING (1994)

Starring Jet Li, Christy Chung, Kent Cheng, Ngai Sing
Directed by Corey Yuen
Golden Harvest/Eastern Productions

This martial arts movie serves as a Hong Kong version of the hit Hollywood film *The Bodyguard* (1992), with Jet Li playing Allan, a highly trained elite security expert in the Chinese army, who is hired by James, a wealthy Hong Kong businessman, to protect his girlfriend Michelle, who is the only surviving witness to a murder.

Initially, Allan's obsessive attention to detail irritates Michelle and the two police officers assigned to protect her. However, it doesn't take long before Allan's professionalism becomes essential in keeping Michelle alive and, as the film progresses, Michelle begins to develop feelings for him. But their romance is quickly sidelined by the arrival of the deadly Killer Wong (Sing), who seeks vengeance against Allan.

Jet Li treats us to a fantastic performance as the skilled and stoic bodyguard Allan, while Christy Chung delivers a convincing performance as Michelle, the woman he is tasked with protecting. The chemistry between the two actors is palpable, adding a layer of emotional depth that is often missing from similar films.

The fight scenes are well choreographed, with Jet Li displaying his impressive martial arts skills. The final battle between Allan and Killer Wong is a standout, showcasing the impressive abilities of both actors, which definitely leaves audiences on the edge of their seats.

A BOOK OF HEROES (1986)

Starring Hu Kua, Yang Hui San, Yasuaki Kurata,
Yukari Oshima, David Tao
Directed by Chu Yen-Ping
Produced by Raymond Wong
Action by Lam Man-Cheung
Cinema City Enterprises/Golden Princess Amusement
Company

Two merry schemers (or cardsharps as they like to be called) learn the whereabouts of an enormous bullion stash. They are joined by two fumbling cops who want to finger Japanese menace Yamashita (Kurata), who also has his greedy little heart set on getting the gold.

This Taiwanese flick's corny gags, mad stunts and great femme-fights make for good, fun viewing!

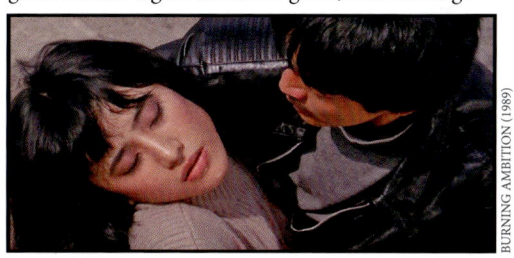

BURNING AMBITION (1989)

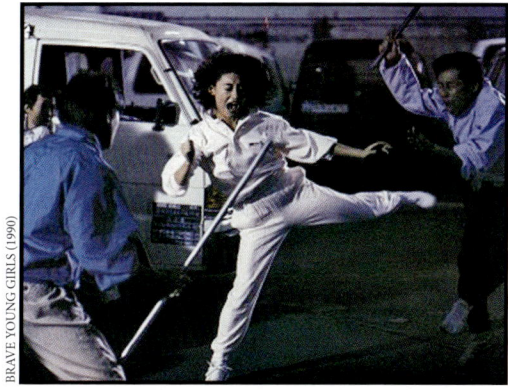

BRAVE YOUNG GIRLS (1990)

BRAVE YOUNG GIRLS (1990)

Starring Yukari Oshima, Kara Wai, Margaret A. Li,
Leung Kar-Yan, Shing Fui-On
Directed by Luk Kam-Bo
Action by Ching Tao, Jimmy Ha
Kam Bo Motion Picture Company

The brave young girls are a heroic trio consisting of a prostitute, a robber, and a Japanese detective. They are on a mission to eliminate a gang of international flesh peddlers. After many confrontations, the bad guys are bashed beyond belief, and the police decide to make a stand for men's rights and arrest the furious femmes.

This is a silly plot made watchable by the likes of Yukari Oshima and Kara Wai. There is the usual smattering of high-kicking fights and gunfire, plus a villainous performance from Leung Kar-Yan, but this is far from the most memorable fighting femme fatale flick.

BURNING AMBITION (1989)

Starring Frankie Chan, Yukari Oshima, Ko Chun-Hsiung,
Eddy Ko, Jeff Falcon, Simon Yam, Dan Mintz,
John Ladalski
Directed by Frankie Chan
Long Shong Pictures/Lusty Electric Industries

Vengeance fuels a bleak tale of gang warfare, as an unscrupulous uncle callously claws his way to the top of the organization. Nobody is safe, not even his own kin. A birthday celebration becomes a bloodbath, a heavily pregnant woman is brutally beaten, feisty babes battle triad terminators on broken glass, and there's a hot pursuit down a fairground's water chute.

The high-velocity hi-jinks in the underground parking garage sequence are awesome enough to have you rewatching to see how they managed the stunts! Director Chan stirs plenty of frenetic punch-ups into a satisfying broth, even allowing a sprinkling of humor before the dark and deadly final course.

BURY ME HIGH (1991)
Starring Moon Lee, Sibelle Hu, Yuen Wah,
Chin Kar-Lok, Tsui Siu-Ming, Corey Yuen
Directed, cowritten and produced by Tsui Siu-Ming
Action by Tsui Sui-Ming
Bo Ho Film Company Ltd/New Dawn Pictures/Tsui Sui Ming Productions

This was billed as the first feng shui (Chinese geomancy) action movie. Some Chinese people believe that the choice of a burial site may influence the fate of younger generations for good or evil.

Two explorers, Wei and Ruan, arrive at a group of mountains with awesome feng shui. There are three auspicious caves: one will bring riches, one wisdom and the other one power . . . to the descendants of those who are buried there. Ruan becomes obsessed with the notion of eternal power and when Wei foresees disaster, Ruan orders his death. Wei escapes with the aid of a boatman, who is mortally injured, so Wei buries the boatman in the cave of wealth, then

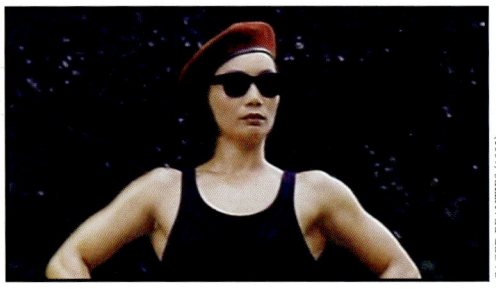

CAGED BEAUTIES (1992)

inters his own father in the cave of wisdom. Many years later, the descendants have all been influenced by the feng shui. Wisely (Kar-Lok), son of Wei, is a computer whiz kid with an outrageously high IQ. He becomes involved with Anna Wong (Lee), daughter of the dead boatman, who has become a computer tycoon. They go on a quest to find out more about the feng shui and witness a coup led by a power-hungry General (played by lean, mean Yuen Wah). From then on it is high-powered thrills all the way, as they join with the locals to destroy the source of the General's power: his father's burial site.

The spectacular fight scenes score high on the adrenaline-ometer and the electrifying cinematography makes this a project to savor on a grand scale.

CAGED BEAUTIES (1992)
Starring Derek Wan, Jeff Falcon, Chan Sing,
Choi Jeong-Il, Hon Kwok-Choi, Chui Ging-Sin
Directed by Yuen Ching Li
Golden Flare Films Company/First Films

The action starts in Thailand, with Derek Wan marrying his sweetheart under the watchful eye of his good friend Jeff. But the celebrations don't last long as communist guerrilla Choi (Kwok-Choi) forces Derek and his wife to go to a "training camp" run by an evil commander (Sing). Derek is repeatedly tortured, while all the female "recruits" suffer the wet T-shirt torture. Jeff Falcon leaps into action and wipes out Choi's cronies, before a bone-crunching acrobatic bout with Choi, which results in his capture. While the commander tries to get intimate with the inmates, Jeff stages an explosive escape, with the vindictive Choi in hot pursuit.

This is a well-shot action movie, although the exploitation scenes mix uneasily with the fight fare. Jeff Falcon uses some awesome Wu Shu moves and Kwok-Choi is an effectively menacing villain with some brutal footwork.

CHEETAH ON FIRE (1992)
Starring Donnie Yen, Carrie Ng, Michael Woods,
John Salvitti, Cheung Man, Lan Hui Kwong, Ken Lo,
Gordon Liu, Shing Fui-On
Directed by Thomas Yip
Action by Chui Fat
Cheung Yau Production Co

The Royal Hong Kong Police is assigned to help three CIA agents extradite a suspected criminal to the US for trial, but this is made much more difficult when the boss of the Gunmen of the Golden Triangle takes an interest in a computer chip from a top secret military weapon, which has been stolen by the criminal. Now the chase is on, in a roller-coaster ride of action with the fighting stars of *Tiger Cage 2* (1990)!

Donnie Yen was one of the brightest talents of the martial arts screen when he demonstrated his ability in *In the Line of Duty 4* and *Tiger Cage 2* and, although he is reunited with old favorites Michael Woods and John Salvitti, *Cheetah on Fire* is regarded as a bit of a lackluster attempt to rekindle the magic. There are several memorable moments, however, including excellent action from Ken Lo, the superb kicker who shot to fame with his end fight scene against Jackie Chan in *Drunken Master 2*.

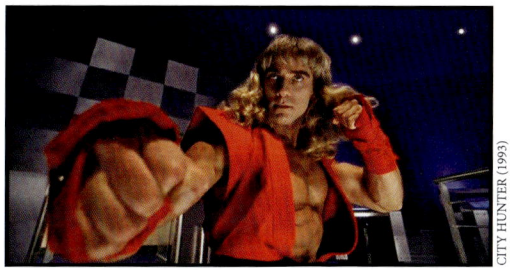

CITY HUNTER (1993)

CITY COPS (1989)
Starring Cynthia Rothrock, Mui Kiu-Wai,
Tong Chun-Yip, Michiko Nishiwaki
Directed by Liu Chia-Yung
Movie Impact Limited

Also known as *Beyond the Law*, this is a cop actioner
with heavy leanings toward the more humorous
aspects of the story. Fighting femme Rothrock is
allowed for once to look a little sexy in a sweat-
soaked vest as she massages a male colleague!

Generous helpings of kung fu fight action, some of
it pretty breathtaking, include a feisty female versus
female scuffle. Brit martial artist Mark Houghton
does his stuff as a bad dude and loads of white-
overall-wearing minions receive bright red blood
splashes during a machine gun battle in a warehouse.

CITY HUNTER (1993)
Starring Jackie Chan, Goto Kumiko, Joey Wong,
Chingamy Yau, Leon Lai, Richard Norton, Gary Daniels,
Ken Lo, Mike Abbott, Louis Roth
Directed and written by Wong Jing
Produced by Chua Lam
Golden Harvest/Golden Way Films Ltd

Jackie Chan plays the part of Ryo Saeba, loosely based
on the girl-chasing detective character from the
popular manga *City Hunter*. With his assistant Kaori
(Wong), he has to track down runaway Japanese
heiress Shizuko Imamura (Kumiko) aboard a luxury
ocean liner. Also on board are beautiful private
detective Saeko (Yau), some crazy entertainers and
a gang of ruthless international terrorists.

Although most of the elements from the original
City Hunter manga are missing, the result is a
hilarious movie, packed full of Jackie's trademark
stunt sequences and fight routines. In a cinema-set
fight sequence, Jackie is given guidance by the on-
screen Bruce Lee, while the excellent *Street Fighter 2*
set piece is definitely the most memorable moment
in the movie, with live action expertly emulating

the video game. And the *City Hunter* theme tune
is unforgettable!

CRIME STORY (1993)
Starring Jackie Chan, Kent Cheng, Christine Ng,
Law Kar-Ying, Chung Fat
Directed by Kirk Wong
Action by Jackie Chan
Golden Harvest

This is based on a real-life event in Hong
Kong, concerning the kidnapping of a Chinese
businessman. Jackie Chan, playing a policeman who
can't deal with killing bad guys, is assigned the job
of tracking down the kidnappers, unaware that his
partner is also a villain.

While it's not Jackie's greatest film, there are some
fine moments, including a cracking car chase, with
the kidnappers trying to revive the businessman's

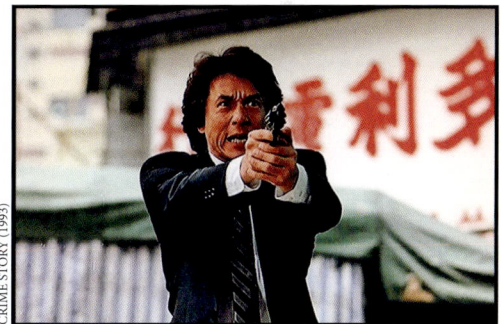

CRIME STORY (1993)

wife after she has a heart attack, using a couple of
jump leads and a revved-up engine (don't try this
at home, kids!) There's also a brutal rooftop brawl
and, of course, the final fight scene, which starts in a
marketplace and ends up in a building's basement.

There's a big gas leak explosion, and we see Jackie
running out of a burning building with a child in his
arms—a great stunt that has got to be seen.

CRYSTAL HUNT (1991)
Starring Donnie Yen, Sibelle Hu, Carrie Ng, Ken Lo,
Hsu Hsia, Fujimi Nadeki
Directed by Hsu Hsia
Cheung Yau Production Co/Golden Sun Film Company

A retired godfather's daughter, Lisa (Ng), hires a
professor (Hsia) to assist in the search for a special
crystal in a forbidden land. Unfortunately, a gang
discover Lisa's plans and kidnap the professor.
With the help of a vengeful lady cop (Hu), a new

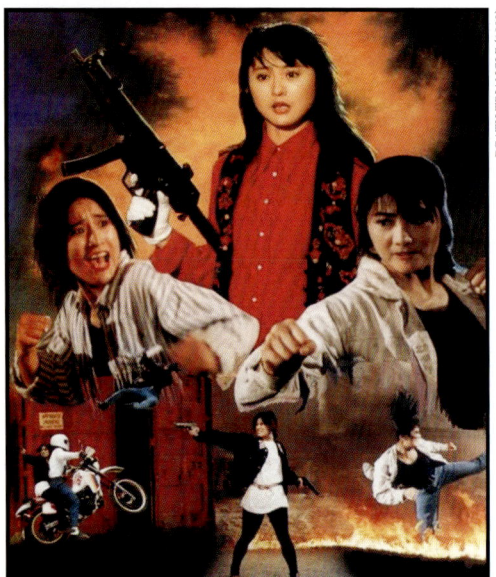

DEATH TRIANGLE (1993)

performance as Carlin in *Scum* (1979) by claiming he is the "daddy," as he perches halfway up the prison wall. But Alexander Lo Rei steals the show, proving that genuine martial arts talent will always shine through, even in a low-budget production like this.

DEATH TRIANGLE (1993)
Starring Yukari Oshima, Moon Lee, Cynthia Khan, Lawrence Ng, Eric Tsang
Directed by Albert Lai
New Treasurer Films Company/Golden Sun Films

Golden Sun Films will never be up for any awards when it comes to story or quality action, but they sure know what ingredients to put into a film to make it sell. They specialize in fighting-femme flicks, and here they go one step further by casting their own heroic trio: the Osh, Moon Lee and Cynthia Khan.

Cops Li (Lee) and Yang (Khan) are lifelong friends who are in love with the same man, Wilson, but only one of them is aware of it. Things come to a head and, in a fit of insane jealousy, Li fights with Yang and knocks her unconscious. She then kills Wilson and frames Yang for the murder. Yang, desperate to prove her innocence, calls on her loyal criminal friend Coco (Oshima) to help her.

Plot holes and poor pacing hinder this film, plus the fight scenes are in fairly short supply, though it all picks up at the very end. Also known as *Yes Madam '92: A Serious Shock* and *A Serious Shock! Yes Madam!*

expedition sets out to reach the prize before it falls into enemy hands.

Crystal Hunt is a well-cast film, but its low budget does not allow it to live up to expectations. As always with Donnie Yen, though, the martial arts action is of reasonable quality, but the magic, which is often worked into his films with Yuen Woo-Ping, is sadly lacking. Having said that, followers of fighting femme flicks will get a kick out of this action movie.

THE DADAH CONNECTION (1990)
Starring Jacinta Lee, Steve Tartalia, J.D. Khalid, Alexander Lo Rei
Directed by Toby Russell
Sunny Film Corporation

Toby Russell's directorial debut is inspired by the true-life story of his longtime friend Nick Masters, who left England for the East with him back in the eighties.

Ex-DEA agent Nick (Tartalia) is sent to track down a drug kingpin, but is mistakenly apprehended by a woman police officer (Lee), who doesn't realize that he is an undercover agent in hot pursuit of Alex (top-notch martial artist Alexander Lo Rei). Alex has been murdering underworld heads to gain total control of the Golden Triangle drug flow from Malaysia to the US, and it is left to Nick and his new cop partner to bring him to justice.

The real Nick Masters puts in a good cameo in a prison scene, paying homage to Ray Winstone's

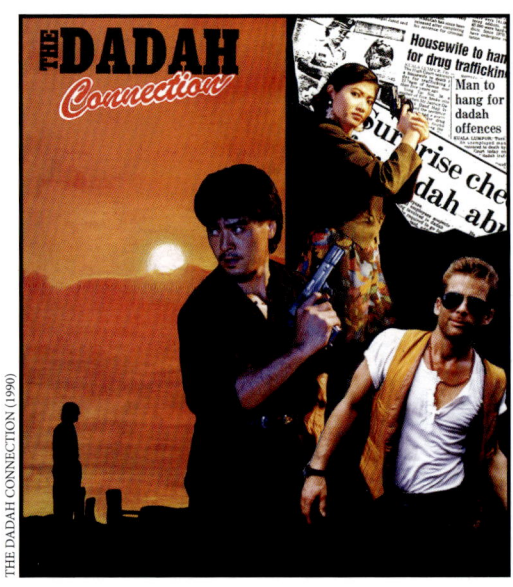

THE DADAH CONNECTION (1990)

DON'T PLAY WITH FIRE (1980)

Starring Lo Lieh, Lin Chen-Chi, Albert Au
Directed by Tsui Hark
Fotocine Film Productions Ltd

Three bespectacled students, one from a rich family, kill somebody in a hit-and-run accident, which is witnessed by Pearl—a would-be urban terrorist. She blackmails them into meeting up with her and finally they all become embroiled in an affair concerning banknote fraudsters and triad gangs.

This early film from Hark, also known as *Dangerous Encounters of the First Kind*, is scattered with violent imagery from beginning to end. During the opening credits, a mouse has a pin forced into its' brain (for real) by Pearl, who places it into a cage full of similar brain-damaged rodents.

Later, when a cat attempts to get at the mice, Pearl grabs the feline and hurls it onto a barbwire-festooned fence, transfixing it on the railings, which mirrors an unexpected death toward the end of the movie. Even a briefly seen clip from a cartoon on a television is a violent one: Sylvester the Cat exploding!

The whole story is basically a series of angry confrontations, including a scene where Pearl steals an American fraudster's stash of banknotes, bites his arm and is helped by the three blackmailed youths, who hurl rocks at the car. But only moments before, Pearl had been attempting to burn one of the students to death for leaving her on her own during a bus hijacking.

It's dog-eat-dog in this black slice of urban life from Hark: Pearl steals checks from the Americans, has the money taken from her by a local scumbag triad boss who, in turn, has his lips sewn together with wire by the Americans. Apart from the policeman brother of Pearl, no one in this movie is an unblemished character: the three students are guilty of a hit-and-run death, plus various other acts of violence, Pearl is a bitter, mixed-up activist, who bombs and hijacks for twisted reasons known only to herself, and the US fraudsters are a bunch of ex–Special Service Nam vets willing to shoot up anyone in their way.

The violent climax occurs in a large cemetery, where the Americans, armed to the teeth with machine guns, confront Pearl's brother and the three students, one of whom has poisoned himself with Dettol! As one would expect from a film that dwells on such bleak subjects, the finale shows the now almost insane

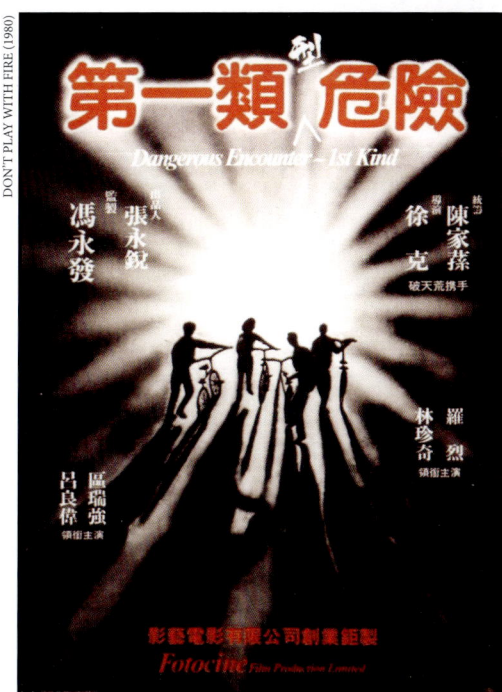

DON'T PLAY WITH FIRE (1980)

survivor firing madly into the graveyard, followed by black-and-white photos of real urban violence in Hong Kong. Angry, mean cinema at its best.

DR. WAI IN THE SCRIPTURE WITH NO WORDS (1996)

Starring Jet Li, Rosamund Kwan, Charlie Yeung, Takeshi Kaneshiro, Collin Cho
Directed by Ching Siu-Tung
Win's Entertainment Ltd/Eastern Productions

Hold onto your hats and get ready for a wild ride with Jet Li! In this action-packed adventure, a kung fu–skilled archaeologist goes on a quest for ancient Chinese artifacts, accompanied by his bumbling sidekick.

From the get-go, the movie hits the ground running with a thrilling mechanical bull ride that sets the tone for the rest of the film. As the dynamic duo infiltrate a posh party in Shanghai, battle ninjas and even fall in love with two unlikely characters, the laughs keep on coming.

The humor is good-natured and will keep you chuckling throughout the film, which has special effects that may be dated now, but that only adds to the hilarity, making for some truly entertaining moments. And let's not forget all the Wu Shu–centric

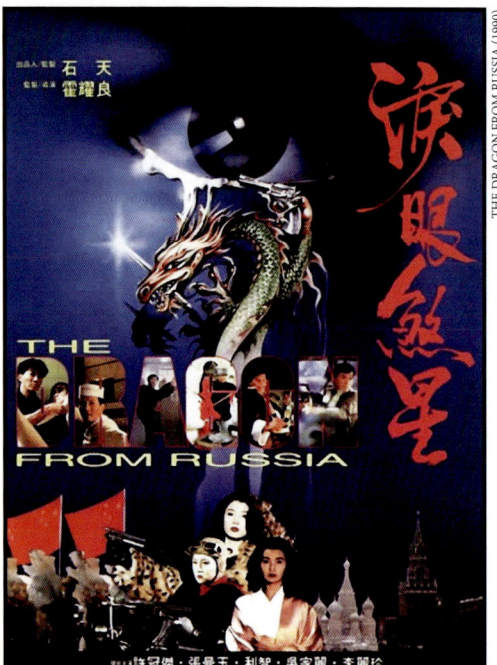

THE DRAGON FROM RUSSIA (1990)

DRAGON FIGHT (1989)

Starring Jet Li, Dick Wei, Stephen Chow, Nina Li Chi,
George Chung
Directed by Billy Tang
Produced by Fong Ping
Lo Wei Motion Picture Company/Grand March Movie
Production Company Ltd

Lee (Jet Li) and Wong (Dick Wei) are touring in New York as part of a troupe demonstrating their Wu Shu martial arts. Wong takes a liking to American culture and decides to abscond from the troupe to become one of America's many illegal immigrants, so Lee tries to reason with him, but misses his own flight home. Unperturbed, Lee is determined to pursue Wong and show him the error of his ways. Wong finds himself working his way through the ranks of the local triads, while Lee befriends Yau (Stephen Chow), who offers him shelter and casual work at his father's shop. Unfortunately, Yau's gambling debts mean that Wong and Lee's paths are destined to cross again in a final conflict of martial arts fury.

Shot entirely in America, this was Jet Li's first attempt to cross over into the modern day genre. It also brought attention to Stephen Chow, who had yet to define his comic persona. After a fast-paced opening, the film drops several gears, lifted again when a killer (played by George Chung) has an impressive backstreet showdown with Lee. It then returns to a fairly slow pace, until the finale, which allows Jet Li, Dick Wei, and a host of extras to light up the screen with some explosive fighting.

fight scenes! They are a real treat to watch and will have you on the edge of your seat.

Jet Li brings a lot of fun and energy to the Dr. Wai character, who comes complete with an arsenal of pen-gadgets, while Keneshiro brings the laughs with his antics.

While the story may not be the strongest point of the movie, this production is a lighthearted nod to pulp heroes like Indiana Jones and is a fun way to spend an afternoon. So, grab some popcorn, settle in, and get ready for a kung fu-filled adventure that'll have you smiling from start to finish!

Note: the original Hong Kong release version features Jet Li as an author who plows all of his frustrations into writing a fictional work, in which he sees himself as a cool adventurer.

THE DRAGON FROM RUSSIA (1990)

Starring Sam Hui, Maggie Cheung, Nina Li Chi,
Carrie Ng, Yuen Tak
Directed by Clarence Ford
Action by Yuen Tak
Cinema City/Golden Princess

This intensely paced, nonstop action-fest, loosely based on the Japanese manga *Crying Freeman*, centers on the relationship between Lung (Hui) and May (Cheung), two Manchurians who have grown up together in Russia. After a fight with a strange masked man on a train to Leningrad, Lung loses his memory and is abducted by a group of assassins known as the 800 Dragons. He is kept captive at their headquarters and trained in martial arts by a disfigured character called the Master of Death (Tak). Lung's back is tattooed, he dons a white mask, and he becomes a super-assassin known as

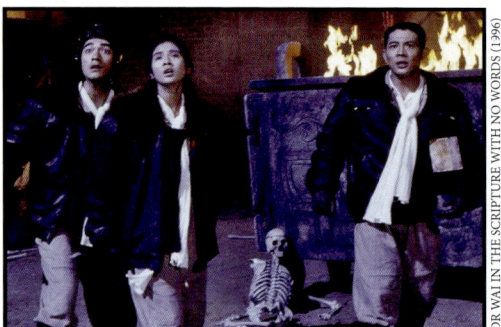

DR WAI IN THE SCRIPTURE WITH NO WORDS (1996)

Freeman. The Master of Death uses him to wipe out his rivals in a series of brutal murders but, when Lung is ordered to kill his old friend and lover May, he begins to regain his memory.

The preposterous plot manages to hold together some remarkable fight scenes, including a blindfold nunchaku battle, a torch fight in a darkened room, and a sequence in a church where Freeman zooms and spins around the steeple, destroying opponents. The fight choreography is sleek, streamlined and stylish, filling the screen with bold strokes and unfettered imagination.

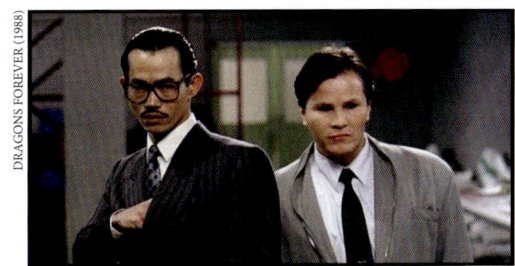

DRAGONS FOREVER (1988)

DRAGONS FOREVER (1988)
Starring Jackie Chan, Sammo Hung, Yuen Biao,
Deannie Yip, Pauline Yeung, Crystal Kwok, Yuen Wah
Directed by Sammo Hung
Produced by Leonard K.C. Ho
Golden Harvest/Golden Way Films Ltd

Jackie Lung (Chan) is hired as a sharp lawyer when chemicals start destroying the local fish farming. When the matter goes to court, Jackie finds himself attracted to the defense's star witness, played by Pauline Yeung. Sympathising with her plight, Jackie decides to go against his client, Hua Hsien-Wu (Wah), and he enlists the help of a psychotic professional burglar (Biao) and an arms dealer (Hung). After a series of encounters, they discover the factory is a front for drug smuggling, so the three unite to destroy the factory and the drug gang.

When Hong Kong's three favorite sons—Jackie, Sammo and Yuen Biao—came together in the eighties, they helped shape and broaden the West's interest in Hong Kong cinema. Alas, *Dragons Forever* was to be their last film together, but it undoubtably ranks as their best.

Sammo Hung's ability to direct Jackie Chan and Yuen Biao highlights the fact that he was the best in the business. The fight choreography in this film set a new precedent in modern day action and some excellent supporting roles from Yuen Wah, Dick Wei, Billy Chow, plus a second outing in a Jackie film for Benny the Jet, make this a firm favorite with Chan fans everywhere.

The stunts in the final reel are far beyond anything conceivable in a Hollywood actioner at the time, and it is hard to believe that the stuntmen were able to get up and walk away from such bone-crushing stunts. This is an ideal movie to introduce someone to Hong Kong cinema. An action classic!

DREAMING THE REALITY (1991)
Starring Moon Lee, Sibelle Hu, Yukari Oshima, Eddy Ko
Directed by Lu Chin-Ku
Produced by Tsui Fat
Action by Lung Sang
Cheung Yau Martial Arts Direction Company/J.S. Productions

Two girls, Black Cat (Oshima) and Silver Fox (Lee), trained as deadly killers under the influential gang leader Fok (Ko), plan to retrieve government evidence which could incriminate him. However, their plan backfires, and the Fox is badly injured, falling into a coma. When she recovers, she begins a new life, completely unaware of her criminal past. But Fok is furious with this state of affairs, and hatches a plan to bring her back home.

This is a well-above-average femme fatale action film, featuring a triple bill of battling starlets, plenty of fight scenes and a good storyline.

EASTERN CONDORS (1987)
Starring Sammo Hung, Yuen Biao, Dr Haing S. Ngor,
Yuen Wah, Joyce Godenzi, Yasuaki Kurata,
Lam Ching-Ying, Billy Lau, Phillip Kao, James Tien,
Dick Wei, Yuen Woo-Ping, Wu Ma
Directed by Sammo Hung
Produced by Leonard K.C. Ho
Action by Sammo Hung
Golden Harvest

Ten soldiers condemned to life-term prison sentences within the army are offered an amnesty if they go behind enemy lines in Vietnam to destroy a munitions dump. As the ten men parachute from the plane, the mission is aborted, but it is too late for them to be warned, and Tung (Hung) and his team begin to tackle the obstacles that lie before them.

If *Police Story* (1985) is Jackie Chan's apex, then *Eastern Condors* is most definitely Sammo Hung's. With a cast featuring some of the top action stars of Hong Kong, it's unthinkable that this film project could fail.

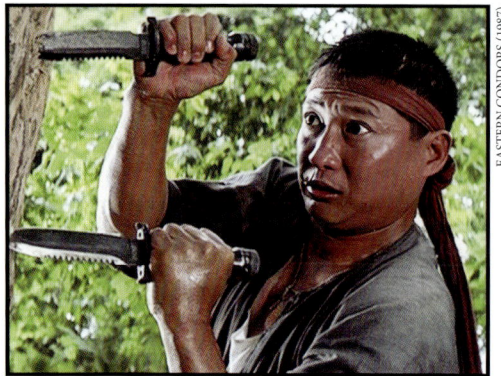

EASTERN CONDORS (1987)

The storyline is very reminiscent of *The Dirty Dozen* (1967) and the skilful direction of Sammo Hung, the powerful music score and some of the best fight action to come out of Hong Kong make this a firm favorite with film fans worldwide.

If there has to be one movie to introduce people to Hong Kong cinema, then this would be an excellent recommendation. Simply incredible.

ENTER THE FAT DRAGON (1978)
Starring Sammo Hung, Yang Chun, Leung Kar-Yan, Meg Lam, Roy Chiao. Lee Hoi-Sang
Directed by Sammo Hung
Produced by Florence Yu
Action by Sammo Hung
H.K. Fong Ming Motion Picture Company

In this, the best of all the Bruce Lee tribute films, Sammo Hung plays pig farmer Lung, a Bruce Lee fanatic who arrives in Hong Kong from the new territories to work in his cousin's cafe. Just like Bruce Lee, he has a run-in with a bunch of local hoods. He sends them running after an all-out *Way of the Dragon* fight, but they return and raze the cafe to the ground. Now destitute, Lung finds work in a dim sum restaurant, where he befriends a couple of waitresses. A millionaire interested in antiques arrives at the restaurant and takes a shine to one of the girls. This angers Lung, who must now face the rich man's hired bodyguards: they include a Western boxer, a pseudo black karate fighter, complete with Jim Kelly afro, and a classical Chinese kung fu fighter played by Leung Kar-Yan.

It's not much of a story, but the film is laced with beautifully choreographed fight scenes. Sammo Hung is, without a doubt, the best Bruce Lee impersonator, as he himself illustrates in a scene

where he plays an extra in a Lee cash-in movie: disgusted by the Bruce double's lack of courtesy and skill, Sammo sends him and the stuntmen packing in true Lee style.

FANTASY MISSION FORCE (1983)
Starring Jackie Chan, Jimmy Wang Yu, Brigitte Lin, Adam Cheng, Sun Yueh
Directed by Chu Yen-Ping
Produced by Shen Hsiao-Yin, Chiang Wen-Hsiung
Action by Lam Man Cheng
Cheung Ming Film

In a movie set in wartime, the Japanese have captured four top military figures from the allied forces. Before the news becomes widely known, a rescue mission is seriously needed, so Captain Don Wen (Yu), an eccentric military figure, is chosen to head the team.

The action is punctuated with cheeky comedy sketches and there are big names aplenty: lovely Brigitte Lin plays a devouring dark angel who packs a mean kick and Jackie Chan delivers some nicely framed fight action.

Wang Yu stalks through each scene with natural style, the action has madcap impact, the jokes keep coming, and it's obvious that when Wang Yu is in a film, everyone who is anyone wants to play.

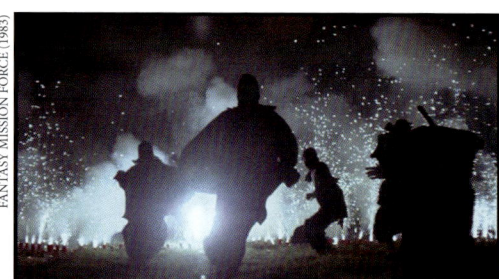

FANTASY MISSION FORCE (1983)

FATAL CHASE (1992)
Starring Yukari Oshima, Waise Lee, Robin Shou, Phillip Ko
Directed by Phillip Ko
Regent Film/Harvest International Films

A senior Hong Kong police officer and an unconventional undercover cop track down a vicious drug dealer in Hong Kong and, together with another senior police officer, Cynthia (Oshima), bring him to the Philippines for prosecution. But when the cops fail to keep their prisoner from escaping, they are put under strict supervision by the Manila Police Department. Meanwhile, the big gang boss villain has plans to eliminate anyone who hinders his criminal activities . . .

Director Phillip Ko seems to be a maestro at turning out good low-budget action films (*Killer's Romance, Ultracop 2000*), and *Fatal Chase* is no exception. It's brimming with high-octane shoot-outs and martial arts skirmishes. Unlike some of his other productions, where he usually depends on Yukari Oshima to sell the film, he attempts to put more than one star name on the screen. Here, in good supporting roles, are Waise (*Bullet in the Head*) Lee and Robin (*Tiger Cage 2*) Shou. A little gem of a film.

FIST OF FURY 1991 (1991)

Starring Stephen Chow, Kenny Bee, Cheung Man, Corey Yuen, Shing Fui-On, Wan Yueng-Ming, Tai Bo, Ng Man-Tat
Directed by Rico Chu
Action by Corey Yuen
Chun Sing Film Company

Stephen Chow plays Lau Ching, a naive immigrant from mainland China, who hopes to start a new life in Hong Kong. However, no sooner has he arrived than his possessions are stolen by Smart (Bee). Ching gives chase, and the two face off in an unorthodox duel, until Ching is forced to unleash

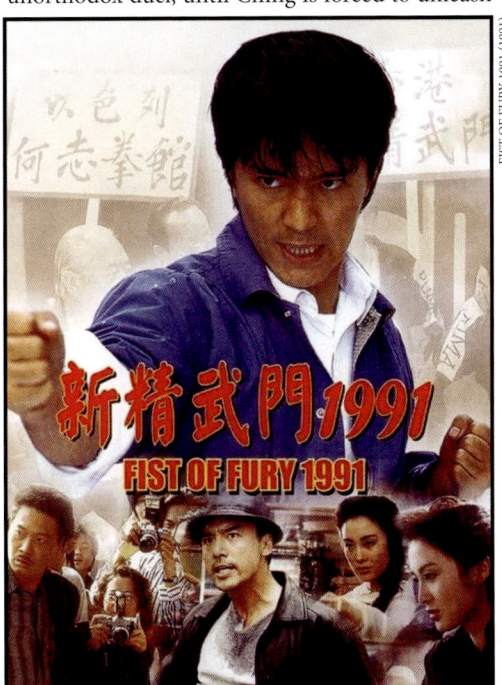

FIST OF FURY 1991 (1991)

his "Fist of Fury." After Smart recovers from its effect, the two become friends and join a martial arts school run by Sifu Fok (Yuen). They both fall in love with his daughter Mandy (Man), much to the annoyance of senior student Wai (Yueng-Ming), who also loves her. But the real trouble starts when a group of Japanese students and their interpreter (Bo) arrive at the school. From here the film goes into overdrive, building up to a climax at the martial arts tournament.

Chow displays some incredible fight prowess that, when combined with his verbal and visual comedy skills, makes his performance reminiscent of Jackie Chan. The humorous references to Bruce Lee, the *A Better Tomorrow* movies, Chow's previous films, and much more, make this vulgar, outrageous and highly enjoyable film eminently watchable.

THE FORTUNE CODE (1990)

Starring Andy Lau, Anita Mui, Alan Tam, Sammo Hung, Eric Tsang, Wilson Lam, Gordon Liu
Directed by Kent Cheng
Movie Impact Limited

The story centers around a POW camp in World War II, with secret agents on the trail of a code to a Swiss bank account containing millions of dollars.

Sammo Hung is really only in a supporting role and, despite many fight sequences, they are second rate for a film with him in it. But there is some first-rate comedy and well-choreographed action, especially from Alan Tam and Anita Mui.

FULL THROTTLE (1995)

Starring Andy Lau, Gigi Leung, David Wu, Paul Chun, Chin Kar-Lok, Elvis Tsui
Directed by Derek Yee
Film Unlimited/Win's Entertainment Ltd

Trust fund kid David (Wu) returns to Hong Kong and joins the local biker community, becoming involved in illegal road races and forming a friendship with ace racer Joe (Lau), who is the rebellious son of Paul, sponsor of a professional motorbike team. After a near-fatal crash, Joe must recuperate in a wheelchair, going from assured street-racer to struggling co-owner of a bike shop. He also tries to cope with a fear of riding at speed and does his best to maintain a loving relationship with his girlfriend Yee, who is scared Joe will eventually get killed or paralyzed. Joe promises Yee that he will quit racing for good, but

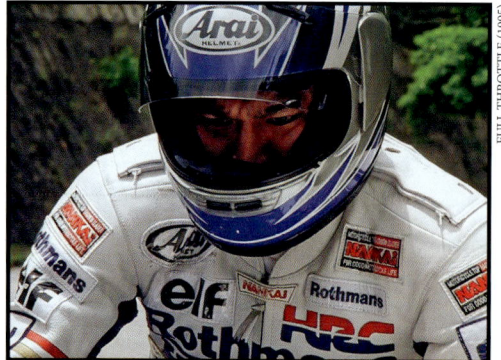

FULL THROTTLE (1995)

when his old buddy Jiale dies in a race with David, Joe ultimately regains his confidence by competing against David, who encourages him to hurry back to Yee before she can leave him.

The competent dramatics tend to take precedence over the biker action, with a little bit of soap opera father/son conflict added to the mix, which is all just fine because *Full Throttle* delivers a decently told, engrossing story.

FUN AND FURY (1992)
Starring Frankie Chan, Kent Cheng, Vivian Chow, Leon Lai, Kim Penn
Directed by Frankie Chan
Movie Impact Limited

The action begins when a cop (Lai) busts an international drug ring at Singapore Airport. A startling fight sequence follows, which allows Leon Lai to flex his ability. But the real action starts when he arrives in Hong Kong with his wife-to-be, who is then kidnapped by her own triad gangster father. Longtime friend Yee (Chan) immediately comes to his aid, and together they pursue the missing fiancée.

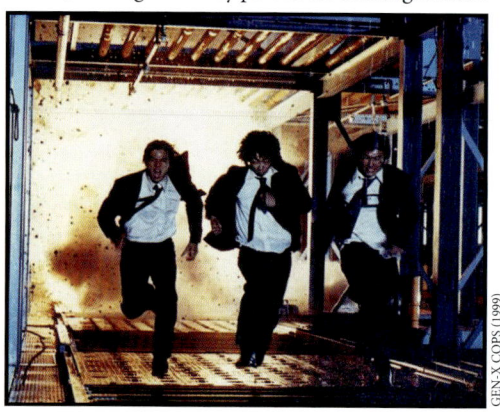

GEN-X COPS (1999)

Frankie Chan tries to return to the formula that found him box office success with *Outlaw Brothers* (1990), this time featuring a sidekick played by recording star Leon Lai. Despite some well-choreographed fight scenes, this film falls short of the standards that made *Outlaw Brothers* such an outstanding movie. Yukari Oshima is replaced with Kim Penn, who sadly lacks the presence of the Osh. But, despite this, the film has many funny moments and, although not memorable, it is entertaining.

THE GAMBLING GHOST (1991)
Starring Sammo Hung, Meng Hoi, Nina Li Chi, James Tien, Lam Ching-Ying, Billy Chow
Directed by Clifton Ko
Action by Meng Hoi
Golden Leaf Film Production Consultant

Sammo and Meng play two of Hong Kong's unluckiest hustlers in search of a shortcut to the easy life, much to the disapproval of Sammo's father, who sees his son heading down the same path that killed his own dad. But the real problems begin when beautiful car thief Nina Li Chi enters their lives. First, she gets them fired from their jobs, then they decide to steal a car for her, only to find themselves facing the irate owner and his triad gang, who take Meng hostage. Sammo blames his ancestors for his misfortune, prompting his grandfather's ghost to appear and offer help. Meng is rescued and the ghost explains that he was murdered and wants them to avenge him, so Sammo and Meng end up facing a gang of thugs, including Thai boxer Billy Chow and veteran bad guy James Tien, in a ferocious fight to the finish.

Sammo is in top form here, playing all three generations magnificently, and the furious final fight scene is reminiscent of *Pedicab Driver* (1989).

GEN-X COPS (1999)
Directed by Benny Chan
Starring Nicholas Tse, Stephen Fung, Sam Lee, Eric Tsang, Daniel Wu, Grace Ip, Francis Ng, Tōru Nakamura and a cameo appearance from Jackie Chan
Media Asia Films

Alien, Jack and Match are young, disobedient, rule-breaking cops who are given the chance to go undercover and solve a case involving stolen, volatile rocket fuel canisters and warring arms smugglers.

Eric Tsang overdoes it a little as the shouty, twitchy

Inspector Chan, heartthrob Stephen Fung inevitably has some clichéd, glossy, romantic moments, Sam Lee, coming across like some kind of skinny, Asian Harpo Marx, is overly silly sometimes, and the mix of Chinese and English dialogue is distracting rather than cool, but the film as a whole is a solid, slick, lively Hong Kong actioner.

Well-handled, kinetic set pieces, a couple of decently sketched villains (Ng & Wu), and several twists ensure the movie remains enjoyable throughout.

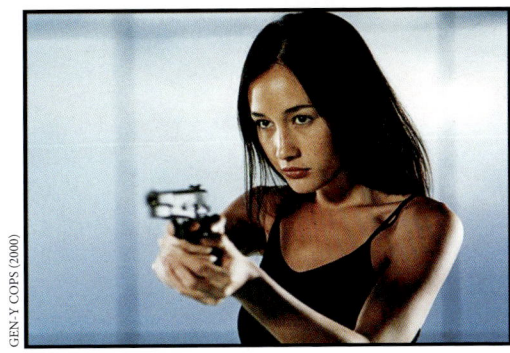

GEN-Y COPS (2000)

GEN-Y COPS (2000)

Directed by Benny Chan
Starring Edison Chen, Stephen Fung, Sam Lee,
Paul Rudd, Maggie Q
Media Asia Films

Undercover cops Match (Fung), Alien (Lee) and Edison (Chen) have to deal with a group of villainous tech guys out to steal the prototype American RS1 attack robot during an international military technology exhibition in Hong Kong, but Edison is injected with a hypnosis drug by former hacker friend Kurt, which compels him to take part in the theft of the American robot. Now the Hong Kong cop trio must attempt to recover the stolen robot while avoiding a bunch of trigger-happy FBI agents, led by Agent Curtis (Rudd), who believe Edison is a willing

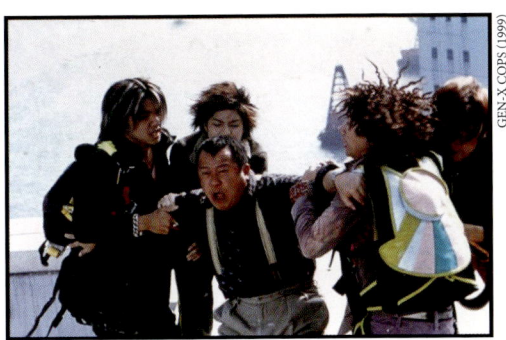

GEN-X COPS (1999)

participant in the heist. Fortunately for the Gen-Y Cops, Jane Quigley (Q), another FBI agent dealing with the case, starts to believe Edison is innocent.

This sequel to *Gen-X Cops* (1999) begins with a demonstration of the RS1's powers, where it withstands flames and heavy machine gun fire, can hit flying objects with pinpoint accuracy . . . and can delicately pick up a piece of tofu with its metal fingers (I'm sure that last ability will always

come in useful for an attack-bot!) The RS1 does get momentarily hacked, however, though this doesn't prevent the FBI from concluding that it's still safe to take this lethal killing machine to Hong Kong for the military tech show.

The technology exhibition itself is wittily handled, introducing such robots as Hong Kong's D1010, which can predict lottery numbers and is repeatedly mistaken for a trash can, France's Jerry L robot, which gets its head ripped off in a fight with RS1, and China's Tung Fung robot, which loses one of its arms during a display and is mockingly referred to as a "One-Armed Boxer."

Gen-Y Cops has its fair share of lowbrow humor, including the moment idiotic cop Alien scrapes his dandruff into the FBI's coffee cups, and any hope the film has of being taken seriously is severely hampered by the fact the protagonists, especially Alien, come across as borderline buffoons much of the time, with scenes of them accidentally blowing up a car and giggling like schoolboys, all of which prevents them from even remotely resembling professional law enforcement officers.

The script makes an effort to use a lot of English dialogue, written by Bey Logan, though it tends to depend too much on generic terms like "hey, man" and "goddamn it," but the movie does finally kick into gear, proving to be a pleasing, amusing sci-fi-tinged actioner, with robot rampages, shots of the heroes diving in slow motion from explosions and a full body burn stunt during the finale.

Mainly brought to life via practical effects, the RS1 has a Transformers-like head and looks really rather good on-screen, using a rocket launcher, machine guns, a flamethrower and even an extendable fist to wreak havoc wherever it goes. It's a shame, then, that a showdown with the Tung Fung robot at the end uses low grade CGI to create the Chinese automaton.

Gen-Y Cops gets an unduly bad rap from many reviewers, but it's a mindlessly enjoyable, throwaway flick that boasts gunfights, flashbacks involving a man dressed as a lobster, kung fu skirmishes and a decent robot adversary. Plus, there's the added pleasure of seeing a youthful Paul Rudd go from potential adversary to good guy, taking part in some Hong Kong–style fighting. He even speaks a little Cantonese!

My advice is to put your brain on hold and revel in the colorful nonsense.

THE GOD OF COOKERY (1996)
Starring Stephen Chow, Karen Mok, Vincent Kok, Ng Man-tat
Directed by Stephen Chow, Lee Lik-Chi
Star Overseas

Stephen Chow plays a lead character called . . . Stephen Chow, who is a top chef hailed as a culinary expert. He is as elitist and cocky as one would expect, and far from humble and kind, but he is debunked as a fraud and loses his title. Chow's downfall finds him landing on Temple Street, a seedy district where a chance meeting of minds with Turkey (Mok), an uncouth noodle cook, sets off what could be Chow's first step to getting back everything he's lost. Chow's riches-to-rags journey eventually leads to him learning the true meaning of humility, through

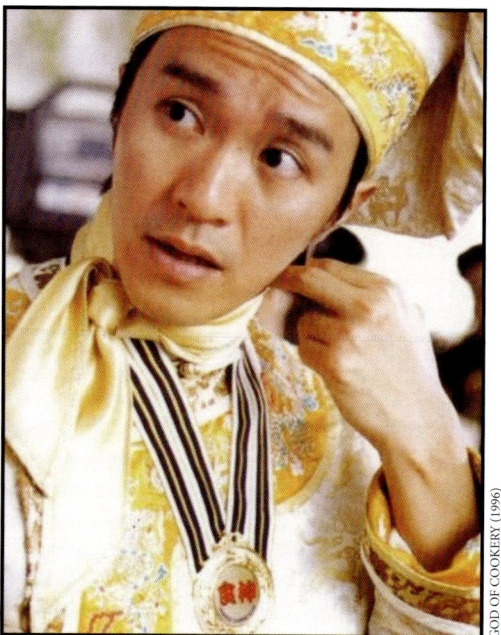
GOD OF COOKERY (1996)

loss and harrowing near-death survival, to eventual enlightenment. It's from here we see the rise of Chow, who is now an understudy, in scenes reminiscent of the old kung fu movies, as he is trained by a no-nonsense master to regain his title.

When watching Chow's comedy with a Chinese audience you feel you miss a lot of the quick-fire gags, as the rest of the audience roars with laughter, mainly due to the poor subtitle translation (the dubbed versions are considerably worse), so you

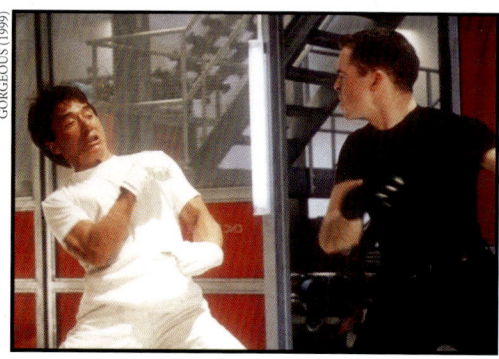
GORGEOUS (1999)

have to watch his expressions and visual comedy to get a lot of the gags. But the fact remains that Chow is a multitalented actor and filmmaker. Ng Man-tat, who often plays Chow's sidekick, puts in an excellent performance too, as Uncle.

Without doubt one of my personal favorites, with Chow delivering a comedy masterclass.

GORGEOUS (1999)
Starring Jackie Chan, Shu Qi, Tony Leung Chiu-Wai, Emil Chau, Ken Lo, Brad Allen, Sam Lee
Directed by Vincent Kok
Golden Harvest/GH Pictures

Written and directed by Vincent Kok and produced by Jackie Chan, the film offers a unique blend of humor, romance and action, telling the story of Bu (Qi), a beautiful young girl from a small Taiwanese fishing village, who discovers a romantic message in a bottle. Her interest piqued, she heads to Hong Kong to find the writer of the note, which was in fact written by Albert (Leung), who is just a lonely man. But by chance she meets wealthy recycling company owner C.N. (Chan) and, as expected, they fall in love. But the plot soon thickens with the rivalry between Howie Lo (Chau) and C.N., who are both businessmen that have known each other since their childhood days.

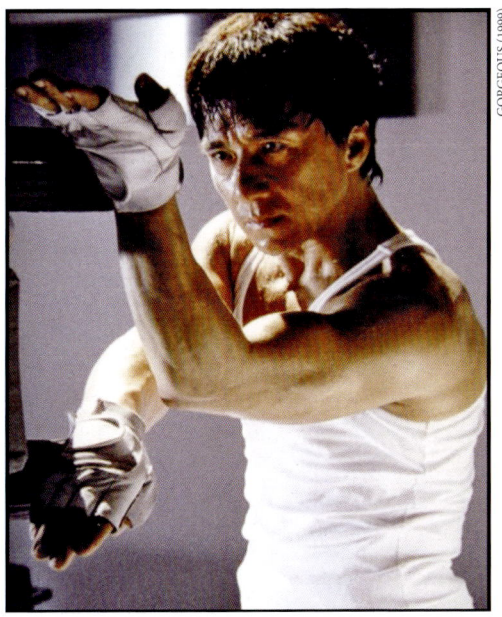

GORGEOUS (1999)

actor and stunt performer Brad Allen. Sadly, Brad passed away in 2021, but his contribution to the film industry is still very much appreciated. He brought an incredible level of energy and excitement to the action scenes in *Gorgeous* and his skills as a stunt performer were truly impressive.

It's worth noting that in the English dubbed version some of the dialogue is changed and a few scenes are edited out of the version I viewed, including an airport scene and a sequence in which Stephen Chow's policeman character comes to investigate after C.N. fights off Howie Lo's masked goons.

This film keeps you entertained from start to finish, with its engaging plot, great performances and occasional action-packed scenes, and is a must-watch for fans of Hong Kong's action-comedy genre.

HARD TO KILL (1992)
Starring Robin Shou, Yukari Oshima, Phillip Ko, Fung Wai-Lun
Directed by Phillip Ko
Regent Film

This merely so-so actioner features the same stars from *Fatal Chase* (1992), in a story about hard-boiled Interpol agent Yukari Oshima undertaking the mission of a lifetime, when she's sent overseas to bring to justice one of Asia's top drug kingpins.

Also known as *Interpol Connection*, it's a rather flat drama, and Yukari Oshima isn't in the film as much as she should be, but there are a few shoot-outs and foot-to-face kicking stunts, accompanied by a decent musical score, which augments the superb end fight scene between Yukari Oshima and a foot-wielding foe.

I have to admit that I really enjoyed this outing from Jackie, even though romantic comedies aren't always the top of my watch list. This certainly isn't your usual Jackie Chan-style movie, but it was definitely something Jackie wanted to do because he helped write the screenplay too. Hey, if Jackie wants to try something different, then his fans will always support him. There isn't a lot of action, but when there is some, it is excellent. The two well-choreographed combat scenes with Brad Allan are some of the best fights Jackie has filmed since the 80s, in my opinion. But, in the end, this really is more of a "feel good" movie than anything else.

One of the highlights of the film is the performance of Australian martial artist, action choreographer,

HEART OF THE DRAGON (1985)
Starring Jackie Chan, Sammo Hung, Emily Chu, Melvin Wong, Yuen Wah, Meng Hoi, Dick Wei
Directed by Sammo Hung
Produced by Leonard K.C. Ho
Bo Ho Film Company Ltd/Golden Harvest

Also known as *First Mission*, this is a heartwarming drama which sees both Jackie Chan and Sammo Hung changing direction from their usual reinvented kung fu comedies to a straight drama. Jackie plays a cop who forsakes his dream of sailing around the world to care for his brother (Hung), who is disabled. His love and devotion is stretched to the limit when Sammo is innocently caught up in a

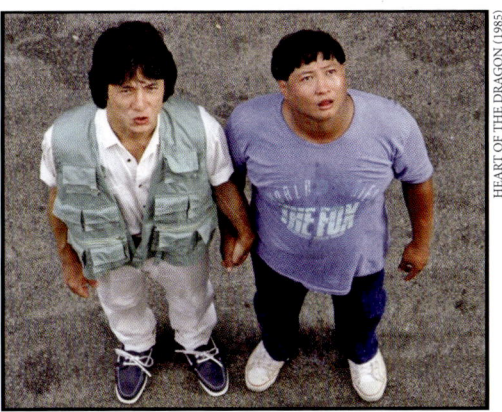

HEART OF THE DRAGON (1985)

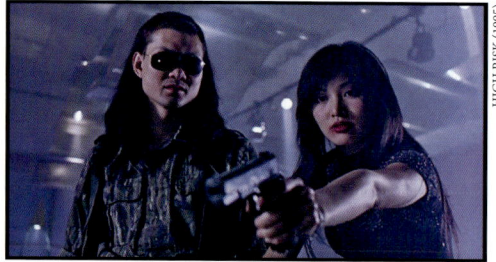

HIGH RISK (1995)

gangland fight over some stolen goods, with Sammo getting kidnapped to force Jackie to hand over a police informant.

Sammo's acting is every bit as good as his martial arts skills, and Jackie carries off his straight role of the brooding cop on the edge with great aplomb. This gripping story leads inevitably to a violent, explosive ending.

Sammo once again proves that he is more competent at directing Jackie than Jackie is himself. People watching the original UK version of this film will find that there is little fight action until the final reel, but it is worth noting that in the Japanese version there are two other major fight scenes: firstly, in the opening, when Jackie fights several assailants in a hospital, and then later on, when he and several friends, including Meng Hoi, have a parking lot battle with a gang. Although the cuts did not affect the storyline, the real tragedy lies in the fact that these twelve or so minutes of footage allowed Jackie to show off some of the fighting skills that won him an army of fans worldwide. They should be seen at all costs.

HIGH RISK (1995)

Starring Jet Li, Chingmy Yau, Jacky Cheung,
Charlie Yeung
Directed by Wong Jing
Golden Sun Entertainment/Upland Films Corporation
Limited/Wong Jing's Workshop Ltd

Former bomb disposal expert Kit Li (Jet Li) works as a bodyguard and stunt double for cowardly action movie star Frankie Lane (Cheung). They both attend an exhibition of Tsarist crown jewels at a big Hong Kong hotel, just as the Doctor, a criminal mastermind behind the death of Kit's wife, invades the place with his well-armed *Die Hard*-style gang. As Kit does his best to take down these killers, Frankie finally finds the courage within himself to be a real hero and, ultimately, Kit gets the chance to make the Doctor pay for his crimes.

High Risk, also known as *Meltdown*, mixes high-

body-count violence with broad comedy that mainly stems from the character of Frankie, who is meant to be buffoonish and amusing, but is generally merely irritating. A lot of obvious dummies are used in various action scenes, unfortunately, but this is a garish, racy actioner that delivers some good fights, especially a brawl between Kit and the Doctor's shades-wearing brother Rabbit, plus there's a decent clash with a big super-mullet henchman called Bond. An over-the-top set piece with an out-of-control helicopter crashing into the building and the gang's preposterous use of a bag full of snakes in a restroom also help keep the proceedings watchable.

HITMAN (1998)

Starring Jet Li, Eric Tsang, Simon Yam and Gigi Leung
Directed by Tung Wei
China Star Entertainment/Win's Entertainment Ltd

Hit men converge on Hong Kong after the murder of a Japanese crime lord triggers a "revenge fund," which will be paid to whoever captures and eliminates the kingpin's assassin, known as the King of Killers. Chinese mainlander Fu (Li), desperate to make money, tries to become a contract killer after teaming up with small-time con man Lo (Tsang). Fu soon finds himself clashing with rival bounty hunters, saving Lo's skin on several occasions, falling for Lo's lawyer daughter, and realizing he's maybe not cut out to be a cold-blooded killer.

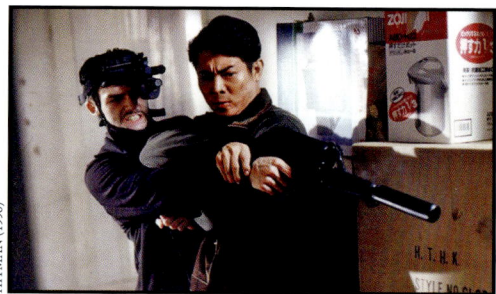

HITMAN (1998)

Also known as *Contract Killer*, this film is certainly entertaining, featuring a lanky Western bad guy equipped with rings and shoes that emit flashes of light to dazzle Fu as they fight, an action scene in an elevator shaft that ain't bad, and a marvelous final showdown. This end battle, involving a katana-wielding Japanese mobster, a kimono-wearing female fighter and the King of Killers (Yam) kitted out in black tactical gear, makes you realize how much better this film could've been if the rest of the movie had boasted set pieces of a similar quality. In fact, once you see Simon Yam in action, efficiently taking down underworld goons, you find yourself wishing the whole story had been about him!

HOW TO MEET THE LUCKY STARS (1996)

Starring Sammo Hung, Eric Tsang, Richard Ng, Stanley Fung, Michael Miu, Françoise Yip
Directed by Frankie Chan
Grand March Movie Production Company Ltd

This is a hilarious and action-packed 1996 Hong Kong comedy film that brings together some of the biggest stars in the industry. Directed by Frankie Chan and produced by Eric Tsang, this final installment of the *Lucky Stars* film series is a must-see for any fan of the genre.

The film features the *"Lucky Stars"* themselves—Sammo Hung, Eric Tsang, Richard Ng, Stanley Fung, and Michael Miu—who deliver their trademark humor and charm in spades. But there are also some new faces, including Vincent Lau Tak as Sammo Hung's younger cousin and Françoise Yip as their love interest. With a number of guest appearances by industry legends, such as Natalise Chan, Chen Kuan-Tai, Cheng Pei-Pei, Chan Hung-Lit and Nora Miao, *How to Meet the Lucky Stars* is a star-studded affair.

The story centers around an international gambling competition, where the King of Gamblers Lui Tin (Chen Kuan-Tai) loses to the psychotic and lascivious lesbian queen of gamblers known as the Gambling Flower (Kung Suet-Fa), leading to his tragic death by suicide. His daughter (Fung Sau-Yin) vows to avenge her father's death and seeks help from Uncle Wah (Cho Tat-Wah), who is a police inspector. Uncle Wah then enlists the aid of the Lucky Stars to assist him in his quest for justice, resulting in a fun, action-crammed adventure.

Director Frankie Chan does an excellent job of balancing the film's comedic and action elements, creating a fast-paced and entertaining ride. The film's action choreography, led by Yuen Cheung-Yan and Mars, is also top-notch and adds an extra layer of excitement to the film. But it's the performances of the movie's stars that really make *How to Meet the Lucky Stars* shine. Sammo Hung, in particular, delivers a standout performance, playing not only his original role but also taking on the part of a cop.

The film is a fitting end to the *Lucky Stars* film series and is sure to entertain and leave you smiling.

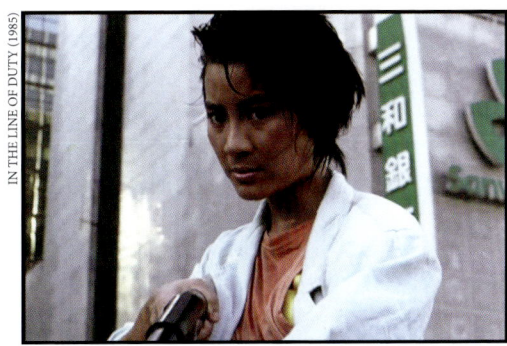

IN THE LINE OF DUTY (1985)

IN THE LINE OF DUTY (1985)

Starring Michelle Yeoh, Cynthia Rothrock, John Sham, Meng Hoi, Sammo Hung, Tsui Hark, Dick Wei
Directed by Corey Yuen
Produced by Sammo Hung, Dickson Poon
Action by Meng Hoi, Corey Yuen
D & B Films Co. Ltd

Originally released as *Yes, Madam!*, this movie launched the successful careers of Michelle Yeoh (then known as Michelle Khan) and Cynthia Rothrock, and was retroactively retitled *In the Line of Duty* to act as the first installment of the movie series. There has always been confusion about the correct title for each part of this franchise, the names of which vary from country to country. The movie can also be credited with triggering the new wave of Hong Kong girls-with-guns flicks that followed in its wake.

Michelle Yeoh plays Inspector Ng, while Cynthia Rothrock plays Carrie Morris, a Scotland Yard Inspector, although there is very little evidence to support this if you were to judge her on accent. The plot involves Strepsil (Sham) and his friends stealing some items, not realizing that there is concealed microfilm, leading to them being pursued by underworld gangsters. Strepsil and his partners thus have no choice but to join forces with Ng and Morris in an attempt to break the gang's secret plot.

An all-round excellent action film, with some notable martial art performances, the film showcased Cynthia Rothrock, who broke new ground to become the first Western female to lead a Hong Kong cast. Sammo Hung puts in an appearance, although this was cut from the UK print. Also of note is the fact that the UK release print does not open with its original footage: in the Chinese version we see Michelle Yeoh browsing through a book in a shop, when she is approached by a flasher. With a quick thrust and clap of her hands, she puts paid to the likelihood of him spawning any new flashers! But in the UK print we are offered the opening five minutes from Sammo Hung's *Where's Officer Tuba?* This has nothing to do with this movie, but D & B felt that the opening action sequence would be more acceptable than Chinese comedy. Whatever your choice of opening scene, *In the Line of Duty/ Yes Madam!* is a superb roller-coaster ride of stunts and martial arts action.

The movie is also known as *Police Assassins 2*.

IN THE LINE OF DUTY 2 (1986)
Starring Michelle Yeoh, Hiroyuki Sanada, Michael Wong, Chan Wai-Man, Bai Ying
Directed by David Chung
Produced by Dickson Poon, John Sham
Action by Meng Hoi
D & B Films Co. Ltd

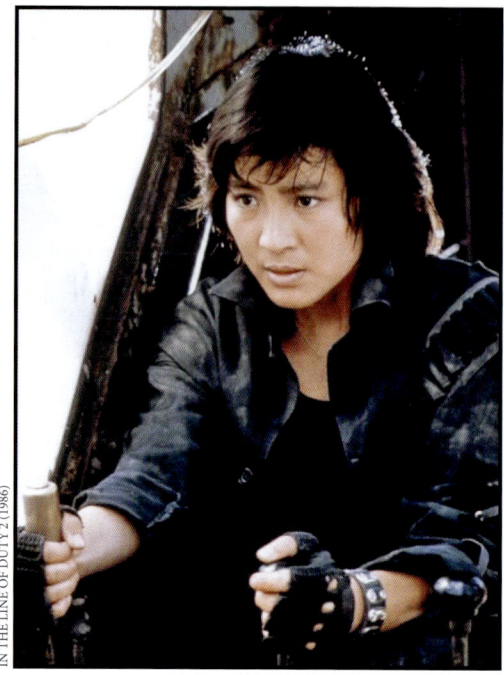

IN THE LINE OF DUTY 2 (1986)

The movie begins with some excellent in-flight combat, where we are introduced to Japanese agent Yamamoto (Sanada) and Hong Kong's most glamorous police woman, Michelle Yip (Michelle Yeoh, who was billed as Michelle Khan). The fight on the plane leads up to a villain's asphyxiation, which is achieved by holding his head out of a smashed window. Gasp! The aftermath of this confrontation leads to a series of revenge attempts, with the breaking point coming when Yamamoto's wife and daughter are murdered in a car bomb explosion. Security guard Michael Wong (Wong), who has the hots for Michelle, joins the two in an attempt to wipe out the gang once and for all.

The story, for the most part, is a fairly lightweight tale of the three protagonists being marked for death by the gang of ex-soldiers, but it is enhanced by superb martial arts scrapping. The action is gasp-inducing, as people are kicked, punched, thrown very heavily against posts and beaten with fire extinguishers. There's a martial arts chainsaw fight, a pickaxe/shovel struggle and an Uzi attack in a disco, leading to a kung fu scuffle that involves the use of a broken bottle and the disco's hanging metal tubes décor. This is a great actioner by any standards, boasting some fine car chases and stunts too.

This second outing for Michelle Yeoh as a fighting femme of the force continued to inspire countless Hong Kong production companies to cash in with a wave of battling babe flicks, although few could compete with her gutsy performance—she also did

many of her own stunts. Even though Yeoh's film career was put on hold when she married producer Dickson Poon, her first two pictures are still regarded as the cream of tough femme fatale movies.

This film's original title was *Royal Warriors*, before it retroactively became part of the *In the Line of Duty* series. In the UK it was released as *Police Assassins*.

IN THE LINE OF DUTY 3 (1988)
Starring Cynthia Khan, Hiroshi Fujioka, Michiko Nishiwaki, Dick Wei, Stuart Ong, Yueh Hua
Directed by Brandy Yuen, Arthur Wong
D & B Films Co. Ltd

Michelle Yeoh's loss was Cynthia Khan's gain. No relation—in fact, the name Cynthia Khan was a result of taking Rothrock's Christian name and Michelle's original surname, Khan. This was ex-dancer Cynthia Khan's first lead role and she was soon winning armies of fans—both Eastern and Western.

Cynthia plays Madam Yeung, who is assigned to help a Japanese inspector investigate a bloody robbery at a jewelry exhibition, which has been held up by two armed gangsters, Nishiwaki & Nakamura. As the film unfolds, we discover that the mastermind is, in fact, the Japanese jewelry designer Yamamoto (Hua) himself, trying to swindle money out of his insurance company. But events take a new twist when Yamamoto is murdered by the two gangsters, forcing Yeung and the Inspector to dispose of the unsavory pair.

Although a weaker film than its predecessors, some fast-paced fights and good stunt work convinced D & B that they had the right actress to continue the series, so a new Asian star was discovered to attract the attention of many Western fighting femme film followers.

Also known as *Force of the Dragon* and *Yes Madam 2.*

IN THE LINE OF DUTY 4 (1989)

*Starring Cynthia Khan, Donnie Yen, Michael Wong,
Yuen Yat-Chor, Michael Woods, Yuen Shun-Yee
Directed by Yuen Woo-Ping
Produced by Stephen Shin
Action by Yuen Shun-Yee, Yuen Woo-Ping, Cho Wing
D & B Films Co. Ltd*

An anti-narcotics bureau detective in San Francisco is pursued for a film he snapped containing evidence of drug trafficking between a certain American intelligence agency and the Green Dragon drug dealers. Before his death, he hands the film over to a Hong Kong immigrant (Yat-Chor), who throws it away when the killer arrives. Madam Yeung (Khan), assigned to San Francisco to help the local police investigating the case, witnesses this. The immigrant, who is now suspected of murder, pleads his innocence to her. She then has the task of trying to prove his innocence with the help of Captain Yan (Yen) and his sidekick (Wong).

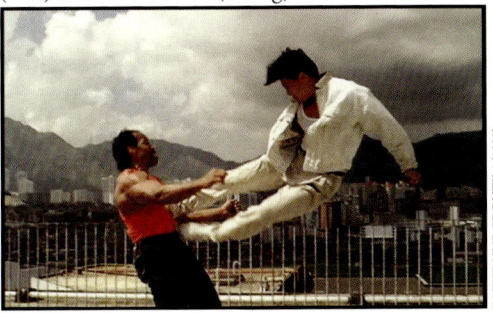

The storyline may sound quite basic and typical of what was being churned out at the time, but this film, although not highly successful, was regarded in the West as one of the best modern day action films to come out of Hong Kong. Yuen Woo-Ping's chemistry with Donnie Yen can be compared with that of John Woo and Chow Yun-Fat. The excellent camera work and creative direction, coupled with

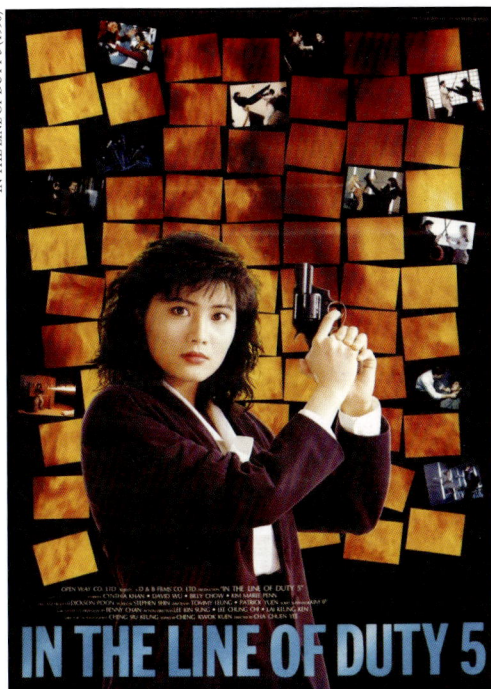

the fighting skills of Donnie Yen, make this film truly a roller-coaster ride of action.

Donnie Yen's end fight scene on top of a high-rise tower against awesome Michael Woods is totally breathtaking, and it is unlikely that any true Hong Kong film fan could find fault with this visual feast of action.

Cynthia Khan, who heads the cast, puts in one of her best performances, especially the incredible fight scene on the moving ambulance. The film is also known as *Witness.*

IN THE LINE OF DUTY 5 (1990)

*Starring Cynthia Khan, David Wu, Billy Chow,
Elvina Kong, Chris Lee, Lo Lieh, Ku Kuan-Chung,
Vincent Lyn, Steve Tartalia
Directed by Cha Chuen-Yee
Produced by Dickson Poon, Stephen Shin
Action by Chris Lee
D & B Films Co. Ltd*

In the fifth episode of the *In the Line of Duty* series, Cynthia Khan continues to play her typecast role of a cute cop with a gun. This time she gets involved in the action after helping her cousin David (Wu), whose buddy has been killed. As a result, attempts are made on both their lives as they find themselves

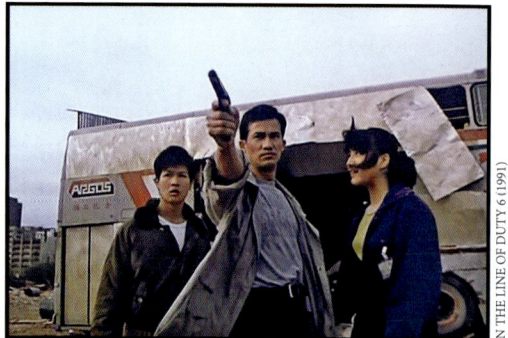

IN THE LINE OF DUTY 6 (1991)

ensnared in a plot linked to the stealing of military secrets. Their only option is to make their way to the villain general's headquarters and eliminate him and his cronies.

This is the usual gun action and martial arts fighting fare, which keeps the otherwise slow plot entertaining. Director Cha Chuen-Yee does not deliver the intense set pieces of his predecessor, Yuen Woo-Ping, unfortunately, though Billy Chow puts in his usual credible performance as the villain with an attitude.

Also *known as Middle Man, Ultra Force II* and *In the Line of Duty 5: Middle Man.*

IN THE LINE OF DUTY 6 (1991)
Starring Cynthia Khan, Waise Lee, Gary Chau,
Robin Shou, To Siu-Chun, Hui Shiu-Hung
Directed by Yuen Chun-Man, Cheng Siu-Keung
Produced by Stephen Shin
Action by Philip Kwok, Paul Wong
D & B Films Co. Ltd

Aka *Forbidden Arsenal*, this entry sees Cynthia Khan return as Madam Yeung, this time tracking down a gang of arms smugglers from across the border, aided by mainland public security officer Hua (Siu-Chun) and Chen, a Taiwanese Interpol detective (Lee). This allows for some humorous interactions as the country bumpkin mainlander is lampooned by his more sophisticated Taiwanese partner.

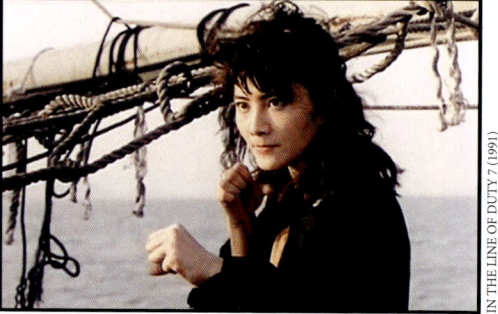

IN THE LINE OF DUTY 7 (1991)

The action scenes are well-staged, including an impressive fencing bout and a battle on top of a moving container truck.

IN THE LINE OF DUTY 7 (1991)
Starring Cynthia Khan, Simon Yam, Gary Chow,
Chim Bing-Hei
Directed by Cheng Siu-Keung
Produced by Dickson Poon, Stephen Shin
Action by Philip Kwok
D & B Films Co. Ltd

Cynthia Khan plays Inspector Yeung, who is assigned to follow Gary, an illegal immigrant (Chow), who is thought to be a cold-blooded killer. But from her observations, she discovers that he is actually suffering from amnesia, and has been framed by John (Yam), the mate of a pirate ship, who has also killed Gary's sister. With the ship bound for Hong Kong, and with insufficient evidence, Yeung stows away on board with Gary in a bid to help him get his revenge.

Also known as *Sea Wolves*, this is a sort of "Die Hard at sea," which finds the *In the Line of Duty* saga running out of steam. Although Simon Yam can always be depended upon to put in an above-average performance, you're likely to become weary of the far-fetched plotlines.

Fortunately, several well executed, violent fight scenes help save *Sea Wolves* from sinking.

THE INSPECTOR WEARS SKIRTS (1988)
Starring Sibelle Hu, Regina Kent, Cynthia Rothrock,
Anne Bridgewater, Sandra Ng, Ellen Chan, Kara Wai,
Jeff Falcon
Directed by Wellson Chin
Produced by Jackie Chan
Action by J.C. Stunt Association
Golden Harvest/Golden Way Films Ltd

A fast-paced *Police Academy*-style action comedy, with a story centered around a top squad of female cops, who are knocked into shape by drill instructor Madam Wu (Hu), a ruthless disciplinarian. When they start faring better than their male counterparts in the SWAT squad, a martial arts tournament is arranged with the women emerging the victors. With this established, everyone resolves their conflicts and join forces to pursue a gang of notorious thieves.

There are enough stars in this flick to fulfill the needs of any fighting femme fatale follower, with a superb finale in which Madam Law (Rothrock)

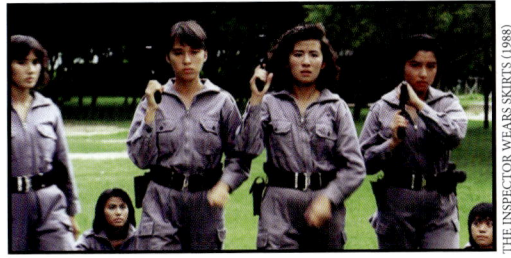

THE INSPECTOR WEARS SKIRTS (1988)

comes fist-to-fingernail with a tough robber leader played by Western martial artist Jeff Falcon.

If the sets look familiar, that's because several of the action sequences were shot on the set of *Project A Part 2* (1987), because Jackie Chan didn't want to see his magnificent sets go to waste!

The film is also known as *Top Squad*.

THE INSPECTOR WEARS SKIRTS II (1989)

Starring Sibelle Hu, Sandra Ng, Billy Lau, Regina Kent, Kara Wai, Fung Shui-Fan, Amy Yip
Directed by Wellson Chin
Produced by Jackie Chan
Action by J.C. Stunt Association
Golden Harvest/Golden Way Films Ltd

This follow-up provides more romance and comic thrills from those femme fatale lovelies. Sibelle Hu returns as the no-nonsense drill instructor Madam Wu, who has ordered the girls back to basic training, where they find themselves once again head-to-head with their male counterparts in the SWAT team.

Meanwhile, Wu is developing a romance with the SWAT leader, Inspector Kan (Shui-Fan), which is disturbed when news comes that the jewel thieves have broken out of jail.

Several well-coordinated stunts, courtesy of the Jackie Chan Stunt Team, help save this film from becoming a run-of-the-mill romance movie. Also known as *Top Squad 2*.

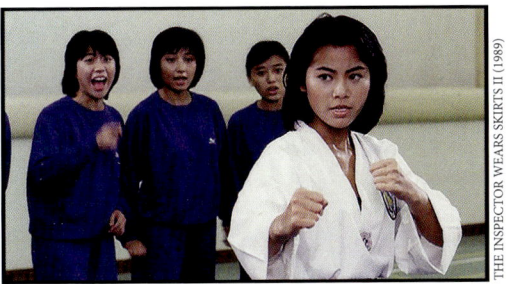

THE INSPECTOR WEARS SKIRTS II (1989)

ISLAND OF FIRE (1990)

Starring Jackie Chan, Tony Leung Ka-Fai, Sammo Hung, Andy Lau, Jimmy Wang Yu
Directed by Chu Yen-Ping
Produced by Wang Yu
Action by Lam Man-Cheung
Blaine and Blake Ltd

Also known as *Island on Fire*, *The Burning Island* and *The Prisoner*, the film's plot follows policeman Wang (Leung) as he gets himself put into a prison run by a corrupt chief warden, in order to discover who is faking the deaths of condemned convicts and then using them as expendable assassins. Also in the jail are prisoners played by Sammo Hung, who keeps escaping to see his son, Jackie Chan, who is there for accidentally killing a gang boss, Wang Yu, the daddy of the prison, and Andy Lau, the brother of the dead gang boss, who is attempting to avenge his brother by bumping off Jackie.

This prison picture has everything: a superstar cast, brutal fights, touching scenes of loyalty-among-thieves and some neat slo-mo sequences. It's well scripted, and it's good to see Jackie Chan in such a heavy exploitation pic. It even culminates in a spasm of heroic bloodshed, John Woo style, as Jackie, Sammo and Andy, all in black jackets and white T-shirts, blast away at a drug baron's private army.

A real Hong Kong winner!

JACKIE CHAN: MY STORY (1998)

Starring Jackie Chan, Willie Chan, Sammo Hung, Michelle Yeoh, Stanley Tong, Yuen Biao
Directed by Jackie Chan
Media Asia

For the avid Chan fan, this documentary will hold very little new information. Jackie's autobiographies delve much deeper, for instance, but for someone wanting to know the basics, then *Jackie Chan: My Story* is certainly a good watch as we navigate our way from childhood to his early film career and on to Hollywood, where his performance in *Rush Hour* made him one of the world's biggest action stars. We can also see his passion and enthusiasm for his work here, as a director, actor and as a stuntman who often risks his life to get the perfect shot with death-defying stunts that have become his trademark.

This documentary would definitely have been better if more was heard from Sammo Hung and some of the fellow actors who worked closely with Jackie after they became friends during their Peking Opera

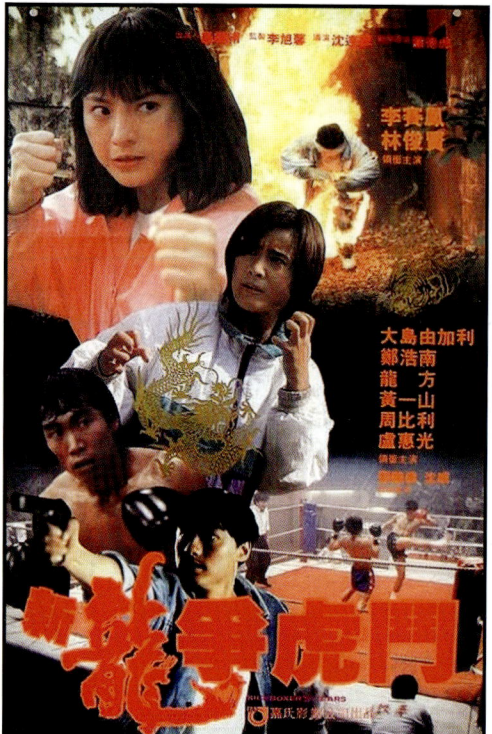

KICKBOXER'S TEARS (1992)

school days, but, alas, we only get small snippets. *Jackie Chan: My Story* is still enjoyable, though, and it's hoped that a more in-depth, updated documentary will be made, that takes a deeper dive into the life of this unique action star.

JACKIE CHAN: MY STUNTS (1999)

Starring Jackie Chan, Ken Lo, Bradley Allen, Andy Cheng
Directed by Jackie Chan, Xavier Lee

Jackie Chan fans and aspiring stuntmen must have rejoiced when Jackie announced that he was making two documentaries, one of which was aptly named *My Stunts* and the other titled *My Story*. This stunt documentary is both informative and entertaining, especially if, like most folks, you've never been on the set of a Hong Kong movie. Jackie takes us on a tour of his "stunt lab" and demonstrates some of the stunts he has perfected over the years. When watching him, you begin to understand the amount of complexity and timing required to achieve such feats, as well as the mindfulness necessary for those performing them. Additionally, Jackie provides workshops on how to execute your own stunts on

a limited budget, for those wanting to create their own action scenes for film projects.

We also get a behind-the-scenes look at Jackie on the sets of *Who Am I* and Brett Ratner's blockbuster hit *Rush Hour*, showing the martial arts superstar actually in the midst of making movies. *My Stunts*, written by Bey Logan, provides an excellent insight into the world of Hong Kong stunt performing. However, once you know some of the secrets, it might take away a little of the magic when watching a Jackie movie in the future. It's similar to a magician sharing the secret of a mind-blowing illusion: it still looks good, but you know it's not real.

This is a must-watch for fans of Jackie Chan and aspiring filmmakers alike. It's a fun and informative look at the world of stunts and the man who revolutionised the genre.

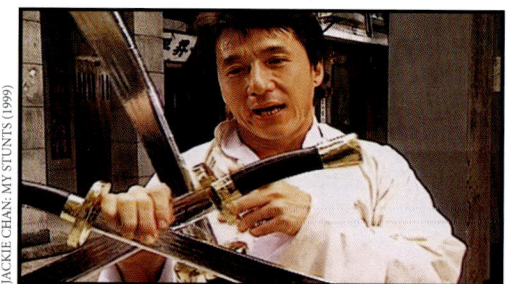

JACKIE CHAN: MY STUNTS (1999)

KICKBOXER'S TEARS (1992)

Starring Moon Lee, Mark Cheng, Wilson Lam, Billy Chow, Yukari Oshima, Lung Fong, Ken Lo
Directed by Shun Daat-Wai
Jin's Motion Picture Company/Regal Films Distribution

This low-budget production attempts to cash in on the kickboxing craze, with a story that sees Moon Lee playing Li Feng, manager of a kickboxing gym. Her brother is tragically slain in the ring by the lethal Billy (Chow), which devastates Li and she lets the gym slide into financial difficulties. Another student (Mark Cheng) enters small kickboxing tournaments in an effort to raise capital for the club, but the insignificant bouts are of little help to Li's cause. She has no choice but to challenge Billy to a rematch and, during the match, Li discovers that Billy used an evil ploy to kill her brother, spurring her on to kill Billy. Li now decides to close up shop and return to her homeland, China, but Billy's boss (Fong) has other plans in store for her. Using his deadly mistress (played by Yukari Oshima) as an opponent, he lures Li into a secret match where they will have to fight it out in a life-or-death struggle.

Even the pretty splendid cast cannot save this underwhelming movie, also known as *Kick Boxer's Tears*, which is hampered by subpar fighting and poor direction.

KING OF COMEDY (1999)
Starring Stephen Chow, Karen Mok, Ng Man-Tat,
Cecilia Cheung, Cheng Man-Fai, Fung Min-Hun
Directed by Stephen Chow, Lee Lik-chi
Star Overseas/Newport Entertainment

Stephen Chow takes a comedic and dramatic look at the trials and tribulations of an aspiring actor, in a story said to be based on Chow's own early career, as he began as a bit-part actor before becoming a successful and popular comedy star. It's interesting to note that the film features a cameo by Jackie Chan, who also got his start as an extra.

The main character, Wan Tin-Sau (Chow), is a wannabe actor who moonlights as a movie extra and teaches acting at his village's community center. He falls in love with one of his students, Lau Piu-Piu (Cheung), and they begin a relationship. As the story progresses, Wan's fortunes begin to change when he lands a leading role in a film next to a legendary actress, Sister Cuckoo (Mok). However, his part is taken away just as he is on the verge of stardom. Then, fortunately, with the help of a misanthropic henchman at the studio, who is secretly a CIA agent, Wan takes part in an undercover operation and saves the day, becoming famous thanks to his performance in his current movie.

King of Comedy ends bizarrely with a marketing plug for Pringles potato chips, in a scene that comes out of nowhere! Overall, this is an entertaining film that is worth watching for fans of Stephen Chow and those interested in a fun, behind-the-scenes look at the struggles of actors.

KNOCK OFF (1998)
Starring Jean-Claude Van Damme, Rob Schneider,
Lela Rochon, Michael Wong, Wyman Wong,
Paul Sorvino
Directed by Tsui Hark
Film Workshop/MDP Worldwide

In Hong Kong, just as it is about to be handed back to China, Marcus Ray (Van Damme) discovers that his business partner, Tommy Hendricks (Schneider), is actually a CIA operative. Ray gets mixed up in a world-threatening scheme involving Russian villains

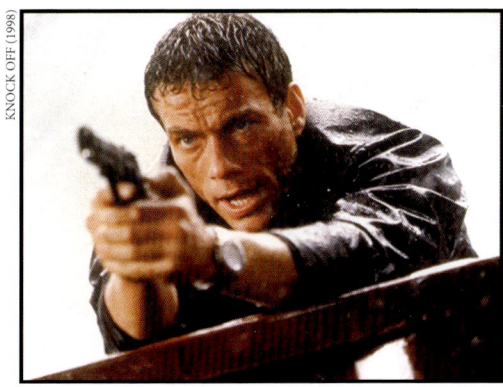

KNOCK OFF (1998)

implanting nano-bombs inside knockoff products like dolls and designer jeans, which they are able to trigger remotely whenever they like.

This hyperactive film, written by *Die Hard* screenwriter Steven E. De Souza, starts with a hectic rickshaw race and never really slackens its pace from there. Rob Schneider, who's something of an acquired taste, is fairly amusing here, while Jean-Claude Van Damme looks like he's enjoying himself a lot, as his character is caught up in a series of preposterous situations, within a story that is forever finding excuses to show him taking off his shirt or trousers.

With green-tinted explosions, a ship-set finale and lots of frenetic camera movements, zooms and extreme close-ups of objects, Tsui Hark's silly, bright and breezy movie comes across as a lightweight knockoff of other, similar, better action thrillers.

LADY SUPERCOP (1993)
Starring Carina Lau, Waise Lee, Teresa Mo,
Chan Wai-Man, May Lo Mei-Mei, Eric Tsang
Directed by Chung Siu-Hung
Produced by Chiu Mei-Bo

A gals with guns action flick about Wenine (Lau) arriving back from Canada to head up a unit in the Hong Kong police force. She is unperturbed by their incompetence in the early stages, but when things

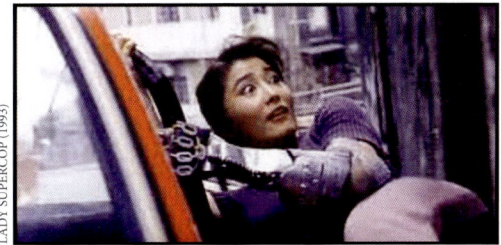

LADY SUPERCOP (1993)

start to go drastically wrong, she decides it is time to knock them into shape.

Some slick female gun action, sprinkled with several ultraviolent moments, including one very graphic dental scene reminiscent of *Marathon Man* (1976), make this run-of-the-mill flick worth watching.

THE MAN FROM HONG KONG (1975)

Starring Jimmy Wang Yu, George Lazenby, Rebecca Gilling, Hugh Keays-Byrne, Sammo Hung
Directed by Brian Trenchard-Smith, Wang Yu
Produced by Raymond Chow
Action by Sammo Hung
Golden Harvest

Long before Jackie Chan was captivating audiences with mind-expanding stunt action, the original king of boxers, Wang Yu, was rocking through one death-defying stunt after another. The action here begins at Ayers Rock in the Australian desert, and ends up in a dramatic hang glider assault on the Sydney headquarters of an arch criminal played by George Lazenby.

Despite the numerous Bond-isms, Wang Yu has a cool power all his own. The bone-crashing stunts are way over the edge, with Wang Yu almost losing his life for real in the outstanding hang gliding sequence.

Also known as *The Dragon Flies*.

THE MASTER (1992)

Starring Jet Li, Yuen Wah, Crystal Kwok, To Wai-Wo, Jerry Trimble, Billy Blanks
Directed and produced by Tsui Hark
Action by Yuen Wah, Yuen Chun-Yeung
Film Workshop/Vast Art Film/Golden Harvest

Shot entirely on location in Los Angeles, this witty and fast-paced action-drama centers around a young kung fu student played by Jet Li, who, while visiting America, decides to look up his old master, Tak (Wah), only to discover that he is having trouble with local hoodlums terrorizing the neighbourhood. Jet then decides to embark on an attempt to train three local teenagers to help him chase off the hoods.

Jet Li had made a name for himself with period-set box office successes like *Shaolin Temple* (1982), *Kids from Shaolin* (1984) and *Martial Arts of Shaolin* (1986) and, after a brief rest, had made a comeback in the modern-day actioner *Dragon Fight* (1989), also shot in America. Although the action scenes are quite slickly shot in both *Dragon Fight* and *The Master*, it is obvious that Jet doesn't look comfortable in his modern-day role.

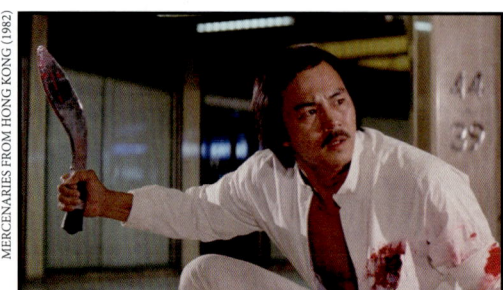
MERCENARIES FROM HONG KONG (1982)

After poor box office receipts, this Tsui Hark project was shelved, but it was reissued in 1992 after Li and Hark teamed-up again to make the internationally successful *Once Upon a Time in China* (1991).

Despite its faults, *The Master* does deliver a great end fight finale, when Jet Li confronts forty or fifty hoodlums on top of a skyscraper in a fight to the death. It's worth watching for this sequence alone.

It is also known as *Wong Fei Hung '92*.

MERCENARIES FROM HONG KONG (1982)

Starring Ti Lung, Michael Chan Wai-Man, Chan Pak-Cheung, Candice Yu, Lai Kam-Sing, Lo Lieh, Wong Yu, Ai Fei
Directed by Wong Jing
Shaw Brothers

Lo Lik (Lung) is hired by Miss Ho (Yu) to head up a mission to Cambodia to capture a top assassin nicknamed the Devil. Lo recruits a team of experts with various skills, succeeds in his mission after much shooting in guerrilla-held territory, but falls foul of a double cross.

Okay, so the traitor in the team is pretty easy to guess and Lo comes across as rather too trusting as the merc leader who's seemingly the last person to suss that Ho is up to no good, but this is a brisk,

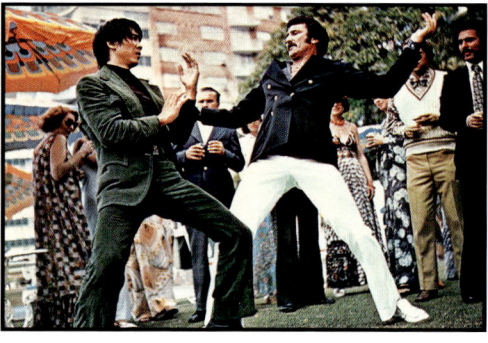
THE MAN FROM HONG KONG (1975)

pulpy, enjoyable, no-nonsense men-on-a-mission movie that delivers shoot-outs, explosions, a baseball bat brawl, smatterings of humor, and a kukri duel.

MIDNIGHT ANGEL (1990)

Starring Yukari Oshima, May Law, Mark Cheng,
Miu Kui-Wai, Melvin Wong
Directed by Chik Ki-Yee
Produced by Ng Ming-Choi
Action by Alan Hsu
New Treasurer Films Company

With law enforcement unable to capture ruthless criminal Bull (Wong), it is left to a black-clad female do-gooder to come to the rescue in this unusual hybrid of kung fu actioner, HK police story and vigilante movie.

Gun battles are mixed with high-energy fights and girls in "bat-capes" and party masks! In one scene the vigilante heroine beats up a guy who has just kicked his pregnant wife, shoving him onto her skateboard and sending him hurtling into a pole. She also utilizes a flamethrower to scorching effect! Soon she is joined by her two sisters, one of them played by Yukari Oshima, who gives the villainous Bull a major thrashing.

In an inventive assassination, two motorcyclists fire harpoon guns at an undercover cop, pulling him out of his car and down the street, where Bull nails his ID tag to his chest! With gratuitous gun action and plenty of high-kicking female fisticuffs, this is a diverting oddity.

MIRACLES (1989)

Starring Jackie Chan, Anita Mui, Bill Tung, Richard Ng,
Wu Ma, Ko Chun-Hsiung
Directed by Jackie Chan
Action by J.C. Stunt Association
Golden Harvest/Golden Way Films Ltd

A reworking of the plot of 1961's *A Pocketful of Miracles* (and therefore 1933's *Lady for a Day*) sees Jackie Chan as Kuo, an opportunist from Canton, who arrives in Hong Kong down on his luck. After buying a rose from a street seller, things take a change of course and, quite by accident, Kuo finds himself the new boss of a vast gangland operation. Opening a fashionable nightclub that features a stunningly talented singer, business starts booming and, not surprisingly, the other gang leaders are hungry for a piece of the action. Feeling he owes his success to the roses that he purchases, Kuo offers to help

the distraught seller when she discloses that her daughter's fiancé and his high-flying father are to visit her, expecting her to be equally rich. Kuo soon finds himself desperately juggling his time between his business, maintaining peace among the gangs and seeing that the biggest con in history is pulled off.

Also known as *The Canton Godfather, Mr. Canton and Lady Rose* and *Miracles: The Canton Godfather*, this production is quite a technical achievement, employing some of the most sophisticated camera work seen in Hong Kong cinema. The comedy and characterisations are spot on, as is the action, which, like the rest of this movie, is on a vast scale, featuring the breathtaking stunts and skirmishes we expect from Jackie Chan. The most notable clash in this film is definitely Jackie's fight with a villainous thug played by Billy Chow.

The original cut of this movie was 127 minutes long, but the UK release was edited down in a bid to

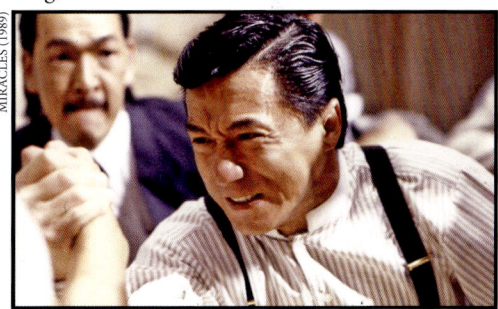

MIRACLES (1989)

tighten up the film's slow pace and present something more in tune with Jackie's expected manic speed of action. Watch out for a cameo from Yuen Biao: blink and you will miss him!

MISSION OF JUSTICE (1992)

Starring Moon Lee, Wong Kwong-Leung, Yukari Oshima,
Carrie Ng, Mark Houghton, Sophia Crawford
Directed by Lu Chin-Ku
Action by Yuen Bo
J.S. Productions/Joe Siu International Film Ltd

Bullet (Oshima) and Moon (Lee) are two tough agents, who are out to bust the biggest drug syndicate in Thailand . . . and they only have ten days to do it! Nothing is beyond these fighting women, as they enter the Golden Triangle, heading through the jungle in pursuit of their prey.

Despite the very so-so storyline, the film at least has several decently choreographed fight sequences featuring Moon and Yukari.

MR. NICE GUY (1997)

Starring Jackie Chan, Richard Norton, Miki Lee,
Karen McLymont, Gabrielle Fitzpatrick
Directed by Sammo Hung
GH Pictures/Golden Harvest

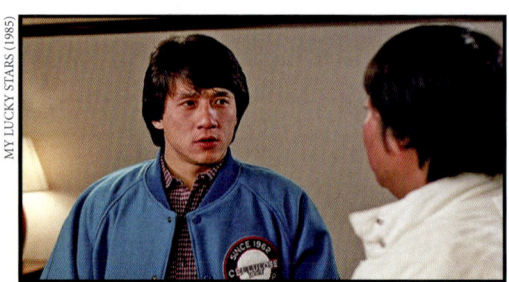

MY LUCKY STARS (1985)

In this action-comedy Jackie (Chan), a television chef, becomes embroiled in a series of wacky and dangerous adventures after he accidentally comes into possession of a valuable videotape.

One of the highlights of *Mr. Nice Guy* is Jackie Chan's signature blend of physical comedy and impressive martial arts skills. The film features numerous impressive and creative action sequences, including a memorable scene in which Jackie fights off a group of attackers using a variety of kitchen utensils. The movie also boasts a talented supporting cast, including Richard Norton as the film's main antagonist and Miki Lee as Jackie's love interest.

Overall, the film's mix of humor, thrilling action and heart make it another great entry in Hong Kong's action-comedy genre.

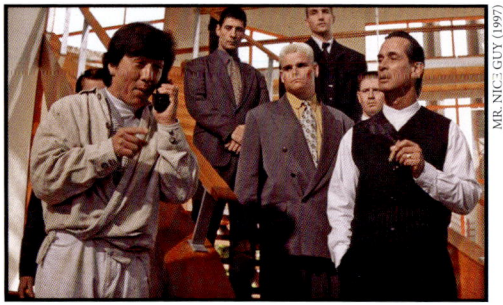

MR. NICE GUY (1997)

MY FATHER IS A HERO (1995)

Starring Jet Li, Anita Mui, Xie Miao, Yu Rongguang,
Ngai Sing, Ken Lo
Directed by Corey Yuen
Produced by Wong Jing, Tiffany Chen
Win's Entertainment Ltd

The film follows the story of young kung fu champ Johnny, played by Xie Miao, who grows up believing his father Wei, played by Jet Li, is a dangerous criminal. However, it turns out that Wei is actually an undercover agent infiltrating a Hong Kong triad gang.

Enter Inspector Fong (Mui), a brazen cop on a mission to dismantle the criminal gang, who investigates Wei's mainland past and uncovers his true identity, leading to her working alongside father and son to bring down the triad. The stakes are

high, as Wei's gravely ill wife passes away and Fong takes Johnny back to Hong Kong with her, but with a criminal empire to topple, the trio is up to the challenge.

What follows is a series of exhilarating action sequences, brilliantly choreographed and executed with precision. But what really sets *My Father is a Hero* apart is the heart and emotion that runs through it. The bond between father and son is palpable, as Wei does everything in his power to protect Johnny, even if it means putting his own life on the line.

The chemistry between Li, Miao, and Mui is fantastic, and the story is well-paced, with plenty of twists and turns to keep you on the edge of your seat.

My Father is a Hero, which also goes by the title *The Enforcer*, delivers both entertaining fight scenes and a compelling emotional core, with Jet Li proving once again that he is a master of his craft. The supporting cast brings their A-game too, making this a standout film.

MY LUCKY STARS (1985)

Starring Sammo Hung, Jackie Chan, Sibelle Hu,
Lam Ching Ying
Directed by Sammo Hung
Produced by Leonard K.C. Ho
Action by Sammo Hung, Lam Ching-Ying, Yuen Wah,
Yuen Biao, Billy Chan
Golden Harvest/Cine-Asia

The cast members of *Winners and Sinners* (1983) are reunited in this well-paced action comedy, set in Japan.

Muscles (Chan) and Ricky (Biao) are two Hong Kong policemen trying to serve an extradition order on a dangerous criminal. When their identities are discovered, Ricky is captured and, in an attempt to get him free, Muscles calls upon his old childhood "orphanage gang" for help. They are happy to travel to Tokyo, especially when it entails sharing a hotel room with the beautiful policewoman (Hu) assigned to help them.

Perhaps the closest Hong Kong has come to

producing a *Carry On*-style film, the simple, childish humor here is as effective as it is shameless.

It is only with the final reel that it really assumes the appearance of a Jackie Chan feature, where top-notch fight action and stunt work abound.

NEW KIDS IN TOWN (1990)
Starring Lau Kar-Leung, Chin Siu-Hao, Moon Lee, Andy Cheng, Sophia Crawford, Karel Ng, Eddie Maher
Directed and produced by Lau Kar-Yung
Lau's Film Production

Two kung fu students from mainland China are selected to travel to Hong Kong to train under a resident master. It is not long before the young men and the master's daughter get caught up in the activities of a major drugs syndicate.

The simple plot to this film, also known as *New Killers in Town*, creates many opportunities for bone-crunching confrontation. Lau Kar-Leung (The Pops) for once succeeds in the modern day setting, and the careful blend of classical martial arts, kickboxing and gunplay makes for an exciting, albeit brainless, adventure film.

The antagonists (Karel Ng and Eddie Maher) are suitably contemptible, while the young heroes are very virtuous, in a movie that's an entertaining example of how there is a place for chivalry in Hong Kong movies set in the modern day.

'97 ACES GO PLACES (1997)
Starring Tony Leung Chiu-Wai, Christy Chung, Alan Tam, Francis Ng, Donna Chu
Directed by Chin Kar-Lok
Crystalfix

This Hong Kong action-comedy marks the final installment of the *Aces Go Places* series. Directed by Chin Kar-Lok, the film boasts an all-star cast, including Alan Tam, Tony Leung, Christy Chung, Donna Chu, Francis Ng and Billy Chow. Although it features different actors and storyline from its predecessors, the film manages to retain the humor and excitement that made the series a hit.

The film follows a group of thieves who attempt to steal a diamond from a wealthy businessman. However, their plan goes awry when they are pursued by a team of police officers led by Inspector Ho (Leung). As the chase ensues, the thieves and the police officers find themselves teaming up to take down a common enemy.

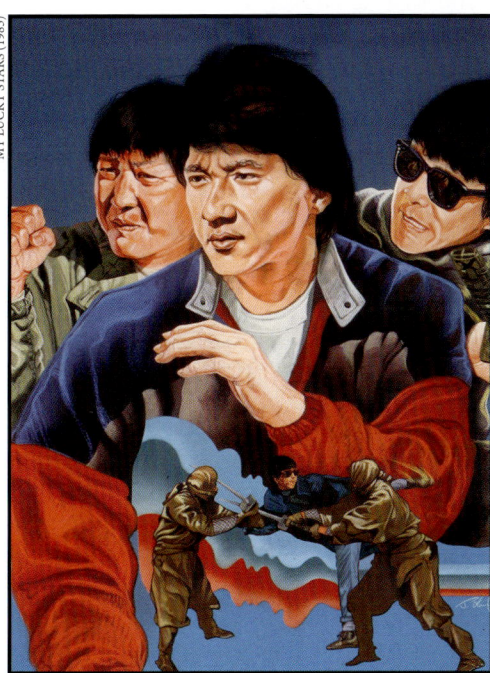

MY LUCKY STARS (1985)

One of the strengths of '97 *Aces Go Places* is definitely its stellar cast, who all deliver strong performances. Tony Leung is particularly impressive in his role as Inspector Ho, injecting the film with a sense of gravity that grounds the comedic elements. Meanwhile, Alan Tam and Christy Chung provide plenty of laughs as the bumbling thieves.

In terms of action, the film delivers, featuring a number of thrilling set pieces that are sure to keep the viewer's attention.

A worthy conclusion to the *Aces Go Places* series, this movie may not offer anything particularly new or groundbreaking, but it delivers on the promise of an entertaining action-comedy, and newcomers to the franchise may find themselves eager to check out the earlier installments.

NINJA TERMINATOR (1985)
Starring Richard Harrison, Phillip Ko, Jack Lam, Jonathan Wattis, Maria Francesca, Hwang Jang-Lee
Directed by Godfrey Ho
IFD Films and Arts

Various ninja factions want to possess the three pieces of the Ninja Golden Warrior statuette.

This is an ace example of spliced-together IFD madness. See Richard Harrison, as ninja hero Harry, use a plastic Garfield phone to talk menacingly with

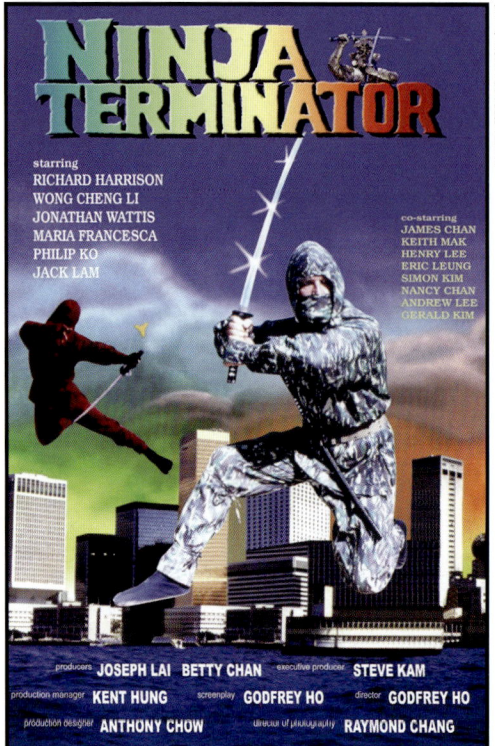

NINJA TERMINATOR (1985)

NOMAD (1982)
Starring Leslie Cheung, Cecilia Yip, Patricia Ha,
Chan Bo-Yeung
Directed by Patrick Tam
Action by Luk Tsun
Century Motion Picture & Dist.

In this well-crafted coming of age picture, Leslie Cheung stars as a teenager who learns about life, love and death during the hot and humid Hong Kong summer. The totally unexpected happens when Leslie offers to harbor a fugitive on the run from the Japanese Red Army. Now the happy lives of four Hong Kong teenagers turn to tragedy.

Rather than just making a teenage exploitation flick, director Patrick Tam handles his material with sensitivity and colorful humor, although at times he does wallow in self-indulgent pretentiousness.

OUTLAW BROTHERS (1990)
Starring Frankie Chan, Yukari Oshima, Miu Kui-Wai,
Michiko Nishiwaki, Mok Siu-Chung, Mark Houghton,
Sheila Chan
Directed by Frankie Chan
Produced by Wallace Cheung, Frankie Chan, Eric Tsang
Movie Impact Limited

This gem of a film casts Frankie Chan (yes, the guy who fights Yuen Biao in *Prodigal Son*) as a professional car thief who, with his partner played by Mok Sui-Chung, specializes in hotwiring top of the range Porsches. But the police are closing in, in the shape of Yukari Oshima. As Frankie Chan tries to stay one step ahead, he finds himself becoming more and more attracted to his deadly foe.

This is the film that firmly established Yukari Oshima as the top lethal lady in Hong Kong, with her looks and excellent martial arts bringing her an instant army of fans. The final reel highlights some of Yukari's best fighting and still stands the test of time.

the leader of the ninja empire! See a small, cheap toy robot used by the bad ninjas to deliver their ultimatums! See a swarm of crabs crawling from a saucepan, scaring Harry's wife (played by Harrison's real-life wife Maria), forcing Harry to skewer one of the crabs with a ninja throwing dart! See various ninjas attack each other with smoke bombs, katana, shuriken and even some sneaky elbow-spikes!

What helps ramp up the enjoyment factor of this particular Ho-tastic offering is the fact the original footage that the ninja scenes have been spliced into is taken from a Korean movie called *The Uninvited Guest of the Star Ferry* (1984), which features really good fight action scenes! Here we get to see Jack Lam (playing a character called Jaguar Wong on the new audio track) kicking ass in a very effective-looking manner, which leads up to his confrontation on a beach with villain Hwang Jang-Lee.

With katana swords that can spray smoke out of their hilts, ninjas able to vanish and then reappear again, Hwang Jang-Lee wearing a blond wig for some unfathomable reason and Jack Lam looking supercool in all of his scenes, this is absurd cut-and-paste ninja movie nirvana!

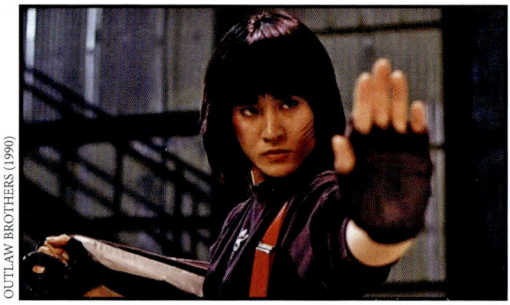

OUTLAW BROTHERS (1990)

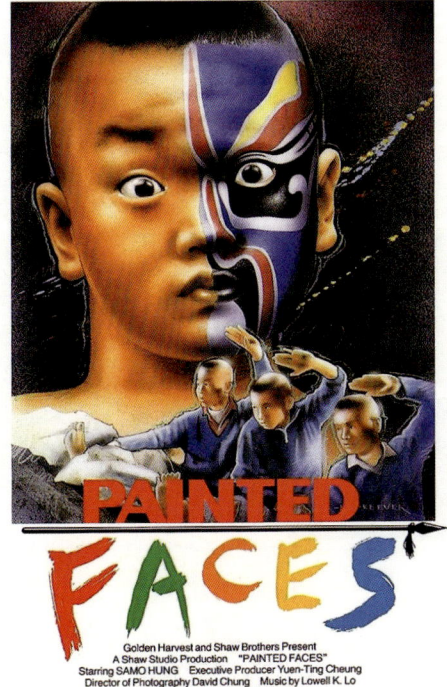

PAINTED FACES (1988)

The critically-acclaimed story of three young men growing from a traditional Chinese theatrical school to stardom in Hong Kong's thriving film industry.

Golden Harvest and Shaw Brothers Present
A Shaw Studio Production "PAINTED FACES"
Starring SAMO HUNG Executive Producer Yuen-Ting Cheung
Director of Photography David Chung Music by Lowell K. Lo
Produced by Leonard Ho and Mona Fong
Screenplay by Alex Law and Yuen-Ting Chung Directed by Alex Law

Owl. When a property developer, who is shielded by a police superintendent, is involved in illegal undertakings, the superintendent loses his upright position in society and has to retire from the force. He decides to trick the two bumbling criminals into helping him locate the property developer in a bid to get even.

Despite several good comedy moments, and an ingenious tap dancing routine from Hung, the film doesn't really exploit Sammo Hung's action-minded genius.

PAINTED FACES (1988)
Starring Sammo Hung, Lam Ching-Ying,
Cheng Pei-Pei, John Sham, Li Tien-Hsing, Wu Ma
Directed by Alex Law
Produced by Leonard K.C. Ho
Golden Harvest/Shaw Brothers

Based on fact, with added fictionalised elements, this film tells the tale of seven boys (the Seven Little Fortunes—Jackie Chan and co.) as they progress through their studies at the famous Peking Opera, under the guidance of Master Yu.

The story highlights the endurance and dedication necessary to survive the rigours of the traditional school, plus the way in which the boys dealt with the growing temptations of infiltrating Western cultural influences during the Sixties.

Sammo Hung plays Master Yu—ironic as the movie is partly based on his own experiences under Yu. The film is sympathetically directed by Alex Law.

PANTYHOSE HERO (1990)
Starring Sammo Hung, Alan Tam, James Tien, Jaclyn
Chu, Philip Chan
Directed and produced by Sammo Hung
Action by Sammo Hung
Bojon Films Company Ltd

Most people's memories of Alan Tam are probably of his wimpy role playing opposite Jackie Chan in *Armour of God* (1986). But Tam, under the watchful eye of Sammo Hung, definitely hardened up his image (see *The Dragon Family* and *The Last Blood* for proof).

Here Sammo and Alan play two cops selected to go undercover to track down a slasher who is running wild in the gay clubs. To get themselves into character, they are given (politically incorrect) lessons on how to act effeminately, learning to mince when they walk and hold their arm on their hip as

The film also allowed several up-and-coming Western talents to demonstrate their ability, as at this time there was a growing trend to have several Western fighters in the end fight scenes. Here we get Mark Houghton, Jeff Falcon, and Vincent Lyn.

With Jackie Chan on the set to help choreograph the fight scenes, this is truly one of the classic femme fatale action films. And if that's not enough, the sleek but deadly Michiko Nishiwaki was drafted in to bring villainous glamor to this stylish production.

THE OWL VS BUMBO (1984)
Starring Sammo Hung, George Lam, Deanie Ip,
Michelle Yeoh, Billy Chan, Philip Chan
Directed by Sammo Hung
D & B Films Co. Ltd

Sammo Hung, the portly kicker whose name is normally associated with quality, here directs a potboiler. He and George Lam play retired criminals who have the underground names of Bumbo and

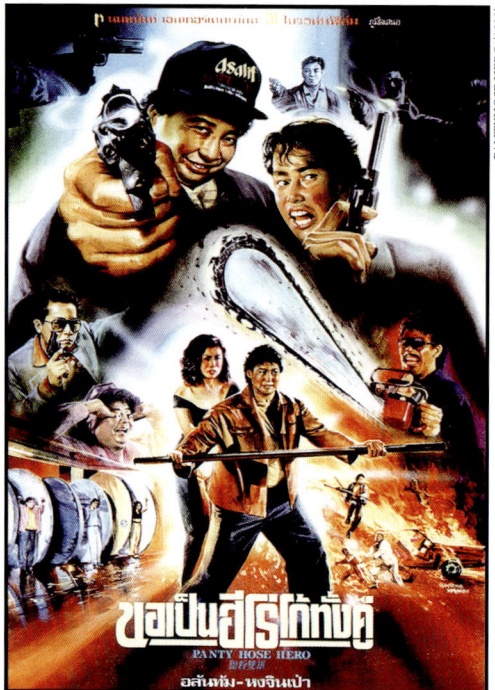

PANTYHOSE HERO (1990)

if carrying wallpaper. Despite their reluctance, they find themselves adapting to their new position quite well, with some hilarious consequences.

Also known as *Pantyhose Killer*, Sammo Hung's silly comedy, full of gay stereotypes and outrageous behavior, also includes, as is the way with Hong Kong films, some harsh, often violent moments, and the superior fight choreography which Hung has become notable for is featured too.

PAPER MARRIAGE (1988)

Starring Sammo Hung, Maggie Cheung, Dick Wei, Joyce Godenzi, Billy Chow, Alfred Cheung
Directed by Alfred Cheung
Action by Yuen Wah
Bo Ho Film Company Ltd/Golden Harvest

Sammo Hung plays a down-on-his-luck Chinese boxer living in Canada. Desperate for money, he decides to accept Maggie Cheung's marriage proposal so that she can get Canadian citizenship. (Sammo Hung must be the only guy who would want money to marry Maggie Cheung!) Unfortunately, Maggie realizes too late that this is part of a complicated con by a so-called boyfriend to cheat her out of her money. Suddenly, Sammo and Maggie find themselves broke, living on the breadline, with Sammo being forced

to go back into the ring. Maggie, wanting to share the burden, finds the only way she can raise a few dollars is to mud wrestle in seedy nightclubs! As the two find their lives becoming more complicated and difficult, they slowly start falling in love.

Sammo Hung seemed to be turning out his best work in the mid-to-late eighties, but *Paper Marriage* was not one of his better showcases, and the combination of romantic comedy, peppered with sporadic fight scenes, makes for a very uneven vehicle. But it is worth the watch, if only to see a groundbreaking kick which only the genius of Sammo Hung could have devised: Billy Chow, fighting a Western assailant, runs at his attacker doing a perfect forward roll and, at the same time, he brings his foot 360 degrees over . . . and cracks his opponent square in the head! It's amazingly physical inventiveness like this that makes the other 89 minutes worth watching.

PEDICAB DRIVER (1989)

Starring Sammo Hung, Mok Siu-Chung, Meng Hoi, Nina Li Chi, Billy Chow, Lau Kar-Leung
Directed by Sammo Hung
Action by Sammo Hung, Brandy Yuen, Meng Hoi
Bojon Films Company Ltd/Golden Harvest

This is an awesome movie, from the opening fight in the cafe, through an excellent confrontation between casino boss Lau Kar-Leung and Sammo Hung, who plays the movie's protagonist Tung, to a classic end clash between Sammo and the highly underrated Billy Chow, in the role of a tough thug, which will really have you cheering!

One of the kings of fight choreography, Sammo really excels himself in this masterpiece of action comedy, which has to be seen to be believed.

Nuff said!

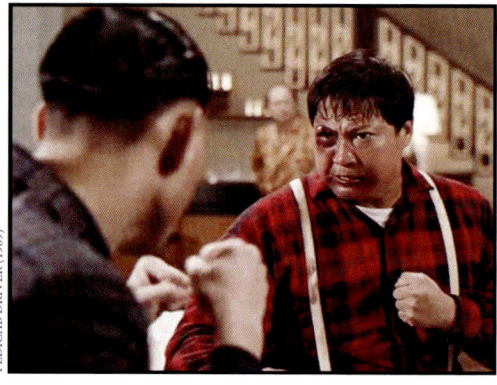

PEDICAB DRIVER (1989)

POLICE STORY (1985)
Starring Jackie Chan, Maggie Cheung, Bill Tung,
Chor Yuen, Mars, Brigitte Lin
Directed by Jackie Chan
Produced by Leonard K.C. Ho
Action by Jackie Chan
Golden Harvest/Golden Way Films

Police Story is regarded by many as the pinnacle of Jackie's film career, breaking new ground worldwide with its breathtaking fights and stunt sequences.

After the explosive opening, where a whole village is demolished, Jackie, playing Sergeant Chan, apprehends a gang boss (Yuen), who is then released on bail despite being caught with a briefcase full of money. To strengthen Chan's case, the police decide to take the boss' beautiful secretary (Lin) and put her into a witness protection scheme, trying to bluff the boss into believing that she will give evidence against him. Chan is put in charge of her, and in an attempt to pressure her into giving evidence, he sets up an attempt on her life by getting a colleague to pretend to be an assassin. But, meanwhile, the boss decides maybe he should have her silenced for real, just in case she cracks under pressure. Chan's persistence and determination, however, forces the

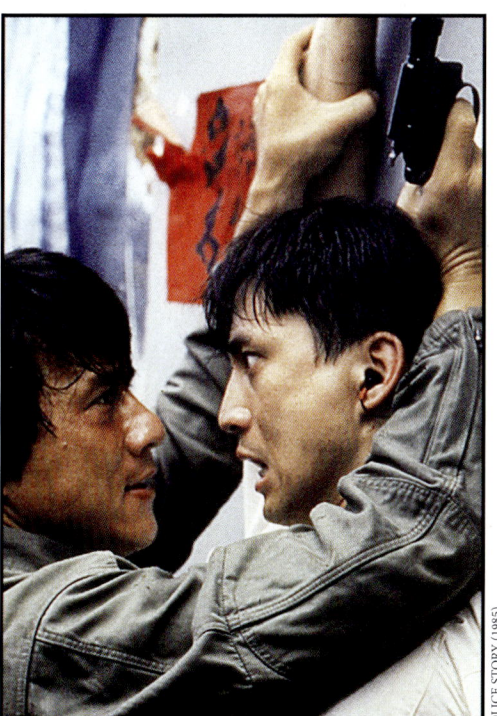

POLICE STORY (1985)

boss to take further steps, and we discover that he has one of Chan's police friends working for him, who the boss then decides to murder so that he can set Chan up. After a desperate battle, Chan finds himself chloroformed and dumped near the airport, knowing he has been framed. Unable to prove his innocence, he takes his commanding officer hostage and pursues the gang boss and his cronies to a shopping mall for a showdown . . .

What starts out as a typical Jackie Chan comedy, with Maggie Cheung as his long-suffering girlfriend, takes a stark turnabout when Jackie finds himself on the opposite side of the law. Jackie's ability to mix a compelling storyline with arguably some of the best Hong Kong stunts and action ever committed to celluloid, demonstrates why he is the number one box office star in his chosen field of action flicks.

This film is the perfect example of why Hong Kong cinema was labeled "over the edge" and it is an excellent introduction to the genre.

POLICE STORY 2 (1988)
Starring Jackie Chan, Maggie Cheung, Lam Kwok-Hung,
Benny Lai, Mars, Bill Tung, Wu Ma
Directed by Jackie Chan
Produced by Leonard K.C. Ho
Action by Jackie Chan
Golden Harvest/Golden Way Films Ltd

It was probably impossible for *Police Story 2* to improve on the original concept, although Jackie, ever the perfectionist, does his best to deliver the goods, but the plot seems to give way to Chan's new designer look, heavily influenced by the *Miami Vice* television series.

This time Jackie, as Sergeant Chan Ka Kui, is pursuing a gang of terrorists that are involved in making explosives. Once more his girlfriend May is in tow, played again by Maggie Cheung.

Police Story 2 does have several stunning fight sequences, including a very well-choreographed fight in a park. The final showdown is great, too, with Jackie allowing his stuntman and longtime friend Benny Lai to steal the limelight in an excellent scene. This skirmish does fizzle, though, when Jackie reverts to throwing little bombs at his attacker, rather than using the skilled fighting that won him so much praise in previous films.

Police Story 2 is a good film taken on its own merits, but not even the genius of Jackie could surpass his own masterpiece.

POLICE STORY 3: SUPERCOP (1992)

Starring Jackie Chan, Michelle Yeoh, Yuen Wah,
Maggie Cheung, Kelvin Wong, Philip Chan, Mars,
Bill Tung
Directed by Stanley Tong
Action by Jackie Chan
Golden Harvest/Golden Way Films Ltd

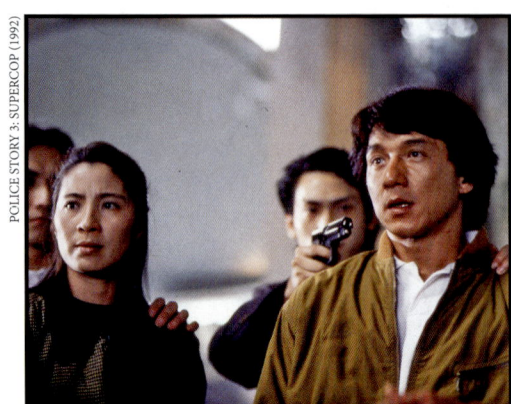

POLICE STORY 3: SUPERCOP (1992)

Jackie Chan returns as the maverick cop Ka Kui, for the third installment of the popular series. In a change of pace from the first two films, Ka Kui goes undercover, infiltrating a gang smuggling arms and drugs between the mainland and Hong Kong. Aiding him in this top secret mission is agent Yang (Michelle Yeoh). Although not one of Chan's most memorable outings, this is nevertheless an astonishing example of the superiority of Hong Kong's action cinema. The skillfully directed action, incorporating fists, feet, explosives, automatic weaponry and every mode of transport imaginable, when added to the nature of Ka Kui's job, makes this the Chan project most similar to a Bond film.

Thankfully, cheesy one-liners are not on hand, but comedy supplied by Bill Tung and Maggie Cheung offers momentary relief from the tension. Stanley Tong's direction is generous, not only making sure Chan looks good, but also ensuring Michelle Yeoh is sufficiently courageous, charismatic, and deadly as Chan's sidekick: there is definitely stiff competition for the limelight in the scenes where they both feature!

No such film would be complete without a classic stunt, and the sight of Chan dangling from a helicopter swooping through Kuala Lumpur fits the bill perfectly. Most Hollywood actioners seem pale in comparison.

POLICE STORY 4: FIRST STRIKE (1996)

Starring Jackie Chan, Jackson Lou, Annie Wu, Bill Tung
Directed by Stanley Tong
Golden Harvest

Jackie Chan is back as Ka Kui, a cop embroiled in an international plot involving the KGB, CIA, and arms dealers. While the film features a number of familiar elements from Chan's previous movies, including chases across continents and outrageous stunts, it also introduces a story that seems geared toward Western audiences.

Although Chan is still in decent form, his age is starting to show, and the action sequences, while impressive, lack the all-out mayhem that made him famous. The film is filled with emotional plot devices, but they serve as filler rather than adding depth to the story. The standout moments include a thrilling central action sequence and a fun shark tank chase, but, overall, the movie fails to reach the heights of its predecessors, especially *Police Story* and *Supercop*.

Despite the fresh performance from female lead Annie Wu, the film lacks the distinct "Hong Kong" qualities that set Jackie Chan apart from other action stars. This film, also known as *Jackie Chan's First Strike* and simply *First Strike*, may entertain Chan fans, but it falls short of being a must-watch for action enthusiasts.

POM POM AND HOT HOT (1992)

Starring Jacky Cheung, Tung Wei, Lam Ching-Ying,
Bonnie Fu, Loletta Lee
Directed by Joseph Cheung
Action by Tung Wei and Kong To-Hoi
New Prima Film Production

Pom Pom and Hot Hot merges wacky slapstick comedy with heroic bloodshed shoot-out moments. Lurking within all the Hong Kong–style humor is a story featuring the leader of an underground gang, who is, without a doubt, one of the slickest gun users in the East. When it all becomes too much for our heroes, they draft in super-hotshot cop Lam Ching-Ying.

Though this is a so-so comedy for the most part, with bursts of action interspersed throughout, the final confrontation erupts into fifteen minutes of sheer high-octane action, a roller-coaster ride of a gun battle with Lam and his two sidekicks taking down the gang members one by one, until we are left with the two main villains. It's an outrageously over-the-top firefight that will have you rewatching it time and time again.

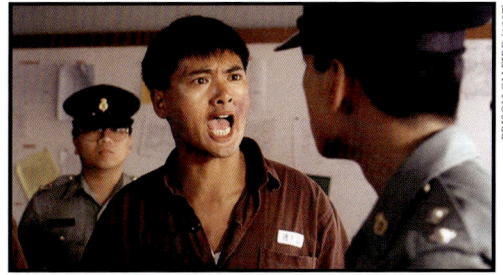

PRISON ON FIRE (1987)

PRISON ON FIRE (1987)
Starring Chow Yun-Fat, Tony Leung Ka-Fai,
Ho Ka-Kui, Victor Hon Kwan, Roy Cheung
Directed by Ringo Lam
Produced by Karl Maka, Ringo Lam
Action by Joe Chi, Liu Chia-Yung
Cinema City

Chow Yun-Fat plays convicted criminal Chung Tin Ching, who befriends mild-mannered Lo Ka Yiu (Leung), the victim of constant bullying. However, when Chung comes to Lo's aid, the bullies turn their focus on Chung, so the two outsiders must use their wits to outsmart the vicious thugs.

Roy Cheung is excellent as the sadistic prison warden, who orchestrates the brutal showdown with Chung. The humorous approach of many earlier scenes is suspended for this bloody confrontation, with Chung fighting most inventively to save himself from the terrible beating.

This excellent drama shows the full range of Chow's extraordinary acting talents.

PRISON ON FIRE II (1991)
Starring Chow Yun-Fat, Chan Chung-Yung,
Elvis Tsui, Wong Kwong-Leung, Yu Li,
Victor Hon Kwan
Directed by Ringo Lam
Produced by Karl Maka
Action by Lin Man-Hua
Cinema City/Golden Princess Film Production Limited

Chung (Yun-Fat) is still in prison, and circumstances there have not improved! Not only is there a growing rift between the Hong Kong and mainland prisoners, but there is also prison officer Zau (Tsui) to be dealt with. Chung finds himself caught in the middle of the conflict and befriends mainland Chinese convict Dragon (Chung-Yung).

Zau is determined to run the prison in his own way, so he tries to keep the inflamed conflict between the prisoners alight. Meanwhile, Chung also has

to face the emotional trauma of having his son committed to an orphanage while contending with the sadistic treatment that he and the other prisoners continually endure, which all leads, once again, to Chung deciding he must stand up to the authorities.

While more lighthearted than the first part, this film still contains incredible action sequences, including a fine finale: a nail-biting, emotionally draining bout of heroic bloodshed. Chow's screen presence, and the subtle blend of humor, menace and dignity which Chan Chung-Yung brings to his character, make this one to watch.

PROJECT A (1983)
Starring Jackie Chan, Sammo Hung, Yuen Biao,
Dick Wei, Mars, Winnie Wong
Directed by Jackie Chan
Produced by Raymond Chow, Leonard K.C. Ho
Action by Jackie Chan, Sammo Hung
Golden Harvest/Authority Films

This could be regarded as the perfect showcase to highlight not only Jackie Chan's extraordinary martial arts ability, but the hilarious way he fuses it with comedy.

Set at the turn of the century, Jackie plays Sergeant Dragon Ma Yue Lung, who belongs to a detachment of marine police that have been far from successful at capturing the notorious pirates and cutthroats that infest the China Sea. Little do they know that there is a traitor in their midst, allowing the pirates to stay one step ahead. To slow matters down even more, the marines are in constant rivalry with the local police, which results in a spectacular barroom brawl. But, finally, the two groups unite against the pirates, mounting an action-packed raid on their lair.

Sammo Hung and Yuen Biao are the extra ingredients that help make this an all-round Hong Kong action-blockbuster, that subsequently broke

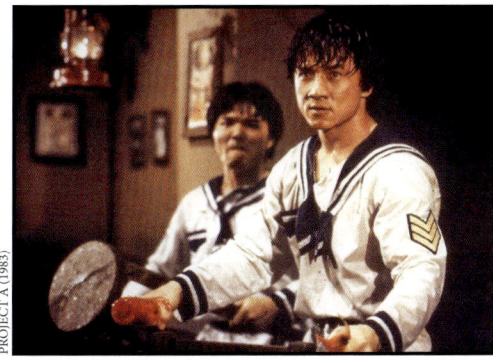

PROJECT A (1983)

box office records in Asia. The movie almost cost Jackie his life too, when a stunt involving him falling from a clock tower, breaking his fall using three canopies, didn't go as planned. Jackie chose not to use safety mats, relying on the last canopy to allow him to land safely, but, as the outtakes at the end show, Jackie landed on his head and was lucky not to have been more seriously hurt than he was.

Highlights include a bravura bike chase through increasingly narrow back alleys and the climactic fight sequence, which sees Jackie, Sammo, and Yuen battling pirate leader Dick Wei.

PROJECT A PART II (1987)
Starring Jackie Chan, Maggie Cheung, David Lam, Rosamund Kwan, Carina Lau, Bill Tung, Mars
Directed by Jackie Chan
Produced by Leonard K.C. Ho
Action by Jackie Chan
Golden Harvest/Golden Way Films Ltd

After the runaway success of *Project A* it was inevitable that Golden Harvest would follow it up with a sequel. At the time, there seemed to be a rift between Jackie Chan and Sammo Hung, which saw Jackie go it alone to make this follow-up film, while Sammo, along with Yuen Biao and a host of other top action stars, made *Eastern Condors*.

In *Project A Part II* Jackie has changed sides, becoming Inspector Dragon Ma, who has been assigned to try and end gangland activities, which leads to yet another exciting fracas inside one of the dens they frequent. In a revenge attempt, the villains hire two revolutionaries, in the beautiful guises of Maggie Cheung and Carina Lau, to infiltrate a party where Jackie and his men are acting as security. They steal the commissioner's most valuable possessions, frame Jackie for the theft and he goes to jail. Fortunately, the same revolutionaries break into the prison in an attempt to rescue one of their comrades and they accidentally release Jackie, who now befriends them and goes in search of revenge.

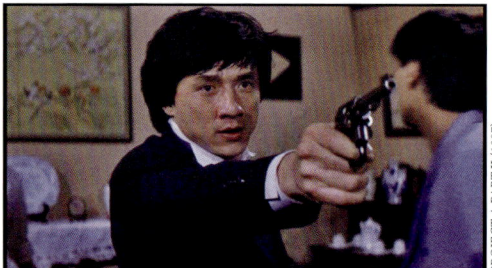
PROJECT A PART II (1987)

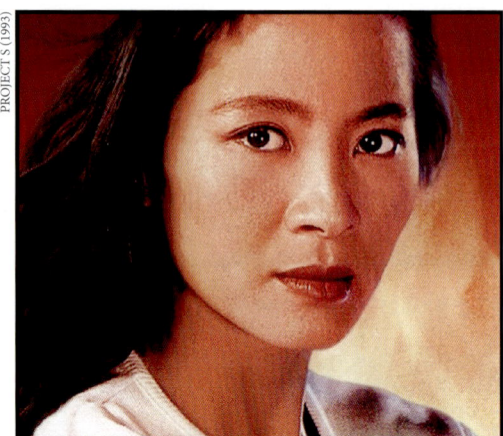
PROJECT S (1993)

Jackie, in an attempt to prove himself to his brothers in kung fu—Sammo and Yuen Biao—plays down the fight action in order to pursue several mindboggling stunts. One sees him fall from the side of a building, bouncing all the way down off bamboo scaffolding, which must be one of the most painful stunts of all time, and then, to top this, in homage to Buster Keaton, his influence from the silent screen, Jackie stands beneath a collapsing building . . . and the camera watches as he strategically places himself directly under the open window and walks away unscathed.

Project A Part II is a fast-paced comedy caper, which, despite its many magic moments, falls just short of the brilliance of its predecessor.

PROJECT S (1993)
Starring Michelle Yeoh, Yu Rongguang, Fan Sui-Wong, Emil Chau, Bill Tung, Yukari Oshima, Dick Wei, Jackie Chan
Directed by Stanley Tong
Action by Stanley Tong
Golden Harvest/Golden Way Films Ltd

While Jackie Chan does make a cameo appearance (in drag!) in a hilarious fight scene, the undoubted star of this movie is Yu Rongguang. He plays David, the lover of Michelle Yeoh, who reprises her role as Yang from *Police Story 3*. David takes up an opportunity to go to Hong Kong and, as the years pass, he becomes the head of a Chinese gang that robs a bank in the central district. Yang is sent to Hong Kong to track the gang down and, after some mind-blowing fights, she realizes that the gang leader is her former lover, who is now attempting to rob the un-robbable Hong Kong Bank. Events, of course, very quickly get out of hand . . .

Despite Jackie not heading the cast, the action here is dynamic, with Yu Rongguang delivering the action goods with great flair. A must-see movie.

THE PROTECTOR (1985)
Starring Jackie Chan, Danny Aiello, Roy Chiao,
Bill Wallace, Moon Lee, Saun Ellis
Directed by James Glickenhaus
Produced by Raymond Chow, David Chan,
Leonard K.C. Ho
Action by Jackie Chan
Golden Harvest/Golden Way Films Ltd

Jackie Chan goes Stateside for the second time, in an attempt break into the Western market. Here he plays Billy, a New York cop working the sleazy South Bronx area. After a series of mishaps, which include his partner being killed and seven million dollars' worth of damage to public property, Billy is demoted to softer assignments in disgrace, with new partner Danny Garoni (Aiello). While Billy is acting as security at an uptown fashion show, the host, Laura Shapiro (Ellis), is kidnapped in a

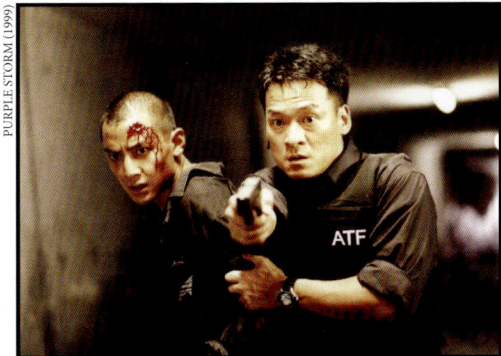

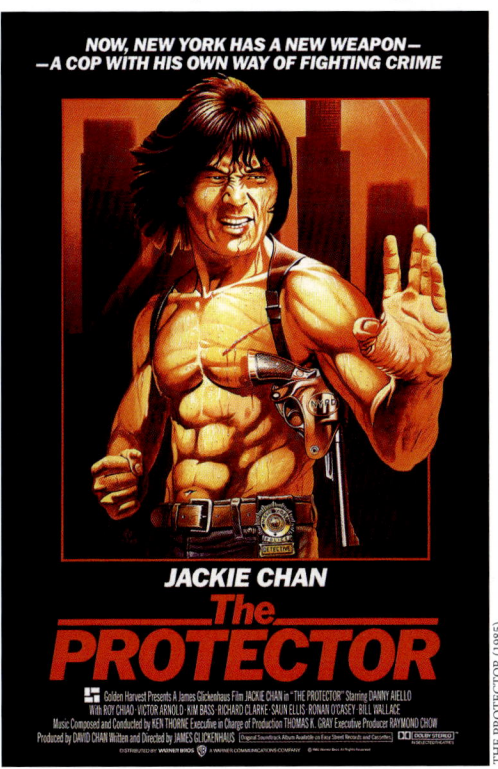

commando-style raid. Once again, the buck stops with Billy. He is about to lose his badge when he comes up with a lead that takes him and Danny to Hong Kong to rescue Laura and, in the process, a huge drug operation is uncovered.

Jackie Chan's rocky relationship with director James Glickenhaus led to him becoming unhappy with the finished version. So, with some remaining members of the crew, Jackie decided to reshoot the second half of the film, dispensing with the nudity and overt American style, replacing it with the "Jackie formula" his Asian fans expected. The result is that there are two versions of the movie: the Western release, which, although quite successful, made very little use of Jackie's skills, and the Asian version, which has at least thirty minutes of new footage, fights, and action. Jackie Chan purists will definitely want to see the latter.

PURPLE STORM (1999)
Starring Daniel Wu, Kam Kwok-Leung, Emil Chau,
Josie Ho, Joan Chen
Directed by Teddy Chan
Media Asia Films

This acclaimed techno-thriller was a breakthrough in Hong Kong movie-making, delivering a high-octane action film that takes its viewers on a roller-coaster ride of espionage and terrorism.

The film follows the story of a group of terrorists linked to Cambodia, who are determined to further the goals of the Khmer Rouge. The opening scene of the film is a brilliantly executed operation that goes wrong, leaving one of the terrorists in police custody with a serious head injury. The police use this opportunity to brainwash him into thinking that he is a counterterrorist agent and force him to help foil the plans of his former comrades.

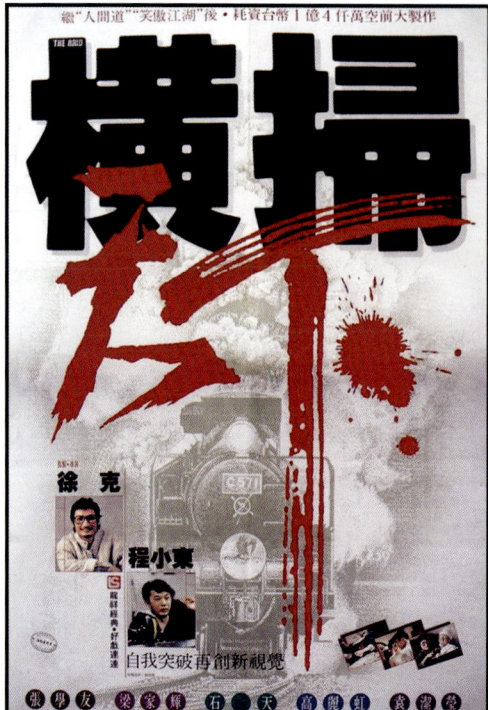

THE RAID (1991)

Purple Storm is visually impressive and follows the modern trend of fancy camera angles and slow-motion shots. While the slo-mo effects are at times overdone, they add to the overall appeal of the film. The movie boasts plenty of visual FX, and while some may appear outdated by Hollywood standards, they are a step in the right direction for Hong Kong cinema.

Despite its flaws, *Purple Storm* keeps you engaged throughout the film, thanks to its intricate plot and adrenaline-pumping action sequences.

THE RAID (1991)
Starring Dean Shek, Jacky Cheung, Tony Leung Ka-Fai,
Corey Yuen, Joyce Godenzi
Directed by Tsui Hark, Ching Siu-Tung
Produced by Tsui Hark
Action by Ching Siu-Tung
Cinema City/Golden Princess

Presented like a live action comic strip, this pretty damn preposterous spy-action-comedy film takes place in Japanese-occupied Manchuria, where the protagonists are caught up in a power struggle for rule of the empire.

Bedroom farce elements and cliff face midair action are combined with some cool martial arts, including

a duel between Joyce Godenzi and a sparky, young spear-wielding Wu Shu opponent, plus a brilliant sword fight involving Commander Masa, played by Tony Leung.

The movie could do with more of this Wu Shu action and less of the unimaginative bloodshed and destruction of inanimate objects, although it remains great entertainment.

THE RED WOLF (1995)
Starring Kenny Ho, Christy Chung, Elaine Lui,
Cho Wing, Woo Fung
Directed by Yuen Woo-Ping
Hsing Bao Art Screen Co

Set on a luxurious cruise ship, where a group of vicious terrorists are on the hunt for a batch of uranium kept in the ship's safe, the story sees Alan (Ho), the head of security, finding himself outnumbered after witnessing the brutal death of his captain as the terrorists take everyone hostage. With nowhere to run except overboard, Alan has no choice but to prevent the terrorists from achieving their mission. His only help comes in the form of a beautiful pickpocket, Linda (Chung), who has overheard the terrorist plan.

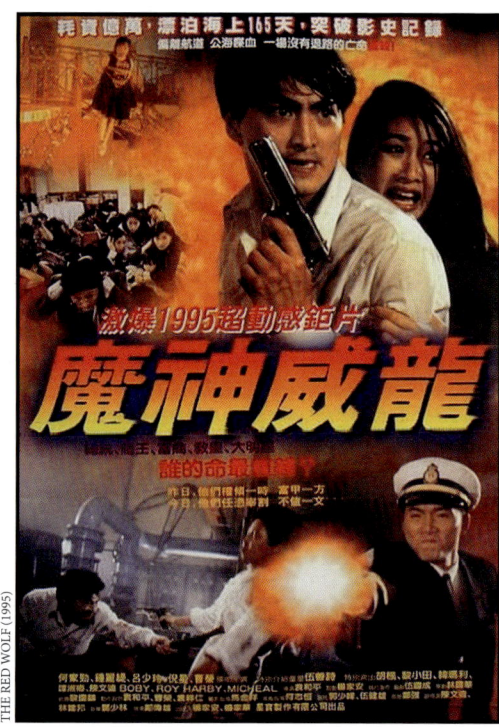

THE RED WOLF (1995)

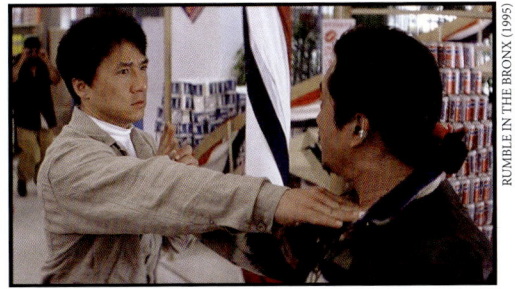

RUMBLE IN THE BRONX (1995)

Yuen Woo-Ping takes the fight action from land to sea, creating a cross between *Under Siege* and *Die Hard*. Despite its thin plot, the action is nonstop, with a brutal body count that you would normally only see in a John Woo or *John Wick* movie. Kenny Ho's martial arts ability stands out on screen with some flashy kicks and hand work, and Elaine Lui also delivers as the sadistic female terrorist, almost matching Kenny Ho's kill count.

As with all Yuen Woo-Ping movies, the film offers a fair amount of wirework, but it's well-choreographed and adds to the film's high-octane feel. This big-budget film was obviously attempting to cross over to an international theatrical audience, which seemed to be the focus of many Hong Kong film companies in the mid-nineties, but it didn't quite reach the mark. Nonetheless, it did well worldwide at the time on video and DVD.

ROARING WHEELS (2000)

Starring Dave Wang, Karen Mok, Moses Chan, Maggie Siu
Directed by Aman Chang
Universe Entertainment

Set against the backdrop of underground motorbike racing, the film focuses on two highly competitive riders. Fred Wong (Wang), admired by all the other racers, boasts an unbeatable record, placing him at number one. On the other hand, Weird Fung (Chan) consistently fails in every race and has to accept second place, but he cannot hide his bitterness toward Wong. Frustrated, he challenges Wong to a final race, which ultimately proves to be a grave mistake. During the final stages of the race, Weird's back wheel comes loose, resulting in a horrifying crash. As the ambulance rushes him to the hospital, Wong has flashbacks of the girl he loves, who is currently giving birth at the hospital. However, tragedy strikes once again as she dies due

to complications during delivery, leaving Wong devastated. His eyes snap open as he passes Weird in the hospital corridor, realizing that his life and hopes have all been destroyed in one tragic night.

We fast-forward three years, Wong, now a single parent, has moved out of the area in an attempt to put the past behind him. However, he is tracked down by Weird, who, through his girlfriend Suki (Mok), blackmails Wong into one final race.

Despite being shot in 2000, the movie has the feel of an 80s or early 90s film with its style and action. They must have filmed the bike scenes in the dead of night to have such little traffic. Aman Chang seems to be at home directing B-style movies as the bike racing scenes are certainly well-executed and he manages to get a good performance from his cast, including Karen Mok and Maggie Siu.

RUMBLE IN THE BRONX (1995)

Starring Jackie Chan, Anita Mui, Françoise Yip, Bill Tung
Directed by Stanley Tong
Golden Harvest/Golden Way Films Ltd

Rumble in the Bronx is an enjoyable, pacy Jackie Chan actioner, showcasing his signature acrobatic martial arts style and prowess in physical comedy. Jackie plays a visitor from Hong Kong, who comes to New York to attend his uncle's wedding, only to find that their South Bronx grocery store is under attack from street thugs and the mob.

Despite the lack of plot, deep dialogue and character development, Jackie's ability to execute flawlessly choreographed fight scenes and death-defying stunts is what makes this movie truly worth watching. So, while the movie certainly isn't a cinematic masterpiece, Jackie Chan's performance here is nothing short of a display of physical genius that rivals the likes of Chaplin and Keaton.

For anyone who loves action cinema, *Rumble in the Bronx* is a must-see.

SECRET POLICE (1992)

Starring Moon Lee, Alex Fong, Yip San, Billy Chow
Directed by Yiu Tin-Hung
The Star Overseas Ltd

Secret Police tells the tale of a man, played by Alex Fong, who is torn between his association with gangsters and his obligations to his girlfriend. Fong's reckless behavior constantly embarrasses his father and stresses out his girlfriend, who yearns for more

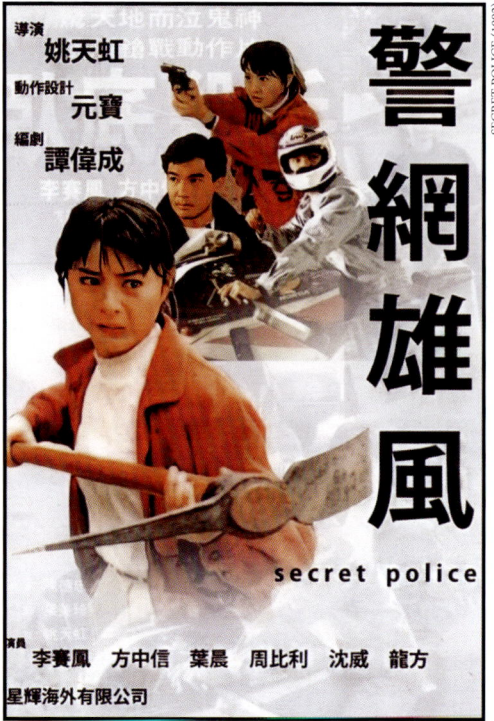

導演 姚天虹
動作設計 元寶
編劇 譚偉成

警網雄風

secret police

李賽鳳 方中信 葉晨 周比利 沈威 龍方
星輝海外有限公司

SECRET POLICE (1992)

that bring their characters to life. Yiu Tin-Hung's storytelling and direction do enough to keep you engaged throughout the film, which has well-choreographed action sequences and some intense dramatic moments.

If you enjoyed the *Angel* movies and liked the femme fatale action flicks that came out of Hong Kong during this period, then this will be one to watch for sure.

SEVEN WARRIORS (1989)
Starring Adam Cheng, Mok Siu-Chung, Jacky Cheung, Tony Leung Chiu-Wai, Lo Lieh, Wu Ma, Sammo Hung
Directed by Tong Kay-Ming
Maverick Film Ltd

Tong Kay-Ming directs a competent cast in his adaptation of Kurosawa's *Seven Samurai*. A village ravaged by local robbers attempts to make a stand by enlisting the help of outsiders who are more used to dealing with unsavory elements.

The story is updated to the 20th century, where our heroes have an almost spaghetti western–style appearance. It's a tense and often gripping film, which allows the characters to develop as they await the inevitable showdown.

Rather than glamorous martial arts choreography, Kay-Ming opts for cruder, more violent actions to create the film's realistic feel.

SHANGHAI AFFAIRS (1998)
Starring Donnie Yen, Athena Chu, Yu Rongguang, Man Choh-Han, Lam Yiu-San, Lee Qui Tam Man-Ying, Kenji Tanigaki
Directed by Donnie Yen
Sam Po Entertainment Production Co.

commitment from him. His sister (Moon Lee) is a cop who works in the same station as their father. She despises her brother's lifestyle and cannot stand his actions.

Tragedy strikes when their father is brutally murdered by a hired hit man. Determined to seek justice for her father's death, the sister sets out on a mission of vengeance.

The film takes its viewers on an adrenaline-pumping ride, as the sister's quest for revenge puts her in the crosshairs of the dangerous criminal underworld.

The film boasts a good cast, with Alex Fong and Moon Lee delivering decent performances

Shanghai Affairs, directed by and starring Donnie Yen, is a decent martial arts film that focuses on Tong Shan, a doctor in Shanghai, who is dedicated to serving his community. Tong Shan's mission to help the less fortunate is challenged by the ruthless Axe Gang, who make it difficult for him to carry out his work. To make matters worse, Tong Shan finds himself falling for the sister of the gang's leader.

The plot of *Shanghai Affairs* has enough twists and turns to keep the viewer's attention and Donnie Yen's direction has improved significantly since his previous films. Fight scenes are well-executed and showcase Yen's martial arts abilities, while the supporting cast delivers solid performances. Man Choh-Han's portrayal of the Axe Gang leader is a

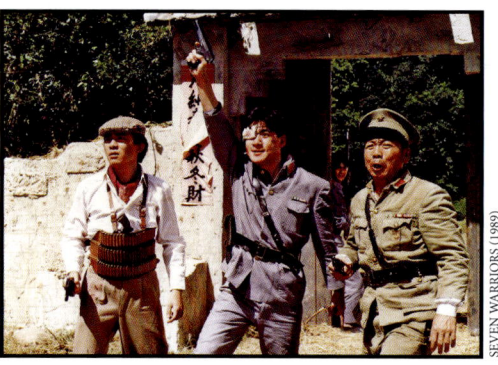

SEVEN WARRIORS (1989)

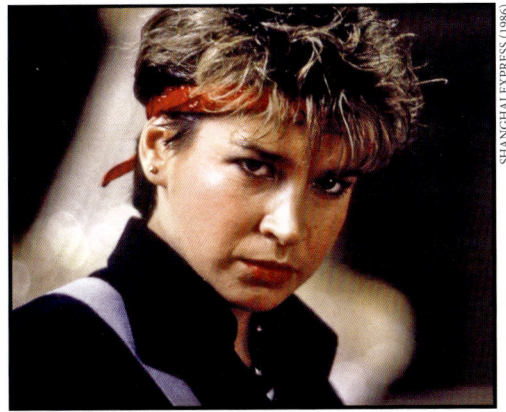

particular standout, bringing an air of menace and intensity to the film.

The film spends time showing Tong Shan's struggles as he tries to balance his professional and personal life, which adds a layer of complexity to the story, and his romance with the gang leader's sister provides emotion to the film. While *Shanghai Affairs* may not be the most groundbreaking martial arts film ever made, it is a solid addition to the genre, with a decent plot, action sequences, and good performances from its cast.

SHANGHAI EXPRESS (1986)

Starring Sammo Hung, Yuen Biao, Eric Tsang,
Olivia Cheng, Rosamund Kwan, Emily Chu,
Cynthia Rothrock, Richard Norton, Yasuaki Kurata,
Dick Wei, Yuen Wah, Richard Ng, Hwang Jang-Lee,
Bolo Yeung, Phillip Ko
Directed by Sammo Hung
Action by Sammo Hung
Bo Ho Film Company Ltd

Once again Sammo Hung surrounds himself with a cast of thousands to put together a classic, providing exposure for several new starlets, including Cynthia Rothrock. Although only a small supporting role, her final confrontation with Sammo helped to establish her as the new force in femme fatale fighting. Yukari Oshima also has a cameo role in her first Hong Kong production, as a swashbuckling samurai, using nifty bladework that made her an instant success.

This lightweight comedy is set aboard a train on its maiden run, which becomes the focal point for several interested parties. Zany Hong Kong humor is integrated with fast-paced action, and the various subplots come together in a finale of superb action, with Yuen Biao and Dick Wei going hammer and

tongs, Cynthia going fist-to-fingernail with Sammo, Yasuaki Kurata exchanging techniques with Richard Norton, and super-kicker Hwang Jang-Lee putting away adversaries with his lethal footwork. Also known as *Millionaires Express*.

SIXTY MILLION DOLLAR MAN (1995)

Starring Stephen Chow, Gigi Leung, Ng Man-Tat,
Paulyn Sun, Elvis Tsui, Joe Cheng
Directed by Wong Jing, Yip Wai-Man
Produced by Wong Jing
Win's Entertainment Ltd

Sing (Chow) is the son of a wealthy businessman who runs the local medical school. Spoiled, he's a bit of an arrogant jerk, acting like a playboy among his friends, pranking and abusing the staff and his schoolmates at every given opportunity. His life is turned upside down, however, after he meets the attractive Chung Chung (Leung). Both worse for drink, she suggests they enter a twist dance competition, which Sing refuses to do, until she offers to sleep with him. As they do their version of the Travolta/Thurman dance routine from *Pulp Fiction*, her husband Fumito (Cheng), the local Yakuza boss, sees them and wants Sing out of the picture, so he arranges for Sing to be blown up.

With only Sing's lips left intact after the explosion (and still able to talk), enter the crazy Professor

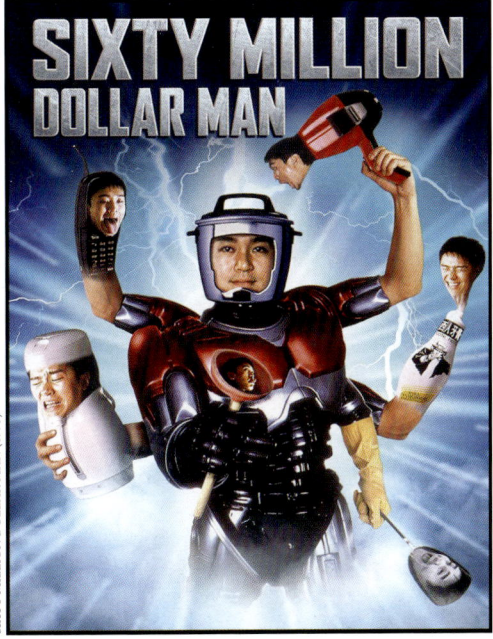

Chang Sze (Tsui), who manages to put him back together, only to discover that Sing has newfound abilities. He can now turn into an array of household objects, including toothpaste, a vacuum cleaner and a toilet, to name just a few. But are these oddball traits enough to get revenge on Fumito?

This film is as bonkers as a Stephen Chow film can get, providing him with the opportunity to make countless visual gags. Director Wong Jing is noted for his pillaging of ideas from American films and *Sixty Million Dollar Man* heavily borrows from Jim Carrey's *The Mask*. This film shows Stephen Chow at his best, delivering outrageous, laugh-out-loud comedy and over-the-top imagery.

SKINNY TIGER AND FATTY DRAGON (1990)

Starring Karl Maka, Sammo Hung, Carrie Ng,
Lung Ming-Yan, Lau Kar-Wing, Wu Fung
Directed by Kau Kar-Wing
Produced by Wellington W. Fung, Andrew Yau
Action by Eric Tsui
Cinema Capital Entertainment Ltd

Skinny and Fatty are two hardboiled cops, known in the underworld as crazy and unpredictable characters. For months they have been tracking a ruthless drug dealer, Wing (Kar-Wing), and they attempt to bust a drug deal in a crowded downtown shopping mall, but Wing's couriers—his beautiful girlfriend and a transvestite—manage to escape. Skinny and Fatty go to the girlfriend's place to look for evidence, but are interrupted when she returns with Wing. The two cops pull stockings over their

faces and, posing as burglars, escape in Wing's limo. Their next attempt to nail the dealer ends in a big fistfight in one of the finest restaurants in town, but, unfortunately, it is being rented by the Police Commissioner for his wedding party. Wing is arrested, but Skinny and Fatty are suspended. Wing, freed on bail, vows revenge, kidnapping Skinny's girlfriend and sending his two transvestite killers to Fatty's house to attack his dad. Now the two cops realize they are sitting ducks and devise a complicated and devious scheme to destroy the whole crime syndicate . . .

Sammo Hung once again pays homage to Bruce Lee and, despite his portly figure, proves that he is by far the best Bruce Lee impersonator out there, as highlighted in *Enter the Fat Dragon* (1978) and again here, with his skilful use of nunchakus and Lee-like war cries.

Also known as *Nutty Kickbox Cops*, this is a film with first-rate action but rather off-putting humor.

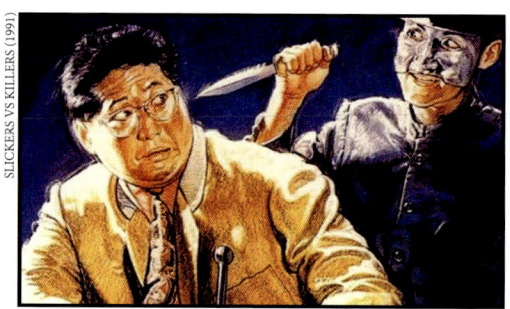

SLICKERS VS KILLERS (1991)

Starring Sammo Hung, Carol Cheng, Jacky Cheung,
Joyce Godenzi, Yu Li, Lam Ching-Ying
Directed and produced by Sammo Hung
Action by Sammo Hung, Brandy Yuen, Yuen Mo
Bojon Films Company Ltd

A salesman gets mixed up in a vendetta between a couple of killers and the triad gang they want to teach a lesson to. To make matters worse, the salesman's wife, a policewoman, is fancied by one of her colleagues, who decides to kill the salesman and pretend the gang did it.

An early fight set piece, when Sammo's character, Success Hung, first encounters the killers Bat (Cheung) and Owl (Ching-Ying) boasts top-notch choreography, and the finale is a madcap affair, as the gang members, Hung, the murderous cop, plus Hung's wife and psychiatrist, all get drawn into the

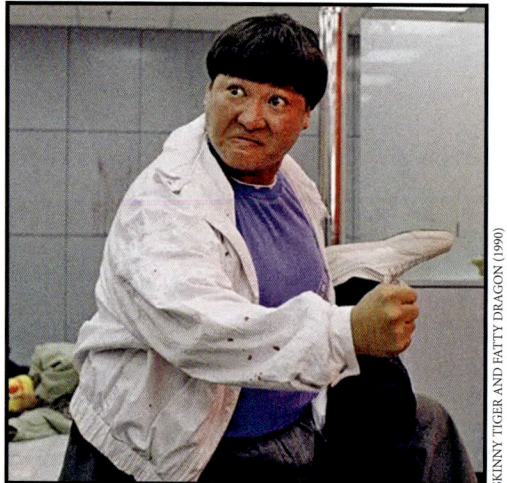

SKINNY TIGER AND FATTY DRAGON (1990)

SLICKERS VS KILLERS (1991)

fight. There's also a nifty all-female catfight and loads more murderous mayhem.

It's a merely adequate Sammo potboiler, but a good showcase for his world-class choreography talents.

THE STONE AGE WARRIORS (1991)
Starring Nina Li Chi, Elaine Lui, Fan Siu-Wong, Chang Kuo-Chu, Dick Wei
Directed, written, produced and choreographed by Stanley Tong
Golden Gate Film Production

When businessman Nakamura (Kuo-Chu) goes missing while hunting for treasure with his guide (Wei) in the jungles of Indonesia, his daughter Eko (Lui) and his insurance rep Lucy Wong (Li Chi) set out to find him, with the aid of martial arts missionary Lung Fei (Siu-Wong).

They have to overcome cannibals, Komodo dragons, insects, the jungle, and kickboxing drug barons! Fan Siu-Wong displays some incredible martial artistry and acrobatics, Elaine Lui lets loose with some high-kicking action and serious swordplay, while Nina Li Chi wears some very psychedelic clothing and provides most of the laughs.

The first film from Stanley Tong as director, it's worth checking out for the promise of greater things to come, including *Police Story 3: Supercop*.

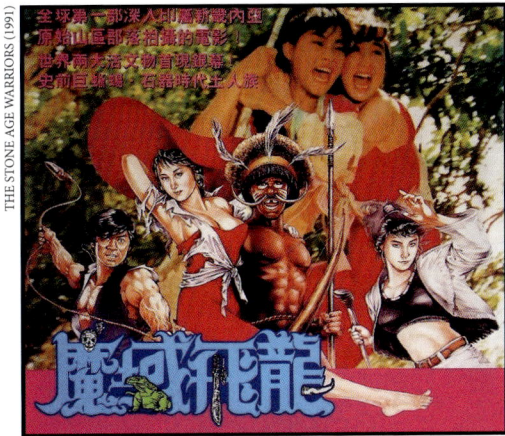

THE STONE AGE WARRIORS (1991)

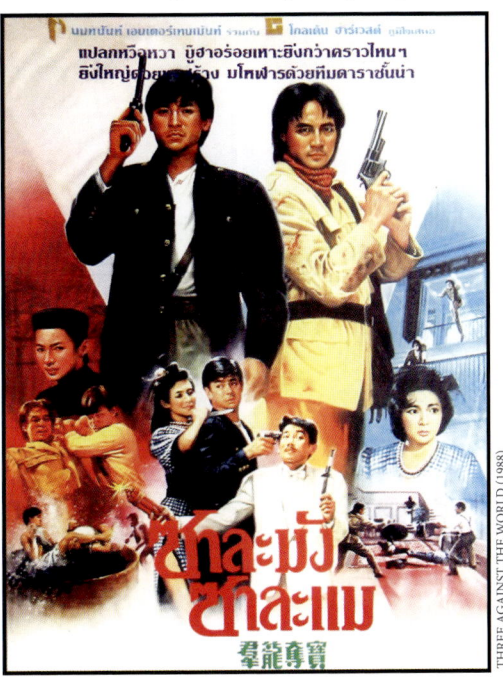

THREE AGAINST THE WORLD (1988)

THREE AGAINST THE WORLD (1988)
Starring Andy Lau, Teddy Robin Kwan, Tsui Siu-Keung, Rosamund Kwan, Shing Fui-On
Directed by Brandy Yuen
Bo Ho Film Company Ltd/Golden Harvest

Shot in sepia tone, this follows a gang of thieves trying to steal a valuable statue, with Andy Lau playing a security chief who must make sure the museum has maximum protection.

The film ticks along as a Buster Keaton–style comedy until the last twenty minutes, when it takes on a whole new dimension with an incredible fight finale. It really makes the most of Andy Lau's fighting skills, here returning to the calibre displayed in *Twinkle Twinkle Lucky Stars* (1985).

THUNDERBOLT (1995)
Starring Jackie Chan, Anita Yuen, Michael Wong, Thorsten Nickel, Chor Yuen, Ken Lo
Directed by Gordon Chan
Golden Harvest

This action flick has stunts and chase scenes, but falls short in terms of plot and dialogue. The story follows Jackie Loh Chan, a motor mechanic with a father who helps the cops take down illegally modified street racing vehicles. When Chan witnesses a car nearly killing a police officer to evade capture, he gets caught up in the chase to capture the notorious criminal and speed freak known as Cougar (Nickel).

While the action scenes are impressive, the pacing and direction of the film leave something to be desired. The film suffers from a weak script and unconvincing dialogue, and the director's use of

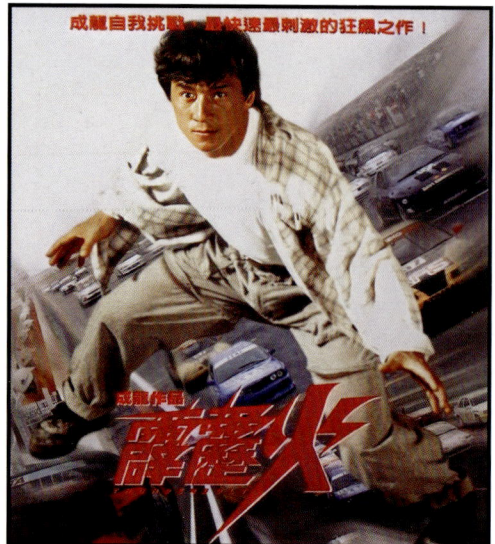

THUNDERBOLT (1995)

quick cuts and overediting spoils some of the fight scenes.

The absence of comedic flair makes the film feel less like a Jackie Chan movie and the acting is also hit-or-miss, with Jackie struggling to bring serious depth to his role and Thorsten Nickel's Cougar character not really given the chance to develop. Anita Yuen, however, is the standout, delivering a natural performance as Amy.

All in all, while *Thunderbolt* may not be one of Jackie Chan's best efforts, it still offers some thrilling action and adrenaline-pumping chase scenes.

TIGER CAGE (1988)

Starring Jacky Cheung, Carol Cheng, Donnie Yen,
Simon Yam, Leung Kar-Yan, Irene Wan
Directed by Yuen Woo-Ping
Action by Yuen Cheung-Yan, Yuen Shun-Yee,
Paul Wong Kwan, Donnie Yen
D & B Films Co Ltd

A dazzling display of courage and skill on the part of the police sees many at the top of a major drug gang either captured or killed. Further investigations into the gang's dealings become personal when one of the cops is mercilessly gunned down by a brutal henchman. The closer the cops get to the truth, the more disturbing it becomes, as senior members of their department are implicated. What follows is a race against time to see the true criminals brought to justice before any more innocents suffer.

Boasting excellent action, both in terms of awesome

martial arts and explosive gunplay, this is an exciting action-thriller, also known as *Sure Fire*, which starts as it means to finish: with gun barrels blazing. Sadly, the film runs out of puff somewhere around the middle, when ace wushu exponent Donnie Yen's character is killed. At the time of production, Jacky Cheung was new to the genre, and his skills as an actor and screen fighter were raw. But despite his (and Carol Cheng's) limitations, he does manage to carry off this stylish cop actioner, which is recommended without reservation.

TIGER CAGE II (1990)

Starring Donnie Yen, Rosamund Kwan, David Wu,
Robin Shou, Cynthia Khan, Michael Woods
Directed by Yuen Woo-Ping
Action by Yuen Cheung-Yan, Yuen Shun-Yee,
Phillip Kwok, Donnie Yen
D & B Films Co Ltd

This actioner's story revolves around the search for a case lost during the robbery of laundered money. The cop-on-the-run tale, though, is simply a convenient and lightweight framework onto which many tough action sequences can be attached.

Pugilistic struggles come thick and fast: Donnie Yen is knocked out countless times, Cynthia Khan takes part in a little martial arts madness on a speeding ambulance and countless fights make it very hectic. However, the final sword duel is better paced and dramatically choreographed, culminating in an excellent confrontation which has hero Dragon Yau (Yen) taking on a huge villain (Woods) with his hands chained together.

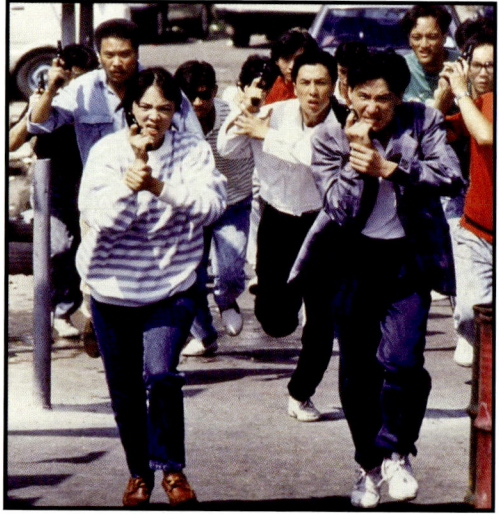

TIGER CAGE (1988)

TIGER CAGE III (1991)

Starring Cheung Kwok-Leung, Sharla Cheung Man,
Michael Wong, Wong Kam-Kong, John Cheung
Directed by Yuen Woo-Ping
Action by Yuen Shun-Yee, Ku Huen-Chiu
D & B Films Co Ltd

When the Commercial Crime Branch suspects business tycoon Mr. Lee (Kam-Kong) of criminal activities, it dispatches inspectors James (Kwok-Leung) and John (Wong) to check him out. With the help of James's girlfriend Suki (Sharla Cheung Man), who works for Lee's accountant, they begin to gather the evidence. But Lee is aware of their investigation and he destroys John's career, kidnaps Suki, and blows up James. John's attempts at revenge are unsuccessful until a horrifically burnt James reappears, intent on rescuing Suki.

The plot is incredibly disjointed, leading to a finale full of quadruple-crossing, but the film does deliver a mighty amount of bone-crushing action. It serves as a showcase for the highly talented martial artist Cheung Kwok-Leung, who comes across as a rough and tough fighter in a brutal showdown with shovels, pickaxes, poles, and flaming torches.

TOKYO RAIDERS (2000)

Starring Tony Leung Chiu-Wai, Ekin Cheng, Kelly Chen,
Cecilia Cheung, Hiroshi Abe, Tôru Nakamura
Directed by Jingle Ma
Golden Harvest/Red on Red Productions

Macy (Chen) is left at the altar by her rich Japanese businessman fiancé Takahashi (Nakamura), who is somehow linked to gang boss Mr. Ito (Abe), so she heads to Tokyo to find her missing boyfriend, helped by interior designer Yung (Cheng) and private detective Lin (Leung), but are any of these people really who they claim to be?

Beginning as it means to go on with an extended, playful action sequence, involving Tony Leung using an umbrella, glue and a telescopic taser to take on a series of bad guys, *Tokyo Raiders* is a slick, enjoyable production, utilizing a catchy, Spanish-influenced score to add to the breezy concoction.

With set pieces including a skirmish with gangsters wielding golf clubs, a chase through the city involving bicycles and a motorised skateboard, a fight atop a car transporter, plus a finale featuring motor boats and a Jet Ski, this lightweight film's many twists and an easy on the eye cast keep viewers entertained.

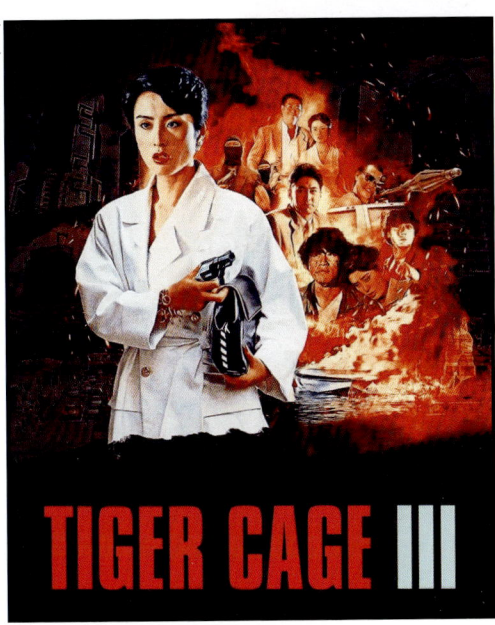

TIGER CAGE III (1991)

THE TRICKY MASTER (1999)

Starring Stephen Chow, Nick Cheung, Sandra Ng,
Wong Jing, Kelly Lin, Suki Kwan
Directed by Wong Jing
B.O.B and Partners

Nick Cheung plays carefree police detective Leung Foon, who is instructed to take down a notorious swindler called Ferrari (Jing). Excited at the prospect of a promotion, he jumps at the chance, but things quickly spiral out of control and he must obtain the help of Master Wong (Chow) to outsmart Ferrari.

The interactions between the two lead characters are pure comedy gold, as they trade insults and jabs while Leung learns the tricks of the trade. Though not one of Stephen Chow's best films, *The Tricky Master* was still a big box office hit. Everyone loves Chow!

THE TWIN DRAGONS (1992)

Starring Jackie Chan, Teddy Robin Kwan, Maggie
Cheung, Nina Li Chi
Directed by Tsui Hark, Ringo Lam
Produced by Ng See-Yuen
Golden Way Films Ltd/
Hong Kong Film Directors Guild

In a hospital back in the sixties there is a triad-related incident which results in the separation of two identical twin babies. Many years later, one is now a small-time hoodlum surviving on the streets

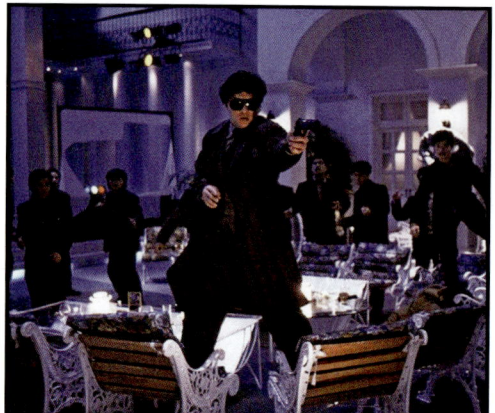

THE TWIN DRAGONS (1992)

of Hong Kong, while the other is a distinguished composer and musician who has been raised in the West. When the musician travels to Hong Kong for a big concert, he is reunited with his brother, much to the confusion of themselves, their girlfriends, the musical community and a hive of crooks.

With a story shamelessly stolen from the Jean-Claude Van Damme movie *Double Impact* (1991), the picture is played strictly for laughs. Although not one of Jackie's best flicks, it still contains some serious action, with Chan performing complex kicks and some of his most dangerous stunt work.

TWINKLE TWINKLE LUCKY STARS (1985)

Starring Jackie Chan, Sammo Hung, Yuen Biao,
Eric Tsang, Andy Lau, Richard Ng, Fung Shui-Fan,
John Sham, Sibelle Hu
Directed by Sammo Hung
Action by Sammo Hung, Yuen Biao, Jackie Chan,
Lam Ching-Ying, Yuen Wah
Bojon Films Company Ltd/Golden Harvest

The *My Lucky Stars* troupe are back!

In Thailand, the cockeyed crime-busters are celebrating the undeserved success of their previous case, but their merrymaking is cut short when they discover that assassins are on their way to Hong Kong to kill a drug boss.

Jackie Chan and Yuen Biao are both in supporting roles, but their presence is most welcome. The warehouse fight scene, which teams Jackie with Yuen Biao and Andy Lau, is an excellently executed fight sequence and contains one of the best kicks in cinematic history: Yuen Biao, coming off the side of a crate in a midair cartwheel, lands perfectly and

performs a 180-degree roundhouse kick, followed by a perfect side kick. It's a moment that will have you endlessly rewatching in disbelief! There's also a great finale, with Sammo Hung destroying Australian martial artist Richard Norton with a pair of tennis rackets.

This is an excellent balance of comedy and kung fu action. How many faces can you spot coming out of the lift at the end of the movie?

2000 AD (2000)

Starring Aaron Kwok, Daniel Wu, Andrew Lin,
Phyllis Quek, James Lye, Ray Lui, Francis Ng
Directed by Gordon Chan
Media Asia Films/People's Production Limited

Greg Li (Lui), an agent and shady computer expert, obtains a program that can wreak havoc in the world's financial banking systems. He is hunted down and assassinated by a splinter group of the Singapore SID, so his brother Peter (Kwok) takes it upon himself to investigate, finding himself spiraling down a rabbit hole of conspiracy, unsure of who he can trust.

Although the plot may be convoluted at times, it can be forgiven as this movie offers lots of eye candy sequences, including impressive *Top Gun*-style action and slick fight choreography: the rooftop martial arts battle between Kwok and Andrew Lin is a standout moment, along with the *Heat*-inspired gunplay. Additionally, the film boasts a talented cast of solid actors, with Aaron Kwok, Daniel Wu, Francis Ng, and Andrew Lin all delivering commendable performances.

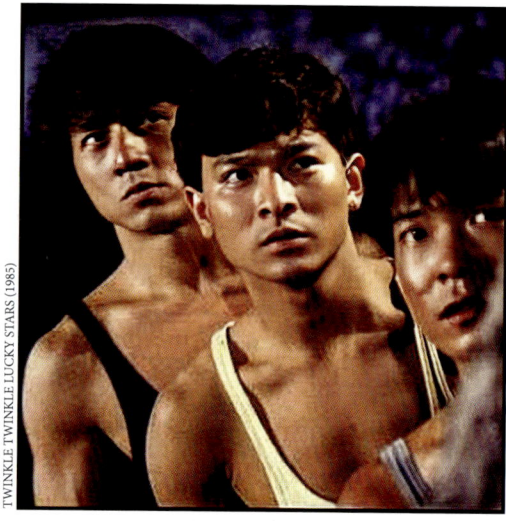

TWINKLE TWINKLE LUCKY STARS (1985)

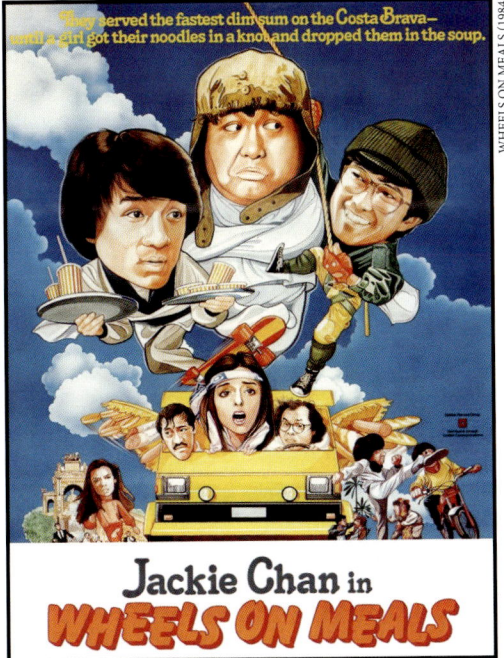

WHEELS ON MEALS (1984)

WHEELS ON MEALS (1984)

*Starring Jackie Chan, Yuen Biao, Sammo Hung, Benny
Urquidez, Lola Forner, Keith Vitali
Directed by Sammo Hung
Produced by Raymond Chow, Leonard K.C. Ho
Golden Harvest*

Two young Chinese men (Chan & Biao), who run a
fast food business in Spain, unite with their private
investigator friend (Hung) to fight the villains that
are hunting for a young heiress (Forner).

 Both the action and the comedy come thick and fast
in this exciting adventure set in Barcelona. The use
of Western martial arts champions as villains gives
a new edge to the fight scenes, which are expertly
choreographed. There's more to this film than just
comedy and kung fu: car chases, skateboarding and
a gang of bikers all feature in this minor epic.

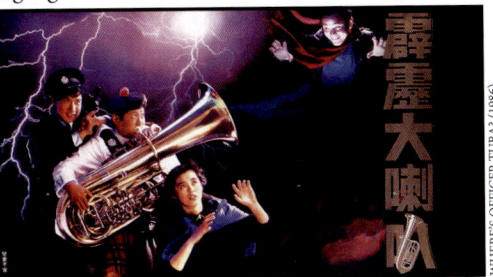

WHERE'S OFFICER TUBA? (1986)

WHERE'S OFFICER TUBA? (1986)

*Starring Sammo Hung, David Chiang, Jacky Cheung,
Joey Wong, Stanley Fung, Hwang Jang-Lee, Yuen Wah,
Woo Fung
Directed by Ricky Lau, Philip Chan
D & B Films Co Ltd*

Tuba (Hung), a trumpet player in the police band,
is infatuated with Joanne (Wong) and seeks help
from beyond the grave from his old buddy Rambo
Chow (Chiang), who was killed in pursuit of an
extortionist played by Hwang Jang-Lee. Rambo
agrees to assist Tuba, but in return wants help to
avenge his own death.

 This movie, a reworking of the old British television
series *Randall and Hopkirk (Deceased)*, is a light
comedy with some sporadic fight scenes, lifted
in quality by the presence of Sammo Hung. The
finale introduces a young Jacky Cheung, whose
character helps Tuba out of a tight corner. Rambo,
meanwhile, proves that there is strength beyond the
grave, as he lifts Tuba and makes him fly through
the air like Superman, to the disbelief of the villains.

 An enjoyable film, although hardly a classic.

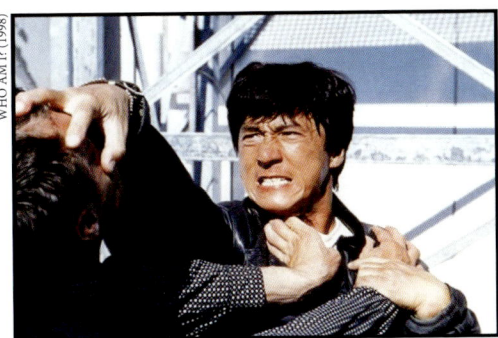

WHO AM I? (1998)

WHO AM I? (1998)

*Starring Jackie Chan, Michelle Ferre, Mirai Yamamoto,
Ron Smerczak, Ed Nelson, Ron Smoorenburg, Ken Lo
Directed by Jackie Chan, Benny Chan
GH Pictures/Golden Harvest*

Get ready to buckle up and be transported back to
the days when Jackie Chan was the king of martial
arts comedies! In this film Jackie delivers yet again
with a high-energy, action-packed adventure that
will leave you gasping.

 As a member of an elite Special Forces unit, Chan
takes on the role of a skilled soldier tasked with
capturing three scientists in South Africa, who've

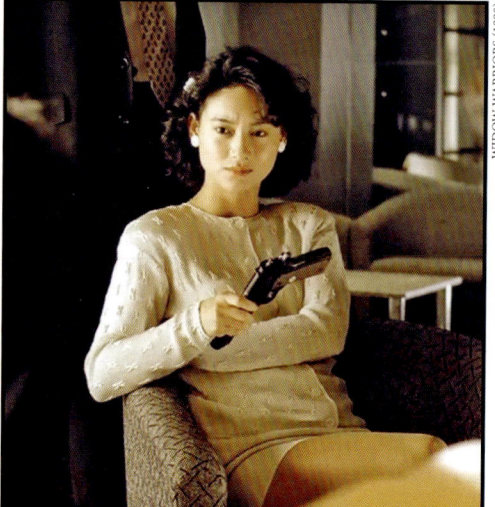

WIDOW WARRIORS (1990)

uncovered a new energy source. But things quickly go awry and Chan loses his memory. The film takes a wild turn as Chan navigates his way through a journey of self-discovery and memory-recovery.

The storyline is tight, and the fight scenes are top-notch, proving that Jackie Chan is still the master of his craft. With a mix of hilarious humor and heart-pumping action, this is a must-watch for fans of the legendary action star.

Jackie defies physics and performs death-defying stunts that will leave you in awe. He battles opponents in original ways, including wooden shoes, skilfully dodges oncoming traffic, and shows he is an animal lover as he saves small dogs, all the while keeping you entertained with his signature brand of martial arts comedy. From battling on top of a skyscraper to transforming everyday items into lethal weapons, Jackie proves once again why he's undoubtedly the king of such movies.

WIDOW WARRIORS (1990)
Starring Elizabeth Lee, Tien Niu, Wei Ying-Hung, Michiko Nishiwaki
Directed by Wong Lung-Wei
Produced by Manfred Wong
Action by Sun Chien, Wong Lung-Wei
Maverick Films Ltd

An excellent lineup of female stars, including Wei Ying-Hung, Elizabeth Lee, and Michiko Nishiwaki, add to the glamor in this femme fatale action flick.

Widow Warriors follows a group of women who are thrown together by circumstance after all the male triad family members are assassinated, forcing the women to take on the crueler elements of the triad world. It's a pretty powerful drama with spectacular fight action.

WINNERS AND SINNERS (1983)
Starring Sammo Hung, John Sham, James Tien, Jackie Chan, Philip Chan, Dick Wei, Yuen Biao
Directed by Sammo Hung
Produced by Leonard K.C. Ho, Raymond Chow
Golden Harvest

When five small-time crooks are released from prison, they try to go straight by setting up a legitimate cleaning business. They find, however, that while they have changed, their luck has not, and one of the homes they clean is the secret headquarters of a counterfeiting operation. When, quite by accident, they gain possession of a duplicating plate, two gangs enter the fray and the sister of one of the protagonists is taken prisoner. A disgraced police officer now aids them in their plight to free the sister and bring the criminals to justice.

With cameos from Jackie Chan and Yuen Biao, this is an enjoyable action-comedy with some of the most incredible stunts you are likely to see.

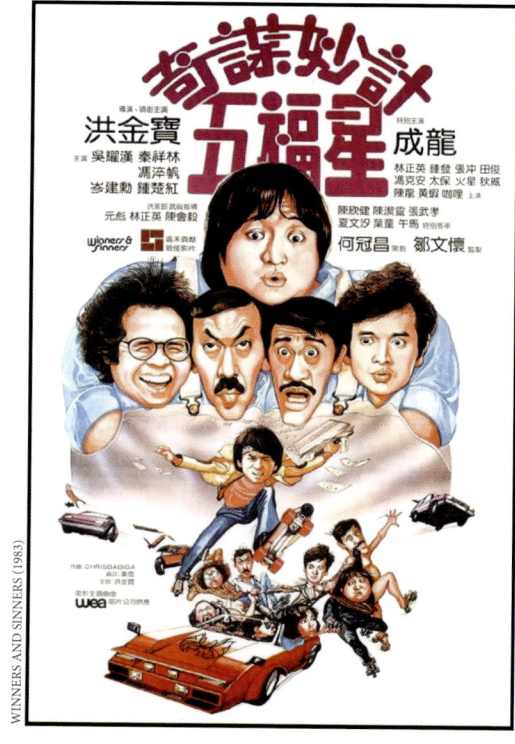

WINNERS AND SINNERS (1983)

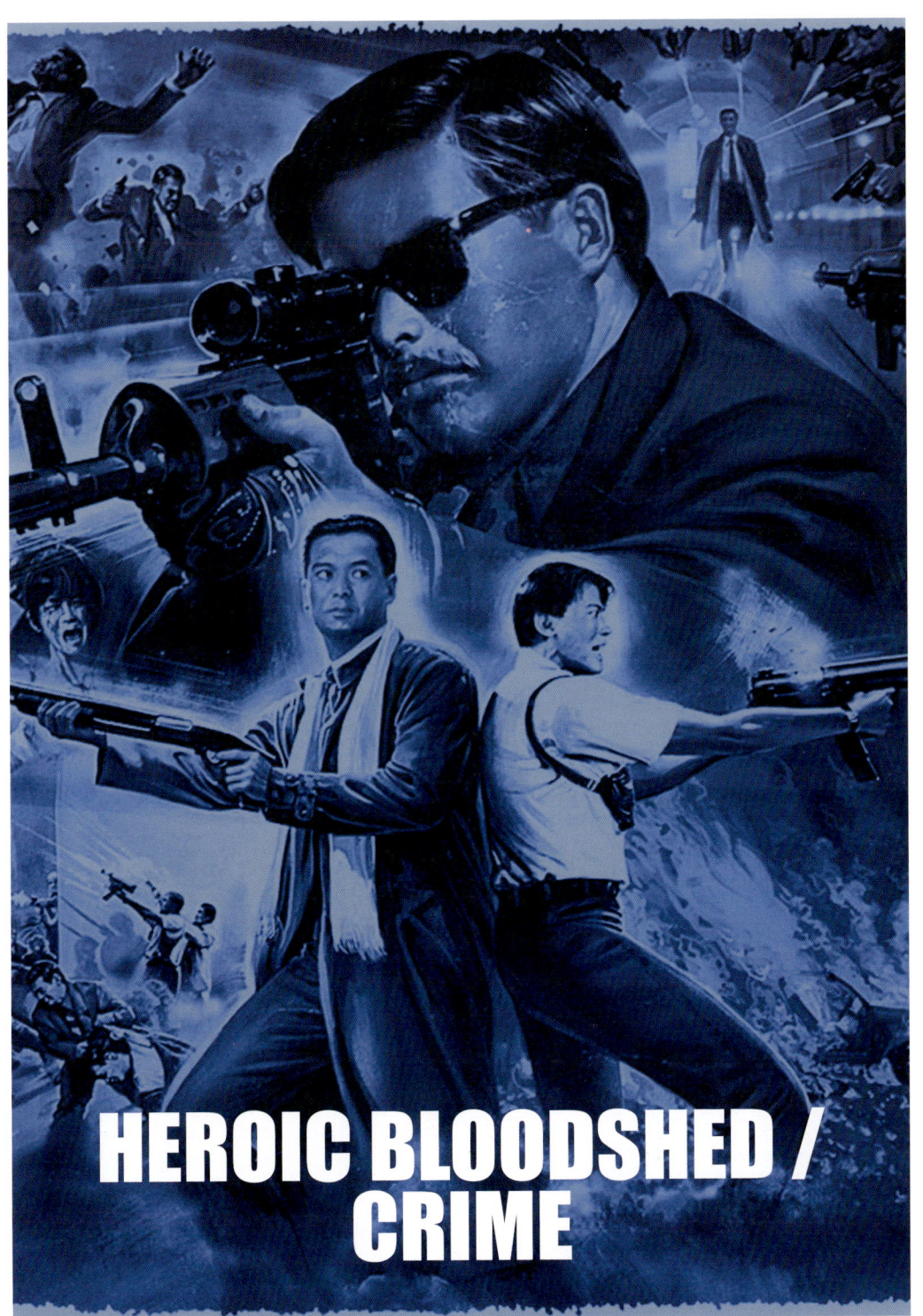

HEROIC BLOODSHED / CRIME

AS TEARS GO BY (1988)

Starring Andy Lau, Maggie Cheung, Jacky Cheung,
Alex Man
Directed by Wong Kar-Wai
Produced by Alan Tang
Action by Tony Poon, Tung Wei
In-Gear Film Production

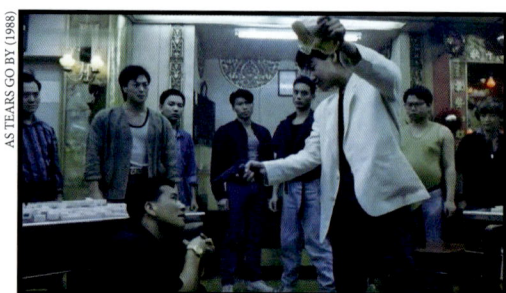

Ah Wah (Lau) and his younger brother Fly (Jacky Cheung) are two lowlife Kowloon thugs working as debt collectors for a local gang boss. Life is harsh and uncompromising, dominated by casual violence and daily brutality. Fly is obsessed with proving how hard he is, quickly making enemies of the other gang members. Ah Wah already has a reputation as a tough guy and is respected, but finds his position complicated by his lack of control over Fly, whose hot temper causes many confrontations. When distant cousin Ah Ngor (Maggie Cheung) arrives on Wah's doorstep he is initially indifferent, but begins to take an interest in her when his girlfriend dumps him after years of neglect. He expects Ah Ngor to fit in around his violent activities, but when she returns home, he begins to realize what life could be like with her, away from the pressures of Kowloon. But any chance of happiness is snatched away by his pride and loyalty to his brother.

An assured directorial debut by Wong Kar-Wai, the film's chilling mood is conveyed in the dark night streets, neon signs, and televisions tuned to dead channels. The violence is swift and bloody with no fancy choreography: the tools of the trade are meat axes, pool cues, and baseball bats. Jacky Cheung gives a fine performance as the psychopathic brother who drags Wah to his destiny, while Andy Lau is the definitive antihero—one moment soulful and vulnerable, the next coldly brutal and frighteningly intense.

BALLISTIC KISS (1998)

Starring Donnie Yen, Annie Wu, Jimmy Wong,
Simon Lui, Vincent Kok, Yu Rongguang
Directed, written and produced by Donnie Yen
Bullet Films/Golden Harvest

Cat (Yen) is a former cop turned hit man vigilante. Carrie (Wu) is a police officer who, while in pursuit of a killer responsible for the deaths of many triad gangs, finds herself becoming conflicted when she discovers that Cat is the one responsible . . . because she is falling for this brooding antihero.

There are some good sequences, such as when Cat enters a nightclub, where he starts to conduct like a maestro, only to inform the gangsters that they are all about to die, even though there are a dozen or more guns pointing at him. He's so fast and proficient that he easily takes out all of the henchmen, and then, wearing shades, he strolls up to the main boss, Chow Yun-Fat–style, to finish his job. It's at this stage we realize that Cat is not a man to be messed with.

This was Donnie Yen's second outing as director and you get the feeling that he was trying to shoot an arthouse movie. The film starts with a scene with no dialogue and just a piano playing some soft classical music, like a moment from a Wong Kar-Wai movie. The film almost feels like an experimental movie, with Donnie trying to explore new ways of creating a visual style and, in the process, losing some of the substance of the characters. The camerawork is choppy and the quick editing makes some of the action confusing.

Despite its flaws, however, *Ballistic Kiss* is a pretty good movie.

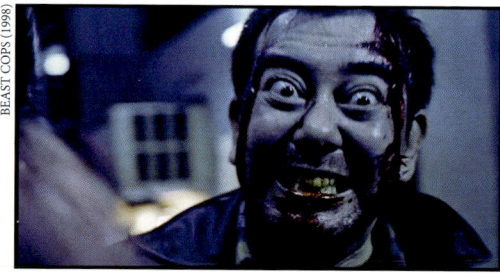

BEAST COPS (1998)

Starring Anthony Wong, Michael Wong, Roy Cheung,
Kathy Chau, Sam Lee, Patrick Tam
Directed by Gordon Chan, Dante Lam
Media Asia Films/People's Production Ltd

Scruffy cop Tung (Anthony Wong) is so broke he rents out his own room to Cheung (Michael Wong), his new straight-arrow boss, who thinks that Tung spends too much time hanging out with underworld characters. After high-ranking triad member Big Brother (Cheung) goes on the run following a shoot-out, his absence causes a deadly power vacuum within the local gangs, tempting upstart Wah (Tam) to ruthlessly take control. Events get deadlier for the cop protagonists when Big Brother returns to discover that his ex-girlfriend is now pregnant with Cheung's child and Tung finally decides to confront Wah, who seems hell-bent on getting to the top no matter what.

Anthony Wong, who won the Best Actor gong at the Hong Kong Film Awards for this role, imbues his compromised character with a mixture of world-weariness, humor, vulnerability, and lowbrow charm. The cast in general is good, but it's definitely Anthony Wong who stands out.

Relationships and characterisation take center stage in *Beast Cops*, with a genuinely amusing, natural kind of humor lightening the drama, but there are spasms of visceral violence too, including a savage street attack and an especially ferocious climax. This finale ramps up the viciousness as Tung transforms into a bloody, brutalized beast of a cop, on his way to becoming a self-respecting law officer once more.

A BETTER TOMORROW (1986)
Starring Chow Yun-Fat, Ti Lung, Leslie Cheung,
Emily Chu, Waise Lee
Directed by John Woo
Produced by Tsui Hark
Action by Tung Wei, Blackie Ko
Film Workshop/Cinema City

Supercool mobster Mark (Yun-Fat) is a man of honor in a world of crime. His partner Ho (Lung) is having second thoughts because kid brother Kit (Cheung) is an ambitious cop. Kit remains blissfully ignorant of his older brother's profession until Ho is double-crossed, their father is murdered and Ho is imprisoned. Mark swears to avenge his friend, but his right leg is shattered in the ensuing shoot-out—a legendary scene of sensationally choreographed

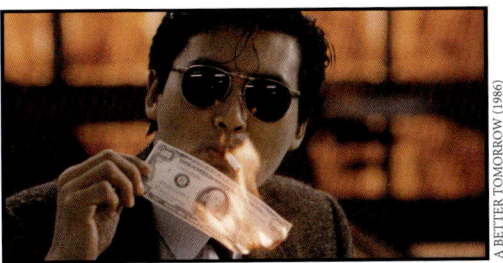

A BETTER TOMORROW (1986)

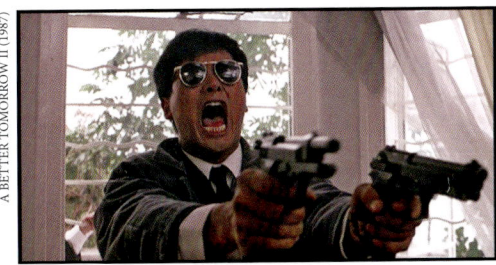

A BETTER TOMORROW II (1987)

gunplay. When Ho leaves the slammer, he finds the crippled Mark reduced to scrubbing dirt off the gang boss' stretch limo. Both are determined to go straight, but neither Kit nor the crime lords are done with them yet. Finally, Mark, Ho, and Kit must face their destinies in a blazing cross fire of conflicting loyalties and hot lead. Who will survive?

John Woo creates a finely tuned balance of strong characterisation and ballistic action, while Chow Yun-Fat is flawless in the role that launched him into superstardom.

One of the finest gangster movies ever made.

A BETTER TOMORROW II (1987)
Starring Chow Yun-Fat, Ti Lung, Leslie Cheung,
Dean Shek, Emily Chu
Directed by John Woo
Produced by Tsui Hark
Action by Ching Siu-Tung
Film Workshop

Though it doesn't seem possible, *A Better Tomorrow II* manages to be more melodramatically intense and more violent than the original!

Chow Yun-Fat returns, this time as Ken, the twin brother of Mark, who was blasted to kingdom come in the first film. In this sequel Ken, together with Ho and Kit, helps Mr. Lung (Shek), a former gang boss, avenge killings perpetrated by two rival gangs.

Merging emotional drama expertly with over-the-top gunplay, the movie intertwines scenes such as the moving one in which Kit dies in a public telephone booth while talking to his wife, who'd just given birth to their first child, with outrageously hyper-destructive shoot-outs. The finale, involving Lung, Ken, and Ho, armed to the teeth with hand-grenades, pistols, and pump-action shotguns, dishing out bloody revenge in a building full to the brim with members of two gangs, is simply astounding. The shootings, complete with blood-squib explosions, go on and on, with one villain getting blasted about 20 times by Ken!

Unlike the main characters in, say, Peckinpah's *The Wild Bunch* (1969), who all die, the bullet-riddled stars of this film still manage to walk over to chairs to await the arrival of the police!

For me this is as good, if not better, than the first in the series!

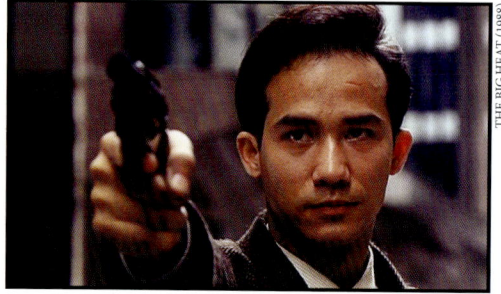

THE BIG HEAT (1988)

A BETTER TOMORROW III (1989)
Starring Chow Yun-Fat, Anita Mui, Tony Leung Ka-Fai, Saburo Tokito, Shih Kien
Directed and produced by Tsui Hark
Action by Lau Fong-Sai, Lau Chi-Ho
Film Workshop/Golden Princess Film Production Limited

Tsui Hark, who produced the first two parts, takes the helm for what is actually a prequel to the original *A Better Tomorrow*. In this story, Mark (Yun-Fat) is not yet the supercool gangster, and it isn't until after much zipping to and fro—from war-torn Vietnam and his meeting with tough, beautiful underworld mentor Kit (Mui)—that he gradually becomes the gun-toting character with shades and long coat.

Though Tsui Hark can't match John Woo for outrageous gun sequences, he does underpin his tale with an interesting subtext concerning the ability

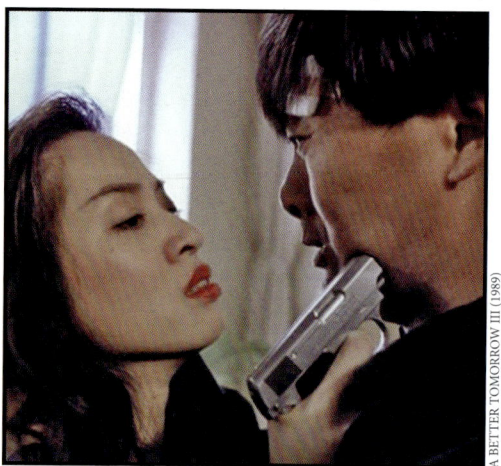

A BETTER TOMORROW III (1989)

(or inability) to leave (or stay in) a country. Hark's obsession with passports, riots, airport customs problems and so on reflects his anxiety about Hong Kong and the 1997 handover. But these subtexts don't overpower the film, which is a glossy, romantic, stylishly lit tale of well-attired hit men, gun fetishism and brief spasms of slo-mo, bullet-spitting death.

Anita Mui is especially striking as Kit, who guns down line after line of Vietnamese soldiers with her semiautomatic. The film is also known as *A Better Tomorrow III: Love and Death in Saigon*.

THE BIG HEAT (1988)
Starring Waise Lee, Philip Kwok, Chu Kong, Joey Wong, Matthew Wong
Directed by Andrew Kam, Johnnie To
Produced by Tsui Hark
Film Workshop/Cinema City

An exceptionally gory production about a policeman investigating a brutal homicide. The evidence leads to a prominent businessman trying to make a quick fortune before 1997. As the cop continues his search for a possible motive, he discovers that the people willing to talk are vastly outnumbered by those prepared to shut them up.

There are human torches, fingers blown off, bodies torn in two, and decapitations, but at no expense to the engrossing plot, which moves swiftly to its highly charged and bloody conclusion.

Performances are of a high standard, especially that of Waise Lee, for once in a heroic role. It's a first-class bullet ballet, but not for the fainthearted.

BLACK CAT (1991)
Starring Jade Leung, Simon Yam, Thomas Lam
Directed by Stephen Shin
Produced by Dickson Poon, Stephen Shin
D & B Films Co. Ltd

This flawed remake of the French classic *Nikita* (1990) marks the screen debut of the lovely Jade Leung. She plays a violent young girl who, after accidentally killing an American police officer, is given an ultimatum: the death penalty or a new identity as a top secret assassin. Choosing the latter option, she undergoes a severe training regime, but, unlike her fellow students, she finds it hard to emotionally detach herself from her work.

What was obviously intended to be a serious, Hollywood-style action film, which puts the lead characters (and therefore the audience) in a moral dilemma, is actually little more than a diverting ninety minutes of action cinema. The actors play their roles with conviction and the action sequences are well executed, but the plot itself is unrefined and the decision to use sync sound was a mistake. An example of wasted potential, but not a waste of time, all the same.

BLACK CAT 2 (1992)
Starring Jade Leung, Robin Shou, Zoltan Buday, Bob Wilde
Directed by Stephen Shin
Produced by Dickson Poon, Stephen Shin
D & B Films Co. Ltd

In this slam-bang sequel to the highly successful *Nikita* rip-off *Black Cat*, micro-skirted & micro-chipped cutie Erica is on the prowl again. With unlikely Chinese CIA agent Robin Shou for a sidekick, she's hoping to prevent a super-soldier from snuffing Boris Yeltsin. Along the way, there's a ski lodge massacre, a bogus sheik, a punch-up in a steelworks, and a motorcycle dash through a sewer. However, when our heroine sprays a granny's brains all over a shopping mall, it seems like she may have slipped a sprocket.

The gorgeous Jade Leung is a lethal cocktail of sensuality, vulnerability and icy determination as she kicks and blasts the bad guys.

BLOOD STAINED TRADEWIND (1990)
Starring Waise Lee, Alex Fong, Carrie Ng, Lo Lieh, Ng Man-Tat, Idy Chan
Directed by Chor Yuen
J&J Film Company

Hong (Lee) and Shing (Fong) are childhood friends who grow up in a triad gang. As an adult, Shing refuses his godfather's request for him to take charge of the organization and leaves town, enabling Hong to take control. Meanwhile, a Japanese gang boss

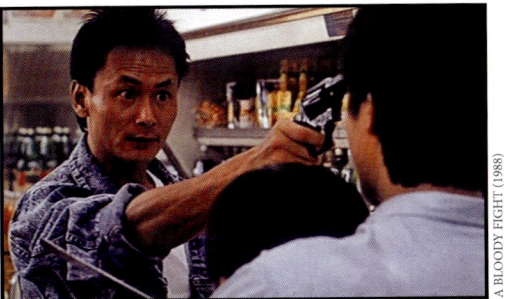

A BLOODY FIGHT (1988)

wishes to secure business deals in Hong Kong . . .

This rather routine gun movie has a fine cast and builds up to one of the most jaw-dropping examples of cross, double cross, and triple cross you are ever likely to see.

A BLOODY FIGHT (1988)
Starring Tsui Siu-Keung, Gordon Liu, Chor Yuen, Lau Kar-Leung, Chan Wai-To
Directed and produced by Wilson Tong
Attraction Film

Chui Keung (Siu-Keung), a long-serving hit man, wants to leave the triads as he fears for his family. His boss seems content to grant him his wish, but then Keung's wife and son are murdered and killers are dispatched to get him. Escaping an attack, an injured Keung is reunited with Lau (Liu), a friend who he has not seen in many years. In the intervening years, Lau has become a police officer, and he is obviously shocked to find that his prime suspect in a murder case is Keung. But with the triads turning their attention from Keung to his own family, Lau realizes that, although on opposing sides of the law, he and Keung share a common enemy, who they now must confront to survive.

Although the plot offers little new in terms of characters and their dilemmas, this is a pleasing enough gangland action drama. The violence comes in bursts, with the highlight being an excellent scene in which Lau Kar-Leung, aided by a baseball bat, demolishes an army of weapon-wielding thugs.

BORN TO BE KING (2000)
Starring Ekin Cheng, Jordan Chan, Sonny Chiba, Shu Qi, Peter Ho, Gigi Lai, Sandra Ng, Jerry Lamb, Chin Kar-Lok, Jason Chu, Roy Cheung
Directed by Andrew Lau
Artwell Productions/B.O.B. and Partners/Golden Harvest

Triad gangster Chicken agrees to an arranged marriage with Nanako, the daughter of Isako Kusaraki, which creates strong ties between the Taiwanese San Luen Gang and the Japanese Yamada gang. But when it becomes clear that unknown players are attempting to set up Chicken and murder anyone else in their way, gangland buddy Nam(Cheng) and his Hong Kong outfit come over to Taiwan to aid Chicken, who is also helped by his tough, wheelchair-bound father-in-law.

This sixth chapter of the *Young and Dangerous* series mainly takes place in Taiwan, with Chicken

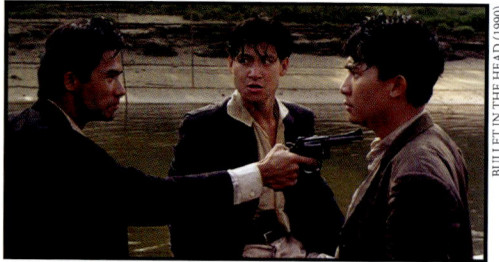

BULLET IN THE HEAD (1990)

(Chan) taking center stage for much of the running time, after being totally absent from part 5. As with previous chapters in the franchise, all of which were written by Manfred Wong, the plot revolves around the protagonists getting framed for murders and used as scapegoats, as shady alliances are formed, gang factions bicker and the real culprits ruthlessly attempt to come out on top. The sexual assault of a main female character also remains a go-to staple for the series, unfortunately, with Chicken's wife Nanako getting attacked this time, in order to give the hero a reason to seek revenge.

A subplot focusing on Nam becoming obsessed with a woman who's a dead ringer of his deceased girlfriend Smartie is unnecessarily protracted and too schmaltzy, but a later scene showing Chicken repeating his wedding vows in front of his wife and Kusaraki is effectively handled and works better emotionally.

The movie's villains include the seemingly pleasant Lui (Ho) and Kusaraki's nasty adopted son Akira, portrayed by Roy Cheung, an actor who has already played two other bad guys in previous *Young and Dangerous* films!

Born to be King is definitely overlong but remains watchable, with Sonny Chiba adding some old-school star power to the scenes he is in.

BULLET IN THE HEAD (1990)

Starring Tony Leung Chiu-Wai, Waise Lee, Jacky Cheung, Simon Yam, Fennie Yuen, Yolinda Yam
Directed and produced by John Woo
Golden Princess Film Production Limited/
John Woo Film Production

Ben (Leung), Frank (Cheung) and Paul (Lee) are good friends, who grow up in the slums of Hong Kong. Frank borrows from a loan shark to pay for Ben's wedding banquet, but local hoodlum Ringo and his gang try to steal the money, and Frank is severely beaten. The three friends confront the gang

and kill Ringo, then flee to Vietnam. Their hopes of establishing a new life are soon dashed in the aftermath of a Vietcong massacre, when they lose the consignment of penicillin and other contraband they had intended to sell. They meet Luke (Yam), a hit man who involves them in a plan to steal gold from the local godfather. Soon they are captured by the Vietcong, who take them for South Vietnamese spies. They are brutally interrogated before Luke rescues them. Paul, crazed by greed and terrified that Frank's hysterical screams will give them away, shoots his erstwhile friend in the head. However, Frank is not dead, just insane and in constant need of morphine to dull the agonies caused by the bullet lodged in his head. Ben seeks out the cause of his friend's suffering and uncovers the shameful secret for which he must somehow seek retribution . . .

Director John Woo forsakes the cool, mythic style of *The Killer* for an altogether harder, more brutal approach in this horrific, spellbinding movie, which starts off as an *American Graffiti*–style story, before rapidly and surely speeding further and further down into the depths of dark emotions and violence.

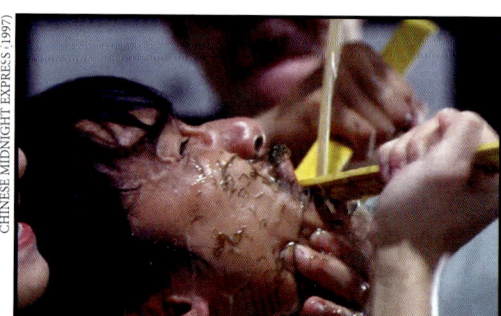

CHINESE MIDNIGHT EXPRESS (1997)

CHINESE MIDNIGHT EXPRESS (1997)

Starring Tony Leung Chiu-Wai, Ng Man-tat, Ben Lam, Ben Ng Ngai-Cheung, Pinky Cheung, Elvis Tsui
Directed by Billy Tang
Cameron Entertainment Ltd/Young Filmmakers Ltd

Tony Leung stars as Ching On, a journalist who uncovers corruption within the police force, but, unfortunately, his good intentions lead to his wrongful imprisonment, after being framed for drug distribution. With his family threatened, On is forced to confess to the crime and endure the harsh and brutal treatment that comes with being a new inmate.

As the gritty story unfolds, On must face new challenges, find allies within the prison walls and try to hold onto hope. Meanwhile, his loyal girlfriend

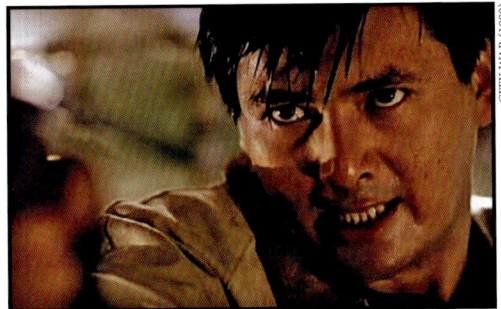

CITY WAR (1988)

Jess (Pinky Cheung) faces her own terrifying battles with the corrupt cops who put On behind bars.

Director Billy Tang does an outstanding job of capturing the harshness and hopelessness of prison life, while Tony Leung delivers a solid and powerful, emotional performance as the falsely accused protagonist.

CHINESE MIDNIGHT EXPRESS II (2000)

Starring Francis Ng, Yung Kam-Cheong,
Lee Siu-Kei, Elvis Tsui, Lung Fong
Directed by Kant Leung
Jing's Production

This gripping prison drama boasts a powerhouse cast, including Francis Ng, Lee Siu-Kei and Lung Fong. Directed by Kant Leung, this film delivers an intense and emotional viewing experience.

At its core, *Chinese Midnight Express II* is a story about the power of conviction and the struggle for justice. Chan Siu-Hong, played by Francis Ng, is a lawyer who finds himself behind bars after a violent altercation with a corrupt police officer. As he adjusts to life in prison, he quickly gains the respect of his fellow inmates for his unwavering commitment to nonviolent conflict resolution.

Kant Leung expertly ratchets up the stakes, infusing the film with lots of tension and suspense, as Chan, wonderfully played by Ng, becomes embroiled in

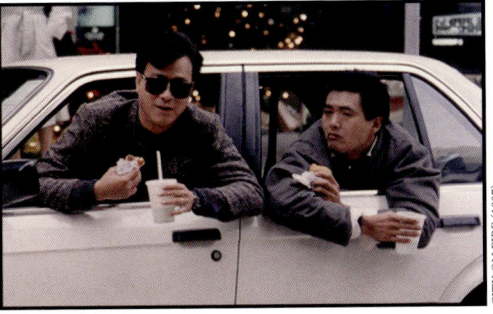

CITY ON FIRE (1987)

dangerous power struggles within the prison walls. The supporting cast shines just as brightly, with standout performances from Lee Siu-Kei and Elvis Tsui.

The film doesn't shy away from the brutal violence and dehumanizing conditions that inmates face on a daily basis, but it also offers a glimmer of hope through Chan's unwavering commitment to his principles.

CITY ON FIRE (1987)

Starring Chow Yun-Fat, Danny Lee, Sun Yeuh,
Roy Cheung, Lau Kong, Carrie Ng
Directed by Ringo Lam
Cinema City

The death of an undercover agent puts the police in a dilemma, since the murder has eliminated a chain of clues necessary to track down a syndicate specializing in jewel robberies. Ko (Yun-Fat) is chosen to take up the mission and goes undercover as a gun dealer. He is put through various rigorous tests under surveillance before he is finally accepted into the gang, but the gang are caught in a police ambush while breaking into the target workshop and, unaware of his identity, the police shoot Ko . . .

Reservoir Dogs fans will notice a strong resemblance to the storyline here, so it's no surprise to know that Quentin Tarantino is a major Hong Kong film fan. The action is forceful, the final showdown, complete with Mexican stand-off, is intense, and Chow's performance is matchless in this must-see Ringo Lam classic.

CITY WAR (1988)

Starring Chow Yun-Fat, Ti Lung, Tien Niu,
Tsui Siu-Keung, Robin Shou
Directed by Sun Chung
Action by Yuen Bing
Cinema City

Chow Yun-Fat plays charismatic police detective Dick Lee and Ti Lung is Ken Chow, Dick's hardnosed partner. They are both forced to turn vigilante when gangster Ted Yiu (Siu-Keung) decides to bump off their ex-partner Ho Ka Ting. During the shoot-out, Ted is rendered impotent by a bullet from Ken, and is subsequently jailed. Ten years later Ted emerges, nursing his vengeance and obsessed with the need to destroy Ken's career. To make matters worse, Dick falls in love with Penny (Niu), Ted's longtime mistress, who is torn between the two. Meanwhile, Ted sends a hit man (Shou) to assassinate Ken, but in a bloody battle the hired killer fails to eliminate his target, murdering Ken's wife and son instead. When Dick discovers this, he is shattered, knowing that he was with Penny when he should have been there to protect his friend's family from this vicious onslaught. Now Dick and Ken find themselves once again having to confront Ted in a final showdown . . .

Hot on the heels of the Chow Yun-Fat/Ti Lung partnerships seen in *A Better Tomorrow, A Better Tomorrow II* and *Tiger on the Beat*, Cinema City teamed them up again for *City War*. Although this is an above-average gangster yarn, director Sun Chung fails to spark the same magic that was apparent under the watchful eye of John Woo. There are some excellent high points, though, including a well-executed gun battle in the final reel and Robin Shou's performance as the manic hit man.

COOLIE KILLER (1982)

Starring Charlie Chin, Yueh Hua, Cecilia Yip, Danny Lee
Directed by Terry Tong
Action by Leung Siu-Hung
Century Motion Picture & Dist. Co. Ltd

Ko Da Fu, leader of a small team of hired killers, is the only survivor of his group when unknown assailants attack them in the night. Could the killers be a foreign gang angry at Ko's refusal to undertake a hit on two of his former Wah Hing gang bosses, or could it actually be the work of another Wah Hing boss? Maybe this boss wanted the other leaders out of the way and decided to put a contract out on them, but became angry at Ko and his men for refusing the job?

Coolie Killer is a tough little movie, which details Ko's hunt for the real culprit responsible for his men's deaths. Finally, after an injured Ko trains himself back to fitness in tried-and-tested Hong Kong movie fashion (lots of shots of him working out, practicing his aim and so on), he confronts the men who betrayed him, which results in him having to take on lots of gang members. This showdown has Ko dealing with the many minions with the help of specially hidden machine guns and even a shotgun hidden in a lead pipe. The set pieces, such as Ko's battle with a group of knife-wielding roller-skaters in his apartment block, are well shot, without being as overly fancy as the later gangster movie clones that followed in the wake of Woo's triad tales in the

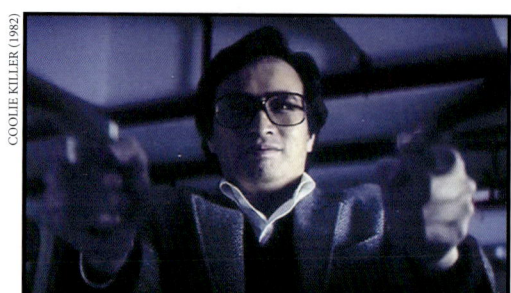

COOLIE KILLER (1982)

mid-eighties. The main characters are fairly well-sketched, with Ko Da Fu coming across as a silently determined man with his own code of honor.

Though the plotting could, at times, have been made a little more lucid, and the deaths of Ko's men at the film's start were achieved rather too effortlessly considering they were professional assassins, *Coolie Killer*, in the main, is solid entertainment. Its use of borrowed music is excellent, such as when a main character's dead body is burnt on a hillside to the accompaniment of the Alan Parsons Project on the soundtrack.

THE CRIMINAL HUNTER (1988)

Starring Danny Lee, Eric Tsang, Dick Wei, Nina Li Chi
Directed by Frankie Chan
Produced by Lo Wei
Lo Wei Motion Picture company

Though, on the surface, this cops 'n' criminals flick would seem to be a humorous comedy thriller, its use of the tragic killing of loved ones as a way of providing Lee and Tsang with sufficiently vengeful motives is somewhat sick. After briefly showing cop Lee playing with his baby, the film serves up the first of several bad-taste scenes by showing scar-faced bad guy Nan (Wei) shooting Lee's wife and baby, with blood shooting up from the pink pram. Tsang has a girlfriend called Lina, who he accidentally stabs as he fights Nan. Discharging herself from the hospital, Lina takes part in a fashion show and is attacked by Nan, who squeezes her bandaged wound, killing her. Then, in a sick romantic scene, Tsang dresses up her corpse in a bridal gown and photographs himself kissing her. Following a gun-and-grenade skirmish, nasty Nan is led into a trap in which Tsang wires up Lina's corpse so that her finger can be yanked to fire off shots at Nan! Lee finishes the job by blasting a few more rounds into the killer.

To provide one final piece of tastelessness, *Criminal Hunter* ends with Tsang laughing because Lee, who is being led to prison, is scared of being "ass-raped." Charming and subtle stuff, eh?

CROCODILE HUNTER (1989)
Starring Andy Lau, Alex Man, Sandra Ng,
Cheung Kwok-Keung, Lung Fong, Elvina Kong
Directed and produced by Wong Jing
Action by Tung Wei, Tony Poon, Kong Tao-Hoi
Win's Film Productions

A policeman (Lau) doesn't agree with his father's view that "the pen is mightier than the sword" when it comes to dealing with violent criminals.

The end portion of the movie has some similarities to *Die Hard*, with a tower block being taken over by criminals led by a high-class villain intent on getting into a hi-tech computer. Unlike that Bruce Willis film, however, *Crocodile Hunter* contains some really rather silly humor, such as the smelly partner of the hero running around naked with a plastic shopping bag on his head for much of the climax.

The movie does provide a novel demise for the lead baddie: with no gun available, our cop hero decides to put his dad's belief into practice by hurling his fountain pen into the antagonist's chest. In slow motion, he does a flying kick and boots the embedded pen through the villain's body, the tip protruding from his back. Yep, the pen does indeed turn out to be mightier than the sword!

CURRY AND PEPPER (1990)
Starring Jacky Cheung, Stephen Chow, Ann Bridgewater,
Eric Tsang, Blackie Ko, Bruce Fontaine
Directed by Blackie Ko
Action by Blackie Ko
Media Asia Films/Movie Impact

Despite the unappealing title, this is an excellent action-comedy-bloodshed movie, which helped launch the careers of Stephen Chow and Jacky Cheung. They play two hardboiled cops known as Curry and Pepper, who have a *Starsky & Hutch* approach to their job. We follow them on a joyride through the busy streets of Hong Kong, often with hilarious consequences. But, like all Hong Kong films, the comedy can often turn into startling action and, as in John Woo's *Once a Thief*, Blackie Ko's direction fuses the black comedy and high-octane action into a potent combination.

The manic pace of the film is very reminiscent of Wong Jing's *The Last Blood* (1991) and is well worth checking out. A sequel was planned for 1991, but,

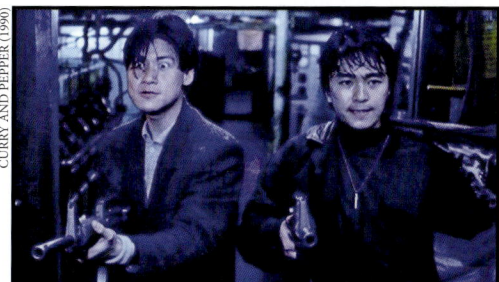

CURRY AND PEPPER (1990)

due to the rising success of both stars, this never materialised. However, Jacky Cheung did return to create a similar role with Lam Ching-Ying in the 1992 movie *Pom Pom and Hot Hot*.

THE DRAGON FAMILY (1988)
Starring Andy Lau, Alan Tam, Mok Siu-Chung,
Tsui Siu-Keung, Ko Chun-Hsiung
Directed by Lau Kar-Wing
Movie Impact

When Lung Ying (Chun-Hsiung), a Hong Kong godfather, believes his underworld business should turn legitimate, he attempts to gain support from the four families around him, but events soon lead to killings and betrayals.

This film is content to be a typical triad drama for much of its running time, interspersed with spasms of violence, but things liven up once *The Dragon Family* reaches the third act, where viewers are treated to an utterly fierce end battle that unleashes blood squibs galore, blasting shotguns, grenades, sword fighting, and kinetic martial arts brawling!

EDGE OF DARKNESS (1988)
Starring Chin Siu-Ho, John Sham, Alex Man, Lo Lieh
Directed by Fung Hark-On
Golden Sun Films Distribution

This might well have been called "Edge of the Seat," for that's where you'll be throughout this suspenseful thriller about Kay, an underground cop who has singlehandedly infiltrated a triad gang and won the boss' favor. Kay's job is so secret his wife and child are kept in the dark, and his only contact with the right side of the law is his nighttime meetings with an ambitious, but careless, sergeant. As Kay continues to tread the fine line between the law and lawlessness, he longs to return to a normal lifestyle, but little does Kay know that the threat of death is far closer to him than he'd dare to imagine, when his senior officer runs into trouble with loan sharks and needs some money quickly . . .

Despite an inadequate opening, this is a tensely plotted film, which casts a critical eye on those whose loyalties are easily bought. The action scenes themselves are mainly the usual stunt-and-guns fare that offer few surprises, but the flawless acting and uncompromising story easily make up for this.

FLAMING BROTHERS (1987)
Starring Alan Tang, Chow Yun-Fat, Patricia Ha,
Jenny Tseng
Directed by Joe Cheung
Produced by Alan Tang
In-Gear Film/Golden Harvest

Alan Tang made a name for himself in seventies gangster films, and when Chow Yun-Fat shot to fame in *A Better Tomorrow*, Tang's In-Gear company cast the pair in this bullet-spitting production.

Chow and Tang play close friends who grow up with not just a bond, but a code of honor. When Chow falls in love, Tang decides to carry on his triad business, but a rival mob moves in. In a desperate bid to help his blood brother, Chow goes to his aid for a brutal Butch Cassidy-style ending.

This movie, written by Wong Kar-Wai, merges extreme action sequences with romantic moments and is definitely worth a watch.

FULL ALERT (1997)
Starring Lau Ching-Wan, Francis Ng, Amanda Lee,
Jack Kao
Directed by Ringo Lam
Brilliant Idea Group/Young Filmmakers Ltd

Officer Pao (Ching-Wan) of the Special Crime Bureau is laser-focused in his mission to prevent criminal Mak Kwan (Ng) from masterminding a big heist, which turns out to be the audacious robbery of the Hong Kong Jockey Club vault.

With assured direction from Ringo Lam, this is a gritty policier punctuated with action set pieces and a couple of moments of visceral violence, culminating in a third-act heist sequence involving scuba diving, high explosives, a double cross, and the nihilistic final showdown between Pao, Kwan, and his girlfriend Chung (Lee).

The acting is satisfyingly unflashy, the film looks good, characterizations are nicely shaded and it all ends with a reminder that it isn't easy to kill someone,

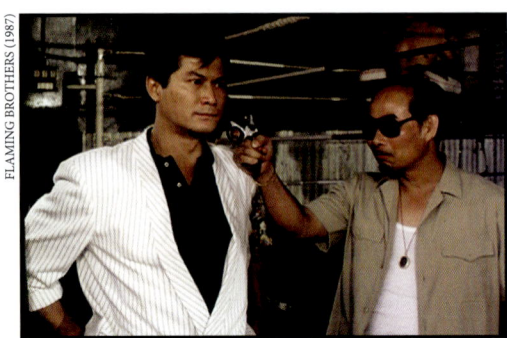

FLAMING BROTHERS (1987)

as Pao struggles with the emotional cost of taking lives while a thunderstorm rages around him.

FULL CONTACT (1992)
Starring Chow Yun-Fat, Simon Yam, Anthony Wong,
Ann Bridgewater, Bonnie Fu, Chris Lee, Frankie Chin
Directed and produced by Ringo Lam
Action by Lau Kar-Wing
Silver Medal Productions Ltd/
Golden Princess Film Production Limited

Jeff (Yun-Fat) and his friends Chung (Lee) and Sam (Wong) team up with Sam's cousin Judge (Yam) in a raid on an arms convoy in Thailand. After the raid, Judge and his gang (muscly yob Deano [Chin] and his lascivious girlfriend Virgin) double-cross Jeff. Chung is killed, and the weak-willed Sam is forced to kill Jeff. Instead, Sam leaves him for dead in a burning house, but Jeff survives and plots his revenge.

Ringo Lam's no-nonsense, brutally efficient direction conveys the sleaze and violence of this dog-eat-dog world. Chow looks leaner and meaner than ever before, slashing and shooting with ruthless style, demonstrating far less of the sensitive side compared to his previous screen characters. Simon Yam is superb as the sadistic killer Judge, who has the hots for Jeff, but won't hesitate to kill him. Judge's party piece is flourishing a handkerchief, which always turns out to conceal a knife or gun, which he uses deftly.

Full Contact is as stylish as a John Woo film,

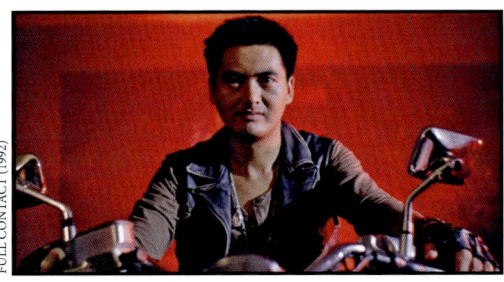

FULL CONTACT (1992)

but without such rigid codes of honor: even Jeff doesn't seem particularly concerned as innocent bystanders are slaughtered in the arms hijack. And, rather than escalating to full-scale massacre, Lam inventively chooses to follow each individual bullet's trajectory in the visually superb nightclub shoot-out.

With excellent action, a gritty storyline and a charismatic and memorable performance from Chow, *Full Contact* is an awesome movie, highly recommended to all bullet ballet fans.

FURY IN RED (1991)
Starring Conan Lee, Robin Shou, Ben Ng Ngai-Cheung, Mark Houghton, Vincent Lyn, Jo-Jo Ngan
Directed by Chong Lei
Regent Film

Take half a movie shot in Hong Kong and half a movie shot in LA . . . and you get *Fury in Red*. Unfortunately, the two films don't slot together too well, but two outstanding performances make this worth seeing. Mark Houghton puts in a great performance as a racist, badass FBI agent, showing his talent both for comedy and fisticuffs, and Robin Shou gives his best as the Night Monster, a depraved psychopathic hit man: poke him in the eye and he'll come back for more!

Conan Lee, unfortunately, doesn't get much to do, apart from one ho-hum fight scene. Shame.

GANGS '92 (1992)
Starring Aaron Kwok, Winnie Lau, Tse Wai-Kit, Ricky Ho
Directed by Cho Kin-Nam
Suen Woo Film Productions Co

Aaron Kwok plays a rich kid who befriends a group of young adults, whose only worry is where the next video arcade can be found. Their simple lives take a turn when they witness a vicious gang murder and a bribed senior policeman holds them responsible.

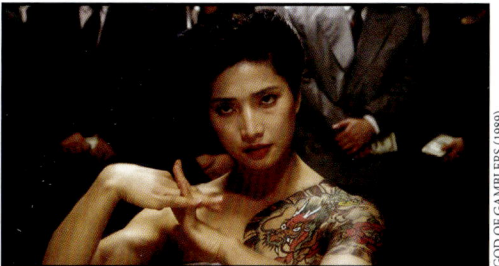

GOD OF GAMBLERS (1989)

Soon their futures are at risk from a powerful triad, its junkie leader, and the policeman he is paying.

Not a full-blooded action film per se, *Gangs '92* is a coming of age flick with cast members that play their characters with conviction, within a pessimistic story that climaxes in a brutal confrontation, with the youths finally corrupted by violence.

GOD OF GAMBLERS (1989)
Starring Chow Yun-Fat, Andy Lau, Joey Wong, Ng Man-Tat, Charles Heung
Directed by Wong Jing
Win's Film Productions

This movie is regarded by some as Chow Yun-Fat's finest moment. Deemed to be the best of the best in the gambling world, Ko Chun (Yun-Fat) finds himself the accidental victim of a stupid prank which leaves him with the mental age of ten and an uncontrollable craving for chocolate. Andy Lau is Knife, the streetwise con artist who discovers that, despite Chow's disability, he has an incredible talent for cards, and tries to exploit this to make money from the local hoods. But it's only a matter of time before Ko Chun regains his senses and blows the lid off Andy's scheming.

Although the action is pretty restrained for a Chow Yun-Fat gangster movie, this really allows him to demonstrate his acting ability, ranging from super-slick card pro, to sad, lost little boy, and back again. There are some fine comic moments, plenty of pathos and, of course, as the charismatic card genius, some mega-cool moments courtesy of Chow Yun-Fat!

GOD OF GAMBLERS II (1990)
Starring Andy Lau, Stephen Chow, Ng Man-Tat, Cheung Man, Charles Heung
Directed by Wong Jing
Produced by Charles Heung, Jimmy Heung
Action by Wong Kwan
Win's Film Productions

Following the huge success of the original *God of Gamblers*, Andy Lau returns in this comic sequel as Knife, the Knight of Gamblers, with Stephen Chow as Sing, the Saint of Gamblers, and Ng Man-Tat as his faithful sidekick. Sing decides to become Knife's student after hearing of his magical powers, but has trouble persuading him. Meanwhile, evil is stirring, and Knife is ambushed in his house. An imposter proclaims himself to be the Knight of Gamblers, so Knife is forced to team up with Sing to outsmart him.

There are some excellent gambling matches before the full-scale fighting breaks out, and Andy Lau gets to display his martial arts skills, while Stephen Chow uses a pair of plungers like nunchakus! Unlike its predecessor, this is more of a comedy than an action film: a wise decision, perhaps, as nothing could measure up to the brilliance of the Chow Yun-Fat original. But with the change of style, this is actually a funny and enjoyable film in its own right.

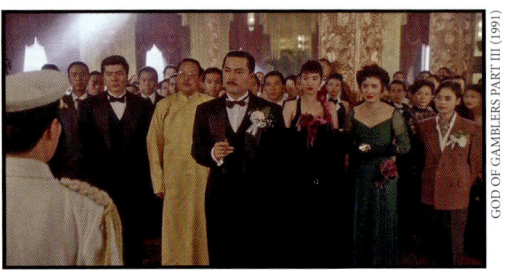

GOD OF GAMBLERS PART III (1991)

GOD OF GAMBLERS PART III: BACK TO SHANGHAI (1991)

Starring Stephen Chow, Gong Li, Ray Lui, Ng Man-Tat, Charles Heung, Sandra Ng
Directed by Wong Jing
Produced by Charles Heung, Jimmy Heung
Win's Film Productions/
Samico Films Production Company Ltd

The Saint of Gamblers (Chow) is transported back in time to Shanghai, 1937, where he meets up with his own grandfather (Ng Man-Tat) and becomes involved in a gangland feud. They are befriended by gang boss Ding Lik (Lui), who has been challenged to a gambling duel. When the Saint of Gamblers uses his powers to defeat Ding's rivals, who are represented by his old enemy Tai-Kun, Ding grants him three wishes. Meanwhile, just to complicate matters, the Saint of Gamblers has fallen in love with Ding's girlfriend Yu San's identical sister (Gong Li, playing both parts), who has a mental age of five. And when a Japanese fighting femme enters the feud, things get totally out of control.

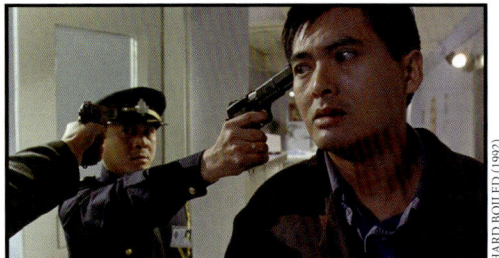

HARD BOILED (1992)

The nonsensical plot gives Stephen Chow plenty of opportunities for much comic tomfoolery and lampooning which have made him famous, and there are some nifty bits of fighting and gun action, but by and large there's little memorable about the movie. It's just a daft, fairly entertaining piece of fluff that's about as far removed from the classic original *God of Gamblers* as you can get.

GUNMEN (1988)

Starring Tony Leung Ka-Fai, Adam Cheng, Waise Lee, Elizabeth Lee, Carrie Ng, David Wu, Elvis Tsui
Directed by Kirk Wong
Action by Fung Hark-On
Film Workshop

Four men bond together during the Civil War in China and, when the conflict is over, go their separate ways. Several years later, Ding (Leung) becomes a member of the Shanghai police force and comes across his old friends, who have been reduced to poverty. In order to help them, he offers them jobs in the police force, but they refuse, having seen enough killing in the war. This changes when they witness how badly Ding is injured in a fierce gun battle against a villain called Haye (Cheng). The four form the Gunmen Squad, tracking Haye to a final confrontation that escalates into a bloody battle, which will determine their ultimate fate.

Produced by Tsui Hark, *Gunmen* is a good to look at period police tale with the usual bouts of male bonding and gun-toting action. Director Kirk Wong, who made the visually arresting sci-fi-actioner *Health Warning* (1983), handles the set piece skirmishes well enough, but they lack that extra something that would've elevated them to the standard seen in a John Woo film.

HARD BOILED (1992)

Starring Chow Yun-Fat, Tony Leung Chiu-Wai, Anthony Wong, Teresa Mo, Philip Chan, Philip Kwok
Directed by John Woo
Action by Philip Kwok
Milestone Pictures/Golden Princess

Chow Yun-Fat plays Tequila Yuen, a maverick cop, who takes the law into his own hands as he battles triad gangsters in this explosively over-the-top gun-fest. Tony Leung is Alan, a brooding undercover cop who is more hit man than policeman now, while Anthony Wong is Johnny, the new-style, ambitious triad boss with no regard for conventions of honor.

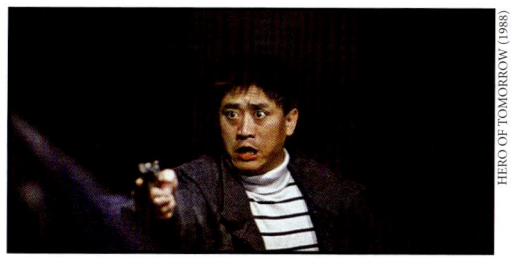

HERO OF TOMORROW (1988)

The action set pieces are John Woo classics, starting with a vicious large-scale firefight in a teahouse, through a classy gangland slaying in a library, to a fast-paced shoot-out in a warehouse and, finally, to the slaughter-packed finale at a hospital, where, if the patients weren't on the critical list when they arrived, they soon surely would be!

The style which lifts Woo's splatter epics into the firmament is much in evidence here and, while the plot's nothing new, the production is an utter joy to watch, with Chow Yun-Fat excelling as the supercool cop with an attitude, though Philip Kwok steals the show as the unstoppable Mad Dog.

The outrageous action sequences, involving multiple actors, stuntmen, guns, slo-mo stylishness, explosions, and squibs, especially in the third act, are mind-blowing, spectacular, and inventive. Nobody does gunplay like John Woo.

HE WHO CHASES AFTER THE WIND (1988)

Starring Alex Man, Elizabeth Lee, Chen Hao,
Stephen Chow, Carrie Ng
Directed by Lai Kin-Kwok
Diamond Cast Films

Hong Kong cop Ko (Man) becomes obsessed by the woman whose diary he is in possession of.

This is an adequate Hong Kong thriller which does have its moments, such as the sequence in which Ko finally shows his real feelings to the object of his desire by kissing her as he shows her how to fire his gun (and a Chinese version of the *Top Gun* theme plays on the soundtrack!)

There is a brilliant bullet-in-the-forehead shot at the start, with blood splattering out in slow-motion, plus a vicious garroting attack in which the boyish Stephen Chow is strangled in a prolonged assault that culminates in suffocation-by-plastic-bag.

The film as a whole could have done with an injection of more action, although there is the usual nihilistic gun duel at the end, where Ko and the villain blast away at one another. During this confrontation Ko is ordered to lower his gun, which Ko does, placing his free hand over the barrel. Then, in a fine example of Hong Kong heroics, Ko fires through his own hand in order to hit the bad guy!

HERO OF TOMORROW (1988)

Starring Mok Siu-Chung, Miu Kiu-Wai, Ho Ka-Kui,
Blackie Ko, Wong Kwong-Leung
Directed by Poon Man-Kit
Produced by Cheung Kwok-Chung
Movie Impact Limited

This film isn't concerned with the John Woo-style designer suits and shades brigade, but with the lives of the Sze Kau, the foot soldiers of the triads. Their lives are spent pursuing debts and collecting protection fees, and they are the ones all too often required to fight for the honor of their gang's name.

Mok Siu-Cheung plays Crow, a young man who joins a gang while his brother-in-law Lee (Kiu-Wai), recently released from prison, is leading a peaceful life and trying to escape his violent criminal past. Initially, life for the ambitious Crow is simple and he finds no difficulty in carrying out the tasks his position entails. It's not long, however, before he finds his deep-rooted loyalties conflicting with his new obligations to his boss, Billy (Ka-Kui).

This film cannot be accused of glamorising the triad lifestyle: here the codes of honor are long gone, and the societies are increasingly money-minded. Old triad leader Uncle Chung is all but helpless and can do little to control the sadistic, greedy and vengeful Billy, as this sour tale moves swiftly along to its tragic, bullet-ridden climax.

HEROES SHED NO TEARS (1984)

Starring Eddy Ko, Lam Ching-Ying, Ma Ying-Chun,
Chin Yuet-Sang
Directed by John Woo
Action by Chin Yuet-Sang
Golden Harvest/Paragon Films Ltd

Originally lensed as *The Sunset Warrior*, the movie was shelved until it was released as *Heroes Shed No Tears*, following the success of John Woo's *A Better Tomorrow*.

In this story, which had changes made to it by Woo before he started filming, the Thai government approaches a retired soldier, Chan Chung (Ko), enlisting him to capture the chief drug baron of the region, a colonel played by Lam Ching-Ying. As he sets out on his hazardous mission, Chan Chung finds himself under threat from both sides.

Although the final cut wasn't edited by John Woo himself, and includes scenes that were not shot by him, some of Woo's traits, which were to become his trademarks in his gangster movies, are in evidence here.

Also known as *Close Call with Death*.

IN THE BLOOD (1988)

Starring Andy Lau, Bill Tung, Wu Ma, Hsiao Hung-Mei, Chin Siu-Ho, Anthony Chan, Sammo Hung
Directed by Corey Yuen
Produced by Wu Ma
Bo Ho Film Company Ltd/D & B Films Co. Ltd/
Golden Harvest

Pei Dan, an accident-prone policeman, hopes to become a good CID officer so that his father, a high-ranking policeman, will respect him.

A couple of tightly choreographed fights can't negate the general slowness of the proceedings in this mediocre cop-socky production. Look out for Sammo Hung in a tiny cameo as a waiter.

ISLAND OF GREED (1997)

Starring Andy Lau, Tony Leung Ka-Fai, Pauline Suen, Annie Wu, Chin Shih-Chieh, Winston Chao
Directed by Michael Mak
Win's Entertainment Ltd/Johnny Mak Productions/
China Star Entertainment

This film features a star-studded cast, including Andy Lau and Tony Leung, and boasts a script written by the director's brother, Johnny Mak. The story follows Fong (Lau), an investigator for the Ministry of Justice Investigation Bureau, as he uncovers a gambling scam involving Chow Chiu-Sin (Leung), a seemingly respectable businessman who is also

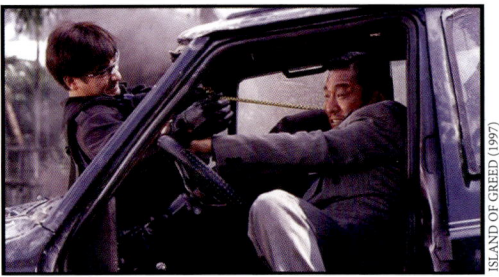

ISLAND OF GREED (1997)

the leader of a triad gang.

Fong attempts to bring Chow to justice, but he soon discovers that the gang leader has connections within the government and can easily get the charges dropped. Frustrated and outraged, Fong begins a bitter battle to take Chow down.

The plot is disjointed in places, as Michael Mak tries to combine political themes with the action-packed elements of a Hong Kong heroic bloodshed movie, but, despite this, the film offers up some big action set pieces. These include a battle between rival cab firms, helicopters firing anti-tank missiles and a thrilling chase scene involving Fong and his men on motocross bikes being pursued by hundreds of real Alsatian dogs.

Island of Greed may not be perfect, but its tale of corruption and greed, peppered with action sequences, makes it worth a viewing for fans of Hong Kong gangster movies.

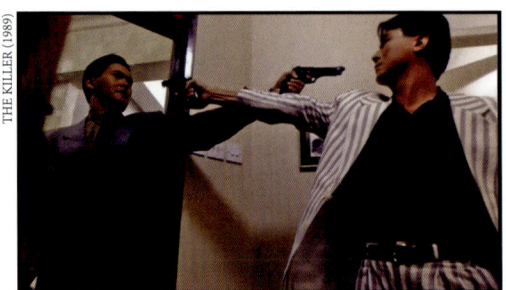

THE KILLER (1989)

THE KILLER (1989)

Starring Chow Yun-Fat, Danny Lee, Sally Yeh, Chu Kong
Directed by John Woo
Produced by Tsui Hark
Action by Ching Siu-Tung, Lau Chi-Ho
Golden Princess Film Production Ltd/Film Workshop

Charismatic superstar Chow Yun-Fat plays Jeff, a hired killer who accidently blinds nightclub singer Jennie (Yeh) during what was to have been his final hit. Unable to live with his conscience, he takes on another job to pay for her cornea transplant, only to find himself caught in a web of deceit and betrayal, with cop Ying (Lee) on his tail. But gradually a bond is forged between the two men, as cop and killer are forced to acknowledge that they are opposite sides of the same coin. Ying discovers that the killer's code of honor reflects his own and the two men end up fighting back-to-back in a desperate shoot-out in an abandoned church, as they take on Jeff's triad enemies in a bloody confrontation.

John Woo's vision and Chow Yun-Fat's masterful performance combine with breathtaking action and a nicely constructed, melodramatic script to make this an all-time classic that displays Woo's directorial skills at their zenith. Once seen, this tale of honor and betrayal, set against a backdrop of incredible violence, can never be forgotten.

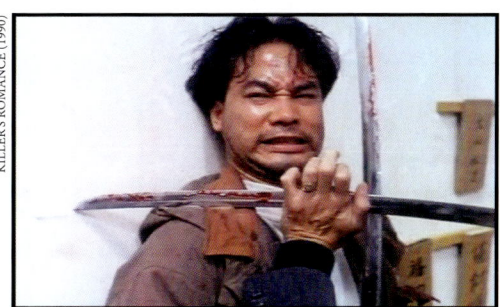

KILLER'S ROMANCE (1990)

THE KILLER'S LOVE (1993)
Starring Carol Cheng, Simon Yam, Anglie Leung,
Wong Chi-Yeung, Jamie Luk
Directed by Jamie Luk
Produced by David Lam
David Lam Films

Using the first twenty minutes as a guide, you'd be forgiven for assuming that this movie was nothing more than a lighthearted comedy. In actual fact it is a flawed attempt at combining elements of comedy and heroic bloodshed.

Carol "Do Do" Cheng plays a village schoolteacher whose uneventful life makes an about-face, when she takes in a tall, dark and handsome stranger as her lodger. He teaches the naive bumpkin what true love is, and their future together looks very rosy indeed. Such a pity, then, that her new beau is actually a professional killer who is bored with the criminal lifestyle and is being pursued by a vicious psychopath intent on filling him with lead!

This is an enjoyable but inconsistent film, which one minute is all laughs and the next is total carnage.

KILLER'S ROMANCE (1990)
Starring Simon Yam, Joey Wong, Phillip Ko, Luk Chuen
Directed and produced by Phillip Ko
Regent Film Limited

Jeffrey (Yam), the adopted son of a UK-based Japanese gang head, seeks revenge on his father's Chinatown killers. Paula (Wong), an innocent bystander, witnesses one of Jeffrey's hits and becomes obsessed with him, falling in love with the silent assassin. It is then revealed that Jeffrey has been misinformed, and the killers are not who he expected them to be: his father's murder was actually the result of the teaming up of Chinatown gangsters and the Japanese, led by the supposedly trustworthy deputy chief, Yoshikawa. Jeffrey, of course, now sets out to blow away both outfits.

Simon Yam is a troubled Chow Yun-Fat–style killer in this film, akin to the Vietnam-based hit man

he played in *Bullet in the Head*, a similarity that is strengthened as both characters are maimed in one arm by the end of both movies.

The earlier section of *Killer's Romance* bears some similarity to the Japanese *Crying Freeman* manga as Jeffrey performs several assassinations, most notably in the scene where he leaps past his victim, shooting him.

The gun battle at the Chinese HQ is a splattery affair, while the final confrontation at the Japanese home base is given an interesting twist with the introduction of some good samurai sword fighting. During the amazing finale it doesn't end well for anyone ... Paula is kneecapped, Jeffrey's arm is lopped off, and Yoshikawa's head gets sliced down the middle!

It's odd to see Hong Kong movie-style posturing and gangland skirmishes in British surroundings, such as when a Chinese kingpin in a wheelchair is terminated in Hyde Park! All things considered, this is a really effective little movie, mixing bloody shoot-outs, sword fights, some kung fu scraps at the end, romance, and a reflective/melancholic atmosphere to good effect.

THE LAST BLOOD (1990)
Starring Alan Tam, Andy Lau, Eric Tsang,
Leung Ka-Yan, May Law
Directed by Wong Jing
Produced by Wallace Cheung, Eric Tsang
Action by Blackie Ko
Movie Impact Limited

A group of Japanese Red Army terrorists attempt to kill the Daka Lama while he is on a goodwill visit to Singapore. They wound him, and also the girlfriend of small-time hood Bee (Lau). Both victims need blood transfusions and share the same extremely rare blood group. As the Lama is protected in a secure hospital, the terrorists try to assassinate all possible blood donors, until only one would-be donor, Fatty (Tsang), is left alive. The security forces,

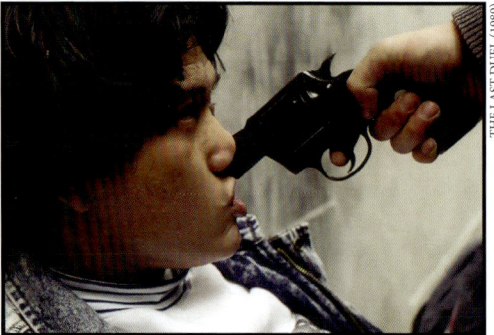

THE LAST DUEL (1989)

led by Lui Tai (Tam), set out to find him, but Bee also enters the hunt, to try and save his girlfriend.

The movie is crammed with frenetic automatic gun action, as the ruthless terrorists blow away men, women and children without hesitation, and the security forces are equally trigger-happy, mowing down gun-toting air hostesses and tooled-up terrorists with the obvious conviction that nothing succeeds like excess.

Cable car fights, mass motorbike attacks, and axe assaults build up to the brilliantly ballistic climax at the hospital in this way-above-average actioner.

THE LAST DUEL (1989)

Starring Alex Man, Rosamund Kwan, Joanna Chan,
Wong Chi-Yeung
Directed by Fan Sau-Ming
Action by Lau Chi-Ho
D & B Film Distribution/Ocean Shores

Ken (Chi-Yeung), a negligent police officer, causes the death of a pregnant woman and frames street trader Suen (Man). After serving a prison sentence, Suen hopes to rebuild his humble life, but, as fate would have it, upon his release he discovers that his new neighbor, Mei Li (Kwan), is dating Ken, who is now a senior inspector. At first Ken is content to taunt Suen with words, but soon rape, arson and murder ensue, as he systematically goes about destroying Suen's life.

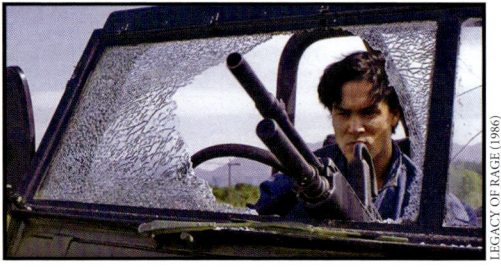

LEGACY OF RAGE (1986)

The action sequences in this progressively pessimistic tale are less stylised and more brutal than is usual in Hong Kong movies, and the performances here are exceptional, particularly Alex Man as the well-meaning Suen and Wong Chi-Yeung as the slick, over-confident cop.

LEGACY OF RAGE (1986)

Starring Brandon Lee, Michael Wong, Regina Kent,
Meng Hoi
Directed by Ronnie Yu
Produced by John Sham, Linda Kuk
Action by Meng Hoi
D & B Films Co. Ltd

Brandon's one and only attempt at Hong Kong action is still considered his best film. He plays Brandon Ma, a righteous guy who is used by his lowlife friend Michael (Michael Wong) to get rid of a police officer. Brandon is sent to prison and Michael finds himself attracted to Brandon's longtime girlfriend (Regina Kent). Unaware of Michael's dirty tricks, she allows him to befriend her, but spurns his advances when he tries to take advantage. Enraged, Michael attempts to rape her and when Brandon finds out he tries to escape from jail, but fails, and has to wait until he has served his full term before he can go after Michael, who by now has become a powerful mafia boss.

It was John Sham who lured Brandon into the world of Hong Kong cinema and, although Brandon was never going to be able to live up to the celluloid image of his father, Bruce Lee, his own on-screen charisma and acting ability allowed him to be cool and impactful in his own way.

Legacy of Rage leans more toward heroic bloodshed than martial arts, but several sequences did allow Brandon to demonstrate that the spirit of Bruce Lee's fighting lived on and a sequel was planned, but Brandon was snapped up by Hollywood, where he was to die tragically on set a short time later.

THE LEGENDARY 'TAI FEI' (1999)

Starring Anthony Wong, Teresa Mak, Benny Lai,
Alex Lam
Directed by Kant Leung
Wong Jing's Workshop Ltd

Hung Hing triad branch leader Tai Fei (Wong) is asked by his dying ex-girlfriend to look after Shin (Lam), the seventeen-year-old son he never knew he had. The problem is Shin is a cocky member of Tung Hing, a different gang branch run by King, a manipulative mobster planning to kill his own boss and frame Tai Fei for a stolen drugs shipment.

This is a passable *Young and Dangerous* spin-off movie, focusing on Tai Fei's attempts at bonding with his son Shin, who is played as an irritating, nose-picking brat by Alex Lam. Benny Lai is more interesting as King, portraying him like a slimy, untrustworthy, womanising pastiche of *Young and Dangerous* gangster hero Nam.

The so-so film mixes in some melodrama with the usual intergang double-dealing and ends with a face-off between triads, as Tai Fei puts his own life on the line to save his son.

LONG ARM OF THE LAW (1984)

Starring Lam Wei, Huang Jian, Chiang Lung, Yeung Ming
Directed by Johnny Mak
Produced by Johnny Mak, Sammo Hung
Bo Ho Film Company Ltd/Johnny Mak Productions

Tung, a Big Circle Gang leader wanted by the police, returns to confer with his gang members: Blockhead, who dotes on his son, Chubby, who is very attentive to his grandmother, Chung, Rooster and Bull's Eye. Tung informs the gang that their new mission involves robbing a jewelry store in Hong Kong and getting back across the border within forty-eight hours. But, as they set out for the border at night, things begin to go wrong.

John Woo's *A Better Tomorrow* may have been seen as the beginning of a new wave of heroic bloodshed movies, but several years earlier Johnny

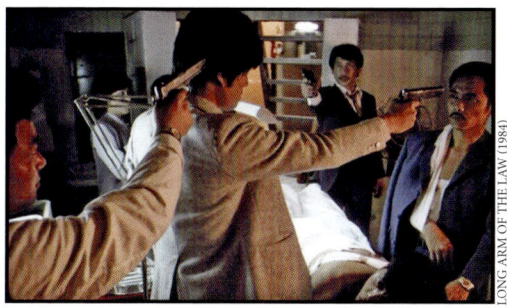

Mak was already shaping this style of cinema with his simmering storylines relating to codes of honor. Mak, like Ringo Lam, tended to base his stories on realism and often dealt with illegal immigrants entering Hong Kong.

Long Arm of the Law was loosely based on a spate of robberies committed by Big Circle Gangs (illegal

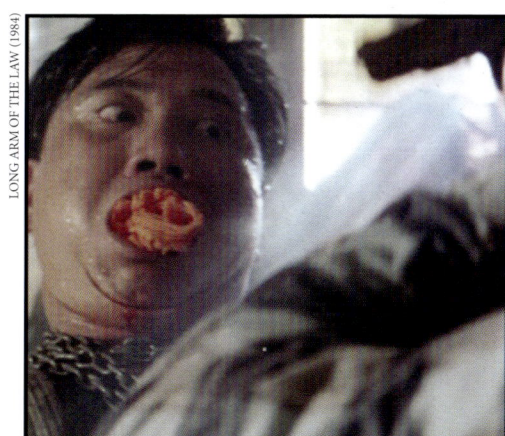

immigrants from Guangdong; often gentle people forced into a life of crime). Johnny Mak interviewed over five hundred people to discover unknown actors, giving the film its gritty, real life look. He also consulted with Big Circle Gangs to establish the film's realism. Although not as stylised as the John Woo movies, the story is compelling and violent, and is without a doubt a fine example of Hong Kong crime thriller.

LONG ARM OF THE LAW II (1987)

Starring Alex Man, Wong Siu-Fung, Elvis Tsui,
Kirk Wong
Directed by Michael Mak
Johnny Mak Productions/Golden Harvest

Not a sequel, but the second installment delving into the lives of mainlanders and their codes of honor. Directing this time is Michael Mak, brother of Johnny Mak.

In this film Big Circle Gang crimes have increased, so a trio of mainland illegal immigrants are recruited to infiltrate the Big Circle underground, because these gangs are always exclusively staffed by mainlanders. They are chaperoned by a local undercover cop, who unfortunately is waylaid by one of the gangsters. The mainlanders do not believe in a swift death, as you might find in a mafia execution and, instead, the poor guy is hung upside down, his head is covered by a sack full of rats and, just before the excruciating pain makes him pass out, his head is chopped off with an axe. Nasty!

Although slightly more glossy than its predecessor, Michael Mak still manages to imbue part 2 with a gritty atmosphere, coaxing an excellent performance from Alex Man.

LONG ARM OF THE LAW III (1989)
Starring Andy Lau, Mok Siu-Chung, Elizabeth Lee,
Elvis Tsui, Kirk Wong, Ken Boyle
Directed by Michael Mak
Action by Leung Siu-Hung
Johnny Mak Productions/Movie Impact

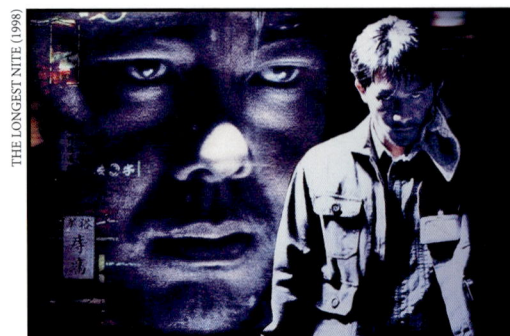

THE LONGEST NITE (1998)

Also known as *Escape from Hong Kong*, Johnny Mak's production is chock-full of superb fighting and gunplay, with a plot focusing on three illegal immigrants from the mainland. Kong (Lau) is on the run from a death sentence, with a Red Army captain hot on his tail, when he meets up with Mun (Lee) and Chicken Heart (Siu-Chung). On their arrival in Hong Kong, they go their separate ways and Kong is set upon by triad members. He beats them in a wicked fight, thus coming to the attention of the bosses, who Chicken Heart now works for. Meanwhile, Kong must rescue Mun from the clutches of the gang, while evading the Red Army captain hunting him down.

For once Andy Lau's unique fighting skills are amply showcased, as he gets to cut through hundreds of gangsters. Add this to his top-notch gun handling and, well, what more could any action fan want?!

LONG ARM OF THE LAW IV (1990)
Starring Elvis Tsui, Ching Siu-Lung, Jacqueline Ng,
Chan Wing-Chung, Frankie Chin, Ken Boyle
Directed by Michael Mak
Johnny Mak Productions/Golden Harvest

Also known as *Underground Express* and *Long Arm of the Law: Part 4*, the story focuses on the corruption between China and Hong Kong and the police. A gang, headed up by Bing (Tsui), exploits the trafficking of students to Hong Kong, taking three female students, including the leader of the student's revolution, Wong Siu Wai, played by newcomer Jacqueline Ng. Their attempt nearly fails as the gang is betrayed at the checkpoint. A fierce gun

battle ensues and they manage to escape on foot, continuing to attempt to cross the border to Hong Kong, facing many perilous trials as they play cat and mouse with the Chinese military in hot pursuit.

Elvis Tsui, often found at home in Category III flicks, always gives a good performance and here, as Bing, he delivers a portrait of a menacing gang leader with a heart. There's a high body count in gun battles between the gang and the military, and brutality too, with one scene showing a captured gang member being brutally tortured as he is told that his old mum has been sent for to take his body home.

The film, as in the three other movies, deals with factual news stories interspersed within the storyline. The shooting seems rushed, and the budget seems to have been reduced, but with Michael Mak at the helm and Johnny Mak on screenplay duties, they do deliver a decent movie.

THE LONGEST NITE (1998)
Starring Lau Ching-Wan, Tony Leung Chiu-Wai,
Maggie Siu
Directed by Patrick Yau (plus an uncredited Johnnie To)
Film City Co/Milky Way Image Company

Brutal cop Sam (Leung), who doesn't think twice about beating and framing people, finds himself being set up as a fall guy, in a scheme to rid Mr. Hung, Macao's top gang boss, of his main rivals, but just what part does mysterious bald dude Tony (Ching-Wan) have to play in these events?

The ways in which Sam is manipulated and coerced into becoming an assassin, due to Tony's elaborate machinations, strains credulity a little too far, but the film remains a hard-bitten crime thriller that uses Giorgio Moroder's track "The Chase" effectively to accompany Sam as he moves about the city, boasts moody cinematography and maintains a suspenseful, tense vibe throughout.

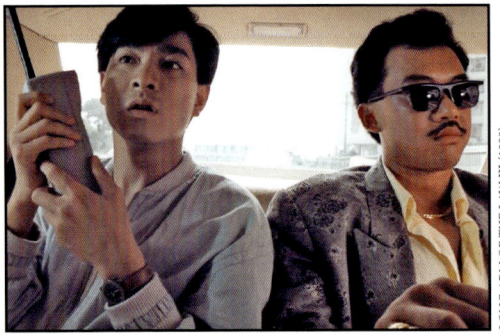

LONG ARM OF THE LAW III (1989)

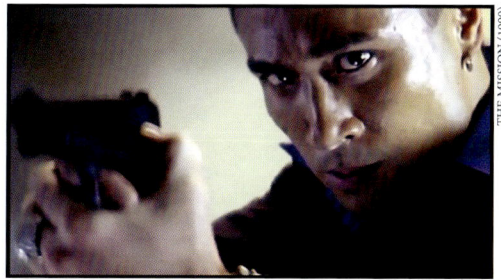

THE MISSION (1999)

Starring Francis Ng, Anthony Wong, Jackie Lui,
Roy Cheung, Simon Yam, Eddy Ko, Lam Suet
Directed by Johnnie To
Milky Way Image Company

Triad boss Lung (Ko) is nearly assassinated, so he hires five bodyguards to protect him, including Curtis (Wong) and Roy (Ng). These efficient dudes are calm under fire and, after some initial friction, bond well together. They now set out to keep their boss safe and take down the bad guys.

Nobody makes these kind of crime movies quite like Johnnie To does. He imbues his films with his own style and one of the components of his style is deliberate, measured pacing. There are, of course, scenes of violence, shoot-outs and confrontations, but they are carefully choreographed and subtle in execution, with moments of stillness as the protagonists hold their nerve and await their enemies' next move.

These dudes are effortlessly cool, they never try too hard, they just exude no-nonsense, methodical professionalism. We then get to see how these characters, who have connected with each other during tense, life-and-death encounters, handle a colleague's indiscretion: do they splinter as a team, or do they dig deep to find a solution that's good for all of them?

The actors playing the five-man team are all good, but Francis Ng really stands out. He's just so damn cool-looking whenever he's on screen!

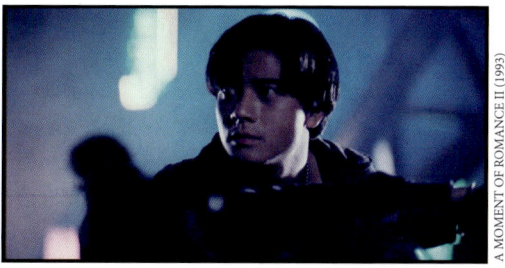

A MOMENT OF ROMANCE (1990)

Starring Andy Lau, Wu Chien-Lien, Ng Man-Tat,
Wong Kwong-Leung
Directed by Benny Chan
Produced by Ringo Lam, Johnnie To, Wong Jing
Movie Impact/Paka Hill Productions

If Andy Lau, among his numerous movies, was to be credited for one piece of superlative acting, then the award must go to his work in *A Moment of Romance*. He has played this delinquent, rebel-without-a-clue character in many movies, but here his performance has real depth.

Andy plays Wah Dee, a small-time hood who is forced to become the getaway driver for the psychopathic Trumpet (Kwong-Leung), his senior gang member. Incompetence abounds, the robbery goes disastrously wrong, and it is only due to Wah Dee's skilled driving that the gang members escape. But, in the confusion, they take a hostage and Wah Dee gradually finds himself becoming attracted to this innocent girl, Jo Jo (Chien-Lien). When Wah Dee refuses to let the gang kill her, so that she cannot identify them to the police, he and Jo Jo must stay one step ahead of the triad members, who cannot accept that she will keep silent. So Wah Dee has only one choice . . . to eliminate his hunters.

This movie rises head and shoulders above most heroic bloodshed movies, with excellence in all aspects of its production, flawless acting from the male and female stars and a powerful soundtrack. A must-see movie.

A MOMENT OF ROMANCE II (1993)

Starring Aaron Kwok, Wu Chien-Lien, Anthony Wong,
Roger Kwok
Directed by Benny Chan
Produced by Johnnie To
China Entertainment Films Production/
Paka Hill Productions

Celia (Chien-Lien), an illegal immigrant from the mainland, becomes a prostitute in a desperate bid to help her imprisoned brother. Her first trick is a triad boss, and she witnesses his brutal murder at the hands of an ambitious subordinate. Fleeing the scene with the deceased man's wallet, Celia is chased by the gang's hoodlums, who believe she is the killer. Noticing her distress, a stranger on a motorbike rescues her and takes her to the relative safety of his flat. The pair fall in love, but their romance is ill-fated: the investigations of an obsessive policeman

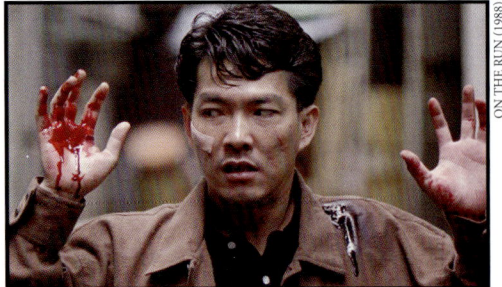

ON THE RUN (1988)

uncover Celia's whereabouts, and soon they are beset on all sides, from both the law and the lawbreakers.

This is not a continuation of events from the classic *A Moment of Romance* (1990), but another drama-romance composed of tragedy, violence, bike racing and conflicting loyalties. Not as good as the original, but it's an entertaining watch nonetheless.

NOBODY'S HERO (1989)
Starring Liu Wai-Hung, Kathy Chow, Lok Ying-Kwan
Directed by Kuk Kok-Leung
Action by Poon Kin-Kwan, Kong To-Hoi
Jan Gong Movie-Making Company

Gun (Wai-Hung) cannot come to terms with the fact his girlfriend ran off with another man and, to add to his woes, as a taxi driver he is sickened by the ugly sight of criminal activity on the streets around him, so he decides to become a policeman, but to his dismay he cannot join the force because he is color-blind. The next best thing is security work at a mall, where he meets a blind girl, though this inexorably leads to a bloody confrontation with a local triad gang that is using the girl to smuggle drugs.

A mix of romantic comedy and gritty, grubby action thriller, this film, which is a riff on Martin Scorsese's *Taxi Driver*, ends in an all-out heroic bloodshed killing spree.

ON THE RUN (1988)
Starring Yuen Biao, Patricia Ha, Charlie Chin, Lo Lieh,
Yuen Wah, Idy Chan, Phillip Ko
Directed by Alfred Cheung
Bo Ho Film Company Ltd/Golden Harvest/
Mobile Film Production

Alfred Cheung's *On the Run* is a superior piece of Hong Kong noir, turning a standard police corruption plot into a stylish chase crime thriller. Patricia Ha puts in a memorable performance as Pai, a professional hitwoman from the Golden Triangle,

who fulfills a contract by murdering the wife of Ming (Biao), a CID officer. Pai then finds herself betrayed and hunted down, forced to become Ming's ally.

Yuen Biao will always be best known for his flips and kicks, but here, under the watchful eye of Alfred Cheung, who is better known for directing inane comedies, he displays an acting ability rarely seen. In fact, he only does one spectacular stunt, and for the rest of the running time he is like Harrison Ford in *The Fugitive*, ducking and diving, trying to stay one step ahead until the final confrontation, which is delivered with extreme violence.

A definite unsung classic.

ONCE A THIEF (1991)
Starring Chow Yun-Fat, Leslie Cheung, Cherie Chung,
Kenneth Tsang, Chu Kong, David Wu
Directed by John Woo
Produced by Terence Chang, Linda Kuk
Action by Philip Kwok
Milestone Pictures/
Golden Princess Film Production Limited

Joe (Yun-Fat) and Jim (Cheung) are a pair of art thieves denuding Paris of its valuable paintings, while vying for the love of Cheri (Chung). They get caught up in the gangland machinations concerning one special painting, and in the getaway after stealing the

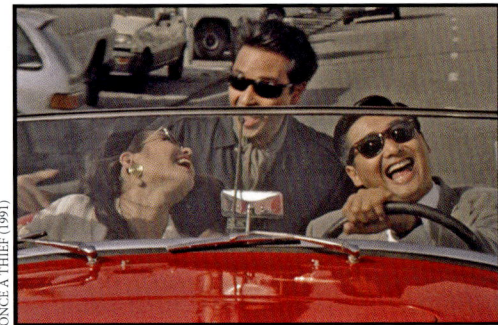

ONCE A THIEF (1991)

picture Joe apparently sacrifices himself so that Jim can escape. Jim returns to Hong Kong, where Joe also miraculously resurfaces, albeit wheelchair-bound. Together they confront their crooked foster father, a triad boss with a fixation on this special painting.

John Woo stages the action scenes as well and as inventively as ever, and there is also a lot of humor here too. Highlights include characters acrobatically dodging laser beams and swinging from chandeliers to overcome a hi-tech security system, a death-by-microwave moment, and playing cards being used as lethal, razor-sharp weapons.

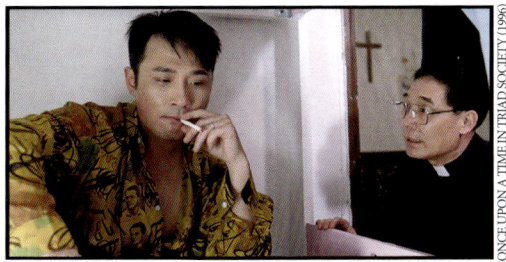

ONCE UPON A TIME IN TRIAD SOCIETY (1996)

The film's plot defies comprehension sometimes, however, due to the film having been hurriedly put together for a Chinese New Year release.

ONCE UPON A TIME IN TRIAD SOCIETY (1996)

Starring Francis Ng, Loletta Lee, Allen Ting, Edmond So, Michael Chan Wai-Man
Directed by Cha Chuen-Yee
Concept Link Productions

Cha Chuen-Yee produced and directed this comedy spinoff of the *Young and Dangerous* series. Brother Kwan (Ng), better known as Ugly Kwan due to his bad attitude toward women, friends, and other gangsters, finds himself on the receiving end of a failed assassination. Rushed to the hospital, none of the doctors or nurses seem keen to save his life due to his reputation. When he falls into a coma, we are taken on an alternative story to discover what made him such a vile character. Here, he is portrayed as a nice, caring guy struggling with the ethics of being a triad dude. After being betrayed by his boss, the girl he loves from afar, and his best friend, he sets up life in Japan, meets a new wife who becomes pregnant, but his happiness is broken when the Hong Kong gang tracks him down and murders his wife by throwing her into the water. Distraught, Kwan jumps after his wife, only to awaken to find himself rescued by a ship close to Hong Kong. Bitter and twisted, he temporarily comes to while having the bullet removed, only to slip back into a coma, which is when we get the caption: "My New Face." Now we embark on the nasty side of Kwan, an unscrupulous, ruthless gangster tormented by his past.

Francis Ng is excellent: his comic timing is on par with Stephen Chow, moving easily from hopeless hero to ruthless triad boss, and there is a great performance from Michael Chan Wai-Man too. The movie moves from funny to very dark and is well-paced with a great funky jazz opening theme tune.

ONCE UPON A TIME IN TRIAD SOCIETY 2 (1996)

Starring Francis Ng, Angie Cheung, Roy Cheung, Cheung Tat-Ming, Ada Choi
Directed by Cha Chuen-Yee
Concept Link Productions

Set against the backdrop of Mong Kok, the movie is told from three different perspectives as two triad gangs battle for control of the streets. In spite of its title, this is not a sequel and the only familiar face is Francis Ng, who plays Dagger.

Despite being a member of the triad and trying to act tough, Dagger seems to shy away from street skirmishes and instead prefers to showcase his skills at mahjong. Dinosaur (Roy Cheung), on the other hand, is a more violent triad boss and through flashbacks we see him killing countless triad guys in violent machete street battles. Dummy (Tat-Ming), meanwhile, is a downtrodden policeman whose girlfriend finds him boring.

Director Cha Cheun-Yee delivers a decent movie that boasts some gritty action and a really great 1980s-style soundtrack that sounds like it was played on a solo keyboard.

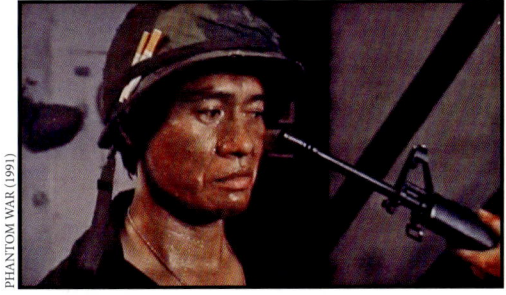

PHANTOM WAR (1991)

PHANTOM WAR (1991)

Starring Alex Man, Ben Ng Ngai-Cheung, Yammie Lam Kit-Ying, Phillip Ko
Directed by Cindy Chow Fung, Simon Yeung Siu-Gwong
Produced by Phillip Ko
My Way Film Company/Regent Film

Nan (Ng), an ex-Vietcong fighter, is reunited with his wife in London and hopes to settle down to establish his own small business. He receives financial assistance from the wealthy Chinese businessman whose life he saved during a triad-related attack. Along with the money, his brave act brings him unwanted attention from the various gangs which, like parasites, are feeding off the Chinese community.

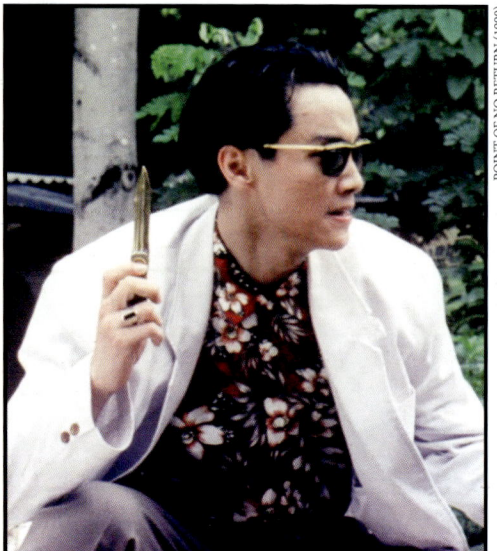

POINT OF NO RETURN (1990)

In pursuit of Nan are an ambitious triad boss, his followers, and a drug dealer, who bears a personal grudge against Nan which spans a decade. In addition to the battle he must now fight, Nan has yet to come to terms with his experiences in Vietnam, and is constantly haunted by the horrors of his past.

This is a well-crafted, pessimistic tale, full of scenes of brutality and mental anguish. The cast play their parts with conviction, overcoming any limitations caused by the tight budget. Recommended.

POINT OF NO RETURN (1990)
Starring Jacky Cheung, Joey Wong, Patrick Tam, Kenneth Tsang
Directed by Guy Lai
Y. C. Lai Film Production Company

Despite not offering anything new in terms of plot or action, this is a competent bloodshed film which concerns two brothers, one of them adopted, and their relationships with each other and their father. In this family, the father is a retired hit man who is less than enthusiastic that his sons are following in his footsteps. When one of them falls for his would-be victim, their troubles really begin, with his brother urging him to act like a professional, but then an angry crime boss despatches two deadly assassins to finish them off, along with anyone else stupid enough to stand in their way . . .

Point of No Return is a violent, well-paced movie which does more than just pass the time.

QUEEN'S HIGH (1991)
Starring Cynthia Khan, Simon Yam, Kenneth Tsang, Hung Kwok-Yeung, Shum Wai, Chris Lee Kin-Sang
Directed by Chris Lee Kin-Sang
Fok Shing Film Company

After the deaths of her father, brother and husband, Kwanny (Khan) takes control of her gangster family and exacts revenge on the killers.

This good-looking heroic bloodshed movie, also known as *In the Line of Duty—the Beginning*, starts in a fairly restrained manner, building up to a great set piece shoot-out at Kwanny's wedding, filmed in slo-mo with no dialogue—just gunshot sound effects and effective background music by Richard Lo. White-suited assailants gun down most of the gangland wedding guests until Kwanny starts fighting back, thus providing the movie with its memorably absurd/marvelous central image: Cynthia Khan, attractively clothed in her wedding dress, dispatching victims with a bullet-spitting uzi! During this high-body-count firefight, a statue of Mary is briefly seen—is this a homage to *The Killer*, maybe?

A fine example of Hong Kong's nihilistic, glamorous, gun-happy gang movies, *Queen's High* possesses good slow-motion combat scenes at the end, though it all lacks the strong emotive undercurrents of John Woo's crime epics.

REQUITAL (1992)
Starring Alan Tang, Jimmy Wang Yu, Amy Yip, Chen Sung-Yung, Lo Lieh, Wu Ma
Directed by Chu Yen-Ping
Action by Lin Wan-Chang
Chang Hong Channel Film & Video

The trials and tribulations of an orphan who is adopted by a Taiwanese gang boss after the boy helps save the gangster in a shoot-out.

With an atmospheric sepia prologue, *Requital* starts as it means to go on, by mixing brutal killings with excellent cinematography. It borrows heavily from several Western gangster classics, to the extent that you have to admire its barefaced cheek! The protagonist progresses from a heartless killer to a man with a certain moral code, but his performance is most striking as he carries out his work, strafing a table full of gangsters from a helicopter and finally taking a one-way plunge from a very tall building.

The filmmakers obviously wanted their gangster tale to be pretty brutal, delivering generous, geyser-like

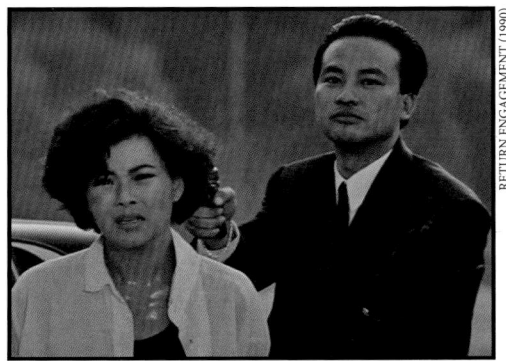

RETURN ENGAGEMENT (1990)

bursts of blood with each bullet impact, a garroting, stabbings, and some pitiless kickings. And then, during the end credits, the most violent moments are replayed!

RETURN ENGAGEMENT (1990)

Starring Alan Tang, Simon Yam, Elizabeth Lee,
Andy Lau, May Law, Carrie Ng
Directed by Joe Cheung
Produced by Alan Tang, Rover Tang
In-Gear Film

Paul, the boss of a Vancouver-based Chinese gang, goes to prison after wiping out the Italian mafia who'd killed his wife. Ten years later he is released and embarks on a search for his daughter, who was sent to Hong Kong as a baby. Once in Hong Kong Paul becomes friends with Susan, who is looking after a girl that might know the whereabouts of Paul's daughter. At the same time, the local would-be gang leader, Harry (Yam), decides that it's time to take over, which means killing-off the old boss, and maybe Paul too. When Susan is kidnapped, Paul calls on some Vancouver triad members loyal to him to help out . . . and the stage is set for an all-out gang firefight.

Return Engagement is a Hong Kong heroic bloodshed movie that takes the tried-and-tested iconographic elements of the genre and boosts them to their absurd extremes. When, for instance, Harry eradicates some drug dealers, his suit-wearing minions appear from every side, firing at the smugglers and showing no concern about being caught in their own cross fire. Together with these almost parodic shoot-outs, the dress sense of the gangsters is also heightened to a major degree, as every member of Harry's mob is a smartly attired, tie-wearing dude in shades! Director Joe Cheung, along with Wong Kar-Wai, wrote the story and

they both obviously set out to make a self-aware heroic bloodshed pic. Whereas Chow Yun-Fat merely dressed smartly in the *A better Tomorrow* movies, the writers here have Andy Lau's character actually talk about how being narcissistically well-dressed is essential to any triad gangster worthy of the name.

The midsection of the movie slackens slightly, and there's some subpar dubbing in the English-language version, but the film soon reaches its high point, which is a finale that sees Paul and his small band of Canadian/Chinese cohorts attack Harry's mob during a funeral in an armor-plated van. As is de rigueur in this kind of movie, the main characters never show any remorse for the numerous gangland members they shoot to pieces!

Also known as *Hong Kong Corruptor*, this is an emotionally lightweight but wonderfully iconic and hyperviolent tale.

RICH AND FAMOUS (1987)

Starring Chow Yun-Fat, Andy Lau, Alex Man,
Alan Tam, Danny Lee, Wong Siu-Fung, Shing Fui-On
Directed by Taylor Wong
Produced by Johnny Mak
Action by Leung Siu-Lung
Win's movie Productions Ltd/Golden Harvest/
Johnny Mak Productions

Kwok (Lau) and Yung (Man) are drawn into a world of crime when Yung forges a betting slip. Their sister Wai (Siu-Fung) is kidnapped by men working for the gambling boss Chu, and things take a serious turn when she is stabbed and Kwok has to give himself up. In desperation, Wai goes to another boss she has just met, Li Ah Chai (Yun-Fat), to ask for help. He takes pity on her and demands the return of Kwok, who has been badly beaten and tortured.

Kwok and Yung, along with friend Mak Ying Hung (Tam) begin working for Chai, and they find favor or disgrace within the gang, depending on how they behave, with Yung finally getting thrown out of the group for messing up and disobeying orders, so Kwok has to leave too after coming to his brother's defense. After various betrayals and underhand dealings, with Chu revealed to be totally focused on killing Chai, matters reach a head at Chai's wedding.

This excellent drama has enough ballistic action to satisfy the most hardened bloodshed fan, with some classy sequences, including Chai storming through throngs of attacking hoods in a van, two guns blazing away as he mows them down, and the suspenseful

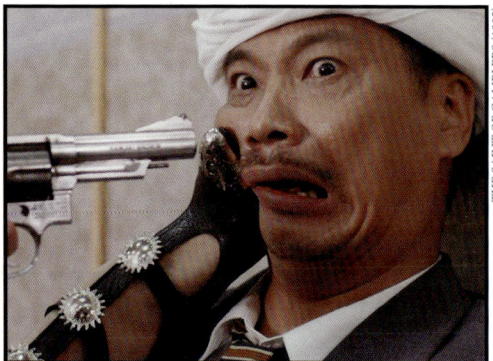

THE SAINT OF GAMBLERS (1995)

wedding shoot-out, but the film never allows the showy set pieces to overpower the enthralling story. Chow Yun-Fat plays the elegant crime boss with his usual charismatic style and Andy Lau and Alex Man are superb as the brothers who must resolve their divided loyalties.

THE SAINT OF GAMBLERS (1995)

Starring Eric Kot, Chingmy Yau, Donnie Yen,
Ng Man-Tat, Diana Pang, Chan Pak-Cheung,
Ashton Chen, Ben Lam
Directed, written and produced by Wong Jing
Wong Jing's Workshop Ltd

The movie starts with gifted child Siu Lung (Chen) taking on the tyrant of gamblers, who doesn't want to lose and orders his guards to kill the kid, but he has some kung fu moves that easily dispatch the attackers. So now a flurry of red ninjas descend from out of nowhere and finally pin the boy against a wall. But, before they can kill him, Yuen Fan (Yau) bursts gracefully through the rice paper shutters like she came straight from the set of *City Hunter*, demonstrating balletic gun skills as she kills the ninjas. She's followed by Ray Thai (Lam), who kills the tyrant of gamblers after an awesome display of martial arts kicking.

Realizing that there will be assassination attempts on his life, Ray Thai decides to seek a mask-wearing decoy who will be trained by Uncle Tat (Man-tat). A perfect stooge is found, "God Bless You" (Kot), who happens to possess the magical powers needed to go up against the many skilled players that Ray would have played to get him to the World Card Championship finals.

Wong Jing tries to continue his run of gambling-themed movies after the success of *God of Gamblers 1 & 2* and *All for the Winner*. The film does offer the usual madcap comedy, but Eric Kot does not really live up to his predecessors, especially in delivering comedy like Stephen Chow. But Wong Jing does add a lot of martial arts action, with some great set pieces, even getting a cameo from Donnie Yen.

SHANGHAI GRAND (1996)

Starring Leslie Cheung, Andy Lau, Ning Jing,
Wu Hsing-Kuo, Almen Wong Pui-Ha, Amanda Lee
Directed by Poon Man-Kit
Win's Entertainment Ltd/Film Workshop

Set in 1930s Shanghai, the story follows Keung (Cheung) and Lik (Lau) as they rise through the underworld ranks to become top-dog mob bosses, but their friendship is torn asunder when Lik realizes that Ching Ching (Jing), the woman he has always adored, is actually the lover of Keung. After an extended flashback, detailing how Ching Ching and Keung met, circumstances lead inexorably toward a showdown between the two ex-friends in a bar on New Year's Eve.

The film begins in the bowels of a grim Japanese-controlled ship, where Keung and other members of the Taiwan People's League are tortured and gunned down by a foxy female assassin (Pui-Ha), in a luridly fun sequence resembling something from an old pulp magazine. A similar pulp-tastic scene occurs later in the film, when Lik is chained to a bed by the same femme fatale, who seems to obtain much pleasure from watching him being constricted by a huge python that slithers from beneath the bedsheets!

The majority of the film is a lavish tale of love, friendship and heartbreak, of gangsterism and collaborators, boasting great production design and attractive cast members who look extra suave and cool in their period costumes. With some well-handled, bloody, slo-mo shoot-out set pieces, *Shanghai Grand* is, by turns, melodramatic, sumptuous, romantic, heroic, pulpy, melancholy, violent and always entertaining.

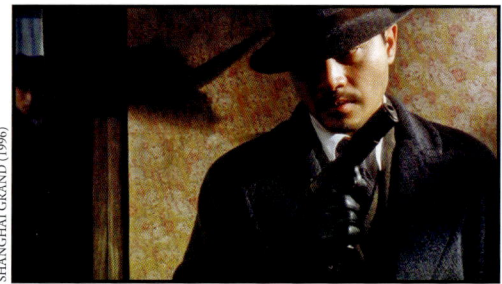

SHANGHAI GRAND (1996)

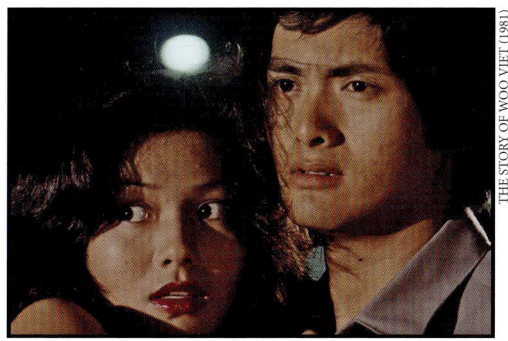

THE STORY OF WOO VIET (1981)

THE STORY OF WOO VIET (1981)
Starring Chow Yun-Fat, Cora Miao, Cherie Chung,
Lo Lieh
Directed by Ann Hui
Action by Ching Siu-Tung
Pearl City Films

Chow Yun-Fat plays Viet, a Vietnamese refugee who takes a boat to Hong Kong where he meets his penfriend, Lee Lap Quan (Miao). A friend in the refugee camp confides in Viet that he has seen a special agent dumping a woman's body in the sea and then, that night, his friend is killed. When, on the following night, an attempt is made on Viet's life, he flees the camp. Lee Lap Quan shelters him and puts him in touch with a man who can get him a false passport so that he can get to the States. He meets a Vietnamese girl, Shum Ching (Chung), who is also buying a fake passport and the pair make it as far as the Philippines, where there is a stopover. While there the pimp, who has been helping Shum Ching escape, rounds up the girls and takes them away. Viet injures a policeman while he is trying to trace her, then Boss Chung, who now has the girls, offers Viet a job, in return for which he will help Viet pay for new passports for himself and Shum Ching. Viet has no choice but to work for Chung, killing and kidnapping, aware that every job may be his last, because Chung can easily double-cross him.

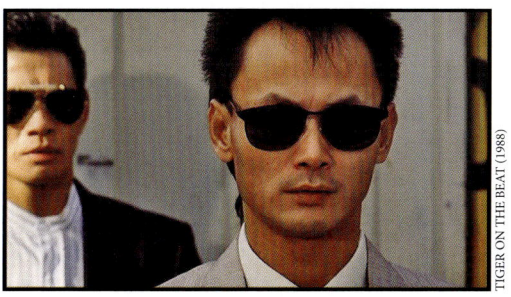

TIGER ON THE BEAT (1988)

This is a rather bleak, depressing and sordid tale which can hardly be called entertaining, but the story is absorbing, and Chow Yun-Fat puts in an excellent performance as the desperate refugee who refuses to abandon his friends or give up hope.

TIGER ON THE BEAT (1988)
Starring Chow Yun-Fat, Conan Lee, Ti Lung,
Nina Li Chi, Shirley Ng, Tsui Siu-Keung, Gordon Liu
Directed by Lau Kar-Leung
Cinema City

Li (Yun-Fat) and Michael (Lee) are the unlikely, mismatched couple of cops who, after a gung-ho introduction, find themselves pursuing the beautiful Marydonna, played by Nina Li Chi, whose brother they suspect is involved in a drugs syndicate. Li's rough approach to Marydonna turns into love, as he realizes she is only trying to help her brother get out of trouble with his triad friends.

The climax comes when Marydonna is gunned down and Li's sister is kidnapped. Li and his muscled friend Michael are forced to take on the gang in a tremendous last reel showcase, which has Conan Lee and Gordon Liu battling with chainsaws!

Even with its offbeat humor, *Tiger on the Beat* is an excellent example of Chow's acting ability, showing he can play both sides of the coin, as adept at portraying a cop as he is a gangster.

TIGER ON THE BEAT 2 (1990)
Starring Danny Lee, Conan Lee, Ellen Chan, Roy Cheung,
Maria Cordero, Gordon Liu, Tsui Siu-Keung
Directed by Lau Kar-Leung
Produced by Karl Maka
Cinema City/Golden Princess Film Productions Limited

Hong Kong cop Lam (Danny Lee) is asked to help his American-born nephew Buffalo (Conan Lee) find a decent Chinese girl but Buffalo falls for Sweet Dream (Ellen Chan), who has witnessed a murder. This would not be such a big problem for a seasoned cop, except that Sweet Dream is a thief herself and the murder involves a ruthless underground cocaine ring.

Once the looking-for-a-wife and meeting-a-hostess sections are over, viewers are rewarded with some slam-bang action scenes, culminating in a punch-up/shoot-out in a bus station. Conan Lee is good as the affable relative from abroad and gets to partake in some *Die Hard*–esque bloody-bare-feet-on-glass action.

Look out for Gordon Liu using a pipe for some staff fighting and Conan Lee performing a stunt where he jumps for a lamppost from a bridge, but he's unable to hang on and falls helplessly to the ground! This stunt-gone-wrong put Conan in hospital and almost wrecked the film, but the cameras were left rolling and the scene does look good!

THE TIGERS (1991)
Starring Andy Lau, Tony Leung Chiu-Wai, Kent Tong,
Wong Yat-Wah, Leung Ka-Yan, Miu Kiu-Wai, Irene Wan
Directed by Eric Tsang
Media Asia Films/Movie Impact

Five policemen accept a bribe from a crazed gangster called Fong (Tong). Each man has a different reason for keeping the money and each one lives to regret it. The bribe destroys their careers, friendship and, in some cases, their lives, as they refuse to work for Fong, and he calls in the Independent Commission Against Corruption. From here the film builds to a blood-soaked finale, sidestepping the moral issue in favor of violent action.

Andy Lau is smooth as silk as one of the bribed cops, while Kent Tong gives a fine performance as the depraved villain.

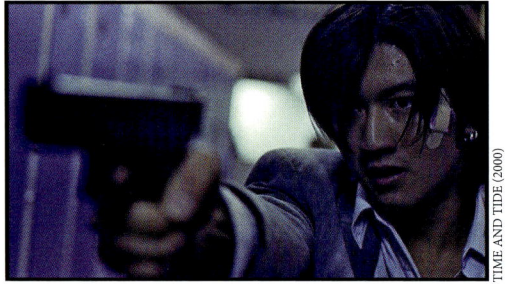
TIME AND TIDE (2000)

TIME AND TIDE (2000)
Starring Nicholas Tse, Wu Bai, Anthony Wong,
Cathy Tsui
Directed by Tsui Hark
Film Workshop/Columbia Pictures

Tyler (Tse), a streetwise young man whose only gainful employment is working at a Hong Kong bar, finds himself in a difficult situation after a fight with his girlfriend. He ends up having a drunken romp with Ah Jo (Tsui), a lesbian cop, and to make matters worse he discovers she is pregnant and wants nothing to do with him as she's already in a relationship with another woman. Feeling responsible and needing

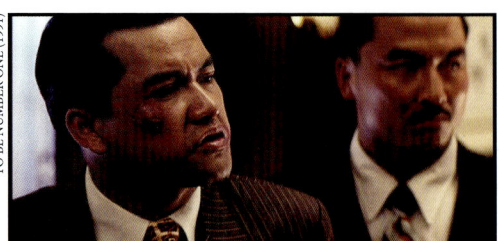
TO BE NUMBER ONE (1991)

cash to give to Ah Jo, Tyler decides to join Uncle Ji's (Wong) unlicensed bodyguard agency to earn some quick money.

Suddenly Tyler is immersed in a world of danger and violence after being assigned to guard a triad boss under threat of assassination. After losing a case of money and being knocked out by an attacker, he finds himself trapped and now at war with a South African drug cartel known as the Angels. Tyler's only option is to reach out to Jack (Bai), a former member of the gang returning from South Africa, and ask him to join forces in this life-or-death crisis.

Directed, produced and cowritten by Tsui Hark, *Time and Tide* is a well-paced, slick thriller with impressive action choreography enhancing some inventive, kinetic and well-executed sequences, which include an outrageous giving-birth-while-having-a-shoot-out moment, vertical firefights in a resettlement block, and a lengthy battle scene that starts at a railway station and ends during a rock concert. Recommended for fans of heroic bloodshed and action junkies alike.

TO BE NUMBER ONE (1991)
Starring Ray Lui, Kent Cheng, Cecilia Yip, Amy Yip,
Waise Lee, Elvis Tsui, Lawrence Ng, Wong Kwong-Leung
Directed by Poon Man-Kit
Golden Harvest/Johnny Mak Productions

This epic gangster pic traces the rise and fall of one of Hong Kong's most sensational criminals, Ng Sik-Ho, aka Crippled Ho, from his arrival in Hong Kong as a penniless refugee in 1962, to his sentencing in 1975 to a thirty-year prison term. In between, Ho reaches the pinnacle of success as head of a powerful crime syndicate.

Frequent bursts of excessive violence are used to preach the old-fashioned moral: crime doesn't pay. Ho, his henchmen and adversaries attack one another with everything from coat hooks, chickens and acid, to electric fans and garden shears. But, eventually, the winners pay for their sins through drug addiction, gambling debts, and so on.

Ray Lui gives the performance of his life as Ho, even gaining weight to portray the mob boss in middle age in this mature version of the old gangland movies.

TONGS: A CHINATOWN STORY (1986)
Starring Simon Yam, Tan Te-Pin, Lau Dan, Ben Chau
Directed by Philip Chan
D & B Film Distribution

This brutally violent and depressing tale follows the fortunes of two brothers who, having escaped from Mainland China to Hong Kong, then move on to New York in order to take advantage of the greater opportunities America has to offer. Both get involved in the underworld: the elder brother becomes a drug dealer, while the younger brother falls foul of organized gangs.

The budget restrictions of this production seriously harm the effectiveness of the plot, but, despite this, the film does make its point, that escaping the restrictions of communism does not automatically set the brothers free and capitalism also has its own inherent problems.

The action is not stylised, but random, reflecting the methods used by such gangs. Also known as *Tongs—Terror in Chinatown* and simply *Tongs*, this is a pessimistic, moral tale, albeit a flawed one.

TRAGIC HERO (1987)
Starring Chow Yun-Fat, Andy Lau, Alex Man,
Ko Chun-Hsiung, Wong Siu-Fung
Directed by Taylor Wong
Produced by Johnny Mak
Action by Leung Siu-Lung
Win's Movie Productions Ltd/Johnny Mak Productions

A sequel to *Rich and Famous*, this gangster film follows the bitter rivalry between two brothers and their opposing criminal gangs. The leads deliver robust performances and, though there's not lots of action, the full-on finale is very well handled, featuring a two-man attack on the psychotic

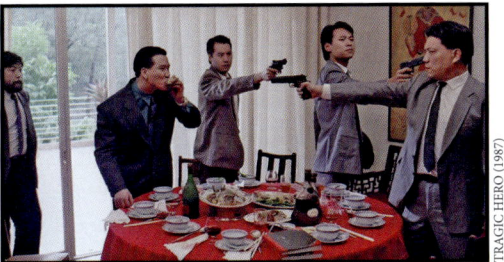
TRAGIC HERO (1987)

boss' mansion, with the anti-hero and his brother unleashing firepower amid a frenzy of explosions.

This terrific conclusion is evidence that Taylor Wong, when he puts his mind to it, can expertly direct engaging heroic bloodshed set pieces like the best of them.

TREASURE HUNT (1994)
Starring Chow Yun-Fat, Wu Chien-Lien, Chin Han,
Roy Chiao, Gordon Liu, Michael Wong, Philip Kwok
Directed by Jeffrey Lau
Action by Philip Kwok
Eastern Renaissance Pictures/
Golden Princess Film Production Limited

This is an odd, slightly incoherent concoction of bloodshed, comedy and romance, that sees Chow Yun-Fat playing an American agent, Cheng, who is sent on a mission to China to bust an antiques-smuggling ring. He ends up staying at the Shaolin Temple, where he falls in love with a strange girl, Mei (Chien-Lien), who has mysterious supernatural powers. Meanwhile, Cheng causes major culture shock among the Shaolin monks by introducing them to the Gameboy, french fries, and baseball. But the bad guys rear their ugly heads, and when Mei gives herself up to the ringleader to save Cheng, our hero is forced to take on a whole army of villains to rescue her.

The action, when it finally comes, is excellent, with Philip Kwok taking on the head monk in a dramatic pole fight, plus Cheng trapping his enemy within a ring of fire. But the comedy and slushy romance, which take up most of the film, won't be of much interest to heroic bloodshed fans.

TRIADS: THE INSIDE STORY (1989)
Starring Chow Yun-Fat, Roy Cheung, Chan Wai-Man,
Tien Feng
Directed by Taylor Wong
Produced by Cheung Kuen
Cinema City

Li Man-Ho (Yun-Fat) is faced with a dilemma when he attends the funeral of his triad boss father in Hong Kong. Although obliged to protect his wife and son, he feels he has an obligation to the gang, and is forced into making a swift choice between a life of peace in the suburbs of New York and one of opportunity in Hong Kong. Beset on all sides by both the law and those with their own ambitions for the gang leadership, Li soon fully understands what his new "job" will entail.

This film, which gives us some glimpses into what goes on in these triad groups, including an induction ceremony, is a fairly glamor-free view of the gang societies. The violence is not of the ballistic variety, but comes from hordes of young men wielding batons and meat cleavers. Chow Yun-Fat, of course, is always worth watching, here playing a role which is the opposite of the cool, gun-toting gangster heroes created by him in movies like *A Better Tomorrow*.

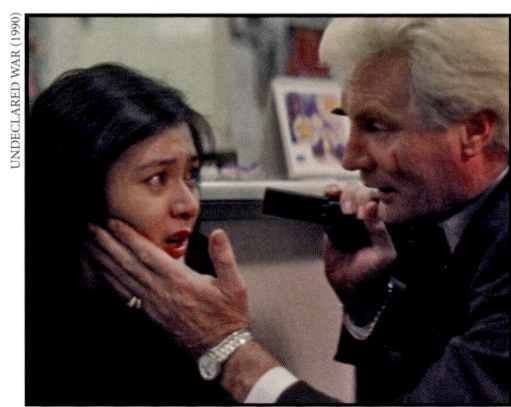

UNDECLARED WAR (1990)

UNDECLARED WAR (1990)
Starring Danny Lee, Olivia Hussey, Peter Liapis,
Rosamund Kwan, Vernon G. Wells, Mars
Directed by Ringo Lam
Produced by Ringo Lam, Karl Maka
Cinema City

Following on from the success of his "On Fire" films, director Ringo Lam tried to break into the international market with this piece of action fluff. A group of international terrorists led by Olivia Hussey head for Hong Kong, where they intend to extort large sums of money from foreign investors residing there. Enter CIA man Peter Liapis and uncouth Hong Kong cop Danny Lee, who hunt down these international menaces and put a stop to their dastardly deeds once and for all.

Though it's far from being one of Lam's best works, the movie is partially redeemed by some manic stunts and impressive, hi-octane, gory, squib-tastic shoot-outs, including a deadly church massacre and a boat chase.

VICTIM (1999)
Starring Tony Leung Ka-Fai, Lau Ching-Wan,
Amy Kwok, Emily Kwan, Lai Yiu-Cheung
Directed by Ringo Lam
Produced by Ringo Lam, Joe Ma
Brilliant Idea Group/Mei Ah Films Production Co Ltd

When Manson Ma (Ching-Wan) is kidnapped, beaten and left hanging in a derelict building, he begins to act very erratically afterward, as if he's possessed, prompting Pit of the Organised Crime Bureau to obsessively dig to the bottom of this mystery.

Boasting a well-sustained sequence showing Pit (Leung) and his cop partner Bee (Yiu-Cheung) stalking through a gloomy, abandoned "haunted" hotel during a lightning storm, a bravura, realistic

car chase, and some signature Ringo Lam spasms of violence, *Victim* keeps the viewer guessing. Skilfully wrong-footing expectations, this supposedly paranormal scenario becomes an elaborate criminal plot involving the Hong Kong Monetary Authority and the Hong Kong Currency Printing company.

It all inevitably leads to a brutal Ringo Lam–style finale and then, cheekily, the film finds time to actually throw in a brief supernatural coda to the tale.

VIOLENT COP (2000)
Starring Anthony Wong, Michael Wong,
Lai Yiu-Cheung, Iris Chai, Astrid Chan
Directed by Steve Cheng
Jing's Production

After accidentally shooting his partner, Inspector Cuba Koo (Michael Wong) teams up with pimp informant Tai Pan Kim (Anthony Wong) to track down a serial murderer called the Cross-Killer. This killer, obsessed with a distorted view of Christian doctrine, removes the genitals of his male victims with a curved blade.

Revealed to be Tse Chun Mao, the tea boy at the police station, the killer starts believing he is actually the son of God, poisons lots of cops with his tea, goes on a shooting rampage and, as the film reaches its climax, ties Kim's adopted daughter Cee (Chai) to a large crucifix on the police HQ roof.

Lai Yiu-Cheung is pretty effective as disturbed killer Mao, playing the character as equal parts underdog, murderer and obsessed religious fanatic, and Anthony Wong effortlessly portrays Kim as a crass pimp with a tarnished heart of gold, so it's a shame that the film seems unfocused story-wise, unsure if it should concentrate on Koo, Kim, Cee or Mao.

WILD SEARCH (1989)

Starring Chow Yun-Fat, Cherie Chung, Roy Cheung,
Wong Kwong-Leung
Directed and produced by Ringo Lam
Born Top Producers/Brandy Film Production/Golden
Princess/Silver Medal productions Ltd

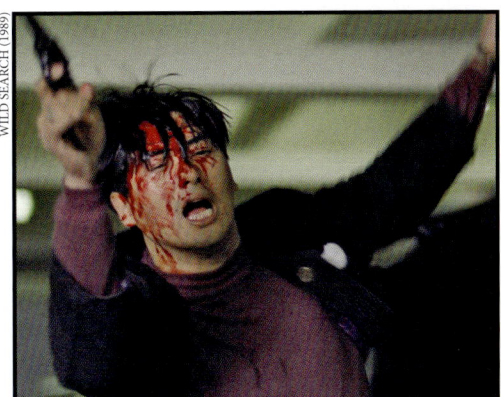

A policeman from the big city finds himself getting
acquainted with a young woman (Chung) way out in
the New Territories as he deals with a case involving
a child witness and violent triad members.

This third Ringo Lam/Chow Yun-Fat collaboration
is a cop-thriller-cum-romance that's not the most
memorable film ever, but it does have its moments,
most notably at the climax, when the mean, mad
hit man (Cheung) launches his attack. Bullets fly, a
gas canister goes off, and the triad killer gets blown
to smithereens.

YOUNG AND DANGEROUS (1996)

Starring Ekin Cheng, Jordan Chan, Gigi Lai, Francis Ng,
Frankie Ng Chi-Hung, Simon Yam, Michael Tse
Directed by Andrew Lau
Art Top Movie Productions Ltd/Jing's Production

Nam, Chicken and their mates are young triad
gangsters, working for Brother Bee (Chi-Hung), a
high-ranking member of the Hung Hing Society.
Their freewheeling daily life involves hanging
out together, dealing with triad business, finding
romance, posturing, fighting and, when needed,
killing other gangsters.

This well-received film, spawning sequels and
spin-offs, glamorizes gangsterism in a way that
only Hong Kong films can pull off: depicting their
leads as sometimes righteous, sometimes brutal,
sometimes sentimental, but always able to keep the
viewer on their side. The movie is punctuated with
comic-style illustrated panels, paying homage to
the popular comic book it is based on, which adds
extra coolness to the production.

Ekin Cheng, as Nan, is the handsome, up-and-
coming member of the group, who plays by gang
rules, falls for stuttering car thief Smartie (Lai),
but is then kicked out of the Society thanks to the
machinations of rival gang boss Brother Kwan.

The tone of the film gets grimmer once Kwan,
played as a truly despicable lowlife by the always-
great Francis Ng, really goes on the offensive, killing
Bee and burying his family alive. After Nan crawls
on his knees at Bee's funeral to pay his respects, in
a melodramatic, tearful moment that, again, only

Hong Kong flicks seem able to make work, the stage
is set for him to reteam with absent buddy Chicken
(Chan), who returns from a profitable self-exile in
Taiwan as a smart-suited mobster. This scene of best
buddies reuniting, accompanied by a Cantopop tune
on the soundtrack, is well-handled and soon makes
way for the protagonists' third act mission to take
down Kwan. And, boy, we really want to see Kwan
get what he deserves!

YOUNG AND DANGEROUS 2 (1996)

Starring Ekin Cheng, Jordan Chan, Gigi Lai, Chingmy
Yau, Anthony Wong, Michael Tse, Jerry Lamb,
Simon Yam
Directed by Andrew Lau
B.O.B. and Partners

This sequel spends a chunk of its running time
detailing Chicken's experiences during his stay in
Taiwan as the new member of the San Luen Gang,
exploring his relationships with triad boss/politician
Mr. Lui and his mistress, Ting Yiu. Zipping back
to the present, the film focuses on Nam, who finds
himself clashing with nose-picking rival Hung Hing
Society boss Tai Fai, while also watching over his
injured, comatose lover Smartie.

Nam and Chicken once more encounter trouble
in Macau, the problem this time centered around
Mr. Lui muscling in on the opening of a new casino,
pushing the Hung Hing gangsters aside. Chicken
feels torn between Taiwanese big boss Lui and his
buddy Nam, but when the duplicitous Ting Yiu
frames Chicken and Nam with Lui's assassination,
events lead inevitably toward a settling of scores
during the opening of the new casino.

Part 2 only uses the comic book panels gimmick
a couple of times and the movie, as a whole, is not

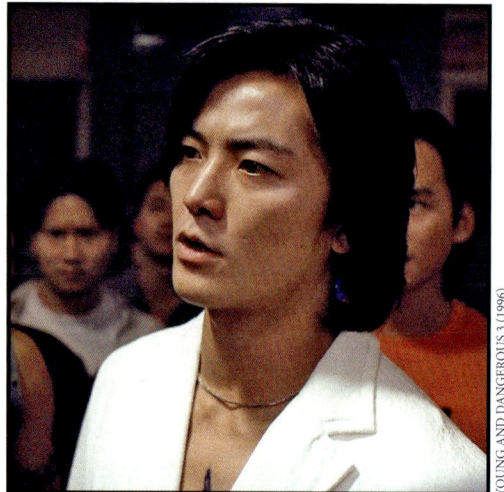

YOUNG AND DANGEROUS 3 (1996)

changes abruptly, however, with a triad assassination and shoot-out in the streets of Amsterdam, as nice boss Mr. Chiang gets wasted! No! Then, in what is a recurring plot development in the *Young and Dangerous* series, Nam is framed, forcing him to keep his head down, but Crow and his slimy, murderous sidekick Tiger won't let up till they've destroyed Nam and his gang. Things can only get nastier now, and the third act sees a likeable main character ruthlessly murdered, ultimately leading to fiery payback during a big, climactic funeral brawl.

YOUNG AND DANGEROUS 4 (1997)

Starring Ekin Cheng, Jordan Chan, Karen Mok, Michael Tse, Roy Cheung, Jerry Lamb, Anthony Wong, Sandra Ng, Pinky Cheung, Jason Chu
Directed by Andrew Lau
B.O.B. and Partners/Golden Harvest/Everwide

After Hung Hing mobster Dinosaur is killed by Tung Sing Society baddie Yiu-Yeung, Chicken is offered the chance to become branch leader of the Tuen Mun district, but he must compete for the position with the thuggish Barbarian. Nam advises Chicken not to go for this role, which he sees as a poison chalice, but Chicken thinks Nam simply doesn't want him

quite as well-crafted as the original, but Anthony Wong is on fine form as the loutish Tai Fai, Ekin Cheng once more plays Nam as a righteous kinda dude, Jordan Chan is great as the brash Chicken, and there are several twists and reveals to keep viewers on their toes.

YOUNG AND DANGEROUS 3 (1996)

Starring Ekin Cheng, Jordan Chan, Gigi Lai, Karen Mok, Roy Cheung, Frankie Ng, Michael Tse, Jerry Lamb, Anthony Wong, Simon Yam
Directed by Andrew Lau
B.O.B. and Partners/Golden Harvest

Nam (Cheng) and his Hung Hing Society group must deal with a series of provocative acts of aggression and intimidation perpetrated by Crow, a volatile member of the rival Tung Sing gang. Meanwhile, Chicken (Chan) falls for local priest Father Lam's independent daughter Shuk-Fan (Mok), Smartie (Lai) wakes from the coma she fell into in episode 2, and Nam joins top boss Mr. Chiang (Yam) on a business trip to the Netherlands.

This second sequel melds posturing, street fighting, subterfuge, sentimentality, and the settling of scores effortlessly, just like the previous two installments, though Ekin Cheng's lead character Nam is a little too passive for much of the story and Roy Cheung, as Crow, overplays his role as the endlessly disruptive, nihilistic, swaggering villain, but, admittedly, he certainly makes you want to see Crow get what's coming to him by the end of the movie.

At first the visit to Holland seems to be just a travelogue sequence, lacking any real point. This

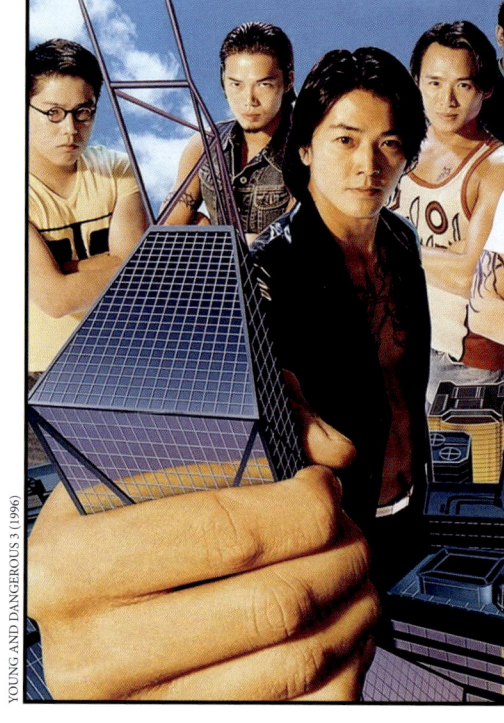

YOUNG AND DANGEROUS 3 (1996)

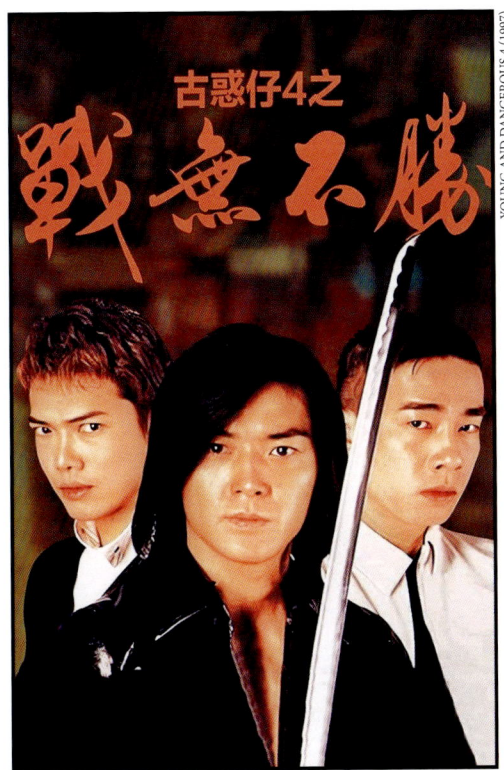

YOUNG AND DANGEROUS 4 (1997)

when Nam competed against Tai Fai, and chaotic mass scuffles are always on the verge of kicking off.

Classical music–loving villain Yiu-Yeung is played by Roy Cheung, which is a slightly jarring casting choice, as Cheung played the main, over-the-top bad guy in part 3 as well. There's also a misjudged sequence where Nam, who Yan Yan believes is a teacher, actually goes to a local school to oversee a class. Nam is a calm, collected and cool sonofabitch, no doubt about it, but it stretches credibility to believe he'd take time out to pretend to be a substitute teacher. With that said, there's stuff this series always handles well: the use of recurring characters like Father Lam and wimpy-looking cop God of Gun, the assured juggling of murders, backstabbing motives and assaults with meet-cute scenes and even a coy, romantic lovemaking interlude, plus the realistically scrappy fights that are refreshingly far removed from the usual slick kung fu face-offs.

YOUNG AND DANGEROUS 5 (1998)
Starring Ekin Cheng, Chin Kar-Lok, Mark Cheng,
Shu Qi, Paul Chun, Jerry Lamb, Jason Chu, Sandra Ng,
Alex Man, Danny Lee, Anthony Wong
Directed by Andrew Lau
B.O.B. and Partners/Golden Harvest/Everwide

to attain this higher rank within the gang, thus a rift once more threatens to spoil their friendship.

With Barbarian secretly backed by double-dealing Hung Hing pornographer Fat Lai and the slightly psycho Yiu-Yeung, Chicken struggles to woo the locals of Tuen Mun, so the newly married Yee (Tse) misguidedly attempts to help Chicken out by assassinating Barbarian at a fish market, but this fails badly. Yee is later killed by Yiu-Yeung, who has a penchant for hurling his victims from high places, and it seems certain that Chicken will not become branch leader . . . but will the secret, deadly alliances behind the recent tragedies finally be revealed on the day of the vote?

Also known as *Young and Dangerous 1997*, this fourth entry in the franchise introduces the new big boss, who is the brother of murdered top-dog Mr. Chiang, a new love interest for Nam called Yan Yan, a new, smarter haircut for Tai Fai, and new gang characters like Sister Thirteen (Ng). Some things, however, remain the same: there's more internecine triad confrontations, the main plot concerning Chicken and Barbarian vying for the same vacant position is very similar to what occurred in part 2,

Szeto (Mark Cheng), branch leader of the Tung Sing Group, vies with Nam for control of Causeway Bay and will do whatever it takes to achieve this.

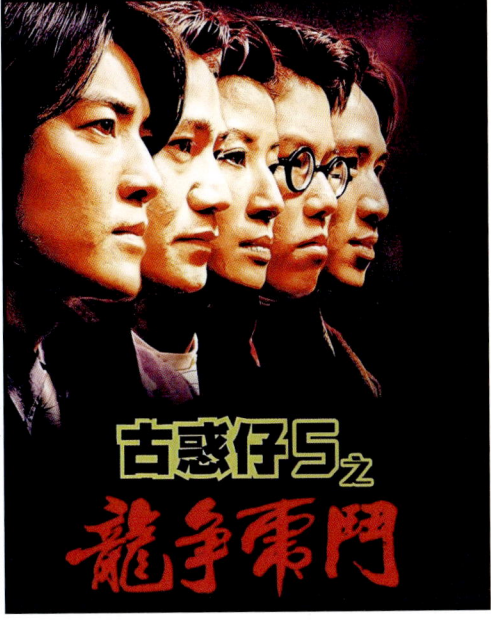

YOUNG AND DANGEROUS 5 (1998)

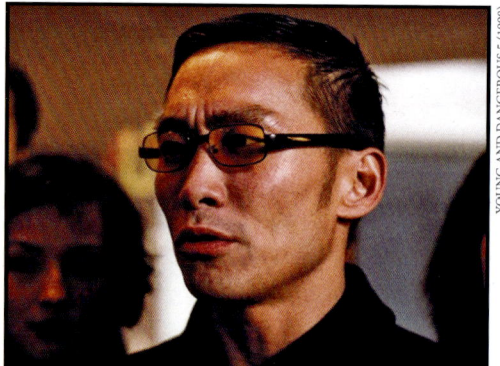

YOUNG AND DANGEROUS 5 (1998)

Meanwhile, Nam has dealings with shady Malaysian businessman Mr. Datuk (Chun), starts a relationship with sexy Mei Ling (Qi), comes to an understanding with tea-loving Officer Lee of the Anti-Triad Bureau and offers to help out former gangster Big Head.

Chicken (Jordan Chan) is nowhere to be seen in this sequel, but Chin Kar-Lok is a good addition to the cast, delivering an assured performance as Big Head, who undergoes a satisfying character arc from picked-on newsstand owner to dependable member of the Hung Hing crew.

Tried-and-tested *Young and Dangerous* ingredients include a typically chaotic street fight, the death of a likeable series regular and the obligatory underhand schemes. Ekin Cheng is, as per usual, effortlessly charismatic, quietly spoken and chilled as heroic gangster Nam. With a big kickboxing event finale, involving Nam slugging it out with Szeto to decide who gets Causeway Bay, this is a solid, enjoyable, well-plotted franchise entry.

YOUNG AND DANGEROUS: THE PREQUEL (1998)

Starring Nicholas Tse, Frankie Ng Chi-Hung, Francis Ng, Shu Qi, Sam Lee, Daniel Wu, Benjamin Yuen
Directed by Andrew Lau
B.O.B. and Partners/Golden Harvest/Fitto Movie Co. Ltd

Set in 1989, the story follows Nam and his friends as circumstances and lack of options lead to them joining up with best buddy Chicken and working for Hung Hing triad branch leader Brother Bee. From being bailed out of jail for street brawling, to committing their first gang-sanctioned assassination, the young friends are soon embroiled in inter-gang rivalries.

Nicholas Tse, who won the Best New Performer gong at the 18th Hong Kong Film Awards for this role, is good as the 17-year-old Nam, Sam Lee comes

across as a little too comical playing the youthful Chicken, and Daniel Wu does a decent job as a younger version of Big Head. The older characters are played by the original actors, which is great because it gives viewers the chance to see Francis Ng being all traitorous again as Kwan and Frankie Ng Chi-Hung shining as the perfectly cast Brother Bee, who is squat, solid, hard, righteous and no-nonsense.

Sentimentality, criminality, unglamorous violence, boisterous hijinks, gangland double crosses and smatterings of twee romance all intersect, as they always do in these *Young and Dangerous* films. This time around the story also includes a cold turkey sequence and a torture scene, where Nam is hung up, severely beaten, then has a bagful of rats shoved over his head! Putting aside the movie's clumsy attempts at somehow drawing parallels between a gangland mass-fight and the Tiananmen Square massacre by intercutting a sprawling triad brawl with actual Tiananmen Square news footage, this is a watchable prequel that proves to be another satisfying entry in the series.

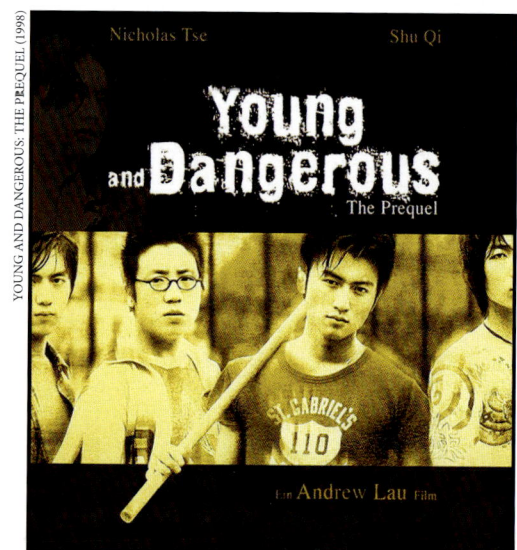

YOUNG AND DANGEROUS: THE PREQUEL (1998)

Nicholas Tse   Shu Qi

Young and Dangerous
The Prequel

ST. GABRIEL'S 110

A Andrew Lau *Film*

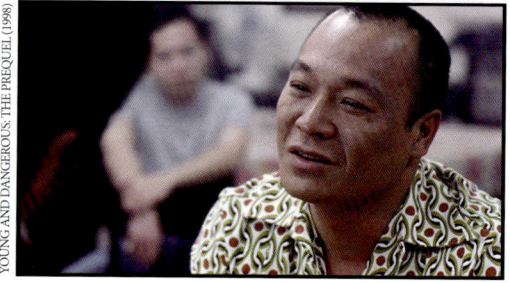

YOUNG AND DANGEROUS: THE PREQUEL (1998)

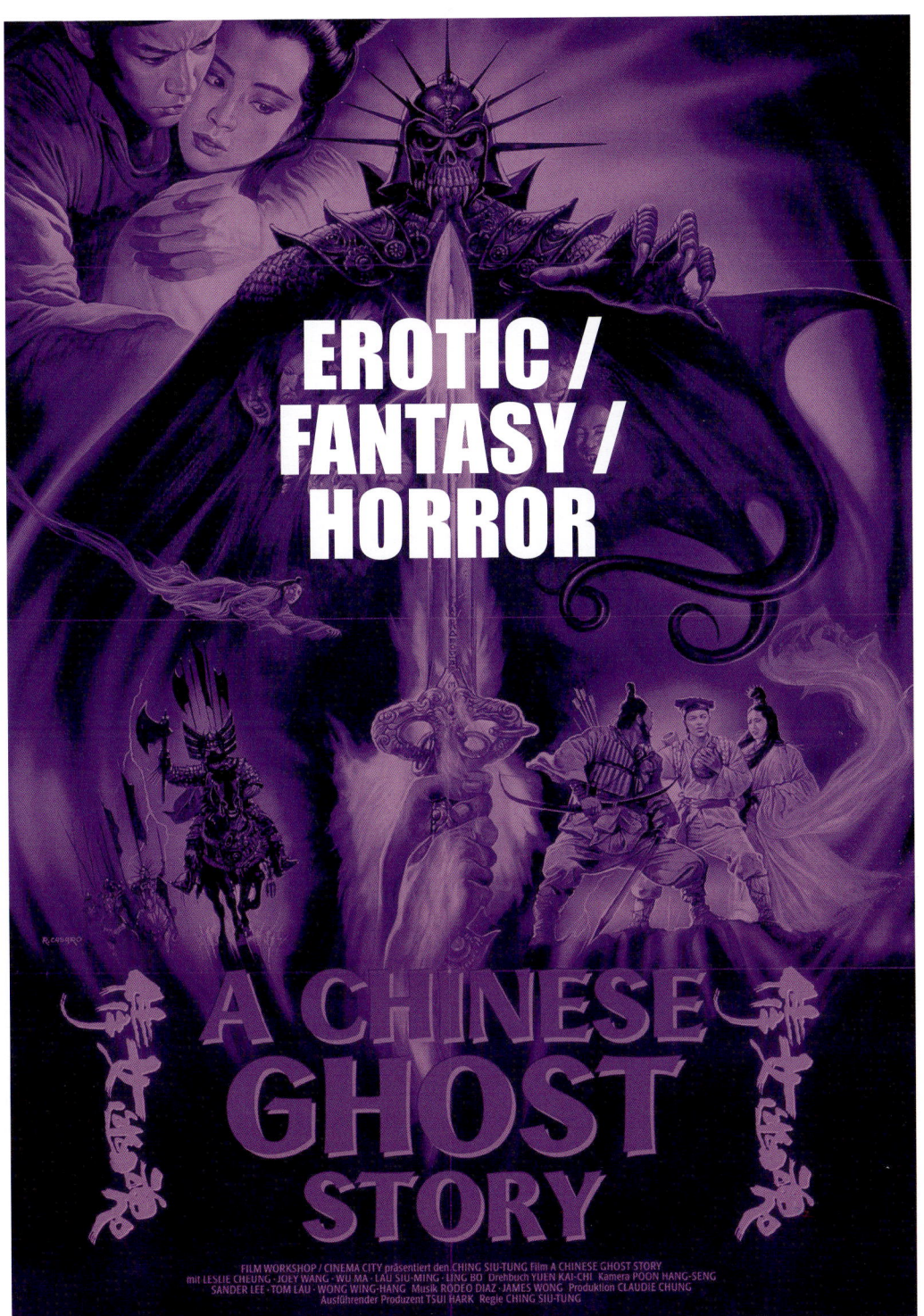

EROTIC /
FANTASY /
HORROR

A CHINESE
GHOST
STORY

FILM WORKSHOP / CINEMA CITY präsentiert den CHING SIU-TUNG Film A CHINESE GHOST STORY
mit LESLIE CHEUNG · JOEY WANG · WU MA · LAU SIU-MING · LING BO Drehbuch YUEN KAI-CHI Kamera POON HANG-SENG
SANDER LEE · TOM LAU · WONG WING-HANG Musik RODEO DIAZ · JAMES WONG Produktion CLAUDIE CHUNG
Ausführender Produzent TSUI HARK Regie CHING SIU-TUNG

ANGEL HUNTER (1992)

Starring Anthony Wong, Vivian Chow, Lau Ching-Wan,
Ng Man-Tat, Carrie Ng
Directed by Sun Chung
Produced by Dean Shek, Wang Ying-Hsiang
Action by Yuen Bun
Flaming Star International Company

Anthony Wong stars as the Bishop, a satanic high priest who preys upon the poor, lost and lonely souls of the Hong Kong middle class. Once sucked into his sordid order, the women are put out on the streets to bring in cash for the Bishop, who is in league with mobsters. The Bishop's flock grows daily, until a curious social worker and a religious studies expert (Ng Man-Tat) set out to bring down the heretics and save Hong Kong from the wicked wrath of the Bishop.

Anthony Wong's effective performance raises this to an above-average satanic cult thriller.

ARMAGEDDON (1997)

Starring Andy Lau, Michele Reis, Anthony Wong,
Claudia Lau, Jessica Chau
Directed by Gordon Chan
Win's Entertainment Ltd

Dr. Tak Ken (Lau), haunted by memories of his dead love Adele (Reis), is asked to help with an investigation into some burnt-out communications systems and also the freakish deaths of other top scientists. It seems that the unfortunate victims were somehow microwaved from the inside out, their organs thoroughly cooked, and Ken theorises that they might have died from spontaneous combustion.

Helped and hindered by James from MI6 and old, grouchy friend CID detective Chiu (Wong), Ken and the team delve into theories surrounding the end of the world, especially beliefs espoused by the major religions. A group called the Brotherhood of Technology seems to be somehow involved in these mysterious goings-on, which become much more strange and more personal for Ken when Adele starts physically appearing to interact with him.

A major plus factor for *Armageddon* is its plotting, which keeps you guessing, wondering if the odd deaths are linked to spontaneous combustion, or a laser-equipped satellite, or maybe something of a more supernatural nature. However, once the moon turns red and the leader of the Brotherhood of Technology is revealed to be endowed with telekinetic powers, it's obvious there's a mystical

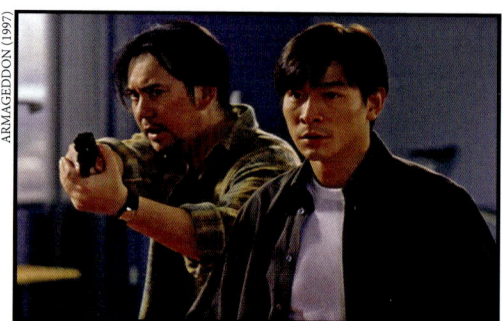
ARMAGEDDON (1997)

origin to everything, which is when *Armageddon* should really have turbocharged the apocalyptic nature of the tale, but the actual resolution is merely so-so, lacking the required oomph. But it's a decent mystery ride up until this point.

THE ASSASSIN (1993)

Starring Zhang Fengyi, Mok Siu-Chung, Rosamund Kwan
Directed by Cheung Siu-Hung
Produced by Chan Yung
Action by Tung Wei and Kong Tao-Hoi
Prosper Film Productions

A young couple trying to flee from the forces of a powerful eunuch are captured. The young man, Tong, is separated from his lover and undergoes severe torture. He is, however, given a slim chance of survival: he must fight and defeat his fellow prisoners. Tong does just this, displaying a natural talent for causing carnage, which results in him being taken on by the eunuch as an assassin specializing in missions of exceptional intricacy. Tong's brutal treatment and his vicious assignments slowly harden him until murder means nothing to him . . . until he is reunited with the love he thought was lost. Then, just as Tong is close to finding his gentle self, his superiors come for him, and he is soon making decisions which will affect not only him, but a large number of innocents.

More than just *Nikita* meets *The Dragon From Russia*, this is a rare gem of a movie that boasts

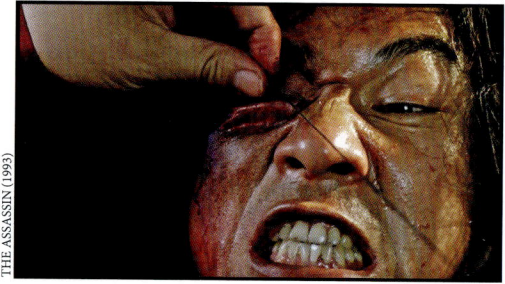
THE ASSASSIN (1993)

unique, powerful visuals, superb camerawork, an appropriately dramatic musical score and expertly handled fight scenes that progressively get more violent, earning the film a CAT III rating for its carnage.

THE BATTLE WIZARD (1977)

Directed by Pao Hsueh-Li
Starring Danny Lee, Tan Nei, Lin Chen-Chi,
Shih Chung-Tien
Shaw Brothers

Saying that this Shaw Brothers movie, based loosely on the novel *Demi-Gods and Semi-Devils*, is off-the-wall is not an understatement . . . The pre-credit sequence features the Emperor's brother sending light beams from his fingers to shoot off the legs of his lover's husband, Wang Yu Win (names vary depending on which film print you watch): yikes!

Twenty years later, Wang (also known as Yellow Robe Man) seeks revenge on the man who crippled him, by attempting to kill his enemy's son, Tuan Yu (Lee). Oh, by the way, Wang now has metal, telescopic, clawed bird feet which he can contract and expand for use in battle! He is aided by his brother, who has dime store fangs, a bald, veined,

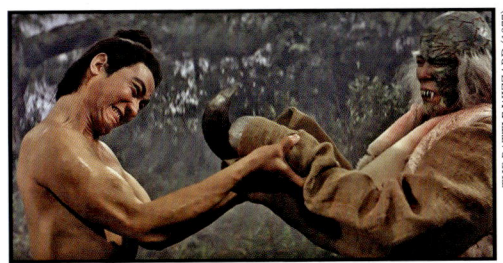

THE BATTLE WIZZARD (1977)

scabby scalp, a metal crab-type pincer in place of one of his arms and a partly mangled face. At one point this dude pinches a guy in the groin with his pincer, lobbing the victim through the air.

Tuan Yu is helped by a woman called Ling Ar, who has the power to make snakes glow and bore into people's bodies, and masked swordswoman Miss Moo, who is revealed to be his stepsister. Tuan Yu wrestles with a giant, red snake that attacks him in the woods. He wins and, because he drank some of the serpent's blood, he attains the power to fire beams from his hands (like his dad) and the ability, at one point, to run up vertical walls.

When Moo and Tuan Yu are thrown into a pit, they are attacked by a kung fu–skilled gorilla (a man in

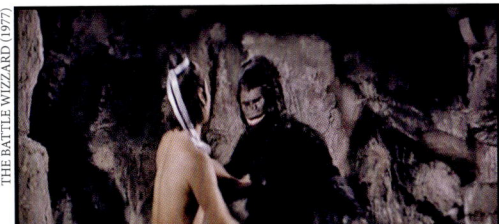

THE BATTLE WIZZARD (1977)

a suit, of course) . . . and Tuan Yu kills the simian adversary by using a hand-strike to chop off one of its arms! Tuan Yu develops even more powers after eating a glowing, green toad. This makes him totally invincible, enabling him to escape the pit.

Tuan Yu, his father and the Emperor, all of whom can fire laser/heat beams, have a final battle with pole-legged Wang and his clawed brother. Tuan Yu, who is now really supercharged, blows the fanged brother's head off and then blasts Wang, who dissolves in multi-colors onto the floor. Miss Moo also dies, and Tuan Yu rides off with Ling Ar.

This oddball production contains lots of optical/cel-animated laser beam/magic effects during the finale and also boasts an oral flamethrower trick: Wang breathes flames onto his foes and, during the final battle, there's a contest between his jet of flame and Tuan Yu's red/green hand laser beams.

The merging of weird storyline, so-so optical effects (Miss Moo fires cartoon darts out of a bone weapon), theatrical, colorful sets, frenzied pacing and a gorilla that knows kung fu does manage to elicit a decent amount of warped respect for this film!

THE BEHEADED 1000 (1991)

Starring Jimmy Wang Yu, Joey Wong, Monica Chan,
Chin Siu-Ho, Wu Ma
Directed by Ting Shan-Hsi
Blaine and Blake Ltd

Retirement is beckoning, as royal executioner Ren (Wang Yu) nears his thousandth beheading. His disciple, played by Chin Siu-Ho, yearns to be his successor, but things get very supernatural, with many souls lurking with no direction to go and the arrival of the vengeful Blood Lotus (Joey Wong).

Featuring ghostly children, Wu Ma as the Guardian of Hell, an imp puppet, cartoon spiders with orange eyes, a lo-fi CGI dragon and floating skulls, the special effects are okay for their time, but it's the coolness of Wang Yu's presence that adds that certain something extra to the production, which is a mix of horror, action, comedy, and fantasy.

BEWITCHED (1981)

Starring Ai Fei, Melvin Wong, Lily Chan Lee-Lee,
Fanny, Hussein Hassan
Directed by Kuei Chih-Hung
Shaw Brothers

Stephen Lam (Fei) is arrested for the murder of his daughter, admits to driving a nine-inch nail through her head, is found guilty, and afterward asks Bobby (Wong), the policeman overseeing the case, to listen to his story, swearing that it was Thai witchcraft that compelled him to do what he did. Intrigued, Bobby looks into these claims and is soon the target of black magic rituals himself.

An extended flashback reveals how Stephen went on holiday to Thailand, had relations with a local woman called Bon Brown (Lee-Lee), returned to Hong Kong and promptly disregarded his promise to return to her, prompting the woman to seek supernatural revenge via Magusu (Hassan), an evil spell-caster.

We're soon witnessing various rituals, including a ceremony invoking a Vegetable Basket Spirit, which is enacted in silence and stillness, helping the scene to stand out when compared to the usual hectic, noisy rituals seen in most Hong Kong horror films. There's also a grisly sequence in a temple mortuary, where the chanting Magusu sticks a spike into the foot of a dead pregnant woman to make her sit up, then uses a candle to make oil drip from the fake-but-grotesque corpse's nostrils. Yet another novel instance of weird witchcraft involves the dark sorcerer burying a needle-transfixed lemon under the tarmac of a street: every time a passing pedestrian steps onto the buried piece of fruit . . . a stabbing pain is triggered in Bobby's chest!

The standout supernatural sequence, however, is the remote confrontation between Magusu and a Buddhist monk. Director Chih-Hung nicely contrasts the bright, clean, expansive look of the monk's Thai temple with the sorcerer's dimly lit, shuttered

shrine room, as the two men utilize different arcane methods to counteract each other's mystical might. With Magusu's veins filling with green gunk, the black magician prays to a bat effigy, which becomes a "real" bat creature that flies off and kamikazes into the monk's ceremonial fan to wreck his ritual! This whole duel of mystic men is really well-handled.

Even though the finale is reliant on the sudden, handy intervention of the monk at an airport, where he causes Magusu to develop blisters and resemble an old woman with a bat puppet crawling from her mouth, this is a continually diverting horror story.

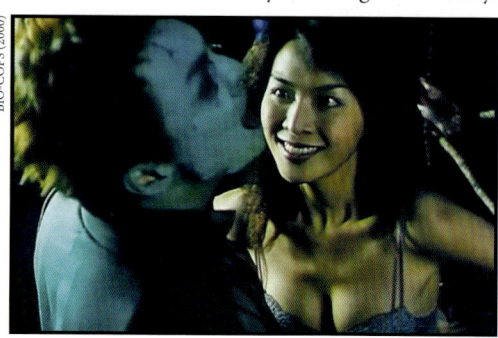

BIO-COPS (2000)

BIO-COPS (2000)

Starring Stephen Fung, Sam Lee, Alice Chan,
Chan Wai-Ming, Benny Lai, Frankie Ng Chi-Hung
Directed by Steve Cheng
Jing's Production

Dr. Harry (Lai) smuggles a sample of weaponised virus from a lab attempting to create "painless warriors," but he is bitten by one of the test subjects (Jude Poyer) and slowly turns into a zombie-like being, triggering an outbreak of the undead at a rural Hong Kong police station.

There's too much extraneous chat and a string of pointless scenes padding out the beginning of this movie. Matters become more interesting once Harry starts drooling green gunk during sex, rips apart the occupants of a police cell, and then becomes a superstrong, scabby-faced "New Human," who can bend bars.

Instead of being a super-soldier thriller, as suggested by the opening sequence, *Bio-Cops* evolves into a zombie outbreak flick and is really rather silly. Quite a few zombies seem to like to hide in lockers, a cop gets his arse bitten by petty hoodlum Cheap (Lee), who's just pretending to be a zombie, and Frankie Ng Chi-Hung simply looks embarrassed playing zombified Hung Hing gang boss Kow.

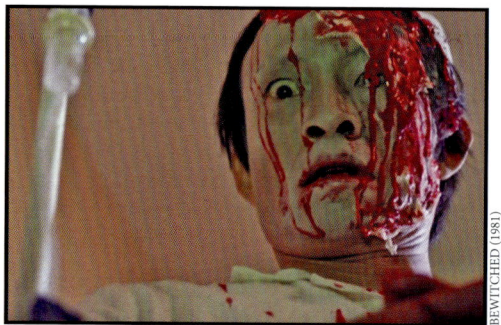

BEWITCHED (1981)

Reminiscent of *Bio-Zombie* (1998) in some ways, this film is nowhere near as good as that flick, though the diverting latter zombie siege moments, involving submachine guns and pump-action shotguns, do enliven the story, but the finale lacks fizz, turning into a talky confrontation between cop hero Marco (Fung), his girlfriend May (Wai-Ming) and Harry, but at least it ends with Harry having a grenade shoved into his mouth. Boom!

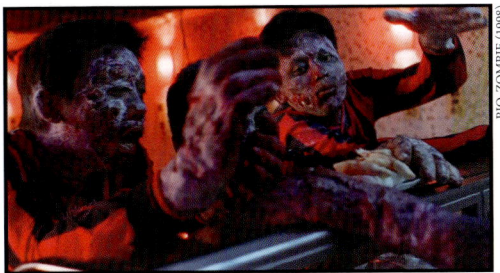

BIO-ZOMBIE (1998)

BIO-ZOMBIE (1998)

Starring Jordan Chan, Emotion Cheung, Sam Lee, Angela Tong
Directed by Wilson Yip
Brilliant Idea Group/Cameron Entertainment Ltd

Lethal chemicals in a Lucozade bottle trigger a zombie infestation in a Hong Kong shopping mall. Nonsense-spouting VCD shop employees, Woody Invincible and Crazy Bee, find themselves trapped in the mall with several other shop workers, as the crazed, scabrous, cannibal undead start multiplying in number.

Horror comedy *Bio-Zombie* begins by introducing us to the lowly, trivial world of slackers Woody and Bee, who think nothing of mugging Rolls (Tong), a pretty fellow mall worker, for her ring and cash. Yet, despite their superficial banter and disreputable ways, director Wilson (*Ip Man*) Yip, who cowrote the script with Matt Chow and So Man-Sing, manages to encourage us to tolerate these two fast-talking, disaffected teens, rather than dismiss them immediately as total scumbags. Actor Jordan Chan, from the *Young and Dangerous* film series, instills a certain amount of rough charm and hints of well-hidden decency into the character of Woody, further encouraging us to give these shirkers a chance.

The arc of another character, Kui (Lai Yiu-Cheung), goes in the opposite direction, however, as he segues from seemingly self-assured, arrogant phone store proprietor to a total coward who is prepared to shove a fellow survivor into the clutches of a mass of zombies to save his own skin.

The zombie makeups vary wildly in quality, and the movie takes its time to build momentum, but it is worth the wait, as we are treated to some interesting sequences, such as the scene where a lovelorn, infected sushi guy (Emotion Cheung) fights his undead urges and tries to protect Rolls from a bunch of zombie footballers . . . by offering them a plate of severed fingers served on rice!

The film retains its irreverent humor throughout, but introduces increasingly bloody encounters, including Woody shoving a cordless drill into a zombie's mouth, and it also includes a couple of unexpected emotional moments, plus some quirky homages to survival horror video games.

Unlike most zombie films, which generally feature characters unaware of the whole mythos surrounding the undead, this movie wittily has Crazy Bee (Sam Lee) suddenly remembering a zombie computer game he'd been playing, prompting him to inform a cop that he needs to shoot an undead attacker in the head.

Woody's transformation from strutting, self-concerned jerk to heroic zombie-fighter is nicely handled, a moment of on-the-nose sentimentality that occurs after Crazy Bee gets bitten somehow works (only Hong Kong films can get away with this kind of scene!) and the ending succeeds in being quite affecting as Woody willingly drinks from the deadly Lucozade bottle after seeing Rolls unknowingly take a sip (although an alternative, more obviously downbeat final shot is featured in the end credits).

BLACK MAGIC (1975)

Starring Ti Lung, Lo Lieh, Lily Li, Ku Feng, an Nei
Directed by Ho Meng-Hua
Shaw Brothers

In Malaysia a black magician called Shan Jianmi (Feng) earns a living by casting love spells and death spells for customers. When Shan becomes involved with rich, pushy Luo Yin (Nei), who wants Xu Nuo (Lung) to desire her, the magician finds himself devising various potions to bump off Xu's wife, fending off supernatural attacks by a mystical archenemy, and leching over Luo Yin.

This good-looking production features various spells that all require exotic ingredients . . . like women's breast milk, parasitic worms, drool from a corpse's mouth, wax effigies, and rice that has been placed in a vagina. The very first ritual we see Shan Jianmi performing involves him cutting a huge slice

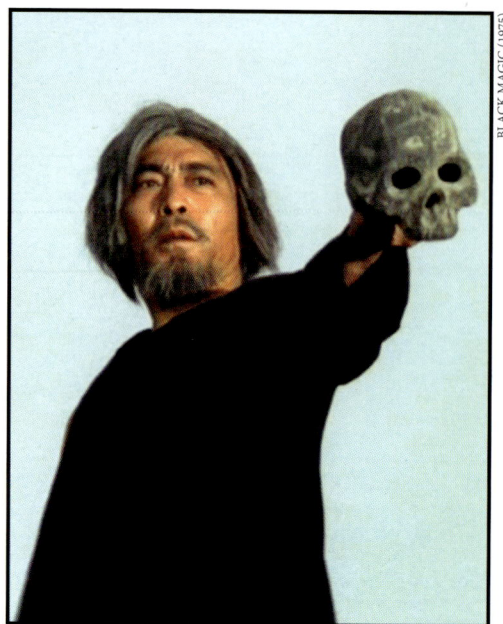

BLACK MAGIC (1975)

of flesh from a dead body, which he grills, along with the corpse's severed head.

The story, much of it revolving around Xu either getting mind-controlled, acting strange, or recovering from a spell only to be hexed once again, reaches a climax atop a construction site building, where the good and bad magicians battle it out, using glittery forcefields, chanting, and blue lightning.

Black Magic is a sound piece of genre filmmaking, though it should have really ramped up the weirdness factor, which is touched upon in the black magician's bizarre rituals, but the film is just not outlandish enough to be as memorable as, say, *Red Spell Spells Red* (1983) or the director's own mind-melter: *The Oily Maniac* (1976).

THE BOXER'S OMEN (1983)

Starring Phillip Kao, Wang Lung-Wei, Bolo Yeung, Elvis Tsui
Directed by Kuei Chih-Hung
Produced by Mona Fong
Shaw Brothers

Southeast Asia has long been Hong Kong cinema's dark continent—a world of barbaric, ominous happenings, a zone impenetrable except to an intrepid few who seek its mysterious secrets. *The Boxer's Omen* is perhaps the typical example of Hong Kong's Southeast Asian voodoo-style movies.

Loosely linked to the film *Bewitched* (1981), a tale partly set in Thailand that was also directed by Kuei Chih-Hung, this movie focuses on a guy (Kao) who goes to Thailand to challenge the man (Yeung) who crippled his brother. Before he can do anything, however, he is led to a temple where he is told he is somehow linked to a dead monk. It is here that the monk begins to teach the boxer a method of repelling hexes and spells.

This wild horror flick, loaded with offal, chanting monks, vomit-eating, rotting bodies, maggots, nudity, eels, laser beam effects, and bats, is well worth tracking down.

THE BRIDE FROM HELL (1972)

Starring Yang Fang, Margaret Hsing Hui, Lui Ming, Carrie Ku Mei, Ko Hsiao-Pao, Chang Feng
Directed by Chou Hsu-Chiang
Shaw Brothers

This Shaw Brothers ghost film tells the tale of a scholar named Yun Peng, who sees a woman named Anu fully naked and feels compelled to marry her. However, Yun Peng discovers that Anu is actually the spirit of a woman who was raped and murdered twenty years ago by one of his relatives . . . and now she wants revenge.

Interestingly, even though Anu is a vengeance-seeking, green-faced ghost, killing her victims in novel ways, she is portrayed as a sympathetic figure, a victim of the masculine world.

While *The Bride from Hell* is definitely not as in-your-face as later Shaw Brothers fantasy-horror films, it is still worth a watch for the Hong Kong gothic vibes and the signature Shaw Brothers sets, which are atmospheric and shrouded in mist.

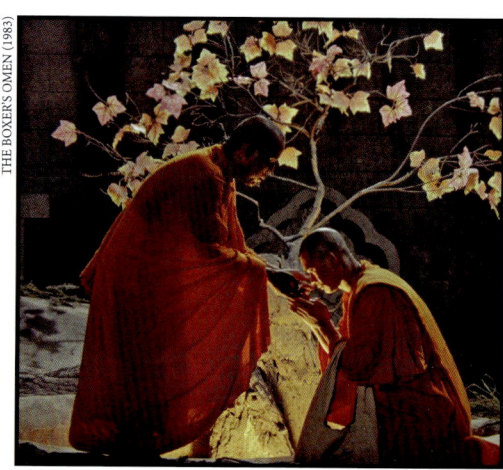

THE BOXER'S OMEN (1983)

THE BRIDE WITH WHITE HAIR (1993)

Starring Leslie Cheung, Brigitte Lin, Francis Ng,
Elaine Lui
Directed by Ronny Yu
Mandarin Films Distribution

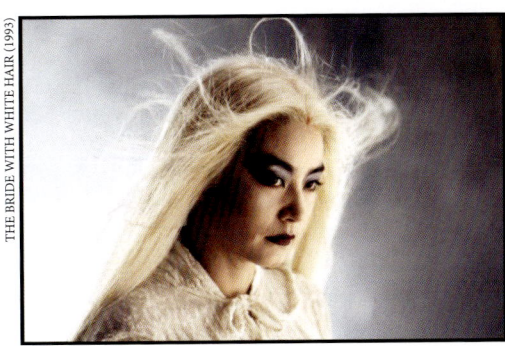

THE BRIDE WITH WHITE HAIR (1993)

This stylish movie combines many of the traits that make Hong Kong fantasy movies so outstanding. It is a lavish, visually stunning production packed with haunting scenes of great beauty, sword fights on a grand scale and, for once, a relatively coherent plot.

Leslie Cheung is the hero Cho Yi Hang, a matchless sword fighter devoting his talents to righting wrongs, who was once, as a mischievous boy, saved from wolves by Lien, a mysterious girl raised by wolves. Now, many years later, he meets up with her again, but by this time she has been adopted by the leaders of an evil cult, a pair of insane Siamese twins. The female twin trains Lien to be a killing machine, while the male twin falls in love with her.

Cho Yi Hang goes up against the evil cult at the same time as he and Lien realize that they love each other, and he swears that if she ever grows old and her hair turns white, he will find her a magical herb that will grant her eternal youth. He also says that he will never doubt her.

The evil Siamese twins are furious that Lien wishes to leave and devise a vicious trial for her. Meanwhile, Cho Yi Hang finds his master slain, and his clan comrades jump to the obvious conclusion as to who the culprit is, with tragic consequences . . .

Every second of this absorbing and beautiful movie is utilized to make it an overwhelming visual treat, so the only disappointment comes with the somewhat abrupt ending, and the realization that we'll have to watch part 2 to find out what happens next!

THE BRIDE WITH WHITE HAIR 2 (1993)

Starring Leslie Cheung, Brigitte Lin, Sunny Chan,
Christy Chung, Joey Meng
Directed by David Wu
Mandarin Films Distribution

This film picks up the story ten years after the first installment. Cho (Cheung) is still waiting in the snow on top of a mountain for the magic flower that will restore youth to Lien (Lin). Meanwhile, Lien continues to wreak vengeance upon Cho's comrades, wiping out all the young fighters capable of carrying on the clan's name.

Cho's nephew Fung Chun Kit (Chan) marries a beautiful girl called Lyre, but on their wedding night white-haired Lien attacks them, wounding many of Kit's friends and kidnapping Lyre. Once in Lien's stronghold, Lyre is bewitched by Chan Yuen Yuen, a woman who has suffered at the hands of men, who encourages Lien to continue her acts of revenge, with the help of a band of women who are sworn to kill men whenever they see them.

Kit is nursed back to health by the tomboy Moon (Chung) and, together with his friends, he vows to rescue Lyre. However, the task is not as simple as they had hoped: their kung fu is no match for Lien, plus they also have to battle Chan Yuen Yuen's women warriors and even Lyre herself. Kit finally learns the secret of his uncle's whereabouts and tries to find him, but fails and realizes his clan will have to challenge Lien again, unaided, in a battle to the death.

This sequel has a rushed feel to it, but it still boasts wonderful effects, atmospheric sets, and a fast pace, and, though the story isn't quite as bizarre this time around, focusing on different characters, it is still a strong enough plot to keep you glued to the screen.

BRUTAL SORCERY (1983)

Starring Lai Hon-Chi, Lily Chan, Kwan Hoi-San
Directed by Pan Ling
Continental King Lung Movie Production

A Hong Kong taxi driver travels to Thailand to rid himself of a troublesome duo of ghosts, only to fall victim to a poison black magic spell there. This causes him to eat live fish, raw liver, and a live chicken, resulting in a distended gut. His wife and his doctor go to enlist the help of a Thai magician called Ping the King of Devils, to reduce the stomach swelling.

Apart from some puking, a head-swelling effect, and a maggot-covered stomach that balloons in size, this movie is somewhat lacking in incident.

The main character suddenly drops out of the movie because he is incapacitated by his big belly, causing the plot to lose its central focus. The film becomes too disjointed and the climactic good versus bad magician duel, even though it includes some cel-animated ghost FX, is a lackluster confrontation.

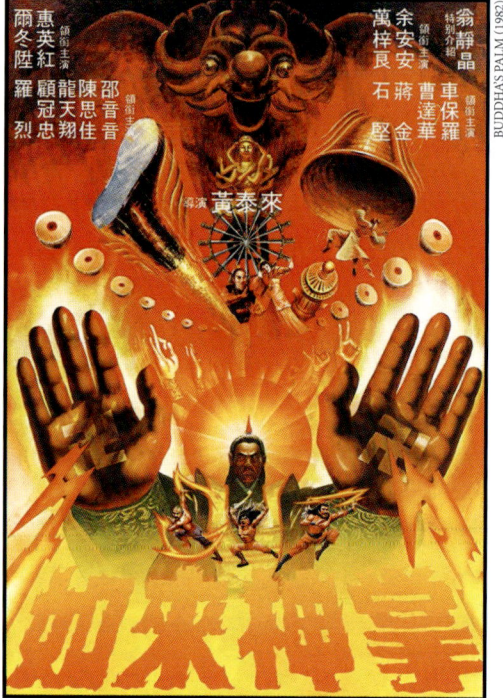

BUDDHA'S PALM (1982)

BUDDHA'S PALM (1982)

Starring Derek Yee, Yu On-On, Kara Wai, Lo Lieh, Alex Man, Shih Kien
Directed by Taylor Wong
Shaw Brothers

Long Jianfei (Yee) gets kicked into a chasm, but he is fortunately saved by a gold-skinned, winged creature called Dameng, which is kind of like a small dragon with the face of a friendly triceratops. Dameng takes Jianfei to its blind master, called Flaming Cloud Devil (Man), who becomes Jianfei's foster father.

Jianfe is taught formidable Buddha's Palm skills by his new dad and he's soon swept along in a series of confrontations, as various old martial arts masters, including Sun Biling and Bi Gu of East Island, settle scores, team up, argue, or are betrayed by others.

With lots of leaping, spinning and flying characters from such groups as Ten Thousand Swords Clan and Dark Moon Clan, that perform outlandish skills like Heavenly Foot and Three Invincible Palms, this production is swamped with colorful cartoon animation force-beams, cel-animated daggers, cartoon flames and so much more!

One character uses Tortoise Style: the ability to fake death, while another master lets loose with the Wrath of Ten Thousand Buddhas Stroke, which results in loads of cartoon Buddhist swastikas flying everywhere, as trees break, lightning flashes and a storm rages! That's quite a technique!

The soundtrack, very often loud and discordant, adds to the wild, off-kilter nature of the movie, helping to complement such over-the-top visuals as the villain known as Foot Monster (Kien) using a super-extendable leg to attack adversaries, a kid with a large facial cyst from which he can squirt acidic fluid, turning his victims into green gunge, plus the unsheathed Golden Dragon Dagger that looks and sounds like a lightsaber!

Buddha's Palm is a riotous amalgamation of sounds, cel-animated power effects, insane fantasy super-fu skills, and larger-than-life characters. Wonderful stuff!

THE BUTTERFLY MURDERS (1979)

Starring Lau Siu-Ming, Wong Shu-Tong, Michelle Yim, Chan Chi-Chi, Eddy Ko
Directed by Tsui Hark
Seasonal Film Corporation

Tien, leader of the Ten Flags clan, investigates the mystery surrounding killer butterfly attacks in the deserted Shum Castle, accompanied by some of his troops and lone woman warrior Green Shadow. Entering the catacombs beneath the castle, they encounter esteemed scholar Fong (Siu-Ming), Master Shum, his wife and a mute maid named Chee. The butterflies continue to kill, hidden rooms are discovered, and renowned fighters known as the Thunders enter the story.

Tsui Hark's first film is an assured, thoroughly engrossing Hong Kong new wave wuxia murder mystery with creature feature elements. The empty Shum Castle itself, often shown from the outside, looming above the long grasses, adds immeasurably to the atmosphere of the film, as does the effective use of Jerry Goldsmith's *Planet of the Apes* score. Wong Shu-Tong is steely, stoic and thoughtful as Tien the clan leader, and Michelle Yim is playful and acrobatic as Green Shadow.

The film offers a realistic reason for characters being able to fly about, by showing them using various line-firing gizmos, but there are still fantastical components to the story, like a fire crow that explodes on contact with people and the notion that butterflies can actually kill a person, though these lethal Lepidoptera assaults are actually explained away as being the result of the use of "butterfly-controlling medicine."

The introduction of a helmeted, armored man becomes the focus of the latter stages of the movie, with the killer butterflies taking a back seat, as fights involving dart-ejecting weapons and explosive projectiles ultimately lead to a nihilistic finale.

The secret plans and rivalries eventually revealed to be the reasons behind the events may fail to be particularly compelling, but *The Butterfly Murders* remains a very moody, intriguing, enjoyable viewing experience.

CALAMITY OF SNAKES (1982)

Starring Hsiang Yun-Peng, Kao Yuen, Wei Ping-Ou,
Lo Pi-Ling
Directed by William Cheung Kei
Kee Woo Film Co

An unscrupulous businessman orders his workers to kill loads of snakes infesting a construction site. After a new apartment complex is built there, thousands of snakes return and attack the building's occupants to get their revenge.

This Hong Kong–Taiwanese movie features the killing of lots of live snakes and unashamedly shows the deaths in loving detail, so be warned before you decide to give *Calamity of Snakes* a watch. If you can stomach these mondo moments of real-life reptile butchery, then the movie certainly delivers on its promise of multiple moments of snake-attack mayhem!

The film starts as it means to go on, with the slaying of various species of snake infesting a pit during the building of a new apartment development in Taiwan, owned by Mr. Chang. Ignoring the protests of his architect, Chang refuses to deal with them humanely, ordering his workers to splat the serpents with shovels instead. Chang himself gets in on the act by using a digger to dice more snakes.

Continuing this theme of snake-related nastiness, we then see a live snake being slit open and skinned alive for its bladder at a market. Not too long after this, the snakes start to strike back, as foreseen by Chang's superstitious wife, beginning with an

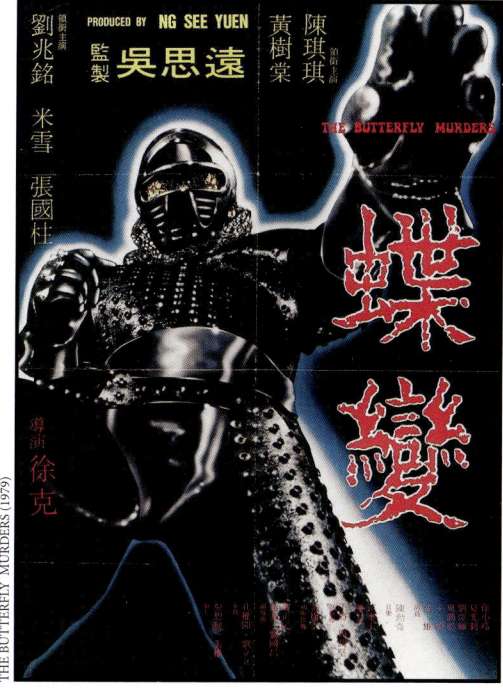

THE BUTTERFLY MURDERS (1979)

attack on a construction worker and a call girl . . . as they have sex!

Attempting to deter any further snake assaults, Chang's uber-geeky right-hand man employs the services of a snake expert, who sprinkles a powdery concoction of cement, tobacco, and sulfur around the place because "all snakes fear these things". After the powder washes away in a rainstorm, the snakes return, so Chang uses mongooses to deal with some of the serpents.

The director obviously believed viewers really, really wanted to watch a lot of mongoose vs snake action, because he presents us with an extended series of close-up mammals-murdering-reptiles shots. This sequence just goes on and on!

Realizing that he needs more than mongooses, Chang calls in a snake-hunting master, a dude with white eyebrows, who we first see performing some kind of stage show, pulling a snake from his mouth and allowing it to bite his tongue. It is theorised that a boa is influencing the other snakes to attack en masse, so the master sets out to kill the ringleader.

In an over-the-top confrontation in a storage building, the master fights the large boa, which bites off some of his fingers, leaps about energetically and roars! This is an enjoyably kinetic, fast-moving scene, shot like a kung fu fight, that sees the master use a rope to finally strangle the big snake. The master leaves, assuming his job is done . . . but it's shown that there's another boa lurking around.

The focus of the movie shifts to the newly opened apartment building now, where we are introduced to various characters, including rich, old guys, a precocious child, and a large lady who loves her food. These stock characters, plus more scenes involving the cost-cutting boss and the idealistic architect, give *Calamity of Snakes* a vibe reminiscent of 70s disaster movies.

There are some incredibly lowbrow comic moments added to the cheesy mix, including a scene where speeded-up footage of the overweight woman eating too much food is intercut with shots of a pig with its snout in a trough, though there fortunately aren't too many of these "funny" scenes!

When snakes start flying up out of the building's basement level and begin to infest the complex, slithering into elevators and overflowing into lobbies and bedrooms, the actors are soon rolling around the place, with loads of real, writhing snakes crawling over their bodies and faces. The snakes in this movie are obviously treated badly, but the actors don't fare much better, as an endless flood of real reptiles are hurled at them! I do hope these thespians were paid well enough!

There are a lot of snakes used during the finale, and I do mean a LOT! Entire corridors are deluged with slithering serpents. There are snakes in punchbowls, snakes in the bath, snakes on the reception desk and a tsunami of snakes that spill from a lift!

Chang, at one point, grabs a samurai sword and the movie "treats" us to a sequence featuring the slow-motion hacking of snakes, complete with close-ups of the various portions of the decapitated reptiles twitching on the floor.

The fire department is eventually called and dudes in snazzy silver boots & helmets come to the rescue, chopping up snakes with fire axes and spraying them with extinguishers. But even the firemen have trouble dealing with the second big, roaring boa, forcing them to resort to using flamethrowers! This, of course, gives the filmmakers the excuse to now present us with shots of various species of snakes being burned alive.

The boss boa is no pushover, however, especially as it fights like a martial arts master! The critter flies around the rooms, slapping away people with its coils (cue loud, kung fu–style punching noises) and it even hurls a large eagle statue and a drum kit at the firemen, then agilely leaps away from their

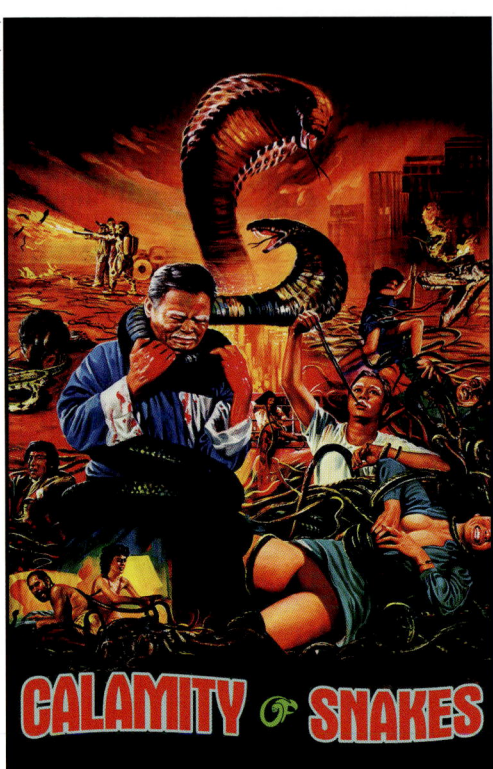

CALAMITY OF SNAKES (1982)

flamethrowers! The big puppet beast is finally set alight, whereupon it wraps itself around Chang, then constricts him and immolates him at the same time!

Calamity of Snakes is an unashamedly exploitative, schlocky, infamous extravaganza that comes across like a mad animals-attack genre film infused with 70s disaster flick trimmings. If you can withstand the many, many mondo shots of snake snuff footage hurled at your retinas (which is kind of hard to do), this is a dumb, fun, subtlety-free, unhinged, revolting-yet-watchable, one-of-a-kind creature feature that you're not likely to forget in a hurry.

THE CAT (1992)
Starring Gloria Yip, Waise Lee, Christine Ng, Philip Kwok
Directed by Lam Nai-Choi
Diagonal Pictures/Golden Harvest

Night after night, eerie and disturbing noises come from an upstairs flat. The man who lives below decides to go and caution the noisemakers and he sees an old man, a young girl, and a black cat, but is shocked the next day when he finds out that the flat has been deserted for some time. When Wisely

(Lee) looks into the matter, he instantly suspects the black cat is the culprit, so he and his partner, an extremely talented dog, set about to try and capture the cat. In an astounding fight sequence, the cat's tail is broken and the tail is taken by Wisely to the laboratory, where it is discovered that it is at least sixty years old. But surely no cat can live that long?

This is definitely a jaw-dropping movie, a strange mixture of sci-fi and *Peacock King*–style fantasy. One extended scene, which is definitely not for animal-lovers, takes place in a scrapyard, where Wisely's dog confronts the cat. With a mixture of puppets and even a bit of stop-motion, plus a real cat and dog, a full-on fight ensues, with the two critters using some of the most ingenious fight moves imaginable to combat each other!

This film really is ridiculously unusual, with the cat revealed to be a good alien that is out to stop an evil life-form known as the star killer!

CENTIPEDE HORROR (1982)
Starring Margaret A. Li, Miu Kiu-Wai, Hussein Hassan, Wang Lai
Directed by Keith Li
Produced by Stephen C. K. Chan
Nikko International Productions & Films

In the murky categories of horror flicks, this one is probably best termed a "squirmy." Certainly, if you're the kind of viewer who can happily sit through mass disembowelment and carnage, yet will freak at a spider in the bathroom, then it's advisable to give this one a miss, as the centipedes in this film aren't your average small fry bugs, but are big enough to give any entomophobe nightmares for a month. However, that doesn't mean the rest of us need rush to see *Centipede Horror*, as it's a fairly lackluster effort. The movie begins intriguingly enough as a kind of Far Eastern *Don't Look Now*, with our hero haunted by the mysteriously creepy-crawly-coated demise of his sister, but which, several liberal dollops of bone-rattling mumbo jumbo later, resolves itself fairly tamely into your standard good sorcerer versus bad sorcerer set-to that we've all seen before in this kind of movie, although the reanimated chicken skeletons are a fairly novel addition, I guess.

Centipede Horror has its moments, though, most notably the climactic, pretty damn disgusting vomiting-up-centipedes scene, but the movie, as a whole, promises more than it delivers and is really rather dull.

CHILD OF PEACH (1987)
Starring Lin Hsiao-Lao, Chin Tu, Huang Chung-Yu
Directed by Chao Chung-Hsing and Chen Chun-Liang
Chin Ke Film Company

High up in the Himalayas is the Peach Garden, an area of eternal springs, flowers and birds, where it never snows, thanks to the natural power absorbed by the Sword of the Sun. But a blue-faced, red-haired, fanged villain called King Devil attacks this tranquil place, steals the sword and kills the master of the garden and his wife, but they manage to save their baby by placing him inside a giant, flying Holy Peach! The huge peach whizzes down from the mountains, causes some trouble at an old couple's home, then splits open to reveal the baby, which the couple adopt and name Peach-Kid.

When King Devil's evil forces begin to attack the land, a fairy helps Peach-Kid grow up superfast, so

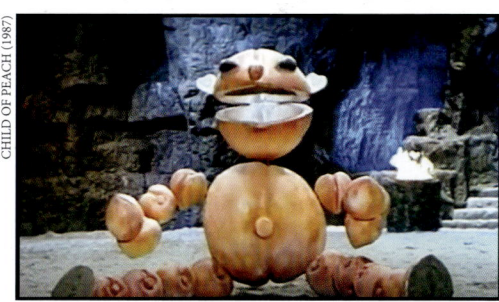

CHILD OF PEACH (1987)

that he becomes a strong teenager (actually played by actress Lin Hsiao-Lao), who is ultimately able to defeat King Devil's horrible army, which includes white-clad minions in fright wigs, a strongman with a spiked mace called Hercules, horned, green-haired warriors, a dude called Aeolus, who uses a big bag of compressed wind to defeat people, and a villainess with a flamethrower staff named Grandma from Devil Island (character names vary according to which print you watch).

This Taiwanese flick, loosely based on Japanese folklore hero Momotarō, boasts *Power Rangers*–style villains with colorful wigs, a lot of fun fantasy fighting, and a bunch of pretty novel moments, like the fight with a group of trident-wielding shark men, who have lumpy craniums and dorsal fins on their backs. As the story progresses, Peach-Kid is aided by hefty dude Melon and the former "guardian angels" of Peach Garden, which are three super-powered kids that can become a bird, a gibbon, and a dog . . . and are called Tiny Cock, Tiny Monkey, and Tiny Dog.

Things to look out for include King Devil's showdown with a puppet creature that's made up of lots of large peaches, some gags involving drinking gibbon urine or getting peed on by a giant peach, and a brief scene where Peach-Kid blows air down a tube into Aeolus' mouth, causing his head to explode! Erm, this is a children's film, right?

Wacky, weird, and fun.

A CHINESE GHOST STORY (1987)

Starring Leslie Cheung, Joey Wong, Wu Ma, Lam Wai, Lau Siu-Ming
Directed by Ching Siu-Tung
Produced by Tsui Hark
Action by Ching Siu-Tung, Philip Kwok, Lau Chi-Ho, Wu Chi-Lung
Cinema City Film Productions/Film Workshop/Golden Princess Amusement Co. Ltd

Ching Siu-Tung gained international success when he directed *A Chinese Ghost Story*: a horror-martial-arts-ghost-comedy-romance that also incorporates a rap musical routine performed by a sword-wielding, ghost-killing Taoist priest!

The story revolves around the love felt for a pretty female ghost (Wong) by Ling Choi San (Cheung), a young, accident-prone tax collector. The main hitch to the relationship is the fact that the ghost is forced, by an evil tree/woman spirit, to lure men to their deaths. As soon as she has an amorous male in her passionate grasp, the ghost allows the tiny bells on her ankle to ring, summoning her wicked mistress. But, when Ling ingratiates himself into the girl spirit's company, she cannot bring herself to cause his demise. So, with the help of a hermit-like Taoist priest (Ma), Ling attempts to free his love from her captor, though this means not only fighting the nasty mistress in her many guises (cross-dressing dame or a gigantic human tongue), but also the dark lord of the underworld, who plans to marry the ghost girl in Hell!

Directed with kinetic panache by Ching Siu-Tung, this film is crammed with atmosphere, emotion, gravity-defying swordplay, and some goofball physical comedy. There are some fun special effects on show too, such as the battle with the mega-tongue, where we see the long, fleshy organ split in two, turning into a sort of narrow, mutated set of alligator jaws that open to reveal the evil tree-spirit's face, which has a mass of tentacles issuing from it!

The film's mix of Hong Kong story elements—beautiful flying ghosts, a Taoist priest-swordsman,

etc.—and Western filming techniques—Sam Raimi-esque roving cameras and some gooey FX—make this production an enormously entertaining watch, with Leslie Cheung, Joey Wong, and Wu Ma all perfect in the leading roles.

Joey Wong is the real standout, playing the sexy-yet-vulnerable ghost, flying about the stylishly lit locations in her flowing silk robes. There is a wonderful moment when she gives Leslie Cheung's character, who is having to hide from her evil 'sisters' underwater, a slow-motion kiss that is also providing

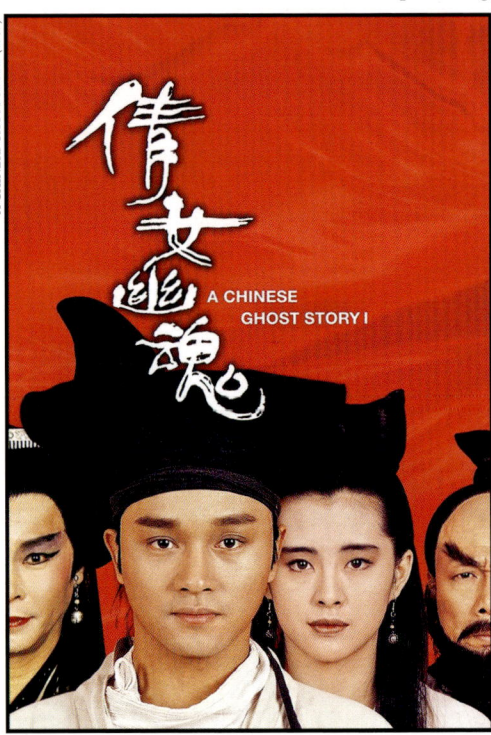

A CHINESE GHOST STORY (1987)

him with much-needed air. This is one of the best ever screen kisses!

And, of course, we shouldn't forget the shriveled stop-motion corpses lurking in the temple that our hero is staying in. These undead dudes shuffle around the building in the early part of the film, trying to get hold of him, but thanks to a series of comedic, lucky mishaps, he remains completely unaware that the zombies are there, eventually killing them with sunlight without ever noticing them!

Produced by the legendary Tsui Hark, this film is a Hong Kong classic, effortlessly merging genres, with a haunting score and a finale featuring the heroes battling it out in the netherworld to save the heroine.

Spawning two sequels, an animated film, a television series and a remake, the first film remains the best. Awesome stuff!

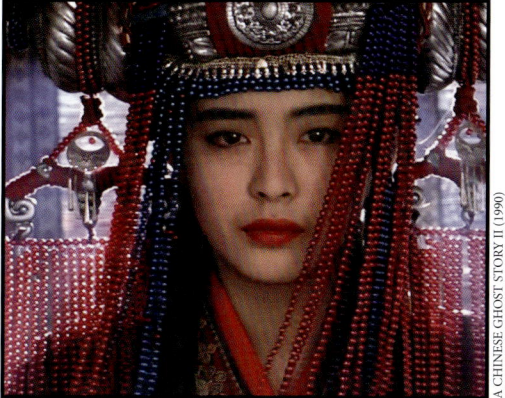

A CHINESE GHOST STORY II (1990)

A CHINESE GHOST STORY II (1990)
Starring Leslie Cheung, Joey Wong, Jacky Cheung,
Wu Ma, Waise Lee
Directed by Ching Siu-Tung
Produced by Tsui Hark
Action by Ching Siu-Tung, Lau Chi-Ho, Wu Chi-Lung
Film Workshop/Golden Princess Amusement Co. Ltd

A scholar (Leslie Cheung) escapes wrongful imprisonment and falls for a beautiful rebel woman, played by Joey Wong, which leads to an adventure involving lots of fights, monsters and action-packed, supernatural encounters.

Ching Siu-Tung's *A Chinese Ghost Story* (1987) is one of my all-time favorite Hong Kong movies. This follow-up, also directed by Ching Siu-Tung, doesn't match the charming, madcap, romantic, stylish heights of the original, but it is enjoyable nonetheless, with scenes featuring a humanoid demon monster and an ending involving a devious High Monk who turns out to be an ancient, giant, flying, monster centipede!

One extended action set piece involves a demon corpse-monster, which is a goofy-looking, full-scale model for a lot of the scenes, intercut sometimes with a man in a creature costume. It gets skewered with spears and swords at one point, but this doesn't stop the monster, even after Imperial Officer Hu (Waise Lee) hacks off the demon monster's arms and head! The demon-monster just keeps attacking and it uses its rib cage like a giant venus flytrap to clutch onto Hu! Wild stuff!

The toothy centipede that provides the conflict for the finale is also a full-scale model for many of the scenes. This critter bursts out of the ground, flies about with the characters clinging to its back, and swallows a couple of them!

Even though *A Chinese Ghost Story II* focuses less on the endearing, romantic scenes featured in the first installment, the sequel does boast lots of fights, magic incantations and flying swords. Wu Ma, returning from the first movie, and Jacky Cheung, playing a young Taoist priest, add to the manic fun.

A CHINESE GHOST STORY III (1991)
Starring Tony Leung Chiu-Wai, Jacky Cheung, Joey Wong,
Lau Shun, Lau Siu-Ming, Nina Li Chi
Directed by Ching Siu-Tung
Produced by Tsui Hark
Action by Ching Siu-Tung, Yuen Bun, Ma Yuk-Sing,
Cheung Yiu-Sing
Film Workshop/Golden Princess Amusement Co. Ltd

Set a hundred years after the events of the first movie, the tree demon is on the loose again, controlling some beautiful ghosts. The hero this time is a Buddhist monk nicely played by Tony Leung, and Joey Wong is once again the ghostly love interest.

This movie features more romantic slapstick comedy and fewer sword fights and monsters. The giant killer tongue is not used much this time, but we do get a temple building that comes to life and the briefly seen giant stone head of a mountain demon.

There's some novel stuff like the master monk stretching his earlobes to cover his eyes when he's caught by the tree demon and a ghost girl who can extend her fingernails superlong, but the movie, ultimately, lacks the verve and visual flair of the original.

A CHINESE LEGEND (1991)
Starring Jacky Cheung, Joey Wong, Cheung Man,
Wu Ma, Lau Shun
Directed by Lau Hung-Chuen
Grand March Movie Production Company Ltd

A highly atmospheric film with stunning visuals, though it becomes disappointing at the end.

Jacky Cheung plays a vagabond swordsman who falls in love with a beautiful damsel-in-distress (Wong), but she is betrothed to the king of ghosts. With the help of a vixen spirit who assumes human form (Man) and a Taoist warrior priest (Ma), he sets out to save his love, defeat the king of ghosts, and save the world from eternal darkness.

The incredible sequences and superb visuals include

a stunning duel between Wu Ma and Cheung Man in an immense temple and the materialisation of the king of ghosts. Sadly, the final battle is ineptly handled and ends abruptly and confusingly. Still, it's worth checking out for the preceding 80 or so minutes.

A CHINESE ODYSSEY PART ONE: PANDORA'S BOX (1995)
Starring Stephen Chow, Ng Man-Tat,
Yammie Lam Kit-Ying, Karen Mok, Law Kar-Ying
Directed by Jeffrey Lau
Color Star Films/Xi'an Film Studio

Joker (Chow), the rather inept leader of a gang of robbers, is oblivious to the fact that he is actually the Monkey King, who was punished for his bad behavior and turned into a human 500 years earlier. The movie begins rather abruptly, as if some of the introduction to this sequence got trimmed down too much, showing the Monkey King disobeying his master, Longevity Monk, and being swiftly chastised for his misdeeds by Guanyin, the Goddess of Happiness. The narrative briskly zips forward hundreds of years and focuses on Joker's comedic, slapstick encounters with a couple of she-demons,

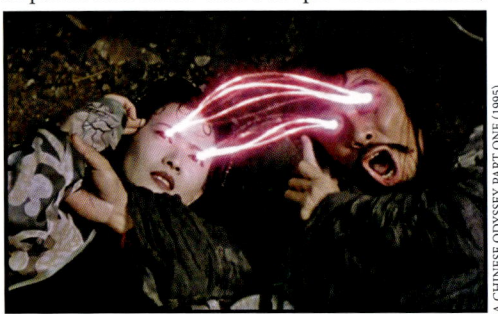
A CHINESE ODYSSEY PART ONE (1995)

who take over his motley crew of incompetent thieves as they await the arrival of Longevity Monk. You see, these monstrous femmes want to eat some of Longevity Monk's flesh, which will make them eternal.

Even though the characters are taken from the classic novel *Journey to the West*, *A Chinese Odyssey Part One: Pandora's Box* has nothing to do with that story.

The earlier portion of the movie is crammed with Chow's usual blend of earthy humor, pratfalls and slapstick, and is followed by loads of enjoyable fantasy-action situations. These include the woman-demon known as Spider Devil going on a well-mounted rampage after transforming into a long-legged arachnid-monster, Joker inexplicably zooming

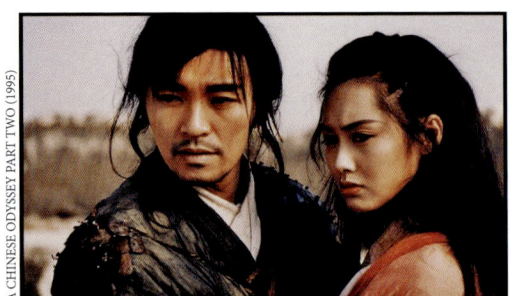
A CHINESE ODYSSEY PART TWO (1995)

around the place using his hands instead of his feet, and encounters with King Bull, who is a huge, bull-headed dude who can also reduce down to human size.

Once the main characters reach the Spider Web Cave, the filmmakers seem to depend too much on the opening and closing of sliding rock doors as a device to propel the plot forward. But, on the plus side, we get to see loads of fun, oddball moments, such as a fight inside King Bull's guts, a time loop sequence and an on-off romance between Joker and the demoness Pak Jing-Jing (also known as Boney M), who can turn from a human-looking female into a robed, strange-faced, white-haired being.

The film ends just as abruptly as it starts, finishing with some action-packed footage from the second film, *A Chinese Odyssey Part Two: Cinderella*.

A CHINESE ODYSSEY PART TWO: CINDERELLA (1995)
Starring Stephen Chow, Ng Man-Tat, Athena Chu,
Ada Choi, Yammie Lam Kit-Ying, Karen Mok
Directed by Jeffrey Lau
Color Star Films/Xi'an Film Studio

In this sequel to *A Chinese Odyssey Part One: Pandora's Box* we follow the comedic adventures of Joker/Monkey King (Chow) after he is sent 500 years into the past. Here he once more encounters characters like Longevity Monk and King Bull.

Our hero is torn between two loves in a story that relies on a lot of body-swapping humor, such as when a female character switches bodies with Pigsy (Man-Tat). There's also a running joke concerning Longevity Monk, who is portrayed as such an insufferably irritating chatterbox that bovine warriors would rather kill themselves than listen to him!

This time around we're introduced to Princess Iron Fan (Choi), a bat-eared villain called Old Black Mountain Devil that can sniff away a person's life, and King Bull's many minions, who have visages resembling dogs and lizards.

With Joker finally becoming Monkey King, he battles King Bull, who uses a magic fan to cause earthquakes and winds, sending the city and everyone within it hurtling toward the sun! Monkey King saves the day, helps the new incarnations of Joker and his lover Zixia find romance, then heads off across the desert with his master. Part two is certainly a mad ride, but the original is funnier, with better-handled set pieces.

CORPSE MANIA (1981)

Starring Wang Jung, Tan Nei, Yu Tsui-Ling,
Lau Siu-Kwan
Directed by Kuei Chih-Hung
Produced by Mona Fong
Shaw Brothers

The discovery of a decomposing, sexually abused female corpse covered in mealworms leads police chief Zhang to hunt for a convicted necrophiliac named Li Zhengyuan. As more people die, and brothel owner Madam Lan (Nei) seems set to be another victim, Zhang must reevaluate his initial suspicions and perhaps look elsewhere for the real killer.

Corpse Mania begins as an artfully filmed necro-horror story, using shots of powder being rubbed into a dead woman's skin with a white fur mitten and close-ups of mealworms writhing on posed, naked corpses to imbue the production with a queasy, perverse vibe, but then, interestingly, it evolves into a well-mounted giallo movie, focusing on a mysterious

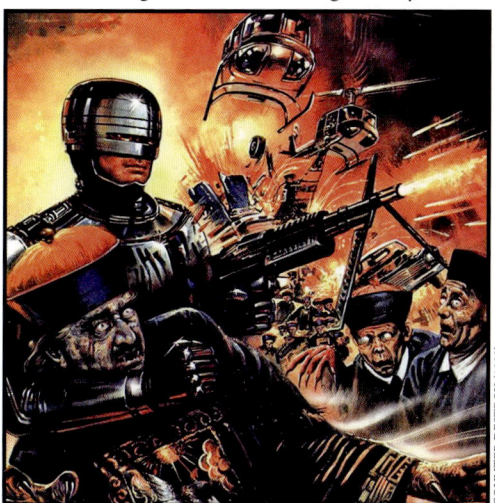

COUNTER DESTROY (1989)

killer with a glinting blade. A blood-spattered attack on a victim in an anachronistically modern-looking car and a chaotic, noisy, effective set piece in a room full of round chicken cages are highlights of the film's crimson shift into giallo territory.

Moody cinematography, first-rate art direction by Johnson Tsao and a controlled, unruffled central performance courtesy of Wang Jung as Zhang help to outweigh the film's later far-fetched twists and turns. Well worth a watch.

COUNTER DESTROY (1989)

Starring Sorapong Chatree, Sun Chien, Michelle Yim,
Fan Chin-Hung, To Siu-Ming
Directed by Edgar Jere
Produced by Tomas Tang
Filmark International Ltd

A scriptwriter called Joyce goes to an isolated villa to write her magnum opus about the last Emperor of China, but other film companies want to prevent this biopic from being made and will resort to murder to get their way. To make matters worse (and weird) the plot also involves hopping vampires, a cross-eyed Taoist priest, a possessed phone, ninjas with automatic weaponry, poisoned lipstick, a razor-fingered spirit, a fortune-telling sacred bird, a muscular zombie-vampire that leaves sparkling footprints, an explosive bouquet of flowers, the ghost of a Ching Dynasty eunuch . . . and the silvery cyborg hero from *Robo Vampire* (1988)!

The dubbing, dialogue and acting in this cut-and-paste mind-warper, which is also known as *Counter Destroyer, The Vampire is Still Alive* and *Robo Vampire 3: Counter Destroy*, achieves levels of cheesiness that other Tomas Tang productions even fail to reach. The voice work for the actress playing Joyce's friend is especially jarring!

The various bits of unrelated footage, some from a Thai film called *Killer Eyelashes*, are tenuously linked, as usual, with new dubbed dialogue "seamlessly" melding it together, but all logical narrative is swept away during a finale involving the robo-warrior, hopping vampires, the Taoist priest and a ghostly vampire kid who bursts from Joyce's rapidly swelling belly! This brat tells a couple of vampires that they are going to pay for killing his "mother," even though it was the kiddy-vamp who actually killed Joyce by erupting from her stomach! The vamp-child then proceeds to urinate on the vampires, but don't worry, folks, the film ends with Joyce somehow still being alive?! My brain hurts . . .

CROCODILE FURY (1988)

Starring Kent Wills, Trudy Calder, Lucas Byrne,
Sorapong Chatree, Sun Chien, Jack Mackay
Directed by "Ted Kingsbrook"
Produced by Tomas Tang
Filmark International Ltd

Master Cooper, who controls people-munching killer crocs from his golden cave, plans to team up with Monica (Calder), the blonde sorceress who is running a "vampire business." Together they hope their crocodiles and hopping vamps will take over the world, but agent Thompson (Wills) is determined to prevent this evil plan from happening.

OMG! Where to start with this incredibly weird cut-and-paste flick?! Well, here's just some of the things that occur . . .

There are multiple crocodile attacks, both in the water and on land, with a high body count and much screaming. Monica performs seemingly pointless incantations, at one point causing several fish to spill from a vampire's mouth, into a fishbowl, which then fly up into a different vampire's mouth. A levitating dude loses his concentration and falls prey to a hungry crocodile. A guy vomits up maggots. A smaller man-in-suit croc does tricks for villagers. Some of the vampires are of the Chinese hopping

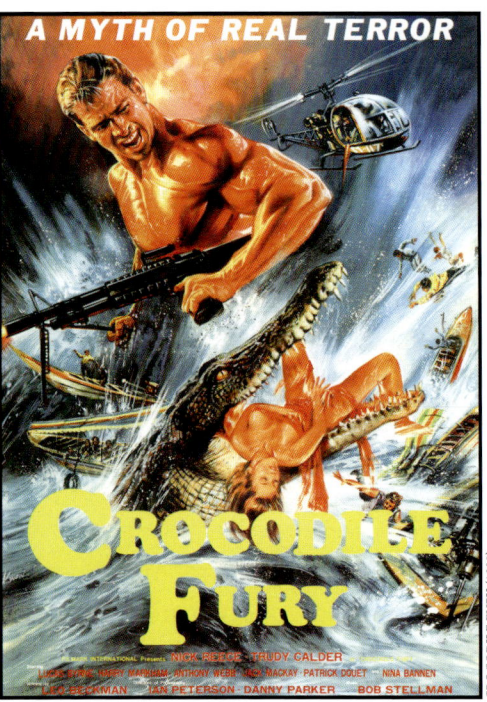

CROCODILE FURY (1988)

variety, while others are more like zombie-vamps with green blood. Oh . . . and the crocodiles are actually the spirits of people who have become reptiles, so they often appear in human form too!

The croc footage stems from a Thai film directed by Sompote Sands, called *Krai Thong 2* (1985), and the main crocodile, though not exactly a Hollywood-standard animatronic creation, is a pretty serviceable full-size model that munches down on many, many extras. The low-tech attack scenes actually possess a pacy verve, as loads of people run, shout and get bitten or carried away. One of the reasons these reptile assaults stand out is because they are never isolated incidents: the various crocs don't bother waiting around to pick off lone victims, they launch onslaughts against groups of people near their homes or at riverside markets. Most of these attacks involve the actors struggling in the reptile's jaws, but there's one particular scene that is quite gory, with limbs being bitten off, and I'm sure actual amputees were cast to portray these legless or armless victims. The film focuses more on the crocodile spirits in their human form later in the story, mainly based in the golden cave, referred to as Sea World. This is the location where two croc-demon guys, one called Donald and the other named Stephen, fight one another, with Stephen hurling small, stuffed-looking crocodiles at Donald!

The film reaches dual climaxes, one involving a croc-fighting hero with a special spear & dagger, the other finale boasting a showdown between Thompson, vampires, and witch-lady Monica, who suddenly develops a fake-looking, throbbing belly, from which bursts a slimy human head!

This Tomas Tang production, often mistakenly credited as a Godfrey Ho film, is utterly batshit crazy, filled with so much incident, including a croc biting the head off a water buffalo, a machine gun assassination attempt, and a crocodile with diamond teeth, that the film actually makes other cut-and-paste epics like *Scorpion Thunderbolt* (1988) look like coherent, perfectly normal movies in comparison!

CURSE (1985)

Starring Li Sua, Kwan Hoi-San, Fang Yeh, Chang Hoi
Directed by Pang Ling
Artview Investment Co. Ltd

This is a pretty outlandish offering centered around the travails (and then some) of Rila, a young woman who suffers the misfortune of being the reincarnation of Sara, an evil sorceress, cursed for all eternity with something rather more than plain bad luck. Her tormentor is the reincarnation of Sara's old foe and, boy, does this one bear grudges! Rila promptly has ten husbands die on her, all through sexual exhaustion it would seem, and becomes a hooker and single mum—but her luck seems to be changing when she meets a pleasant chap who wants to marry her, were it not for the fact that Rila is being nightly ravished by ghosts. Realizing this could put a strain on any future wedded bliss, Rila visits the obligatory venerable old monk who, after an effects-filled dust-up, seems to have banished the curse . . . or has he?

Pretty damn tawdry at times (Rila takes more showers than you'd think were artistically necessary), *Curse* does have a script that includes interesting information on the myths and practices of Chinese witchcraft.

CURSE OF EVIL (1982)
Starring Tai Liang-Chun, Ai Fei, Lily Li, Wang Lai, Eric Chan, Yu Tsui-Ling
Directed by Kuei Chih-Hung
Shaw Brothers

The story takes place in a mansion in a quiet back alley, where the members of the dysfunctional Shi family and their servants act very superstitiously on the 1st and 15th day of each month, because this is when freaky stuff can happen, due to the fact that thirteen members of the family were killed by bandits and thrown into a dry well many years ago. When a weird, pink, toothy "bloody frog" is encountered, this is seen as a bad omen for sure, as this amphibian always presages ominous events. Terrible things do begin to happen, with a slimy, horned monster crawling out of the well, intent on raping and killing.

Kuei Chih-Hung, director of luridly memorable Hong Kong horror opuses like *The Boxer's Omen, Corpse Mania, Bewitched,* and *The Killer Snakes,* clearly decided not to hold back when making this demented, gooey weird-fest, choosing to merge murder mystery plotting with creature feature imagery, adding exploitative sexual abuse scenes to make the movie that little bit more sleazy.

The story somehow manages to combine: a subplot involving certain relatives trying to kill off the Shi family's wheelchair-bound matriarch (Lai) in order to inherit her house, footage of a demon-headed well-monster with two tentacles instead of hind legs that sexually assaults its female

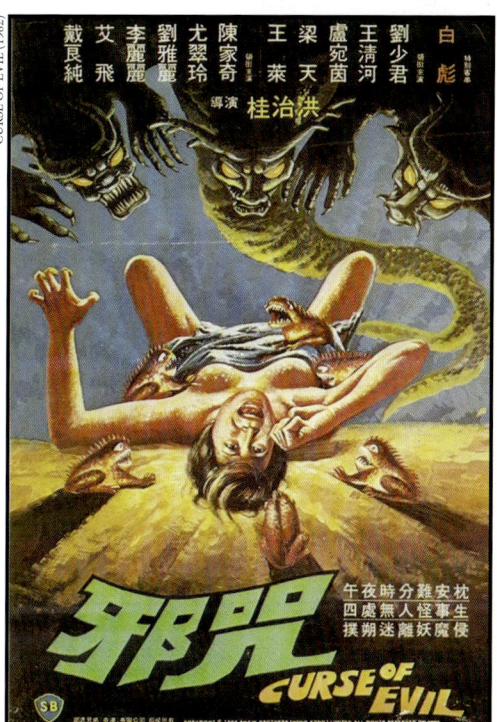

CURSE OF EVIL (1982)

victims and kills them with its flesh-ripping steel teeth, shots of a mystery figure secretly feeding offal to a pit full of spiky bloody frogs, and scenes of abusive cousin Jinhua (Fei) hypnotising one of the maids so that he can have sex with her, resulting in an unwanted pregnancy. As you can see from this list of unhinged elements, Kuei Chih-Hung obviously believes that enough is never enough!

We get close-ups of the tentacle-monster's extendable appendage as it sucks out the eyeballs of elderly manservant Quan and see the critter cover its female victims with pink, gelatine-like slime . . . and yet . . . it's eventually revealed that this beast is actually fake, just a guy in a suit! This is all an elaborate setup, of course, involving fake identities, obscure secondary characters and the matriarch herself, who is not really disabled and can become an unstoppable maniac . . . until she is beheaded! The unimaginably preposterous denouement would have us believe that all of the strange happenings were fabricated and nothing supernatural actually occurred, yet the film never provides a real-world explanation for the existence of the flesh-eating bloody frogs, which chow down on several people, including a bound-up maid. Did these amphibians mutate purely because they were fed lots of offal? Does it matter, really? This is a loopy film where logic takes a backseat, so that the director can focus on extremely crazy stuff like a mad granny secretly sewing costumes for a kid's skeleton in the attic, perverted amateur hypnotism, and outrageously far-fetched murder schemes.

DANCES WITH SNAKES (1993)
Starring Tsui Man-Wah, Fan Lai-Chau, Dick Wei, Wong Shun-Kwan
Directed by Lee Kin-Hing
Produced by Wong Tak-Lung
Action by Wong Shun-Kwan
New Sam Po Film

Expecting a rip-off of a certain Kevin Costner flick? Bad luck. Then again, if you fancy a smutty period romp focusing on a trio of comely serpent-women out to suck the essence of a Christian missionary, then you came to just the right place!

The sexy threesome are engaged in perpetual struggle with a nasty monster dude, who craves their own special essence. Things become more complex when they happen upon a rich tavern owner, who, having worn out his member in four-girl naked oil-wrestling orgies, allows them shelter and the pick of any passing virgin males, whose essences they require to fight their monster foe.

Where things get really deranged is when two Christian missionaries arrive, a Westerner and Richard, who is the anglicized brother of the impotent host. Richard is revealed to have revitalizing properties stashed between his legs, and the movie gets back to being a whole lot of silly, saucy fun, which is the level at which it operates best.

Wholly recommended, with the Hermit Tim gag worth the admission alone.

THE DEAD AND THE DEADLY (1982)
Starring Sammo Hung, Wu Ma, Lam Ching-Ying, Cherie Chung
Directed by Wu Ma
Produced by Raymond Chow and Sammo Hung
Action by Sammo Hung, Yuen Biao, Lam Ching-Ying, Billy Chan
Golden Harvest/Bo Ho Film Company Ltd

A supernatural pic starring Sammo Hung, who allows a ghost to enter his body so it can take revenge upon its murderers, but the ghost has to flee Sammo's body when a woman puts her knickers on his head!

Knickers, of course, are a way of protecting yourself from spirits in Chinese movies! In *The Haunted Cop Shop* (1987), for instance, the heroes become invisible to a vampire because they put their underpants on their heads! Anyway, back to this movie: the finale has Sammo's wife attempting to get Sammo's own life force, which is being watched over by three ghost guards, back into his body. The ghost guards are fed on wine and eggs, which sends them to sleep, then Sammo's spirit appears as an insect, which his wife wraps up in a sanitary towel so the guards can't detect it! The reawakened, angry guards transform into cel-animated incorporeal spirits, but are trapped by the wife in a blocked-off chimney, thus saving Sammo—until he has a child . . .

Sammo Hung's performance recaptures the magic displayed in *Encounters of the Spooky Kind* (1980), making this a must for followers of Sammo's brand of Hong Kong action-fantasy flick.

DEADFUL MELODY (1994)
Starring Yuen Biao, Brigitte Lin, Carina Lau, Wu Ma, Lam Wai, Chung Fat
Directed by Ng Min-Kan
Super Class Production Ltd

This is an enjoyable but hopelessly convoluted tale of a magic lyre—a Chinese harp—which causes wholesale destruction in the right hands. A kung fu master and his wife are killed when they try to protect the lyre, but their children survive. Their daughter becomes a revenge-obsessed witch, in whose skilled hands the lyre is a deadly weapon. Their son Lun (Biao), who has no idea who his real family are, is adopted by the head of a security firm.

Lun accepts the task of delivering the lyre to kung fu master Hon Suen (Fat), not realizing that he will be ambushed on all sides by the heads of the six schools, all of whom want to wield the power of the lyre for their own ends.

Sounds simple so far? Well, on his journey Lun is attacked continually, aided by a female student of one of the weird kung fu masters, who ends up falling for him even though she set out to steal the lyre. He is also helped by a mysterious, androgynous figure (Lin), who turns out to be his sister in disguise. But when he finally delivers the lyre to Hon Suen, he discovers the case in fact contains the head of Hon Suen's cowardly son! It turns out he has been duped into gathering the six kung fu masters together by none other than . . . his sister! The stage is set for a major showdown between Lun's sister and her supernatural weapon, and Ghost Master (Wai), the spooky ringleader of the bad bunch.

Lun, meanwhile, must choose a side, but that's not so easy when all he wants is to see an end to the ceaseless revenge killings. After the umpteenth wire-aided aerial fight, it's tempting to just give up on the plot, which is no great loss, and sit back to enjoy the spectacle. Although the wirework is excessive and the fighting not really that exceptional, there are some funny moments, notably an ingenious beheading that leaves the victim with a pretty surprised expression on his face!

DEADLY SNAIL VS KUNG FU KILLERS (1977)

Starring Candice Yu, Tony Wong, Little Unicorn, Tien Ching
Directed by Heung Ling
Spring Film Company/Chyo Tare Film Company

Nice guy Cheng Fu (Wong), who his bullied by his uncle's family, picks up a sea snail shell, takes it home, and has a dream, in which a small fairy implores him to drip some blood into the shell. Cheng Fu wakes from his dream and does, indeed, dribble some blood from his finger into the snail's shell.

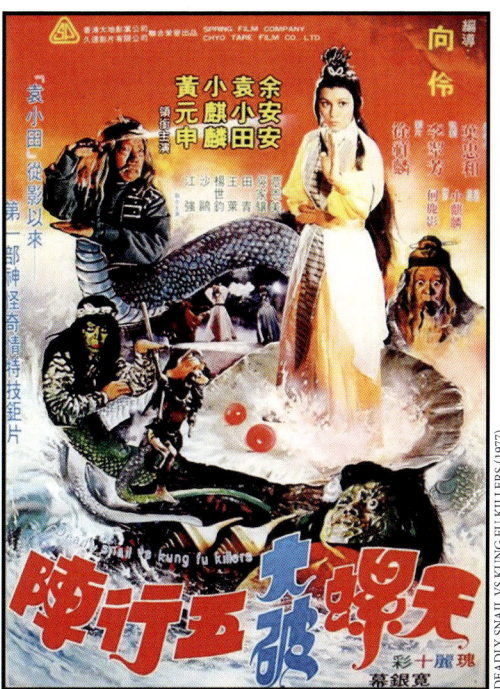

DEADLY SNAIL VS KUNG FU KILLERS (1977)

The snail fairy, now in the form of an attractive woman (Yu), falls in love with Cheng Fu, starts providing him with lovely meals, then magically tidies-up and repairs the shack-like home that his mean-spirited uncle has banished him to. The mollusc fairy and Cheng Fu eventually decide to get married. Ah, how sweet!

But the couple must deal with Cheng Fu's nasty relatives, especially a slimy, obnoxious cousin (Ching), who hires thugs to kidnap the fairy. The pair also come under threat from a snake demon villain (Unicorn), who can take on the form of an actual snake, a larger (puppet) serpent, a frog-eating monk or a snake-human.

The very cheap budget means that the snake-human is basically actor Little Unicorn with face makeup of the standard seen at a children's birthday party, the trick effects are achieved by such simple methods as double exposure, music is "borrowed" from various movies, including *King Kong* (1976) and *Carrie* (1976), and the undersea world of the snail fairies is a realism-free set with lots of bubbles floating about in it.

A moderately interesting moment involves Cheng Fu becoming a skilled fighter when his fairy love's spirit enters his body, enabling him to beat his adversaries using different styles of kung fu, plus there's a diverting sequence in a theatrical-looking cavern, where the snail fairy's two sisters combat several supernatural demon fighters, including a gold dude, a red dude and a "wood" dude, who creaks when he moves and can transform into multiple flying logs.

Extreme money limitations, however, mean that what ends up on-screen definitely fails to do justice to the ideas, but the tale is actually quite charming in a fairy tale kind of way, ensuring that you keep watching as the put-upon hero and his snail fairy bride overcome all obstacles and live happily ever after.

DEMON OF THE LUTE (1983)

Starring Chin Siu-Ho, Kara Wai, Philip Kwok, Kei Kong-Hung, Jason Pai Piao, Yuen Tak, Lung Tien-Hsiang
Directed by Lung I-Sheng
Shaw Brothers

Feng Ling (Wai) is sent by her master to locate the special fiery bow and arrows, which are the only treasures that can stop a mystery villain from using the lethal Six-Stringed Demonic Lute to wreak havoc everywhere. Along the way she teams up with her brother Old Naughty (Tak), a likeable thief (Kwok) and his son, a good guy called Yuan Fei (Siu-Ho) and a powerful martial artist known as the Woodcutter (Tien-Hsiang).

This fantasy wuxia is lots of fun, crammed with loads of exotic characters. Let's look at just some of them: there's Red Haired Evil, who rides a small chariot drawn by German shepherd dogs and hurls his Thunder Flying Wheel weapon like a frisbee, Eagle Man, who can flap his costume's wings to fly like a bird, Skinny Elf, who has a misshapen forehead and likes to sit on people's shoulders, Long Limb Evil, who can super-extend his arm, and Fatty Elf, who can entangle folks in his lengthy beard.

Utter strangeness abounds throughout this production, with warriors erupting from a giant silver ball, Feng Ling using her rainbow sword like a guided missile, a horseless wagon whizzing around with the deadly lute inside, some trees momentarily becoming monsters, Old Naughty riding his horse backward and a kitschy killer lute that glows with LED strip lights when it's played.

Though some of the music and on-screen antics become rather too childish, *Demon of the Lute* has much to offer, including Kei Kong-Hung, who's surprisingly good as the thief's plucky young son Xiao Ding Dong.

DESCENDANT OF THE SUN (1983)
Starring Yee Tung-Shing, Cherie Chung, Ku Kuan-Chung, Lung Tien-Hsiang, Ai Fei
Directed by Chor Yuen
Shaw Brothers

Shue Sang is found as a baby in an ice cave and later discovers that he is actually Yuen Ying (Tung-Shing), a being from the Da Lor fairyland, a place situated between the spiritual and physical worlds. Imbued with special powers, he falls in love with a princess (Chung) and battles an evil villain, also originating from Da Lor fairyland, who has reincarnated on Earth.

There are the usual spacious Shaw Brothers sets on view, but these don't really make up for the shoddy direction and lackluster action choreography. Some of the effects are pretty poor too, including store-bought dolls on wires used to represent transcendence.

Even so, there's stuff that keeps you watching, like the unexpected, ghoulish introduction of the Intelligent Kingdom, where babies on conveyer belts are checked

over and, if it's deemed their brains are too small, are nonchalantly tossed away into a furnace! Plus, there's Yuen Ying's bizarre powers including the ability to turn into a giant pair of scissors, duplicate himself and transform into a large axe to chop down the villain, who has transformed into a monster tree!

It's also fun to see a Chinese mythological riff on the Superman/Clark Kent/Lois Lane story, complete with a clumsy alter ego for the hero and his own version of the Fortress of Solitude.

If nothing else, *Descendant of the Sun* really pulls out all the stops for an ending chock-full of cel-animated hand beams, flame-breathing, flying, stormy winds and an attack by ghostly corpses that chew on the golden-garbed hero before they all explode. This finale is not quite well enough done but, damn it, the result overflows with a crazed energy that manages to make it entertaining anyway!

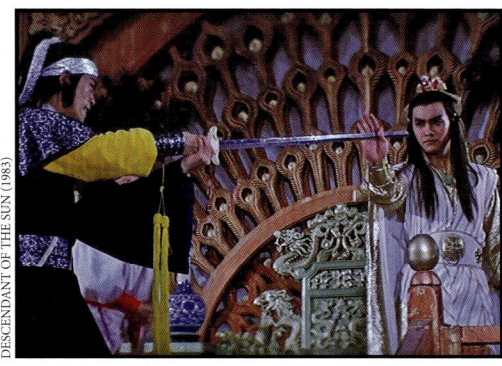

DESCENDANT OF THE SUN (1983)

DEVIL FETUS (1983)
Starring Eddie Chan, Leung San, Lau Dan, Au-Yang Sha-Fei
Directed by Liu Hung-Chuen
Produced by Lo Wei
Action by Mai Kei
Lo Wei Motion Picture Company

Possessions, supernatural occurrences and death await a rich family following the purchase of a jade vase.

The somewhat phallic-looking ornament, which is smashed early on in the movie, is really just an excuse for a string of occult happenings, including levitation, the vomiting of birthday cake and worms, the eating of a recently exhumed dog's guts, and rape by a white-haired, slimy demon. As the title suggests, there is the brief shot of a green fetus-thingy bursting from a dead woman's stomach, plus a face-ripping that reveals maggots beneath the flesh and the bravura on-screen head-crushing of one of the characters trapped in a shrinking room.

The standard of the special FX varies: a shot of a holy man, who is twisted into the earth by grasping hands, is achieved simply by using double-exposed images, as are shots of the possessed younger son gliding about the place. However, the scene of the son splitting in two down the middle, as a demon bursts out of him, is a novel effect. This devil critter is beheaded almost immediately and, in a show-stopping example of Hong Kong weirdness, a succession of human heads on long necks streak from a severed neck, followed by a fountain of fluid! After an *Evil Dead*-style shot of the demon head decomposing (via jerky animation), the toothy skull zips toward the camera for a freeze-frame ending.

Making little sense, this film becomes more and more ludicrous, but it remains an enjoyable spectacle throughout, eschewing the usual Hong Kong filmmaking tendency to include comedic interludes.

DEVIL GIRL 18 (1993)

Starring Mark Cheng, Woo Fung, Ga Ling,
Yukari Oshima
Directed by Lam Wah-Chuen
Toy Hing Films

Pretty lowbrow fare, *Devil Girl 18* is a cheapie sexploitationer that throws in a pinch of Taoist numerology to inflate a somewhat limp tale of horny demons assuming human form to better enjoy the pleasures of the flesh, a state they can only maintain by capturing the essences of fifty souls, all of them belonging to victims born on 6/6/66 (the "Extreme of Masculinity") or 9/9/69 (ditto for femininity), a device which, remarkably, means all are young, good-looking and more than capable of submitting to carnal advances—what a surprise!

The bulk of *Devil Girl 18* relies more on cheap thrills, cheap laughs (such as armored bras, oversized male appendages, AIDS gags) and even cheaper filmmaking: watch out for the sudden explosion of stock footage flashback exposition!

Though the film obviously has very low aspirations, and Yukari Oshima only appears briefly in a cameo, there are a few things to pique the interest, notably the Taoist exorcist who, for reasons best known to himself, dresses like Lee Van Cleef cruising a gay bar, plus the curious sight of a pinup picture in the bordello of none other than British topless model Samantha Fox. Mind you, noticing something like that surely speaks volumes about *Devil Girl 18* itself . . .

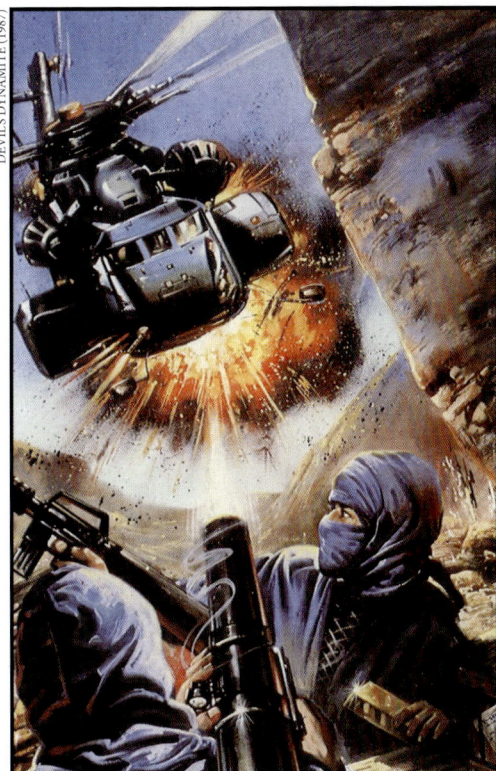

DEVIL'S DYNAMITE (1987)

DEVIL'S DYNAMITE (1987)

Directed by "Joe Livingstone"
Starring Suen Kwok-Ming, Sun Chien,
Wang Kuan-Hsiung, Angela Mao
Produced by Tomas Tang
Filmark International Ltd

Newly shot footage of hopping vampires, a silver-suited hero called Shadow Warrior and various ninjas is intercut into an older gambling movie called *Giant of Casino*, which features Angela Mao and Wang Kuan-Hsiung. The freshly concocted plot involves blue-faced vampires used as part of a smuggling operation and ninjas sent on a mission to eliminate Steve Cox, the Gambling King.

Points of interest include ninjas getting turned into grinning hopping vampires, Shadow Warrior using a bell to distract a bunch of bouncing vampires during a breakneck skirmish, a holy man performing a ceremony to heal injured vamps that seems to involve sticking sparklers into them, and a voodoo doll used to control a priest.

Just as this film seems to be on the verge of being almost coherent, the movie cuts to a shot

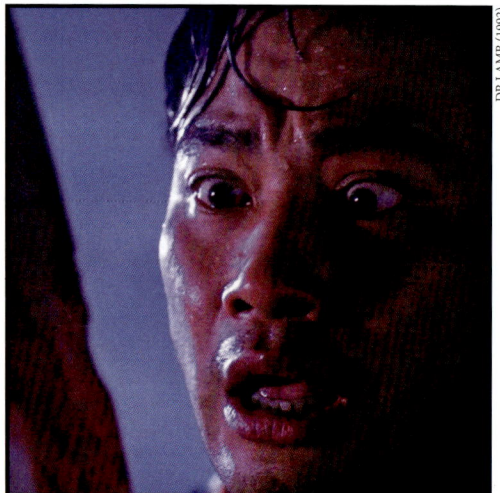

DR. LAMB (1992)

of a ghost girl skipping, before jumping back to more Shadow-Warrior-versus-vampires action. Alex, aka Shadow Warrior, undergoes a ceremony involving a yellow-robed priest painting special symbols on his torso and then throwing shrine dolls into his body. Alex becomes a more powerful version of the helmeted Shadow Warrior and, at one point, with the help of the priest, starts doing some moonwalking, before he batters his vampire foes with explosive punches and kicks!

Often erroneously listed as a Godfrey Ho opus (nobody seems to know who definitely directed it, perhaps it was Tommy Cheng), this cut-and-paste Tomas Tang production is a cheap, cheesy, cheerful challenge to every viewer's sense of narrative logic. This brain-blaster is also known as *Devil Dynamite* and, cheekily, *Robo Vampire 2: Devil's Dynamite,* obviously in an attempt to pass off silver-garbed hero Shadow Warrior as the infamous "Robo-Warrior."

DR. LAMB (1992)
Starring Simon Yam, Danny Lee, Kent Cheng, Eric Kei
Directed by Danny Lee
Produced by Danny Lee
Grand River Film Ltd/Heroes United Films Ltd

This is based on the true story of a Hong Kong taxi driver, who, while working nights, cruised the streets preying upon young girls. After murdering them, he took photographs of their mutilated bodies, and he might still have been at large if he had not taken his prints to be developed in a nearby photo store! The assistant, horrified by what he saw, contacted the local

police. The story was front-page news in all the Hong Kong newspapers and led to a TV movie called *Hong Kong Criminal Archives—Female Butcher,* which told the gruesome story of the killer, portrayed by Simon Yam, who reprises the role for this Danny Lee movie.

Dr. Lamb is definitely not for the squeamish, with the camera showing every nauseating detail of the crimes during flashbacks, which unfold as the killer is interrogated. The film is sometimes hilarious, sometimes revolting, and Simon Yam is excellent as the psychotic murderer, another in his series of deranged killer portrayals!

DON'T STOP MY CRAZY LOVE FOR YOU (1993)
Starring Simon Yam, Michael Wong, Yvonne Yung Hung, Law Lan
Directed by Hon Wei Tat
Golden Power Productions

This is a film with a deceptive title, indicating a tale of softcore passion, but it turns out to be a sexploitationer, with Simon Yam playing Fred Suen, a disturbed and obsessive fan pursuing TV presenter Kitty (Yvonne Yung Hung), who has played more than his fair share of jittery sleazeballs, gets down to business as Fred the

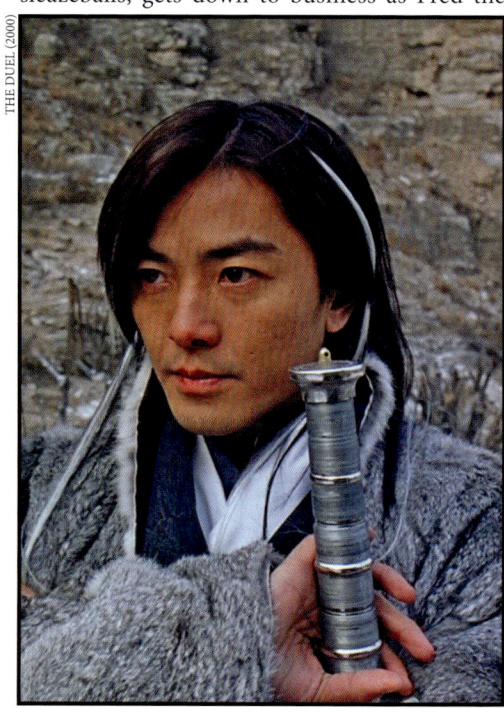

THE DUEL (2000)

psycho, who is in a room with a view of Kitty, using a telescopic lens so that he doesn't miss her undressing. He also has a dummy replica of her, which he writhes around on the bed with, whispering sweet nothings about his crazy love . . .

When Fred meets Kitty and her lover at a gun club, things get really out of hand. Soon she is receiving strange phone calls, but when she decides to improve home security, she goes to a firm run by Fred himself! This culminates in the gruesome murder of her fiancé and a climactic scene which will have all but the most insensitive squirming in disbelief.

The film makes up for its small quota of shocks with an unrelentingly oppressive atmosphere and the convincing, unhinged performance from Yam, who is Hong Kong's equivalent of Anthony Perkins.

THE DUEL (2000)

Starring Andy Lau, Nick Cheung, Ekin Cheng, Zhao Wei, Kristy Yeung
Directed by Andrew Lau
China Star Entertainment/Win's Entertainment Ltd/B.O.B. and Partners

Imperial Agent Dragon 9 must deal with the events leading up to a duel between top-fighters Cool-Son Yeh and Simon the Snow Blower atop the Forbidden City. Bets are made and everyone wants an invite to the much-anticipated clash, but is there more to this face-off than just a fight to see who's best?

As with Andrew Lau's *The Storm Riders* (1998), the warriors in this movie can fly, spin very fast, levitate, and use super-skills like "Telepathic Microsteps" and "Buddha's Pointer."

Highlights include Simon the Snow Blower's scrap with living terra-cotta warriors, Dragon 9's gadget-filled umbrella and a sequence in a pit equipped with dart-firing booby traps, scorpions, and closing walls.

Nick Cheung is an easygoing, fun lead as the dreadlocked Imperial Agent Dragon 9, Zhao Wei is appealingly quirky as lovelorn Princess Phoenix, Andy Lau, as Cool-Son Yeh, is his usual suave self, playing a half-royal coup-planner who likes to make impressive entrances as maidens and dragons float in orange-tinted clouds, and Ekin Cheng is chilled and restrained as Simon the Snow Blower.

More should have been done with the climactic duel after all the buildup, but this wuxia fantasy-adventure is laced with humor, is easy on the eye and is always watchable, though it is not quite as fantastical or exciting as it should have been.

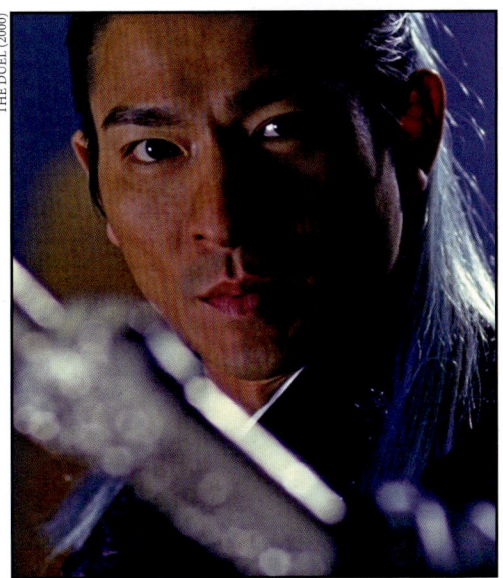

THE DUEL (2000)

EBOLA SYNDROME (1996)

Starring Anthony Wong, Marianne Chan, Wong Tsui-Ling, Shing Fui-On
Directed by Herman Yau
Jing's Production

Kai (Wong) leaves Hong Kong after a confrontation with his boss turns into a multiple homicide, moves to South Africa and gets a low-paid restaurant job. After raping an infected tribeswoman during a visit to a Zulu village to buy pig meat with his new boss, Kai contracts Ebola, becomes a carrier of the disease, and eventually heads back to Hong Kong after yet another brief murder spree at the restaurant. Back in his home city, Kai unknowingly spreads Ebola to prostitutes and then hooks up with his ex-wife, but he's been recognized by a woman he attempted to burn alive years ago . . . and now the police are focused on catching him.

Yikes, where to begin with this CAT III sleaze-fest?! Well, let's start with the film's opening, in which Kai is caught having sex with his boss' wife, is beaten up by the angry husband and one of his goons, is urinated on by the fretful wife and is threatened with castration. Kai retaliates, using pruning shears and a folding table to attack his abusers, with the situation getting very bloody as he smashes the boss to a pulp and cuts off the wife's tongue with the hand pruners! Just when you think this introductory sequence can't get any nastier, Kai spots the boss' young daughter cowering in another room, ties her up and pours petrol over her! Fortunately for her, Kai is forced to escape the apartment before he can immolate the child.

Anthony Wong, star of infamous CAT III classic *The Untold Story* (1992), cements his claim as king of lowlife, foul, reprehensible, murderous characters with this movie. In a string of awful acts, we see him: sexually assault an ill Zulu woman and bludgeon her to death with a rock after she sprays Ebola-spit into his face, use meat from the restaurant kitchen to masturbate into (and then serve to a customer later), suck out the eyeball of the restaurant owner's wife he has just raped, and kill his new boss by ramming toothpicks into his face. He is the scumbag of scumbags in this movie!

Kai dismembers his victim's bodies and, just like in *The Untold Story*, he uses the flesh as the secret ingredient in the "African Buns" he feeds to his clientele. Unlike *The Untold Story*, however, no attempt is made to tell this tale in a way that elicits any sympathy for Wong's character. Kai is a conscience-free psychopath with a bullying complex, lacking empathy for men, women, and children, reacting impulsively to satiate whatever urge he is currently feeling and violently striking out in confrontations that his own actions have instigated.

For the most part, the filmmakers are content to simply fill the movie with a string of grotesque, violent and sleazy sequences, but they do try to inject some tension into the plot once Kai flees back to Hong Kong and reunites with his wife and daughter. Here we get a series of scenes in which Kai almost infects his wife and child when he sneezes, then nearly passes on the virus to them by sharing food, etc., and all the while we are shown the Ebola particles in close-up, floating around inside his mouth! As this is a CAT III film starring Anthony

Wong, Kai's unfortunate family doesn't stand a chance, with the wife dying from Ebola and the daughter getting strangled accidentally by Kai during a face-off with the police, in a finale that has Kai spitting Ebola into the faces of anyone who gets close to him!

Featuring shots of frogs and chickens being killed for real, casually racist dialogue, plus a graphic, skin-peeling autopsy scene, *Ebola Syndrome* sets out to be an unapologetic, in-your-face CAT III exploitation flick . . . and succeeds.

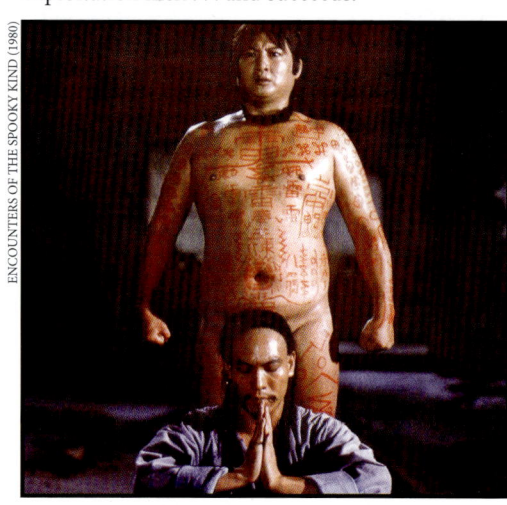

ENCOUNTERS OF THE SPOOKY KIND (1980)

ENCOUNTERS OF THE SPOOKY KIND (1980)
Starring Sammo Hung, Chung Fat, Wu Ma,
Lam Ching-Ying, Chan Lung
Directed by Sammo Hung
Produced by Raymond Chow
Action by Sammo Hung, Yuen Biao
Golden Harvest/Bo Ho Film Company Ltd

Sammo Hung has been immortalised in many classic martial arts films, and his switch from traditional kung fu to fantasy-horror confirmed him as probably one of the best all-rounders in Hong Kong cinema.

In this film Sammo plays Bold Cheung, whose speciality is sleeping overnight in haunted houses. His wife, who is having an affair, decides to rid herself of Cheung and hires a Taoist priest to lure him into a trap, which will either scare him to death or result in Cheung being killed by corpses. Luckily, a rival to the priest discovers the evil plan and decides to help Cheung battle the corpses.

Sammo blends his kung fu mastery with effects and horror, making this the perfect crossover movie,

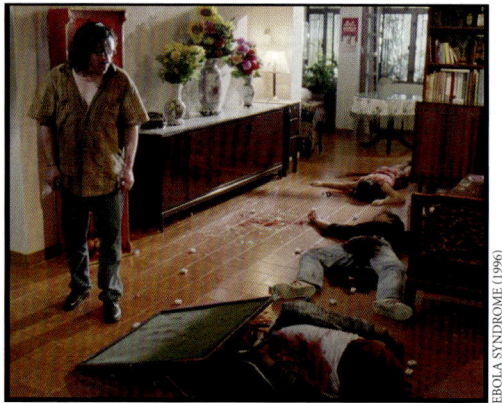

EBOLA SYNDROME (1996)

with lots of classic hopping vampire action. The film broke new ground in Hong Kong cinema, leading to many other horror-fantasy-comedies, including *The Dead and the Deadly*, the *Mr. Vampire* series and an excellent sequel to this movie.

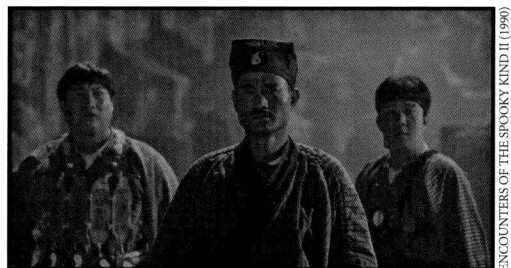

ENCOUNTERS OF THE SPOOKY KIND II (1990)

ENCOUNTERS OF THE SPOOKY KIND II (1990)
Starring Sammo Hung, Meng Hoi, Lam Ching-Ying
Directed by Ricky Lau
Action by Sammo Hung
Bojon Films Company Ltd

Sammo Hung returns for this enjoyable follow-up, this time becoming friends with a female ghost and wreaking havoc in the spiritual world as he contends with yet another evil Taoist priest.

Along with Meng Hoi and Lam Ching-Ying (in full vampire-buster mode), Sammo takes on kung fu mummies, cockroach-filled zombies, demons, possessions and, in an incredible all-out fight finale, two highly skilled fighting snake men.

Also known as *Spooky Encounters*, this is an entertaining blend of humor, martial arts fantasy and supernatural shenanigans.

EROTIC GHOST STORY (1990)
Starring Amy Yip, Man So, Hitomi Kudo, Tan Lap-Man, Manfred Wong, Chan Wai-To
Directed by Nam Nai-Choi
Diagonal Pictures

The movie that sired a trilogy is a tackily lavish potboiler, centered around three pulchritudinous females and their sex-filled encounters with a supposed scholar, who turns out to be none other than the god Wu Tung, who is one extremely horny little devil indeed.

Our heroines are actually wolves in petticoats: shapeshifting "fairies" who are determined to stay pure for 36 days in order to achieve immortal human forms. It's a process you just know is about to come

unglued when a Taoist warns against "lustful thoughts" and, shortly thereafter, the girls discover Wu Ming (Lap-Man), a humble shack-dwelling scholar. They take him, rather too literally, to their bosom, which is when the film's obvious selling-point comes to the fore, amid oodles of sensual writhing, allowing all performers to display their, um, talents. Of course, no good is going to come from this, and it doesn't take long before Wu Ming's real identity is revealed in a crude but pretty deranged burst of special effects.

Though at times unevenly made, *Erotic Ghost Story* lives up to its billing and is pretty raunchy stuff, even for a CAT III. Okay, so there are moments that simply don't make sense, but with the largely undraped cast giving it their all, you might not be too bothered about that . . .

EROTIC GHOST STORY II (1991)
Starring Anthony Wong, Charine Chan, Ichijo Sayuri, Kwok Yiu-Wah, Tsang Siu-Yin, Amy Yip, Man So
Directed by Peter Ngor
Action by Kong To-Hoi, Tony Poon
Diagonal Pictures Ltd

If you missed part one, don't worry, as you get a full resumé of events to date before the credits and, thus, we learn that horny ol' devil Wu Tung (Wong) is now inhabiting the body of Chiu Sheng and seriously in love with the beautiful Hsiao Yen, a fellow spirit who hopes to reform the lustful demon of his satanic influences. A start could be made, we feel, with the guy's looks: with an obviously phallic tail and a humungous blond wig, the fellow looks like David Bowie's Goblin King character from *Labyrinth* on bad drugs! When Hsiao Yen gets rubbed out by a heavenly hit squad, Wu Tung soon reverts to type and sets up home in a cave with his new main squeeze, a slinky demoness with a passion for essence of virgin. This odd couple's needs are assuaged by the fearful local villagers, who sacrifice Wu Tung a monthly maiden to keep him sweet. However, after Hsiao Yen lookalike Yu-Yin escapes the demon's clutches and marries handyman Shan-Ken (Yiu-Wah), all hell breaks loose, as anarchic lust descends, courtesy of one mightily displeased Wu Tung, and we learn that Yu-Yin and Hsiao Yen might conceivably be related.

On a par with the original, nookie-wise, *Erotic Ghost Story II* benefits from a larger budget, some nifty FX-work and production values that strive for atmosphere along with the you-know-what. And, by the way . . . what is that guy doing with that pig?

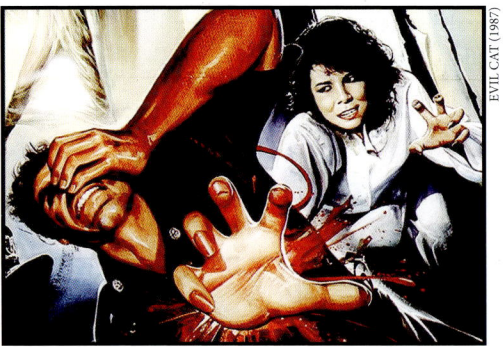

EVIL CAT (1987)

EROTIC JOURNEY (1993)
Starring Chan Wing-Chi, Cheng Yuk-Hing,
Wong Yuet-San, Melvin Wong, Dick Wei
Directed by Liu Kuo-Hsiung
Long Shong Pictures

Gangster and women-in-prison genres meet in this cheapie CAT III thriller about three girls in Thailand, who are in the wrong place at the wrong time during a drug bust, and end up in a remote prison run by sadistic prison wardens. Salvation lies with a permanently drunk doctor, who helps the trio (and the rest of the camp for that matter) to escape.

While sleaze fans will no doubt go for the various punishments meted out on our femmes, including liberal whippings and one poor gal forced to bite a snake's head off, those who appreciate really bad cinema will love the complete incoherency of the plot and the director's attempt to slot some really bad martial arts and gun battles into the storyline.

ESCAPE FROM BROTHEL (1992)
Starring Pauline Chan, Billy Chow, Sofia Crawford,
Rena Murakami, Alex Fong
Directed by Wang Lung-Wei
Produced by Hung Leung-Tak
Ocean Shores Entertainment

This is a sleazy Category III exploitation flick, focusing on a Happy Valley hooker, Hung (Chan), who is sold into prostitution to pay off her feckless husband's debt. Together with her "sister," Ann (Murakami), she endures the ceaseless attentions of lowlife clients, until her life is thrown into turmoil by the sudden arrival of her ex-boyfriend, Sam (Fong), with the mob and the cops hot on his tail. Sam is an escapee from the mainland, smuggled into HK to participate in a fake jewel heist, which is part of an underworld insurance scam. When the robbery

is bungled and a passerby is blown away, the mob demands Sam's head. Seeking refuge with true-love Hung, Sam discovers the sordid secret of her real profession and, though devastated, persuades Hung to flee to the mainland with him.

Consistently downbeat and often grimly nasty, this movie provides interesting, and sometimes poignant, comments on the exploitation of illegal immigrants by the Hong Kong underworld, all the while, of course, featuring enough sex and violence (naked kung fu, even!) to delight the most rabid Category III fan. There are several moments of jaw-dropping nastiness, involving electrocution and the improper use of a baseball bat, that push *Escape from Brothel* toward the realms of a genuine shocker.

ESPRIT D'AMOUR (1983)
Starring Alan Tam, Ni Shu-Chun, Philip Chan,
Tang Pik-Wan, Cecilia Yip
Directed by Ringo Lam
Cinema City

This Hong Kong fantasy-comedy flick, which was Ringo Lam's directorial debut, is an amiable affair, about a young insurance investigator, Chi Ming (Tam), who summons a recently dead girl with a Ouija board and falls in love with her.

Cute Ni Shu-Chun plays the ghost and, surprisingly, though the movie is a pretty generic supernatural

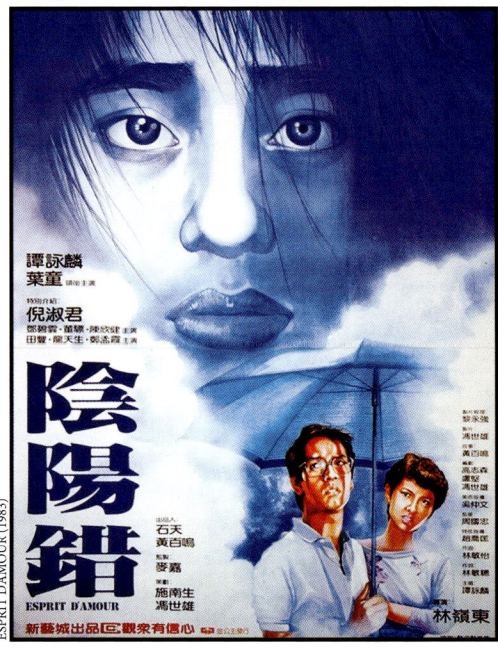

ESPRIT D'AMOUR (1983)

romance for the most part, it has a rather more serious finale, as an exorcist banishes the ghostly gal from the mortal world after much exploding glass and flames. Chi Ming attempts to help her, but fails as she is sucked away from him forever. Sob!

EVIL CAT (1987)
Starring Lau Kar-Leung, Tang Lai-Ying, Mark Cheng, Wong Jing, Hsu Shu-Yuan, Stuart Ong
Directed by Dennis Yu
Cinema City/Dennis Yu Film Production Company Ltd

An evil cat demon-spirit reappears every fifty years and a descendant of the demon-fighting Cheung family has always been there to combat it, in a cycle of events that spans the past 400 years. Now the final cat spirit has been set free on the Earth and Master Cheung, who is suffering from cancer, enlists the help of young chauffeur Ah Long (Cheng) to destroy the evil once and for all. Armed with a bow and three charmed arrows, Long & Cheung hunt down the energy-absorbing feline entity, which first possesses Long's boss Mr. Fan and then his personal assistant, Tina.

Evil Cat is standard 80s Hong Kong horror-fantasy fare, with the requisite amounts of humor, suspense,

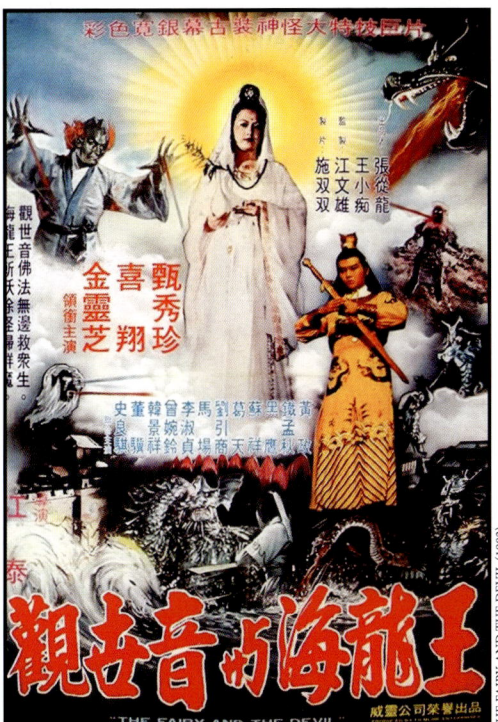

THE FAIRY AND THE DEVIL (1982)

and decent action scenes overseen by master martial arts director Lau Kar-Leung, who also plays spirit-fighter Cheung.

Written by Wong Jing, the film gains momentum once Tina (Shu-Yuan) gets possessed, triggering scenes in which she bites off the tongue of a pop star during sex in a car, rams her hand through a policeman's body, and withstands multiple gunshot hits when cops blast at her during an energetic police station rampage.

The plot's supernatural lore is patchy at best, with the cat-demon easily jumping from host to host, even when it is stabbed by the supposedly lethal magic arrows, but the movie doesn't worry itself too much about the fuzziness of its mythology, concentrating instead on supplying incident after incident, intent on reaching its climax, where the evil spirit finally reveals its true form: a pale, white-haired cat-woman.

Evil Cat doesn't really stick in the memory, but it is never dull and certainly passes the time nicely enough.

THE FAIRY AND THE DEVIL (1982)
Starring Chen Hsiu-Chen, Hsi Hsiang, Chin Ling-Chih, Hei Ying
Directed by Chiang Tai
Wai Leng Film Company

Yun Chung Lung, also known as Prince 3, is a golden dragon deity. He is banished to the human world as penitence for causing catastrophic flooding during a battle with another, evil dragon. Lung, now in human form and aided by a young, lovestruck couple, takes on the devils causing problems in the kingdom, including one flesh-hungry villain disguised as an ill, old lady.

Also known as *Mother Goddess Vs the Sea Demon*, this Taiwanese fantasy production uses stock footage from *The Founding of the Ming Dynasty* (1971) and *Exorcising Sword* (1975), plus music purloined from the likes of *Star Trek: The Motion Picture* (1979), and is of most interest when giant monsters take center stage. These creatures include a colossal, red-haired, fanged demon-dude with reptilian hands & feet, a massive white ape, two serpentine (marionette) dragons, a bat-eared lake monster that resembles a kind of gigantic gill-man, a large (puppet) cobra and a huge, humanoid monster with long white hair and bulging eyes. Oh, there are various giant, floating heads, too!

These beasties, mainly men-in-suit creations, possess varied powers, including the ability to breathe flame, shoot electrical power beams from their eyes and, at one point, flip from one monster form to another.

Miniature sets get flooded, animated energy bolts fill the screen, suicide is treated very lightly, the human drama moments tend to drag and, generally, the movie comes across as a cheap, sometimes plodding merging of fairy tale, sub-Toho kaiju flick and baffling mythological yarn.

FEARLESS KUNG FU ELEMENTS (1978)
Directed by Chen Chiu
Starring Chan Sing, Barry Chan,
Charlie Chin Chiang-Lin and Lin Ping

Five diverse characters, including a fighting femme restaurateur named Miss Lotus, an upbeat undertaker and a young warrior called Dragon, discover they are actually the children of the murdered Song Dynasty Emperor. They join forces with an old Song general and a monkey-man to seek their revenge against the current, very ruthless rulers, who are able to mobilise supernatural allies against the heroes, thanks to the fact the Empress (Ping) is actually a kind of wolf/ fox demon in disguise!

This cut-rate Taiwanese kung fu fantasy romp features such fantasy creatures as a friendly, white-furred monkey-guy with a blond hairdo, a fox demon that resembles a shoddy bear suit with a horse-like face, and a briefly seen orange-haired, horned

monster-dude. These critters are brought to life by guys in extremely crude costumes, while the other "demons" working for the villainess tend to be human-looking, with the ability to go transparent, disappear and reappear. At one point a squad of staff-wielding supernatural fighters wearing fur tunics are summoned to fight the heroes and, when they're killed, they become empty fur tunics lying on the ground.

The five heroes possess elemental powers, meaning they can emit fire or bursts of water, fly through the air, or crawl speedily through dirt and sand, but these powers are used rather sparingly. One dude even briefly hitches a ride on a big puppet bird.

This all sounds great, but the film's choppy editing makes some sequences downright confusing to follow and the budget is so very low the movie cannot hope to deliver the fantasy spectacle that the story requires. But, hey, it features a lot of fights!

FINGER OF DOOM (1972)
Starring Ivy Ling Po, Chin Han, Chen Feng-Chen,
Hung Sing-Chung, Tung Li
Directed by Pao Hsueh-Li
Shaw Brothers

A spike-fingered woman with black hair and white robes stabs men in the back of their necks with her poisoned metal talons, turning them into zombie-like minions, who dutifully carry her around in a coffin. Other men are also attacked, becoming members of the undead after their female assailant shoots metal pins into their necks. Meanwhile, three brothers decide to take on the local villains, including a hunchback and Chang Kung Chin, but two of the brothers are transformed into undead vassals, leaving just Lu Tien Bao to avenge them.

Interestingly, the spike-fingered woman is revealed to be the heroine, sleeping in her coffin merely to seem spooky, and the minions she has zombified are actually bad men. Her sister, however, is really nasty and will turn anyone into the living dead with her metal pins. Lu and the good sis join forces to rid the land of this evil, which is headquartered in the temple of Chang Kung Chin.

Atmospheric, evocatively lit sets and the story's horror trappings definitely help this early 70s Shaw Brothers wuxia stand out. I love the cheeky ending too, where the heroine finally tells Lu what her name is . . . but the shot freezes, so we never learn what she's called!

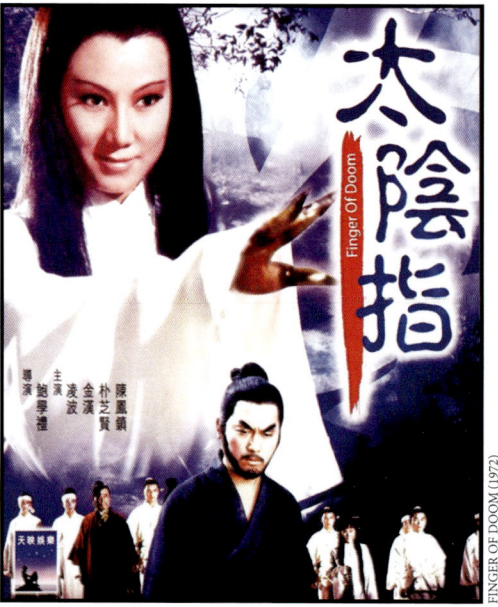

FINGER OF DOOM (1972)

FUNNY GHOST (1989)

Starring Chan Pak-Cheung, Sandra Ng, Elvina Kong,
Billy Lau, Wu Fung
Directed by Yuen Cheung-Yan
Action by Yuen Cheung Yan
D & B Films Co. Ltd

A hostess who comes into possession of a magic pot containing the ghost of a dead, pregnant Malaysian woman has various misadventures.

This comedy-fantasy starts with jokes about two girls attempting to commit suicide, goes on to show them using the magic pot to win at gambling, and reaches a climax in which the pot breaks, releasing the ghost.

Though she's portrayed as a vicious entity once freed from her container, one can't help but find the ghost's fate to be somewhat nasty: blood is dripped into the small pot which houses her unborn child's ghost, causing her stomach to expand until it explodes!

The film is very lightweight for the most part, although the final confrontation scene is just what you'd ask of a Hong Kong ghost pic.

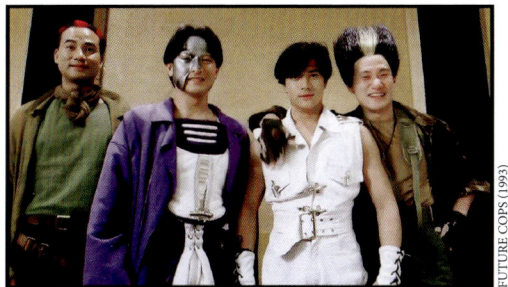

FUTURE COPS (1993)

FUTURE COPS (1993)

Starring Andy Lau, Simon Yam, Jacky Cheung,
Aaron Kwok, Richard Ng, Chingmy Yau,
Directed by Wong Jing
Produced by John Higgins
Action by Ching Siu-Tung
Fantasy Productions/Wong Jing's Workshop Ltd

Half a dozen of Hong Kong's leading male stars dress up as members of Capcom's *Street Fighter II* gang, with the good guys including Vega (Lau), Dhalsim (Yam), Guile (Cheung) and Ryu (Kwok).

The Future Cops come to do battle in the present day in the guise of schoolkids, who use their abilities to impress their classmates. The story, involving the heroes trying to prevent the bad guys from releasing their boss from prison, also features cameo appearances from that green bundle of fury Blanka (Ng) and a character who doesn't come from *Street*

Fighter II, but is popular in Hong Kong and Japan: Goku from the *Dragon Ball* franchise.

All in all, it's a video gamer's dream, and the next best thing to virtual reality. Attention was definitely paid to the skills of each character, although there are some slight name changes from the game. Wong Jing, who also directed *City Hunter*, another film featuring *Street Fighter* characters, handles this movie's special effects well. They are pretty impressive, actually, especially during the opening sequences and the finale, although much of the middle section is padded out, maybe to balance the budget.

Future Cops is a good idea, then, with a big cast, but it is lumbered with a plot urgently in need of propping up in the middle.

GHOST BALLROOM (1989)

Starring Gordon Liu, Tsui Siu-Keung, Tai Bo, Ngai Suet,
Ken Lo
Directed by Wilson Tong
Action by Wilson Tong
Attraction Film Co. Ltd

A murdered prostitute comes back as a ghost to take revenge on her killers.

The narrative leaves a lot to be desired, as the movie switches from one storyline (brothel bodyguard has to fight thugs) to another (taxi driver is cheated at cards), with the ghostly hostess' vengeance-seeking tale providing just one narrative thread in the film.

There is an attack by the ghost-girl's disembodied hand, some bonking in a swimming pool and some spectral vomiting, but, by and large, the patchy story ruins the movie's chances of becoming particularly memorable.

GHOST BUSTING (1989)

Starring Chan Pak-Cheung, Sandra Ng, Sharon Kwok,
Chingmy Yau
Directed by Lau Sze-Yue
Grand March Movie Production Company Ltd

A school for learning magic is threatened by a bunch of evil beings.

Together with lots of gags and pratfalls, the movie boasts some novel fantasy elements. For instance, a group of the students attempt to beat the supernatural foes by reincarnating into various "foreign gods." So, one by one, they turn into Chinese versions of Elvis, Charlie Chaplin, and Jesus . . . with the tune "Jesus Christ Superstar" playing in the background! The hero also turns into "Bruce Lee," complete with *Game of Death* orange tracksuit. The most imaginative reincarnation occurs when four of the students merge into one being: a multi-faced Hindu god. Neat idea!

One of the villains bares his torso to reveal a chest covered with screaming visages à la Freddy Krueger and another antagonist turns into a particularly nice cel-animated bat/ghost.

In one scene guaranteed to make you grimace, a guy in a bunk bed dreams of branding a chained-up girl while dressed up like Hitler . . . and as he enjoys his dream, he begins to dribble pints of spittle, which drips down into the mouth of the man sleeping in the bunk below him. Subtle Hong Kong humor at its best!

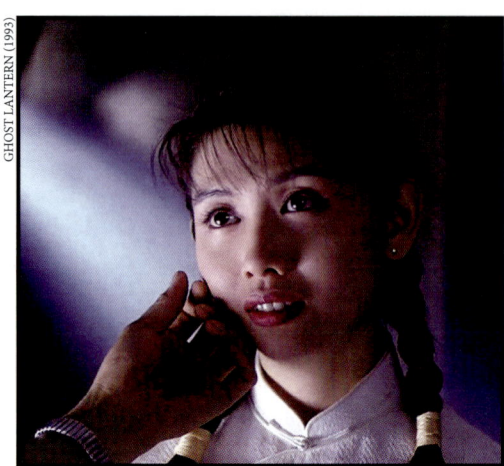

GHOST LANTERN (1993)

GHOST LANTERN (1993)
Starring Tony Leung Ka-Fai, Chingmy Yau, Roy Cheung
Directed by Andrew Lau
Produced by Wong Jing
Wong Jing's Workshop Ltd/Scholar Films Company

A young hawker (Leung) discovers that he is the reincarnation of an eminent lawyer, who, together with his young lover, was brutally murdered by a sadistic gangster and practitioner of the deadly Sun Ta (God skill). The girl's skin was stripped from her back and used to cover a lantern, thus keeping her soul trapped within, denying her the chance of reincarnation. The young hawker locates the whereabouts of the lantern and must face the sadistic maniac who keeps it, in a do-or-die battle of the supernatural.

Another excellent performance by Roy Cheung makes this supernatural offering better than it should be.

GHOST NURSING (1982)
Starring Tsui Siu-Keung, Shirley Yim, Melvin Wong,
Chin Yuet-Sang, Billy Chan
Directed by Wilson Tong
First Films

Jackie (Yim), distraught after her boyfriend is murdered by angry debt collectors, goes to Thailand, where she meets a Buddhist witch doctor, who suggests a morbid but highly effective remedy to bring her better luck. Jackie is given a jar containing a pickled foetus and is informed that she must pray and feed the foetus every day, and in return he will grant her every wish. Jackie takes the bottled foetus back

to Hong Kong and soon things start to work out for her, until, one day, she forgets to give it a drop of her blood. The devil child grows angry and gives Jackie a wicked warning not to forget his offering again. After a while, Jackie meets a nice guy called Raymond (Siu-Keung) and falls in love with him. The foetus gets extremely jealous of Raymond and taunts him in the most gruesome ways imaginable, forcing Jackie to confront the evil that she has nurtured so lovingly . . .

After a long and successful run in the kung fu genre, Wilson Tong tried his hand at horror with this film, with surprisingly decent results. *Ghost Nursing* has good performances from Shirley Yim and Tsui Siu-Keung (who actually got married shortly after making this picture) and boasts some quite decent special effects.

GHOSTLY LOVE (1989)
Starring Austin Wai, Emily Chu, Lam Wei,
Lung Tien-Hsiang, Mark Long
Directed by Chang Jen-Chieh
Winson Entertainment/Film City

Ghosts and fantasy have long been popular themes in Hong Kong cinema, but the Category III classification allowed directors and producers to take the underlying sensuality of the stories one step further, making the eroticism the main theme. This Taiwanese movie blends the erotic with visual effects and martial arts action to give a less restrained emphasis to the more familiar spiritual goings-on seen in movies like the *A Chinese Ghost Story* trilogy.

Some excellent supernatural battles, plus a lingering scene between Hui Tien Chee, his concubine, and a loofah, make for a most entertaining viewing!

GHOSTLY VIXEN (1990)

Starring Chan Pak-Cheung, Sandra Ng, Amy Yip, Wu Ma
Directed by Wellson Chin
Golden Flare Films Company

A female supernatural spirit from Thailand, enclosed in a mah-jongg tile, is taken to Hong Kong, where she attempts to find two virgin men born on a certain date. If she manages to give these final two men blow jobs (she's already given 98), she will gain an immortal body. A Thai wizard, dressed in black leather and chains, follows the spirit in order to destroy her with his glowing sword.

Trust a Hong Kong movie to have the accident-prone male virgin getting raped by two male robbers and treat it as a joke! The same man then develops a four-foot-long penis, thanks to a spell, which he has to strap to his leg until the spell is negated. His leg rises every time he sees an attractive girl!

This disjointed but watchable ghost comedy has very "Hong Kong" humor, with the ghost girl taking out her eyeballs, the main protagonist's penis turning into a flower, and similarly silly moments.

GREEN SNAKE (1993)

Starring Maggie Cheung, Joey Wong, Wu Kuo-Chiu,
Vincent Zhao, Wu Hsing-Kuo
Directed and produced by Tsui Hark
Seasonal Film Corporation/Film Workshop

Two women turn heads wherever they go, because of their astounding grace and beauty. But they conceal a bizarre secret: they are both really snakes who have learned to change their shape and pass as human. A naive scholar, Hsui Xien (Hsing-Kuo), falls in love with White Snake (Wong) and she seduces him, concealing her secret even though she is challenged by priests. Green Snake (Cheung), who is less practised at shape changing, is jealous and does her best to seduce Hsui Xien too, but, unlike her sister, she cannot feel human emotions. During the Dragon Boat Festival, Green Snake is forced to show her true shape and literally scares her sister's lover to death! The only cure is a special herb, but the way is blocked by Fa-Hai (Zhao), a priest whose self-appointed mission in life is to destroy all nonhumans. What follows is an epic battle between snakes and humans, with the elements utilized as magic weapons.

Tsui Hark, the master of Chinese fantasy, evokes an enchanting, erotically charged atmosphere here, with every scene stunning to look at. The plot is

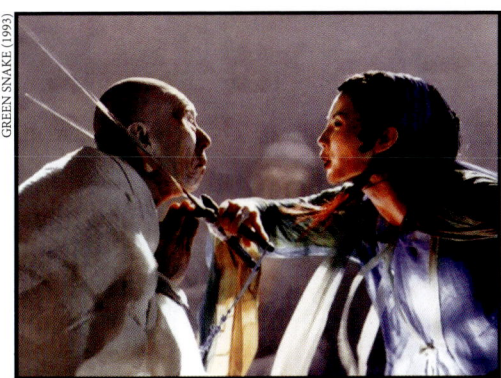

GREEN SNAKE (1993)

absorbing, and the two leading ladies shine as the seductive and mischievous snake sisters. A must-see movie for fantasy flick fans.

GUYS IN GHOSTS HAND (1991)

Starring Kara Wai, Ku Feng, Alex Fong, Wu Ma
Directed by Ma Shao-Wei
Tai Ying Audio Visual Company

Though it sometimes strays close to the realms of true Z-grade filmmaking, *Guys in Ghosts Hand* is never sufficiently inept to fall into the "so-bad-it's-good" category and, it being nowhere near good enough to be anything else, remains mired in a bog of turgid plot and pedestrian exposition that some low-rent special effects are never going to salvage.

This Taiwanese horror film begins promisingly enough, with the dismembered corpse of a long-murdered woman stalking the Hong Kong hills accompanied by its flying head, in search of revenge on her assassins' descendants. A few cases of vampirism later, the cursed family call in the exorcists, and the battle is joined. Now, all this could be plenty of fun, but it's hard to become engrossed after the umpteenth scene of the ghost stalking slowly through the woods toward some hapless victim, only for her then to dispatch said unfortunate soul in a manner that, frankly, wasn't worth the wait.

Once the evil is known to be at large, the exorcism team arrives and there's suddenly some hope that they, at least, will kick a little ass. They do, but only after they've sat around for ages discussing things, by which time the viewer really can't give a damn.

Students of Chinese exorcism techniques might like this, but the rest of us will simply yawn our way through a flick in which even a detailed discussion on the efficacy of urine types in combating demons fails to stir any interest. What a pity.

THE HAPPY GHOST (1984)
Starring Raymond Wong Pak-Ming, Bonnie Law,
Loletta Lee, Sandy Lamb, Teresa Carpio
Directed by Clifton Ko
Cinema City

Bonnie (Law) brings a ragged piece of rope back to her boarding school, unaware that a failed Ching Dynasty scholar called Pik (Pak-Ming) had used this noose to hang himself . . . and his soul still lurks within the rope! After being initially scared by the somewhat nerdy-looking ghost, Bonnie becomes friends with Pik, who aids and hinders Bonnie and her friends Juliet (Lee) and Venus (Lamb) as they deal with school dances, boys, and exams. When the head nun teacher Sister Lee (Carpio) realizes that there's a ghost in the school, she has the rope burnt to dispel Pik's spirit, upsetting Bonnie and her teenage buddies, but they do get the chance to say farewell to Pik, who vows he will be reincarnated.

This amiable, easygoing fantasy-comedy flick, aimed at teenagers, is pretty lightweight fun, only getting a little more serious when tackling Venus's exam pressures and a teenage pregnancy subplot involving Juliet. Raymond Wong Pak-Ming is good as the ghost Pik, who uses his spectral skills to help Bonnie win a school athletics championship and make fun of the pompous Sister Lee. He even dresses up as Boy George at one point!

This was a hit film and sequels followed.

HAPPY GHOST II (1985)
Starring Raymond Wong Pak-Ming, Fennie Yuen,
May Lo Mei-Mei, Gigi Fu, Charine Chan, Jeanne Kanai,
Tsui Kwong-Lam, Chen Man-No
Directed by Clifton Ko
Cinema City

Pik, the "Happy Ghost" from the first film, is reincarnated as Mr. Hong, a teacher at an all-girls school, who must deal with his unruly class by using his superpowers.

This time around there's a swimming competition, where Hong uses his magic abilities to supercharge his team, plus the usual pratfalls, pranks, and juvenile humor. Mr. Hong (Pak-Ming) is quite a fun creation: an unremarkable, put-upon, gawky character with enough smarts and magic skills to enable him to usually have the last laugh. He does lose his powers for a while and gets fired because of a prank orgy invite letter written by his pupils,

but Hong is eventually reinstated, earns the respect of the kids, and comes to an understanding with his inner ghost-self, regaining his special talents in time to help his class win a crucial volleyball match.

With a song-and-dance finale, *Happy Ghost II* is a harmless, silly and superficial yarn that is an entertaining watch, just like its predecessor.

HAPPY GHOST III (1986)
Starring Raymond Wong Pak-Ming, Maggie Cheung,
Danny Poon, Charine Chan, Chen Man-No
Directed by Johnny To
Cinema City

The ghost of Tsui Pan-Han (Cheung), a failed singer who committed suicide, vows to make life hell for hapless teacher Hong (Pak-Ming) after he inadvertently prevents her from reincarnating.

Written and produced by Raymond Wong Pak-Ming, who plays the lead character once more, this sequel features some new magic powers, including the ability to freeze time and possess people, adds more jeopardy with the inclusion of triad bad guys and is not as teen-oriented as the first two films.

Adding an extra ghost in the shape of cute, impish Maggie Cheung to the plot gives *Happy Ghost III* a different story structure, though the film does lack the quaint vibe of its forerunners. To make up for this, the production's larger budget means it can deliver a more elaborate third act, with a trio of gangsters getting magnetized by Tsui, followed by a well-handled multi-vehicle chase finale, boasting car crashes and decent miniature effects, as Pik the Ching Dynasty ghost drives a taxi vertically across the city's buildings in an attempt to get Tsui to a hospital in time for her reincarnation.

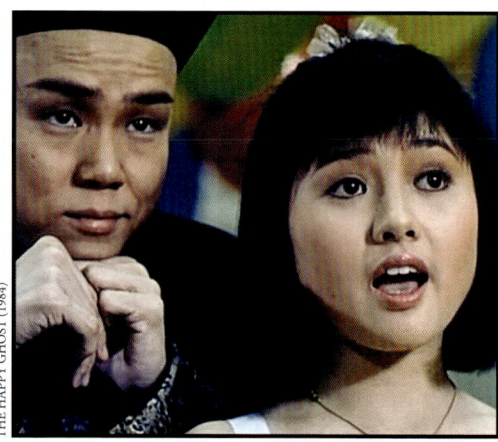
THE HAPPY GHOST (1984)

HAPPY GHOST IV (1990)

Starring Raymond Wong Pak-Ming, Pauline Yeung,
Lau Shun, Yip Sai-Wing
Directed by Clifton Ko
Action by Leung Siu-Hung
Pak Ming Films/Ko Chi Sum Films Company Limited

When mild-mannered schoolteacher Hong is pursued by an ancient warrior, the ghost of his ancestor comes to the rescue. With members of the Hong Kong rock band Beyond adding to the zany humor, *Happy Ghost IV* proved to be another popular hit for the series.

Tsui Hark's Cinefex Workshop team, who provided visual effects for *Happy Ghost III*, here lend their magical skills to a fun FX scene that mixes live action with animation for some *Who Framed Roger Rabbit*–style antics.

HAPPY GHOST V (1991)

Starring Raymond Wong Pak-Ming, Kris Aquino,
Roger Kwok, Wong Kwong-Leung
Directed by Norman Chan, Raymond Wong Pak-Ming
Mandarin Films Distribution

Magic, an Old English Sheepdog, saves a temple from burning down, so the Happy Ghost (Pak-Ming) grants the dog's wish to become a man, but the pooch can only remain in human form for 49 days.

Even for a film series that has silliness baked into the DNA of every installment, *Happy Ghost V* is still by far the silliest of the lot. The first act revolves around Magic the dog, his owner Kathy (Aquino) and her boyfriend Jack (Kwok), who is jealous of his girlfriend's total devotion to her pet. There's not really much of a plot until Magic is transformed into a man by Happy Ghost, with Raymond Wong Pak-Ming (who codirected this film) playing both the ghost and the dog-in-human-form.

As a human, Magic can still communicate with dogs, which comes in handy when he gets a job at a veterinary clinic. He retains certain doggy behaviors, like sniffing food, sleeping in a dog basket and biting bad guys, though he tries his best to act like a human, with Happy Ghost helping him from time to time, such as when the friendly spook takes on Magic's unpleasant coworkers during a supermarket burglary. Magic starts to really enjoy being a person, becomes attracted to Kathy, but is persuaded by Happy Ghost to try and get Jack and Kathy back together again after they split up.

With an armed bank robbery finale, Pak-Ming, who

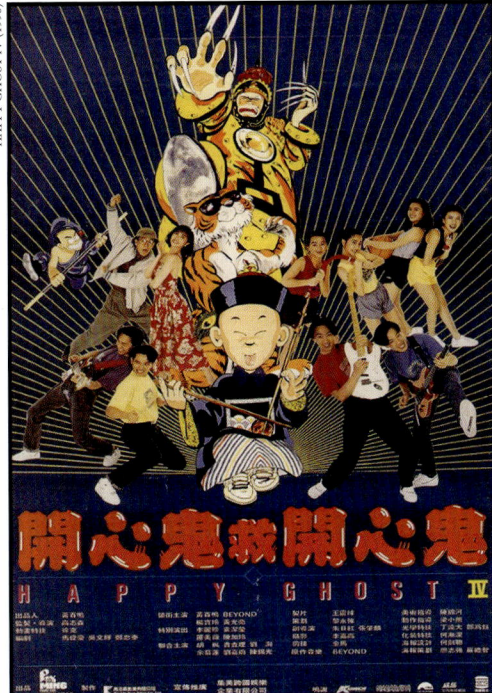

HAPPY GHOST IV (1990)

開心鬼救開心鬼
HAPPY GHOST IV

wrote the script, makes the interesting decision to kill off Magic as he tackles the gun-toting robber, though this does allow the story to show Magic's spirit return to his owner Kathy in the form of a cute puppy, who urinates in Jack's face for a final lowbrow joke!

Insubstantial, cheap, foolish, but kinda pleasant.

HAUNTED MANSION (1998)

Starring Gigi Lai, Anthony Wong, Shirley Cheung,
Law Lan
Directed by Dickson To
Wong Jing's Workshop Ltd

Journalist Gigi (Lai) goes back to her family home in Hong Kong's Yuen Long District with her cop husband Fai (Wong), to help her mom (Lan) and sister (Cheung) deal with various problems, including hauntings and several attempted acts of sabotage perpetrated by lowlifes working for Mr. Chin, a shady businessman.

Starting out promisingly with a dead dog being strung up outside the mom's home and a guy getting transfixed by a television aerial, the movie unfortunately soon becomes a rather pedestrian, underachieving affair, lacking suspense or any sense of dread. The story seems content to plod along with scenes of Gigi and Fai's easygoing, unexceptional marital life, interspersed with the occasional glimpse of a creepy kid or similar underwhelming incidents.

Gigi becomes increasingly concerned about what is happening at the family home and is given various snippets of advice and pearls of occult wisdom by one of her work colleagues, Uncle Ming, which includes his theory that the weird phone calls she's been getting in the middle of the night are from ghosts that are "on the same frequency" as Gigi.

Events become stranger when Fai's soul is trapped in an endless mah-jongg game and the ghostly young girl becomes more of an ongoing presence at the property. Gigi, with the help of Uncle Ming, eventually gets to the bottom of what is happening, after her mute mom's soul is released from her body (thanks to the application of electricity!) so that she can explain everything. The mother's soul reminds Gigi that she'd had an abortion several years earlier . . . and the spectral girl is actually her unborn daughter's spirit, which is causing Fai and Gigi's sister Fen to become possessed by other ghosts.

Gigi allows the ghostly girl to stick her hand right through her body, but this doesn't happen in reality, and Gigi's willingness to sacrifice herself placates her aborted daughter's angry spirit. Now Gigi teams up with her wraith daughter in an attempt to extricate Fai's soul from the ongoing ghostly mahjong game . . .

Haunted Mansion does improve toward the end, but it suffers overall from poor plotting choices, including sidelining Anthony Wong's interesting, slightly loutish & clumsy character for a large chunk of the second half of the movie, and never explaining the reason Mr. Chin, the businessman villain, is so desperate to get hold of the property he's willing to kill for it. There's a jarring shift in tone, too, when the film momentarily veers into CAT III territory, as Mr. Chin's wife gets stripped and assaulted in their office by an unseen entity. Chin is then attacked and strangled by the possessed wife, leaving his whole subplot hanging.

A decent moment involves the blue-lit, long-nailed ghost girl jumping onto the back of one of Mr. Chin's minions when he attempts to burn down the house, plus there are a couple of scenes featuring cut-out figurines from the mansion's elaborate shrine that seem to move around of their own volition, though this cool concept is soon forgotten, which is a shame, as they added a novel visual aspect to the story.

HE LIVES BY NIGHT (1982)
Starring Sylvia Chang, Eddie Chan, Kent Cheng, Simon Yam
Directed by Leong Po-Chih
Cinema City

A transvestite strangler/slasher (Chan) attacks women who wear silk stockings, which trigger his urge to kill.

A jokey subplot concerning an overweight policeman's adoration for a girl DJ dissipates the film's atmosphere whenever it arises, but the attacks themselves are suspenseful. Especially effective is an attack on two women in a house: one girl is slashed up as her friend sings obliviously in the bath. Another well-handled scene is a giallo-like retractable knife assault on a woman walking through an alleyway filled with red and yellow sheets hanging from clotheslines.

When the killer fights his desire to kill a neighbor's young daughter, who wears silk socks, quelling his murderous urges because he likes the girl, this helps make him more than just a one-dimensional character. As with Italian giallos, the murderer has a flashback to explain his kinky killing sprees.

The movie ends with outtakes during the credits, which seems odd for a suspenser like this. There's even the return of the cross-dressing killer for a freeze-frame smiling encore, rather than the usual shock ending!

HEALTH WARNING (1983)
Starring Wang Lung-Wei, Eddy Ko, Yuen Tin-Wan, Elvis Tsui
Directed by Kirk Wong
Bang Bang Film Productions/Verdull Film Dept.

In the near future, when society is breaking down, a martial arts school attempts to stick to the old ways by vigorous training and eschewing drugs. Unfortunately, the neo-nazi Ex Gang wipes out most of the school, so its two remaining members, Master Lau and pupil Ah Wei, decide to go on a revenge mission.

After Ah Wei recovers from an attack in which a handful of rabies-infected syringes (!) are stabbed into his back, he sneaks into the Ex Gang's HQ with Lau. Inside, an electro band plays to an audience, while two drug-taking female villains, dressed in stockings and pink tutus, club a girl with truncheons and drown her in a tank of water as part of the entertainment.

This cyberpunk martial arts actioner, as can be gleaned from the above description, is surprisingly dour, with none of the usual humor found in similar sci-fi-tinged Hong Kong offerings.

Health Warning, also known as *Flash Future Kung Fu* and *Digital Master*, improves as its story progresses, with nearly every scene awash with strong backlighting, flickering television screens, neon tubes, smoke, vid games and an incessantly fast, continual background synth score.

Ah Wei tackles baldies with swastika armbands, computer-controlled assailants wearing leather bondage masks and then, finally, takes on the leader of the Ex Gang, who fights Ah Wei in a boxing ring surrounded by nazi banners. This fight is very vicious, culminating in Ah Wei madly beating his fallen opponent in an uncontrollable fit of rage.

With Master Lau dead from an axe wound, Ah Wei escapes in an ether-powered car, departing the Ex Gang's headquarters with one of the villainesses, which makes this a somewhat amoral ending, considering that Ah Wei is leaving with a woman who has regularly committed murder as part of a musical act!

THE HEROIC TRIO (1993)

Starring Anita Mui, Maggie Cheung, Michelle Yeoh, Anthony Wong, Yen Shi-Kwan
Directed by Johnny To
Action by Ching Siu-Tung
China Entertainment Films Production/
Paka Hill Productions

A villainous Evil Master (Shi-Kwan) dwelling in the sewers below a city sends an invisible assailant out to kidnap children, one of whom may be the preordained "King" of China. Together with the police, two superheroines, Wonder Woman (Mui) and the Thief Catcher (Cheung), attempt to thwart these baby snatchers. The unseen intruder turns out to be their friend, the Invisible Woman (Yeoh), who is being forced to carry out the kidnappings. Teaming up, this Heroic Trio take on the Evil Master and his bird-eating sidekick Kau (Wong).

Despite some clumsy wirework and a confusing plot, it's a fun film. The pace rarely slackens, the fighting femmes are a treat to watch, and some of the action scenes are over the top, such as when the Thief Catcher's motorbike is sent spinning through the air like a rotating weapon! A novel ongoing gag sees the villainous Kau losing his fingers one by one, but he doesn't seem too worried: he's already eaten one of them himself!

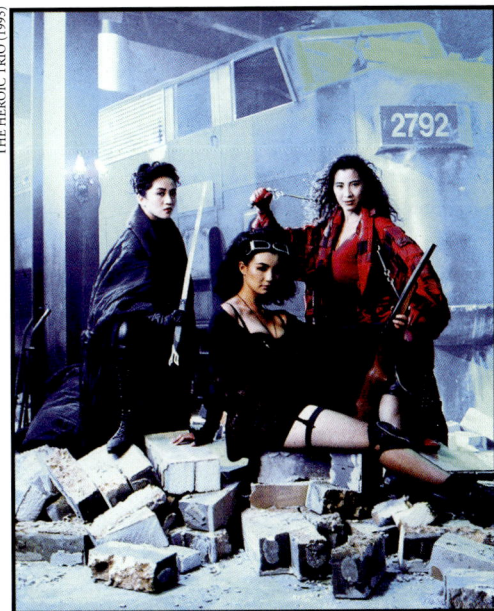

THE HEROIC TRIO (1993)

The end battle, with the Trio taking on the Evil Master, who is a living skeletal corpse-being, features a pretty memorable fighting technique: the withered, staring corpse latches onto the Invisible Woman, wraps its limbs and rib cage around her, and forces her to punch and kick her colleagues!

Ending with a multi-flashback/brain-exploding climax, *The Heroic Trio*, due to its total nuttiness, will probably make you like it whether you want to or not.

HEROIC TRIO 2: EXECUTIONERS (1993)

Starring Michelle Yeoh, Anita Mui, Maggie Cheung, Damian Lau, Anthony Wong, Lau Ching-Wan
Directed by Johnny To and Ching Siu-Tung
Action by Ching Siu-Tung
China Entertainment Films Production/
Paka Hill Productions

Also known as *Executioners*, this follow-up once again sees our kickass trio of fighting femmes tackling the forces of evil, but where the original was cool and wacky, this sequel is far moodier, grungier and bleaker.

Set in post-holocaust Hong Kong, which is in thrall to the disfigured Mr. Kim (Wong), who is the twisted genius behind the water company that regulates the all-important H_2O supply, the plot sees Kim attempt to destabilize the government and seize control. When Wonder Woman's police commissioner husband is killed, the girls swing into action, intent on thwarting Kim's fiendish scheme.

With great performances from Mui, Cheung and Yeoh, the film certainly doesn't attempt to simply emulate its madcap predecessor, delivering a far more pessimistic story that culminates in a surprisingly downbeat finale.

HEX (1980)
Starring Tan Nei, Wang Jung, Chen Szu-Chia,
Han Kuo-Tsai, Ma Chao, Yu Tsui-Ling
Directed by Kuei Chih-Hung
Shaw Brothers

Bullying, violent husband Chun Yu (Jung) is drowned in a water-filled pot when his sickly wife Sau Ying (Nei) and helpful houseguest Yi Wah (Szu-Chia) fight back. But Chun Yu's bloated corpse returns to scare Sau Ying to death . . . triggering a series of further apparitions, twists and strange goings-on.

The start of the film does a good job of making the viewer utterly despise the bitter, obnoxious, woman-beating Chun Yu, who seems to die himself, only to return for his wife's funeral in a *Les Diaboliques*–like twist. The plot then sees him and coconspirator Yi

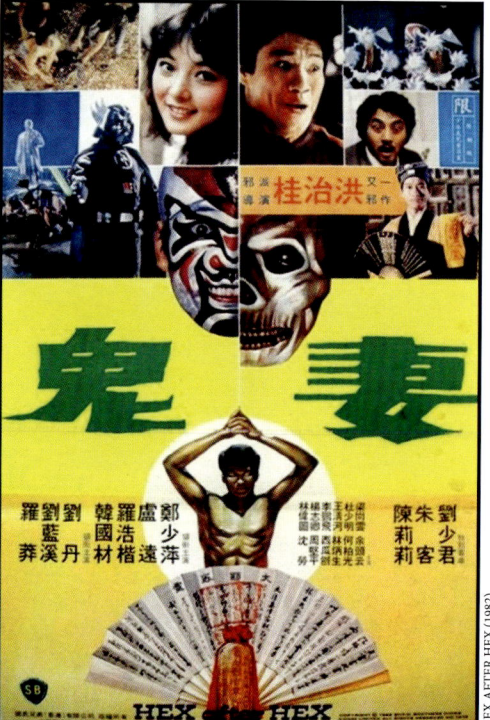

HEX AFTER HEX (1982)

Wah haunted by Sau Ying's fanged ghost, leading them both to become stressed and unhinged.

The tone of the film falters with the introduction of a silly, cross-eyed furniture mover (Chao), though the film is generally a competent ghost yarn, featuring shots of a severed hand crawling about and a well-handled sequence involving a bald street trader attempting to avoid the maddened Chun Yu, who stalks around the nicely lit mansion with a razor-sharp meat cleaver.

And then . . . the movie climaxes with a kind of expressive dance-ritual, performed by a naked woman covered in painted symbols and letterforms. This woman, bathed in light shining through colored window-glass, capers about and is slapped by an older exorcist lady with a shoe, as the prolonged dance routine simply goes on and on. With the camera lingering on the woman's nakedness, and the exorcist spitting dog's blood onto her cleavage in close-up, it's as if another director has taken over, turning *Hex* into a more arty, exploitative affair, which ends with a nude, shaven-headed Yi Wah having spells written all over her skin, *Kwaidan*-style.

Boasting a final (admittedly far-fetched) plot twist, *Hex* is a film that gets better as it progresses.

HEX AFTER HEX (1982)
Starring Lo Meng, Lily Chan, Lau Dan, Ma Chao
Directed by Kuei Chih-Hung
Shaw Brothers

A ghost (Chan) purposefully causes a car crash so that she can inhabit the body of the dead neighbor of Ma Su (Meng). Calling herself Pok Pok, she begins a relationship with the muscly Ma Su, who is at first unaware of her supernatural origins.

Hex After Hex begins immediately after the events of *Hex Vs Witchcraft* (1980) and contains the same kind of broad humor, slapstick and silly, jumbled, undisciplined storyline. Ma Chao, who is never one to knowingly underact, returns for a third time, playing a cross-eyed arsonist who has the Shaw Brothers logo branded on his backside. Other briefly diverting moments involve Pok Pok taking on the likeness of a lo-fi Yoda, then invoking a Darth Vader lookalike called Black Knight, who strikes at demolition workers with his lightsaber, magically making their clothing vanish!

The film's main subplot focuses on the heartless, stingy boss of a property business, who Pok Pok sets out to bankrupt after he evicts everyone from the building that she and Ma Su were living in. Pok Pok's scheme involves becoming the company secretary, hanging out with the boss when he gambles, then making him think the worthless horse statuettes he is purchasing are actually made of solid gold. This storyline, however, is protracted, not particularly interesting or funny, and sidelines the Ma Su character for a big portion of the running time.

Matters become more engaging after Ma Su discovers that Pok Pok is a ghost, studies skills to allow the Tai Sheung God to enter his body, and tries to banish his spirit girlfriend. Ultimately, Ma Su retains feelings for Pok Pok and saves her from a ritual which causes a statue of Thomas Jefferson to become animated, controlled by a priest's movements, forcing Ma Su to invoke the Monkey God into his body and fight the automaton. This scene, using a quite impressive statue costume, is way more professional looking than the special makeup effects seen earlier in the movie, such as Pok Pok's cheap ghost mask. To cap off this encounter, the statue, bizarrely, reveals itself to be a kind of slot machine and starts spitting gold Krugerrand coins out of its mouth?! Everyone gets rich! Hooray!

HEX VS WITCHCRAFT (1980)
Starring I Lei, Pei Ju-Hua, Liang Chen-Ni, Chan Shen, Lo Meng
Directed by Kuei Chih-Hung
Shaw Brothers

Unlucky gambler Cai Tou (Lei) loses his wife and is ordered to commit suicide by the gangsters he owes money to, but he agrees to marry the ghost of an elderly man's dead daughter instead, and she eventually helps him to win big.

This charmless, unfunny comedy non-sequel to *Hex* (1980) begins with main character Cai Tou purposefully getting his wife drunk so that she'll unknowingly have sex with the gangster he owes money to. When this ploy fails, we are presented with a series of attempted suicides that are played for laughs. Matters improve slightly after Cai Tou agrees to wed the ghost, who possesses various women so that she can have sex with her new husband, resulting in scenes of a nude air hostess (Ju-Hua) soaping herself down to a disco tune and Cai Tou being forced to go to bed with a ghost-controlled garbage lady. He's even sexually pestered by a cross-eyed house painter, played with a lack of restraint by Ma Chao, who was also in *Hex*.

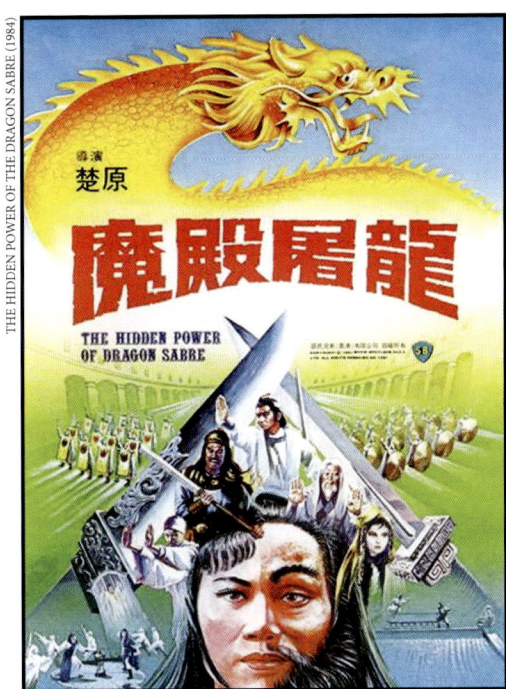

THE HIDDEN POWER OF THE DRAGON SABRE (1984)

If *Confessions of a Window Cleaner* (1974) had been filmed as a Hong Kong gambling-ghost-sex-farce . . . it might well have ended up looking like this movie. With its guileless, crass central character, cheap production values and overly broad acting, the film is decidedly lacking, but does become moderately more interesting during the gambling den finale, where Cai Tou is aided by his spirit-spouse to beat the casino's top witch-croupier to rake in the cash.

THE HIDDEN POWER OF THE DRAGON SABRE (1984)
Starring Derek Yee, Ti Lung, Alex Man, Cherie Chung, Ku Feng, Lo Lieh
Directed by Chor Yuen
Shaw Brothers

The Emperor (Feng) wants to keep Ming hero Zhang Wuji's legendary Heaven Sword and Dragon Sabre at his imperial temple, but Zhang (Yee) isn't a fan of this idea, so Song Qingshu (Man), the Emperor's Grand Tutor, formulates a plan to attain the weapons.

The plot is, as usual, far from straightforward, with Song advising the Emperor to send troops disguised as Ming Cult members to strike at Mongolia, in order to provoke General Tieh (a stoic Ti Lung), known as the Mongolian Hawk, into attacking Zhang. Song also plans to journey to Ermie Mountain, to steal a sacred sutra guarded by his ex-wife Zhou Ziruo.

This Shaw Brothers production is an extremely colorful wuxia that merges traditional-looking period sets, that are dripping with dry ice mists, with visual elements indebted to Western sci-fi films. So, we get special swords firing laser beams, hologram-like glowing columns of light, power rays shooting from hands and, when the protagonists venture under Heaven Mountain, they encounter a subterranean zone resembling a *Star Wars* spaceship interior!

There are pyrotechnic detonations galore in *Hidden Power of the Dragon Sabre*, plus exploding priestesses, masses of optical effects, a small, bearded child warrior, a kidnapped Mongolian princess and a villain who, once he attains the two magical Perspex-like blades and the knowledge contained within a pair of special sutras, transforms into a half-man/half-woman yin-yang super-being!

HOCUS POCUS (1984)

Starring Lam Ching-Ying, Tung Wei, Alice Lau,
Lo Ho-Kai, Chin Yuet-Sang
Directed by Chin Yuet-Sang
Produced by Sammo Hung
Bo Ho Film Company Ltd/ Golden Harvest

Hot on the heels of the success of *Encounters of the Spooky Kind* and *The Dead and the Deadly*, Sammo Hung produced yet another gem, telling a tale of

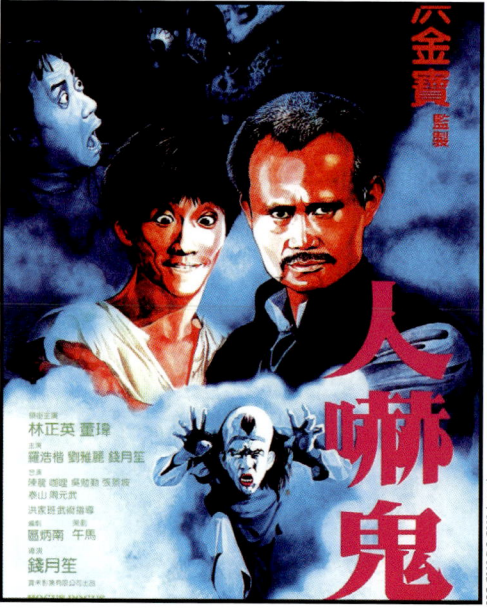

HOCUS POCUS (1984)

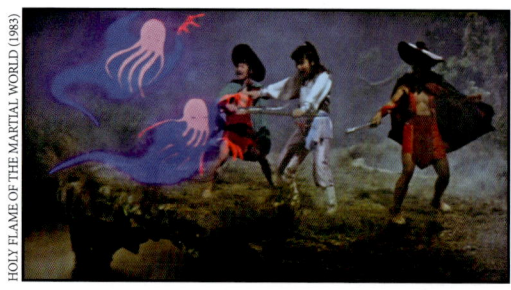

HOLY FLAME OF THE MARTIAL WORLD (1983)

a traveling Chinese opera troupe who want to get back at the unpopular prima donna of the show, Master Sheng (Ching-Ying). They dress up as ghosts and try to frighten him by haunting his house, but during all these spooky shenanigans they attract the attention of a real good-natured ghost (Yuet-Sang), who comes to haunt the haunters. They decide to find the remains of the ghost's former body and lay the spirit to rest by giving the corpse a proper burial. Unfortunately, they bury the wrong remains and when one of them urinates on the grave, they disturb a far from friendly spirit, who seeks revenge.

Hocus Pocus may be a little weak on plot, but some excellently choreographed scenarios and funny fantasy frolics confirm Sammo Hung's genius in mixing Chinese mythical culture with martial arts mayhem.

HOLY FLAME OF THE MARTIAL WORLD (1983)

Starring Leanne Lau, Mok Siu-Chung, Philip Kwok,
Yeung Ching-Ching, Yung Jing-Jing, Jason Pai Piao
Directed by Lu Chin-Ku
Shaw Brothers

Wan Tien Sau (Siu-Chung) and Yi Dan Fung (Ching-Ching) are actually brother and sister, who were orphaned as babies after the murder of their parents by baddies Grand Master (Lau) and Monster Yu (Piao). Wan is fortunate enough to be brought up by a good-natured elder known as The Phantom, but Yi is raised by the brusque Grand Master, who twists the facts surrounding the demise of Yi's parents.

Wan becomes adept in the use of a mystic weapon known as Holy Flame but, unknown to him and The Phantom, it transpires that there's a matching Holy Flame, which Yi is able to use expertly upon reaching her 18th birthday. After being manipulated and lied to, Yi finally learns the truth about her past, joins forces with her brother and deals with Grand Master and Monster Yu in a super-fu-powered finale.

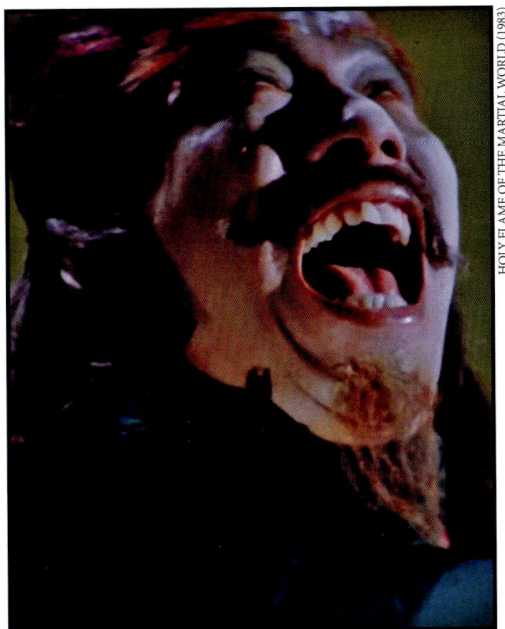

HOLY FLAME OF THE MARTIAL WORLD (1983)

HOLY VIRGIN VS THE EVIL DEAD (1991)

Starring Donnie Yen, Pauline Yeung, Ben Lam,
Chui Hei-Man, Kathy Chow, Ken Lo, Sibelle Hu
Directed by Lu Chin-Ku
Action by Tsui Fat
Cheung Yau Martial Arts Direction Company/Chung
Ngai Movie Production

In modern day Hong Kong, a teacher's female student guests are all murdered by an evil Cambodian being called the Moon Monster (Lo), who is a long-haired dude similar to Dick Wei's character in *Return of the Demon* (1987). The teacher, played by Donnie Yen, is suspected of the murders at first, until the Moon Monster assaults a policeman's wife and receives several bullets in the torso before being electrocuted. After pulling out the guts of a mortuary attendant, the undead Monster returns to Cambodia, followed by Yen, his brother, a policeman, and his wife . . .

A Cambodian princess (Yeung) of the High Wind Tribe is introduced halfway into the film. She is able to fly and helps the protagonists with her magical sword that can fire yellow lightning!

In the fun climax, machine gun action mingles with magical mayhem, as the Monster suffers from a bad case of facial blisters when the sword is driven into the top of his head.

This movie mixes supernatural shenanigans with shoot-outs and some good fisticuffs from Yen, but, okay, so it doesn't quite have that extra something to ensure it lives up to the promise of the title, but it still entertains.

HOLY WEAPON (1993)

Starring Michelle Yeoh, Sandra Ng, Maggie Cheung,
Cheung Man, Carol Cheng, Damian Lau, Simon Yam,
Ng Man-Tat, Charine Chan
Directed by Wong Jing
Action by Ching Siu-Tung
Scholar Film Company/Win's Film Productions

This is a fantasy fighting flick with a plot so convoluted it's virtually impossible to follow, but it has humor and action that's so diverting you don't much care.

Expert sword fighter Mo Kake (Lau), known as Heaven's Sword, takes on the evil Super Sword (Yam), using a powerful drug which gives him the strength to combat the Long Life Evil Sword technique, which is a move whereby the villain transforms himself into a blade of light to slash off his opponent's head. Mo Kake is victorious, but the drug has such a dreadful

This is the kind of colorful fantasy-wuxia you need to go into expecting to see all kinds of outlandish exploits and mad skillz. If you do this, you're going to enjoy such feats as the Phantom's special Ghostly Laugh, which can cause strong, hurricane-like winds, or the chief of the Blood Sucking Clan's ability to make illustrated fighters with Halloween mask–like faces pop out of their tapestries to become flesh and blood adversaries.

A fun sequence involves Wan battling some fluorescent cel-animated ghosts before flying through the mouth of a cavern behind a green-lit waterfall to subdue large, spinning Chinese letterforms that shoot from the mouths of stone faces on the walls of a dark chamber. Wan also melts an acrobatic, bodystocking-wearing, reanimated corpse with his Holy Flame blade, a young woman called Juan Er (Jing-Jing) acquires the power to fire lasers from her red finger, there's a semi-comical bunch of masters from such groups as the Cung Tung Clan and Miu Shan Clan, and we get the chance to see Grand Master & Monster Yu combine their evil energies to produce force beams capable of making people explode, leaving just their bloody skeletons behind!

Philip Kwok delivers a likeable performance as the mega-laughing, helpful Phantom, and the knowing streak of humor permeating the production helps make the movie enjoyably absurd and amusing throughout.

effect on him that another fighter must be found to combat Super Sword on his return. Well, to be exact, seven fighters are needed, who must all be female virgins. But gender issues become extremely clouded here: one fighter is Mo Kake's fiancé (Yeoh), who has been disguising herself as a man to attack heartless men who treat women badly, another fighter is the beautiful but bitchy princess Tin Heung (Cheung), who is accompanied by her bodyguard, another male impersonator. A beautiful maiden (Man) can transform herself into an evil spiderwoman to trap male pursuers and her sister, Butterfly (Chan), falls in love with Mo Kake's fiancé, believing her to be a man. There is also the would-be-wife of an innocent peasant boy, who becomes the object of the female bodyguard's attentions when a love spell goes wrong. But the peasant boy himself saves the day by transforming into a girl to complete the troupe of fighting femmes! Did you follow all of that?!

Throw in a green-haired, slimy zombie vampire, Super Sword's flying lackeys and some spectacular wirework directed by the emperor of fantasy choreography, Ching Siu-Tung, and what you get is an absolute riot of stylish silliness and inspired action.

HUMAN LANTERNS (1982)
Starring Liu Yung, Chen Kuan-Tai, Lo Lieh, Tan Nei
Directed by Sun Chung
Produced by Mona Fong
Shaw Brothers

A lantern maker, Chao Chun Fang (Lieh), kills several women to get revenge on a rich man. In an atmospheric room of large cog wheels, the mad artisan slices a cross onto his victims' heads, then pours mercury into the wound, which allows him to peel the skin off more easily!

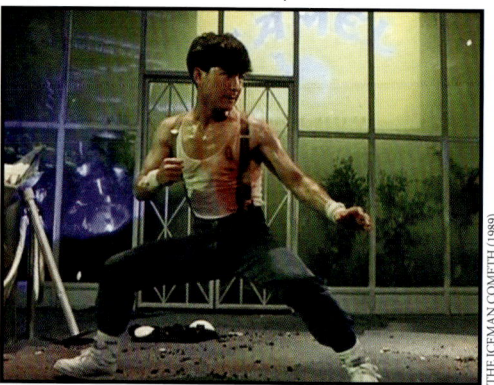
THE ICEMAN COMETH (1989)

Also going by the title *Human Skin Lanterns*, this traditional-style Shaw Brothers film boasts good production values, a couple of brief skinning scenes and loads of martial art confrontations. The fighters can hop on lily pads without sinking and walk along handheld paper fans. "Money and fame are hollow," says the villain, who meets a fiery end.

I LOVE MARIA (1988)
Starring Tsui Hark, Sally Yeh, Tony Leung Chiu-Wai, John Sham, Lam Ching-Ying, Dennis Chan
Directed by David Chung
Produced by Tsui Hark, John Sham
Action by Ching Siu-Tung
Film Workshop/Golden Harvest/Golden Princess Film Production Limited

This light, wacky sci-fi-comedy-actioner is packed full of fighting, robots and firepower. The story concerns the Hero Gang: a group armed with robots and Transformer-type machines that is set on taking over the city. Research Department cop Curly (Sham) teams up with Whiskey (Hark), an ex–gang member, and they try to stop the Hero Gang from achieving their goal.

Along with Pioneer 1, a twenty-foot killing machine, there is Pioneer 2, a female human-sized robot with machine-gun fingers, rocket-powered feet, superstrength, and missile-firing arms. Pioneer 2 is destroyed and then put back together by Curly, after which she joins their team. With the sides more even, the battle soon begins and robots battle it out with rockets, extending arms, rocket-propelled flying, and just about anything else you can think of.

Also known as *Roboforce*, this pacy film has special effects that are decent enough for the time and budget, a pretty simplistic plot, plus Sally Yeh playing two roles, looking especially lovely as the *Metropolis*-inspired Pioneer 2!

THE ICEMAN COMETH (1989)
Starring Yuen Biao, Yuen Wah, Maggie Cheung
Directed by Clarence Fok
Produced by Raymond Chow, Stephen Shiu
Golden Harvest/Johnny Mak Productions

Yuen Wah plays a renegade swordsman who murders a princess and steals a black jade buddha. The buddha can activate a time wheel, allowing those who use it to travel across the ages. It is the job of Yuen Biao's hero to recover the buddha and bring the swordsman to justice. But while battling in the snowbound mountains, Yuen Wah manages to activate the time wheel, and the two of them are instantly transported to the present day, where they are locked into a glacier, until archaeologists accidentally free them. The two warriors then continue their fight across modern day Hong Kong.

The fights are stylishly choreographed, the acting is excellent and Maggie Cheung adds glamor as the call girl who befriends Yuen Biao. Whether you're a fantasy fan or a fight fanatic, this is seriously recommended.

Also known as *Time Warriors*.

THE IMPERIAL SWORD KILLING THE DEVIL (1981)

Starring Meng Fei, Ching Li, Chang Yi, Hsia Ling-Ling
Directed by Fang Hao
Ch-Shyan Film Company

A group of men traverse a booby trap–filled series of caverns littered with (not very realistic-looking) skeletons, contending with acid water, some kind of mini flying snake monster and explosions, so that they can retrieve a sought-after treasure map, which becomes the focus of nice guy Hung, the villainous Lung Wu, and others.

The nonstop, very loud soundtrack, comprised of umpteen "borrowed" tunes, including tracks from *Flash Gordon* and *Once Upon a Time in the West*, plus synth & rock riffs and other ill-fitting-yet-apt pieces of music, melds with the continually weird imagery to make this movie an audio and visual deluge of oddness. That isn't to say this Taiwanese film is particularly good, but it's certainly never dull or ordinary.

Where else can you get to see a female fighter wield a spinning, light-covered umbrella weapon that can also function as a sort of mini-motorboat?! Craziness continues as we watch Lung Wu become a master of the Great Illusion feat, gaining the power to multiply

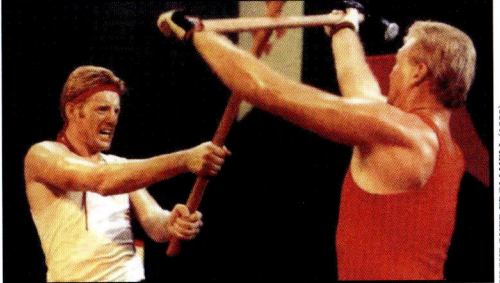

KICKBOXER FROM HELL (1990)

himself in order to confuse his enemies. In the ultimate showdown, however, Hung is given a special potion, becomes a shooting bolt of light, and wipes out all of Lung Wu's Great Illusion doppelgängers . . . then flies right through Lung Wu himself, who is left standing with a huge, perfectly round hole in the middle of his torso!

KICKBOXER FROM HELL (1990)

Starring Mark Houghton, Nora Miao, Wayne Archer, Richard Edwards
Directed by Alton Cheung
IFD Films and Arts

Also known as *Zodiac Power 3: Kickboxer from Hell*, this is a chop-and-paste IFD movie that intercuts new footage featuring Western martial arts actor Mark Houghton with a 1976 Hong Kong/Korean supernatural movie called *The Obsessed*, starring Nora (*Way of the Dragon*) Miao.

The film begins with a woman called Sophia being chased by sackcloth-wearing bad guys. She stumbles upon a kickboxer called Sean (Houghton), who saves her. Back at Sean's home there is a funny conversation on the couch as Sophia explains things to Sean: "It's a long story—I'm a nun, actually—but my partner and I are working undercover against Lucifer." Excellent stuff! This explanation works as a tenuous link to the existing footage from *The Obsessed*, with the newlywed heroine in this 1976 production, played by Nora Miao, being passed off as Sophia's partner, who has now given up being a nun and has married a stocky guy called Robert. I hope you're following all this!

In this part of the plot, we see creepy things begin to happen, such as a broken clock start to work again in the family home and a scene where Robert and his wife are given their wedding photos . . . and each shot features the ghostly face of his dead first wife Lisa! Soon, of course, Lisa's ghost makes an appearance and causes trouble.

Back with the newly shot IFD footage, we cut to the dark HQ of the Lucifer-worshippers, who like to wear face paint and sackcloth. After some amusing trash-talk bickering (the dialogue in the new scenes is priceless), the two dudes who failed to catch Sophia are forced to fight to the death in a martial arts ring.

The ghost-themed thread of the plot culminates with Robert, who has been taunted by Lisa's ghost for murdering her, getting captured by the authorities. The Sean-vs-satanists section of the film reaches its climax as the hero confronts the Lucifer-worshipping bad guys at their headquarters, where Sophia the young undercover nun is being held prisoner. Sean and the main henchman fight each other with sledgehammers, as the theme from *Re-Animator* (1985) plays, with the hammer duel ending when Sean breaks the guy's neck. The cult leader, who sports face paint that the rock band Kiss would love, brings the broken-necked main henchman back to life, but Sean dodges a swinging sledgehammer blow and a sacred skull gets shattered, causing the cult leader to die. And then . . . we get an abrupt IFD-style finish: the end!

The scenes from *The Obsessed* are well enough done, with the story possessing at least a little bit of mystery, but not much effort is made by IFD to make this plotline seem at all relevant to the satanists story.

THE KILLER SNAKES (1974)
Starring Kam Kwok-Leung, Li Lin-Lin, Chen Chun,
Lin Feng, Ko Ti-Hua
Directed by Kuei Chih-Hung
Shaw Brothers

Zhihong is a poor, gawky, bullied youth living in a shack next to a snake bladder store in a rundown Hong Kong neighborhood. When an injured cobra slithers through a crack in the store wall, entering Zhihong's ramshackle home, he decides to stitch up the serpent's wound and look after it, triggering a set of circumstances that will lead to Zhihong using his killer cobra, plus more reptiles liberated from the store, to avenge himself against those who have treated him badly.

Unlike *Willard* (1971), however, which this film is obviously inspired by, Zhihong is a far more disturbed protagonist compared to the rat-obsessed main character in the American original. In a scene where Zhihong carries a prostitute who'd tried to mug him back to his shack, *The Killer Snakes* queasily merges Zhihong's desire to get back at his tormentors with his disturbed sexual urges, showing him take advantage of the woman by tying her up and licking her. Though Zhihong himself has been a victim of bullying, he does far worse, allowing his snake friends to violate his captive in a sweaty, seedy scene that uses black and white flashbacks to suggest that Zhihong's dark urges stem from childhood memories of abuse and voyeurism.

Starting with mondo-style footage of live snakes having their gall bladders cut out, this film is sordid

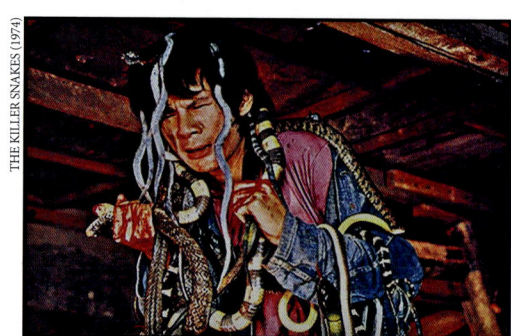

THE KILLER SNAKES (1974)

and repellent in many ways, but it is well shot and lit, juggling its exploitative components expertly. Bondage fantasies, scenes of Zhihong letting monitor lizards scratch his latest tied-up female victim, a set piece involving an abusive character chopping up snakes for real with a sword before he's constricted to death by a huge python, plus other grindhouse elements, show how this movie set its sights on offending and disturbing its viewers, a goal it obviously succeeded in achieving with sleazy ease.

KUNG FU FROM BEYOND THE GRAVE (1982)
Starring Billy Chong, Lo Lieh, Sung Gam-Shing,
Fang Mien
Directed by Lee Chiu
The Eternal Film Company

During the annual Ghost Festival, bare-chested hero Chun (Chong) is visited by the eyeless, green-faced spectre of his dead dad, who informs his son that he was a victim of murder. Chun decides to go to Yellow Dragon Town to get revenge for Pops, but it won't be easy as the villain controls a bunch of henchmen and is aided by a black magician priest (Gam-Shing). After Chun is pestered by hopping undead corpses in a playful scene, he's inspired to go back to the location of a book of magic, which he uses to raise a group of mangle-faced undead to do his bidding.

This film is a great deal of fun! Just to illustrate this, let's look at what happens in a nicely mounted confrontation between Chun and his ghosts versus the bad priest: the magician uses a magical cape and two long-tongued spirits in pointy hats to fight Chun's ghosts, but Chun stands his ground and retaliates, using his glowing magic book to turn the black magician's spirits into puddles . . . but the movie's weird factor is suddenly turned up a notch as the priest piles on the pressure . . . by summoning Count Dracula! Wonderful stuff!

Billy Chong's fight moves are a joy to watch, we get a deadly ghost with stretching arms, a long-range flamethrower breath attack, women's underwear thrown at the wizard to weaken him, and the main villain (Lieh) being chased by the burning scalps of his victims! These surreal elements, added to fine action courtesy of martial arts directors Alan Hsu and Sung Gam-Shing, make this a very entertaining kung-fu-horror-fantasy yarn.

KUNG FU VS. ACROBATIC (1990)

Starring Andy Lau, Joey Wong, Yuen Wah,
Chan Pak-Cheung
Directed by Taylor Wong
Action by Yuen Wah
Win's Movie Productions Ltd

Andy Lau releases a centuries-old (but still very attractive) princess and her servant from a cave. The long-dormant princess is played by Joey Wong, an actress who must be able to play ghostly gals and supernatural babes in her sleep!

Unfortunately for Andy's character, he also releases a nasty, evil dude (Wah) from the cavern, who follows them back to Hong Kong . . .

This wild comedy-fantasy-actioner has supernatural magic battles with spectral feet and fists smashing into one another and even finds time to include a cartoon ghost turtle.

Ultimately, the film is silly and superficial, but passes the time.

KUNG FU WONDER CHILD (1986)

Starring Lin Hsiao-Lan, Yukari Oshima, Jack Long,
Chang Shan
Directed by Lee Tso-Nam
Action by Alexander Lo Rei, Li Hai-Hsing
Poly Film

The head of a school for magical young priests is really an evil holy man.

If you can ignore the constant, chaotic babble of ranting kids on the soundtrack in the first section of the picture, this theatrical-looking yarn of flying priests and spells does contain some quite diverting ingredients, including spirits kept in burial jars, hopping vampires, a blue-faced spirit, the bad priest transmuting into a cel-animated dragon and even something that resembles a flying draft excluder with teeth!

Although low budget and a little convoluted, with rather too much scatological humor (there's a pissing

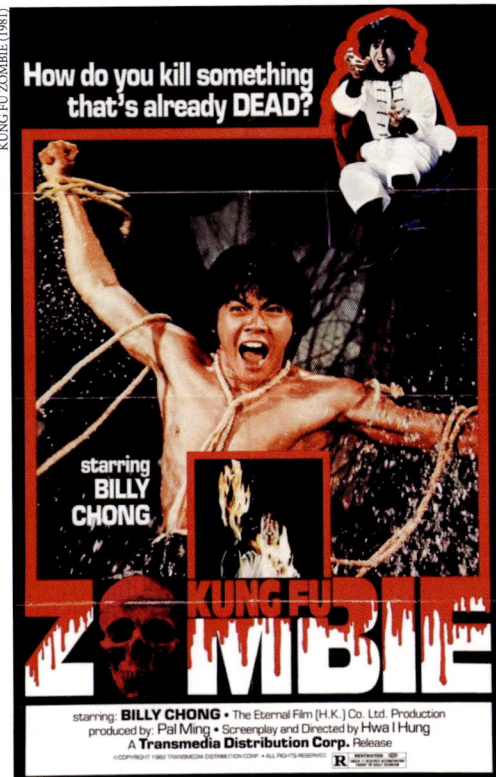

KUNG FU ZOMBIE (1981)

How do you kill something that's already DEAD?

starring **BILLY CHONG**

starring **BILLY CHONG** • The Eternal Film (H.K.) Co. Ltd. Production produced by: Pal Ming • Screenplay and Directed by Hwa I Hung A **Transmedia Distribution Corp.** Release

dog, some farting, someone urinates down their own leg), this Taiwanese movie has some decent fight choreography and culminates in a pyrotechnical finale. Just don't expect it to be as well directed as a Ching Siu-Tung or Tsui Hark movie.

KUNG FU ZOMBIE (1981)

Starring Billy Chong, Chan Lau, Cheng Ka-Ying
Directed by Hua Shan
The Eternal Film Company

A renegade priest brings the dead back to life as eyeless, hopping zombies to help a bad guy called Mu Tai kill his opponents, but the villain dies in one of his own booby traps, so his ghost demands to be reincarnated in another body. Mu Tai's spirit ends up residing in the corpse of the father of hero Pang (Chong), but a faulty ritual turns the dead dad into a white-faced part-human and part-ghost being, who is hell-bent on murdering several folks. To make matters worse, Pang is also targeted by scar-faced undead villain Long, a guy so tough he even carries on fighting when his hands and feet catch fire! Fortunately for Pang, the handy intervention of a Buddhist monk imbues him with the power to defeat Long, who is finally lynched with prayer beads and stabbed to death with a tree branch.

This Eternal Film Company production is a comedic fantasy-horror-actioner, starring the likeable Billy Chong, which merges lively bouts of kung fu, humor, and supernatural hijinks with music borrowed from *Moonraker* (1979) and *Exorcist II: The Heretic* (1977). The movie informs us that spirits need to be nailed to the corpses they are going to inhabit and reveals the fact that a hat constructed from leaves can make its wearer invisible to the living dead!

There's some superfast editing for several fight scenes, plus speeded-up farcical chases, though this all actually works out fine within the context of this film, which is, after all, an exaggerated comedy kung fu horror flick.

LABORATORY OF THE DEVIL (1992)
Starring Chu Kong, Wan Man-Ying, Andrew Yu
Directed by Godfrey Ho
Produced by K.P. Cheung, Ricky Wong Ka-Kui
My Way Film Co

In the spring of 1945, Japan established secret base Unit 731 in Manchuria, where many innocent Chinese, Korean, and Mongolian people were killed in grotesque experiments. An idealistic young doctor is horrified by the experiments being performed in the camp, and when his fiancé arrives disguised as a Chinese prisoner, he sets out to liberate the camp.

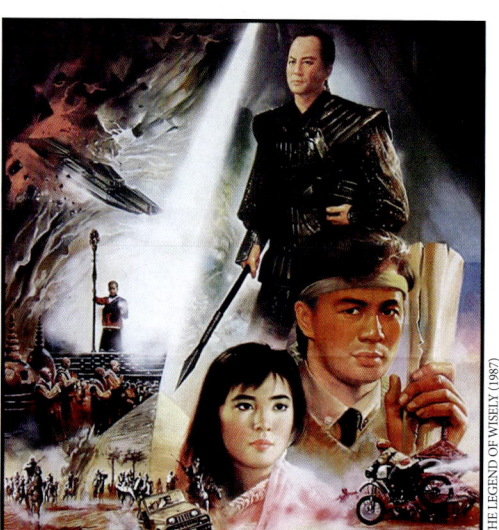

THE LEGEND OF WISELY (1987)

This is a stand-alone sequel to the notorious *Man Behind the Sun* (1988) and includes the same kind of gross, gory, explicit scenes of experiments and autopsies. Also known as *Maruta 2: Laboratory of the Devil*, *Unit 731: Laboratory of the Devil* and *Man Behind the Sun 2: Laboratory of the Devil*, this very exploitative film should probably only be sought by those who have an interest in such subject matter.

THE LEGEND OF WISELY (1987)
Starring Samuel Hui, Ti Lung, Teddy Robin Kwan, Joey Wong
Directed by Teddy Robin Kwan
Cinema City

Also known as *The Legend of the Golden Pearl*, the film's hero, Wisely (Hui), helps a very short mate steal a sacred pearl from some monks in Nepal, which involves lots of acrobatic fighting. Wisely, who is an adventurer-photographer-science-fiction-writer, then becomes linked with an underworld boss and his sister.

The middle portion of the movie is, unfortunately, rather uninteresting, though things get livelier once the action returns to Nepal. Here we get a monk-burning, humanoid alien, who wants the pearl back because it is, in fact, a solar piloting computer for his spaceship. Finally, the stellar vessel bursts out of the side of a mountain, in the shape of a dragon, and flies the nasty alien home.

The film boasts some decent sets and includes novel action moments, such as a fight atop an aircraft that's ready to take off, but the mishmash of genre elements, including kung fu, car chases, exotic location-hopping, science-fiction & adventure, doesn't really come off and, even though a lot of effort was put into the production, the story just runs out of steam. At least effects designer Yiu Yau-Hung's fleetingly seen dragon ship is rather nice to look at.

LOVE TO KILL (1993)
Starring Danny Lee, Anthony Wong, Elizabeth Lee
Directed by Chung Siu-Hung
Produced by Kirk Wong
Heroes United Films Ltd/Uniden Investments Ltd

Relentlessly brutal and often downright nasty, *Love to Kill* picks up where psycho-dad offerings like *The Stepfather* (1987) leave off, in a production that veers from straightforward sexy cop drama to near-unwatchable scenes of spousal degradation and abuse.

This film features Anthony Wong in virtually a reprise of his deranged family man role seen in *The Untold Story*, but, whereas his antisocial activities were pretty indiscriminate in *The Untold Story*, here it's definitely a family affair, as his character, Sam Wong, makes life a misery for wife Jade and their infant son. Jade has it especially bad, forced to submit to any number of her hubby's sick sex-and-bondage fantasies. Sympathetic cop Fireball Hung (Lee) intervenes to provide sanctuary for Jade and her son, but this move only serves to further fuel Wong's depraved fantasies and stir him into a final frenzy of savagery, culminating in an appropriately bloody finale, with nail guns featuring prominently.

On graphic shock value alone, *Love to Kill* matches *The Untold Story*, and Wong's portrayal of a dad so psychotic he makes Jack Nicholson from *The Shining* look like Santa Claus is never less than chillingly convincing.

MAGIC COP (1990)

Starring Lam Ching-Ying, Wilson Lam, Billy Chow,
Michiko Nishiwaki, Frankie Chan
Directed by Tung Wei
Movie Impact Limited

Lam Ching-Ying plays a police officer who favors more traditional methods of fighting crime. His two assistants are very much of the modern school and are sceptical about his ways, but when a deadly vampire arrives from the other world seeking a mystical shield of power, the mystically powered cop has the perfect opportunity to demonstrate his skills to the full, in order to save everyone from this dreadful adversary.

A perfect mix of traditional spooky shenanigans and modern-day action, *Magic Cop*, also known as *Mr. Vampire 5*, makes the most of Lam Ching-Ying's vampire-busting persona.

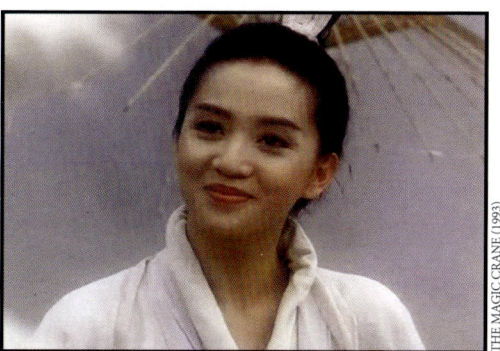

THE MAGIC CRANE (1993)

THE MAGIC CRANE (1993)

Starring Anita Mui, Tony Leung Chiu-Wai, Rosamund
Kwan, Lawrence Ng
Directed by Benny Chan
Produced and written by Tsui Hark
Long Shong Pictures/Film Workshop

Pak Wan-Fai (Mui) is a mysterious woman who rides a giant magic crane. When she encounters kung fu disciple Kwun-Mo (Leung) and his master on the way to a gathering of all the kung fu schools, they become embroiled in a revenge saga that began twenty-five years earlier, when Pak Wan-Fai's master sacrificed his lover and child to save her life. The daughter, Butterfly Lam (Kwan), is determined to have her revenge on Pak Wan-Fai, who attempts to defend herself from Lam and help Kwun-Mo to calm things at the gathering at the same time. The schools, it's revealed, are disputing territorial boundaries, while the vicious leader of the Tien Lung tribe (Ng) stirs things up, sending in a flock of bloodsucking bats to poison the kung fu masters! The only cure is the gall of a giant thousand-year-old tortoise, which Pak Wan-Fai cuts from the creature's body. Then the two beautiful female fighters must battle it out to settle old scores . . . but there are plenty of others who are happy to use this duel for their own ends.

The Magic Crane may not be a particularly pioneering production, but it's a visual treat just the same, packed full of the stylish effects, impressive animation and atmospheric sets one would expect from fantasy king Tsui Hark.

MALEVOLENT MATE (1993)

Starring Wong Kwong-Leung, Bonnie Fu, Lam Ka-Wah,
Rita Ching, Yip San
Directed by Lin Chi-Fan
Fortune Star Films

There's something about this grim crime saga that suggests it was based on fact. Unfortunately for us, that something is the idea that genuinely true crime is rarely as exciting or dramatic as the fictionalized version, as *Malevolent Mate*, which opens intriguingly enough with a graphic (if heavy on the rubber limbs) dismemberment, constantly promises unlimited carnage, only to dwell on the more mundane aspects of the plot, which is centered around a police investigation of the disappearance of a restauranteur's wife and their interrogation of the chief suspect, the husband's mistress.

If indeed this movie is rooted in fact, then the one overwhelming impression you'll carry away from it is that you sure as hell don't ever want to fall under suspicion of murder in Hong Kong. Though the cops are our heroes, these boys will do anything to extract a confession, including electrocution, scalding and torching the teddy bear of the accused's kid.

The film plays like a whodunit, but, given that we know who did from the start, the only real interest is in whether the supposed killer will crack under pressure.

Yes, there's a twist in the tale, but it comes too late to impact on the sluggish pace or increase the intensity you initially expected.

MAN BEHIND THE SUN (1988)

Starring Wang Gang, Wu Dai-Yao, Wang Run-Shen, Tian Jie-Fu
Directed by T. F. Mous
Produced by Fu Chi
Sil-Metropole Organisation Ltd

This vile movie tells the story of a Japanese biological experiment camp that was in occupied China at the end of World War II.

A group of boys are sent to the camp to learn how the Chinese are nothing but fodder for experiments for the Japanese. The film is grim, serious, well made and contains some sickeningly real effects. Some of them, a little too harrowing to mention here, seem far too convincing to be done purely with special FX.

Only for the strongest stomach and mind: if you're prone to spew, don't view!

THE MIGHTY PEKING MAN (1977)

Starring Danny Lee, Evelyne Kraft, Ku Feng, Lin Wei-Tu
Directed by Ho Meng-Hua
Shaw Brothers

An expedition brings back a gigantic ape-man to Hong Kong, where he (surprise) runs amok. His jungle girl companion (Kraft) tries to help the hairy vandal, but it all ends in tears.

Shaw Brothers released this fantasy flick in the wake of 1976's *King Kong* remake and did rather a good job. Though the special effects have been ridiculed in such publications as The Psychotronic Encyclopedia of Film, I found the sets and model work to be on par with similar scenes in Toho's Godzilla movies. The Hong Kong city set is pretty large and decently detailed, with the usual pyrotechnical destruction occurring at the movie's climax.

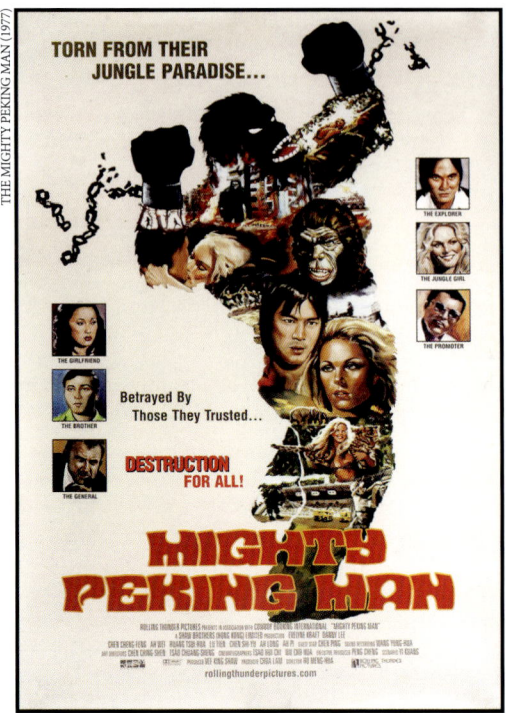

THE MIGHTY PEKING MAN (1977)

Though the titular Peking Man is obviously a man in a costume, of a standard far below that of Rick Baker's simian creation seen in the '76 *King Kong*, the model face used for close-ups of Peking Man's visage is up to snuff.

One of the movie's plus points is Evelyne Kraft who, as the loincloth-wearing amazon, is a fetching addition to the cast. Other ingredients include an elephant stampede and a man who has his leg bitten off by a tiger!

Surprisingly, a certain amount of pathos can be found in Peking Man's plight because, generally,

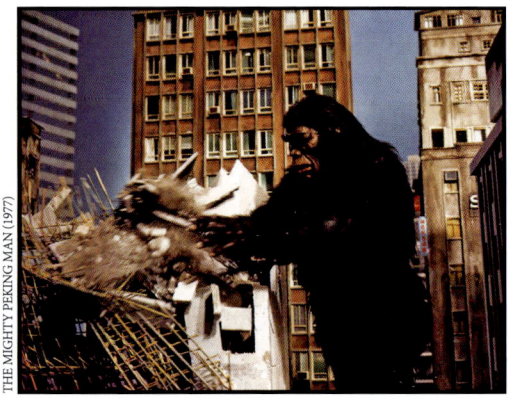

THE MIGHTY PEKING MAN (1977)

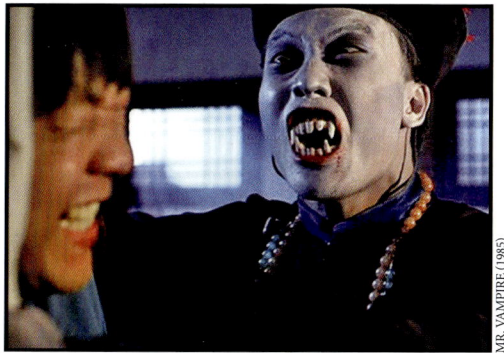

MR. VAMPIRE (1985)

the ape-man is shown to be friendly, at least in the company of Kraft, thus adding to the tragedy of the finale, as the furry fury and his diminutive dame companion come under fire from buzzing helicopters.

THE MIRROR (1999)
Starring Nicholas Tse, Ruby Lin, Lillian Ho, Law Lan, Xu Fan, Jack Neo
Directed by Siu Wing
Mandarin Films

This portmanteau horror film uses a dressing table with a cursed mirror as the link between a series of stories, set in 1922 Shanghai, 1988 Singapore and 1999 Hong Kong.
The first tale, about Mary (Fan), a wheelchair-bound woman suffering from mirror-induced flashbacks that remind her of how she poisoned her husband, is the best of the bunch.
The story set in Singapore begins in a more humorous manner, with the mirror this time influencing a solicitor (Neo) to commit murder to win his current court case, and it finishes with a briefly seen ghost (played by the movie's scriptwriter) and a rather silly twist ending involving plastic surgery.
The third yarn concerns a young guy called Ming (Tse) bringing Judy (Lin), his new girlfriend, back to his home, where he lives with his rich grandmother and his cousin, Yu (Ho). He marries Judy, but unpleasant events start to occur, culminating in the death of the grandmother. It is eventually revealed that Judy framed Yu in order to make sure Ming inherited his grandmother's fortune.
In addition to these three main stories, there is a brief pre-credits sequence set in a Ming Dynasty brothel and an even shorter teaser ending, based in Taiwan.
The film lacks any real suspense or scares, the mirror is only tenuously involved in the second and third

stories, and the tales, written by Raymond Wong Pak-Ming, are just not very engaging, though the Hong Kong segment at least boasts a dead-puppy-in-granny's-sink moment and an absurd scene in which the grandmother's severed head gets flung about.
The Shanghai-set story is the most successful at intertwining the mirror into the actual plot, has a well-sustained atmosphere and some decent period details, plus there's a scene where the dressing table slides across the room menacingly, echoing a similar moment with a "living piano" in the British anthology film *Torture Garden* (1967). The mirror's ability to move is only a figment of Mary's imagination, unfortunately, and the dressing table remains an inanimate, rather passive presence for the remainder of the movie.

MR. VAMPIRE (1985)
Starring Lam Ching-Ying, Ricky Hui, Chin Siu-Ho, Moon Lee, Huang Ha, Wu Ma
Directed by Ricky Lau
Bo Ho Film Company Ltd/Golden Harvest

This enjoyable fantasy horror flick depends heavily on comedic set pieces involving a zombie's thirst for living prey and the hilarious responses used to ward it off. The zombie in question is the father of a rich landowner in the early days of republican China. Consulting a feng shui master, the landowner is advised to move the corpse of his father away from its present grave. He sets about hiring a priest for this purpose, played by Lam Ching-Ying, along with his bumbling disciples. They manage to botch the job and the corpse turns into a murderous zombie.
The success of *Mr. Vampire* spawned four sequels and numerous parodies and copies, establishing Lam Ching-Ying as the Van Helsing of the Far East.

MR. VAMPIRE II (1986)
Starring Lam Ching-Ying, Yuen Biao, Moon Lee, Chung Fat, Billy Lau
Directed by Ricky Lau
Action by Sammo Hung
Bo Ho Film Company Ltd/Golden Harvest

For round two of the hugely successful series, Golden Harvest golden boy Yuen Biao is drafted in to add that extra-special martial arts touch.
Lam Ching-Ying reprises his role as the Van Helsing of Hong Kong, and glamor is supplied in the supernatural shape of Moon Lee.

An often-hilarious romp among the quick, the dead and the somewhere in-between, the film is not quite as good as its classic predecessor, but is still hopping fun for Chinese vampire film lovers.

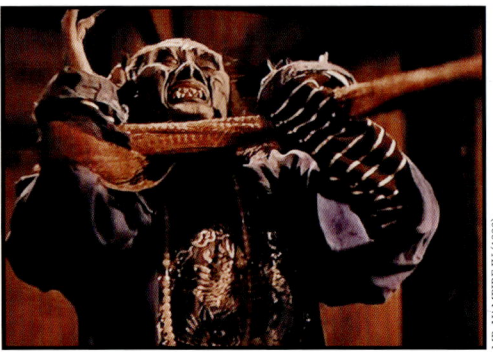

MR. VAMPIRE IV (1988)

MR. VAMPIRE III (1987)

Starring Lam Ching-Ying, Lui Fong, Richard Ng, Billy Lau
Directed by Ricky Lau
Bo Ho Film Company Ltd/Golden Harvest

Also known as *Mr. Vampire Part 3*, this third installment of the series boasts fine primary colors and blue lightning, and is chockablock with inventive supernatural confrontations from beginning to end. Glowing rocks are sucked from the ground to be flung at Lam Ching-Ying and his crew, a child vampire hops about and a lizard is beheaded in this racy ghost fantasy.

Sammo Hung pops up as a waiter, a ghost gets its arm torn off, a supernatural girl spits up maggots and cockroaches, and an angry female spirit whizzes about seeking revenge.

It's fun all the way, give it a go.

MR. VAMPIRE IV (1988)

Starring Wu Ma, Anthony Chan, Chin Kar-Lok, Loletta Lee, Yuen Wah, Wu Ma
Directed by Ricky Lau
Bo Ho Film Company Ltd/Golden Harvest

Ricky Lau once again directs, but Lam Ching-Ying, busy with countless *Mr. Vampire* cash-ins, is a no-show, replaced here by veteran actor Wu Ma. Loletta Lee plays a disciple, Chin Kar-Lok brings his martial art mastery to the screen and Yuen Wah camps it up as one of the vampires.

The gags and visuals are fast-paced and, although this movie, known also as *Mr. Vampire Saga Four*,

seems to be running out of steam, lovers of the franchise will find the usual amount of enjoyment and Hong Kong tomfoolery to make this a pleasing watch.

MR. VAMPIRE 1992 (1992)

Starring Lam Ching-Ying, Ricky Hui, Chin Siu-Ho, Sandra Ng, Suki Kwan, Billy Lau, Tsui Man-Wah
Directed by Ricky Lau
Grand March Movie Production Company Ltd/Lau Kun Wai Production

Lam Ching-Ying returns as . . . Master Lam Ching-Ying, an expert in vampirism looking into an outbreak of the undead in an area overseen by a General (Lau), who is married to Lam's former love. Lam and his two assistants (Hui & Siu-Ho) really have their hands full, however, because they also need to deal with an evil maidservant's plot to grow the spirit of an angry aborted child in the belly of the General's pregnant wife. Running out of options, they call on exorcist Birdie (Ng) to help out, and she's more than happy to aid them, since she really has the hots for Lam!

Mr. Vampire 1992 uses the notion that the spirits of aborted children remain in the form of kids as a major supernatural element to the story, with certain child-spirits becoming frustrated and dangerous due to the fact their mothers had several abortions, thwarting any chance of the spirits getting reincarnated. But this interesting concept is

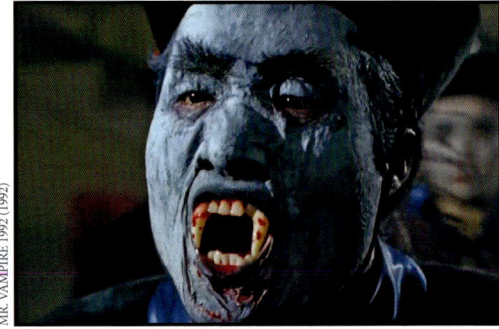

MR. VAMPIRE 1992 (1992)

not really explored and is shoved aside in favor of loads of scatological humor and general silliness.

A midpoint sequence in a village entirely overrun by hopping vampires looks like more effort was made to ensure that it was well-lit and atmospheric, plus there's a slo-mo parade of spirits in the woods that is nicely handled. Billy Lau enjoys himself playing the vamp-infected General who can't stop doing little vampire-hops every now and then, Sandra Ng is amusing as the Lam-obsessed Birdie, all the stuff about having to grind down vampire teeth to make a curative powder is fun, and the final-reel showdown, where Lam and co. battle an electrically powered, bald, veiny demon-child, the acrobatic, tough-fighting maidservant and another bunch of hopping vampires, is diverting and decently done, which compensates somewhat for the parts of the film that are flatly lit, pointless, or tiresomely obsessed with pissing and shitting jokes.

MY BETTER HALF (1993)

Starring Yip Sin-Yi, Lee Yuet-Sin, Lee Chung-Ning
Directed by Lam Yee-Hung
Ka Wah Films

This is a Category III trilogy of terrors, mixing eroticism with murderous relationships.

Story one has a concubine who marries a respectable master, but when he dies before they can consummate their relationship, she is forced to go back to her old occupation, where the ghost of her husband returns to protect her from an obnoxious customer's advances. Similar stylistically to *Rouge* (1987), except that it has a jaw-dropping punchline: her husband's ghost is given a second chance, except that he has to perform ever more complicated sexual positions with his living wife before dawn, or return to the underworld.

Story two involves a family made destitute by the husband's illness. When he is forced to go into surgery, his wife is forced to sell her body to a lecherous chicken merchant, but when the husband finds out, he kills her and himself.

Story three is a study of paranoia and madness told in flashbacks by a woman confessing the murder of

her husband (complete with chainsaw and cooking pot!). The psychotic woman gets carried away, going into graphic CAT III descriptions of their sex life before a policewoman can tell her to shut up! The tale is told with tongue firmly in cheek, but without sacrificing the gruesomeness of its subject matter.

NA CHA AND THE SEVEN DEVILS (1973)

Starring Yu Lung, Ching Li, Tina Chin Fei, An Ping, Wei Hung, Chen Hung-Lieh
Directed by Tetsuya Yamanouchi
Shaw Brothers/Jih Mao Film Company

After eating a sacred peach and accidentally knocking the other seven peaches down to the mortal world, young Na Cha must deal with the human-looking devils that have appeared on Earth after various animals have chowed down on the mystical fruit.

This seems like a kids' fantasy film to begin with, but soon we're presented with shots of groping couples making out and scenes of folks being killed by the devils, who have a penchant for turning themselves into the likenesses of loved ones.

There's a decent kaiju moment when a giant dragon burns down a village, plus a subplot involving the devils attempting to prevent a military fleet from setting sail and an airborne skirmish too, between Na Cha, a devil eagle and the dragon. To even the odds in this fight with the puppet predators, Na Cha grows in size and becomes multiarmed for a while!

Na Cha and the Seven Devils is a watchable Hong Kong–Taiwanese fantasy adventure coproduction that, just like similar mythical tales, continually introduces extra characters as the story progresses, including a snake dude, a bull dude and a goat dude, plus an immortal hero with a third eye called Yang Jian, who is aided by Celestial Dog: a canine companion wearing its own natty yellow costume!

NAKED KILLER (1992)

Starring Chingmy Yau, Simon Yam, Carrie Ng, Yao Wei, Madoka Sugawara
Directed by Clarence Ford
Produced by Wong Jing
Wong Jing's Workshop Ltd

The trouble with a lot of sex 'n' violence flicks is that there's usually not enough of either. However, that's a dilemma that *Naked Killer* remedies with a vengeance, as a simple tale of a traumatized cop

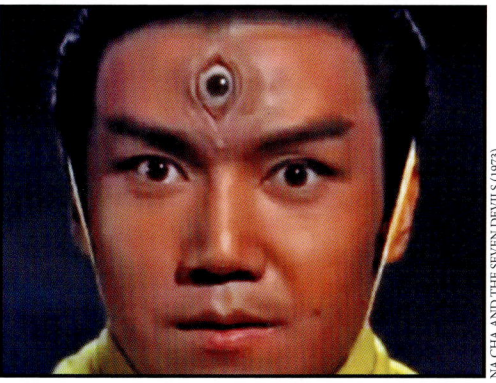

NA CHA AND THE SEVEN DEVILS (1973)

with a past meeting a feisty femme fatale spirals off deliriously into a sizzling "roughie," that's high on ultraviolence and low on plot, with enough stylish sleaze to more than compensate.

Simon Yam plays Tinam, a cop so haunted by his involvement in the death of his brother cop that he vomits at the sight of guns. He falls in love with Kitty (Yau), but when she seeks bloody retribution against her dad's killer, she finds herself under the wing of expert hitwoman Sister Cindy and working as a contract killer under her tutelage. Things hot up when Tinam reappears on the scene, still head over heels for Kitty, and when a slinky, kinky lesbian ex-pupil of Cindy's arrives in Hong Kong with a contract on both hitwomen, you just know this one ain't gonna end peacefully.

If the storyline is somewhat free-form, then there's more than ample compensation in some major martial arts action, wild gunplay and devilish nastiness, from poisoned lipstick to inadvertent penis-munching, which makes *Naked Killer* a treat not to be missed.

NIGHT CALLER (1985)
Starring Melvin Wong, Wong Siu-Fung, Philip Chan, Patricia Ha
Directed by Philip Chan
D & B Films Co. Ltd/Pyramid Films Production

A carving knife killer claims several victims and a policeman tracks him down and discovers that *he* is a *she*. The policeman is held prisoner and repeatedly beaten while his colleagues endeavor to find him.

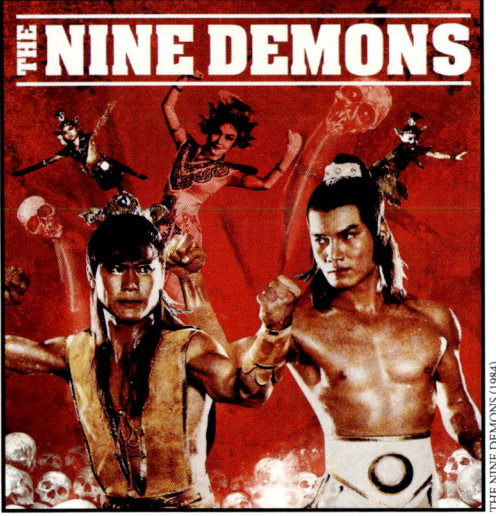

THE NINE DEMONS (1984)

The action centers more on the exploits of the cops than the killer, although the creepier scenes are pretty atmospheric.

The opening sequence is gripping, as an attractive woman is slashed by an assailant wearing black gloves and brandishing a gleaming carving knife. A girl holding a doll fitted with a tape recorder witnesses her mother's demise before hiding in a wardrobe. The killer is unaware of the girl's presence, until she accidentally causes the doll to start playing a tune . . . It's a pity the rest of the film doesn't live up to this opening, although the captured policeman's incarceration is effectively handled, with the good-looking killer indulging in some mud-bathing, reminiscences and grievous bodily harm.

THE NINE DEMONS (1984)
Starring Ricky Cheng Tien-Chi, Chiang Sheng, Lu Feng, Lee Kim-Sang, Chang Fu-Chien, Wang Quen
Directed by Chang Cheh
Chang He Film Company

Joey (Tien-Chi) does a deal with the Black Prince of Hell (Fu-Chien), allowing nine demons into his body in exchange for the chance to save his friend Gary (Kim-Sang) and avenge himself against those behind the violent takeover of family estates. Gaining a fancy caped costume, Joey uses the demons, who take the form of either nine small skulls or eight acrobatic kids & a woman, to destroy all his enemies, which include various uncles and cousins conspiring against him. Unfortunately for Joey, these nine demons must drink human blood every day, so he becomes a compromised character, seeking righteous revenge but also needing victims to feed his demons.

The many studio sets help give the production a Shaw Brothers vibe. The movie is sometimes garishly lit with reds and greens, and its bizarre ingredients include floating, smoking (obviously plastic) skulls zipping about the place and smiling demon-kids, all dressed in traditional Thai-style garb, chowing down on people's throats.

Additionally, this crazy fantasy-horror-martial-arts-actioner culminates in an unconventional battle between Joey and warriors wearing mini water skis. These guys nimbly scoot around the surface of a shallow pool, until Joey uses his powers to freeze the water, prompting his opponents to use long lengths of bamboo to create a framework above the ice, allowing the fight to continue, with Joey letting loose his demons once again and his adversaries brandishing flaming torch weapons against him. Ultimately, the power of Buddhism prevails, Joey rids himself of the demons and promptly explodes, freeing his spirit to be reincarnated. Bloody weird!

NINJA: THE VIOLENT SORCERER (1982)

Starring Simon Reed, Harry Carter, Henry Steele, Joe Nelson, Chiang Tao, Lu Feng, Chen Hung-Lieh, Angela Mao, Danny Lee
Directed by "Bruce Lambert"
Produced by Tomas Tang
Filmark International Ltd

Two dice, taken from hopping vampires, will help Mr. Baker, known as the Gambling King, take over the whole gambling world! But Roger, the brother of a gambler forced to kill himself, promises to get revenge, which he does dressed as a white-clad ninja!

You've got to grudgingly admire the don't-give-a-f*ck plotting in producer Tomas Tang's spliced-together specials from Filmark International. This particular film sticks new vampire & ninja content (probably shot by action director Chiang Tao and not Godfrey Ho, who is always credited as director for these kind of movies) into footage from another film called *The Stunning Gambling* (1982), which stars Danny Lee and Angela Mao, featuring gamblers betting their lives on the outcome of games, including a superfast card-dealing challenge.

With ninjas being taught anti-sorcery magic by a priest, seemingly unconnected scenes located on a war movie set and in a rowdy barroom, green & white ninjas with the ability to vanish and reappear, and a briefly seen female ghost called Rose, *Ninja: the Violent Sorcerer* ends with the two ninja heroes and a good priest combating multiple hopping vampires and an evil priest in a normal-looking suburban living room.

NINJA VAMPIRE BUSTERS (1989)

Starring Nick Chang, Kent Cheng, Stanley Fong, Jacky Cheung
Directed by Norman Law Man, Stanley Siu Wing
Foo Ong Film/In-Gear Film Production

Known also as *Vampire Buster*, this film follows the story of a vase, which contains the spirit of an evil vampire who was exorcised 500 years ago and sealed in the vase with a paper seal. The vase is sold in present-day Hong Kong at an auction and the

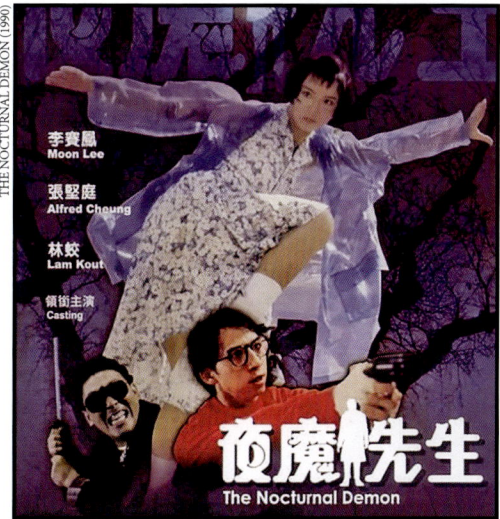

THE NOCTURNAL DEMON (1990)

seal is broken, letting the spirit loose, allowing it to go from body to body to avoid being caught by the exorcist, who has been sent to return it to its resting place. So, at one time or another, most of the leading characters are possessed for a while.

The film is not exceptional until the excellent last half hour or so, which is packed with flying, walking up walls, fast fighting, and a touch of gore. One poor nurse gets his arm pulled off and most of the hospital patients get flung all over the place via some terrific wirework.

THE NOCTURNAL DEMON (1990)

Starring Alfred Cheung, Moon Lee, Lam Kau, Yuen Wah, Cho Wing, Tsui Sui-Ming, Billy Lau
Directed by Ricky Lau
Gold Double Productions/Lau Kun Wai Production

A taxi driver (Wing) turns out to be a psychotic killer who vomits at the smell of perfume. Sniffing lighter fuel, the bespectacled killer uses a knife with a retractable blade to slash up buxom female victims.

Moon Lee plays Wawa, a scatty girl from the sticks who comes to visit her relatives in the city. Wawa is a terrific martial artist, and her roller skate scrap and pole fighting sequences are real crowd pleasers.

Fight action, farce, and deadly serious murder are mixed in a crazy combination, leading to a final scene with Moon Lee dressed preposterously in orange hotpants, wig, and thigh-high leather boots, as she teams up with her blind grandfather to take on the mad murderer and hurl him around the room.

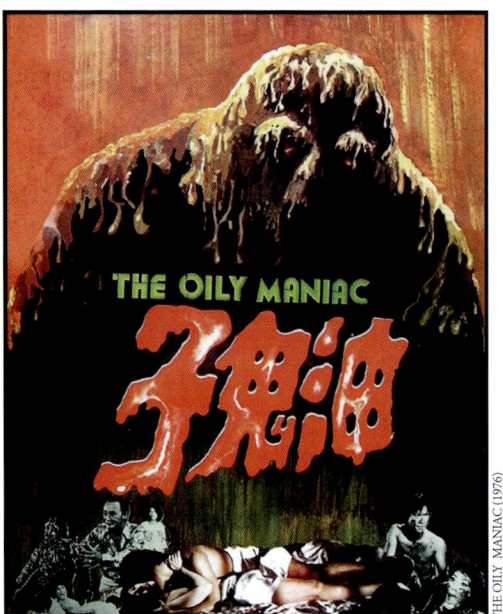

THE OILY MANIAC (1976)

THE OILY MANIAC (1976)
Directed by Ho Meng-Hua
Starring Danny Lee, Chen Ping, Lily Li, Hua Lun,
Wang Hsieh, Angela Yu Chien
Shaw Brothers

Written by Chua Lam, this Malaysia-set story revolves around disabled seeker of justice Sheng Yung, who works for a law firm and finds himself compelled to use a spell that turns him into a supernatural, oily being, enabling him to protect his childhood sweetheart Little Yue (Ping) from lowlife characters.

Yung, however, begins to use his sludgy alter ego to inflict muddy vigilante justice on various other deceitful characters, including an unlicensed female surgeon who botches boob jobs and an actress who accuses an innocent neighbor of rape in court. Once Yung discovers that his corrupt, sleazoid boss is in cahoots with Yue's new boyfriend, in a scheme that will eventually lead to Yue's rape and suicide, events rapidly spiral out of control, climaxing in confrontations with machete-wielding thugs and the local cops.

This Shaw Brothers release, sporting pretty decent production values, is a crazy blend of 1970s-style exploitation, horror and action, with some courtroom dramatics added to the mix.

The movie's unique selling point, of course, is the Oily Maniac himself, initially brought to life when Sheng kneels at the bottom of a pit he's dug in the center of his living room, chanting a special spell as the hole fills with water. Sheng is submerged beneath the muddy waters . . . then rises back into view, transformed into a yellow-eyed, mud & oil-coated humanoid monster . . . as the music from *Jaws* plays on the soundtrack! This bizarre, grungy creature has an exposed, red beating heart and emits an echoey roar similar to the kind of sounds the monsters made in the cartoon series *Scooby Doo, Where Are You!*

The Oily Maniac can turn into an animated, not particularly realistic mud puddle, which slithers around the place, before forming back into a slime-covered humanoid. We see this cartoony splash of goo zipping about floors and walls quite a few times in the movie, accompanied by the *Jaws* music! After his various attacks, the Oily Maniac always changes back into Sheng, who wakes up lying on the floor of his home, covered in oil splotches.

Whenever Sheng wants to become the monstrous maniac, he must coat himself in oily substances to trigger the transformation, so we get to see him do such things as pump diesel over his body at a gas station or submerge himself in a barrel of boiling oil near a road construction site.

Once he's the Oily Maniac again, he can either slither about as that squirmy puddle or go on the rampage as the lumbering, blobby beast. Interestingly,

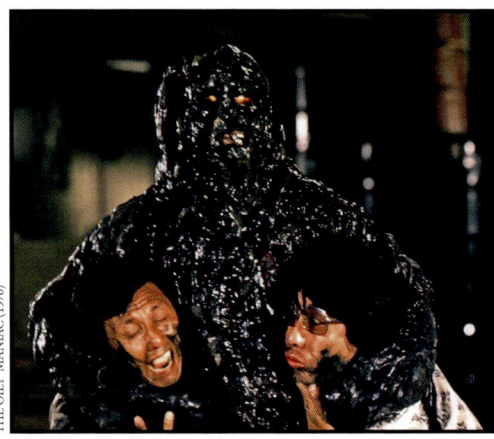

THE OILY MANIAC (1976)

when it suits him, the Oily Maniac ceases his slow, cumbersome mode of walking and becomes able to leap around very agilely indeed, dashing across rooftops and running over the top of vehicles. Memorable set pieces include the glistening, oil-coated monster rising from a pink bathtub to attack a victim and a rampage through an operating theater that specializes in restoring women's hymens!

Danny Lee, years before starring in John Woo's *The Killer* (1989), dabbled in several fantastical Shaw Brothers productions in the 1970s, including *The Mighty Peking Man* (1977), *The Battle Wizard* (1977) and *The Super Inframan* (1975). But it's in *The Oily Maniac* that Lee gets to really immerse himself in an oddball, weirder-than-weird tale. As Sheng, who is disabled (due to contracting polio as a child), he is initially a browbeaten character inspired to become a powerful, avenging pile of slime to protect Little Yue, but his motivations become increasingly muddled, leading to him killing nurses simply because they happen to work for an unlicensed surgeon.

Constantly finding excuses to include bare female breasts and various misogynistic moments, *The Oily Maniac* is certainly sleazy much of the time, intermingling these exploitative sequences with avenging monster action that predates Troma's *The Toxic Avenger* (1984).

The scenes featuring the vengeful mud-man are actually not particularly gory, but they're certainly outlandishly enjoyable to watch, culminating in a couple of large-scale showdowns, where we see the Oily Maniac transfixed with blades and shot at by the police. But there's no stopping this sebaceous mound of muck, who can always turn into a pool of cartoon sludge, so when his slimy arm and his oily head get chopped off at one point . . . they simply regrow again! Finally, it is a coworker, who loves Sheng, who ends the Oily Maniac's reign of vigilante terror by setting him on fire.

This is a colorful, cruel, crazy Shaw Brothers B-movie gem.

OPERATION PINK SQUAD II (1989)

Starring Sandra Ng, Billy Lau, Cheung Man, Woo Fung, Ann Bridgewater, Suki Kwan, Shing Fui-On, Yuen Cheung-Yan
Directed by Jeffrey Lau
Golden Flare Films Company

Female cops go undercover to crack a forgery case and, while they wait to meet up with the counterfeiter bad guy (Fui-On), they stay at an almost deserted apartment block that is haunted by ghosts.

Aka *Thunder Cops*, this movie is crammed with very broad, farcical humor, much of it centered around a buffoonish, newlywed policeman (Lau) believing that his cop wife (Ng) is having a fling with her boss, Inspector Shin (Fung).

Meanwhile, in the ghost-infested building, a monk (Cheung-Yan) captures the various spirits and stores

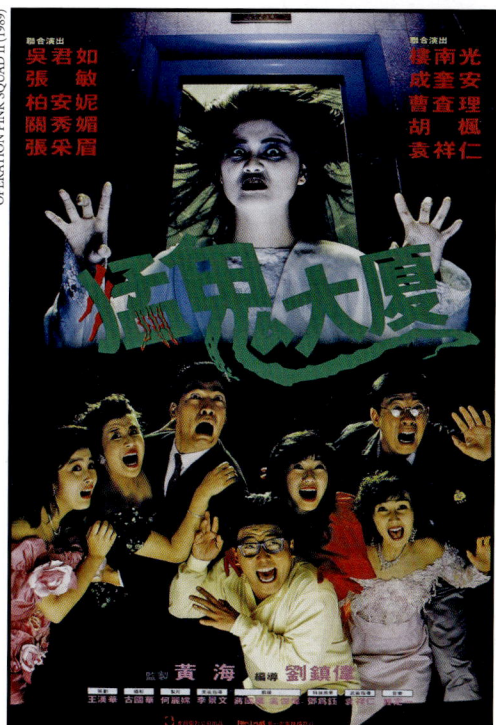

OPERATION PINK SQUAD II (1989)

them in drawstring bags covered in Buddhist swastika symbols. These bags are then placed behind a sealed "Door of Hell," but one of the bags is accidentally dropped, enabling the blue-lit female ghost to escape and begin to terrorize the place. Oh, this ghost can be nasty, but also likes to have her toes sucked!

The overly slapstick film gives us such silliness as Inspector Shin posing as a cross-dressing pimp, a parody of the slo-mo Chow Yun-Fat corridor moment from *A Better Tomorrow* and a scene where two of the guys take part in a literal pissing contest. The flick properly kicks into gear, however, once the monk returns and everyone teams up to tackle the nasty girl ghost, who eventually gets beheaded.

But now matters really become strange, as the headless body chases after everyone, as does the ghost's floating severed head! To tackle this flying fiend, the heroes use remote control toy helicopters, equipped with mini-rockets, to chase the gliding head! The female ghost's cranium is finally cornered by the helicopters . . . so it explodes! The blood from the head splatters onto the characters, which attracts even more ghosts, who storm into the building, resembling shambling, long-haired zombies.

After a farcical sequence involving the monk suggesting that one of the men should be castrated to save the day, the situation is finally solved with the invocation of Buddhist mythological characters, who magically deal with the spirits.

Yes, it's very strange.

OUT OF THE DARK (1995)
Starring Stephen Chow, Karen Mok, Wong Yat-Fei, Lee Lik-Chi, Lo Hung, Ben Wong Chi-Yin, Lee Kin-Yan, Heung Dip, Chow Chi-Fai, Tam Suk-Mui, Hau Woon-Ling, Leung Kar-Yan
Directed by Jeffrey Lau
Cosmopolitan Film Productions

This is a comedy-horror film featuring Steven Chow as Leon, a disturbed mental patient with delusions that make him feel fearless. He claims to be a ghost hunter and has a look that is loosely based on Jean Reno's character in Luc Besson's *Léon: the Professional* (1994). Throughout the film, in fact, Leon wears a similar outfit and carries a plant pot, which he talks to for comfort as he wanders around.

The movie is set in an apartment building, where the evil spirit of a woman who was killed by her son and daughter-in-law is causing spooky shenanigans. Leon decides to investigate, but his involvement only makes matters worse. He accidentally assists the killers in their suicide, as the couple do not want to face responsibility after being spooked by the spirit. This death escalates the situation because, in Hong Kong culture, if you die wearing red you are cursed to return to cause havoc as a revenge-seeking poltergeist.

To rid the building of these unwanted spirits, Leon enlists the help of Kwan (Mok) and two flaky security guards. The jokes come thick and fast, although some may not be understood by viewers who have little knowledge of Hong Kong culture and references to Hong Kong movies.

Despite a slow beginning, fans of Steven Chow will appreciate his zany, impromptu comedy and madcap action, including playing pass the parcel with dynamite!

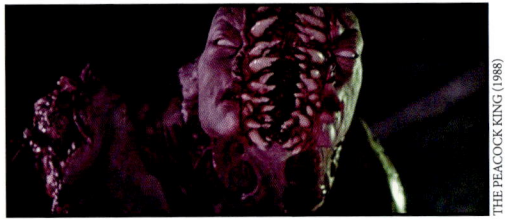

THE PEACOCK KING (1988)

THE PEACOCK KING (1988)
Starring Yuen Biao, Hiroshi Mikami, Wong Siu-Fung, Narumi Yasuda, Gloria Yip, Eddy Ko, Gordon Liu, Philip Kwok
Directed by Nam Nai-Choi
Golden Harvest

Two young monks, Peacock (Biao) and Lucky Fruit (Mikami), must prevent the Hell King from destroying the world. Supernatural forces are able to enter the world via four holes to Hell, and the bulk of the tale concerns the hunt for these entrances. In fact, the film's main weakness is that too much time is given over to whizzing to Japan, Hong Kong, and Tibet, fracturing what chance there is of linear plot development.

However, the movie's fun special effects more than compensate . . .

Early on we see small, many-eyed crawly thingies called "womanising ghosts," which resemble more interesting versions of the stop-motion models crafted for the hologram chess game in *Star Wars*. Another animation model comes into play when Hell's Envoy Raga, played by Wong Siu-Fung, gets injured. Raga arches her back, develops telescopic, insectoid forearms and claws, and then, best of all, causes her now reptilian, elongated face to split lengthwise into a gaping, vertical, toothy maw! This very cool monster acrobatically leaps around the place as it battles the protagonists, with full-scale props and animatronics used in conjunction with the stop-motion puppet to bring this beast to the screen. This is definitely the standout sequence in the movie!

Other special effects moments include a dinosaur model coming to life at a prehistoric exhibition, a genie-type giant, various optical magic effects and a flaming phoenix of light.

Also known as *Legend of the Phoenix*, this modern-day fantasy-action flick is flawed but great fun!

PICTURE OF A NYMPH (1988)
Starring Joey Wong, Yuen Biao, Wu Ma, Lam Wai, Lawrence Ng, Yuen Wah
Directed by Wu Ma
Golden Harvest

To the untrained eye, it's almost like watching a sequel to *A Chinese Ghost Story*. Joey Wong, who is to beautiful ghosts what Lam Ching-Ying is to vampire-hunting, stars with Wu Ma, who, of course, appeared in *A Chinese Ghost Story* with Wong. Martial arts marvel Yuen Biao takes on the Leslie Cheung-style role, in a story that tells of a spiritual love set in ancient China, where a sensitive scholar (Biao) falls in love with a beautiful ghost (Wong) . . . yup, that does sound familiar!

After a demon is accidentally released from centuries of captivity, he must trap the scholar's lover to regain his evil powers. The scholar decides to paint her portrait, in which she hides from the demon. Thwarted, the demon captures the scholar instead, but the ghost surrenders herself to save him.

This is actually a delightful romantic fantasy, with some good special effects and plenty of fluid camerawork, making it one of the more watchable *A Chinese Ghost Story* copycats, although it lacks that certain je ne sais quoi that makes the Ching Siu-Tung original the best of the best.

POWER OF LOVE (1993)

Starring Suen Tong, Rena Otomo, Hsiao Yu-Lung, Lui Lee
Directed by Leung Chi-Wah
Success Film Production Co

Here's a pleasingly nutty sex thriller that not only succeeds in pandering to our most base instincts with lashings of on-screen writhing, enthusiastically performed by a choice selection of HK's most beautiful actresses, but it also manages to insert a plotline so deliciously dumb it'll keep you watching even between the sexy scenes.

What that plot consists of is far too complicated to go into in detail here, suffice to say it concerns a foxy housekeeping lass with a penchant for novel uses of a vacuum cleaner, who finds herself inheriting a fortune in her lecherous boss's will. The old man's son and his pushy missus are most unhappy, of course, and vow to snuff the usurping vixen. Various assassins-for-hire are contracted, one of whom, a heavily armed nymphoid, seems unable to control

her hormones long enough to ever be in a position to rub anybody out.

It all starts getting a bit complicated from then on, as the scenes of undulating and ultraviolence lead inexorably toward a satisfyingly insane climax. Well worth a look.

RAPED BY AN ANGEL (1993)

Starring Chingmy Yau, Simon Yam, Mark Cheng, Jacqueline Ng
Directed by Andrew Lau
Produced by Wong Jing
Wong Jing's Workshop Ltd

Known also as *Naked Killer 2*, this is a pretty nasty Category III thriller centered around a serial rapist terrorizing girls in an apartment block. In fact, it plays more as a straightforward Western rape/revenge number, only minus some of the bloodier aspects you might have expected from a traditional "roughie." Despite its iffy subject matter, *Raped by An Angel* doesn't pack much of a punch: any shock value is too often defused by an overlong courtroom scene and too much exposition regarding the heroine, Yuk-Nam (Yau), and her dalliance with good guy Tat (Yam). We know he's a good guy, as he can be persuaded to practice safe sex on a first date! Speaking of which, that seems to be something of a theme in this one; references to AIDS and the importance of wearing latex protection abound.

What *Raped by An Angel* lacks is anything distinctively "Hong Kong." It's as though the intention was to make a conventional Hollywood thriller, leaving out those moments of jaw-dropping inspirational derangement that make Hong Kong flicks so fascinating. Only in its mindboggling climax does the film lurch into madness and, even then, the twist is so implausible that it'll leave you shrugging. Alas, the same can be said for the rest of the film too.

RED PANTHER (1983)

Starring James Yi Lui, Margaret Li, Chang Kuo-Chu, Philip Chan
Directed by Chiang Lung
H.K. Fong Ming Motion Picture Company

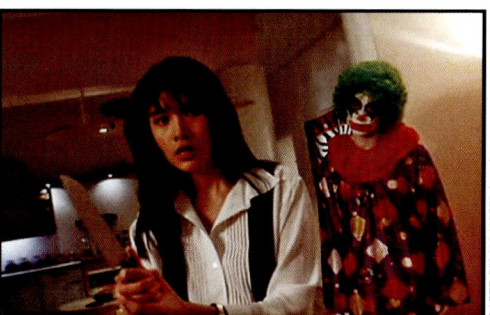

RAPED BY AN ANGEL (1993)

Who is the madman going around with a doctor's bag, killing off victims who have medical problems? Is it the bespectacled geek who makes stew out of corpse-guts? Or is it the local doctor with nervous problems? A policeman suffering from "posterior ulcers" looks into the matter.

This Hong Kong medical thriller places the policeman protagonist into several sticky situations. He eats some of the geek's "special recipe" before realizing he's just swallowed stew à la intestine. He later finds himself trapped in an industrial washing machine and, as a climax, is tied-up on an operating table by the maniac, who wants to deal with his ulcers using a scalpel!

The film is not particularly gory, but it is well done, and the identity of the killer is not as obvious as it first appears.

RED SPELL SPELLS RED (1983)
Starring Kent Tong, Poon Lai-Yin, Lun Chia
Directed by Titus Ho
Nikko International Productions & Films

A film crew sneaks into an off-limits burial place in Borneo, releasing a Red Dwarf ghost, triggering a murderous curse that will only be halted when a gray-haired sorcerer and a Buddhist lama finally intervene.

This unashamedly exploitative release from Nikko International Productions & Films presents us with the typical Hong Kong horror movie staples of arcane rituals and chanting monks, mixing them into a salacious brew heavily indebted to Western movies.

Mondo footage of the slaughter of real pigs, a meddling documentary crew and the depiction of indigenous tribespeople as cruel savages hint at the influence of *Cannibal Holocaust* (1980), while a set piece involving main protagonist Stella being assaulted by a possessed bamboo bed that forces her legs wide open above an oil lamp is undoubtedly inspired by *The Evil Dead* (1981).

Red Spell Spells Red is definitely full of incident! Memorable moments include the very gross spectacle of a Borneo tribesman eating the innards of a still-alive chicken, Stella's possessed period blood provoking a supernatural occurrence, death-by-jungle-vines, people succumbing to scorpion infestations and a finale in which the gray-haired holy man allows himself to be covered in scorpions and then immolated.

Let's just spare a moment to consider put-upon documentarian Stella (Lai-Yin), who finds herself in multiple situations that inevitably result in her clothes getting wet. She is also plagued with a Scorpion Spell that causes her to exude these black arthropods from a wound near a red birthmark, making her deadly to anyone who gets too close to her. Even when the helpful sorcerer is trying to cure her, this calls for

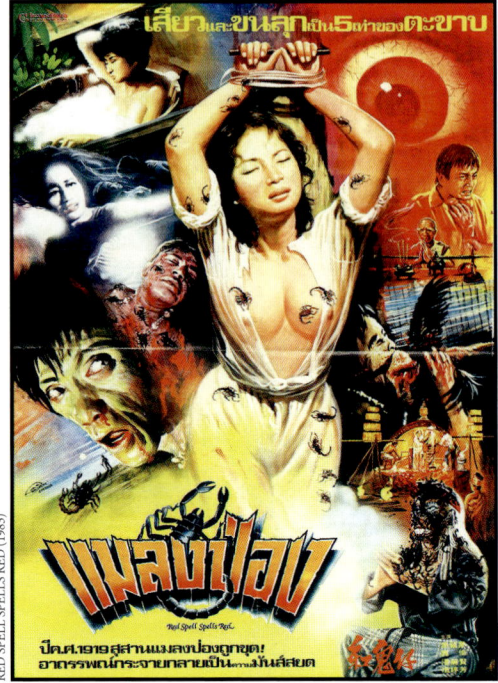

RED SPELL SPELLS RED (1983)

the poor woman to be bound to a rotating water wheel (cue more wet clothing shots), then sprinkled with powder made from the ground-up skull of the sorcerer's dead daughter, before having a chunk of possessed flesh ripped from her shoulder. This is definitely a location shoot Stella will want to forget!

The bottom line is that *Red Spell Spells Red* is a gonzo, shameless piece of brazen Hong Kong exploitation filmmaking that lovers of vulgar, mad & muddled mondo horror movies will love.

RETURN OF THE DEMON (1987)
Starring Charlie Cho, Shing Fui-On, Dick Wei,
Emily Chu, Wu Ma
Directed by Wong Ying
Produced by Charles Heung, Wong Ying
Eagle Film Production

Only a person born in the "Hoi" year, month, and day can get the treasure hidden in the hands of a certain Buddha statue. But it's all an evil trick to enable a superhuman, soul-sucking character known as the Monster to escape from the statue in which it is trapped.

Shing Fui-On's character is big, tough and somewhat stupid, while Dick Wei plays the scabby-faced, brain-sucking villain as a real ass-kicker, in a movie that's generally a surface-deep excuse for loosely connected scenes involving spells, a female ghost, zombies, dog piss–drinking, and fights.

A lynching torture is treated as an opportunity for comedic acrobatics, a boulder is revealed to have a pulsing central core, broken eggs are used to age a spell-making Master (who also turns into a fun weredog), and a blue-lit cavern houses a large wheel on which zombies toil. There's also a network of tunnels set in the rock walls of the cavern, from which the zombies shoot out if a bell is rung. These zombies have a needle in the center of their heads: pull it out and they die.

Return of the Demon is an enjoyable, lightweight serving of relentless Hong Kong action-horror goofiness.

ROBO VAMPIRE (1988)

Starring Robin Mackay, Nian Watts, Harry Myles,
Sorapong Chatree
Directed by "Joe Livingstone"
Filmark International Ltd

Tom, an anti-drug agent, is mortally wounded while taking on narcos, who are using Chinese hopping vampires as weapons and as a means to smuggle their heroin shipments. Tom dies on the operating table, but it is decided to transform him into an android . . . enter the robo-warrior!

Robo Vampire, a cut-and-paste movie courtesy of producer Tomas Tang's Filmark International, closely resembles the kind of productions made by director Godfrey Ho, the king of such chimeric flicks, which is why the film is often falsely attributed to him. So, who is director "Joe Livingstone," then? I don't know the answer to that, but the owner of IFD Films & Arts Ltd, Toby Russell, assures me that it isn't Mr. Ho. Let's move on . . .

Much of the footage in *Robo Vampire*, especially the hostage rescue mission sequences, is sourced from the Thai actioner *Paa Lohgan* (1984). The new spliced-in material is all the hopping vampire and robo-dude stuff and, interestingly, these additional scenes are actually better lit than the original movie footage, which usually isn't the case.

The main character, a stomping, low-tech, silver-suited dude with a big gun, is not actually a vampire, as you might have expected considering the film's title. He's just a cut-price android, though he does skirmish with many scabby-faced, hopping bloodsuckers throughout the film's running time.

In one action sequence, the robo-warrior battles armed bad guys on a beach, where they attempt to immolate him, but when this fails he is assailed by vampires that pop-up from the sand. This is a shoddily shot, gloriously cheesy set piece that ends with a tinfoil-covered dummy, representing the android protagonist, being blown up by a rocket launcher! But don't you worry, the tech guys weld robo-warrior back together again pretty quickly and easily.

Though the jungle-based rescue subplot is a mainly underwhelming series of shoot-outs, fights and explosions, with far too many characters being introduced into the story, a lot of the other incidents in the movie are quite memorable, including drugs being hidden in a real dead cow's slit-open belly, romantic interludes between a ghostly woman and her gorilla-faced super-vampire lover, a bloody eye-poking, fireworks being fired from the ape-mask-vampire's sleeves, and a fight between the now-topless female ghost and a priest! Once the she-spirit defeats the evil holy man, our android hero then scorches the gorilla-vampire with his machine gun, which is now in flamethrower mode (cue burning dummy on a wire)!

Strange, trashy, cheap and cheerful nonsense.

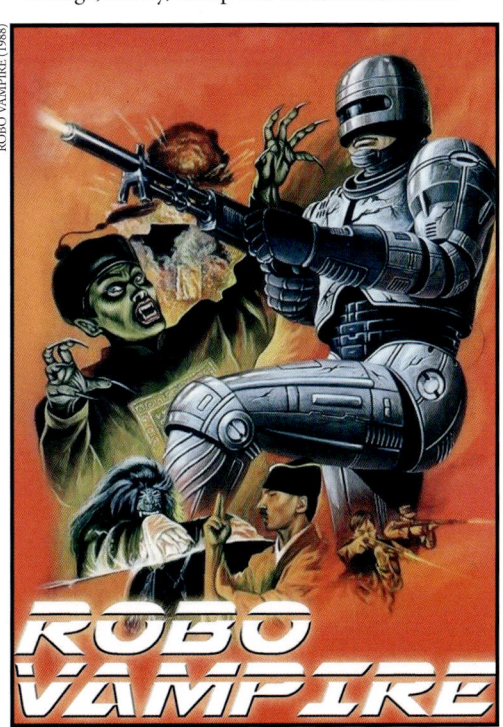

ROBO VAMPIRE (1988)

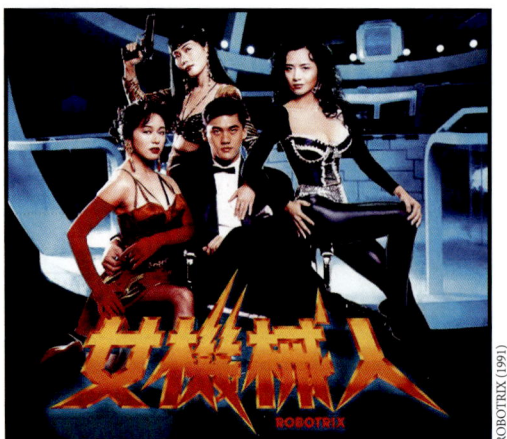

ROBOTRIX (1991)

ROBOTRIX (1991)
Starring Aoyama Chikako, Amy Yip, David Wu,
Billy Chow, Ken Goodman
Directed by Luk Kim Ming
Golden Harvest

This Category III futuristic movie looks like a Chinese *RoboCop* (1987) invested with the spirit of Russ Meyer! Its over-the-top, outrageous humor makes it a camp cheese-fest that mixes gratuitous, graphic moments with nudity, special effects and martial arts.

Doctor Sara, a curvaceous scientist, and her two skimpily attired robots help the police try to find a kidnapper, who is a mad Japanese scientist that commits hara-kiri and transfers his mind into a sex-mad rapist robot. It's man against woman and machine against machine, as good and evil battle it out with every weapon in their arsenal.

The way the juvenile naivety in *Robotrix* mixes with its often very explicit trashiness causes rapid shifts in tone and, although the possibilities of the science fiction theme are barely explored, the heady brew of softcore sex, sci-fi, violence and action does help the film stand out from other CAT III entries.

RUN AND KILL (1993)
Starring Simon Yam, Kent Cheng, Danny Lee,
Melvin Wong, Esther Kwan, Wang Lung-Wei
Directed by Billy Tang
Come On Film Co

Cheung (Cheng) is a mild-mannered businessman who arrives home to find his attractive wife in bed with another man. He about-turns and heads for the nearest music bar, where he drinks himself into a stupor. It is here that he is befriended by Fanny (Kwan), a club girl who operates as a go-between for some small-time hoods. She introduces Cheung to one of her bosses, who persuades Cheung to have his cheating wife killed. Cheung is so drunk he has no idea what is going on. When he returns home, a nightmarish scene is played out in front of him, as his wife is brutally killed by the Vietnamese gangsters. Cheung cannot come to terms with the predicament he has created for himself, and neither can Man (Lee), a cop who finds the whole case utterly absurd.

The police decide that if they give Cheung a long enough rope he will hang himself, so they tail him back to his flat. Cheung comes face-to-face with the Vietnamese gang leader, who demands the balance of payment. He informs Cheung that if he doesn't honor his end of the bargain, they will destroy his shop. When Cheung fails to raise the money, he finds his shop torched, then the gang double the fee for the inconvenience! In desperation, Cheung flees to his hometown in China to seek help. When he arrives at his village, he finds his house occupied by members of the Black Mouse Gang, a bunch of ruthless Vietcong renegades, headed by Ching Fung (Yam). Ching's brother decides to help Cheung, to impress his older brother, so he sets up a meet in a Category III cinema, where he has agreed to make a payoff to the Vietnamese gang boss. Ching's brother takes several of his gang members along to ambush the boss, but a bloody, violent fight breaks out, with Cheung and Ching's brother getting captured and taken to a refugee camp, where they suffer grotesque torture. Ching takes off on a one-man rescue mission, and with a ten-inch bowie knife, exterminates the guards one by one. But Ching's brother soon dies from blood loss and Ching, now completely demented, blames Cheung.

There then follows a personal vendetta, with Ching pursuing Cheung, slaughtering his daughter in the most gruesome way imaginable and, finally, confronting Cheung for a protracted and very inventive end fight scene.

Simon Yam is superb as the utterly insane Ching and Kent Cheng, as poor ol' Cheung, puts in a sympathetic performance as a gentle man whose entire life falls apart due to one unfortunate drunken misunderstanding.

The combination of black humor and extreme violence, plus its willingness to cross lines viewers do not think it'll cross, makes *Run and Kill* a CAT III must-see and, believe it or not, just like *Dr. Lamb* (1992), this film is actually based on a true story!

ROUGE (1987)
Starring Anita Mui, Leslie Cheung, Alex Man, Emily Chu,
Irene Wan
Directed by Stanley Kwan
Produced by Jackie Chan, Leonard Ho
Golden Harvest/Golden Way Films Ltd

This is the sensitive, poignant, romantic and stylish story of Fleur (Mui), a ghostly courtesan who searches for her long-lost lover in modern day Hong Kong. In the 1930s she had made a suicide pact with her opium-addicted lover (Cheung), but he lost his nerve at the last minute and, when he doesn't meet her in the spirit world, she returns to the mortal world to find him.

Fleur is finally reunited with her loved one on the set of a movie about ghosts. One lovely touch has Fleur ascending a staircase as a fake movie ghost silently flies by on a wire behind her. This is a really fine, elegant, supernatural film that doesn't require over-the-top action or FX to leave a lasting impression. *Rouge* was voted best film at the Eighth Hong Kong Film Awards. Recommended.

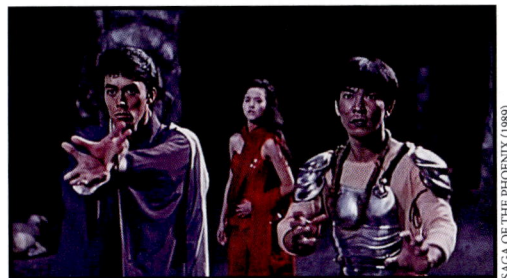

SAGA OF THE PHOENIX (1989)

SAGA OF THE PHOENIX (1989)
Starring Yuen Biao, Gloria Yip, Loletta Lee,
Shintaro Katsu, Hiroshi Abe, Ngai Suet
Directed by Lam Nai-Choi, Lau Sze-Yue
Action by Yuen Bing
Golden Harvest

This not-so-hot sequel to *Peacock King* has Ashura (Yip), aka Hell's Virgin, walking the earth, while Peacock (Biao) gets frozen in a block of ice in Hell.

Look out for (iffy) Buddhist lion statues that come to life, a Mogwai-like imp (which farts yellow gas), a matter transportation device and a huge gargoyle.

For much of the movie the imp is merely a rubber, hand-operated model, but, thankfully, in later scenes an animated, more effective version of the critter

is used. The gargoyle that Hell Concubine (Suet) transforms into is an off-the-wall, full-scale model creation. The big beastie has wings, an external rib cage, a glowing eyeball in its abdomen and Hell Concubine's face situated in its forehead!

All in all, the action and effects in the original film were better than what is on show here.

SATAN RETURNS (1996)
Starring Chingmy Yau, Francis Ng, Donnie Yen,
Wong Chi-Wah
Directed by Lam Wai-Lun
Upland Films Corporation Limited/
Wong Jing's Workshop Ltd

Officer Ching (Yau), who works for the police complaints division, is investigating Nam (Yen) to decide if he is mentally fit to carry out his police duties, but she is asked to team up with Nam instead, to help investigate a serial killer case.

This murderer is not just some typical killer, however. He is called Judas (played in a full-on fashion by Francis Ng), he's an envoy of Satan, and he's trying to track down the Devil's Daughter, who he claims is a woman born at 6 a.m. on June 6, 1969. To test if a woman is, indeed, the devil's offspring, Judas ties his female victims to a cross and surgically removes their hearts: if one of them doesn't die after this procedure she will be proven to be the true one. Though most of what happens is merely suggested, we do see Judas take a bite out of his latest victim's removed heart.

Writer Wong Jing mixes too many comedy elements into the story, mainly centered around inept cop Ka-Ming (Chi-Wah), who is cowardly, terrible at surveillance work, and a pathetic womanizer. Wong also inserts some throwaway dialogue about the impending Chinese takeover of Hong Kong into the movie, though this isn't really gone into. He does put a certain amount of thought into how Judas locates his victims, revealing that Judas compels a woman working at a credit card company to divulge the details of all female customers born on June 6, 1969, but, generally, Wong fails to keep the plot coherent and focused.

With Ching starting to realize that she might actually be the daughter of Satan (she can compel people to hurt themselves by saying "go to hell") and Judas continuing to madly claim that he's doing the devil's bidding, you expect the movie to kick up a gear and become more horror-oriented, but

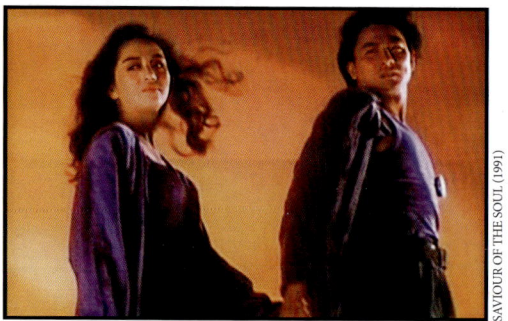

SAVIOUR OF THE SOUL (1991)

Satan Returns, also known as *Shaolin vs. The Devil's Omen*, remains unsure whether it's a comedic police procedural, an action film or a supernatural story.

Ultimately, though director Lam Wai-Lun handles the occasional blue-lit set piece with a certain amount of verve, the film fails to be tense, funny, scary or properly exciting.

It doesn't help that Donnie Yen, playing a hardboiled cop who tends to punch first and ask questions later, is underutilized as Nam. He just should have been featured in the movie more, rather than the useless and irritating Ka-Ming. Though it is a case of too little, too late, the finale does treat us to the spectacle of Nam first brandishing a chainsaw, to cut down some reanimated cop-corpses, and then using a nail gun to pin Judas to a toppled-over cross . . . before the villain is immolated with a Molotov cocktail!

SAVIOUR OF THE SOUL (1991)
Starring Andy Lau, Anita Mui, Aaron Kwok, Kenny Bee, Gloria Yip
Directed by Corey Yuen, David Lai, Jeffrey Lau
Teamwork Productions, 1991

Andy Lau and Kenny Bee play city mercenaries who are both in love with fellow warrior Anita Mui, a martial arts genius. Mui plays her own twin sister too, a shrewish hypochondriac who invents weapons, including the fantastic breathless bullet, which sucks all the air from its victims, causing them to suffocate.

In an ultraviolent and dramatic scene early into the movie, Aaron Kwok, as the supernaturally powered Silver Fox, tries to assassinate superheroine Mui in a ladies' toilet, but Bee comes to her aid. He dies saving her life, but manages to inflict a wound on Kwok's face, which forces him to adopt a Phantom of the Opera–style mask. Lau is left taking care of Bee's cute young sister, portrayed by Gloria Yip, and trains her as his assistant, unaware that she is forming a puppy love attachment to him, but his

love for woman-warrior Mui, who has gone into hiding, blinds him to her feelings. Eventually there's a dramatic final confrontation, as Andy desperately seeks a way to terminate the supernatural killer.

The movie has a vibrant, comic strip feel, with stylishly lit set pieces and very imaginative use of wirework. Although made on a fairly low budget, the film's quality look and well-handled action moments soon gained it a loyal fan following.

SAVIOUR OF THE SOUL II (1992)
Starring Andy Lau, Corey Yuen, Shirley Kwan,
Rosamund Kwan, Richard Ng, Won Jin
Directed by Corey Yuen, David Lai
Action by Yuen Tak
Teamwork Production House

This sequel to the highly successful *Saviour of the Soul* bears little relation to the first part and was obviously scripted at speed. Andy Lau reprises his city soldier–style character, joined by veteran actor/director Corey Yuen.

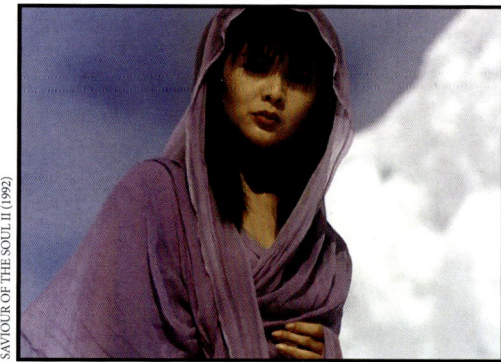

SAVIOUR OF THE SOUL II (1992)

After an impressive opening scene, showing Andy working out with his flexible sword on top of a mountain, we discover the sequel depends far more on elements of comedy than the stylish anime/manga-like violence of part one. Joined in his quest by a young boy, Andy sets out to find a mysterious woman, encountering many obstacles along the way, including a *God of Gamblers*–style situation where, with the use of a magnifying glass, things can appear very big or small.

Shot mainly on location in Canada, part II just doesn't have the same evocative, stylised studio look of the original. So, while the fast pace and comedy make this an entertaining, throwaway watch, make sure you're not expecting anything as good as part one!

SCORPION THUNDERBOLT (1988)

Starring Richard Harrison, Li-Yun Chen, Philip Ko
Directed by Godfrey Ho
IFD Films and Arts

The enjoyability of Godfrey Ho's cut-and-paste movies can depend a lot on how interesting the older source movies are that he cuts his new material into. With *Scorpion Thunderbolt* he utilizes a lot of footage from the Taiwan-set Korean horror film *Grudge of the Sleepwalking Woman* (1983). Also known as *Snake Woman*, this Korean film featured lots of fun cop and monster scenes that greatly enhance the watchability of Godfrey Ho's "new" movie.

Scorpion Thunderbolt begins as it means to go on, using music taken from *Star Wars*, then quickly intercuts between shots of a spiky-fingered witch and Richard Harrison playing a character called, well, Richard, also including clips of a blind flute player. We then move on to a night scene, where a woman is pursued by a madman. We assume he is intending to attack her . . . but no, he leaves her alone, and it is a snake monster that kills the woman instead! The local cops start to investigate the murder and a couple of them try to figure out what the creature might look like by constructing a papier-mâché model of a snake-tadpole critter wearing lipstick. Yeah, that'll be a great help, guys!

As the film progresses, it becomes evident that the witch (often seen slapping a drum with her spiky hands) and the blind flute player are the people who cause someone to transform into the rubbery snake-beast.

Alternating between scenes from *Grudge of the Sleepwalking Woman* and the new footage, we get to watch such things as Richard fending off an assassination attempt by a sexy, killer hitchhiker who has a blade hidden in her lipstick, see young women attacked by the snake beast in their apartment, witness Richard's fight with a possessed plumber and watch a journalist called Helen transform into the rubbery serpent critter and go on a murder spree in a hotel.

Richard finally decides to find out why various people are trying to kill him, so he heads up into the hills to chat with a fortune teller. He is informed that there is a witch who lives in a red castle: she is thoroughly evil and only a magic ring, owned by Richard, can destroy her powers. Richard is given a golden sword and a mystical mirror and is told that, on the 15th day of this month, he must go to the gates of the castle, place the ring on the mystic mirror, chop it with the sword, then throw it into a fire.

After a flashback that reveals Helen is the result of a union between the "Prince of Snakes" and the daughter of a snake-killer, we get a showdown between the cops and the serpent-monster, which, after gliding about on wires, is gunned down by the police team and dies, transforming back into Helen.

The Richard plot thread culminates with him finally reaching the gates of the castle. Here he breaks the ring on the mirror with the golden sword, the witch's home bursts into flames and she dies, as music from *Raiders of the Lost Ark* starts to play! The film ends with a freeze-frame of Richard Harrison smiling at us, victoriously holding up the golden sword. Classic!

The bizarre amalgamation of intercut scenes somehow, at times, transcend their cut-and-paste origins to make *Scorpion Thunderbolt* a thing of jaw-dropping wonder. As an example, the encounter with Richard and a murderous hitchhiker in a screening room features shots of the manic, spike-fingered witch intercut with Richard Harrison performing some softcore sex, intercut with a red-lit shot of frogs in a bowl, intercut with projected body-painting footage. This whole sequence comes across more like an avant-garde art short featuring unrelated

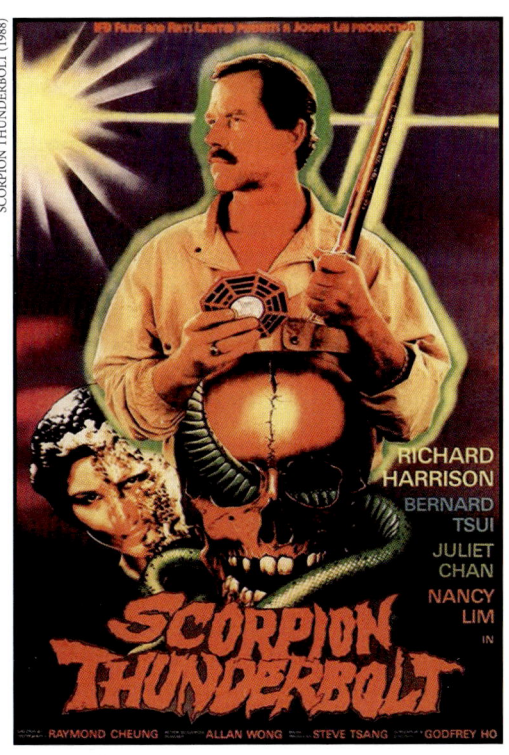

SCORPION THUNDERBOLT (1988)

imagery, rather than what it is: Godfrey Ho splicing together footage to concoct yet another one of his patchwork flicks!

After watching *Scorpion Thunderbolt*, you will either end up being someone who thinks this is a film that must be loved and cherished, or you will be someone who is wrong!

SECRET OF THE WATER TECHNIQUE (1984)
Starring Roc Tien, Leung Kar-Yan, Yuan Shen,
Jason Pai Piao
Directed by Roc Tien
Hua Kuo Film Studio

Commander Lin (Tien) is framed and condemned to ten years in jail so that the son of a local bigwig can take his wife. But with the help of Ruh, a big, ex-brigand monk, Lin eventually avenges himself against the wrongdoers, though this will require a showdown in a cellar full of bizarre adversaries.

Aka *The Legend of all Men Are Brothers*, this Taiwanese production, inspired by the Water Margin novel *All Men Are Brothers*, offers us the chance to see a prison assassination attempt, an aggressive style of massage, a knife in the groin moment played for laughs and a farcical bedroom scene interspersed among the usual martial arts antics.

But this film really becomes interesting and sticks in the memory once it reaches the finale, set in a large cellar . . .

Here we see a confrontation with a fighter in a wheelchair, who only pretends to be disabled and is armed with a razor-sharp fan and metal hoops. A crossdressing antagonist is next, skilled at hurling metal spikes, but he dies after chunky monk Ruh shoves a pole where the sun don't shine. A hopping, curly-haired dead dude, who picks at the rotting flesh on his face, enters the fray to combat the monk now, flicking maggots into Ruh's mouth! Our monk hero is badly wounded, but Commander Lin arrives to battle the ghoul, and then the fourth combatant joins the fight. Going by the name of Never Drunk, this dude sleeps in a barrel of alcohol and seems capable of breathing beneath the booze. Never Drunk leaps from the barrel, takes on Lin and, of course, he does so in a drunken martial arts style.

Okay, so this ongoing cellar skirmish seems pretty offbeat, but circumstances suddenly ratchet up to batshit crazy levels when the dead ghoul's belly begins to distend . . . and a red, raw-skinned, phallic critter

bursts from it! The slimy beastie, with its snapping jaws, tiny forelimbs and snakelike tail, is like some alien monster that has strayed into this kung fu actioner from a sci-fi horror flick! If the animated pork sausage mascot from the Peperami television ads and the chestburster from *Alien* (1979) got together and had a lovechild . . . it would resemble this slimy penis-tadpole! It can talk, too! Madness!

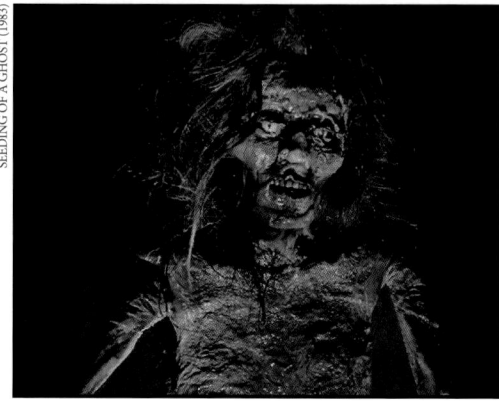

SEEDING OF A GHOST (1983)

SEEDING OF A GHOST (1983)
Starring Tsui Siu-Keung, Philip Ko, Maria Jo, Tien Mi
Directed by Yeung Kuen
Produced by Mona Fong
Shaw Brothers

As rather unpleasant little tales of ghostly vengeance go, this one's pretty gross. When Chou (Ko), a dim bulb cabbie, has the misfortune to run into a witch-dude one night, he scoffs at the creepy weirdo's assertion that disaster will befall him. An unwise move and, before he knows it, his croupier wife, Irene (Jo), is having a steamy affair with Anthony, a married smoothy, and, after that ends, she's set upon by two teen thugs and is raped and killed. Efforts at revenge via the normal channels bring no result, so in desperation Chou seeks out the black magician and persuades him to help. This leads to oodles of disgusting effects, as the corpse of Irene is disinterred and a ghost is "seeded" within the cadaver. This leads to something rather nasty happening to Anthony's wife, who is also pregnant . . .

Though the pace tends to drag, and there's far too much incomprehensible mumbo jumbo for its own good, this flick features enough cheery madness—worm regurgitation, innards-munching, possessed toilets, flying corpses, womb-explosions, and, capping it all, bizarre double necrophilia—that the movie definitely becomes twistedly memorable.

SEMI-GODS AND SEMI-DEVILS (1994)

Starring Brigitte Lin, Gong Li, Cheung Man,
Frankie Lam, Tsui Siu-Keung
Directed by Chin Wing-Keung
Action by Tony Poon
Win's Movie Productions Ltd

Also known as *The Maidens of Heavenly Mountains*, this film uses Jin Yong's novel *Demi-Gods and Semi-Devils* as its source material, telling the story of the power struggle between two sisters who have fiery martial arts skills (Lin and Li). Ting (Siu-Keung) seeks to acquire the martial artistry, for whoever has the power, rules the land. His not-so-loyal disciple Purple (Man) realizes that if she gets the power for herself, she could get rid of her master and rule the martial world herself.

This film is pretty complicated. It's as if you've walked in halfway through a long-running soap opera, only plucking bits of information as you fly along. But, story aside, fans of female fighters will sit quite contentedly watching the leading ladies battle it out.

The atmospheric, rocky setting is reminiscent of *Zu: Warriors from the Magic Mountain* (1983), with the action depending heavily upon wirework, though this is perfectly in keeping with the style of the movie, complementing rather than detracting from the overall impression. In fact, there's so much wirework that the actors' feet barely touch the ground!

The highlight of the movie comes when Ting rips through his own carcass and, to the disbelief of the female onlookers who had assumed he was dead, says: "I have mastered the reborn technique!"

THE SEVENTH CURSE (1986)

Starring Chow Yun-Fat, Maggie Cheung, Chin Siu-Ho,
Dick Wei, Sibelle Hu, Elvis Tsui
Directed by Nam Nai-Choi
Golden Harvest

Adventurer Yuan (Siu-Ho) must return to North Thailand and confront the chief of the Worm Tribe in order to look for the cure to a spell that is slowly killing him. Tagging along with him is pushy reporter Tsai-Hung and, later, his mentor Mr. Wei (Yun-Fat).

After a shoot-'em-up/kung fu punch-up/police siege start, the film soon settles down to the proper tale it intends to tell. This means lots of cave sets, guttering torches, masses of mad tribesmen, fighting and slimy monsters.

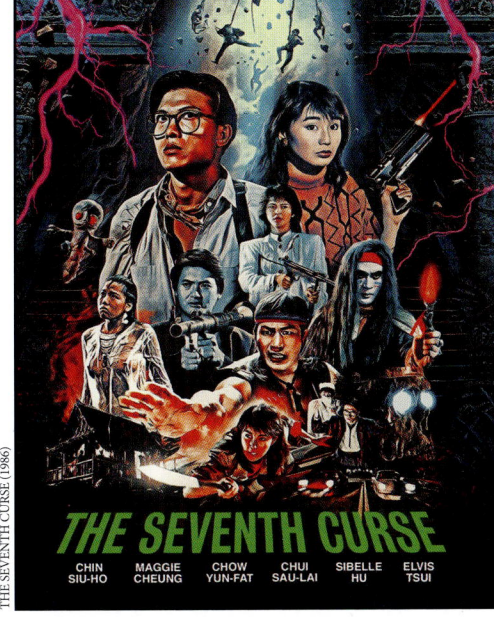

THE SEVENTH CURSE (1986)

THE SEVENTH CURSE

CHIN SIU-HO · MAGGIE CHEUNG · CHOW YUN-FAT · CHUI SAU-LAI · SIBELLE HU · ELVIS TSUI

Though it's not a fighting-oriented film to the extent that, for instance, *We're Going to Eat You* (1980) is, *The Seventh Curse* does boast very good choreography when a brawl starts.

The wirework is really over the top: whenever someone is kicked, or shot, they fly about a quarter of a mile backward! In one amazing scene Yuan blasts a guy with his gun at the same time as his partner Lung shoots the same tribesman with an arrow in slow motion.

When Yuan finds out that he needs the stone eyeball from a Buddha statue to prevent the onset of the Seventh Curse that will kill him, it gives the filmmakers a fine excuse to have some neat stunts on top of an impressively large statue. Rope-swinging, saffron-robed assailants, booby traps, and crumbling chunks of stone confront our heroes as they ascend the Buddha. The sequence becomes more outrageous once the stone eyeballs have been removed from the statue. Blood spurts from the Buddha's sockets as the head falls off and rolls after Yuan à la *Raiders of the Lost Ark!*

This Hong Kong horror-adventure weird-fest includes two oddball critters, called Old Ancestor and Little Ghost.

Little Ghost is the product of a spell utilizing the blood of a hundred children. It has a strange head that is attached to a slimy tail and also has a pair of little arms. This odd "ghost" is captured with the aid of a pregnant cow's placenta! This could only happen in a Hong Kong film, right?

Old Ancestor dwells in his stone coffin in a cave and, when he originally appears, is in the form of a glowing-eyed, clacking-jawed skeleton covered in dry skin. Operated, I assume, as a full-scale marionette, it closely resembles the Japanese skeleton seen in 1986's *The Ghost Snatchers* (also directed by Nam Nai-Choi). Once it drinks the blood of a victim, Old Ancestor does a bit of transforming, becoming a huge beastie with an elongated head. Unlike the really nifty "split head" monster in 1988's *The Peacock King* (also directed by Nam Nai-Choi), which looked good in both long shots and close-ups, Old Ancestor only really impresses during the close-up shots of the head and hands distorting. As soon as we see the complete creature, with its webbed wings, the man-in-a-suit monstrosity is reminiscent of the rubbery Dagoth god-monster seen at the end of *Conan the Destroyer* (1984). In other words . . . Old Ancestor looks kinda cheesy, but it is fun to watch as it whirls about the cavern! The first person we see get killed by Old Ancestor does what probably many victims confronted by a monster would do: he voids his bladder! Finally, it is left to Chow Yun-Fat to deal with the toothy adversary . . . by blowing the critter away with a rocket launcher! Way to go Chow!

All things considered *The Seventh Curse* is a fine ripping yarn.

(Oh yeah, look out for the action scene where Yuan crashes his jeep through a Worm Tribe hut in slow motion: one unfortunate stuntman fails to get out of the way and is hit! I'm sure it was an accident and was not intended that way, but . . . ouch!)

SEX AND ZEN (1991)
Starring Lawrence Ng, Kent Cheng, Lo Lieh, Amy Yip, Isabella Chow, Carrie Ng, Elvis Tsui
Directed by Michael Mak
Golden Harvest/Johnny Mak Productions

If your pleasure in Hong Kong movies lies in their continual power to amaze and flabbergast you, to the point where you cling to your seat, unsure of whether you're crazy or whether it's just the movie, then, at all costs, seek out *Sex and Zen*. Essentially, it's little more than a sex comedy, a kind of 'Carry On Canton' (though heaps more explicit, hence the CAT III status). It's a madcap romp following the amorous antics of a medieval scholar, who sets out to disprove the worth of the Zen philosophy of sexual abstinence. However, when, about twenty minutes in, he decides

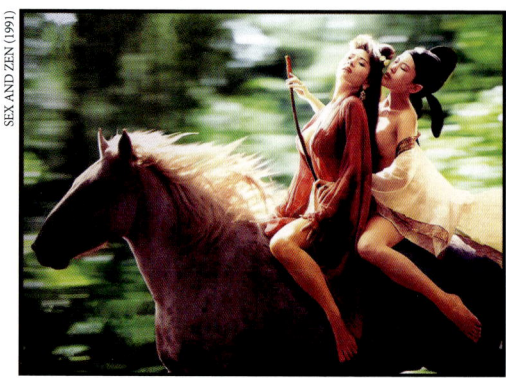

SEX AND ZEN (1991)

this mission would be best served by trading in his undersized member for that of a stallion, well, that's the time to check your brains in at the door and settle back to enjoy some seriously outlandish capers!

Our hero gets involved in any number of farcical encounters, until he receives his ultimate comeuppance at the hands of a couple of S&M practitioners, who cure satyriasis using fiendish tickling devices, whips, and, well, watch the movie to find out.

Sex and Zen is a splendidly loony and lewd entertainment. The transplant scene alone makes this movie worth seeking out!

SEXUAL DEVIL (1991)
Starring Lawrence Ng, Yik Gon-Ha, Cheung Mo-Hau, Paul Che
Directed by Ho Lin-Chow
Sun Tat Bo Film Company

This movie turns out to be one of those productions that has a lurid, provocative title attached to a rather anemic, flavorless story. Basically, the story concerns a fashion photographer and a ghostly girl, with some magic spell-making scenes added.

Shot on video, this enterprise begins with some footage of animal cruelty (a lizard is stabbed in the mouth by a holy man) before, very quickly, becoming exceedingly dull.

Video trick effects are used toward the end of the flick, of a white-robed girl spirit whizzing about the trees, but this only reminds you of how cheap 'n' TV-ish this pic is compared to bona fide Hong Kong cinema releases such as *A Chinese Ghost Story* or even *Esprit D'amour*.

The one novel thing to occur in *Sexual Devil* is the silly scene in which an evil man uses lizards as projectiles, hurling 'em onto an attacker!

SHOCKING ASIA (1981)
Produced by Wong Hoi
First Films Organisation

Kung fu movie producer Wong Hoi decided to cash in on the mondo shockumentaries from Italy, and the result is a highly colorful, sometimes morbid, often exaggerated look into South East Asian culture.

This is basically the movie version of a sideshow, rather than a bona fide documentary, focusing on strange, disturbing and odd subject matter (at least for 1981), though much of what is on screen is staged.

SILVER HERMIT FROM SHAOLIN TEMPLE (1980)
Starring Roc Tien, Meng Fei, Chen Sing, Tien Ho, Wang Ping
Directed by Roc Tien
Kao Sheng Production Company

Also known as *The Silver Spear*, this Taiwanese wuxia production begins like a murder mystery, with several warriors dying of poisoning in a mountain valley. The hero, Silver Hermit, is accused

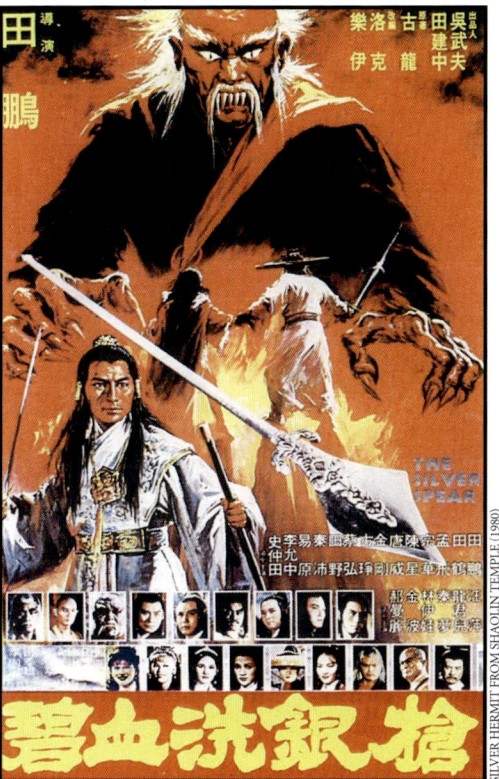

SILVER HERMIT FROM SHAOLIN TEMPLE (1980)

of the killings and becomes embroiled in a story that encompasses concealed identities, Buddhist monks, hidden allegiances, secret siblings, the search for a tunnel to the much-desired Green Jade Villa, the destruction of an entire town and the return of a vampiric villain called Immortal . . .

This movie starts really well, with a nicely paced first act located in misty, snowy valley sets that mix together artificiality and atmospherics effectively. However, after the villain Silver Spear reveals that he poisoned the victims as part of his plan to ensure he inherits Green Jade Villa, the movie becomes more and more confusing, thanks to choppy editing, many over-dark sequences, and the introduction of a multitude of characters, many of whom are concealing their real identities.

Silver Hermit From Shaolin Temple is based on a novel by Gu Long, so perhaps the filmmakers tried to cram too much of the book's plot into the movie. Whatever the reason is for the semi-incoherence, by the time the bloodsucking bad guy Immortal is introduced into the tale you do begin to wonder whether the story is actually being made up as it goes along. On the plus side, the involvement of this villain, who sports a wild, Albert Einstein–esque haircut and is referred to as "a beast from Persia," does mean you get the opportunity to watch a tall, clawed, pale-faced, fang-mouthed monster-man rampage about the place during the enjoyably hectic finale!

SKIN STRIPERESS (1992)
Starring Lam Ching-Ying, Chan Wing-Chi, Billy Lau, Chin Shih-Erh
Directed by Billy Chan
Produced by Kam Cheung-Kuen
Hatract Films Limited

Lau is the owner of a run-down island resort which needs a licence to open. An official, Officer Yung, promises Lau a licence if he is allowed to have sex with Lau's protege, Miss Cheung, in three days' time. Lau's schemes are ruined, or so it seems, when there is a storm, causing electrical cables to fall onto Miss Cheung, hideously scarring her. Lau, needing Cheung to look lovely again for her meeting with Officer Yung, calls in a holy man to reinstate her beauty. Lau is told that he must find an attractive woman so that the holy man can use her unblemished skin . . .

Skin Striperess is a Hong Kong ghost potboiler, which attempts to stand out from the crowd by spicing-up the yarn with a skin-stripping ritual performed by the holy man on a girl killed by Lau. The holy man, later in the movie, actually finds himself also on the receiving end of some flesh peeling.

A major portion of the running time centers on the annoying exploits of six irritating teens, who travel to the island for some typical pranks 'n' petting activities, and so it is left to Lam Ching-Ying to inject some decent, controlled acting into the proceedings. It's just a pity that Lam doesn't have more screen time.

The film is well enough shot, but not many scenes stick in the mind, although the mildly sadistic coupling of Officer Yung and Cheung is one sequence that looked as if it had some time spent on it, so it's a pity that it is intercut with shots of those constantly babbling, charmless teens.

As with *The Nocturnal Demon* (1990), this film includes a somewhat tasteless (if one considers the rather lightweight nature of most of the production) shot of a female victim being urinated on after she's been murdered. Eventually, the film progresses to a typical Hong Kong ghost film finale, as a vengeful, white-robed female spirit glides through the trees, various actors and actresses run around screaming and Lam Ching-Ying (in, of course, Taoist priest gear) dispenses magic scriptures and incantations.

Skin Striperess is a watchable time-waster, but don't expect this to be some kind of cross between *Human Skin Lanterns* and *A Chinese Ghost Story* because, folks, this film just ain't in their league.

SPOOKY SPOOKY (1988)
Starring Alfred Cheung, Wu Ma, Joyce Godenzi,
Anthony Chan, Chung Fat, Mars, Yuen Wah, Richard Ng
Directed by Sammo Hung
Bojon Films Company Ltd/Golden Harvest

This schlocky horror has been compared to *The Evil Dead* (1981), and there certainly are a few parallels with Sam Raimi's classic in terms of makeup, humor, and zombies who won't stay dead. But where Raimi's movie overflowed with kinetic verve, *Spooky Spooky* isn't quite as well made, not that it should be overlooked because it has its moments and the laughs translate quite well for an English-speaking audience.

The film kicks off very much like a zombie version of *Jaws*, as a vengeful "nix," or ghost, haunts a popular resort, picking off the odd unwary swimmer, before moving inland to wreak mayhem in a protracted munch through the cream of the local constabulary, zombifying a good percentage, before finally being spectacularly wasted through the old reliable traditional magic techniques.

With severed heads, projectile ectoplasm and a nutty pathologist called "Queency," *Spooky Spooky* succeeds in giving you a fun-filled 90 minutes, with enough gloop and gore to keep any fan of the undead more than content.

THE STORM RIDERS (1998)
Starring Aaron Kwok, Ekin Cheng, Sonny Chiba,
Kristy Yeung, Michael Tse, Roy Cheung, Anthony Wong
Directed by Andrew Lau
Golden Harvest/Tianshan Film Studio

Lord Conquer (Chiba), power-hungry leader of the Conquerer's Clan, raises two boys called Wind (Cheng) and Cloud (Kwok) as his sons, after it is foretold that they will bring him good fortune. Together with Conquer's adopted son Frost (Tse), youngsters Wind and Cloud grow up to become powerful fighters under their Lord's tutelage, bonding with each other and Conquer's daughter Charity (Yeung). But when the Lord instructs Charity to wed Wind, rather than Cloud, who is the man she actually loves, the stage is set for a confrontation that leads to Charity's accidental death at the hands of her father. Matters become even more dark and deadly after Wind and Cloud learn that Conquer killed their parents and now wants to murder them too.

The Storm Riders, based on the comic book series by Ma Wing-Shing, is a big Hong Kong action-fantasy wuxia movie full of prophesies, characters with super-powered skills, betrayals and legendary weapons with names like Blizzard Blade, Ultimate Sword, Fire Unicorn Sword and Unchallenged Sword.

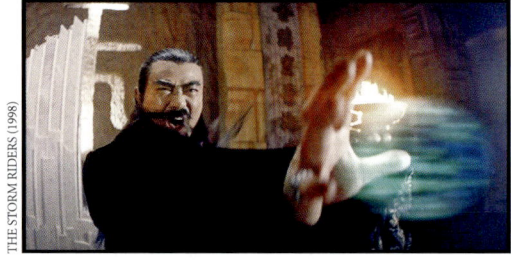

THE STORM RIDERS (1998)

Aaron Kwok, as Cloud, is good at pop-dramatic posturing, whether he's moodily sitting on a rooftop with a billowing cape, standing under a waterfall as he angrily shouts at the sky, or screaming in heartbroken anguish as he detonates plumes of water in a lake. Meanwhile, Sonny Chiba, as the single-minded, driven Lord Conquer, is regal, ruthless and looks the consummate badass at all times.

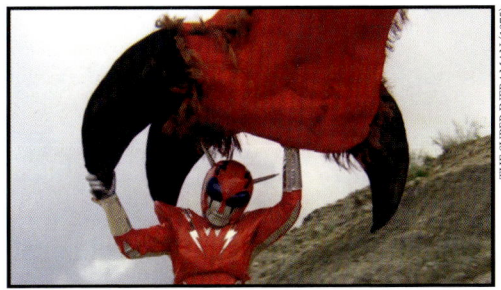

THE SUPER INFRAMAN (1975)

There's a not-too-convincing CGI cave dragon and a less-than-photorealistic special effects-laden duel on and around a giant, stone Buddha, but these moments are acceptable as they exist within the comic book world of this movie. Far more impressive elements include the splendid Sword Grave set and the many scenes showing the characters creating energy spheres, manipulating water, spinning at super-velocities and generating shock waves. The inclusion of surprising plot ideas, such as Cloud ripping off his arm so that he can use the blood as a weapon, and a doctor realizing he must sever his own "Fire Beast Arm" and transplant the limb onto Cloud's body, help keep the movie exotic and fantastical.

Watch out for a hectic bamboo forest fight and a showdown between Lord Conquer and Sword Saint, where we get the chance to see Anthony Wong floating into action like a glowing amalgamation of Moses and Obi-Wan Kenobi, giving off an aquamarine light as he immobilises everyone in his path!

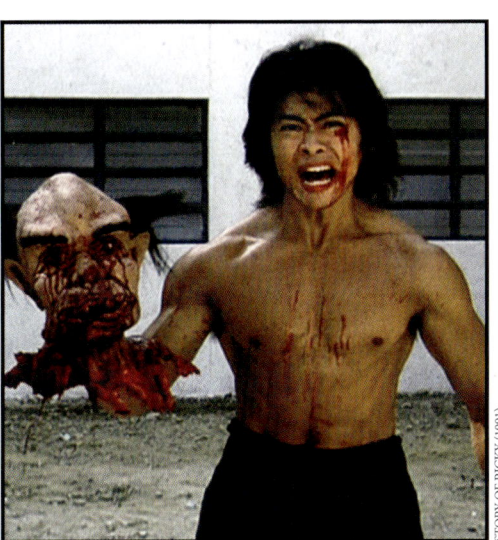

STORY OF RICKY (1991)

STORY OF RICKY (1991)

Starring Fan Sui-Wong, Gloria Yip, Yukari Oshima, Frankie Chin, Philip Kwok
Directed by Nam Nai-Choi
Action by Philip Kwok
Diagonal Pictures/Golden Harvest

Ricky (Siu-Wong), a man of almost supernatural strength, is locked up for avenging his girlfriend's death, much to the pleasure of the sadistic prison warden who is in charge while the governor is away. The warden runs the prison on fear, using a select group of heavies known as the Gang of Four: a dwarf, a musclebound martial artist, a transexual played by Japanese starlet Yukari Oshima and a giant. One by one they taunt Ricky by sadistically beating his friends, until he finally snaps and takes his violent revenge.

There are no punches pulled in this cartoonish gorefest, as you see, in gruesome detail, a guy's face being sliced in half, Ricky tying the sinews of his own arms together to help him fight, eye-gouging, crucifixion and the musclebound freak slicing his guts open so that he can strangle Ricky with his own entrails!

Loosely based on the Japanese manga *Riki-Oh*, this movie is full of enough gory-but-unrealistic violence to please any gorehound!

THE SUPER INFRAMAN (1975)

Starring Danny Lee, Terry Liu, Dana, Wang Hsieh, Yuan Man-Tzu
Directed by Hua Shan
Shaw Brothers

Surfacing from within her lair inside the volcanic Mount Devil, evil Princess Elzebub vows to conquer Earth. To stop her, Professor Liu initiates the BDX plan, using special devices and hormones to transform Rayma (Lee) into the savior of mankind. The logic and science behind this process is sketchy at best, but Rayma is duly turned into a red-suited hero with a bug-man robo-face . . . yes, it's Inframan!

The foes that Inframan must contend with include Witch Eye, a scantily clad villainess with a cone bra, horned helmet, knee-high boots, and clawed glove-hands with eyes in their palms, Mutant Drill, a blobby dude with one shovel hand and one drill hand, Fire Dragon, a fire-breathing bad guy with a red moustache, green scales and a gold helmet, and Plant Monster, a man-in-suit creature with tendrils and the ability to sink into the ground. One monster,

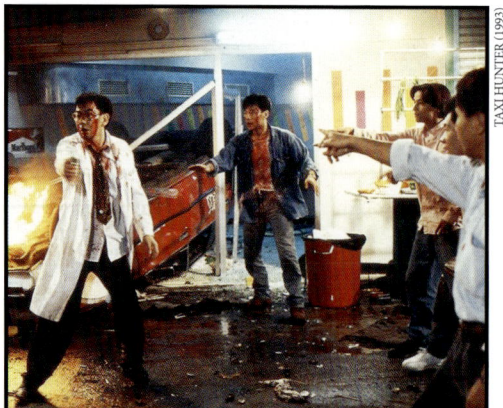

TAXI HUNTER (1993)

looking like a manic version of Cousin Itt from *The Addams Family*, can fire laser beams and cackles a lot.

Visually, the film is a riot of over-the-top art direction, with some wonderful comic book-esque sets featuring dragon fountains, skeletons, skull-faced decor and machinery with blinking lights. The carved entrance to Elzebub's HQ, for instance, resembles a monster's mouth.

There are loads of fun sequences to watch out for, one highlight being Plant Monster's attack on Professor Liu's research building, where the vegetable-beast becomes a mass of giant, fast-growing rubber vines! The massive plant envelopes the place and the battle that follows is a real hoot, with Hong Kong stunt guys getting knocked around by the terrible tendrils!

Another cool moment features a red bug-dude who rapidly enlarges, so Inframan (just like his Japanese Tokusatsu hero counterparts) grows in size too! This is all done using forced perspective, seen from a low angle, with some slo-mo shots, making this giant showdown an effectively handled, standout scene in the film.

The plot may be inconsequential, but that doesn't really matter, as *The Super Inframan* is nonstop fun from beginning to end. You get to see a mass fight between the silver-suited good guys and Princess Elzebub's Skeleton Warrior minions in a studio set full of skull carvings and creature skeletons, then get to witness a fight between Inframan and two mechanical monster-men, who can launch their extendable heads and propel mace-hands at him on retractable metal springs! Inframan has his own special tricks too, of course: he can eject his Thunder Fist gloves, enabling him to punch stuff from a distance, plus he can fire laser blade beams, which, during one confrontation, slice off both of Witch Eye's hands!

For fans of Japanese-style Tokusatsu action, this Chinese take on the genre is an awesome addition, with the folks at Shaw Brothers really putting a lot of effort into this: you get kung fu fights galore with acrobatic flips, somersaults and loud punching sound effects, pyrotechnics, cel-animated laser beams, brainwashing, some iffy flying shots, lots of extras in costumes, a fiery lava pit, a glacial cave set, and a finale in which Elzebub turns into a winged monster that can regrow its head when Inframan cuts it off!

TAXI HUNTER (1993)
Starring Anthony Wong, Ng Man-Tat, Yu Rongguang, Athena Chu, Lai Hoi-Shan
Directed by Herman Yau
Galaxy Films Ltd

Following on from the enormous success of *The Untold Story* (1993), Anthony Wong strikes back in the same year with another tour de force performance as Kin, a young, passive architect, pushed over the edge by annoying taxi drivers who caused the death of his wife and unborn child.

Kin transforms from passive underdog to the hardened avenger "the Taxi Hunter": a vigilante ridding the city of rude and unscrupulous taxi drivers. Eventually the cops are onto him and start driving taxis as a cover, trying to lure him in, only to become hunted themselves.

More of a black comic satire than a thriller, this offbeat movie is lifted to the realms of a minor classic thanks to the performance of the talented Anthony Wong.

THE THRILLING SWORD (1981)
Starring Liu Shang-Chien, Chang Yi, Hsia Ling-Ling
Directed by Chang Hsin-Yi
Lusty Electric Industries

A small fireball zips from space, falls to Earth and enters the belly of a pregnant queen during childbirth. This kills the queen, unfortunately, as a large, red, veined blob of flesh instantly shoots from her womb. The distraught king chooses not to destroy the meaty ball and has it floated away down a river in a basket instead. Seven dwarves living in Happy Forest discover the throbbing flesh-glob, which splits open and becomes a cute baby, who the dwarves adopt and call Yaur-gi. Years later Yaur-gi, now an attractive young woman, encounters Prince Yur-juhn, who is traveling through the forest on his way to visit the king of the Ku Shien kingdom. Yaur-gi falls in love with the prince and eventually discovers that she's the daughter of the Ku Shien king, but many trials and tribulations lie in store for her and the prince, as foxy witch-exorcist Gi-err and shifty sorcerer Shiah-ker set out to usurp the kingdom and take over Yaur-gi's mind.

Also known as *Thrilling Bloody Sword*, there's much to enjoy in this Taiwanese fantasy flick, including a cyclopean demon-monster and a multi-necked, fire-breathing dragon-beast known as the Nine-Headed Siren, which are actually the creations of Gi-err and Shia-ker, who secretly unleash the creatures so that they can look like saviors by destroying them. We also have a fun development involving the prince being turned into a bear, then transformed back to his normal self, after which he attains some flamboyant black armor and a weapon called the thunder sword. He subsequently goes on a quest to retrieve a magic box, which involves him fighting a winged monster resembling a low-rent Mahar from *At the Earth's Core* (1976), some folks with flippers called Frog Sirens, some immortal warriors who all have a fatal weak spot, a kind of ghost-blob, a giant, floating, gnashing pair of teeth and a couple of disembodied, fleshy monster feet! After a pacy fight with these feet, the limbs finally connect with other body parts to become a bizarre flying figure . . . that is blown up!

There's a real crudeness to the effects, that's for sure, but this doesn't really detract from the quite charming fairy-tale nature of the colorful production, which borrows some story beats from Snow White and adds outlandish elements including a genie-like character with a head resembling butt-cheeks, a rabbit that turns into a fairy, a giant devil statue with glowing eyes, plus some Perspex weapons you'd expect to see in a *Thundercats* show.

THUNDER OF GIGANTIC SERPENT (1988)

Starring Pierre Kirby, Edowan Bersmea,
Danny Raisebeck, Chi Kuan-Chun, Paul Chang Chung
Directed by Charles Lee
IFD Films and Arts

In Lab 707 scientists are working on the Thunder Project, experimenting with a formula that can make plants and animals grow to large proportions. This formula is never really shown, though: it seems to depend more on using a see-through box and electricity, rather than vials and fluids.

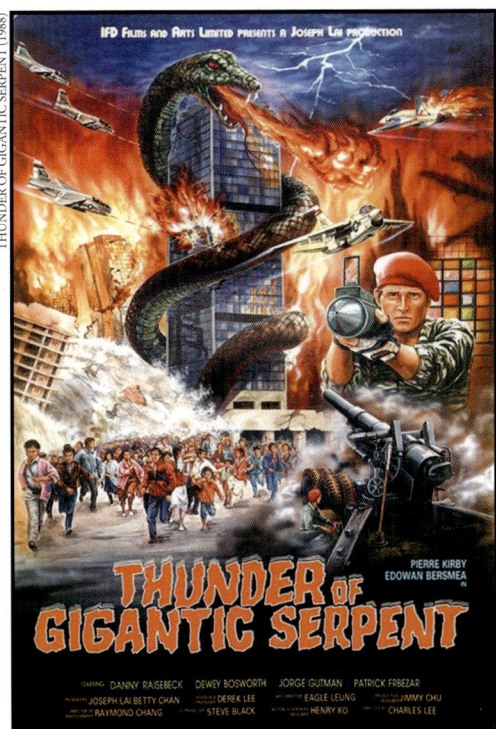

THUNDER OF GIGANTIC SERPENT (1988)

Terrorists attack the army-run lab facility to acquire the formula, there's a bloody shoot-out, but several scientists run into the countryside with the special case, which gets lost after a car crash, and it is discovered by a young girl called Ting Ting. She decides to put her pet snake Mosler in the see-through box, switches on the case's "lights," the serpent is electrified . . . and then it begins to grow!

Thunder of Gigantic Serpent is a cut-and-paste IFD Films and Arts movie that uses lots of footage from the earlier Taiwanese monster movie *King of Snake* (1984) with added film material featuring martial arts actor Pierre Kirby.

For several scenes we see Ting Ting having fun with the semi-large Mosler: they play hide-and-seek and play catch with a ball, and the snake also helps Ting Ting win a Rollerblade race against a couple of other kids. Mosler, it is revealed, can understand what Ting Ting says and reacts to her by nodding or shaking its head. It also makes a sound like a parrot. Meanwhile, we are introduced to Pierre Kirby's military agent character, Ted Fast: now there's a heroic name! Tough Ted is sent on a mission to hunt down the terrorist group's leader, Solomon (Bersmea).

Some cops and army dudes in red berets also feature in the story, so we get various cops/Ted Fast/gangsters/army confrontations. There is a bunch of shoot-outs, then we get a scene where the terrorists try to capture the snake, but their electrified trap makes Mosler grow much larger. Now the huge serpent makes a deep, roaring sound like a lion!

The film does get rather preoccupied with terrorists and cops having firefights, but then we get monster snake action too! First Mosler attacks a road bridge and then destroys a train bridge, including the train crossing it. Yikes! The formerly nice and playful Mosler is now a large-scale killer! The snake proceeds to break a dam, causing mass flooding and more deaths. Jeez, Mosler is a real psycho-killer now!

After some Ted Fast martial arts action we cut back to Ting Ting, who is being held captive by a bad guy in a tall building. Jets finally arrive, shooting at the snake, which glows around the edges of its body each time it is hit. After one of the jets crashes into Mosler's face, the huge snake falls to the street below and dies.

There's a final showdown between terrorist leader Solomon and Ted Fast: "Go ahead, shoot, make my day, punk!" And then the movie finishes!

Thunder of Gigantic Serpent, as with *Gamera: the Giant Monster* (1965), features a kid who continually pleads for her pet monster to be left alone, even after it causes untold destruction and death! Mosler, it must be said, does start off as a rather nice critter, but after it goes on its binge of dam-busting and train-wrecking it becomes rather difficult to regard the great serpent as anything but a menace.

The effects are definitely not of Toho quality, that's for sure, but this silly, cheesy film remains oddly enjoyable throughout.

THE UNDERGROUND BANKER (1994)
Starring Anthony Wong, Lawrence Ng, Wong Chi-Yeung, Dave Lam Ching, Ho Ka-Kui, Wong Chi-Yeung
Directed by Bosco Lam
Produced by Wong Jing
Win's Film Productions/Wong Jing's Workshop Ltd

In this CAT III cash-in, Anthony Wong plays a working-class truck driver, Tong Chi Ming, whose fate changes when he is rehoused by the government in a plusher apartment. Things start to go wrong for the Tong family when they realize that living in an adjacent apartment is none other than the dastardly Doctor Lamb (Ng), who has just been released from a psychiatric hospital-prison. Mrs. Tong gets involved with an old flame of hers, Canner (Chi-Yeung), who lives on the estate. After being conned into playing the stock market by Canner, Mrs. Tong realizes she has a debt she can't pay. Canner takes her to the underground banker (Ka-Kui), who gives her a loan with extortionate interest rates which she could never repay. She is forced into prostitution to pay the underground banker, but he will not accept her payments or her husband's pleas, and torches their apartment, killing Mrs. Tong and burning their son beyond recognition. Now the passive Tong changes into a physical weapon with the help of his neighbor Dr. Lamb, who has befriended his son. They take on the mobsters with the aid of a surgical kit!

Also known as *Physical Weapon*, this low-budget flick is lifted by the Dr. Lamb cameo, especially the finale, where he slices and dices the villains.

THE UNTOLD STORY (1993)
Starring Anthony Wong, Danny Lee, Emily Kwan, Parkman Wong, Shing Fui-On, Julie Lee
Directed by Herman Yau
Produced by Danny Lee
Golden Harvest/Heroes United Films Ltd

Also known as *The Eight Immortals Restaurant: The Untold Story*, this film is one of the most notorious CAT III films. The movie starts as it means to go on, with our antihero beating up and then burning alive the latest unfortunate soul to upset him. From then on, it gets more and more grotesque, with amputated limbs turning up on the beach and human flesh being passed off as barbecued pork!

Jerky, unusual camerawork makes the ultraviolent flashback scenes all the more shocking. The story is set in a restaurant in Macau, where a new owner, Wong Chi-Hang (Wong), is claiming to have bought the property from the previous owner, Cheng Lam, who has now disappeared. Wong has trouble getting the restaurant signed over to himself, as he has no legal papers, and then, when Cheng Lam's brother Poon (Fui-On) writes from prison to question the sudden disappearance of his entire family, police chief Lee, played by Danny Lee, begins to investigate the restaurant. Wong's reaction to the police investigation makes them suspect foul play, and with good reason, as Wong has a violent temper, lashing out at anyone who gives him a hard time, such as the employee who catches him cheating at mah-jongg.

In true Sweeney Todd tradition, Wong kills and dismembers his victims in a variety of graphically filmed and ingenious ways, then cooks them into "pork" buns. He then takes great pleasure in watching the police officers, who are investigating him, stuff their faces with the cooked human remains! The police eventually guess that Wong has slaughtered Cheng Lam and his family, but when he won't confess, they put him in jail with the sole survivor, the brother Cheng Poon. Wong is brutally beaten but he won't confess, and his insane determination to get his own way, despite the degradation he suffers, makes him much more than the one-dimensional, mindless serial killers of Hollywood tradition. Only after the most inhuman treatment from the police and prisoners does he finally confess . . . and then the sickening details concerning the slaughter of Cheng Lam's whole family, including his small children, is shown, which dramatically switches the viewer's sympathy once again away from Wong, back to his victims.

Like the equally sick *Dr Lamb* (1992), which was directed by this film's star and producer, Danny Lee, *The Untold Story* was based on a true story. By turns funny, gruesome and fascinating, *The Untold Story* never takes the easy option, and Wong, despite his vicious temper and murderous nature, emerges as having as much twisted, personal integrity as the brutal police officers, though he, obviously, is far more adept with a meat cleaver!

VAMPIRE VS VAMPIRE (1989)
Starring Lam Ching-Ying, Chin Siu-Ho, Lui Fong,
Billy Lau, Sandra Ng, Yip So
Directed by Lam Ching-Ying
Taiwan Film Center

One-Eyebrow Priest, played by Lam Ching-Ying (who also directs the movie), has his hands full with bat infestations, ghosts, and vampires in his neighborhood.

Okay, there isn't really a central plotline to *Vampire Vs Vampire*. Rather, it presents us with a series of occult happenings for our hero priest to deal with.

An early set piece involves a "palm tree spirit," which is enticed from its green-leafed abode by tying some string to the toe of one of the priest's disciples. Once attracted to the disciple's room, the spirit is revealed to be a red-garbed woman, who can become an animated red shadow. The spirit is dealt with, but more headaches lie ahead for the one-eyebrowed Taoist priest.

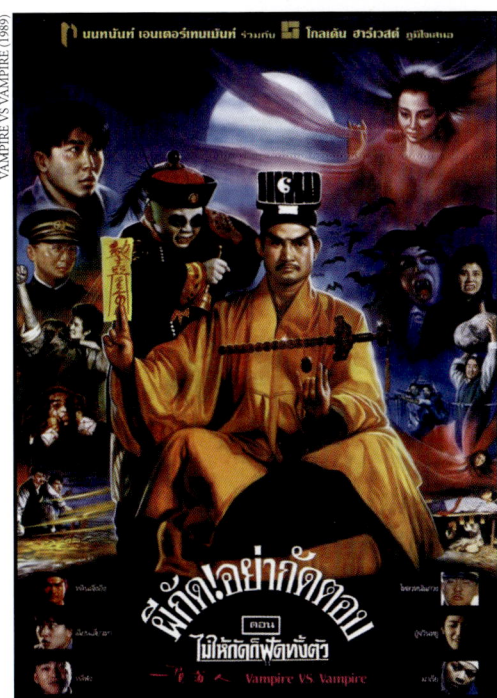

VAMPIRE VS VAMPIRE (1989)

A withered corpse becomes a Western-style bloodsucker once the ruby hilt of a sword that transfixes it is removed. Gulping down the blood of a girl (there's a close-up shot of the corpse's Adam's apple bobbing up and down that is a novel-looking special makeup effect), the dried-up cadaver rapidly transforms into a fanged, caped European vampire. One-Eyebrow Priest gets involved, of course, and gives the undead dude a battering. He jams a coin sword into its eye socket, burns it with a flaming log, boots it . . . and then lobs a large nun onto the bloodsucker, so that it gets forced under the surface of some oily quicksand!

Together with the westernized vampire, this Hong Kong picture adds several other Hammer-esque elements. For instance, a group of Christian nuns are introduced, living in a church. There are bats too, of the Hammer hanging-on-a-wire variety.

Actually, though most of the bats are obviously fake, there is a well-mounted bat siege involving the nuns in the old church. Trapped in the room, the nuns must block off a doorway with planks, as the flying fiends attempt to bite their way in. Individually, the set pieces are quite novel and enjoyable, but the film is too haphazard, lacking a central focus to the story. About the only ongoing narrative thread is the

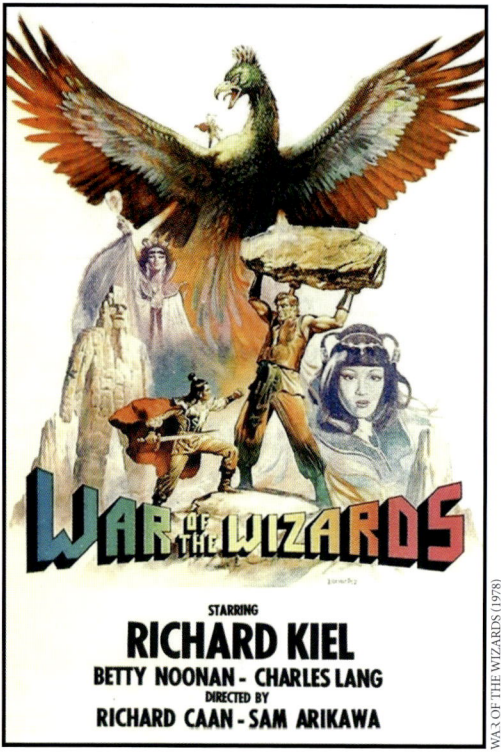

WAR OF THE WIZARDS (1978)

STARRING
RICHARD KIEL
BETTY NOONAN - CHARLES LANG
DIRECTED BY
RICHARD CAAN - SAM ARIKAWA

a-boulder-suit thingy and the big peacock-on-a-wire, which only ends when the rock-man has his head blown off! After beating big Richard Kiel (who would go on to appear in *Mad Mission 3: Our Man from Bond Street*), Ty has to fight ghostly replicas of himself generated by the vessel of plenty. Tidal wave miniature effects and a heat ray-projecting sword also find their way into the movie, but these cool elements aren't enough to outweigh the rather prosaic direction and flat lighting.

THE WEB OF DEATH (1976)
Starring Yueh Hua, Lo Lieh, Ching Li, Lily Li
Directed by Chor Yuen
Shaw Brothers

Members of various sects, including the 5 Venom Clan, Qingyi Clan and Holy Fire Clan, hunt for the hiding place of a legendary weapon. One of these warriors is swordsman Fei (Hua), intent on finding this deadly device before it gets into the hands of those who would use it for evil purposes.

The Web of Death, directed by Chor Yuen, features such fantastical elements as acid pit traps and characters able to unleash energy beams from their hands. The highlight of the film, though, is undoubtedly the secret weapon at the center of

continued reappearance of a "good" hopping vampire child, who regularly helps out One-Eyebrow Priest and his two pupils, although this kiddy-corpse only really serves as light relief.

Watchable fun while it's on, *Vampire Vs Vampire* is not in the same league as other Hong Kong vampire flicks, such as *Mr. Vampire* (1985).

WAR OF THE WIZARDS (1978)
Starring Liang Hsiu-Shen, Richard Kiel, Betty Pei Ti
Directed by Sadamasa Arikawa, Chang Mei-Chun
21st Century Film Corporation

Also known as *The Phoenix*, this Taiwanese production, detailing the discovery of a magic "vessel of plenty" in old China, is theatrical and pantomime-like, with brightly colored sets, cel-animation magic FX and a multi-colored phoenix.

The movie starts slowly, but the finale is an enjoyably silly spectacle, as Ty, the hero, rides the phoenix (a stiff-winged cross between a stuffed peacock and *The Giant Claw*) to the island retreat of the evil Flower Fox. Here the silver-caped, sword-wielding do-gooder confronts a giant rock monster! A Toho-esque battle ensues between the man-in-

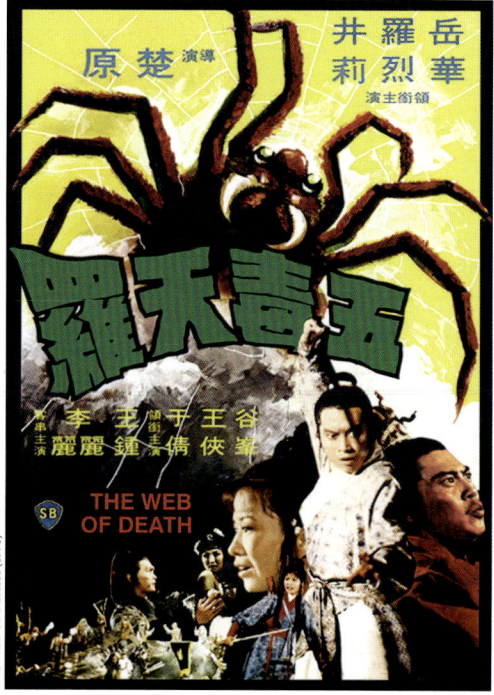

THE WEB OF DEATH (1976)

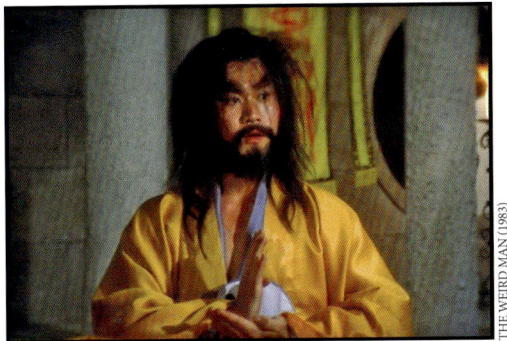

THE WEIRD MAN (1983)

the tale, known as the Spider. This is a handheld smoking lantern containing a glowing tarantula that makes roaring sounds, emits deadly poisonous gas, and creates massive webs that can trap its victims. The use of this curious device, which causes some casualties to develop blackened faces as they expire, adds a layer of surrealism to the film and helps make the finale very strange, absurd, and spectacular.

Though the story is unduly complicated at times, the film remains entertaining, with colorful costumes and wonderful eye candy sets, the most impressive of which is a voluminous chamber containing stone balconies and a large, red spider sculpture.

THE WEIRD MAN (1983)
Starring Ricky Cheng Tien-Chi, Chao Kuo, Wang Li,
Liu Yu-Po, Chu Ko
Directed by Chang Cheh
Shaw Brothers

Set at the end of the Han Dynasty, when the three kingdoms of Shu, Wei and Wu were facing-off against each other, we follow the ever-stranger events that occur when Sun Jia, the Little Conqueror, takes such a dislike to Taoist priest Master Yu Ji (Tien-Chi) that Sun has the do-gooder executed . . . but Yu returns as a mischief-making spirit.

The film is overly convoluted at the start, cramming in too much information concerning who is allied to who, which character plans to usurp the throne, who has married who, who is planning to betray their master, etc, so it's a relief when the plot eventually boils down to the back-from-the-dead Yu taking-on Sun and his devious magistrate Xu Gong (Li).

Highlights include the oiled, youthful-looking spirit of Yu appearing after a blast of steam jets out of his mortal body's severed neck, Sun beating multiple opponents after being shot full of arrows, and the scene where a smiling Yu is transfixed on

a spear, but only bubbles float from his wound . . . and it can be clearly seen that some of the larger bubbles are actually inflated latex gloves!

This is a fun, oddball Shaw Brothers fight-fest that does become rather repetitive, evolving into a series of scenes showing the ever-grinning, red-lit spirit of Yu messing with various characters, making tables fly around and entering the bodies of people, resulting in skirmishes, awkward marital situations, and other hijinks.

WE'RE GOING TO EAT YOU (1980)
Starring Tsui Siu-Keung, Eddy Ko, Michelle Yim,
Melvin Wong
Directed by Tsui Hark
Produced by Ng See-Yuen
Action by Corey Yuen
Seasonal Film Corporation

The fast, frantic pace, action and movement constantly filling the frame add a lot of zip to this cannibal tale.

Tsui Siu-Keung is Agent 999, who is on a mission to apprehend a dangerous criminal hiding out in an island community. Agent 999 discovers that the island is run by a security department, whose head rations meat to the inhabitants. The meat is human flesh, the inhabitants are cannibals, and the security department are responsible for hunting strangers, killing them and chopping them up for meat!

This black comedy is a mixture of martial arts and horror, aiming at satire, but not quite hitting the target. Still, it's well worth a watch.

WICKED CITY (1992)
Starring Leon Lai, Jacky Cheung, Michelle Reis,
Tatsuya Nakadai, Yuen Woo-Ping, Roy Cheung,
Carmen Lee
Directed by Mak Tai-Kit
Produced by Tsui Hark
Film Workshop

Acid rain pours down on a neon-lit futuristic city skyline. The city is peopled by evil shape-shifting mutants and valiant heroes, who wage battles between the forces of good and evil in the streets, the sewers and even the stormy skies, in this live-action adaptation of Yoshiaki Kawajiri's anime, which itself was based on Hideyuki Kikuchi's novel *Wicked City: Black Guard*.

The earth is being invaded by shape-shifting reptilians called Raptors (referred to as Reptoids in some dubbed versions). Taki (Lai) and Ken

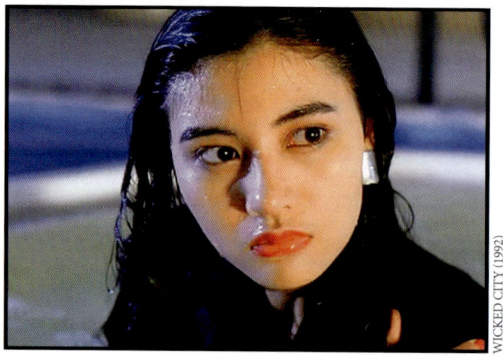

WICKED CITY (1992)

(Cheung) are Raptor hunters, but their mission is complicated by the fact that Taki is in love with a good Raptor (Reis), while Ken is the offspring of a mixed marriage: he's half-human, half-Raptor. The two protagonists discover a plot by an evil Raptor (Cheung) to disrupt peace plans and find themselves having to battle Raptors, treacherous humans and their unsympathetic superiors.

Although the plot is somewhat muddled, the visuals are terrific, with eerie locations, ambitious SFX and some excellent sequences, like the opening Raptor attack and the striking finale, which involves a 747 and the China Bank building. The high weirdness quota, including a woman transforming into a spider and a sex-hungry pinball table, make this one to watch.

A WICKED GHOST (1999)
*Starring Gabriel Harrison, Francis Ng, Gigi Lai,
Mok Ga-Yiu
Directed by Leung Hung-Wah
Times Production*

A group of friends, with names like Big Bee, Rubbish, and Biggie, perform a ritual to enable them to see ghosts. This is meant to be a fun game to pass the time, though it does involve drinking from a bowl of water mixed with fresh blood and using a tealight to burn "oil" taken from a dead person's body! Ming is the only member of the group to refuse to take part (saying that the blood might have AIDS), but his girlfriend Annie joins in the odd game, which does unleash a creepy female ghost, who starts to kill off the friends one by one.

Rubbish is the first to die and Ming's reporter sister Cissy starts to look into the case, along with her fiancé Jack. Cissy's ex-boyfriend Mr. Mo, a drama teacher, also takes an interest in what is going on, and he's the one who comes up with most of the theories, including the idea that the group is being haunted by the ghost of the person whose 'oil' had been burned in the ritual.

Characters continue to die, with one of them tricked into stepping off the top of a high building and Biggie compelled to strangle her own mother before committing suicide. Ming becomes more and more concerned that Annie will soon become a victim too, so he teams up with Mr. Mo to break the curse and discover the origin of the ghost. Their research leads them to the deserted Yellow Hill Village and they eventually learn that the black-haired, vengeful ghost is the spirit of a murdered woman called Cho Yan Mei.

More deaths ensue, including an old man who gets bumped off when a long metal pole falls from a roof and skewers him to the ground via his gaping mouth, in an *Omen*-style moment. Mr. Mo, meanwhile, realizes that it isn't the "oil" that connects all these victims to the spirit, so the search for a way to halt the killings continues, but time is running out for Annie, so a desperate Ming intensifies his efforts to find the resting place of Cho Yan Mei's body.

A Wicked Ghost is a pretty run-of-the-mill Hong Kong supernatural flick, directed in a competent fashion by Leung Hung-Wah. Wah also wrote the script and he does a better job here, supplying enough backstory to the curse and nuggets of new information to keep you watching.

One of these revelations involves Mr. Mo's supposition that Cho Yan Mei's murdered body is actually buried beneath a pond near Yellow Hill Village, which is linked to the local water supply somehow. Ming then realizes that the angry ghost-force of Cho Yan Mei must have entered various victim's bodies "through the medium of water".

Though Mr. Mo (Ng) is the character who uncovers most of the facts, it is Ming (Harrison) who is the film's main character, but he proves to be such a frustratingly hesitant protagonist! In one sequence Annie, possessed by Cho Yan Mei, fills a bowl with prescription drugs and starts wolfing the tablets down like they're sweets. Rather than physically trying to stop his girlfriend from munching all the pills, Ming just ineffectually looks on, asking her to wake up and stop eating the drugs. In a later scene the ever-hesitant Ming is in a position to actually stop the murders when he discovers a special bracelet that is capable of negating Cho Yan Mei's powers . . . but he is so slow to take action, reaching out to Cho Yan Mei's wrist in such a tentative manner, that she has time to evade the bracelet and attack him. Very frustrating!

The inspiration for the look of the malevolent spook in *A Wicked Ghost* is Sadako from *Ring*, which

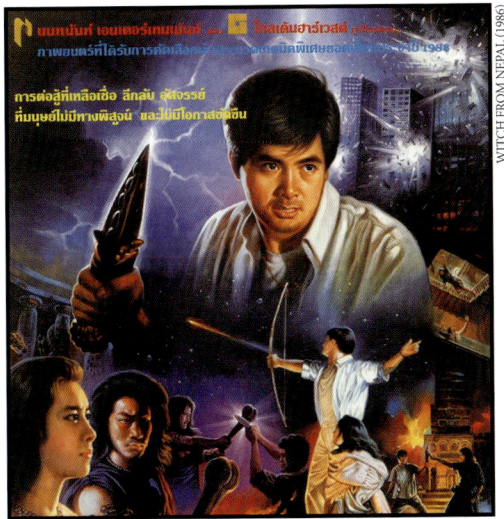

WITCH FROM NEPAL (1986)

was released the previous year and triggered the production of a whole bunch of Hong Kong *Ring* knockoffs. There's an okay moment involving the ghost walking directly behind a female character in a bar, and there's also a fun scene in a bathroom, where Jack sees Cho Yan Mei's hair, and then her hand, poking from a toilet bowl.

Most of the ghost scenes in this low-budget film are achieved using actors in pale makeup, with very few optical effects, though this is acceptable because this kind of story works just fine with brief glimpses of long hair hiding a ghost's face or quick shots of a dark figure passing by doorways. But Leung Hung-Wah fails to include enough supernatural encounters in his tale, meaning the film ends up sadly lacking in decent scares and tension.

With a plot that's burdened with several extraneous characters (Cissy & Jack) and direction that's rather lackluster, *A Wicked Ghost* is, ultimately, a Hong Kong paranormal flick that is watchable but also quite forgettable.

A WICKED GHOST II: THE FEAR (2000)

Starring Ken Wong, Alice Chan, Joey Meng,
Cheung Wei-Yee, Joyce Chen
Directed by Francis Nam
Matrix Productions Company Ltd

An angry spirit triggers illusions in its victims, prompting the sufferers to either kill themselves or others. As the main characters, including cops Li (Wong) and Peanut (Chan), try to stop the supernaturally induced body count, they uncover a case of wrongdoing from the past, involving adultery, rape and murder . . . perpetrated by some of their own ancestors.

You'd think that a film featuring a *Ring*-inspired long-haired female ghost, a bespectacled rapist who chops off his own legs, and audio recordings of creepy spirit noises, plus a scene where a woman in a toilet cubicle sharpens a mop handle so that she can ram it through her own head, might be scary or at least memorable, but this sadly isn't the case.

A floating female ghost's head covered in gloopy, white flesh makes a brief, effective appearance toward the end of the film, but this simply highlights how this lackluster movie needed more of this kind of imagery if it wanted to stick in viewers' minds.

WITCH FROM NEPAL (1986)

Starring Chow Yun-Fat, Emily Chu,
Yammie Lam Kit-Ying, Dick Wei
Directed by Ching Siu-Tung
Action by Ching Siu-Tung, Alan Hsu
Golden Harvest

While in Nepal, Joe (Yun-Fat) meets a mysterious girl who follows him back to Hong Kong. He discovers that he now has supernatural powers and, after the death of the attractive witch, has to combat an evil warrior (Wei) who wants the glowing pendant that Joe wears around his neck.

Featuring the blue-lit photography, slow motion, and romantic atmosphere found in the best Hong Kong fantasies, this film, also known as *The Nepal Affair* and *A Touch of Love*, is for much of its running time simply a tale of a ménage à trois spiced up with some telekinesis and other minor feats of magic. But the film shifts gears toward the end as Joe, his girlfriend, and some children are trapped in a graveyard by zombies who've just crawled out of the mud. A section of railings then bends toward a car and flies into the side of the vehicle like a series of iron spears!

Joe and the bad dude, who growls like a panther, have a final fight, which sees them knocking each other through buildings, culminating with the villain getting speared on a ceremonial dagger, causing his teeth and eyes to plop out and his skin to fly off his skull!

A decent modern-day Hong Kong whimsy, it is a shame that the evil character's ability to transform into a cel-animated panther, shown at the very start of the film, isn't reintroduced during the latter stages of the tale—and the scene where Joe makes sparking electricity cables draw two hearts in the night sky for his love is far, far too twee!

THE WITCH WITH FLYING HEAD (1982)
Starring Chen Hsiu-Chen, Ma Sha, Liu Shang-Chien
Directed by Chang Jen-Chieh
Chia Yu Film Company

This is a rare gem with a high level of bizarre gross-out images, the highlight, of course, being the flying head, which comes complete with impossibly long fangs and a set of internal organs attached!

The movie is packed with insane visuals, including *Exorcist*-style head-spinning, magic duels, an abundance of oozing effects and the flying-head-with-organs diving onto its enemies and chomping their necks.

Absurd fun.

WOMEN ON THE RUN (1993)
Starring Farina Cheung, Tamara Guo, Wong Wai-Tak, Corey Yuen, Won Jin
Directed and produced by Corey Yuen, David Lai
Joe Siu International Film Ltd

When Siu-Yin (Guo) hits the big, bad city of Guangzhou seeking fame and fortune as a kung fu star, only to end up hooked on smack, being pimped by her boyfriend, then killing him and fleeing to Hong Kong—all within the first five minutes—you know that this is definitely an actioner proud of its CAT III classification.

Though ostensibly centered on a tangled plotline concerning cross-border drug dealing and police corruption, the main focus is on Ah Hung (Cheung), the nice-but-naive police officer assigned, at the instigation of Ah Hung's boyfriend David, to engineer a sting on mainland narco-baron King Kong (Jin), using junkie Siu-Yin as bait for her foray into the Guangzhou vice dens. However, when the scam unravels and our heroines find themselves in Vancouver, Canada, with enough dope planted on them to satisfy Keith Richards for several decades, scheduled for termination by the mob, left high and dry by David and then victims of a brutal assault by a pack of bums, you know these women are due some major payback . . .

If some of the script gets daft at points—our junkie heroine launches into a kung fu frenzy after she's had

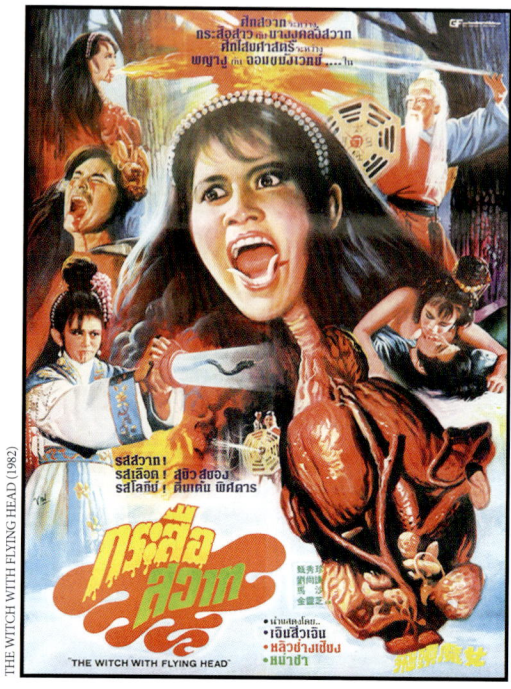

THE WITCH WITH FLYING HEAD (1982)

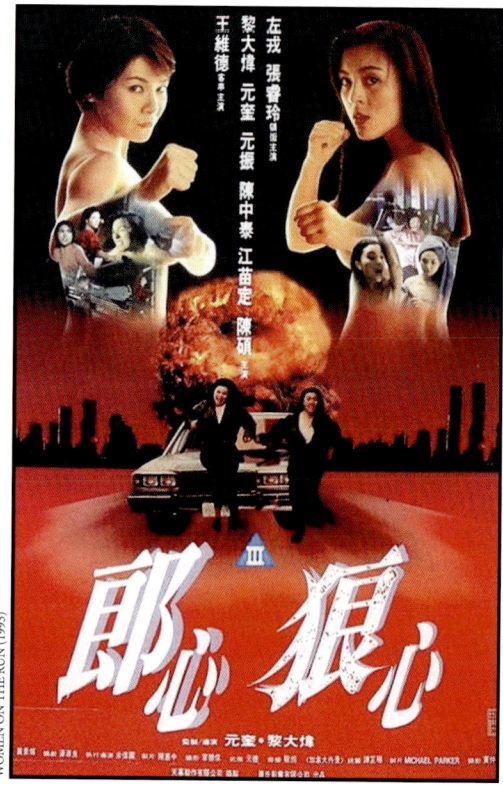

WOMEN ON THE RUN (1993)

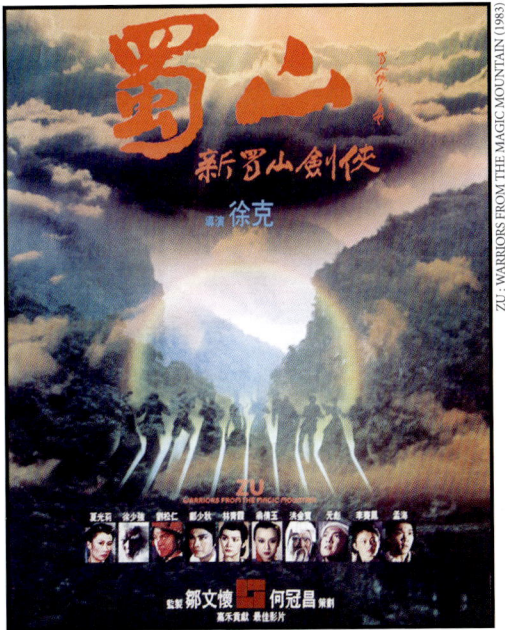

ZU : WARRIORS FROM THE MAGIC MOUNTAIN (1983)

her fix—any quibbles can be overlooked thanks to good performances from the female leads and its lashings of action, boasting the ultimate on-screen kick, when Won Jin does a 180-degree roundhouse with both feet together without the help of wires! It has to be seen to be believed.

ZU: WARRIORS FROM THE MAGIC MOUNTAIN (1983)

Starring Yuen Biao, Adam Cheng, Meng Hoi,
Sammo Hung, Moon Lee, Brigitte Lin, Tsui Siu-Keung
Directed by Tsui Hark
Produced by Raymond Chow
Action by Corey Yuen, Meng Hoi, Yuen Biao,
Fung Hark-On
Golden Harvest

This fine fantasy flick, based on a 1932 book called *The Legend of the Swordsman of the Mountains of Shu* by Huanzhulouzhu (the pen name of Li Shoumin), is so fast, frantic, absurdly action-gorged, fantastical and odd that it makes pretty much any film made in the West look snail-paced in comparison to it.

Set in a region called Zu, the film tells the tall tale of Ming (Biao), an army private, who becomes disillusioned with the civil war ravaging his land. He escapes to the Magic Mountains, which is a grim area plagued by demons and evil disciples. Meeting up with some magical warriors, Ming attempts to prevent the Blood Monster from ending the world.

By far the best portion of this movie, for me, is Ming's initial venture into the mountainous region, a zone of misty boulders and temples, where the private encounters virgin-sacrificing cult members and demons that resemble blue-eyed Jawas with stretching bodies.

After teaming up with three good monk-fighters, Ming confronts the Blood Monster, which first appears as a cascade of blood, then becomes an entity covered by a red sheet. To the aid of the heroic foursome comes Long Brows (Hung): a gray-haired mystic who manages to keep the Blood Monster in check by clasping it with his magically extending eyebrows and beard! The Blood Monster protects its soul, though, by surrounding itself with the skulls of sacrificial virgins and tusks! Ming and his three companions go in search of two powerful swords capable of finally destroying the Blood Monster before it grows too powerful to be restrained by Long Brows.

Tsui Hark adds so many fights, mystics, flying skirmishes, animated magic effects, arguments, twisting Buddha statues and multiple scene-changes that the cumulative effect of this nonstop, energetic assault to the senses is that you feel like your head might explode! By the time the heroes are flying through red, swirling skyscapes, armed with glowing, magic swords, you wonder if you're hallucinating it all!

Hark maybe tries to cram just too many optical effects into the finale and the end results are often less effective than, say, the mainly practical special effects seen in *A Chinese Ghost Story* (1987), but there's so, so much to enjoy here, why bother to quibble? And, let's face it, what other movie contains a fight between a man and a woman zooming about on levitating large elephant statues and a stone griffin?!

Note: The English dubbed version starts off in the modern day, and is edited to suit a more Western market.

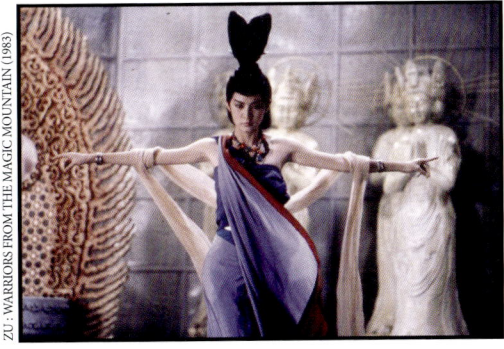

ZU : WARRIORS FROM THE MAGIC MOUNTAIN (1983)

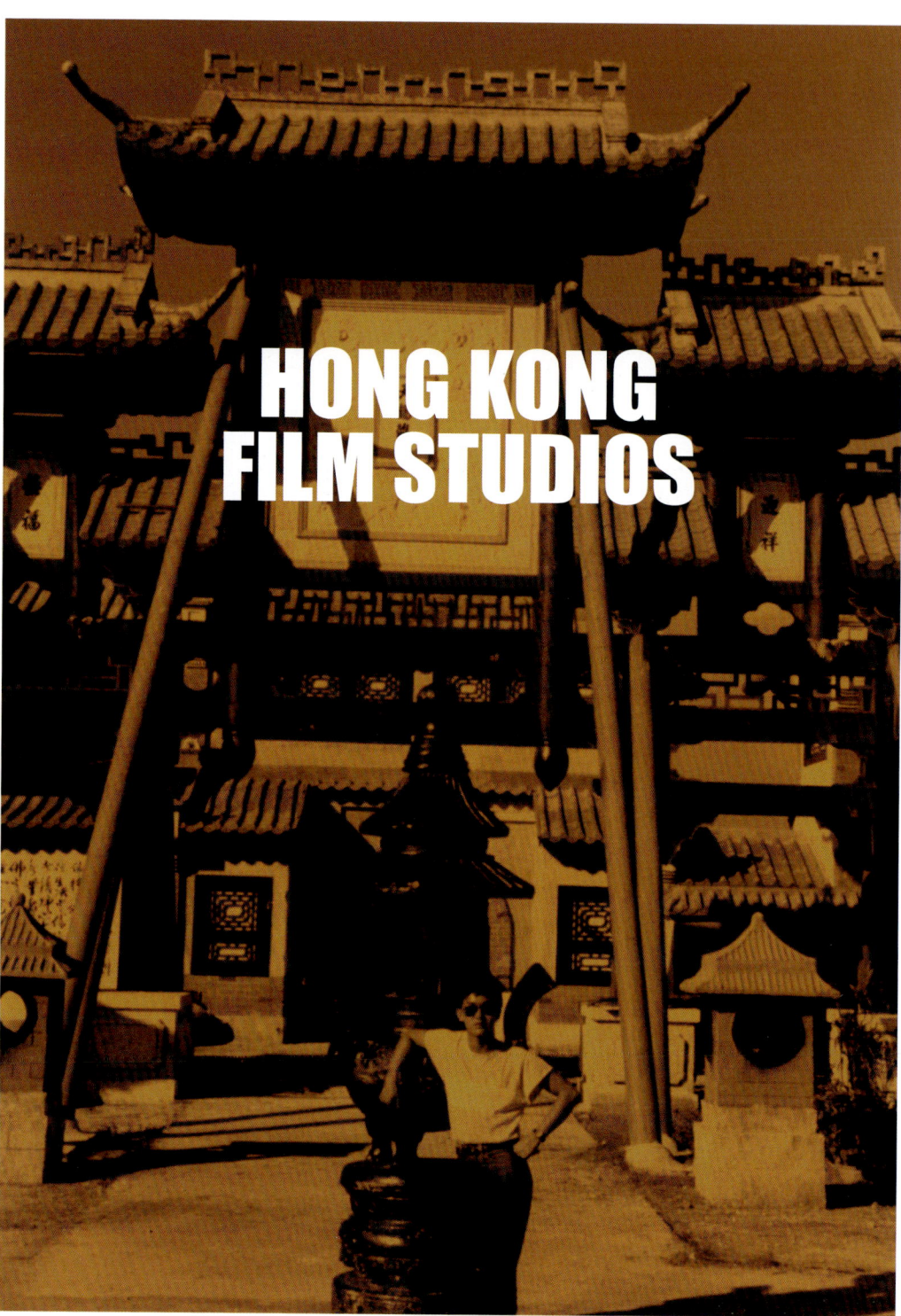

HONG KONG
FILM STUDIOS

STUDIOS THAT MADE HONG KONG'S FILM INDUSTRY SO AMAZING

Perhaps you're watching the Golden Harvest logo's four rectangles slowly come into view, or maybe you're looking at the Cinema City and Film Workshop brand idents appear during the opening credits of *A Better Tomorrow*, but whatever the logos are, there's a good chance that simply seeing these company names will send tingles down your spine before the film has even started!

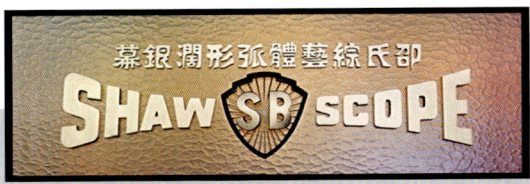

SHAW BROTHERS STUDIO

From a modest beginning in 1925, the company's operation was initiated by the entrepreneurial genius of the Shaw brothers: Runje, Runde and Runme (with Run Run playing a big role later). Their vision, determination, and acute understanding of the local entertainment industry rapidly propelled them to the forefront of the Asian film industry, with a business that included film-processing facilities, sound stages, screening rooms, and a major Southeast Asian chain of cinemas.

In the 1950s the company set up a new studio complex in Hong Kong's Clearwater Bay area, and it was here that Shaw Brothers Studio really began to blossom in the 1960s, when it was able to leverage its dubbing, film processing, special effects, and editing departments, its army of full-time staff, its many stars, and its multiple large sound stages, to begin producing the kind of distinctive releases it is famous for. This was the period that saw the rise of stars like Jimmy Wang Yu in *Tiger Boy* (1966) and Chen Pei-Pei in *Come Drink with Me* (1966). These films, with their unique, stylised blend of action, drama and suspense, drew viewers into a world of fascinating characters and thrilling adventures.

In the ensuing years Shaw Brothers continued to introduce an array of new talent, producing films like *The New One-Armed Swordsman* (1971) with David Chiang, *The 14 Amazons* (1972) with Lily Ho, and *Four Riders* (1972) starring Ti Lung. By the early 1970s the company was internationally famous thanks to movies such as *King Boxer* (aka *Five Fingers of Death*).

Shaw Brothers crafted their films in a house style, made by directors and stars under studio contracts similar to those of the old Hollywood system. These films, very often sporting a heightened theatricality thanks to the regular use of sound stages rather than location photography, definitely had a signature look that added a uniqueness to its output.

The 1980s saw Shaw Brothers agree to dub, pan-and-scan, and edit some of its martial arts movies for US company World Northal, which sold the broadcast rights to independent TV stations as part of a package called Black Belt Theater, which ran successfully for five seasons.

However, thanks to stiff competition from other movie studios (especially the major success of Golden Harvest's Jackie Chan releases), pressure from the Hong Kong government to split up their production and exhibition connection, plus their employees' calls for participation in profits, ultimately led to Run Run's decision to close down the Shaw Brothers film units in the mid-80s, though the company remained active with its television production arm.

Then, in the early 2000s, the renaissance of the Shaw Brothers Studio began, when Celestial Pictures, owner of the film library, took on the mammoth task of remastering the company's classics. The renewed vibrancy and detail of these restored films meant they were not just preserved for nostalgic reasons but thrived in new territories worldwide, with boutique DVD label releases proving that the appeal of these films is truly timeless, ensuring that the movies, with their famous Shaw Scope logo and fanfare, will continue to enthral new generations of viewers.

SIR RUN RUN SHAW

Sir Run Run is something of an enigmatic figure, a pioneer who irrevocably altered the landscape of Asian cinema. His influence, stretching beyond borders and cultural divides, propelled Hong Kong's film industry into the international limelight.

Born in the city of Ningbo, China, in 1907, Run Run was destined for a life steeped in cinema. Moving to Hong Kong in the late 50s, Run Run overhauled his family's Tianyi Film Company, which laid the foundations of Shaw Brothers Studio, a venture that was to become an unrivalled powerhouse of movie production in Asia.

Run Run's vision was as grand as it was groundbreaking. His approach to film production was inspired by Hollywood's golden age studio system: a conveyor belt of film content with dedicated in-house teams. However, the Shaw Brothers version was a more intricate machine, a fully integrated studio-city complex named Movietown. Every cog, from set designers to cinematographers, worked under Shaw's no-nonsense, precise direction. The studio's output was astonishing, with as many as forty films produced annually. Run Run's genius lay in his uncanny ability to identify the pulse of the masses. From martial arts epics such as *The One-Armed Swordsman*, to romances like *Love Without End*, Shaw's films exhibited an extraordinary range that continually defied expectations. His flair for spotting talent was legendary, cultivating and showcasing stars like Jimmy Wang Yu, Lo Lieh and Gordon Liu, and director Chang Cheh.

Shaw's influence wasn't limited to the silver screen. An astute businessman, he expanded his empire into the burgeoning world of television with Television Broadcasts Limited (TVB), pioneering what would become a mainstay of Hong Kong's daily life. TVB gave birth to countless Asian stars, fuelling the careers of household names like Chow Yun-fat, Maggie Cheung, Anita Mui, and Andy Lau.

Shaw's contributions to the film and television industry were monumental, but they were part of a larger philanthropic tapestry. He used his considerable wealth to support educational and medical advancements, and even established the coveted Shaw Prize, often referred to as the "Nobel of the East." Run Run was awarded the Commander of the Order of the British Empire (CBE) in 1974 and was knighted by Queen Elizabeth II at Buckingham Palace in 1977.

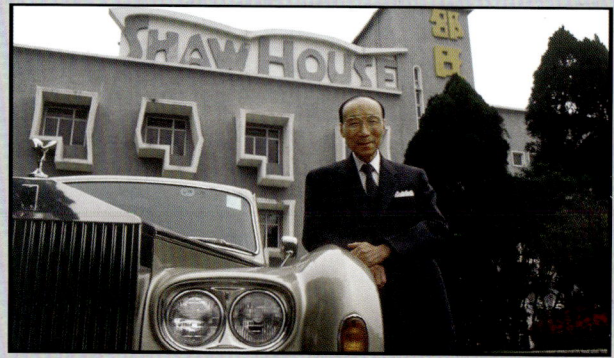

SIR RUN RUN SHAW OUTSIDE SHAW HOUSE

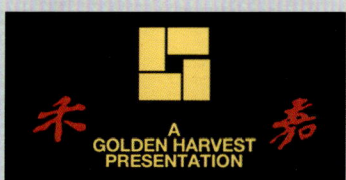

GOLDEN HARVEST

Golden Harvest Studios, officially known now as Orange Sky Golden Harvest, is undeniably a cornerstone of Hong Kong's movie industry. Established in 1970 by former Shaw Brothers executives Raymond Chow and Leonard Ho, Golden Harvest came into being as a challenge to the dominance of Shaw Brothers Studio in Hong Kong's movie industry. Its success wasn't immediate, but everything changed with the release of *The Big Boss* in 1971. Directed by Lo Wei, *The Big Boss* was the first significant venture by Golden Harvest into the international film market, starring a young and dynamic Bruce Lee, launching him as a kung fu superstar. The film's massive commercial success propelled Golden Harvest to new heights and established it as a major player in the industry.

The studio became a haven for nurturing and promoting talent, creating a platform that launched the careers of several martial arts and action cinema icons. Jackie Chan, Sammo Hung, plus directors like John Woo and Tsui Hark, are some of the illustrious names that owe their early career growth to the studio. Jackie Chan and Sammo Hung, with their unique combination of martial arts and comedy, became international stars, while John Woo, with movies like *Hand of Death* (1976) and *Last Hurrah for Chivalry* (1979), emerged as an innovative director.

Golden Harvest was not just a male-dominated arena, of course, with the studio being instrumental in promoting female action stars like Michelle Yeoh and Cynthia Rothrock, ensuring Hong Kong films were just as likely to feature a tough woman protagonist as they were to have male leads.

The Studio also played an essential role in the rapid expansion of Hong Kong cinema with the advent of the video market in the 1980s, which further amplified their reach, with their extensive library of films finding its way into homes worldwide, making Hong Kong cinema a global phenomenon.

Focusing on film financing, distribution, and cinema management now, Golden Harvest's legacy does continue to reverberate with the remastering and reissuing of many of their classic films in 4K. These high-definition releases are introducing a new generation to the gems of Hong Kong cinema, ensuring the studio's enduring relevance.

RAYMOND CHOW

Among the influential figures who have left an indelible mark on the Hong Kong film industry, Raymond Chow sparkles with a special radiance. To many, he was simply a successful movie producer, but for those familiar with his work, he was the guiding hand that launched Eastern cinema into the stratosphere, bringing Hong Kong's vibrant filmmaking culture to the global stage.

Born in 1927 in British Hong Kong, Chow embarked on his cinematic journey with Shaw Brothers, then a formidable force in the local movie industry. However, the seeds of rebellion were sown early. Uncomfortable with the factory-like system that prized quantity over quality, he left Shaw Brothers to establish Golden Harvest in 1970.

Golden Harvest became an embodiment of Chow's vision: he stood as a veritable underdog against the established studios, with the unique ability to blend business acumen with artistic sensitivity, distinguishing him from his contemporaries. His philosophy centered on giving his artists creative freedom, a stark contrast to the more hierarchical structures of traditional studios.

By signing Bruce Lee, Raymond Chow bestowed upon him his first leading role in the Thailand-shot movie *The Big Boss*, an endeavor that not only put both Bruce Lee and Golden Harvest on the global map but also set the stage for their future triumphs. Together, they embarked on a creative journey that resulted in the creation of the iconic films *Fist of Fury* and *The Way of the Dragon*. Co-producing *Enter the Dragon* with Warner Brothers shattered cultural barriers and propelled Lee to the status of a global superstar.

In many ways, Chow's brilliance extended beyond being a filmmaker: he was a star-maker with an exceptional talent for identifying potential, as demonstrated by his discovery of Jackie Chan, which propelled the kung fu star and the genre to unprecedented heights. Jackie Chan himself acknowledged the debt he owed to Raymond Chow's help in a *Variety* interview back in 2000. "Mr. Chow gave me a chance to follow my dreams. I think today that without Golden Harvest, there is no Jackie Chan."

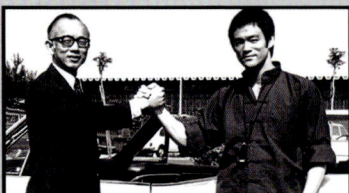

RAYMOND CHOW WITH BRUCE LEE

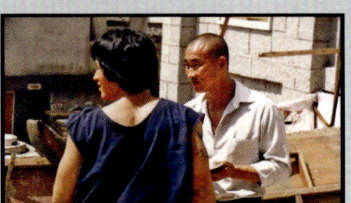

CASANOVA WONG VISITING KWON YOUNG-MOON
ON THE SET OF PROJECT A

FILM WORKSHOP

The Hong Kong film industry has been significantly influenced and developed by numerous other film studios, and one that was instrumental in molding and evolving the distinctive landscape of Hong Kong cinema is Film Workshop.

Spearheaded by the visionary cofounders Tsui Hark and Nansun Shi, this studio played a significant role in popularizing the renowned Heroic Bloodshed genre. The indelible impact of the company's films, such as *A Better Tomorrow* and *The Killer,* extended far beyond the boundaries of Hong Kong, resonating even within the realms of Hollywood.

Other films of note made under the Film Workshop banner include *Swordsman*, *Once Upon a Time in China*, *The Blade*, and the glorious *A Chinese Ghost Story*.

CINEMA CITY

Formed by Karl Maka, Dean Shek, and Raymond Wong, Cinema City (originally named Warriors Film Company) made substantial contributions to the vibrant landscape of Hong Kong cinema through the 1980s, with the company's final releases coming out in 1991.

Cinema City's diverse range of productions spanned various genres, from fantasies like *Esprit D'amour* and *The Legend of Wisely*, to comedies like the *Aces Go Places* series, capturing the hearts of audiences both in Hong Kong and abroad.

Some of the company's other releases include the humorous, very popular *Happy Ghost* franchise and the gritty action-crime flicks *City War*, *The Big Heat*, and *City on Fire*.

WIN'S FILM PRODUCTIONS

Founded by producer Charles Heung and his brother Jimmy, Win's Film Productions consistently contributed to the golden era of Hong Kong cinema in the 80s and 90s. As well as producing, Charles Heung would also sometimes appear in his company's productions in supporting roles, most famously in the *God of Gamblers* series.

The studio backed a significant number of action and martial arts films, including *Crocodile Hunter* and Jet Li's *Kung Fu Cult Master*, doing their bit to enhance the colorful, exciting moviemaking tapestry that was Hong Kong cinema during its glory years.

SEASONAL FILM CORPORATION

Established by Ng See-Yuen, Seasonal Film Corporation's releases included well-regarded fu flicks like *Secret Rivals*, but the company really hit its stride when it produced Jackie Chan's breakthrough films *Snake in the Eagle's Shadow* and *Drunken Master*, which solidified Chan's career, had a huge impact on martial arts films and cemented Season Film Corporation's place in the kung fu movie-making firmament.

The company also produced Tsui Hark's first two films as director, *The Butterfly Murders* and *We're Going to Eat You*, and was responsible for fan favorites like *Ninja in the Dragon's Den* and the American-set Jean-Claude Van Damme starrer *No Retreat, No Surrender*.

BO HO FILM COMPANY LTD

Sammo Hung had previously set up Gar Bo Motion Picture Company with Lau Kar-Wing and Karl Maka, but it didn't release many films. Then, in 1980, when Raymond Chow pulled one of Sammo Hung's films from local cinemas after just a fortnight, Sammo decided to retaliate by forming a new production company: Bo Ho. While smaller in scale compared to many other studios, this company was a solid presence in the Hong Kong film market.

Thriving from the mid-80s to the very early 90s, Bo Ho's influence stems from the fact it made some really good films, including hugely enjoyable comedy-horror flicks like the *Mr. Vampire* series, *Encounters of the Spooky Kind*, and *The Dead and the Deadly*, awesome action movies like *Eastern Condors* and *The Blonde Fury*, and the cool kung fu film *The Scorpion King* (aka *Operation Scorpio*).

D & B FILMS CO. LTD

Along with John Shum and Dickson Poon, Sammo Hung cofounded this production company in 1983. D & B was a prolific producer of entertaining movies throughout the 80s and was operational until 1992.

Some of its noteworthy releases include high-octane girls and guns flick *Yes, Madam!*, which spawned the *In the Line of Duty* series of movies, actioners like the *Tiger Cage* trilogy and two *Black Cat* films, plus Brandon Lee's only Hong Kong film, *Legacy of Rage*.

B.O.B AND PARTNERS

This production company was established by Wong Jing, Andrew Lau and Manfred Wong. They had the finances to set it up thanks to the huge success of the *Young and Dangerous* film franchise.

Along with those hip gangland *Young and Dangerous flicks*, which include several of the spin-offs and *Young and Dangerous: The Prequel*, the company is also known for the action comedy *The Tricky Master* (1999) and the slick, lavish, Andrew Lau–directed sword-fantasies *The Storm Riders* (1998) and *The Duel* (2000).

IFD FILMS AND ARTS

Founded in 1973 by Joseph Lai, IFD Films and Arts carved a niche for itself by producing and distributing low-budget martial arts, war, animation and exploitation films that quickly gained a cult following, especially during the 80s video rental boom.

Many of IFD's releases were cut-and-paste movies, such as *Scorpion Thunderbolt*, *Kickboxer from Hell* and *Thunder of Gigantic Serpent*. Watching these can become an addiction, especially ninja actioners like *Ninja Terminator*, *Ninja Thunderbolt*, and *Cobra Against Ninja*, many of which starred Richard Harrison. In 2017 the IFD film catalog was sold to a British distribution company.

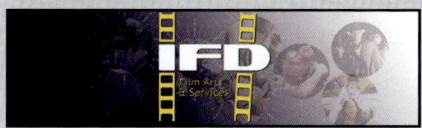

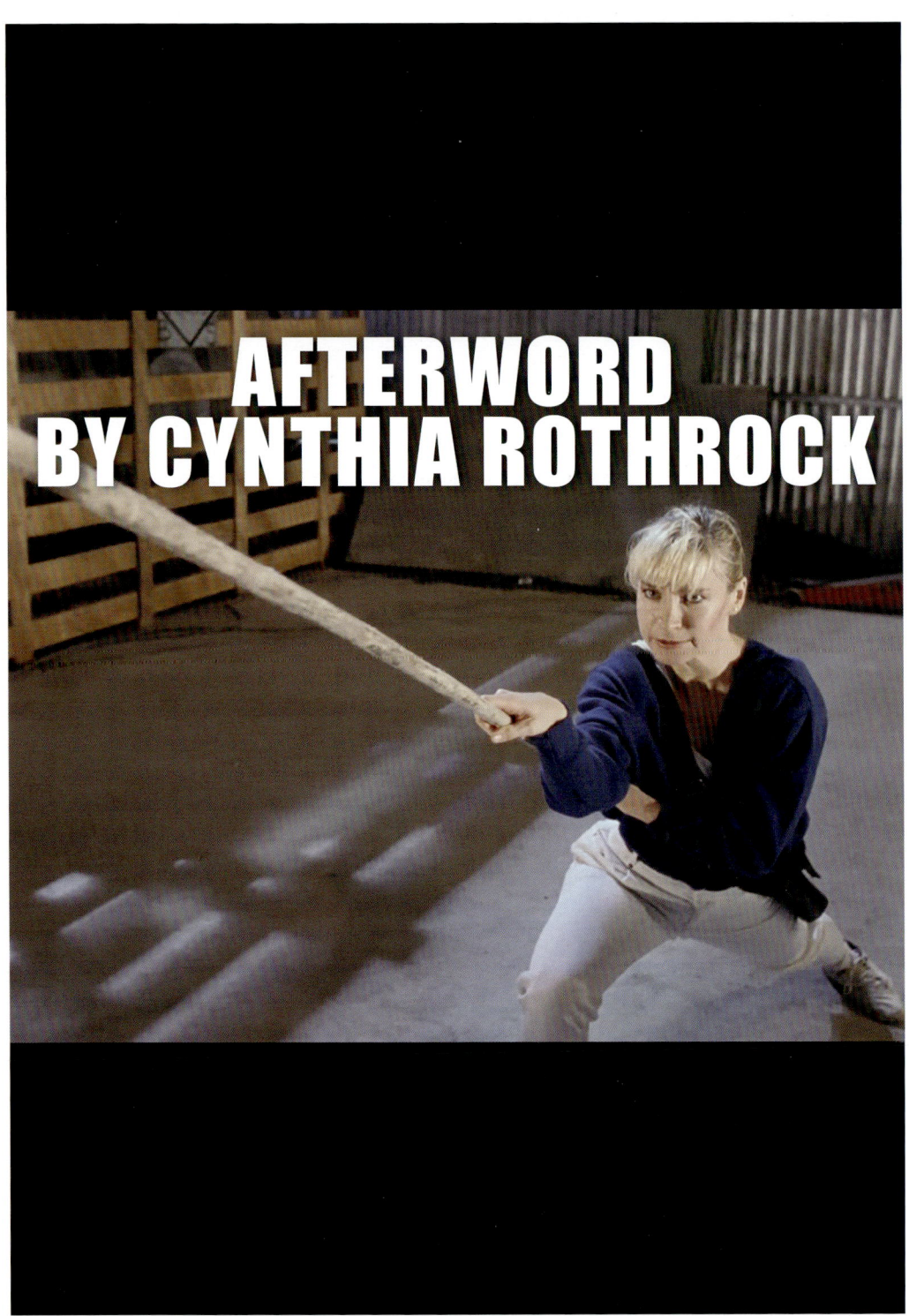

AFTERWORD
BY CYNTHIA ROTHROCK

In 1985 I traveled to Hong Kong to do my first film, *Yes, Madam!* I didn't know what to expect. When flying in, I thought I was landing on Han's Island from *Enter the Dragon!* I was curious to know what I was getting into and to learn about Hong Kong movie production. I was so green and naive at that time, so I assumed I would be doing a period film, dressed in Chinese outfits (which I loved), and perhaps they would give me a wig with black braids and razor blades in them. I was surprised to learn I would be playing a character called Cindy, a Western cop from the United States. My first night of filming was the airport fight, one of the opening scenes of *Yes, Madam!* On the set, I was told, "Whatever you do, try to get your lines to match the Chinese so it doesn't look like bad dubbing." I knew they would dub me in Chinese and that not too many people spoke English. To my surprise, I found no one cared what I actually said, and I was given directions to just open my mouth and say "1-2-3-4."

Welcome to Hong Kong cinema! I wanted to do more and said that I didn't want to do it this way, so I asked for my Chinese dialogue and proceeded to make up the same syllables to appear as if I was actually speaking Cantonese. The director, Corey Yuen, then wanted me to speak in Chinese . . . yikes! Well, I tried, and when I just kept stuttering a syllable, they still assured me it was great. What I had said sounded like, "Humma, humma, humma," but I learned that it didn't matter; all Hong Kong movies were filmed with no sound!

I also learned that Corey Yuen wanted me to hit hard and get hit hard. Eddie Maher, in the airport fight scene, only had a tank top on, so he couldn't use any padding on his arms or chest. During the scene, Eddie was saying, "Not so hard," to me, and Corey kept asking me to do harder hits . . . and I'm wondering who do I listen to? I chose the director!

Shooting action scenes in Hong Kong was complicated, dangerous, brilliant, and so worth all the bruises and injuries I received in each film. I thought, is this how action movies are made? But I just went with the flow. When I did my first US movie, the stuntmen told me I didn't have to hit so hard or get walloped, so it was much easier fighting for me with fewer injuries.

Of all the seventy-plus movies I've done, none of the fight scenes compare to my Hong Kong films. My first movie took almost eight months to shoot.

I learned to be tougher, stronger, and braver than I'd been in any previous training sessions or even in competitions. In each Hong Kong movie I filmed, I thought, "This may be my last movie because I'm going to get killed or seriously injured on set!" The production would end and, eventually, my on-set injuries would heal, and I'd be eager to shoot the next movie. To be an action fighter in a Hong Kong movie, you have to be a bit crazy, you need to always do your best and never complain about your injuries. Even when you get hit in the nose with a sword and tears are automatically coming from your eyes . . . you don't stop.

I recall doing a scene in *Lady Reporter* (aka *Blonde Fury*) where I had to jump two stories onto cardboard boxes that were cushioned only with a mattress on top, while holding a fake baby in my hands, wearing heels, and a real explosion behind me. Before filming the scene, Corey Yuen said, "If you don't jump when I say action, you will get burned from the explosion." That's just one example of many, and I was definitely never taught how to do this in my martial arts training!

I look back at the 80s to 90s as the golden age of action films, when the very best action was captured. Even though many of these movies are over thirty years old, they are currently being remastered, and they all still hold up today as having some of the top fight scenes ever filmed. Why? Because there was no CGI, doubles were rare because we did most of our own stunts and fighting, and you were doing all the wirework.

You see the best of the best in these films. Brilliant choreography, insane stunts done by the actors, the best action direction you will ever find—all done for small budgets with a passion to make a great action film. It's not like today's film budgets, where you have hundreds of millions of dollars to create an action film; these gems were created on half-million-dollar budgets.

I am so happy that this book has come out, so everyone can be reminded of all the hard work that went into Hong Kong film making, where creating the best scenes one could do was done by the actors themselves. I am so blessed to have started filming in the Golden Age of Hong Kong action movies!

All the best,

Cynthia Rothrock

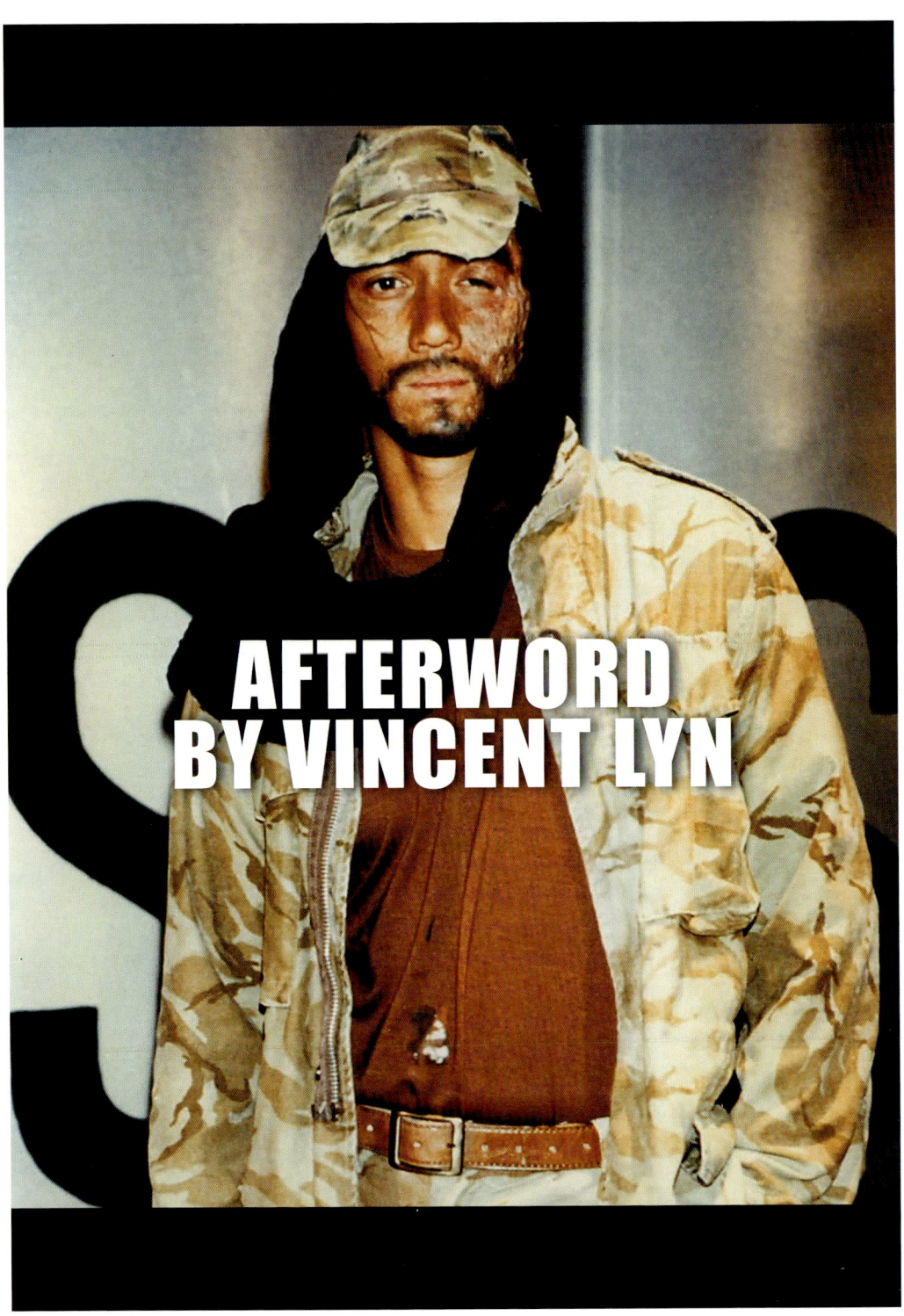

AFTERWORD
BY VINCENT LYN

In February 1988 I had my very first encounter with Jackie Chan. It happened at the Hong Kong Regent Hotel coffee shop. Jackie entered the place surrounded by four bodyguards. When I saw him, I couldn't help but blurt out, "Holy shit, it's Jackie Chan!" I approached his table with my portfolio in hand, determined to get his autograph. However, the bodyguards quickly asserted their authority. I asked Jackie to sign one of my photos, which showed me in a martial arts pose. He inquired if I was a martial artist, and I explained that I was trying to break into the film industry in Hong Kong. Jackie wished me good luck, signed the photo, and was very gracious.

Years later, I was invited to audition for *Armour of God II: Operation Condor* and I got the part. The film's production turned out to be chaotic, plagued with mishaps, changes, and delays. I was told I would only be needed for ten days, but it turned out to be much more grueling than expected! I endured long hours, injuries, and the challenges of a demanding shooting schedule.

The character I was portraying was a cruel and disfigured individual with severe burns and scars on one side of his face, and the first ten days on set were nothing short of a makeup nightmare. Each day I endured the arduous process of having my makeup redone repeatedly. To make matters worse, Jackie would drop by daily and express his dissatisfaction with the makeup crew, exclaiming, "Makeup's no good!"

This ordeal was particularly harsh on my skin, and I couldn't help but feel the toll it was taking on me and, for a while, it seemed like a futile endeavor, with precious time getting wasted. Each day dragged on for eight hours as they attempted to perfect the makeup and every day Jackie would make them change it, saying that they should make me more ugly because, "He's too good looking to be a villain!"

Despite these difficulties I made it through the filming and *Operation Condor* was completed, becoming the most expensive Hong Kong film made at the time.

The film had its US premiere the next year in Los Angeles, which was a grand event, and Jackie and I had a chance to catch up. Then, a few years after *Operation Condor* hit the screens, I decided to take a trip back to Hong Kong for a well-deserved holiday. While there, I made sure to pay a visit to Jackie, and to my delight he was thrilled to see me and extended a warm invitation to his private office; a sanctuary that very few people ever got to witness. As we hung out together, Jackie playfully said, "I'm very upset with you." Naturally, I was taken aback and asked, "Why? What did I do?" He jokingly replied, "Every time I turn on the television, I see your face—actually, I see your face more than mine." We had a good laugh about it, and I explained that it wasn't my fault; it's just that many of the movies I starred in were now being shown on Hong Kong TV frequently!

Fast-forward to 22nd January 2019 where, after a twenty-year hiatus, fate brought me face-to-face with Jackie Chan once again. He was in New York City at the Barnes & Noble bookstore, conducting a book signing event for his new autobiography, *Never Grow Up*. A friend of mine, HBO-sponsored producer Demetrius Angelo, called me and asked if I'd like to meet Jackie. I jumped at the opportunity, and as soon as Jackie saw me, he immediately recognized me. He greeted me with a warm hug, and the cameras were flashing from all corners of the room; it felt like the good old days!

We had a wonderful time catching up and reminiscing. Meeting Jackie again after so many years was truly a memorable and heartwarming experience. Our paths crossed a few more times over the years, and I am now honoured and humbled to be recognized as part of the golden age of Hong Kong cinema: an action-packed moviemaking period that spawned many of the films reviewed in this Guide.

—Vincent Lyn

Jackie Chan said that Vincent Lyn was one of the best fighters he had ever worked with in his book *I am Jackie Chan: My Life in Action*, and it's certainly a fact that the climactic wind tunnel fight scene from *Armour of God II: Operation Condor*, where Jackie battles the scar-faced, high-kicking villain played by Vincent, is regularly listed as one of Jackie Chan's top ten best fight scenes.

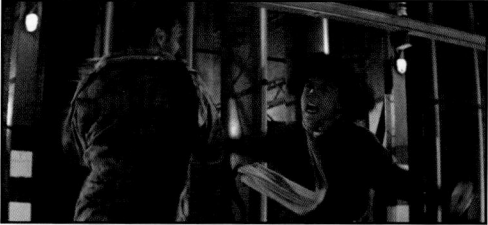

INDEX